From Plato to Platonism

From Plato to Platonism

LLOYD P. GERSON

CORNELL UNIVERSITY PRESS
Ithaca and London

Copyright © 2013 by Cornell University

All rights reserved. Except for brief quotations in a review, this book, or parts thereof, must not be reproduced in any form without permission in writing from the publisher. For information, address Cornell University Press, Sage House, 512 East State Street, Ithaca, New York 14850.

First published 2013 by Cornell University Press
First paperback printing 2017

Printed in the United States of America

Library of Congress Cataloging-in-Publication Data

Gerson, Lloyd P., author.
  From Plato to Platonism / Lloyd P. Gerson.
    pages cm
  Includes bibliographical references and index.
  ISBN 978-0-8014-5241-3 (cloth: alk. paper)
  ISBN 978-1-5017-1063-6 (pbk.: alk. paper)
  1. Plato. 2. Platonists. I. Title.
  B395.G47 2013
  184—dc23   2013010926

Cornell University Press strives to use environmentally responsible suppliers and materials to the fullest extent possible in the publishing of its books. Such materials include vegetable-based, low-VOC inks and acid-free papers that are recycled, totally chlorine-free, or partly composed of nonwood fibers. For further information, visit our website at cornellpress.cornell.edu.

To the memory of two teachers of integrity

Hippocrates G. Apostle
and
John M. Crossett

Contents

PREFACE ix

ACKNOWLEDGMENTS xi

PART 1. PLATO AND HIS READERS

1. WAS PLATO A PLATONIST? 3
   Plato and Platonism 6
   Ur-Platonism 9
   From Plato to Platonism 19

2. SOCRATES AND PLATONISM 34
   The 'Socratic Problem' 39
   Gregory Vlastos 53
   Terry Penner 62
   Christopher Rowe 68

3. READING THE DIALOGUES PLATONICALLY 73
   Plato and Developmentalism 75
   Plato the Artist, Plato the Philosopher 83
   Plato's Self-Testimony 91

4. ARISTOTLE ON PLATO AND PLATONISM 97
   Aristotle and Ur-Platonism 102
   Aristotle's Testimony on the Mathematization of Forms 113
   Aristotle's Criticism of the Mathematization of Forms 125

PART 2. THE CONTINUING CREATION OF PLATONISM

5. THE OLD ACADEMY 133
    Speusippus and First Principles 134
    Speusippean Knowledge 143
    Xenocrates 154

6. THE ACADEMIC SKEPTICS 163
    What Is Academic Skepticism? 165
    Skepticism, Rationalism, and Platonism 172

7. PLATONISM IN THE 'MIDDLE' 179
    Antiochus of Ascalon 181
    Plutarch of Chaeronea 187
    Alcinous 195

8. NUMENIUS OF APAMEA 208
    On the Good 210

PART 3. PLOTINUS: "EXEGETE OF THE PLATONIC REVELATION"

9. PLATONISM AS A SYSTEM 227
    The First Principle of All 229
    Intellect 237
    Soul 242
    Matter 245

10. PLOTINUS AS INTERPRETER OF PLATO (1) 255
    Matter in the Platonic System 257
    Substance and Becoming 263
    Categories in the Intelligible World 270
    The One and the Indefinite Dyad 276
    The Good Is Eros 280

11. PLOTINUS AS INTERPRETER OF PLATO (2) 283
    Human and Person 284
    Assimilation to the Divine 293
    Moral Responsibility 299

CONCLUSION 305

BIBLIOGRAPHY 311

GENERAL INDEX 329

INDEX LOCORUM 335

Preface

In 2005, I published a book titled *Aristotle and Other Platonists*. In that book, I explored the idea, virtually ubiquitous in late antiquity, that Aristotle's philosophy was in "harmony" with Platonism. Although I did try to explicate the harmonists' account of the nature of Platonism, I had little to say about whether that account was accurate. In short, I largely sidestepped the tendentious question "Was Plato a Platonist?" The present work is an attempt to answer that question, or at the very least to show that an affirmative answer is not nearly as implausible as it is often taken to be. In searching for an approach to my question that is minimally non-question-begging, I have been led to reconsider a number of modern assumptions regarding the Platonic dialogues and their relation to Platonism, the relation between Platonism and a putative Socratic philosophy, and the direct and indirect testimony of ancient philosophers regarding Platonism, in particular that of Aristotle. The first part of the book is taken up mainly with the critical examination of these assumptions. In part 2, I examine the "construction" of various versions of Platonism in the Old Academy, and among the 'Middle' Platonists. In these chapters, I face the problem of why, indeed, there are different versions of Platonism if Plato's disciples were in fact aiming to be faithful to the teachings of the master. For anyone inclined to the affirmative answer to my main question, this problem cannot be avoided. As Sextus Empiricus said of dogmatists in general, their disagreement among themselves is one of the best possible arguments for skepticism. So, too, if Platonists disagree, does this not at least suggest that with regard to the question of whether Plato was a Platonist, there is in fact no truth of the matter? There is a considerable literature that takes the dialogues as ink blots for a philosophical Rorschach test. And it cannot be denied that among some self-described followers of Plato, contradictory views about certain matters are held. Nevertheless, I aim to show that behind such disagreements as existed there was a profound agreement about first principles and that assent to the elements of *that* agreement is what Platonism was always thought to be. In part 3, I try to show that in Plotinus we have, as Proclus insisted, the most authentic and insightful "exegete of the Platonic revelation." This is true, I argue, both in his construction of the Platonic system and in his demonstration of how that system is the ultimate basis for many of the solutions that Plato gives to the philosophical problems he raises.

The tenor of this work undoubtedly amounts to swimming against some currents of contemporary scholarship, although probably not as much as it would have a generation ago. It amounts to challenging some orthodoxies of Platonic interpretation, especially as these are still found in North America. And it amounts to a willingness to explore a hypothesis according to which 'Platonism' is the name of a well-articulated philosophical position and not just the label for the "sum total" of Plato's literary product. As much as this book is explicitly rooted in the minutiae of the history of ancient philosophy, its constant overarching goal is to bring history and philosophy into fruitful collaboration.

All translations are my own except where noted.

Acknowledgments

It is a considerable pleasure for me to acknowledge the gracious assistance of numerous colleagues in the writing of this book. George Boys-Stones, John Dillon, Rafael Ferber, Franco Ferrari, Francesco Fronterotta, Jens Halfwassen, Brad Inwood, Debra Nails, Dominic O'Meara, Jan Opsomer, Nicholas Smith, and Harold Tarrant read either the whole of the draft of the book or significant portions of it, and many of them corresponded with me regarding particular technical matters. I very much doubt that any one of these learned colleagues agrees with all or most of what I have written. I know—and they certainly know, too—that they have saved me from many egregious errors. What better definition of a colleague is there than this? As always, I am indebted to my beloved wife, Asli Gocer, who never let her love dampen her professional criticism, or vice versa. This book is dedicated to the memory of two former teachers, Hippocrates G. Apostle and John M. Crossett, who gave me all the best that a small liberal arts college has to offer. Finally, this book was written with the generous support of the Social Sciences and Humanities Research Council of Canada.

PART 1

Plato and His Readers

CHAPTER 1

Was Plato a Platonist?

Was Plato a Platonist? A cheeky question, perhaps. If by "Platonist" we mean "a follower of Plato," then the question is entirely captious. Plato was no more a Platonist than Jesus was a Christian. The question is only marginally more illuminating if we take it to mean "Would Plato have agreed with one or another of the historical, systematic representations of his philosophy?" Naturally, this question, like all questions about counterfactuals in the history of philosophy, is unanswerable. But if the question means "Do we possess evidence that supports the view that Plato's own philosophy was in substantial agreement with that of one or another soi-disant Platonists?" then, according to many scholars, we are in a relatively good position to give a definite answer to the question. And the answer is unequivocally no, Plato was not a Platonist. In this book, I present the case that the correct answer is more likely to be yes.

The term 'Platonism' is used today in roughly three ways. One of these refers to a philosophical position in the philosophy of mathematics and in contemporary metaphysics that is only loosely connected with any historical philosophical view.[1] This use of the term I will mostly leave aside. The term 'Platonism' is, second, also used to refer loosely to whatever is found in Plato's dialogues. It is important, as I will explain in a moment, that those who use the term in this way both mean to refer exclusively to the dialogues and do not necessarily make the claim that 'Platonism' used in this way refers

---

1. See Brown 2012, 98–107, for a contemporary defense of what Brown calls Platonism in mathematics over against naturalism. Brown concentrates on the immaterial and eternal existence of "mathematical objects and facts."

to one consistent philosophical position. Thus, 'Platonism' is the label for whatever Plato said or can be gleaned to have meant through the use of his literary characters—Socrates and the rest. Those who use the term 'Platonism' in this way divide over whether Plato's views ever changed or "developed" throughout the course of his literary career. Those who claim to discern some development are, typically, referred to as 'developmentalists,' and those who deny that there is any or any substantial development are called 'unitarians.' I will have a good deal more to say about these two positions and their common use of the term 'Platonism' in the next chapter. For now, it is sufficient to distinguish this use of the term from another. In its third use, 'Platonism' refers to a consistent or at least comprehensive philosophical position maintained by followers of Plato, or 'Platonists.' Followers of Plato perhaps started declaring themselves to be Platonists—or were so designated by others—beginning in the first century BCE.² By the first century CE, the self-designation was not uncommon. But even prior to the first century BCE, the absence of the term 'Platonist' (Πλατωνικός) certainly does not indicate that there were no followers of Plato who embraced 'Platonism' in this sense. What distinguishes this use of the term from the previous use is, among other things, the belief that Platonism extends beyond the dialogues. That is, elements of Platonism can be found in the testimony of Plato's disciples—especially Aristotle—and also possibly within an oral tradition handed down from Plato himself through a chain of Academy members or "heads."³

The use of the term 'Platonism' in this third sense is not in itself especially contentious. Contention immediately arises, however, if it is claimed that Platonism in this sense has anything to do with Platonism in the second sense. For to claim that the self-declared Platonists of antiquity embraced a philosophical position that is in essence the position that Plato himself embraced is to immediately open oneself to a barrage of criticisms. Though it may be conceded that 'Platonism' thus used may be inspired by or in some way have its roots in the Platonism of the dialogues, the idea that these are

---

2. See Cicero, *ND* 1.73, where the interlocutor Velleius refers to a pupil of Plato as *Platonicus*. According to Glucker (1978, 206–25), philosophers began to call themselves 'Platonists' in the second century CE. Prior to that, disciples of Plato were typically called 'Academics.' This term poses a problem when used both of a 'dogmatic' follower of Plato, like Antiochus of Ascalon, and of the so-called Academic Skeptics. In what sense, if any, were the latter followers of Plato? See below. Glucker (ibid., 225) postulates as an explanation of the change from the use of the term *Academici* to *Platonici* in the second century the connotation of skepticism associated with the former during the last three centuries BCE.

3. Efforts to "connect the doxographical dots" between Xenocrates or Polemo and, say, Antiochus of Ascalon face an almost insurmountable wall of evidentiary silence. On the other hand, neither Philo of Alexandria, Plutarch of Chaeronea, nor Alcinous—all systematic Platonists in some sense—give the impression of being particularly original in their constructions of versions of Platonism. It is, in my opinion, difficult to maintain the view that Stoics and Academic Skeptics were the sole transmitters of Platonic doctrine to these admittedly rather distant disciples of Plato.

identical or nearly so seems far-fetched. In fact, the basically vacuous term 'Middle Platonism' and the originally pejorative term 'Neoplatonism' were coined to mark the putative difference between Plato's own Platonism and what his disciples made out of that.[4] It is perhaps worth stressing, though not with the intention of special pleading, that Plato's disciples grouped under these two labels did not think of themselves as innovative or revolutionary or revisionist; they thought that they were articulating and defending and perhaps applying to new philosophical and religious challenges the philosophy found in the dialogues and, as indicated above, beyond the dialogues as well.

A not unreasonable response to this observation is that what these disciples thought they were doing need not impede us in a correct assessment of what they were actually doing, which is, from one perspective, something quite different from providing an exposition and defense of the pure stream of Plato's thought. Indeed, we may plausibly add that in antiquity innovation was not especially valued; on the contrary, it was often held suspect. Accordingly, what may in fact have been innovative may either not have appeared so to proponents of the innovation or, if it did, there was motivation enough to conceal this. Nevertheless, if we could arrive at a perspicuous articulation of the Platonism of the disciples, we might be in a better position to see exactly where they went off the rails, so to speak. But, of course, to express the task in this way makes evident the obvious problem, namely, how do we articulate the "authentic" version of Plato's philosophy found in the dialogues for the purposes of comparison?

One view has it that there are no philosophical position in the dialogues—at least none that reflect the beliefs of their author—and on this view, it would be vain to seek for Platonism there.[5] That this view is, prima facie, an extreme one hardly counts against it. Perhaps it only appears to be extreme in comparison with views that only seem (incorrectly) reasonable or moderate. Though I will argue in the next chapter that this view is in fact untenable and incoherent, it does at any rate intensify the force of the challenge to show that there is any one philosophical position in the dialogues. By contrast, the developmentalists and the unitarians are in principle congenial to hearing an exposition of Plato's philosophy (or, in the former case, perhaps we should say "iterations of Plato's philosophy"), though they are more than a little resistant to the idea that this exposition will turn up

---

4. See, e.g., Gadamer (1985, 2:508), who declares bluntly: "Platon war kein Platoniker." Dodds (1928, 129) sees in the failure to distinguish Platonism from Neoplatonism the source of multiple misunderstandings of the philosophy of Plotinus. Ryle (1966, 9–10) writes, "If Plato was anything of a philosopher, then he cannot have been merely a lifelong Platonist." Ryle here takes a particularly narrow view of what Platonism is.

5. See, e.g., Press 2000, the subtitle of which is "Studies in Platonic Anonymity." In the introduction to this collection of essays, Press provides a useful survey of various scholarly positions that take "Platonic anonymity" to be virtually equivalent in meaning to the "non-doctrinal" nature of the dialogues.

something that is identical to a position held by philosophers some fifty or two hundred or five hundred or even eight hundred years later.[6]

I want to distinguish the above challenge from the challenge that developmentalists and unitarians set for themselves in offering expositions of Plato's philosophy. For when they refer to 'Platonism' they typically mean something that, by definition, can be found only in the dialogues. According to the other use of the term, Platonism is indeed found in the dialogues, but these dialogues are a record or expression of Platonism understood more broadly; Platonism is not an inductive generalization from the data of the dialogues. This makes a considerable difference, as we will see. The claim that "Plato's philosophy" is just the "sum" of what we find in the dialogues is fundamentally different from the claim that the dialogues are the best evidence we have for Plato's philosophy. It is my contention in this book that the former claim is false and the latter is true. In addition, if Platonism is the philosophical position that Plato expressed, it does not follow that Plato was even the first to express it or that all subsequent expressions come from him or that he expressed it best (though I know of no Platonists who did not think *that*). It is only a trick of language that leads us to believe that Plato could not be a Platonist in this sense. For 'Platonism' substitute 'wisdom' or 'truth about the world' and it becomes immediately obvious that from the perspective of self-declared Platonists, it is reasonable to claim that Plato was a stellar Platonist.

Henceforth, for the purposes of clarity I will substitute for the term 'Platonism' the term 'Plato's philosophy' when using it to refer to what is believed to be found exclusively in the dialogues. My central theme is, then, how Platonism is related to Plato's philosophy.

Plato and Platonism

I have hitherto used the vague descriptors 'position' or 'view' for what I am now calling 'Plato's philosophy,' ignoring the obvious objection that there is a multitude of philosophical positions in the dialogues. After all, a 'philosophical position' can be a bare philosophical claim more or less limited in scope or one argument for that claim. In this sense, there are countless philosophical positions in the dialogues, including those held by Socrates' interlocutors. On the view of developmentalists, there is no direct historically justified inference from the discovery of one of these positions to any other anywhere else in the dialogues. It may be the case that Plato maintained A in one dialogue; it is an open question whether he continued to maintain A in any other dialogue, or at least in any other dialogue in some antecedently postulated subsequent phase of his writing career. For example—and most obviously—to argue that in *Phaedo* and *Republic* Plato maintained something

---

6. See Brittain 2011, 530–41, for a helpful survey of the traditional periodization of the history of Platonism.

called a 'theory of Forms' is one thing; to maintain that this theory is part of the philosophical position that later came to be embraced and defended by disciples of Plato and that Plato was himself always a Platonist because he embraced Platonism thus understood is quite another. To take another obvious example, Socrates in *Apology* seems to evince agnosticism about the afterlife; Socrates in *Phaedo* argues for the immortality of the soul. Are either (or both) of these 'positions' attributable to Plato?

There does not seem to be an obvious non-question-begging way of distinguishing Platonism from Plato's philosophy inductively by examination of the dialogues. Indeed, the problem of question-begging infects the inductive approach itself, since the salience that one gives to one claim rather than another must itself rest on some antecedently arrived-at view of what Platonism is. The epitome of this approach is paraphrase masquerading as philosophy. But failing to make such a distinction, the question of whether Plato was a Platonist has a banal positive answer. If, though, we are able to see our way to such a distinction, then the question of whether Plato was a Platonist at least becomes a substantive one.

In 1908, the great French scholar Léon Robin published a book titled *La théorie platonicienne des idées et des nombres d'après Aristote*.[7] The book was an attempt to reconstruct Platonism entirely from evidence outside the dialogues, specifically, from Aristotle's testimony. This methodology was intended precisely to avoid a question-begging inductive approach to the doctrines of the dialogues. One of Robin's most notable conclusions is that, in line with Aristotle's testimony, there are strong indications that Plato was tending toward what Robin calls 'Neoplatonism,' which is exactly what I am calling 'Platonism.'[8] I will in the third chapter have more to say about this conclusion and a number of others reached by Robin.

For now, I want to focus only on a problem with Robin's methodology. That problem is that by deriving an account of Plato's thought based exclusively on Aristotle's testimony, Robin necessarily occludes the distinction between Platonism *tout court* and Plato's own version of Platonism—if that is a suitable term for Plato's philosophy. There is no doubt that Platonists of antiquity

---

7. Robin (1908) thinks that Aristotle's testimony applies specifically to Plato's philosophy after his writing *Parmenides*. Hence, Robin's view is developmentalist.

8. See Robin 1908, 600: "Aristote nous a mis sur la voie d'une interprétation néoplatonicienne de la philosophie de son maître." The conclusion is echoed by De Vogel 1953, 54: "The studies of the last generations concerning the sense of later Platonism, and especially of the doctrine of Ideal Numbers, has led us to the insight that Platonism must be understood in a Neoplatonic sense, and that Neoplatonism should be regarded, in its essence, as a legitimate Platonism." For a complete repudiation of this conclusion, see Dörrie 1976, who argues that Platonism was reconstructed in a new phase after a break in the tradition more or less stretching 150 years from Cicero to Plutarch. Consequently, the rise of Neoplatonism really does constitute an innovation. Dörrie (45–47) sees the "rediscovery" of Plato's *Timaeus* and the focus on its apparent creationism as crucial for providing a foundation for the innovation. Dörrie appears to give no weight to the Aristotelian testimony as providing the sought-for "bridge" between Plato and Neoplatonism.

assumed such a distinction as odd as it might sound to us. The apparent oddness of speaking of Plato's version of Platonism disappears once we realize that the term 'Platonism' is not one the self-declared followers of Plato used, at least at first. If one maintains that Platonism as described by Aristotle is identical with Plato's philosophy, then there is nothing to occlude. If, though, as I maintain, 'Platonism' and 'Platonist' are just labels for a basic or general philosophical position and an adherent of that position, then it is absolutely crucial to distinguish Plato's version of this from the position itself. As we will see, one of Robin's other conclusions—namely, that Aristotle misinterprets Plato on a number of basic points—rests on the conflation of Platonism and Plato's version of it. Indeed, as Robin himself concedes, Aristotle's criticism of Plato frequently rests on Aristotle's own Platonic assumptions. On the hypothesis of the proprietary nature of the label 'Platonism,' we can distinguish Platonism from Plato's version of it, at which point the seeming paradox of Aristotle criticizing Plato from a Platonic perspective disappears.

Aristotle's testimony is indispensable for determining the nature of Platonism as distinct from Plato's version of it for the simple reason that Aristotle was himself a Platonist.[9] Admittedly, this claim is not self-evident to everyone. I hope it will appear closer to being obvious rather than nonsensical once we make the above distinction. Aristotle's version of Platonism is indeed at odds with Plato's on many points. This does not even begin to undermine the claim that they were both Platonists. Take the following comparison. Martin Luther was certainly at odds with the Roman Catholic Church on many issues. This opposition has for a long time obscured the deep underlying harmony of Lutheranism and Catholicism on fundamental theological principles. Nevertheless, within the last two decades experts on both sides of this divide have come to the conclusion that there has always been an underlying harmony of principles despite the divergence in their application. Similarly, Aristotle's 'Protestantism' can be understood as set in opposition to Plato's 'Catholicism.' Often, this has been the case for extraneous reasons of a polemical nature. Yet if our aim is to understand the philosophical position that dominated philosophy for the largest part of its history, it certainly behooves us to step back from polemics and concentrate instead on the harmony that underlies the multitude of expressions of this position. If we can do this, one immediate bonus, or so I will attempt to show, is a better understanding of these various expressions.

So, if it turns out that Platonism is, to put it modestly, not a distortion of Plato's philosophy, this will require us yet to distinguish Platonism from Plato's philosophy, showing how the latter is actually one version of the former.

---

9. This is the thesis argued for in Gerson 2005. Among later Platonists, Aristotle's preeminence in matters of natural philosophy was recognized even though he contradicts Plato on numerous points. Therein is to be found an important clue as to how these Platonists thought of the nature of Platonism.

Ur-Platonism

As a preliminary to the examination of Aristotle's testimony, I want to begin with a hypothetical reconstruction of what I will call 'Ur-Platonism' (UP). This is the general philosophical position that arises from the conjunction of the negations of the philosophical positions explicitly rejected in the dialogues, that is, the philosophical positions on offer in the history of philosophy accessible to Plato himself. It is well known that Plato in the dialogues engages critically with most of the philosophers who preceded him.[10] Some of these, like Parmenides and Protagoras, exercise his intellect more than others, including probably some unnamed ones as well as some unknown to us. All of these philosophers, with the exception of Socrates, are represented as holding views that are firmly rejected in the dialogues either explicitly or implicitly.[11] It matters little for my purpose if Plato misrepresented or misunderstood some of these philosophers, though I do assume that he did neither of these things. I am not claiming that anyone, including Plato, simply embraced UP. I am, however, claiming that Platonism in general can be usefully thought of as arising out of the matrix of UP, and that Plato's philosophy is one version of Platonism.[12] So, in a manner of speaking, UP is a *via negativa* to Plato's philosophy. To be a Platonist is, minimally, to have

---

10. D.L. 3.25, says that "since Plato was the first to attack nearly all of his predecessors, one wonders why he did not mention Democritus." In the subsequent chapter on Democritus (9.36), Diogenes quotes Democritus as saying that "I came to Athens and no one knew me." At 9.40, however, Diogenes, relying on an account of Aristoxenus, says that Plato did in fact know of the works of Democritus but was unwilling to controvert him in writing owing to Democritus's eminence. Herrmann 2005 argues that Democritus does appear—anonymously—in Plato's *Timaeus,* particularly as a representative of those who think that necessity (ἀνάγκη) governs all change. Herrmann (2007, 239–43 and 332–34, n. 467) adds an argument that *Phd.* 95E–105E is responding to an (unidentified) account of causality in Democritus and to the older philosopher's use of the term ἰδέα. If Herrmann is right, then virtually all of Plato's illustrious predecessors do in fact make appearances in the dialogues, even if some do so anonymously. See Magrin 2010, who shows that Plotinus's analysis of the nature of the receptacle in Plato's *Timaeus* and of its relation to cognition assumes that Plato is using Democritus as a foil in that dialogue. See also Morel 2002. Hussey (2012, 36) presents a suggestive argument that Aristotle initially undervalued the work of the Atomists himself and came only in his later works to see the full force of the Atomist position. If this is the case, it is not implausible that Plato, too, underrated the Atomists.

11. In *Tht.* 183E, Socrates declines to criticize Parmenides' claim that all change is unreal after criticizing extreme Heracliteanism. The criticism of Parmenides is taken up again in *Soph.* 244B–245E, which, though not directly a criticism of the claim that change is unreal, is a criticism of the claim that "all is one," which would, it seems, have as a consequence that change is unreal.

12. D.L. 1.20, says the term αἵρεσις ("sect" or "school of thought") is used for those "who in their attitude towards appearance (τὸ φαινόμενον) follow or seem to follow some principle." He adds that the term is also used for "a bias (πρόσκλισιν) in favor of coherent positive doctrines." Diogenes refers to the earlier historian Hippobotus who lists nine αἱρέσεις including the Old Academy. What I am calling UP may be understood in this context as a proto-αἵρεσις. The "unity" of the Old Academy (and those who came after) is a unity of a proto-αἵρεσις. I thereby leave room to account for the specific differences among individual

a commitment to UP. It is only a slight step further to recognize that this basic commitment is virtually always in fact conjoined with a commitment to discover the most consistent, integrated, positive metaphysical construct on the basis of UP. That is what Platonism is.

Since I am not claiming that Plato was an Ur-Platonist simpliciter, or merely an Ur-Platonist, I do not think I am subject to the above question-begging objection. What I want to show is that the substance of Plato's thought as inductively arrived at by both developmentalists and unitarians can be seen to be built up from UP. More contentiously, and potentially more important, I will argue that we can give a better account of Plato's philosophy than either developmentalists or unitarians can give if and only if we see that as a working out of the positive side of UP, that is, as a working out of what follows positively from the conjunction or unification of the denials of the positions of his predecessors. My hypothesis will also enhance our understanding of differences among Platonists, for as we will see, the further we go along a deductive line from the central idea of a first principle or principles of all, the less are the consequences or implications uniquely determined. Thus, it is perfectly possible that some Platonists should agree on first principles but disagree on what follows from these for, say, ethics or human psychology. It is equally possible that some non-Platonists, for example, Stoics, should arrive at conclusions about such matters that are similar or even identical to those of some Platonists even if they start from diametrically opposed principles.

UP is an ahistorical or theoretical framework for analysis, potentially open to a charge of being anachronistic. It should be noted that Plato himself employs such ahistorical frameworks for considering the views of his predecessors. For example, in *Republic* "lovers of sights and sounds," apparently referring to no one in particular, are contrasted with philosophers; in *Sophist* pluralists and monists, idealists and materialists are lumped together ahistorically for criticism; and, indeed, the term 'sophist,' famously made a pejorative by Plato, is used to refer to those who actually held different views. In this regard, Aristotle just follows Plato in his categorization of various philosophical positions in order to submit them to criticism. The justification for my ahistorical hypothesis will, I hope, emerge as we proceed. Adherence to UP and to an integrated, systematic construct on its basis is what all Platonists share. Disagreements among these same Platonists are, I will try to show, best explained by the fact that this systematic construct does not decisively determine the correct answer to many specific philosophical problems raised especially by opponents of Platonism.

The elements of UP according to my hypothesis are antimaterialism, antimechanism, antinominalism, antirelativism, and antiskepticism. Much more will be said about the details of each of these 'antis' and their conjunction. For the present, a rough sketch will suffice.

---

philosophers despite this unity. See Glucker 1978, 166–92, on the uses of the term αἵρεσις in antiquity.

Antimaterialism is the view that it is false that the only things that exist are bodies and their properties. Thus, to admit that the surface of a body is obviously not a body is not thereby to deny materialism. The antimaterialist maintains that there are entities that exist that are not bodies and that exist independently of bodies. Thus, for the antimaterialist, the question "Is the soul a body or a property of a body?" is not a question with an obvious answer since it is possible that the answer is no.[13] The further question of how an immaterial soul might be related to a body belongs to the substance of the positive response to UP, or to one or another version of Platonism.

Antimechanism is the view that the only sort of explanations available in principle to a materialist are inadequate for explaining the natural order. What, then, distinguishes materialism from mechanism? It would be possible to be an antimaterialist yet still believe that all explanations are mechanical. Such might be the position of an occasionalist. Conversely, it would be possible to believe that materialism is true, but also maintain that there are nonmechanical explanations of some sort, say, at the quantum level.[14] Antimechanism, though, seems to be derived from antimaterialism. That is, having rejected the view that everything that exists is a body or an attribute of a body, the way is open to propose non-bodily explanations for bodily or material phenomena. One way to understand antimechanism is as the denial of one version of what we have come to call "the causal closure principle," that is, the principle that physical or material causes are necessary and sufficient for all events in the physical world.[15] Although contemporary denials of this principle are generally

13. See esp. *Soph.* 246A–248A; *Lg.* 891C1–4. Cornford (1934, 231–32) thinks that when Plato is criticizing materialists in *Sophist*, he means to include Atomists, who are nowhere explicitly named in the dialogues. I agree with Cornford that it is unlikely that Plato did not know about Democritus and Leucippus or that their materialism is not implicitly rejected in the *Sophist* passage.

14. Plato in *Phaedo* seems to hold that Anaxagoras tried to be an antimechanist but failed because he was a materialist. The "simple hypothesis" of Socrates in response to Anaxagoras (99D4–100A3) is an especially clear example of the beginning of an effort to construct the positive response that is based on UP. It combines all the elements of UP including, implicitly, antirelativism.

15. It is a version of the causal closure principle that is implicitly rejected at *Tim.* 47E–48B, where it is νοῦς that overrules ἀνάγκη in the generation of the cosmos. I take it that Stoic incorporeals, namely, place, void, time, and sayables, precisely because they do not causally interact with anything, do not provide a means of separating materialism and mechanism. See Cicero, *Acad.* 1.39 (= *SVF* 1.90); Sextus, *M.* 8.263 (= *SVF* 2.363); Cleomedes (= *SVF* 2.541) on how the positing of incorporeals by the Stoics does not undermine causal closure. For the most explicit statement of the Stoic causal closure principle, see Stobaeus 1.138.14–139.4 (= *SVF* 1.89 and 2.336): ἀδύνατον δ' εἶναι τὸ μὲν αἴτιον παρεῖναι, οὗ δέ ἐστιν αἴτιον μὴ ὑπάρχειν (it is impossible for the cause to be present and that of which it is the cause not to exist) (1.138.15–16). Here, of course, τὸ αἴτιον refers exclusively to material or corporeal efficient cause or causes. Cf. Alexander of Aphrodisias, *De fato* 22.191.30–192.8; 21–24. Seneca, *Ep.* 65.11, includes time and place as necessary conditions for causal interaction, criticizing Platonists for not including these. See Plato, *Phd.* 99A–B. Seneca does not think these necessary conditions are real causes, but he thinks that Platonists in their expansive understanding

focused on supposed mental events having at least no sufficient physical causes, antimechanism takes the stronger position that even admittedly physical events are not comprehensively accounted for by physical causes.

An antimechanist in antiquity generally relies on the principle that an ultimate or adequate explanation for a phenomenon must be a different sort of thing from that which is in need of an explanation. Thus, the principle of number, one, is not a number. Accordingly, one might argue that since the properties of bodies are not bodies, there is nothing in principle amiss in using bodies for accounting for these properties. Helen's beauty, say, is accounted for by her body, perhaps by emerging from or supervening on it. In order to make this work, and to remain within the confines of the principle that that which explains must be different from that which is explained, it is necessary to maintain that the body itself, and not *other* properties of the body, is the explanation for the beauty. If it were other properties, then the original principle would be violated. But of course this way leads to shipwreck. For we either continue to explain properties by properties or we explain properties by bodies, but since the bodies are only differentiated by their properties, the explanation for Helen's beauty will be the same sort of explanation as the explanation for Socrates' virtue. Antimechanism and antimaterialism are distinct views, though within the versions of Platonism that arise from UP, they are always held to be mutually supporting.[16] Along with antimaterialism, the exploration of the nature of explanation in an antimechanist framework belongs to a positive construct on the basis of UP.

Antinominalism is the view that it is false that the only things that exist are individuals, each uniquely situated in space and time.[17] Nominalism can be local or general, denying the existence of anything other than individuals within one kind of thing or denying their existence generally. It can also be extreme, by denying that there can even be a multiplicity of individuals, since in that case each one would be the same as the other in virtue of the fact that it is one. The antinominalist thus allows that two or more individuals can be the same and still be unique individuals. He thus allows 'conceptual space' for sameness that is not identity. By contrast,

---

of causality should include them. Sedley (1993, 317) argues that "the Stoic causal nexus, far from being mechanical, exhibits to a quite astonishing degree the meticulous workings of an intelligent teleology." Similarly, Bobzien (1998a, 48) finds in Chrysippus's account of determinism "an element of teleology, rationality, organization, and order," though she goes on to argue (53–56) for the "combination" of the teleological and mechanistic aspects of Stoic determinism.

16. Thus, the acceptance of the existence of immaterial entities strengthens the challenge to the causal closure principle.

17. As I will explain at greater length below, I take the Eleatic monism in *Parm.* 127D–128D as the central target of Plato's antinominalism. The target is absolutely clear since Eleaticism is unqualified nominalism—not even two things can exist if from this it follows that they will be the same in each being one. Antisthenes may also be a target. See *Soph.* 251A–C. See Allen 1983, 79–80 on Eleaticism as a form of nominalism.

the nominalist maintains that if two things are the same, then they are identical; if two things are not identical, they cannot be the same. An antinominalist could insist on the reality of the phenomenon of sameness in difference and yet deny that there is an explanation for this, claiming rather that it is just a brute fact. Platonists generally associate the acceptance of the phenomenon with at least the possibility of giving a substantive causal explanation for it.[18]

Antirelativism is the denial of the claim that Plato attributes to Protagoras that "man is the measure of all things, of what is that it is and of what is not that it is not."[19] The claim is expressed in two forms in the dialogues: one epistemological and one ethical. Epistemological relativism is not skepticism; hence, the denial of this form of relativism is not a denial of skepticism. One may, after all, be skeptical of the possibility of acquiring knowledge about properties that may well be objective. Relativism is the view that 'true' just means 'true for me' or 'what appears true to me' or 'true for some particular group.' The ethical form of relativism maintains that 'good' just means 'good for me' or 'good for the group' where good is determined by or constituted by a mental state or states, roughly, pleasure broadly conceived. Thus, ethical relativism is virtually hedonism in some variety. The denial of ethical relativism—individual or social—holds that what is good is determinable independently not of what is good for someone, but of what appears to that person as good for him. Thus, the antirelativist can maintain that 'good' is the same as 'good for x' so long as she insists that 'good for x' is not equivalent to what x claims is good for x. A similar point can be made about epistemological relativism. An alternative way of expressing ethical antirelativism is to maintain that goodness is a property of being; for epistemological antirelativism, the analogue is truth is a property of being. For the Platonist, the logical connection between goodness and truth is accounted for by being itself.

Antiskepticism is the view that knowledge is possible. Knowledge (ἐπιστήμη) refers to a mode of cognition wherein the real is in some way "present" to the cognizer. The skeptic does not maintain that cognition generally is impossible, but only that knowledge is. According to the argument we get in the dialogues, if either materialism or nominalism were true, skepticism would follow because it would not be possible for the real to be present to any cognizer; there could only be representations of some

---

18. The rejection of nominalism presupposes the falsity of extreme Heracliteanism. If everything were always in flux in every way, things could not have properties. I do not, however, list the rejection of extreme Heracliteanism as one of the central elements of UP because Plato agrees that sensibles are in some sense always becoming if not becoming in all ways. To be able to show that an account of sameness in difference is possible is, along with the evidence of the senses, sufficient to remove any reasonable motivation for extreme Heracliteanism.

19. We learn from Sextus Empiricus, *M.* 7.60 (cf. Plato, *Tht.* 161C3) that this claim comes from Protagoras's book *On Truth*.

sort of the real, representations whose accuracy would be indeterminable.[20] Throughout the dialogues, Plato has Socrates rail against sophists, rhetoricians, and various demagogues who share at best a cavalier attitude toward the need for knowledge of any sort.[21] Plato's antiskepticism assumes the legitimacy of such attacks.

There is, as I have already admitted, no way of decisively proving that Plato, apart from the dialogues, actually embraced these elements of UP. The best I can do is show how much of the actual form and content of the dialogues make sense when we see them as built on a conjunction of the above five 'antis' and an attempt to unify them in some way. But it is worth here pointing out, I think, that if Plato is, say, a crypto-materialist, masquerading as an antimaterialist, that would make him the worst kind of sophist. It would make his apparently relentless condemnation of sophistry and 'counterfeit philosophy' in the dialogues more than ironic. It would suggest a man with a psychological makeup that can be characterized only as pathological. And more to the point, it would suggest that the man for whom Aristotle had the greatest respect was basically a fraud. Yet there is no evidence whatsoever that Aristotle thought this to be the case or that he took Plato as anything other than a serious philosopher, indeed, the touchstone of his own philosophy.

Obviously, there is a large but not infinite range of possible positions consistent with being antimaterialist, antimechanist, antinominalist, antirelativist, or antiskeptic. For example, an antinominalist is not necessarily an antimaterialist, as I have defined that. The antinominalist position known as 'conceptualism' does not entail that concepts are immaterial entities as opposed to properties of material entities. Nor is an antimaterialist necessarily an antinominalist, as is evident, for instance, in the philosophy of, say, William of Ockham. Nor is an antimechanist necessarily an antinominalist. If, though, we begin to explore logical or explanatory connections among the five 'antis,' the range of positions begins to narrow. Thus, if one is an antimaterialist because one is an antinominalist, a number of possible positions are eliminated. For the UP of the dialogues, antimaterialism is, for example, entailed by the only possible explanation for the supposed datum of two nonidentical things nevertheless being the same.

Continuing along this line of thought, ethical or epistemological antirelativism does not require the embrace of antimaterialism or antinominalism.

---

20. The so-called Recollection Argument in *Phd.*72E3–78B3 provides a sort of transcendental argument against skepticism, showing that certain cognitive acts in which we manifestly engage would not be possible if we did not already possess ἐπιστήμη. I take *Theaetetus*, despite its aporetic conclusion, to attempt to provide the necessary foundation for an adequate response to the skeptic. That response begins, naturally enough from a Platonic perspective, with an account of what ἐπιστήμη is.

21. *Phdr.* 259E–274B is a particularly vivid and wide-ranging attack on those who disregard knowledge in the practice of their craft. As we learn from 272D2–273A1, the pursuit of 'the likely' (τὸ εἰκός) is not an acceptable substitute for the pursuit of knowledge.

If, however, it turns out that the only way to make plausible the justification for a claim about the objectivity of the good or of reality itself is to hypothesize the existence of an immaterial entity, commitment to antirelativism at least provides one reason for commitment to antimaterialism.[22] And antinominalism is thereby supported. As we have already seen, antimaterialism at least opens the way for antimechanist explanations. Finally, though antiskepticism is itself the basis for a host of "dogmatisms," among which are many contradictory positions, antiskepticism yields an increasingly focused range of options for one who is also an antimaterialist, antinominalist, and antirelativist.[23]

The appropriate context for connecting all the elements of UP is explanatory. That is, the general reason why Plato rejects nominalism, materialism, etc., is that these positions render impossible the explanation for the phenomena they are supposed to explain. So, for example, the phenomenon of two or more things having an identical property cannot be explained by nominalism. Or the existence of human cognition cannot be explained by materialism. Or the objectivity of human nature cannot be explained by relativism. The elements of UP belong to an explanatory framework. In constructing this framework, Plato is in one respect perfectly in line with his Pre-Socratic predecessors. That is, he assumes that the true explanatory framework will converge on the minimum number of principles.[24] Thus, Plato assumes that nature (φύσις) is an orderly arrangement of its parts (κόσμος). As we will see, this reductivist tendency is a key facet of Platonism. It serves as a constraint on philosophizing within the framework of UP. So a multitude of principles—especially principles that are unrelated—are prima facie suspect with regard to their explanatory power. Just as modern theoretical physics assumes that the four 'fundamental' forces in nature must be explanatorily connected, so those who embraced UP assumed that the elements of their positive constructs needed to be unified in some way. The default unifying framework will be a fundamental metaphysical theory of some sort. Indeed, the principal reason that later Platonists attributed a metaphysical theory to Plato was the assumption that without that it would

---

22. At *Tht.* 186A–E the refutation of Protagorean relativism and hence of the thesis that knowledge is sense perception turns on showing that the possibility of knowledge—that is, cognition of what is objectively—entails the falsity of relativism, the view that what is is reducible to what is for one person or another. Thus, relativism makes knowledge impossible.

23. See *Tim.* 51B–E where the proof of the falsity of materialism goes like this: if νοῦς (intellection or knowledge) is different from true belief, then Forms must exist. But if Forms exist, then materialism is false.

24. Atomism is not really an exception to this, since the reduction of all phenomena to atoms and the void is far more important than the fact that the atoms are infinite in number. See Krämer 1969, 15–18 and 1994, 5–6, who argues that Plato's doctrine of first principles is exclusively the result of his encounter with Eleaticism, and is not a product of general Pre-Socratic reductionism. This seems to me to be implausibly narrow.

not be possible to unify the elements of UP. And without such unification, the positive doctrines would lack a highly desirable mutual support.[25]

Another way to characterize UP is as fundamental antinaturalism, that is, the philosophical position according to which naturalistic or bottom-up explanations for all problematic phenomena are in principle insufficient.[26] The positive construct on the basis of UP may be aptly termed, following Norman Kretzmann, 'Grandest Unified Theory.'[27] Kretzmann's subject is the natural theology of Thomas Aquinas in his *Summa contra Gentiles*, what he characterizes as a "rational investigation of the first principles and most fundamental aspects of reality in general and human nature and behavior in particular" (23). But this characterization aptly expresses the task all Platonists share. UP simply articulates the opposition to the set of philosophical positions that would make this task impossible or at least radically different from what all Platonists took it to be.[28]

The assumption that a positive response to UP will be a unified explanatory framework has an immediate and portentous consequence. This consequence is that the explanatory framework will have to be in some sense hierarchical. The unification will consist in showing that which is in need of an explanation other than itself is explained by that which is not—the 'heteroexplicable' requires the 'autoexplicable,' the 'stopping point' of explanation. As a principle of metaphysics, this means that the autoexplicable has ontological priority over the heteroexplicable. All versions of Platonism

---

25. Cherniss (1936, 456) thinks that the theory of Forms itself provides the requisite unification: "That the necessary and sufficient hypothesis for this sphere [the sensible world] turns out to be the very one needed for ethics and epistemology makes it possible to consider the three spheres of existence, cognition, and value as phases of a single unified cosmos." It is historically implausible in the extreme that any Platonist supposed that the cosmos was "unified" by a multiplicity of Forms. See, contra Cherniss, Krämer 1964b, 85–88.

26. See Brown (2012, chap. 2, "What Is Naturalism?"), who, in the course of an argument for Platonism, understood very roughly along the lines of UP, characterizes naturalism as the position holding that "all facts are natural facts and only natural science can discover and explain them." For Brown, the existence of eternal mathematical truths is the key premise in the argument rejecting naturalism. As Brown goes on to point out (94), "the principal objection to Platonism is epistemic." That is, the denial that ἐπιστήμη, as defined by Plato, is possible. As we will see at various points in this book, part of the reason for the centrality of antiskepticism in the development of versions of Platonism is that the assertion of the possibility of ἐπιστήμη ties together the other elements of UP as does no other.

27. See Kretzmann, 1997, 23–27.

28. The early Stoa represents, in part, an attempt to retain antirelativism and antiskepticism while abandoning the other elements of UP. Later Platonists rejected such an attempt. Thus, Stoics might well make true claims in ethics following from their antirelativism, but the antirelativism was taken to be arbitrary without a consistent metaphysical framework, including antimaterialism, antimechanism, and antinominalism. Porphyry, in his *Life of Plotinus* (14.4), says that "Stoic and Peripatetic doctrines are blended into his writings, though they are not obvious" ('Ἐμμέμικται δ' ἐν τοῖς συγγράμμασι καὶ τὰ Στωικὰ λανθάνοντα δόγματα καὶ τὰ Περιπατητικά). Plotinus, however, also rejects many Stoic doctrines because they rest on false principles, especially materialism.

introduce some sort of hierarchy into the explanatory framework.[29] The basic hierarchy posits the ontological priority of the intelligible realm to the sensible. But this leaves open the difficult question of hierarchy *within* the intelligible and sensible realms. Throughout the history of Platonism, as intrahierarchical analysis proceeded, the complexities pertaining to unification seemed to multiply.

To claim that the elements of UP belong to an explanatory framework over against the frameworks provided by the positions UP rejects leaves open the essential question of the *explananda*. Thus, for example, antinominalism adheres to a principle that nominalism cannot explain the phenomenon of sameness in difference or, stated otherwise, the phenomenon of 'things' possessing properties that they do not exclusively possess. Nominalism is not an alternative explanation for this phenomenon, since it rejects its existence, even its possibility. The positive constructs that constitute the versions of Platonism do not generally engage directly with their opponents over the existence or possibility of such a phenomenon. Indirectly, Platonists seek to show that, in the above example, sameness has a nature different from identity that, if true, makes it at least intelligible how two things that are not identical can yet be the same.

With respect to skepticism, the phenomenon to be explained is obviously not knowledge, but rather rationality, as Sextus Empiricus would so clearly see. Knowledge is not the *explanandum* for the simple reason that even one who believes that knowledge is possible (like Socrates) might well claim not to possess it. The Platonists want to argue that our ability to reason or make rational judgments could not be explained unless we either already possess knowledge or we are capable of possessing knowledge. Knowledge is here the *explanans*, not the *explanandum*. Another way of indicating the phenomenon is to say that humans possess a mode of cognition that animals do not. This mode of cognition—which even the Skeptic manifests in reasoning to the denial of the possibility of knowledge—cannot, the Platonists maintain, be explained unless we are knowers.[30]

The materialist denies the existence of any immaterial entities. The proponent of UP holds that the only possible explanation for the above phenomena requires the rejection of materialism. In this sense, antimaterialism is a derivative or second-order element of UP. It does not offer an explanation for an independently ascertainable phenomenon.[31] Similarly, the mechanist

---

29. See Merlan 1953, 166–77 on the evidence for such hierarchy in Plato, Aristotle, Academics, and later Platonists. Halfwassen (2002b) argues that the very idea of metaphysics as an explanatory science is, according to Plato and all Platonists, based on the necessity of positing an absolutely simple first principle of all. Cf. Reale 1997, 95–107, who finds in *Phd.* 96A–102A "the Magna Carta of Western metaphysics."

30. Heraclitus or Cratylus would seem to deny that the objects of knowledge must be stable. The Platonist's claim that the objects of knowledge cannot be *un*stable is as much a claim about what the ne plus ultra of cognition must be as it is a claim about the nature of the objects of such cognition.

31. At *Soph.* 247B–C, the 'reformed materialists' are said to allow that justice or wisdom, for example, exist and that it is not reasonable to say that they are bodies. But their concession

denies the phenomenon of purpose in nature, something that could be possible only if there were a being or beings capable of making judgments about the future, which in turn is possible only if they possess knowledge or the possibility of acquiring it. Teleology in nature, which is what antimechanism seeks to explain, appears to be a real phenomenon only if antimaterialism is true. And antimaterialism follows from the explanations for the phenomena that constitute antinominalism and antiskepticism.

Finally, antirelativism is supposed to be the starting point for accounting for the phenomena of objective or interpersonal reality. To deny that 'true' is equivalent to 'true for me' is as much as to claim that there is a world independent of any judgments made about it and that things in this world have the property of objective truth.[32] To identify objective reality as a 'phenomenon' that needs to be explained is problematic on at least two counts. First, a phenomenon, as Protagoras would no doubt point out, must be contrasted with reality. Second, what are the grounds for assuming that reality needs any explanation at all? The proper response to the first problem is to show that there is a distinction between epistemic and nonepistemic phenomena. The former entail the existence of objective reality; the latter do not. What Plato and later Platonists maintain is that epistemic phenomena are explicable only if relativism is false. So it is not reality that needs explaining but epistemic phenomena; objective reality is the explanation for these phenomena. The particular task of the Platonist is to show that the explanation for these phenomena so defined is not circular. Naturally, the Platonist will be able to recur to the argument that concludes to the possibility of knowledge to support the noncircularity of the claim that only objective reality explains epistemic phenomena.

A pertinent objection to the above analytic framework is that it is otiose. If, indeed, Plato is a systematic philosopher, we need only start from the elements of the system—in the dialogues and in the indirect tradition—not from a putative matrix, UP, out of which the system arises. In reply to this

---

need not be taken to constitute their abandonment of materialism as I have defined it. For these might be properties of bodies or supervenient on bodily states or dispositions of bodies functionally related to them. The 'hard-line materialists' at 247C–E would be, we are told, inclined to accept the proffered principle of being: whatever has the power (δύναμις) to affect or to be affected in any degree, by the most insignificant agent, even once. These hardliners could accept the existence of justice and wisdom and so on if their ability to affect anything is taken as a corporeal power. This is apparently the Stoic position, perhaps responding to this passage of the dialogue. See Brunschwig 1994, 119–22. Contra Brunschwig, Vogt (2009, 143–45) denies that the Stoics held that being is power; rather, power is taken as a property of bodies. The question "What is being?" is, according to Vogt, not even on the Stoic agenda. I tend to agree with Vogt that speaking of 'Stoic metaphysics' is at best misleading unless, of course, we grant that 'metaphysics' can refer not to a science of being but to the study of ultimate principles and causes. It is the inseparability of the question "What is being?" and the search for ultimate causes and principles that characterizes Platonism.

32. I will discuss Platonism's distinction between truth as an ontological property and a semantic property below.

objection, the main problem with coming to grips with Platonism is arriving at a non-question-begging definition of it. Assuming, charitably, that Plato is himself consistent, how is it that philosophers who disagree about doctrine can both rightfully declare themselves to be followers of Plato? Indeed, how is it that apparent differences in doctrine in the dialogues can all be held to be elements of Platonism? One considered response to the first question is to maintain that fidelity to Platonism is actually a multifarious fidelity to Plato himself.[33] The usual response to the second question is to maintain either that (a) there is no systematic unity throughout the entire corpus; or else (b) that the 'system' is localized to a particular set of dialogues; or that (c) it is detachable from the dialogues altogether. As I will argue, (a), (b), and (c) are unsustainable based on both the indirect evidence and the dialogues themselves. But this fact does not preclude changes in doctrine across dialogues. Nor does it preclude disagreements among Platonists. These changes and disagreements all occur within the commitment to UP and to the construction of a unified system on its foundation. Not only is a commitment to UP what Plato and virtually all Platonists share, but recognizing this commitment allows us to see what in fact underlies the many disputes we will encounter.

From Plato to Platonism

In this book, I am going to explore the hypothesis that self-proclaimed followers of Plato or 'Academics' took Plato's philosophy to be a positive, integrated response to UP.[34] It is perhaps somewhat disingenuous to attribute to Platonists the view that Plato held merely *a* positive construct out of UP as opposed to their really claiming that Plato expounded "the very best possible construct that any philosopher has hitherto delivered unto mankind." Nevertheless, the point that Plato's philosophy is a response to UP and not UP itself is crucial for the simple reason that no one supposed that a philosophical position could be constituted in the negative, as it were. This is so because a philosophical position was generally thought to follow from a particular "way of life" (βίος), whereas the opposition to, say, nominalism

---

33. See, e.g., Boys-Stones 2001, chap. 6, esp. 99–105. He argues (102) that "the particular doctrines held by particular Platonists are (obviously related, but actually) incidental to what they were: I want to argue that they held the doctrines they held *because* they were Platonists rather than vice versa. And Platonism at root seems to me to be this: the belief that Plato's philosophy was dogmatic and authoritative. Everything else follows from that." Brittain (2011, 527) thinks that the 'Platonic tradition' has three essential characteristics: (a) a belief in the authoritative status of Plato's work; (b) a shared set of assumptions about the inadequacy of empirical experience for understanding the world; and (c) an increasing interest in a range of religious practices.

34. Aristotle, *Meta.* A 6, 987a29–31, says that Plato followed (ἀκολουθοῦσα) the Pythagoreans "in many ways," though his philosophy also had distinctive features (ἴδια). Aristotle adds that these distinctive features arose under the influence of Heraclitus, Cratylus, and Socrates.

in itself does no such thing.³⁵ The interesting exception that proves this rule is Pyrrhonnian Skepticism, which alone held that a total rejection of commitments to any beliefs did actually constitute a way of life, but only in the special sense that absence of commitment produced an otherwise unobtainable psychic tranquillity. For this to work, however, the rejection of belief had to be complete; a rejection of some or many beliefs in favor of others was simply another form of dogmatism.

Thus, I am maintaining that UP is the matrix out of which Plato's version of Platonism arises. Stated otherwise, UP provides the initial set of principles on the basis of which Plato proposed to address the gamut of philosophical problems and puzzles that he had inherited from his predecessors. It is sometimes easy to forget that the philosophical 'schools' of antiquity were in substantial agreement about what philosophy aimed to accomplish despite their differences about methods and results. The shared affirmation of wisdom (σοφία) as life-enhancing understanding of the cosmos underlies the divergent views and arguments. For this reason, it would be astonishing if the elements of UP as found in the dialogues were not intended by their author to serve as the substructure for the systematic superstructure that the abundant direct and indirect evidence reveals.

It might be objected that terms like 'materialism,' 'mechanism,' 'nominalism,' 'relativism,' and 'skepticism,' as well as those terms that indicate their opposites, can only be anachronistically attributed to Plato. I concede the truth in the claim that Plato would not have called himself an 'antinominalist.' I deny, however, that it is misleading to say that UP has antinominalism as a constituent part. As in the present case, such terms need only serve as labels, the contents of which must be specified. When such specification occurs, calling the Megarian position nominalist or Zeno's defense of Parmenides extreme nominalism need occasion no distortion. In any case, UP is no more Plato's position than is "Romance" the name of the language spoken by Dante, Pascal, and Cervantes.

In attempting to assess the relationship between Plato's philosophy and Platonism, we must confront the following issue. A historian of philosophy must acknowledge that if a philosopher S makes a claim A, and if, in fact, A entails another claim B, it does not follow as a historical fact that S actually embraced B. Another philosopher, T, disciple of S, may grant the above historical point yet at the same time insist that those committed to A, like S and T, are also committed to B whether they are aware of this or not. Now, where S = Plato, A = one element of UP, and B = one element of Platonism, the question of Plato's commitment to Platonism becomes ambiguous according to whether our question is about the history of philosophy or about philosophy itself.

---

35. See Hadot 2002, 64, writing of the "unity" of the Academy: "I think we can say that although Plato and the other teachers at the Academy disagreed on points of doctrine, they nevertheless accepted, to various degrees, the choice of the way or form of life which Plato had proposed." I am not so sure, though, about the causal connection between this way of life and the positive construct out of UP, that is, which one is prior.

I provide here two particularly revealing examples of an A and a B from *Republic* and from *Timaeus*. In subsequent chapters, we will meet many others. The first example concerns the Divided Line of *Republic* book 6.[36] As Socrates describes the bottom section of the Divided Line, he terms 'images' (εἰκόνες) things like shadows and reflections in water, and the originals of which these are images are animals, plants, and manufactured things. In the top section, he says that mathematicians use sensible originals as images of those things for which they are seeking understanding, namely, things like the Square or the Diagonal themselves.[37] Socrates does not actually say that there are 'Mathematical Intermediaries' that are the images of Forms. That is, he does not say that there is an ontological class corresponding to the mode of cognition that is διάνοια, that which the mathematicians employ.[38] Aristotle does not hesitate to claim that Plato believed in Mathematical Intermediaries or objects, and virtually the entire Platonic tradition is in agreement that these objects do have an ontological status, which is that of images of Forms.[39] Leaving aside for the moment the issue of whether Aristotle's testimony is an inference from a reading of *Republic* or, what is more likely, based on discussions with Plato himself, are Platonists correct to infer that Plato is committed to mathematical intermediary objects and to the equally portentous proposition that these objects are images of Forms? The former inference sets us squarely before the problem of the nature of mathematical intelligibility, as we will see. The latter inference, if sound, seems to entail that imagery is a fundamental ontological notion for Platonism, not merely localized to shadows and reflections in mirrors.

The second example is from *Timaeus*. Timaeus says of the motive for Demiurge producing the cosmos, "He was good, and in that which is good no grudging ever arises with respect to anything. So, since he is ungrudging, he desired that all things should come as near as possible to being like himself."[40] Just one page further on, the motive is again addressed, "for the god, wishing to make this cosmos most nearly the same as the intelligible thing that is best and in every way complete, constructed it as one visible thing, containing within it all living things in nature that are of

---

36. See *Rep.* 509D–510A.

37. *Rep.* 510B–E.

38. Cf. 534A3–5 where διάνοια is said to be analogous to εἰκασία, the mode of cognition that is named at 511E2 as that which has as objects the images in water, etc.

39. See Aristotle, *Meta.* A 6, 987b14–18. Cf. Z 2, 1028b18–21. Since these Intermediaries are not explicitly mentioned in the dialogues (but see *Rep.* 525E–526A, 534A), these passages seem to be a clear case of Aristotle assuming that Platonism is only accidentally, as it were, contained in the written works. For the later Platonic position, see, e.g., Syrianus, *In Meta.* 82.20; Proclus, *In Parm.* 1057.20–25; *In Euc. Elem.* 4.18, 11.5–7. Though the matter is controversial, the weight of scholarship since Adam (1902, 2:68, 161–63) has been in support of Aristotle's interpretation. See most recently Denyer 2007; Miller 2007, 318–28; and Franklin 2012.

40. *Tim.* 29E1–3: ἀγαθὸς ἦν, ἀγαθῷ δὲ οὐδεὶς περὶ οὐδενὸς οὐδέποτε ἐγγίγνεται φθόνος· τούτου δ' ἐκτὸς ὢν πάντα ὅτι μάλιστα ἐβουλήθη γενέσθαι παραπλήσια ἑαυτῷ. Cf. Aristotle, *Meta.* A 2, 983a2–3, on the ungrudgingness of the divine.

the same kind as it."⁴¹ A seemingly simple inference made from taking these two statements together is that the Demiurge and the model that the Demiurge uses are identical or the same. This inference is reinforced by the description of the intelligible model as itself "an intelligible living animal" (νοητὸν ζῷον), containing within it all the living creatures that are to be the specific models for the living creatures in this cosmos.⁴² We may interpret the inference to mean that the cosmos will be like the Demiurge because if it contains instances of all the kinds of animals, it will be like the Demiurge, who has within himself thoughts of all of these kinds. Or we may interpret the inference to mean that the cosmos will be like the Demiurge because if it contains instances of all the kinds of animals, it will be like the Demiurge, who is identical with the living creature.

Which of these two interpretations—leaving aside the possibility that there may be others—is likely to be the one that Plato would endorse? More to the point, what are the hermeneutical and philosophical principles that should be applied in deciding the matter? It may seem obvious that one principle at least is that we should opt for the interpretation that is consistent or most consistent with what Plato says elsewhere. But this is far from uncontentious. First, the use of such a principle assumes that Plato's views are more or less consistent throughout the dialogues, something that developmentalists would deny. Second, consistency is a weak hermeneutical criterion. Both of the above interpretations might well be consistent with what Plato says elsewhere. In particular, Plato might not have had himself a settled notion of how, given that the cosmos is to be made like the Demiurge and also like the Living Animal, the Demiurge is related to the Living Animal.

It is my contention that the appropriate criterion to apply in deciding on the correct interpretation of implications of the two *Timaeus* texts is consistency with UP. I mean that the proper question to ask—proper in the sense that it is the primary question that self-declared Platonists asked in coming upon difficult or ambiguous claims in Plato—is which interpretation is going to be part of the maximally consistent positive construct one can make on the basis of UP. Since the matter very quickly becomes quite complicated, conscious employment of this criterion would likely account for many of the variations in doctrine within Platonism. We should also not ever forget the obvious but somewhat sobering fact that not all self-declared Platonists were equals in philosophical acumen. The fact that they thought one interpretation to be the authentic part of the positive construct is hardly sufficient for our thinking it so. Nevertheless, in the present example, a

41. *Tim.* 30D1–31A1: τῷ γὰρ τῶν νοουμένων καλλίστῳ καὶ κατὰ πάντα τελέῳ μάλιστα αὐτὸν ὁ θεὸς ὁμοιῶσαι βουληθεὶς ζῷον ἓν ὁρατόν, πάνθ' ὅσα αὐτοῦ κατὰ φύσιν συγγενῆ ζῷα ἐντὸς ἔχον ἑαυτοῦ, συνέστησε.

42. Also, at 37A1–2 we learn that the body of the universe was brought into being by "the best of things intelligible and eternal" (τῶν νοητῶν ἀεί τε ὄντων ὑπὸ τοῦ ἀρίστου), namely, the Demiurge.

commitment to antiskepticism—that is, to the possibility of knowledge—will, I believe, be seen to favor one interpretation over any other, assuming of course that the Demiurge is, paradigmatically, a knower. I mean that given an adequate account of knowledge, we can infer that the Demiurge's knowledge of the Forms guarantees his identity with them in some sense.

In subsequent chapters, I will try to show that UP is itself consistent and that Plato's dialogues reveal him working out what he takes to be the necessary consequences of commitment to UP. It is no exaggeration to say that many of these consequences are extreme, at least from the perspective of anyone who holds one or more of the positions Plato rejects. It is, though, no part of my story that adherence to UP can consistently produce only one set of results. Indeed, one of my main conclusions is that Platonism is a big tent and that within that tent are found parties disputing numerous issues. A salutary exercise for anyone supposing Platonism to be a monolith is a perusal of Proclus's survey of Platonic interpretations of Plato's dialogue *Parmenides*, a work that is for Platonists a central text used for finding the correct path from UP to Plato's version of a positive construct.[43] In his commentary, Proclus catalogs an impressive number of mutually inconsistent interpretations of that dialogue offered by *Platonists*. When Plotinus averred—ruefully, I imagine—that Plato sometimes spoke "enigmatically" about human freedom and the soul, he was indirectly confirming that adherence to UP did not automatically yield answers to basic and even urgent philosophical questions.[44]

We can assure ourselves that the Platonic 'tent' is not infinitely large or perhaps even very large merely from the 'anti' pillars that support it. For example, Atomism is excluded by UP's opposition to materialism and to nominalism. So, apparently, is the philosophy of Anaxagoras, or any other of the so-called pluralist responses to Parmenides. A philosophical position that took hedonism to be the most plausible version of ethical relativism would also be excluded. A Pyrrhonist could embrace neither the antiskepticism of UP nor the positive assertions that constitute the contradictions of the other 'antis.'

There is, though, one philosophical position that might be thought both to endorse UP and to be opposed to Platonism at the same time. That is the philosophical position of Aristotle. Aristotle's supposed anti-Platonism might be thought to follow from a rejection of one or more of the elements of UP. Yet in fact there is abundant evidence in the Aristotelian corpus that Aristotle argued strenuously for each of the five 'antis.' On what grounds, then, are we to suppose that he is an anti-Platonist as well? Perhaps it will be maintained that his opposition to a theory of Forms is

---

43. See Proclus, *In Parm.* 630.15ff; 1083.1–1088.3.
44. See *Enn.* III 4, 5.4ff. At IV 4, 22.10–12, Plotinus actually complains that Plato's looseness in language exacerbates and certainly does not alleviate the problem being considered, which is in this passage the sense in which the earth may be said to have a soul.

sufficient to warrant his anti-Platonism. In that case, given that Aristotle is committed to UP, we would have to say that Aristotle did not believe that a theory of Forms is entailed by UP. If this is so, then we will have to ask if there is any sense in claiming that a philosophical position that rejects a theory of Forms can be said to be a version of Platonism, particularly if some Platonists at any rate want to insist that UP does entail a particular theory of Forms. Before we can answer this question, we will have to consider what exactly Plato's own commitment to a theory of Forms amounts to. It is, for example, evident from a passage in *Sophist* that Plato did not endorse every theory of Forms.[45] In addition, we have to contend with the possibility that Plato's views about Forms changed, so that it is not possible to speak of 'the' theory of Forms and Plato's view about its derivation from UP.

More generally, we have to be clear about how any theory of Forms stands in relation to the basic or generic justification for the claim that nominalism is false. I am here referring to the core commitment of anyone who holds that sameness is distinct from identity, that is, that two or more things can be the same though they are not identical. Indeed, since sameness is a two-term relation, the nonidentity of things that are the same necessarily follows. If Aristotle may be assumed, like Plato, to believe that nominalism is false—Aristotelian science, which is of the universal, would not be possible if this were not so—then Aristotle must share this core commitment.[46] From this core commitment follows the particular justification for the possibility of sameness among things that are nonidentical. No doubt, there are incompatible justifications possible. We need to ask whether any proposed justification amounts to a theory of Forms. Alternatively, we might ask whether a theory of Forms follows from UP. If the answer to either question is no, then Aristotle's commitment to UP is not shaken by his rejection of one or more theories of Forms.

Consider the matter from a slightly different perspective. Aristotle in his *Nicomachean Ethics* delivers a multifaceted sustained argument against the existence of an Idea or Form of the Good.[47] And yet Aristotle apparently sees no incompatibility with this position and his claim in his *Metaphysics* that the unique primary referent of 'being' is also the unique

---

45. See *Soph.* 248A–249D, where the position of the 'friends of the Forms' is rejected whoever these 'friends' may be.

46. Although Aristotle's commitment to the possibility of a universal scientific about natural kinds is sufficient to class him as an antinominalist, any suggestion that this characterization is anachronistic should be dispelled by his dismissal of Antisthenes' claim that nothing could be used to refer to something other than its own formula (οἰκεῖος λόγος). See *Meta.* Δ 29, 1024b32–33. If, as Aristotle believes, terms other than a thing's own formula *can* be used to refer to it, then that thing can have properties that do not identify it unqualifiedly and so can be the same as the properties of other things.

47. See *EN* A 6.

primary referent of 'good.'[48] We may well want to insist that this primary referent, the Unmoved Mover, is not the Idea of the Good. If, though, the Idea of the Good is a hypothetical entity postulated to explain certain phenomena, and if the Unmoved Mover is also a hypothetical entity postulated to explain the same phenomena, the fact that they are not identical does not gainsay the fact that they are doing the same sort of explanatory job.[49] If that is the case, one might well wonder what the addition identity conditions are that would lead us to hold that they are *not* identical. As we will see, the early history of Platonism abounds with examples of philosophers *variously* explaining or accounting for phenomena that anyone committed to UP will want to explain and anyone not committed to UP will think require no explanation at all. Aristotle's Unmoved Mover, it will turn out, is not the starting point for an anti-Platonic system, that is, for a system that rejects UP, but rather the starting point for a version of Platonism that assumes UP.

There were self-proclaimed disciples of Plato whose attachment to any theory of Forms seems to have been no stronger than Aristotle's. And yet these Academics evinced an unalloyed commitment to UP. The usual accounts of Speusippus's rejection of Forms and of Xenocrates' identification of Forms with Numbers assume a deviation from Platonism, including, implicitly, a rejection of UP. It will, I hope, be more illuminating to see the Old Academy as engaged in an ongoing debate about the implications of a commitment to UP. In particular, this debate surrounds the nature of the nonmaterial or intelligible realm and its relation to the material realm. The antimaterialist claim is inseparable from some claim about the identity conditions for nonmaterial entities. In other words, it must provide an account of just what makes intelligibles intelligible. That this problem is at the foundation of one of the central themes in Platonism is incontestable. Equally incontestable, in my opinion, is Plato's growing awareness that the solution to this problem had to be set within mathematical terms. I mean that at some point—perhaps quite early in his career—Plato came to hold that intelligibility was essentially a mathematical concept. Thus, Xenocrates' apparent claim that Forms are Numbers is, minimally, to be seen as a continuation of the Academic discussion about the lineaments

---

48. See *Meta.* Λ 10, 1075a11–13: Ἐπισκεπτέον δὲ καὶ ποτέρως ἔχει ἡ τοῦ ὅλου φύσις τὸ ἀγαθὸν καὶ τὸ ἄριστον, πότερον κεχωρισμένον τι καὶ αὐτὸ καθ' αὑτό, ἢ τὴν τάξιν. ἢ ἀμφοτέρως ὥσπερ στράτευμα; (We should examine in which of two ways the nature of the whole has the good, that is, the highest good, whether as something separate and itself by itself or as the order of the whole; or does it have it in both ways, like an army?) Aristotle's answer is the latter. So the highest good, that which is 'itself by itself' in the familiar Platonic language, is separate. The response to this that maintains that Aristotle's and Plato's positions on the highest good are essentially different is superficial. They are in fact variations based on shared principles with the same systematic explanatory goal.

49. When Plato in *Republic* hypothesizes the Good as an *unhypothetical* principle (510B7), he is clearly using the term 'hypothetical' in two ways: in the first, he is making an abductive inference; in the second, he is claiming that this inference is to a self-explicable or autoexplicable first principle. So, too, Aristotle's Unmoved Mover may be accurately described as a hypothesized unhypothetical first principle of all.

and applications of a positive construct on the foundation of UP. By contrast, our knowledge of the philosophy of Speusippus is so meager that we can scarcely arrive at a firm judgment about what his Platonism might have amounted to. Nevertheless, his assumption of a mathematized theory of the intelligible realm seems likely from the Aristotelian evidence. As I will argue, his so-called epistemological holism is in line with what Plato himself thought knowledge must be if knowledge is of intelligibles and if intelligibles are mathematical. And, as already mentioned, if knowledge so construed is not possible, explanatory adequacy within the ambit of materialism and mechanism remains untouched. So, too, for relativism.

The Skeptics of the New Academy, as it was called by doxographers, provide an interesting test case for the usefulness of UP as an analytic tool.[50] How can one be a Skeptic *and* an adherent of UP? We should admit at once that there is no guarantee that self-proclaimed members of the Academy are bound to follow Plato in any regard. We know so little about the operation of the Academy, whether in Plato's own time or after, that it is purely speculative to treat any philosopher said to be a "member" of the Academy as obliged to adhere to any philosophical position. And yet there was presumably some point in associating oneself with the Academy and hence with its founder. For the Academic Skeptics, the point was, I take it, that there was in Plato's written works or in his philosophy as known from outside the works something thought to be congenial to skepticism. The first thing that comes to mind in this regard is 'Socratic ignorance,' as explicitly claimed by Socrates in the dialogues.[51] But ignorance is not skepticism. Socrates in fact nowhere claims that it is not possible for a human being to know the things that he claims not to know, such as the definitions of the virtues.[52]

There is, however, an important passage in *Phaedo* in which Socrates seems to agree that it is not possible for human beings while embodied to attain knowledge.[53] That is, a separation of soul from body is required in order for knowledge to be acquired by us. This assertion is made prior to an argument that we already possess knowledge as a condition for our making

---

50. See D.L. 4.28–67.

51. As Sedley (1996, 98–99) points out, at least one Platonist in antiquity, the author of the anonymous *Commentary on Plato's Theaetetus,* argued that Socratic ignorance was methodological, that is, it was a position assumed for "dialectical or didactic purposes." Socrates is made to assume a sort of principled ignorance, so that he could get his interlocutors to strive to arrive at the correct answers themselves. A related and obvious point, not mentioned by Sedley, is that if this interpretation is correct, it is Plato who makes Socrates methodologically ignorant, presumably based on an antecedent doctrine about knowledge and how it is achieved. This interpretation was standard among later Platonists. Cf. Proclus, *In Alc.* 170.28–171.6; Olympiodorus, *In Alc.* 12.12–14; anonymous *Prolegomena to Plato's Philosophy* 10.57–72.

52. Vogt (2012, 189) offers a Pyrrhonian Skeptic "reading" of Socratic ignorance as the exercise of caution in formulating beliefs. Such laudable caution, however, does not prevent Socrates from acting on the beliefs he arrives at after argument, including, for example, his belief in *Crito* that he should remain in prison.

53. See *Phd.* 66E4–67B2.

certain judgments we do actually make about the properties of things.⁵⁴ So, obviously, the knowledge we possess now is something distinct from the knowledge that we are supposedly unable to acquire here below. In another dialogue, *Theaetetus*, the distinction between the two sorts of knowledge is made abundantly clear: it is the distinction between the knowledge we "possess" (κεκτῆσθαι) and the knowledge we "have" (ἔχειν).⁵⁵ The former is somehow "in" us; the latter is the realization or actualization or awareness of the former.

Should we take Academic Skeptics to be arguing for skepticism on the grounds that we do not "have" knowledge or we do not "possess" it? One might well wonder how one could argue for the former conclusion without arguing for the latter. But to argue for the latter requires at least that we confront the Recollection Argument, which maintains that we must "possess" knowledge if we are to make judgments that even a Skeptic would find difficult to gainsay. Indeed, as it will turn out, the Skeptics' argument against the possibility of knowledge is directed against a Stoic account of "having" knowledge, not a Platonic account of possessing it. An argument against a Platonic account of the possibility of having knowledge might be at the same time an argument against possessing it. This is just the sort of argument that Pyrrhonists employed. But it might not be that. The Skeptics' argument against the possibility of having knowledge is different from the reasoning employed in *Phaedo* against our having knowledge while embodied. My aim is not the forced recruitment of Academic Skeptics into the ranks of Platonists, but rather that understanding what a commitment to UP involves requires that we set aside contemporary presuppositions about knowledge. To say that Plato was an antiskeptic is not anachronistic; to say that he was an antiskeptic on behalf of a contemporary understanding of empirical knowledge is. Plato's antiskepticism will, as we will see, turn out to be inseparable from his antimaterialism. And a commitment to UP will be seen to be broad enough even to include a certain sort of skepticism, namely, that which we find in *Phaedo* regarding the having of knowledge while embodied. It will also be seen to be compatible with the sort of skepticism that labels the account of the sensible world in *Timaeus* merely a "likely story."⁵⁶

The construction of versions of Platonism among the so-called Middle Platonists presents us with a number of problems. Certainly, not the least of these is the distressing dearth of textual evidence. Two paths of Middle Platonism, though, stand out as particularly useful for understanding the possibilities within UP. The first is found principally in the works of Antiochus of Ascalon (130–68 BCE), who wanted to show that Platonic ethics and Stoic ethics are really the same thing. The second is found principally

---

54. *Phd.* 72E3–77A5.
55. *Tht.* 197B–D.
56. See *Tim.* 29D2, 68D2, εἰκὸς μῦθος.

in the works of Numenius (second half of second century CE), who sought out an integrated Platonic account of the intelligible world.

Stoic ethics has been viewed, even in antiquity, either as Socratic-inspired or Platonic-inspired. When these two views are seen to be distinguished, Socratic ethics is being contrasted with Platonic ethics; in the second way, as with Antiochus, no distinct Socratic ethics is discernible. This dispute raises an important question about positive implications of antirelativism in ethics. Moreover, it invites us to consider how the other elements of UP contribute to these implications.

In a text of Aristotle to which we will return at some length, Aristotle says that Plato's commitment to a separate intelligible realm began as a youth (ἐκ νέου).[57] Without doubt, then, this commitment antedates any of the dialogues supposed to reveal an account of Socratic ethics that is distinct from Platonic ethics. Given this, we have to decide if the claims made by Socrates in these dialogues are claims that entail no such commitment. Granted, it is possible that Plato's commitments are irrelevant to his exposition of Socratic ethics and that these commitments actually constitute an unwarranted adumbration. We might, for example, want to maintain that the firm commitment to all the elements of UP or to things that entail these elements in *Republic* do not necessarily have anything to do with Socratic ethics. It might be supposed, for instance, that in *Republic* Plato's tripartitioning of the soul allows for the sort of irrational acting that is not possible in Socratic ethics. We might want to argue that Plato's outlandish belief in the immortality of the soul has no bearing on unalloyed Socratic insights. Socrates' apparent agnosticism about the afterlife in *Apology* in contrast to Socrates' argument for it in *Phaedo* might be thought sufficient in itself to separate Socratic ethics from Platonic ethics. In order to arrive at this conclusion, we would have to suppose that Plato went through a 'Socratic phase' before he transformed Socrates into a representative of his own Platonic position. This is not an unreasonable approach, though it requires a commitment to some type of developmentalism, a commitment that may on other grounds be found difficult to maintain. For example, it requires a certain amount of waffling in regard to *Gorgias*, in which Socrates directly expresses a belief in the immortality of the soul (as part of his ethical argument), and *Meno*, where a commitment to immortality—or at least to preexistence—is implied by the theory of recollection. Are *Gorgias* and *Meno* 'early' Socratic dialogues or 'middle' Platonic dialogues or works that are 'transitional' from one phase to the other?

Antirelativism in ethics is, for Plato, obviously going to have something to do with the positing of an Idea of the Good. Is this true for a

---

57. See *Meta*. A 6, 987a32–b1. I am aware of no parallel text in which the words ἐκ νέου are used to refer to "early works" or "things written when young," or something like that. They seem always to be used, by Aristotle and others, to refer to the early stage of the life of a human being or animal or plant.

putatively distinct Socratic ethics? Presumably not, according to Aristotle, who claimed that Plato, not Socrates, separated the Forms.[58] But then we must ask how a 'nontranscendent' or 'this-worldly' Socratic ethics is supposed to work. That is precisely the question that a Stoic would feel needed to be answered if he wanted to claim Socratic as distinct from Platonic inspiration.

One of the most difficult facets of the philosophy found in the Platonic corpus is the articulation of the intelligible realm leading up to (and down from) the Idea of the Good. The combination of antiskepticism with antimaterialism yields the problem of what entities populate the intelligible realm and how these entities are distinguished among themselves. As we will see, the variety of versions of Platonism can be arrayed along a quantitative axis wherein at one end a unique intelligible entity is posited, and at the other end an actual infinite number of entities are maintained. In order to see this range as other than arbitrary, we have to inquire into the criterion for the positing of intelligible entities in the first place. Broadly speaking, the criterion is explanatory adequacy, that is, the postulation of the necessary and sufficient causes of phenomena needing to be explained. Thus, for example, if the phenomenon is sameness in difference, the criterion will lead the Platonist to hypothesize a cause that can only be intelligible, that is, nonmaterial. If the phenomenon is the intelligibility of sensible reality, then, according to one interpretation of the meaning of 'intelligible,' the criterion indicates an intellect as cause. If the phenomenon is cognition itself, then the criterion leads us to explain the nature of the objects of cognition such that cognition is possible. And so on.

There is, it appears, a problem with adequacy and redundancy in such explanatory criteria. I mean that it is not clear why more than one intelligible entity is required for any and all explanations. Thus, Plato hypothesizes an eternal intellect, an array of intelligible objects, and a superordinate Idea of the Good. Aristotle collapses into one entity the three functions that these three hypothetical entities are intended to serve. Aristotle's Unmoved Mover does what Forms, the Demiurge, and the Idea of the Good are supposed to do, according to Plato. Conversely, later Platonists will argue how and whether to reconstruct a dyad or a triad of intelligible entities in spite of Aristotelian arguments to the contrary. It is my contention that these

---

58. See *Meta.* N 4, 1078b30–1079a4 (mainly repeating the historical observations made at A9, 990a34–990b9), where Aristotle says that Socrates did not posit Forms as separate (χωριστά), the implication from the context of this discussion being that Plato (and others) did. I take the unspecific reference to those who separated the Forms to encompass a variety of views regarding what was no doubt an unsettled matter in the Academy. However, at *Meta.* Δ11, 1019a1–4 Aristotle says that the meaning of 'prior' by nature and essence (κατὰ φύσιν καὶ οὐσίαν) originates with Plato. If A is prior by nature and essence to B, then A can exist without B, but not vice versa. I take it that this is what Aristotle means when he attributes the separation of Forms to Plato. See Λ1, 1069a34 with Z 2, 1028b19.

arguments occur within the framework of UP and the further commitment to a unified positive construct on its basis.

Consider the rather narrow question of whether the virtues are one or whether we need to hypothesize an intelligible entity for that which each virtue's name names. The issue seems to have puzzled Plato in his *Protagoras*. That there be *some* intelligible entity to explain the possibility of someone possessing the property of, say, courage, is not in question. Whether this is the same entity as that which explains the possibility of someone possessing the property of temperance or not is what is at issue. It might seem obvious that if there is a justification for positing a Form of Courage, then there is equally a justification for positing a Form of Temperance. And yet if both Courage and Temperance are virtues, perhaps only a Form of Virtue is needed. Or perhaps a Form of Virtue is needed in *addition* to separate Forms of Courage and of Temperance. How are we to decide this question? The fact that there is no one obvious way to settle the matter, one way that excludes all others, should lead us to predict that philosophers seriously committed to UP may arrive at differing conclusions.

Among the so-called Middle Platonists like Numenius and others, it was evidently not thought that the first superordinate principle of all could itself be bereft of intellect. But at the same time, its intellectual properties did not lead to the collapse of a secondary demiurgic intellect into it. If the first principle of all actually is an intellect, then apart from all other considerations, the Platonic bona fides of Aristotle is enhanced. It is extremely difficult to say if Numenius believed that in making the first principle an intellect he was interpreting Plato or drawing out the consequences of UP regardless of what Plato himself might have actually held. Indeed, it is difficult to say whether Numenius would have distinguished these two options. This possibility always exists owing to the tentative nature of the dialogues and the well-established existence of an oral doctrine of Plato.

One of the arresting features of the fragmentary evidence of Middle Platonism is the consensus that some sort of divine and separate intellect or νοῦς is the key positive doctrine reflecting antimechanism. And yet the relation between such an intellect and the Forms that are the focus of the positive doctrine following from antimaterialism is disputed. This is equally the case for the relation between this intellect and the Idea of the Good, the focus of the positive doctrine following from antirelativism. As we will discover, many of the debates among the Platonists themselves arise from different understandings of what an intellect is and what its distinctive role is, not just in relation to the material or sensible realm, but within the intelligible realm as well.

When Proclus declared in his *Platonic Theology* that Plotinus was one of the great exegetes of the Platonic 'revelation' (ἐποπτεία), he meant more than that Plotinus was an exceptional interpreter of the dialogues.[59] He meant

---

59. See Proclus, *PT* 1.1.16ff. On Plato as unquestioned authority for Plotinus, see Krämer 1964a, 292; Armstrong 1970, 213–14. By contrast, Dodds (1960, 2) thought that for Plotinus

in addition that Plotinus systematized on the basis of the dialogues, the oral tradition, and Aristotle's testimony, the most coherent and comprehensive version of a positive philosophy based on UP. Even this extraordinarily high praise does not prevent Proclus from criticizing Plotinus on many more or less central points. Still, it was Plotinus, according to Proclus, who narrowed the number of logically supportable versions of Platonism. Stated differently, he narrowed the range of issues that were debatable. Some of these issues arise from circumstantial disputes of which Plato could not but be ignorant. Others regard the properties of the intelligible entities that Plato himself posited.

Plotinus tells us that he considered himself to be nothing more than an exegete of Plato; he would certainly have eschewed the title of 'original' philosopher. Scholars are rightly puzzled that Plotinus could actually think that some of the things he says are in fact authentically views shared by Plato. There are several reasons for this puzzlement. First, like the Middle Platonists, Plotinus does not limit his Platonic sources to the dialogues alone. Although the dialogues are primary, the Aristotelian testimony and the oral tradition are also taken to be relevant. Second, the fact that Plotinus represents himself as a *defender* of Platonism as well as an expositor of it means that he has to apply Platonic principles to the solution of problems that are outside the direct concern of fourth-century BCE philosophy. Third, in addressing problems about the construction of the material realm, Plotinus does not hesitate to apply Aristotelian arguments and distinctions. Plotinus evidently thinks that the employment of these is at least consistent with a Platonic framework, although this means that sometimes he gives the impression that he has detached himself from that framework. It is sometimes difficult, though by no means impossible, to reconnect his use of these distinctions both with claims made in the dialogues (Plato's version of Platonism) and ultimately with UP. Finally, the very idea of a systematization of Plato's thought may seem to be ipso facto distortive. To appreciate the case that this is not so, we need to see systematization both as arising out of UP and as underlying the positive arguments made in the dialogues. It is necessary to see systematization as inseparable from unification, that is, 'reduction' in some sense to a first principle of all.[60] For example,

---

Plato's authority was mainly decorative, not substantial. Dodds says, "Formally, but only formally, the philosophy of Plotinus is an interpretation of Plato; substantially, I should call it an attempt to solve the spiritual problems of his own day in terms of traditional Greek rationalism." Both positions in my view fail to adequately distinguish the 'level' at which Plotinus is in complete accord with Plato, that is, UP, despite divergences in detail.

60. It is precisely for this reason that I resist the efforts of many scholars to locate the systematization of Plato's philosophy no earlier than in the early imperial period. See, e.g., Dörrie 1976; Bonazzi and Opsomer 2009, 1; Donini 2011; Ferrari 2012. Opsomer (2005c, 164–75), however, argues that Plutarch was committed to the 'unity of the Academy' thesis, a unity of doctrine from Plato onward, including the Academic Skeptics. In positing an unhypothetical first principle of all, Plato announces the systematic project. Aristotle's testimony only confirms this.

the argument or arguments for the immortality of the soul in *Phaedo* are thought by Plotinus to rest upon a systematic expression of what UP entails, ultimately a unified doctrine of first principles. Plotinus's implicit attribution to Plato of a systematic expression of UP is admittedly itself a sort of abductive inference. But this in itself is hardly a criticism of it.

The pejorative neologism 'Neoplatonism,' which has its origin in eighteenth-century German academic histories of ancient philosophy, cuts two ways.[61] In supposing that the 'Neoplatonism' of Plotinus or of anyone after him is different from Plato's philosophy, one necessarily supposes the obverse. That is, Plato's philosophy must be viewed as containing none of the elements of Neoplatonism. This can mean one of two things. First, it can mean that specific doctrines found in Plotinus are absent from Plato's philosophy. Just to take perhaps the most contentious example, it might be supposed that the positing of a first principle of all above 'being' is Neoplatonic and emphatically not Platonic. Accordingly, the Idea of the Good in *Republic* has to be interpreted in such a way that it does not fit this description. In addition, Aristotle's testimony that Plato identified the Good with a first principle of all named 'One' has to be discounted. The justification for so doing is no doubt that the superordination of the Good and its identification with the One constitute deviations from Plato's true philosophy. But then, of course, only one who has independent access to what this is can be in a position to make this claim. As we will see in the next chapter, the only apparent vehicle for independent access is the dialogues. But to employ some dialogues to interpret others already implies a criterion of relevance, say, developmental ordering or theoretical cogency. But this brings us once again into question-begging territory.

Perhaps more profoundly, setting Neoplatonism over against Platonism naturally leads to the supposition that the systematic nature of the former must be seen in contrast to the relatively unsystematic nature of the latter.[62] Thus, some scholars arrive at a patently circular argument: Plato's philosophy is unsystematic because Plotinus's philosophy *is* systematic and

---

61. See Büsching 1772, 2:471ff., who uses the term to describe what is in comparison with the philosophy of Plato "eine unklare mystische Schwärmerei." Although the term '*Neuplatonismus*' belongs to the latter part of the eighteenth century, the wholly negative judgments on the fidelity of Neoplatonists to Plato is at least a generation earlier. See Brucker 1742, cited in Tigerstedt 1974, 58, 100–101, nn. 437 and 452. Tigerstedt quotes Brucker as claiming that "they are all—from Plotinus to Proclus and Olympiodorus—madmen, liars, imposters, vain and foolish forgers of a most detestable and false philosophy." Instead of 'Neoplatonists,' he calls them 'pseudo-Platonists' and proponents of 'syncretism.' Dörrie (1976, 45) follows this tradition closely, especially in his insouciance regarding Aristotle's testimony. He concludes his examination of Platonism after Plato by saying, "Den eigentlichen Aufbruch in eine Ontologie, die alle Anschaulichkeit abstreifte, vollzog erst Plotin." See Szlezák 2010a for an illuminating sketch of the course of Platonic hermeneutics from Brucker to Schleiermacher.

62. See Krämer 1964b, 69 on the contrast between the systematic interpretation of Platonism from Aristotle onward and modern and contemporary efforts to jettison systematization altogether.

innovative (i.e., un-Platonic).[63] Perhaps the weakness in this argument will be evident merely by pointing out its circular nature. Nevertheless, there is still the positive case yet to be made, the case that Plotinus, and many others going back to the Old Academy itself, were neither innovating nor fantasizing when they set out Plato's philosophy in a systematic format. The various systematic constructs out of UP, including Plato's own, constitute Platonism.

---

63. See Tigerstedt 1974, 6, who quotes Wilamowitz as declaring that Schleiermacher had discovered the real Plato and had thereby put an end to the 'Neoplatonic Plato.'

CHAPTER 2

Socrates and Platonism

In this chapter and the next, I want to consider some of the central hermeneutical issues facing any interpreter of Plato. In particular, I will address the questions of (1) the relation of the historical Socrates and his philosophy to the Socrates of the dialogues; (2) whether the philosophy in the dialogues—Socrates' or Plato's—developed in any way; (3) the relation of the literary form of the dialogue to any putative philosophy found therein; and (4) how two apparently self-revealing passages in the Platonic corpus (*Phaedrus* 274C–277A and *Seventh Letter* 341C–D) impact our understanding of the dialogues in general. The responses of Platonists prior to the nineteenth century to these four questions are fairly straightforward: (ad 1) the philosophy in the dialogues belongs entirely to Plato, though Socrates' inspirational role is recognized; (ad 2) there is no substantial development in Plato's thought indicated in the dialogues; (ad 3) the literary form of the dialogues sometimes makes Plato's philosophical position difficult to ascertain but in no sense does that literary form occlude or alter the philosophy; and (ad 4) Plato's distrust of the written word or disinclination to put his most serious thoughts in writing does not negate the philosophy in the dialogues, though it makes all the more important Aristotle's testimony about Plato's unwritten teachings. A substantial segment of Platonic scholarship over the last two hundred years or so has been devoted to the refutation of these responses and to construction of different ones.[1]

---

1. The modern separation of Plato from Platonism begins with Friedrich Schleiermacher, who argued that the literary form of the dialogues produced a kind of firewall between Plato and the theoretical constructions of later Platonists. See Schleiermacher 1836. For a compact and authoritative account of the scholarship inspired by Schleiermacher, see Erler 2007, 1–8.

A good question to begin with is whether in the two diametrically opposed views of Plato's dialogues we simply have inconsistent paradigms or whether there is some argumentative basis according to which we can decide between the superiority of one approach to the other. After all, if one is inclined to maintain that the Platonism of Xenocrates or Numenius or Plotinus is in no way an accurate representation of Plato's thought, then this is very likely going to be because one has accepted one or more versions of the contemporary answers to the above four questions. Conversely, the plausibility of one or another of these versions of Platonism is dependent on *their* answer to these four hermeneutical questions.[2]

There is no doubt that the weight one gives to Aristotle's testimony is a strong determinant of one's position on these questions. I will focus on that testimony mainly in chapter 4. Here, I want to consider these questions apart from that testimony—with the exception of a couple of relatively uncontroversial bits of evidence. As we will see, it is not easy to give a firm answer to one question without at least going some way to a commitment to answers to the others. For example, if one maintains that the dialogues contain Socratic philosophy as well as Platonic philosophy, then, naturally, one will deny that the literary form of the dialogues precludes the ascription of philosophical positions to Plato (and to Socrates). Again, if one does not believe that Plato's thought developed, then it becomes more difficult to separate the Socratic philosophy in the dialogues from the Platonic philosophy. If one believes that the literary form of the dialogues prevents us from knowing what Plato's philosophy is, then it would seem both that one cannot distinguish Socratic philosophy from Platonic philosophy in the dialogues and that if there is any development in the dialogues, that development is not one of a philosophical position.

It should be clear from the above that questions about Plato's putative Platonism are distinct from questions about the nature of Platonism

---

An extensive and very helpful account of Schleiermacher as a scholar of Platonism is found in Lamm 2000. Reale (1997, 38–39) lists the three fundamental principles of the 'Schleiermacher paradigm': (a) form and content are inseparable in the Platonic dialogues; (b) the dialogues have a doctrinal unity and a plan of instruction, ascending from an elementary level, proceeding to an intermediary constructive level, and finally reaching a systematic level; and (c) the dialogues are self-sufficient for understanding Plato's philosophy, that is, the indirect tradition has no evidential value. Reale goes on (39–47) to explain how Schleiermacher used these principles to try to solve various problems in Platonic hermeneutics, how scholars in the nineteenth century elaborated the paradigm, and how during the same period other scholars began to question the adequacy of this paradigm, particularly with regard to (c).

2. D.L. 3.51.7–8 states: Ἐπεὶ δὲ πολλὴ στάσις ἐστὶ καὶ οἱ μέν φασιν αὐτὸν [Plato] δογματίζειν, οἱ δ' οὔ... (Since there is much disagreement between those who say that Plato dogmatizes and those who say that he does not...). Diogenes goes on to claim that all of the principal interlocutors in the dialogues (Socrates, Timaeus, the Athenian Stranger, and the Eleatic Stranger) represent Plato's own views. The principal proponents of the view that Plato does not "dogmatize" seem to be Pyrrhonian and Academic Skeptics. See D.L. 9.72 for the former; Cicero, *Acad.* 1.46 for the latter. Sextus, *PH* 1.222 denies that Plato is in any sense a Skeptic.

in other philosophers and that the answer to the former follow from the assumptions that are brought to the reading of the dialogues. Where do these assumptions come from? It is sometimes suggested by a scholar that he or she is dedicated to a completely unprejudiced response to the dialogues. This unprejudiced response requires taking every word into account, without falling into the absurd position of giving equal weight to every word. It requires above all that one be true to the artistic integrity of the dialogue, which means, among other things, that it is illicit to bring in material from one dialogue to interpret another.[3]

This is a desperately hard row to hoe. It requires us not to "privilege" the arguments of Socrates over those of his interlocutors, even when Socrates' argument is a refutation of the views of those interlocutors. It requires us to give equal weight to the mise-en-scène of a dialogue and to the arguments therein. For on what basis are we to privilege the arguments? Jokes, puns, personal remarks, sexual innuendos, vivid characterizations of persons, elaborate dramatic framing—all have as much to do with the literary product as do the arguments and philosophical claims made by Socrates or by the other figures traditionally thought to be the "leading" figure in the works. If one's response to, say, *Phaedrus* is determined as much by a remark about listening to cicadas as by an account of the metaphysics and psychology of love, then we can acknowledge the authenticity of that response at the same time as we can reject it as inadequate on other grounds. What I mean is that conceding that the literary integrity of the dialogues is inviolate does not even begin to preclude one from analysis and interpretation

---

3. See Tejera 1984 for an attempt to follow the methodology of "one-dialogue-at-a-time." A somewhat less rigid application of the same method is found in Shorey 1933. Shorey claims in the preface to his work (vi), that "the synopsis of any dialogue in this book can be understood without reference to the others." At the same time, Shorey's synopses contain abundant cross-references to other dialogues in the margins of his text. It is clear from the references that Shorey is using them to support his own interpretations of the text. For example, when discussing the Idea of the Good in *Republic*, Shorey appeals to *Timaeus* to support the interpretation of the Good as a benevolent deity. See Beversluis 2006, 87, n. 8, who mentions the "non-dogmatic" interpretation of George Grote (1865, 1:237–39), according to whom the dialogues contain no doctrine of Plato. But as Beversluis has no trouble showing, Grote goes on to attribute ethical and cosmological views to Plato based exclusively on the dialogues. Grote (3:244) proclaims, for example, that in *Timaeus*, "the Platonic system is made known to us." See Griswold 1986, 15: "Each dialogue, I hold, is the primary whole relative to which the parts of the dialogue are to be judged.... Some interpreters believe, however, that the Platonic corpus is the relevant whole. Thus, in analyzing a specific passage in one dialogue, they appeal to evidence from another dialogue as a basis (and not as correlative evidence) for their interpretation. That approach is implausible, in my view, because the corpus simply does not possess the degree of organic unity each dialogue possesses." Of course, from the fact that the corpus alone does not present a high degree of "organic unity" it does not follow that Plato's philosophy does not possess such unity. Cf. Gill 2002, 153–61, who argues that each dialogue must be considered as a "dialectical encounter [having] its own integrity and significance." So Trabattoni 2003, who firmly resists the view that the dialogues express anything like a systematic philosophical position.

of the arguments. More important, it does not preclude one from adducing material from other dialogues on behalf of that analysis and interpretation.

Apart from these considerations, to which I will return, it is simply false that even the most rigorous effort to exclude philosophical doctrine from the interpretation of the dialogues can succeed. Assuming that one wishes to go beyond mere paraphrase, one must formulate one's interpretation with a view about what point the dialogue is trying to make.[4] Even the anodyne claim that the dialogues aim to show the importance or desirability of philosophy assumes that Plato has some idea about what philosophy is.[5] It seems to me that there are two possibilities here: Plato had no discernible view about what philosophy is, or he did. If the former, then we are in the embarrassing position of admitting that Plato could not or wished not to distinguish philosophy from sophistry. If that is the case, then a strong emphasis on the literary character of the dialogues should lead us to conclude that Plato was anything but a great literary artist, since one of the strongest impressions that anyone could get from the dialogues is the author's contempt for sophistry.

In response to this argument, one might say that Plato's authorial anonymity precludes us from attributing to him contempt for sophistry. Socrates might have such contempt, but as for the author's position, we simply cannot say.[6] We are in no better position to say what Plato actually thought about sophistry and its relation to philosophy than we are regarding the position of some other Greek citizen who is completely unknown to us beyond the fact that his name was unearthed on some Athenian boundary stone. Let us say, then, that Plato probably did have a view about sophistry and philosophy, but that, for whatever reason, he concealed it in the dialogues. I suppose that the only sane response to this view is to say, "Some concealment."

So we might seize the other horn of the dilemma and admit that Plato probably knew very well what he thought philosophy and sophistry are and that he probably had a strong view about the superiority of the one to the other. On this view, the dialogues are simply protreptic; they are enactments of philosophical interaction whose purpose is to invite or entice

---

4. Ancients generally assumed that each dialogue had a σκοπός, or goal, which was to impart a particular lesson. Hence the ancient titles of the dialogues, which were indicative of the substance of that goal.

5. Cf. Nehemas 1999, 117–19, who argues that the very distinction of philosophy from sophistry in a Platonic manner implies a metaphysical substructure. Nehemas, however (115–16), accepts uncritically the differentiation between the Socratic philosophy of the early dialogues and the Platonic philosophy of the middle dialogues.

6. See Mulhern 1969, 639: "instead of saying what he believes, the author of philosophical dialogues portrays arguments." Cf. Mulhern 1971; Nails 2000, 17. Mulhern argues that there is no entailment from "this character says x" to "Plato believes x." This is uncontestable and would no doubt be the safe approach if there were not such a cornucopia of evidence regarding what Plato believed apart from what is said in the dialogues.

readers to the practice of philosophy.[7] The problem with this view is not that it is false; the problem is that it is too obviously true. But though it is obviously true, it is inadequate. A protreptic is hardly going to be effective unless there is some suggestion about what the activity is toward which you are being led and what the purpose is that is going to be achieved. There is, as we all know, much material in the dialogues about what philosophy is and what the goal of the philosophical life is, beginning with the arresting claims in *Phaedo* that philosophy is the "practice for dying and death," and in *Apology* that the unexamined life—that is, the unphilosophical life—is not worth living.[8]

Whether one takes the words "philosophy is the practice for dying and death" literally or not, I suggest that, without a metaphysical foundation, this claim is nonsense and, more to the point, without force as a protreptic device. But, of course, there *is* a metaphysical backing provided in *Phaedo* for this view. It is irrelevant that one might well find this backing inadequate. It is, however, utterly gratuitous to claim that Plato exhorts the reader to the philosophical life, having a definite idea of what that is, but that the reasons found in the dialogue for pursuing that life are not attributable to him. By contrast, if we accept the argument or arguments for the immortality of the soul as likely to be attributable to Plato as is his belief in the superiority of philosophy to sophistry, then we already have before us a central building block of Platonism. And as Bertrand Russell once remarked apropos the existence of universals, if you allow one, what is the nonarbitrary ground for limiting their number at all?

Generally, if we find it legitimate to attribute to Plato the minimal doctrinal claim that philosophy is different from and superior to sophistry, and if we associate this claim with the things that are actually said about philosophy and sophistry in the dialogues, we arrive at a fairly rich array of beliefs; in fact, something that begins to look like a version of Platonism. These are, however, by no means uncontroversial in their content or obviously consistent. Such observations naturally encourage efforts to differentiate the philosopher Socrates *in the dialogues* from the philosopher Plato who wrote them. They also serve as an invitation to developmentalism as a hypothesis about the apparently inconsistent content. It is not surprising, then, that in contemporary scholarship we frequently find a rejection of antidoctrinalism in favor of developmentalism, wherein the latter focuses principally on the differentiation of Socrates from Plato.[9] I proceed to examine the

---

7. See, e.g., Griswold 1988, 162: "Plato does not so much have a 'philosophy' as a philosophy about making philosophical claims." Rowe (2007, 2) assumes that Plato either intended readers to "think for themselves" *or* "intended to impart doctrines" (my emphasis). Why not both? See Press 2007, 154–58, on the dialogues as "enactments." As I will argue below, there is a sense in which the dialogues can well be understood as enactments, but according to this sense, philosophical doctrine is not appropriately prized apart from them.

8. See *Phd.* 67E; *Ap.* 38A.

9. See Nails 1995, 53–135, who offers a far-ranging largely skeptical account of various developmentalist hypotheses. Also, see Beversluis 2006, 96–101, who, after a dissection of

'Socratic problem' and the views of some outstanding interpretations of a putative 'Socratic philosophy.' In the next chapter, I turn to developmentalism and related hermeneutical issues in the dialogues. My goal is to begin to remove some unnecessary obstacles standing in the way of an accurate appraisal of Plato's Platonism.

The 'Socratic Problem'

Leaving aside for the moment the problem of sorting out authentic dialogues of Plato from those that were falsely attributed to him or from those whose provenance is dubious, there are only five places in the traditional set of nine tetralogies where Socrates is not the leading interlocutor—*Parmenides, Timaeus, Sophist, Laws,* and the *Letters*.[10] It is not an insignificant fact that later Platonists took the first two to constitute the culmination of Platonic teaching, though the reason for this is not that Socrates is therein subordinated to others. He is for the most part represented as refuting the positions of others, never having his own positions refuted, and as the one offering complete arguments, the assumptions of which are one or more of the elements of UP. Socrates himself will recount arguments of those who maintain the opposite of UP, and sometimes Plato will have their proponents speak in their own voice. Virtually all of the texts to which one can point as evidence for the assumptions of UP are texts in which Socrates is speaking.

Despite this fact, some maintain that in some dialogues postulated as 'early,' Plato is representing the philosophy of Socrates and not his own philosophy. It is only in the 'middle' and then in the 'late' dialogues that Plato 'develops' his own philosophical position.[11] It does not seem

---

the antidoctrinal view, seems to opt for developmentalism, arguing that "the early dialogues" represent the view of the historical Socrates.

10. It is worth noting that *Laws* is the only dialogue in which Socrates does not appear at all, though Aristotle (*Pol.* 2.6.1265a10–13) apparently assumed that the Athenian Stranger just is Socrates, possibly unnamed because the dialogue takes place not in Athens but in Crete. See Halliwell 2006, 190, 202–3, who makes a case for a qualified acceptance by Aristotle of the Socrates of the dialogues as representative of Plato's own views. The qualification is in effect based on Aristotle's recognition that there is more to Plato's philosophy than is found in any one dialogue or, indeed, in all the dialogues put together.

11. See Nails 1995, 8–31, and Dorion 2011, for useful reviews of the nature of the Socratic problem, the history of the scholarship, and the arguments for holding that its solution is impossible. The central argument is that the genre of λόγοι Σωκρατικοί, as Aristotle recognizes (*Poet.* 1447a28–b13; *Rhet.* Γ 16, 1417a19–22), contains 'imitation' (μίμησις) of character, not necessarily of philosophical doctrine. But Aristotle's remarks do not specifically mention Plato, although his dialogues are no doubt included in the some two hundred works on Socrates we know of written within the first generation after his death. That the dialogues 'imitate character,' including that of Socrates, tells us very little or nothing about the philosophical positions therein. The context of *Poetics* and *Rhetoric* and the discussion of literary genre make it unsurprising that no mention is made of the dialogues as a repository of philosophical doctrine. See Penner and Rowe 2005, 223, who want to distinguish sharply the philosophy of Socrates and the philosophy of Plato (in large part based on psychological doctrine). They

to me inappropriate to note that among those who take this view, Plato's development is often not viewed favorably. He is viewed as somehow undermining or rejecting the Socratic position, typically with no warrant and with no happy result. Before looking more closely at what this Socratic philosophy is supposed to be and how Plato is supposed to have betrayed it, it is important to emphasize that the character Socrates of *Republic* or *Philebus* or *Theaetetus* is represented by Plato no differently from the Socrates of *Euthyphro* or *Apology*, although the latter are held on this view to contain Socrates' philosophy and the former to contain Plato's philosophy. Indeed, considered dramatically the two latter dialogues are later than the former. In the same vein, whereas *Phaedo* is supposed to contain Platonic philosophy and *Crito*, along with *Apology*, to contain Socratic philosophy, the dramatic connection among these three is even closer.[12] They constitute a dramatic trilogy (to which we can add *Theaetetus* and *Euthyphro* as 'prequels') recounting dialogues over the last few days or weeks of Socrates' life. It is certainly possible that Plato wrote *Phaedo* long after he wrote *Apology* and *Crito*, and that his decision to insinuate non-Socratic doctrine into dialogues that are dramatically in close connection with dialogues that supposedly contain Socratic content was an unfortunate attempt to conflate the two. There is, however, no evidence for this interpretation apart from that supposedly contained

---

assume that when Socrates and Plato agree, they are speaking "in their own person." That is, they assume that we can discover in some dialogues (e.g., *Gorgias*) Socrates speaking in his own person, and in others (e.g., *Republic* and *Laws*) Plato speaking in his own person, albeit through the mouth of Socrates. This seems to me a completely gratuitous distinction.

12. Griswold (1999) argues for what he admits is the limited relevance of the 'fictive chronology' of the dialogues, that is, of their ordering in terms of the dramatic dates in the life of Socrates. But Griswold's explanation (388) for Plato putting a theory of Forms in the mouth of a very young Socrates in what would be the 'first' dialogue in the fictive chronology, namely, *Parmenides*, is unhelpful. He thinks that the subsequent dialogues in which Socrates expresses that theory show that Plato intended the criticisms not to be taken too seriously. This may well be the case, but surely not because Plato intended for *Parmenides*, a dialogue probably written long after many other 'Socratic' dialogues, to be read first, that is, retrojected, so to speak, into the pedagogical order. According to Griswold, *Theaetetus* should have the same or similar role in preparing the reader for reading *Euthyphro*. The problem with this entire approach, I believe, is that it assumes that Platonic philosophy is just what is contained in the dialogues and that, accordingly, we need to seek to discover Plato's cues to the reader as to how to approach their orderly exposition. This is pure 'Schleiermacherism.' For if Plato's philosophy *is* just in the dialogues, then it would be natural to identify that with the philosophy of the fictional Socrates. This is actually more hopeless than the identification of Plato's philosophy *through* the fictional Socrates. For example, no proposed dramatic chronology by any scholar places *Republic* before *Protagoras*. See Nails 2002, 324–26. And yet in the latter dialogue, Socrates argues against the possibility of ἀκρασία, while in the former he argues for its possibility and the psychological apparatus for explaining this. On the 'fictive chronology' view, Plato is telling the reader that Socrates was 'for' ἀκρασία before he was 'against' it. But then, of course, Plato himself was evidently 'for' it again in *Timaeus* and in *Laws*. See Kahn 2000 for a critical response to Griswold along similar lines.

in the doctrinal content itself.¹³ For this reason, even if it is true that Plato misunderstood or otherwise somehow lost sight of the Socratic philosophy he represents in the 'early' dialogues, it certainly does not follow that Plato thought this. Indeed, it does not follow that he in fact thought that the philosophical claims that can be gleaned from these 'early' dialogues are in any way in conflict with the claims made in 'later' ones.¹⁴

Among the outstanding proponents of a Socratic philosophy that is different from a Platonic philosophy are Gregory Vlastos, Terry Irwin, Richard Kraut, Christopher Taylor, John Cooper, Nicholas Smith and Tom Brickhouse, Terry Penner, George Rudebusch, Hugh Benson, Mark McPherran, and Christopher Rowe.¹⁵ According to these scholars, the Socratic philosophy from which Plato has deviated is, broadly speaking, found encapsulated in the so-called Socratic paradoxes. Thus, the seemingly paradoxical claims that 'virtue is knowledge', 'no one does wrong willingly' and 'it is better to suffer than to do evil' provide a good starting point for further analysis. To these we can add the theme of 'Socratic ignorance,' that is, his profession of ignorance of the answer to the questions he poses for his interlocutors. Ignorance, so the argument goes, is a hallmark of Socratic philosophy, not the philosophy of Plato.

The claim that no one does wrong willingly is a convenient place to start.¹⁶ The ambiguity in the words οὐδείς ἑκὼν ἁμαρτάνει is the source of a number of problems. First, the verb ἁμαρτάνειν suggests an error made in attempting to reach a goal or hit a target. If you aim your arrow at the heart of a deer and miss, the correct word to use in ancient Greek is ἁμαρτάνειν. But that implies that you did not miss on purpose or intentionally. In that case, it is an analytic truth that no one does wrong, that is,

---

13. See Thesleff 2009, 288–92, who thinks the writing of *Apology* and *Phaedo* is separated by at least ten years and that the dramatic connection of these dialogues "has little or no relevance to chronology." Thesleff, however (355–57), doubts the authenticity of *Crito*, speculating that it was written *after Phaedo*. I do not accept this hypothesis, but if it were true, then indeed the dramatic connection between *Apology* and *Phaedo* would be irrelevant.

14. The dramatic date of *Theaetetus*—immediately preceding *Euthyphro*—must be in the last year of Socrates' life. There seem to be good reasons to believe that Theaetetus in fact died in the Corinthian War in 392 or 391, not, as some scholars have thought, in a later battle in 369. See Nails 2002, 275–77. So at least one reason for dating the dialogue after 369 seems mistaken. But the classification of *Theaetetus* as a 'middle' dialogue presenting Plato's own views about knowledge, and *Euthyphro* as an 'early' dialogue presenting Socrates' own philosophical views seems also to be undermined by the dramatic ordering of the two dialogues. Those who take the dramatic context as crucial do not take into account the juxtapositioning of the two dialogues.

15. See especially Irwin 1977 and 1995; Kraut 1984; Vlastos 1991; Taylor 1992; Brickhouse and Smith 1994; McPherran 1996; Cooper 1999; Benson 2000; Penner and Rowe 2005; Reshotko 2006; Rowe 2007; Rudebusch 2009. Most of these works contain substantial discussion of the literature on the question of Socratic philosophy in the dialogues.

16. See *Ap.* 37A5–6; *Gorg* 488A3; *Protag.* 345D8, 358C6–7; *Rep.* 589C–D; *Tim.* 86C7–D1; *Lg.* 731C–D.

errs, willingly.[17] If you missed on purpose, you did not ἁμαρτάνειν. On the other hand, if we read ἁμαρτάνειν as indicating not what you intend to do but what you really want to do, then if you do not achieve this, it might be said that you did not do it willingly. Thus, in the famous passage in *Gorgias* in which the paradox is presented, Socrates says that tyrants do what seems (δοκεῖ) best to them, but not what they want or will (βούλεσθαι).[18] This is because, though acts of tyranny seem best to them to do at the time they do them, they do not actually will them because acts of tyranny always have consequences that the tyrants do not or perhaps could not will. If the tyrants actually knew these consequences at the time they chose to engage in tyrannical acts, they would not willingly do them. Hence, they do not do wrong willingly. If this is the way to understand the claim, we clearly no longer have an analytic truth. If, though, it is in fact true that tyrannical acts always have consequences that the agent would (or could?) never want, whence the paradox? Presumably, it is to be found in whatever makes it true that whatever seems best to you is always what you want—if you know what you want. When you know what you want, *that* will seem best to you to do.[19] In this way, the paradox that no one does wrong willingly is associated with the paradox that virtue is knowledge. If doing tyrannical deeds is never what you want, assuming that you know that these deeds will produce consequences you do not want, then this knowledge will be sufficient (and perhaps necessary) for virtue.[20]

What, though, is it that guarantees that tyrannical deeds always produce consequences that the tyrant does not want, so that if he knew this too, it would never seem best to him to do them? It is no accident that Socrates uses a tyrant in his argument. A decent human being may need only to be

---

17. No doubt, this is why Socrates at *Protag.* 345D5ff., in his interpretation of the words in Simonides' poem to the effect that no one willingly does anything shameful, assumes that he is saying something that all educated people agree with. See, e.g., Sophocles, *Women of Trachis* 1123: ἥμαρτεν οὐκ ἑκουσία, the words spoken by Hyllus regarding her mother.

18. See *Gorg.* 467C5–468E5.

19. Some claim that only the tyrant and other evildoers do what seems best to them and not what they want, whereas virtuous people such as Socrates do only what they want and not what seems best to them. At *Cr.* 49C10–E3, Socrates announces his absolutist prohibition of evildoing. He concludes that this has before now and still is what seems (δοκεῖ) to him to be true. Hence, wanting only his own good, it seems to him that not escaping from prison is better than escaping. It appears to me more than odd to insist that *because* he wants only his good and he knows what this is, it does *not* appear to him that his good is attained in this way. But if this is true, then the difference between the vicious and the virtuous is *not* that one does what seems best to himself and one does not; both are doing what seems best to themselves. The difference is that what seems best to the virtuous is in fact so, whereas what seems best to the vicious is not.

20. See Irwin 1977, chap. 3, for evidence for the view that knowledge is both necessary and sufficient for virtue in Plato's "early and middle dialogues." Irwin maintains that in these dialogues Plato's view is identical with the view of Socrates. It is in *Gorgias*, claims Irwin (7), that Plato's view begins to diverge from that of Socrates. Hence, for Irwin, developmentalism is needed to account for the philosophy in the dialogues.

shown that a deed will have bad consequences for someone in order to agree that that is not what is wanted. Once such a person realizes this, it will no longer seem best to do the bad deed, that is, to do things that have such consequences. But the tyrant is a much harder case, for presumably he is concerned only about consequences for himself. Given this, we certainly cannot think that the tyrant will forbear on being shown that his acts of tyranny will have bad consequences for someone else. In that case, he will have to be shown that it is never in his *own* interest to act tyrannically. Once again, what is it that makes this certain or even plausible?

It seems to me that there are two possible answers to this question. The first is a prudential argument to the effect that "crime does not pay."[21] This approach has the perhaps appealing virtue of requiring no fancy metaphysical apparatus whatsoever for it to be understood. Given human nature and the ways of the world, the life of crime is not likely to be a happy one in the long run. Just ask incarcerated hardened criminals. Unfortunately, "not likely" is not the modality apt to deter the tyrant. Such a plea might well be met with the response that this might be so for petty and stupid criminals, but it is far from a certainty for those with the capacity for epic tyranny.[22] Moreover, tyrants and other criminals, petty or otherwise, do in fact sometimes escape punishment. They do sometimes die in their beds, surrounded by loving family members. Just ask hardened criminals who never get caught. If, though, Socrates' paradox is to contain the truth that wrongdoing *never* benefits the wrongdoer, he must eliminate even the possibility of a tyrant making a rational or defensible bet on likely outcomes, that is, on the likelihood of escaping retribution that outweighs the benefits of tyranny. Is it really *never* the case that such a bet turns out in favor of the tyrant? If we admit that it is false that the bad consequences of tyranny will always outweigh the good in the eyes of the tyrant, then it is also false that the tyrant never does what he wants. I conclude that the prudential argument will not work as an interpretation of the paradox that no one does wrong willingly. It does not account for the absoluteness of the claim.[23]

The second answer seeks to show that 'good' and 'good for me' are necessarily identical, where the words 'for me' are purely indexical. That is, 'good' and 'good for anyone' are identical. If this is so, then it could never be the case that, assuming that tyranny is bad for someone, it could be good for the tyrant. If it can never be good for the tyrant, then it can never be the case that the tyrant will want it. And, indeed, it will follow from this that if the tyrant knows this, it will never seem best to him to be a tyrant.

---

21. See Santas 1979, 183–94; Penner 1991, 2004, 2005, 2011; Reshotko 2006; Seel 2006, 43–47; and Brickhouse and Smith 2010, 44–49, for defenses of various versions of prudentialism.

22. Or superhuman powers, as in the case of Gyges in *Republic*.

23. Reshotko's (2006, 155) account of the putative Socratic ethics concedes that there is only a "contingent and nomological connection between virtue and happiness," and (174) that the claim that no one benefits from harming another is "empirical." But if this is so, it surely is not without exceptions, as the supremely gifted tyrant would no doubt insist.

For tyrants, like everyone else, do what seems best to them, that is, what they think will be in their own interest.

How, then, are we supposed to show that 'good' and 'good for me' are necessarily identical? There are two claims essential for concluding this. Both of these claims are found plainly in the dialogues, but according to the proponents of a 'Socratic philosophy' that is different from 'Platonic philosophy,' they are claims that belong to the latter and not to the former. If, though, the Socratic paradox that no one does wrong willingly does not work without these claims, then, assuming we are arguing for a Socratic philosophy, we would have to say that Socrates does not have the resources to defend the paradox. But this would mean that when Socrates utters this paradox in dialogues that contain the claims that are supposed to be Platonic and not Socratic, either Plato has shifted its meaning or Socrates has somehow acquired Platonic 'baggage' that he did not previously possess. This seems quite hopeless. There is no basis for maintaining that the Socratic paradox means something different in *Republic, Timaeus,* and *Laws* from what it means in *Gorgias, Apology,* and *Protagoras*. And if it means the same thing in all these dialogues, then assuming that Plato, too, could see the inadequacy of the prudential argument, one naturally supposes that he has Socrates insist on the truth of the paradox because he (Plato) does actually adhere to the claims that would make true the identity of 'good' and 'good for me.' But even if Plato somehow missed the fact that tyrants sometimes do triumph, that is no basis for attributing the paradox to Socrates as opposed to Plato. Only if Socrates can be shown in the paradox to express a truth unburdened by Platonic 'baggage' do we have a reason to posit that paradox as a cornerstone of an independent Socratic philosophy.

The two claims that lead us to identify 'good' and 'good for me' are (1) that there is a superordinate Idea of the Good, and (2) that a person is the sort of thing whose good could never in principle be had at the expense of the good of another. This sort of thing is an immaterial soul, separable from the body.[24] Its good, unlike the goods of bodies or of composites of bodies and souls, is an immaterial good, and so the pursuit of such a good is not a zero-sum game. My good could never diminish or inhibit your good any more than my knowing a truth could prevent you from knowing it, too. Two obvious questions immediately arise. First, why does the soul need to be immaterial in order for (2) to be true? Second, what does (1) add to (2)? The two questions are especially relevant to my purposes since it is generally held that Socratic philosophy, unlike Platonic philosophy, is not committed to an immaterial soul that could be in principle separated from

---

24. See Gerson 2003, 80–89, 122–24, on the immateriality of the person.

the body, nor is it committed to the existence of separate Forms much less a superordinate Idea of the Good.²⁵

The answer to the first question is that if the soul is not separable from the body, Socrates' insistence in *Apology* and elsewhere that 'soul care' is of paramount importance for a human being is something of a bluff.²⁶ For unless the soul identifies me in a way that the body does not, then soul care need not take precedence over body care in principle. In a dialogue the authenticity of which has long been disputed, but whose provenance among the early Socratic dialogues is not, the identification of the self and the soul is explicitly made.²⁷ Yet the identification that Socrates makes of the soul and the self and the claim that the body is a possession of the soul or self is not argued for. It is assumed that soul care is self care. By contrast, an argument for the immortality of the soul along with an argument that the soul is the self would presumably suffice to make the point about the priority of soul care to body care. Socrates in *Apology* evinces agnosticism about the disposition of the soul at death; in *Phaedo* he argues for the soul's immortality and, by implication, for the identity of the soul with the self.

So the hermeneutical situation is this. We can decide that either the arguments in *Phaedo* are necessary to make good the soul care doctrine and in turn the doctrine that no one does wrong willingly, or else they are not. If they are, then it seems we must count them as part of 'Socratic philosophy,' along with the doctrine of separate Forms that *Phaedo* claims is logically connected with the proof for the immortality of the soul.²⁸ If, though, we

---

25. Aristotle testifies that these are Plato's views. He does not identify any particular set of dialogues as containing Plato's views as opposed to the views of Socrates. Aristotle and modern proponents of the view that there is a Socratic philosophy in the dialogues differ on the question of whether the Socrates who does not share these views is the Socrates of the dialogues or the historical Socrates. Sedley (2004, 10) assumes that Aristotle's testimony, especially in *Meta.* N 4, about the views of the historical Socrates must have been taken from the so-called early dialogues. But I see no evidential basis for this assumption. Indeed, the context of this chapter is clearly a historical account of the views of Aristotle's historical predecessors, including Socrates, Plato, Democritus, and the Pythagoreans. When Aristotle goes on, N 4, 1078b27–29, to give Socrates credit for 'inductive arguments' and 'universal definitions,' it is extremely unlikely that he is referring to the literary character.

26. See *Ap.* 36C5-7: ἐπιχειρῶν ἕκαστον ὑμῶν πείθειν μὴ πρότερον μήτε τῶν ἑαυτοῦ μηδενὸς ἐπιμελεῖσθαι πρὶν ἑαυτοῦ ἐπιμεληθείη ὅπως ὡς βέλτιστος καὶ φρονιμώτατος ἔσοιτο (trying to persuade each of you not to care for any of your possessions before you care for yourselves in order that you should become as good and wise as possible). Cf. 29D7–E3, 31B5; *Cr.* 47E–48A.

27. See *Alc.* I. See Pradeau 1999, 219–20; Erler 2007, 290–93, for surveys of various opinions on authenticity. See Annas 1985, 131–32; Denyer 2001, 14–26, for arguments on behalf of authenticity. Smith (2004) argues against authenticity. Denyer suggests (12 and 152) on the basis of some admittedly slight internal evidence, that the dialogue was written by Plato in the early 350s, that is, likely long after most of the so-called middle dialogues were written. If this 'Socratic' dialogue is authentic and late, then, as Denyer says (24), "the standard chronology [of the dialogues] must, in large part, be abandoned."

28. Cf. *Phd.*76E on inseparability of the theory of Forms and proof for the immortality of the soul from recollection.

want to maintain that the arguments in *Phaedo* are not necessary to support the doctrine of soul care and so the paradoxical version of the doctrine that no one does wrong willingly, we will be burdened with the task of showing how this is possible. Part of this burden requires showing why, in a dialogue supposedly representing Socratic doctrine, namely, *Gorgias*, Socrates offers a myth about the immortality of the soul and divine retribution. We do not have to deny that myth is not argument to insist on the relevance of the belief in the immortality of the soul to the success of the Socratic paradox.

This, however, still leaves us with the paradox in *Apology* where is found Socrates' apparent unwillingness to link a belief in the immortality of the soul with a belief in the primacy of soul care.[29] This unwillingness, we will recall, dramatically precedes *Phaedo* by only a couple of weeks, and again, dramatically, succeeds *Gorgias*. One possibility is that an argument for the immortality of the soul on behalf of the doctrine of soul care would be obviously out of place in the circumstances of Socrates' trial and before his immediate audience.[30] My point is not that Socrates did believe in the immortality of the soul and that this is why he believed in soul care and in the paradox that no one does wrong willingly. My point is rather that nothing in the dialogues, apart from *Apology*, encourages us to believe that anyone held a doctrine of soul care and of the paradox that no one does wrong willingly without also holding that the soul is immortal and that it is the separate immortal soul whose good is never achieved by harming another soul. I offer no opinion on the beliefs of the historical Socrates in this regard, since I am here confining my remarks to the dialogues as a basis for constructing Platonism.

The second question I posed above is what does the hypothesis of a superordinate Idea of the Good add to the doctrine of the priority of the soul to the body as support for the Socratic paradox? This is a much broader and more difficult question since the role of the Idea of the Good obviously goes beyond providing support for a Socratic paradox. Plato is certainly not unique among ancient philosophers in using 'good' (ἀγαθός) as a second-order predicate indicating an ultimate or final end or goal. To say of something that it is 'good' is always to invite the questions "What is good about it?" or "What does its being good consist in?" The answer to those questions will be the first-order predicate or goal being sought. Thus, someone might aim for wealth or power or pleasure, thinking that this is good. That is *why*

---

29. This was already noticed by Panaetius, frr. 127–29 = Asclepius, *In Meta.* 90.

30. See *Phd.* 63B4–5: [spoken to Cebes and Simmias] "Let me try to make my defense to you more convincing than it was to the jury." Cf. 63E8–9. Socrates' defense is not against the charges made at his trial; rather, it is his apology for the philosophical life. This includes the claim that philosophy is practice for dying and being dead (64A), a claim that makes sense, as Socrates proceeds to show, only if the soul is immortal. So, at least, Plato is connecting the Socrates of *Phaedo* with the Socrates of *Apology*. The connection between the two dialogues suggests no contradiction in Socrates' views at all if in the latter he is speaking to a lay jury and in the former to philosophers, indeed, to Pythagorean philosophers.

these are sought. We might suppose that desiring, say, pleasure 'in itself' is equivalent to desiring it because it is good. This cannot, for Plato, be quite right, since he has Socrates lead his interlocutors into agreeing that pleasure, among other things, is good only if it does not bring adverse consequences.[31] If it is the enjoyment of a pleasure that led to your downfall, then the pleasure was not good, though it is still a pleasure. Even someone like the tyrant, who maintains that pleasure is for him always without adverse consequences, does not gainsay this point. The argument that what seems good to the tyrant is not what he wants seeks to show that there is at least a possibility of adverse consequences, in which case the tyrant does not want what seems good to him. This possibility alone guarantees that 'good' is a second-order predicate, not identical with any first-order predicate or goal.

The view that 'good' is a second-order predicate means that it cannot be identical with the content of any first-order predicate. Indeed, part of what it means to say that the Idea of the Good is 'beyond essence' (ἐπέκεινα τῆς οὐσίας) is that the Good does not have a unique substantive nature. But it is, somehow, an ultimate end. To this point we will return. The superordination of the Good indicates its status as a second-order predicate. We may ask, though, the more basic question of why any Form—especially this one—is needed in order to make this point. The answer is simply that all predication rests on a thesis born out of that element of UP that is antinominalism, namely, that the very possibility of saying that one thing is another ('A is B') where 'B' is a predicate of 'A,' depends on the existence of a separate Form for 'B.' Nothing could have 'good' as a predicate unless an Idea of Good exists. But because 'good' is a second-order predicate, this Idea must be superordinate to any Form for any substantive predicate. If something is good for anyone, then this second-order predicate is instantiated in whatever it is that is so. But since the Good is one thing, a state of affairs can never be good for me when that state of affairs is not good for someone else. If it is good for me that I have something now, then it cannot be bad for you that I have that thing now. Therefore, anything that is supposedly good in a zero-sum game is not so. This does not mean, of course, that money is necessarily bad for me; it means only that it is not good for me when and only when my possession of it is bad for me or for someone else.

It might be suggested that the virtues, unlike the 'external' goods of wealth, beauty, power, etc., are not first-order predicates distinct from their goodness. Justice, for example, is unequivocally and absolutely good. This is true, but beside the point. First, the necessary connectedness of justice and goodness does not undercut their distinctness any more than the necessary connectedness between threeness and oddness undercuts their distinctness. Second, because justice (and the other virtues) and goodness are necessarily connected, it can never be bad (i.e., not good) for anyone that

---

31. See, e.g., *Gorg.* 497D8–499B3 for the argument that pleasure is not the good. Cf. 499B4–500A6 where it is argued that some pleasures are not good.

justice is instantiated. Finally, the fact that Plato takes seriously the demand of Glaucon and Adeimantus in *Republic* to show that justice is good in itself and for its consequences is evident in the fact that the first part of the demand is met at the end of book 4, but it takes us until the end of *Republic* to conclude the answer to the second part. And, we may note, the discussion from book 5 to the end of the work introduces, among other highly relevant considerations, the Idea of the Good. It is the superordinate Idea of the Good that the philosophers aim at and are educated to know. The unequivocally good consequence of being a just person, that is, being one in whom reason rules absolutely and unconditionally, is that one ceases to identify one's good as distinct from attaining the Idea of the Good. I mean attaining it in the only way that an immortal disembodied soul attains anything, that is, by knowing it.

That one should so identify one's good without the above two principles hardly makes sense in a putative nonmetaphysical Socratic philosophy. As much can be said, too, for the paradox that it is better to suffer than to do evil. This absolutist prohibition is not defensible for reasons analogous to the prudential version of 'no one does wrong willingly.' Thus, there might be occasions in which doing evil is a better plan of action than suffering it unless the wrongness of 'doing evil' is understood analytically. If that is not the case, then doing evil, even though it harms my soul, might be a more rational choice than the evil done to me were I to suffer it, even if that evil is done merely to my body. Only if the doing of evil is a kind of ontological 'third rail' such that I could not possibly survive as the person I am were I to do it does the absolutist prohibition make sense. And this ontological third rail is manifestly only intelligible in regard to an immaterial soul. Obviously, human beings, as opposed to souls, sometimes survive quite well in the wake of their evildoing. If they are psychically diminished by this, how does the absolutist prohibition trump the decision by the evildoer that on balance the choice to do rather than suffer evil was a good one, psychic harm be damned?[32]

A 'Socratic' interpretation of the paradox that virtue is knowledge brings with it special problems. For on this interpretation, the fact that virtue is knowledge seems to entail the impossibility of incontinence (ἀκρασία).

---

32. Penner (2002, 193) says, "I think Socrates no proponent of moralism," meaning that Socratic intellectualism is a form of psychological egoism. If this were the view that Plato is representing Socrates as holding, absolutism about virtuous behavior hardly seems to follow. Nor, contrary to Penner (199), does a science of good and evil seem possible. Penner acknowledges that the crucial distinction is between real and apparent goods. But it is difficult to see why, on this view, someone's real good could not be in line with what all, including Socrates, seem to consider immoral behavior. Consider a thief who, in the course of a burglary, is surprised by someone who clearly recognizes the malefactor. On what grounds could we say that it is not in his interest to kill the eyewitness? The cautionary tales about guilt and the unending anxiety regarding capture hardly seem to be pertinent since these must always be probabilities. They necessarily fall short of establishing an absolutist prohibition of wrongdoing.

The denial of the possibility of ἀκρασία seems to be the point of Socrates' argument in *Protagoras* that the idea of being overcome by pleasure is nonsense.[33] And yet in *Republic*, the possibility of ἀκρασία seems to be what is being demonstrated in the argument for a tripartite soul.[34] It is, to be sure, possible that Plato changed his mind between the writing of *Protagoras* and *Republic*. This is, indeed, what some developmentalists would argue. The proponents of a 'Socratic' philosophy, however, want to argue that the denial of the possibility of ἀκρασία is a reason for maintaining that no one does wrong willingly.[35] So, since Plato continues to maintain the latter, we must hold that he does so for other reasons than that ἀκρασία is impossible. The fact that these other reasons are thought to include especially the existence of a tripartite soul is beside the point. Socrates, over against Plato, does not need a tripartite soul or the attendant possibility of ἀκρασία to defend his claim that virtue is knowledge.

Perhaps the Socraticist has a point. If the argument for a tripartite soul is necessary to make good the possibility of ἀκρασία, then this possibility might belong to Plato's philosophy. Socrates' philosophy need not be saddled with it and with the tripartite soul. For it is the *denial* of the possibility of ἀκρασία that seems to be used to support the paradox in *Protagoras*. This leaves us with the problem of why Plato apparently continues to have Socrates insist that no one does wrong willingly after he has established, apparently to his own satisfaction, that the soul is tripartite and that ἀκρασία is possible. If it should turn out, however, that no one does wrong willingly, including acratics, we have to ask again why we should conclude that Socrates' understanding of the paradox is different from Plato's. By contrast, if Plato's understanding of the paradox depends on the psychological analysis that makes ἀκρασία possible, we should hesitate to conclude that the paradox in the dialogues has an independent, Socratic foundation.

The paradox that virtue is knowledge is, as we have already seen, ambiguous. Is knowledge merely necessary for virtue or sufficient as well? It would seem that if it is sufficient as well as necessary, then, if ἀκρασία is supposedly acting against knowledge, and such acting is not virtuous, ἀκρασία is, after all, impossible.

---

33. See *Protag.* 352A8–D3.
34. See *Rep.* 439E6–440A2.
35. Seel (2006, 32–39) argues that Xenophon, in his *Memorabilia* 4.5.6–11, gives what is likely to be a more accurate account of the historical Socrates' position on ἀκρασία. For Xenophon says that Socrates believed that one could act contrary to one's own interests, even as he sees them, owing to ἀκρασία, but apparently only in the sense that such a person has impetuosity (προπέτεια). This form of ἀκρασία is distinct from another, that of weakness (ἀσθένεια). Cf. Aristotle, *EN* H8, 1150b19. The former precedes deliberation; the latter follows deliberation. It is only the latter that is impossible, according to *Protagoras*. The recognition of the existence of impetuosity does not require an elaborate metaphysics for its defense. The recognition of the latter, however, does. It may well be that the historical Socrates did not make a clear-cut distinction between the two, as does Aristotle.

Let us consider the sad, conflicted Leontius who, in *Republic* book 4, seems to know that indulging his prurient interests by gazing on the naked corpses is wrong. Yet he does it anyway. How would the Socraticists' Socrates (*not*, obviously, the Socrates of *Republic*) analyze Leontius's plight? What has he really done? Presumably, he does wrong, but not willingly. He would have done wrong willingly only if he knew that what he was doing was not good for him. But if he had known that, he would not have done it. Let us suppose, then, that Leontius only has a strong belief that he should not gaze. What is supposedly missing from his cognitive base such that if it were present, he would not act? It seems that what is missing is his knowledge that what he is about to do is not good for him. It is not, I think, open to the Socraticist to rely on *Republic*'s subsequent strong separation of knowledge (ἐπιστήμη) and belief (δόξα) in order to insist that what Leontius is missing is an entirely different mode of cognition.[36] For according to *Republic*, knowledge is of separate Forms, and it is not belief, which is only of things that simultaneously 'are and are not.' That is, there is no knowledge of the things of which there is belief.[37] Even if the Socraticist agreed that the separation of Forms from sensibles and the attendant separation of knowledge from belief can be accommodated within Socratic philosophy, she is unable to show that such knowledge would be relevant to the belief that Leontius has that gazing on corpses is wrong. That knowledge might produce an even stronger belief in him that it is wrong, but how does this help?

Perhaps what should be said is that if Leontius really knew that what he was doing was bad for him, he *could no longer* have the desire to gaze. Such an a priori stipulation, however, simply assumes that tripartition is false, that is, that one could not desire that which, all things considered, one thought was wrong because there are not different sources of desire in the soul. Desire, so the Socraticist position goes, is thoroughly rational, such that one's desires flow from one's consideration of what is best for one to do. If, by hypothesis, one considers it best not to gaze on corpses, then one cannot but desire not to do so.

The fallacy here, I think, is in supposing that a tripartite soul implies an irrational or nonrational source of desire or appetite (ἐπιθυμία).[38] Leontius's desire to gaze may be said to be irrational in one sense; but in the most relevant sense it is not. It is irrational in the sense that it conflicts with the deliverances of his calculation about the best thing to do. It is, though, rational in the sense that the desire to gaze requires, among other things, a conceptualization of what sort of thing he is doing and a belief that doing

---

36. See *Rep.* 476A9ff.

37. See Gerson 2003, 148–73, where I have tried to show that this claim is far more controversial than it ought to be. In fact, it is a view shared explicitly by Aristotle. See *Post. An.* A 33, 88b30–37. Cf. A 8,75b24; A 18, 81b5–7; *Meta.* Z 15, 1040a1–2; *EN* E 3,1139b19–24.

38. Cf. *Phdr.* 254D1 and 256A6 where the 'appetitive' part of the soul (i.e., the 'bad' horse) complains to the charioteer about breaking their 'agreement' (ὁμολογία), and the 'spirited' part of the soul (the 'good' horse) resists the requests of the beloved with 'reason' (λόγος).

such a thing is pleasurable. In short, his desire is nothing like a bodily reflex; it is not beyond the control of reason. The simple and decisive proof of this is that Leontius quarrels (albeit briefly) with himself about the desire, or, more poetically, he quarrels with the desire.[39] The very possibility of such a quarrel, and the possibility that reason could have won the debate with appetite—in which case Leontius would turn out to be an encratic instead of an acratic—makes nonsense not of the view that the desire, abstracted from its conceptual shell, is not in some sense nonrational, but that it is nonrational as a source of action. That desire is only a source of action when the agent, Leontius, acts, and Leontius is a rational agent. He acts against the normative authority of reason, but he does not act contrary to what he (rationally) desires. And in desiring to gaze and acting on that desire, he does not become something other than a rational being.

This is to say that Leontius is a divided self, someone who in his embodiment is capable of acting as reason alone dictates or as his own rational desire dictates, even against the decision of reason alone. That an embodied person is capable of such conflicts is actually not surprising, when these persons are set within an ontology according to which instances of 'disembodied' Forms manifest contrary properties simultaneously. In fact, what would be surprising is that, given that 'is and is not simultaneously' is a property of sensibles or τὰ φαινόμενα generally, embodied persons would be excluded. We do not, however, need to speculate on the application of Plato's metaphysics to his psychology. Plato tells us in fact that the person is ideally identified with his intellect, but that embodiment compromises this identification.[40] Leontius fails to act virtuously not because he does not know or, at any rate, because he does not believe strongly enough that what he is doing is wrong, but because he does not completely identify himself, and hence his own good, with what his intellect determines he ought to do.

On this interpretation—and only on this interpretation, in my view—the paradox that no one does wrong willingly is separable from the denial of the possibility of incontinence, or ἀκρασία. The reason Leontius does not do wrong willingly, despite the fact that he acts on his desire to do what he believes to be wrong, is that willing (ἑκών) is a property of rational desire, which is the only sort of desire that human beings have. But because Leontius is an embodied person, he is a locus of disparate, even conflicting desires. Leontius does what his embodied self wills, not what his real self wills, which is the possession of good alone. He is, however, different from

---

39. Cf. *Phd.* 83D7 where the soul is said to 'have the same belief' (ὁμοδοξεῖν) as the body regarding its desires. Also, 92E4–93A10, 94B4–95A3, the refutation of the argument that the soul is an 'attunement.' At *Rep.* 442A10–D1, temperance (σωφροσύνη) is defined as the two lower parts of the soul 'having the same belief' as the highest part of the soul about who should rule. Rudebusch (2009, 71–73) rightly argues that the so-called brute desires are no such thing but in fact require conceptual contextualization.

40. See *Tim.* 90A–B. The proof for the immortality of the soul from recollection in *Phaedo* assumes that the immortal soul *is* the subject of rational activity.

the tyrant because the tyrant does not even believe that what he is doing is wrong. Still, 'what seems best' to the tyrant is analogous to Leontius's desire to gaze on the corpses. The diagnosis of the precise flaw in each man's character is different, but the underlying metaphysics is the same. Neither man recognizes that his good cannot be achieved by acts that are not good for others. This recognition would not be possible were there not a superordinate Idea of the Good and were it not the case that the ideal person is an intellect.

My target here is not those who deny that this is the correct interpretation of Plato. Indeed, some Socraticists might concede that it is. My target is those who want to claim that the paradoxes no one does wrong willingly and virtue is knowledge make sense without the metaphysical apparatus provided by Plato.

This still leaves us with the problem that Socrates in *Protagoras* denies the possibility of ἀκρασία, while Socrates in *Republic* affirms it via his postulated tripartite soul. Perhaps the easiest solution is to suppose that Plato changed his mind in the time between the writing of the two dialogues. But if that is so, then we must suppose that he once believed that no one does wrong willingly and virtue is knowledge are defensible claims without tripartition and the separability of the soul or true self from the body. As I have already argued, this seems doubtful. What seems more likely is that *Protagoras* and other dialogues deemed by Socraticists to contain exclusively Socratic doctrine actually give us a Socrates who expresses the paradoxical face of Platonic doctrine. Just as we may assume that, owing to Aristotle's testimony, Plato when he wrote *Euthyphro* believed in the existence of separate Forms even though they do not appear as such in that work, so we may assume that when he wrote *Apology* or *Crito* or *Protagoras* he believed in a tripartite or at least divided soul. Similarly, when he has Socrates express agnosticism about the afterlife in *Apology*, we may assume that he himself believed in the immortality of the soul.[41] If this interpretation seems itself to be doubtful, we should recall that on *any* interpretation, if Socratic philosophy is different from Platonic philosophy, and if Plato wrote both *Protagoras* and *Republic*, then there is no doubt that Plato has no difficulty in having Socrates say apparently contradictory things. After all, it is not Plato but Socrates who in *Republic* offers the argument for the possibility of that which in *Protagoras* is claimed by him to be impossible. The Socrates of *Philebus* is markedly different in his metaphysical claims from the Socrates of the 'early' dialogues. And the young Socrates of *Parmenides* is represented as maintaining a theory of separate Forms, a theory that Aristotle explicitly

---

41. See Slings 1994, 216–22, following De Strycker 1950, for a detailed argument that Plato presents Socrates as in fact maintaining the latter of the alternatives "dreamless sleep or change to another place." This is consistent with my view that the extensive argument for the immortality of the soul in *Phaedo* would be out of place in *Apology* but not out of mind for its author.

refrains from attributing to Socrates but which he evidently attributes to Plato and to others. Finally, this theory of Forms is evidently presented to the mature Socrates as a revelation in *Symposium*, whereas the theory is attributed to him as a youth in *Parmenides*.

The Socraticist seems committed to the untenable position that some of Plato's representations of Socrates contain accurate accounts of his specifically personal philosophy whereas other representations employ the same character Socrates to argue for philosophical positions that are not part of that personal philosophy. The more tenable position is that the Socrates of the dialogues is from first to last the creation of Plato, representing Plato's philosophical position. Beyond Aristotle's rather vague testimony about what the historical Socrates held, there is little basis for speculation about his philosophical views.[42] Socrates *may* have believed in the paradoxes and he may even have believed in a prudential defense of them. Nevertheless, in the light of the above, it is entirely unsurprising that Platonists did not discover in the dialogues a substantial philosophical view other than Plato's and the views of his opponents.[43]

Gregory Vlastos

The doyen of modern Socraticists in the English-speaking world is unquestionably Gregory Vlastos. In a number of widely influential articles and then in his book *Socrates: Ironist and Moral Philosopher* (1981), Vlastos provided a sustained argument for the claim that the early dialogues

---

42. See Irwin 1995, 8–11, who gives a useful accounting of all the philosophical views that Aristotle apparently attributes to the historical Socrates. These include the claim that definitions are of universals, the denial of the possibility of incontinence, and the identification in some sense of knowledge and virtue. As Irwin notes, these views are found in dialogues generally regarded as early in apparent contrast to dialogues in which Socrates expresses different if not contradictory views. What is not clear, however, is that the arguments that we find for these views in the dialogues—for example, the argument against the possibility of incontinence—are the arguments of the historical Socrates as opposed to those of Plato. See Prior 2006 for a similar view. As I will argue, the arguments that Plato does generally provide are based on metaphysical assumptions that everyone including Aristotle himself denies are those of Socrates. See also Cooper 1984, 3, n. 1, for a listing of those passages in *Magna Moralia, Nicomachean Ethics,* and *Eudemian Ethics* where Aristotle repeatedly attributes to the historical Socrates the claim that virtue or the virtues are in some sense knowledge.

43. See Morrison 2000, 107–10, who argues convincingly that the philosophical commitments of the historical Socrates are, based on our evidence, sufficiently vague to make the imputation of the actual arguments or justification for these views highly problematic. We simply do not know why, for example, the historical Socrates held that care for the soul should be paramount or what exactly he was ignorant of or why one should embrace an absolutist commitment to doing the good. By contrast, Plato does provide metaphysical and epistemological reasons for these views. To cut the historical Socrates off from these is one thing, justifiable by the evidence or lack thereof; it is quite another to concoct a non- or anti-Platonic justification for them. See also Kennedy 2011, 249; and Dorion 2011, 17–18, arguing against the use of *Apology* as evidence for the views of the historical Socrates.

contain a philosophical position different from the middle dialogues; the first is Socratic and the second, Platonic. That is, the first belongs to the historical Socrates and the latter to Plato himself.[44] In fact, according to Vlastos, "[these philosophical positions] are so diverse in content and method that they contrast as sharply with one another as with any third philosophy you care to mention, beginning with Aristotle's."[45] Vlastos proceeds to list ten theses, "each of which marks a contrast between a feature of Socratic philosophy found only in the early dialogues and a feature of Platonic philosophy found only in the middle dialogues."[46] Of course, if only one of these differences could be established, that would be sufficient to show that there is a distinctive Socratic philosophy in the early dialogues, even if that one putative feature were trivial. Since, though, in these matters certainty is far from being within our grasp, the weight of Vlastos's argument must be considered to grow with the assembling of such a large number of putative contrasts.[47] If Vlastos is right, then those Platonists who mined all the dialogues for Platonic philosophy were misguided. This would not, of course, invalidate their reconstruction of Platonism entirely. But it would at least suggest that the way they tended to connect the undisputed Platonic metaphysics and epistemology of the middle and late dialogues with the putative Socratic ethics of the early dialogues led them to misunderstand the latter. So, as above, attempts to justify the Socratic paradoxes by adducing the Idea of the Good and the immortality of the soul must fail.

Here is Vlastos's list of contrasts. Instead of talking about Socratic versus Platonic philosophy, Vlastos refers to S_E and S_M, indicating the Socrates of the early dialogues and the Socrates of the middle dialogues, though it is clear that the latter is to be identified as representing Plato's philosophy as opposed to Socrates'.

1. S_E is exclusively a moral philosopher; S_M is a metaphysician, epistemologist, philosopher of science, etc.
2. S_M has a grandiose metaphysical theory of separate Forms and of a separate soul; S_E has no such theory.
3. S_E seeks knowledge elenctically, claiming to have none; S_M seeks demonstrative knowledge, and claims to have found it.

---

44. See Nails 1995, 75–96, for a critique of Vlastos's separation of the "two Socrateses" along lines similar to what is presented here. See Baltzly 2004 for a recent defense of Vlastos's position. Irwin (2008, 78–79) just assumes without argument that Aristotle's distinction between the views of Socrates and those of Plato reflect distinctions between the 'early' and 'middle' dialogues.

45. See Vlastos 1991, 46.

46. Ibid., 47.

47. Indeed, Vlastos (ibid., 82) goes on to claim that he could have listed many more "if [he] were trying for completeness."

4. S_M has a theory of a tripartite soul; S_E has no such theory, which would have undercut his belief that incontinence is impossible.
5. S_E has no interest in mathematics; S_M has mastered the mathematical sciences of his time.
6. S_E's conception of philosophy is populist; S_M's is elitist.
7. S_M has an elaborate political theory; S_E no such theory.
8. S_E's homoerotic attachments figure prominently in his conception of love, but in S_M they have a metaphysical grounding in love for the Form of Beauty.
9. For S_E, piety is the service to a deity who is rigorously ethical in its character and in the demands it makes on men. His personal religion is practical. For S_M, religion centers on communion with Forms. It is mystical, focused on contemplation.
10. S_E's method of doing philosophy is adversative; S_M is a didactic philosopher, expounding truth to his interlocutors. His metaphysical theory is subjected to criticism in *Parmenides*, which in turn leads to a fresh start in *Theaetetus*.

Vlastos is well aware that, relying on the dialogues alone, it would not be possible to show that S_E and S_M represent the philosophies of two different historical figures as opposed to two different philosophies that Plato held at two times in his life. Accordingly, Vlastos in the next chapter of his book appeals to the evidence of Aristotle and Xenophon to support the claim that S_E represents the historical Socrates.[48] In fact, Vlastos argues only that the testimony of Aristotle and Xenophon support the first four theses; on the latter six, he offers no supporting external evidence. This testimony—especially that of Aristotle, which I will have more to say about in the fourth chapter—undoubtedly indicates that the historical Socrates did have views that we might perhaps designate as 'doctrines' or perhaps less tendentiously, as 'teachings.' But this is not enough for Vlastos's case. For he must also show that S_E *is* that historical figure, that is, that the philosophy represented in the early dialogues is the philosophy of the historical Socrates. Since everyone assumes that Plato wrote the dialogues in perfect awareness of what he was doing, we must suppose that the philosophical position expressed by S_E is and was intended by Plato to be identical with the philosophical position of the historical Socrates. Thus, to cite Aristotle's testimony that Socrates sought universal definitions of the virtues, whereas

---

48. Ibid., 81–106. See Dorion 2011, 14–16 on Vlastos's misuse of the evidence from Xenophon and Aristotle to bolster his hypothesis that S_E is the historical Socrates. According to Aristotle, *Soph. El.* 183b6–8, the historical Socrates claimed not to know the answers to the questions he himself put. By contrast, the Socrates of the dialogues—S_E and, of course, S_M—claims to know many things. For example, at *Meno* 98B1–5 he claims to know that true belief is different from knowledge. If the historical Socrates did not know the definitions of Forms, e.g., Forms of belief and knowledge, he would hardly regard himself as in a position to know that they are different.

Plato separated the Forms, does not even begin to show that what is true for the historical Socrates is also true for S_E. This is an especially acute problem for Vlastos, given that Aristotle also says that Plato arrived at the view that there was no knowledge of sensibles "starting in his youth" (ἐκ νέου).[49] Presumably, Plato's "youth" indicates a time prior to 399 BCE, the terminus a quo of at least some, and probably all, of the early dialogues, including those Vlastos cites as indicating Socrates' distinctive position.[50]

49. See *Meta.* A 6, 987a29–b9. Cf. N 4, 1078b9–12. Vlastos (1991, 94, n. 51) cites part of this passage but omits mention of the words ἐκ νέου from the previous sentence. Kahn (1992, 237–38), though critical of Vlastos's distinction between the Socrates of the early dialogues and the Socrates of the middle dialogues, and of his further assimilation of the former to the historical Socrates, bizarrely thinks that Aristotle's testimony about the "young" Plato must refer to what are in fact generally held to be the middle dialogues. So the attribution of the search for universal definitions by Aristotle to Socrates must refer to the early dialogues. Kahn's main point is that there is no reason for relying on Aristotle's testimony for the historical Socrates' views. It seems to me far more plausible that Aristotle is reconstructing these views from the dialogues corrected and supplemented by Plato's own oral communication. In the passage concerned, Aristotle is contrasting the views of Plato and Socrates. It is difficult to see how this can be taken to be a contrast between the Socrates of the early dialogues and the Plato of the middle dialogues, given that Socrates appears in all of these. In addition, it would be exceedingly odd if Plato, who would have been at least forty years of age at the time of the writing of the middle dialogues, were to be referred to by Aristotle as a "youth." Neither Vlastos nor Kahn assumes that Plato wrote *any* dialogues before thirty. Schofield (2000, 52) translates the words at 987a34–b1, ταῦτα μὲν καὶ ὕστερον οὕτως ὑπέλαβεν, "This is a position [that perceptibles are in flux and there is no knowledge of them] he later subscribed to in these terms." Kahn (1996, 81) translates similarly, "and this is what he later believed." These misleading translations, which in the one case omits the καί and in the other gives it the wrong emphasis, leave the impression that Plato did not subscribe to this position in his youth but only later took it up. But two lines later the text says that Plato followed Socrates in focusing on definitions and reasoned that the definitions were of Forms. If Plato did not hold this in his youth, then the words ἐκ νέου would have to refer to the 'early' dialogues, which, given the most likely dating of the dialogues and the usual meaning of the word νέος, is unlikely. The claim that Aristotle's reference to the separation of Forms is actually a reference to the middle dialogues goes back to Jackson 1882–87, especially the first article of 1882 (295–98), where Jackson, ignoring the reference to Plato's 'youth,' identifies the separation of Form as a 'development' that occurs in *Republic* and *Phaedo*. See the revised Oxford translation, which is better: "these views he held even in later years." Steel (2012, 171–74) argues that Aristotle's testimony is most likely not based on a direct report from Plato but rather is based on a reading of *Cratylus* 440B4–C1, where Socrates instructs Cratylus that unless Heraclitean flux doctrine is given up and stable entities are accepted, then knowledge is not possible. The *Cratylus* passage does indeed mirror the substance of Aristotle's testimony about Plato. But Steel's hypothesis does not account for the words ἐκ νέου. And the fact that Socrates is instructing Cratylus in the dialogue does not undermine the claim that Plato himself in his youth came to postulate Forms as a result of Heraclitean influence. The Socrates of the dialogue is, as Aristotle assumes, Plato himself. In the dialogue, Plato has a relatively mature Socrates represent a young Plato. In *Parmenides*, it is an immature Socrates who represents Plato.

50. Xenophon, *Mem.* 1.2.35, seems to suggest that the uppermost limit at which one can be called νέος is thirty. Even assuming that this is correct, Aristotle presumably got his information about Plato's early views from Plato, who, one would think, would not have used the word νέος to mislead, which he surely would have been doing if it was in fact the case that he had already written 'Socratic' dialogues prior to arriving at his metaphysical view about Forms. The

Moreover, Aristotle's testimony regarding the views of a man who died more than twenty years before Aristotle was born and more than thirty years before he arrived at the Academy must have either come in part from Plato himself or at least was not contradicted by Plato in conversation with Aristotle. So, if Vlastos is right, we should probably suppose that when Plato wrote the so-called early dialogues, he kept in check his own metaphysical views—views that, we recall, supposedly differ considerably from those of the historical Socrates—while attempting to represent other views through S_E.[51]

This is no doubt a possible scenario, but it is also a highly implausible one. There is no real evidence for it at all. For the scenario to work, we must suppose, as do all Socraticists, that *Phaedo*, which by Vlastos's own admission

---

nineteenth-century view, held by Hermann (1839) among others, that some of the dialogues were written prior to Socrates' death, has been largely abandoned since then. But see Sider 1980, who argues only against claims that the dialogues could not have been written while Socrates was still alive. See Heitsch 2002 and Rossetti 1991 for rather unconvincing arguments for *Ion* and *Hippias Minor* as possible candidates. Also, see Tomin 1997, who argues, like Schleiermacher (1836, 44–46), that *Phaedrus* is the first dialogue, but that its composition antedates the death of Socrates. Tomin relies on D.L. 3.38, who cites a tradition that *Phaedrus* was the first dialogue. Tomin argues further that this dialogue is a response to Aristophanes' attack on Socrates in *Frogs*, a play produced in 405 BCE and that, further, the positive reference to Polemarchus in *Phdr.* 257B must antedate his execution by the Thirty in 404. Tomin thinks that the dialogue is particularly directed against Isocrates and his rhetorical school (279B). This argument for the relative position of *Phaedrus* depends on the indirect historical evidence Tomin adduces. None of this evidence seems to me to point to a dating of the dialogue in 404. And if one of Plato's motives for writing the dialogue was to counter Isocrates' school, it would seem that this motivation would spring from the founding of his own Academy. The point about Polemarchus hardly seems probative since he appears in *Republic* 1 as philosophically inclined, and the writing of that work postdates his death in 404, even according to Tomin.

51. See Wolfsdorf 1999, who assumes that the distinction between early and middle dialogues is crucial for separating Plato's representation of Socratic philosophy from his own. So, too, McPherran 1996, 14–19. See Brickhouse and Smith 2010, 13–30, who argue, against Vlastos, that their separating the Socratic philosophy in the early dialogues from the philosophy of the historical Socrates shields them against arguments that the dialogues cannot be used as evidence of the latter. I agree. Nevertheless, they are still vulnerable to the argument that the Aristotelian evidence (which they appear at least in part to accept; see 30) suggests that Plato's philosophy is present in all the dialogues. In my view, this fact at least severely diminishes the plausibility of the claim that the early dialogues are intended to represent the philosophy of Socrates as opposed to showing the application of Platonic philosophy to certain ethical problems. That the historical Socrates' response to these problems can, roughly, be expressed in terms of the Socratic paradoxes seems not unlikely. In contrast to Brickhouse and Smith, Rudebusch (2009, 30–46) argues for a very robust and precise connection between the Socrates of the dialogues and the historical figure. He maintains that the dialogues are intended to show three actual stages of Socrates' life corresponding to his activity prior to hearing the Delphic Oracle, his "notorious" gadfly existence in Athens until he solves the riddle of the oracular utterance, and the last stage until his death. Imagining Socrates' life prior to and after his search for a refutation of the oracular claim that he is the wisest of men in Athens is an engaging idea. But it assumes that *Apology* is historically accurate on the point of the Oracle, whereas it arbitrarily dismisses the historical accuracy of dialogues like *Parmenides*. For if that dialogue is taken as historically accurate, it makes a teenage Socrates a proponent of separate Forms.

contains the metaphysical views that belong to Plato and are anathema to Socrates, was written at some distance from *Euthyphro, Apology,* and *Crito.* That is why it is supposed to be a 'middle' dialogue. Otherwise, we would have to suppose that Plato was representing S_E in the first three dialogues, but then for some obscure reason shifted to S_M. But this is inherently implausible. The only reason, apart from stylistic considerations, for distancing the composition of *Phaedo* from these other dialogues is to inoculate S_E from contamination by S_M.[52] But once again we know from Aristotle that the "young" Plato held at least the view that the Forms were separate, even if he did not then hold the view that the soul is immortal. So, distancing the composition of *Phaedo* from these other dialogues does not automatically protect S_E. And unless we are already committed to the hypothesis of a radical distinction between S_E and S_M—the former being represented in *Euthyphro, Apology,* and *Crito,* and the latter being represented in *Phaedo*—we would hardly be inclined to think that the composition of the four dramatically unified dialogues was interrupted in this odd manner. In other words, if separating the composition of *Phaedo* from the other dialogues does not keep Socrates safe from metaphysics, then why do it? Indeed, on the basis of Aristotle's testimony alone, the idea that Plato's philosophy (middle-period and later-period dialogues) developed out of Socrates' philosophy (early-period dialogues) seems just as likely to be exactly backward. Rather, Plato, steeped in a metaphysical view of his own, attempted in these early dialogues to apply that metaphysical view to ethical questions, in particular those that arose from the antirelativism of UP. It *may* nevertheless also be the case, of course, that these ethical views are similar to those of Socrates.

Still, despite this consideration, Vlastos, or someone following him, might have taken the following line. In *Euthyphro, Apology,* and *Crito,* as well as in other early dialogues, Plato may have wanted simply to represent the philosophy of the historical Socrates in the person of S_E. He could have inserted his own metaphysical views at any time, but he chose not to out of fidelity to the memory of Socrates and to his distinctive philosophy. Let us grant this possibility. But as has been argued recently by a number of scholars, it is simply false that Socrates in, say, *Euthyphro,* is just S_E, a philosopher concerned only with the search for universal definitions and oblivious

---

52. See Ledger 1989, 222–24, on the relatively close proximity of the composition of *Apology* and *Phaedo* on stylometric grounds See Kahn 2002, 94, on the stylistic similarity of *Phaedo* to *Apology, Charmides, Crito, Cratylus, Euthydemus, Euthyphro, Gorgias, Hippias Major, Hippias Minor, Ion, Laches, Lysis, Menexenus, Meno, Protagoras,* and *Symposium.* Peterson (2011, 166–95) makes an extraordinarily implausible effort to inoculate Socrates (the historical Socrates) from contamination by metaphysics in *Phaedo.* Her contention is that the arguments for the immortality of the soul and the claims made about separate Forms are not to be attributed to Socrates or even to Plato but are merely the consequences that Socrates draws from assumptions made by the Pythagorean-inspired Simmias and Cebes.

to metaphysics.[53] For example, Socrates in *Euthyphro* does not just want to know what the Form of Piety is; he also believes that there is such a thing as Piety that is the instrumental cause of the piety in pious things.[54] This is exactly the mode of causality attributed to the Form of Largeness and the Form of Beauty in *Phaedo* by the supposedly different philosopher, S_M.[55] So the Socrates of *Euthyphro* must have believed that Piety and Beauty exist, at least in a sufficiently 'substantial' manner that they can be the distinct causes of the existence of the attributes of piety and beauty in things. *This Socrates is not metaphysically innocent, as Vlastos would have it.* To argue, as Vlastos does, that S_E eschews a 'separately existing' Form of Piety and Beauty supports nothing more than the conclusion that the ontological status or mode of existence of Piety and Beauty is left open in *Euthyphro*.[56] Since, though, we have already seen that at the time of writing *Euthyphro* Plato in all probability believed in the separate existence of Forms, the appearance that the question is left open is explained as least as well (or far better, in my view) by the exigencies of the dramatic dialogic structure as it is by the hypothesis that Plato wants to represent the position of the historical Socrates. It may, indeed, be the case that the historical Socrates was uninterested in metaphysics, but the Socrates of the so-called early dialogues is not that philosopher.[57]

Vlastos himself thinks that 'elenctic knowledge,' the search for which is characteristic of S_E but not S_M, is "foundational for his interpretation of Socrates."[58] Elenctic knowledge supposedly consists in the moral beliefs derived from the exposition of the inconsistencies and contradictions in the views of Socrates' interlocutors. Apart from the problem of attributing to

---

53. See Krämer 1973; Prior 2004; Fronterotta 2007. See Fine 1993, 116, who assumes that when Aristotle says that Plato separated the Forms and that Socrates did not, Aristotle means the Socrates of the 'early' dialogues, not the historical Socrates. This assumption produces a strange reading of the passage in *Metaphysics*, given its historical references to Plato and to his predecessors without any mention of the dialogues.

54. See *Eu.* 6D10–11. In addition, this instrumental cause is a 'model,' as in *Parm.* 132D2.

55. See *Phd.* 100D7–8, E5–6. See Politis 2010 for a recent account of how essences or Forms are causes in *Phaedo*. In his cogent account, Forms serve as explanations in exactly the way they do in *Euthyphro*. Cf. *Euthyd.* 301A1–4.

56. See Vlastos 1991, 92–95.

57. Cf. Kahn 1996, 384–85, "From early on Plato's conception of philosophy is guided by a strong metaphysical vision. . . . I conclude then that Plato never wavers in his metaphysical vision." I think consistency demands that, pace Kahn, *Apology* not be excluded from this claim. Blondell (2002, 387), referring to the so-called later dialogues, says that for Plato, "philosophy is now greater than Socrates." But Blondell simply assumes without any evidence that this is not true for the early and middle dialogues.

58. See Vlastos 1991, 111, n. 23. Cf. 115, n. 39, "commitment to the elenctic method as the final arbiter of truth in the moral domain is common and peculiar to the ten dialogues which, for miscellaneous reasons, have been often thought by a wide variety of scholars to constitute the earliest segment of the Platonic corpus which I have called Plato's 'Elenctic Dialogues' in contradistinction to the 'Transitional' ones, in which the elenctic method is discarded while consistency of moral doctrine with their predecessors is maintained."

Plato two different concepts of knowledge—one for moral beliefs and one for demonstrative science—it seems simply false that any of the moral beliefs we might attribute to Socrates in the early dialogues are actually derived from the examination of the beliefs of his interlocutors. But as Kahn argues in his review of Vlastos's book, though this characterization of Socrates' moral beliefs fits the argument with Polus and Callicles in *Gorgias* and with his argument against Thrasymachus in *Republic* 1, it does not fit the use of elenchus in any of the definitional dialogues.[59] For in these dialogues, what are revealed by Socrates' examination of his interlocutors are not moral falsehoods, the opposites of which are the moral truths, knowledge of which Socrates is seeking, but rather ignorance of the definitions of moral Forms, like Piety, Temperance, Courage, and so on. More fundamentally for my thesis, insofar as the moral philosophy of the dialogues held to be early can be summarized in the Socratic paradoxes, though in some sense these may be thought to be derived by the negation of the contradictory claims made by the interlocutors, the reasons or arguments for their truth come from elsewhere, specifically from Platonic metaphysics. For example, in *Gorgias*, the refutation of the claim that doing injustice is better than suffering it, is based on Callicles' lack of acceptance of the claim that cowards are as good as brave men and that catamites live a happy life.[60] But the reason for Callicles' unwillingness to accept these claims is that he is ashamed to do so. Consequently, the reason for believing that the contradictory claim is true, if it is to be more than a moral intuition—in which case the elenchus is irrelevant—must be more than that it is shameful to believe that cowards are as good as brave men. If this is indeed shameful, that is because there is something about the nature of goodness and of human beings that makes it shameful. But in order to discover what this is, we need to have recourse to dialogues that Vlastos firmly identifies as containing the doctrines of S_M, not those of S_E.[61]

---

59. See Kahn 1992, 251.
60. See *Gorg.* 499A–B, 494E.
61. Benson (2000, 9–10), following Vlastos in making a fundamental distinction between S_E and S_M, thinks that the core of the philosophy of the former is epistemological. That is, his distinctive philosophy is found in his "elenctic method, his views concerning definition and definitional knowledge, his professions of ignorance and his view that knowledge is a *dunamis*" (220). Cf. Woodruff 1992, who identifies as 'Socratic' Plato's early theory of knowledge. According to this theory, 'knowledge' is what an expert in a field has as opposed to a novice or a sophist. It is substantially equivalent to true belief and/or τέχνη. Also, Wolfsdorf 2004. Given Aristotle's testimony about Plato's early commitment to a view about the nature of ἐπιστήμη, I find this interpretation implausible. Plato's view about knowledge is of a piece with his view about the objects of knowledge, that is, separate Forms, which, as Aristotle notes, is not Socrates' innovation. Cf. Irwin 1995, 27–29, on Socratic 'knowledge' as justified true belief. It is unclear to me how, in the so-called early dialogues, Socrates or anyone else would go about providing a justification for a belief, thereby guaranteeing that it is true. And if there is no guarantee, in what sense is this knowledge? Indeed, in what sense is it more than a lucky guess if the belief turns out to be true?

The Socraticist might seem to draw support from the historical fact that Stoics were inspired by what they took to be Socratic philosophy at the same time as they rejected the separate intelligible realm of Plato. Perhaps the Stoics' central ethical claim—that virtue is sufficient for happiness—is a better or more accurate representation of the true Socratic philosophy than is anything Plato made of it. Plato seems to base his support for the Socratic paradoxes on an array of metaphysical claims, including the immortality of the soul, that the Stoics reject. Plato's tripartitioning of the soul and his consequent recognition of the phenomenon of ἀκρασία are, too, rejected by the early Stoics, at least. Perhaps their own paradoxical claims such as "all fools are mad" (and everyone but a sage is a fool) and "all errors (ἁμαρτήματα) are equal," claims made without support from Platonic dualism or immaterialism of any kind, express what might be termed a version of Socratic philosophy or at least a conclusion logically drawn from it. As we will see, it is even possible to appeal to a self-declared follower of Plato—Antiochus of Ascalon—who seems to have maintained the harmony of the Stoic position with what he took to be the Platonic one in ethics. We would only need to add in this respect that Antiochus would have been exactly right if only he had distinguished the Socratic position from the Platonic one and identified Stoicism as being in harmony with the former.

The principal flaw in this approach is evident if we consider that the Stoics do not adopt a pragmatic or prudentialist interpretation of the Socratic paradoxes. Indeed, what is most distinctive about Stoicism in antiquity is its absolutely uncompromising rigorism or absolutism. Someone who does not act as the sage would act, say, in the situation in which Socrates found himself in prison, is a fool and utterly mad. One can see that this view follows from Stoic metaphysical principles; a similar view follows, as we have seen, from Platonic metaphysical principles. Indeed, we have only Platonic metaphysical principles to explain Socrates' actions. It is arguable that the Stoic principles are preferable to the Platonic. It does not seem to me to be arguable that without either the Stoic or the Platonic principles, Socrates' ethical absolutism would make sense. For Plato, metaphysical principles turn an indefensible pragmatic version of the paradoxes into a defensible one.[62]

---

62. D.L., 7.38, in the introduction to his general account of Stoic doctrines says that he will include all Stoic doctrine under the life of Zeno since he was the founder of the school. This might suggest that Cleanthes and Chrysippus could have provided the metaphysical backing for Zeno's ethical doctrines analogous to the way that Plato provided the metaphysical backing for Socrates'. If the analogy holds at all, Zeno is to be compared to the historical Socrates, not to Vlastos's S_E, who is Plato's creation.

Terry Penner

A different approach to the establishment of a distinctive Socratic philosophy has been pursued by Terry Penner in a number of subtle and powerful papers. Penner, like Vlastos, assumes that the relatively early dialogues of Plato contain a distinctive philosophical position, what Penner calls 'Socratic intellectualism.'[63] So the Socrates of the early dialogues is close to or identical with the historical Socrates. His position is in crucial respects rejected by Plato in his middle dialogues, where Socrates is now representing Plato's philosophy, not that of the historical Socrates.[64] Penner, like Vlastos, provides a list of contrasts between the early dialogues and the middle ones.[65] Some of the items on the list do not necessarily indicate a difference in philosophical position, such as the contrast between aporetic and non-aporetic structure, the length of the dialogues, and the lightheartedness of the early dialogues versus the somberness of the middle ones. Substantively, Penner finds in the early dialogues the treatment of virtue purely as a τέχνη, whereas in the middle and late dialogues, the acquisition of virtue requires emotional training. Similarly, in the early dialogues Socrates believes that persuasion comes only from teaching, whereas in the middle and late dialogues Plato maintains that appeals to emotion can persuade without Socratic teaching. In addition, in the early dialogues mathematics is not given a special role in the attainment of knowledge, whereas in the middle and late dialogues it is.

The remaining and most important differences, according to Penner, concern the intellectualism of Socrates versus a markedly different concept of human psychology and ethics in Plato. Socratic intellectualism is the view that human wrongdoing and human happiness are entirely dependent on knowledge of the good that all humans seek. Since all desire the good, if one knows what that is, then one cannot but strive to attain it. Thus, in this sense virtue is knowledge. Since this knowledge of good (and evil) is one thing, all the virtues are different names for this one knowledge. Intellectualism also informs the theory of desire. Thus, the desires of everyone, including those who are not virtuous, are for the good, that is, for whatever is best for oneself. What differentiates the virtuous from everyone else is

---

63. On Socratic intellectualism, see Nehemas 1999, chap. 2; Penner 2002, 195–99; Penner and Rowe 2005, 216–30; Burnyeat 2006; Seel 2006, 21–30. Contra: Kahn 1996, 311, 319–20, "In effect, I deny the existence of a distinct Socratic moral theory in the dialogues."

64. See Penner 1992, 130, who seems to assume that the early dialogues were written in Plato's "youth when he was under the influence of Socrates." But Aristotle's testimony reveals that in Plato's "youth" he held at least one important metaphysical position that Penner thinks the historical Socrates did not. See also Penner 2004.

65. Penner 1992, 125–30. Penner (2011, 287–88) actually appeals to *Rep.* 505A–506A in support of his 'Socratic' account of the psychology of action at the same time as he rejects the psychology of action found in *Rep.* book 4, that according to which the phenomenon of incontinence is acknowledged and explained.

that they know how to obtain this.⁶⁶ Accordingly, no one can act contrary to what he believes to be best and so ἀκρασία is impossible. By contrast, Plato rejects most of the tenets of Socratic intellectualism. Plato believes or came to believe that more than knowledge is necessary for virtue; one must be trained emotionally as a precondition for the acquisition of knowledge. In addition, Plato in the middle and late dialogues rejects the unity of virtue precisely because he denies that virtue is nothing but knowledge of good and evil.⁶⁷ Perhaps most important, Plato's tripartitioning of the soul leads him to assert the existence of irrational desires and therefore the possibility of ἀκρασία. He will, then, interpret the doctrine that no one does wrong willingly differently from Socrates. For Socrates, wrongdoing is entirely owing to ignorance; for Plato, although ignorance can lead to one type of wrongdoing, other types flow from the actions of the two lower parts of the soul and from bad bodily constitution or bad upbringing.

Aristotle's testimony does support Penner on two points: Socrates (presumably, the historical Socrates, not the Socrates of the dialogues) thought that (a) the virtues are forms of knowledge, and (b) ἀκρασία is impossible.⁶⁸ The question now becomes whether this testimony may be supposed to tell us about the Socrates of the early dialogues as well as the Socrates of history. That the former maintains that virtue is knowledge in some sense and, in *Protagoras*, that ἀκρασία is impossible, is relatively clear. Can we, then, construct some form of 'Socratic (that is, anti-Platonic) intellectualism' out of these two doctrines alone?

In order to do so, we need to be able to provide an account of knowledge (ἐπιστήμη) that underlies both (a) and (b) inasmuch as the impossibility of ἀκρασία means that one cannot act against what one knows to

---

66. Penner 1992, 127–29.
67. Brickhouse and Smith (1994, 68–72) and Brickhouse and Smith (2010, 154–67) agree with Penner that Socratic philosophy requires the unity of virtue and that the unity consists in there being one knowledge of good and evil. They gloss this as "the expert knowledge of how to live" (2010, 180). Such knowledge includes, for example, knowing when to call a physician (and a skilled one?) in order to remove an evil and replace it with a good, namely, health. It is difficult, though, to see how this 'know-how' and countless others that are seemingly unconnected, such as the 'know-how' of proper religious practice, constitute a unity, the unity that is required to make all the virtues one thing. In any case, true belief would seem to work as well as knowledge here.
68. For the identity of virtue and knowledge in some sense, see *MM* A 1, 1182a15–23; A 20, 1190b28–32; A 34, 1198a10–12; *EN* Γ 8,1116b3–5; Z 13, 1144b17–21, 28–30; *EE* A 5, 1216b3–8. For the denial of the possibility of incontinence, see *EN* H3, 1145b25–26. Presumably, these two claims are supposed to be logically connected on the grounds that incontinence is impossible because of ignorance or an absence of knowledge, so that if knowledge is present, then so is virtue. On the hypothesis that the presence or absence of a definite article in reference to Socrates indicates a distinction between the Socrates of the dialogues and the Socrates of history, see Ross 1924, 1:xxxix–xli. Tarrant (2000, 47) is skeptical of this hypothesis, though, as he suggests, the fact that Plato could have his character Socrates actually maintain views—like the denial of the possibility of incontinence and the identity of virtue and knowledge—that the historical Socrates might well have held, too, does muddy the waters.

be good for oneself. This account will, presumably, differ from the middle dialogue account of knowledge, according to which there is no knowledge of the sensible world. This must be the case since one who knows what the virtuous thing to do is or one who knows that to act in a certain way is to act against his knowledge of the right way to act will have knowledge of that which in *Republic* is available only for belief (δόξα), not knowledge. That is, he will have knowledge of particular or contingent states of affairs. The importance of this point will emerge in a moment.

Penner, rightly in my view, brings (a) and (b) together in the doctrine that no one does wrong willingly (οὐδείς ἑκὼν ἁμαρτάνει). He argues that the meaning of this doctrine is different for one who denies the possibility of ἀκρασία and for one who affirms it. Thus, when Plato (or, more correctly, Socrates in the middle and late dialogues) expresses the doctrine, it means something different from what it means in the Socratic dialogues, where the philosophy of the historical Socrates is supposedly being articulated. The issue is whether this putative 'Socratic' meaning is intelligible apart from the metaphysical apparatus to which Plato evidently adheres even when he is supposedly articulating Socratic doctrine.[69]

Thus, 'no one does wrong willingly' is interpreted by Penner to mean that if anyone errs, it is owing to ignorance.[70] But if this means merely that no one acts counter to the goal they are seeking when they are aware of what does and what does not conduce to this goal, then this Socratic paradox seems to be an analytic truth. Penner, though, wants to argue that 'no one does wrong willingly' is a substantive doctrine.[71] Tyrants, Penner argues, really do evil unwillingly because they do not know that evil is bad for them, that is, that by doing evil they will not achieve the good that they seek.

The problem with this interpretation is that it seems to reduce Socrates' paradoxical and astonishing doctrine to a platitude of prudentiality, similar to 'crime does not pay' or 'honesty is the best policy.' But this is not the way Plato has Socrates' interlocutors take the doctrine or the way that Plato himself takes the doctrine, even if he is representing the historical Socrates when he expresses it in the early dialogues. For one thing, a tyrant might well take a calculated risk that the benefits of wrongdoing will in the end outweigh the benefits of refraining from wrongdoing. Who is to say that

---

69. See Penner and Rowe 2005, 196–97, who claim that in supporting the attribution of 'Socratic intellectualism' to the Socrates of the dialogues there is "an entire web of interlocking claims about knowledge, desire, love, and the good. All of these claims—we propose—are involved in the argument of the dialogue [i.e., *Lysis*], and if we are fully to understand that argument, we need to take cognizance of all of them." At 195, n. 2, Penner and Rowe maintain that the only fundamental difference between Socrates and Plato is in regard to the psychology of action. But this supposed difference in the psychology of action itself rests upon differences with regard to knowledge and the good—differences that they claim are not present in the early dialogues although they may be present later on.

70. Penner 1992, 129.

71. See especially Penner 1991.

this risk is *never* warranted? And yet, in *Crito* Socrates is made to urge an absolutist prohibition of wrongdoing.[72] This absolutism is at odds with the prudentialist interpretation of 'no one does wrong willingly.' We should not, therefore, attribute that interpretation to the claim made by the Platonic Socrates. It may well be the case that the historical Socrates would have accepted this interpretation, but the Socrates of the early dialogues is different.[73]

Penner also associates (a) and (b) above with the doctrine of 'soul care' expressed in *Apology*.[74] His claim is that soul care is what leads to the happiness or good that all seek. Hence, the knowledge that is virtue is the knowledge of how to care for one's soul. Moreover, if no one does wrong willingly, it is because 'doing wrong' is the opposite of caring for one's soul.

---

72. See *Cr.* 49B8: Οὐδαμῶς ἄρα δεῖ ἀδικεῖν. Cf. 49A6–7; *Ap.* 29B6–7; *Gorg.* 469B13–C2, 508C4ff.

73. See Santas 1979, 183–94, who distinguishes what he calls the 'prudential paradox' from the 'moral paradox.' The former derives from the doctrine that no one desires evil things and that all who pursue evil things do so involuntarily. The latter derives from the doctrine that virtue is knowledge and that all who do injustice or wrong do so involuntary. Santas argues that the first doctrine seems paradoxical only to one who fails to distinguish the good that we truly desire from the evil that we unintentionally desire: we really want the former though we mistakenly opt for the latter. The moral paradox arises from the counterintuitive notion that if someone knows what the virtuous thing to do is, he will necessarily do it. As Santas shows, the paradoxes are actually mutually supportive if in fact it is the case that doing the virtuous thing is always in one's interest, though Santas insists (191) that there is nothing in the dialogues to support the claim that Plato accepted the moral paradox. But this leaves Socrates or Plato with the problem of explaining why it is necessarily the case that virtuous behavior is always beneficial. I do not think that there is anything in the dialogues to suggest that Socrates—the historical Socrates—has an answer to this question; Plato's answer requires a metaphysical apparatus that seems quite alien to anything our sources tell us about Socrates. Penner (2002, 195) explicitly identifies the types of belief in his 'belief-desire' account of Socratic intellectualism as including an array of practical beliefs about the actions that will achieve one's own good.

74. Penner 1992, 134–37. See *Ap.* 20A–B, 24C–25C, 36C. See Brickhouse and Smith 2010, 44–49, for a defense of a version of prudentialism. They argue that Socrates' view is that (a) x is good = x is conducive to the securing of what is in the agent's interest; (b) what is in our interest is an objective matter of fact, and not simply a matter of the agent's subjective desires or satisfactions; and (c) we always and only want what is really in our ultimate interest. I think this is correct, but this analysis of the argument draws its apparent plausibility from an ambiguity underlying the use of the term 'objective.' It may well be an objective matter whether or not thievery is in one's ultimate interest, but it is far from obvious that the correct answer is that it never is. What Brickhouse and Smith need 'objective' to mean here is 'universal,' such that regardless of the objective circumstances pertaining to a particular individual, thievery never can be in one's ultimate interest. The defense of such an absolutist position falls within the ambit of Platonic metaphysics, that is, the metaphysics of the Idea of the Good. I take it that the famous ring of Gyges in *Republic* is meant to provide an example of someone for whom on prudentialist grounds unjust behavior is not contraindicated. Nevertheless, Plato wants to maintain that the misuse of the ring could not possibly be in Gyges' interest. I maintain that Socrates, as characterized by Penner and Smith and Brickhouse, has no explanation for this uncompromising modality. But if they wish to soften the modality to 'probably but not necessarily not in their interest,' what sort of philosophical argument does that leave Socrates with?

According to Penner, the reason one should care for one's soul is that it is the *instrument* of human happiness.[75] No doubt, in some sense this is true, but this does not gainsay the fact that the body, and bodily possessions, are also instruments of human happiness. The crucial consideration regarding soul care is whether that should be an absolutely overriding consideration for any human being. But surely that is the case only if the soul is not an instrument of the human being but somehow constitutive of the human being whereas the body is *merely* an instrument. Unless this is so, then one might well make the prudential judgment that in a particular case body care ought to take precedence over soul care. Thus, one might well argue that, contrary to what Socrates repeatedly maintains, it is sometimes better to be the one who harms rather than the one who is harmed.[76]

The identity of the person with the soul (and the 'demotion' of the body to an instrument) is explicitly made by Socrates in *Alcibiades* I.[77] Penner does not mention this text, presumably because he believes the dialogue spurious. But the identity of the person with the soul also seems to be implied by the passage in *Apology* in which Socrates exhorts those who have condemned him to care not for their possessions but for themselves.[78] It also seems to be implied in *Crito* where Socrates claims that the body is inferior to the soul.[79] With the identity of soul and person or self established, one would have the elements of an argument for the conclusion that soul care is of paramount importance for any sane human being. Without this identity, the exhortation to soul care above and beyond everything else in

---

75. The main text cited by Penner for this, *Hip. Mi.* 374E3–4, is odd. The point of the text is not to make the claim that the soul is an instrument or possession but that in general it is better to have an instrument that operates voluntarily rather than involuntarily.

76. See *Cr.* 49A–E and esp. *Gorg.* 472C–481B.

77. See *Alc.* I.130C1–3: Ἐπειδὴ δ' οὔτε σῶμα οὔτε τὸ συναμφότερόν ἐστιν ἄνθρωπος, λείπεται οἶμαι ἢ μηδὲν αὔτ' εἶναι, ἢ εἴπερ τί ἐστι, μηδὲν ἄλλο τὸν ἄνθρωπον συμβαίνειν ἢ ψυχήν (Since the human being is neither the body nor the composite [of body and soul], I think it remains that either he is nothing or, if he is something, then he is nothing other than a soul). Cf. C5–6; *Meno* 86A3–4.

78. See *Ap.* 36C5–7: ἐπιχειρῶν ἕκαστον ὑμῶν πείθειν μὴ πρότερον μήτε τῶν ἑαυτοῦ μηδενὸς ἐπιμελεῖσθαι πρὶν ἑαυτοῦ ἐπιμεληθείη ὅπως ὡς βέλτιστος καὶ φρονιμώτατος ἔσοιτο (trying to persuade each of you not to care for any of your possessions before you care for yourselves in order that you should be the best and wisest possible). Cf. 29D7–E3; 31B5. Hence soul care appears to be 'self care,' something that could never be trumped by 'body care.' If soul care is not self care, then, presumably, the self is the soul plus the body, or more precisely, the subject of psychic states plus the subject of bodily states. Why should we accept that privileging the one over the other is always in our benefit?

79. *Cr.* 47E6–48A1. In this passage, 'body care' is regarded as highly important, though inferior in importance to 'soul care,' presumably because the soul is not a mere possession. The words ἢ φαυλότερον ἡγούμεθα εἶναι τοῦ σώματος ἐκεῖνο, ὅτι ποτ' ἐστὶ τῶν ἡμετέρων, περὶ ὃ ἥ τε ἀδικία καὶ ἡ δικαιοσύνη ἐστίν; (or do we think that whatever it is of ours that is concerned with justice and injustices is inferior to the body?) in reference to the soul may seem to make it another possession like the body, but I think the partitive genitive must be taken in a looser sense, i.e., 'among the parts constituting a human being,' which would include the subject of wicked and just acts, namely, the person or self.

all circumstances is, in my opinion, mostly rhetorical. That Plato in the so-called middle and late dialogues maintains the identity of the person with the soul is clear enough.[80] Even if *Alcibiades* I is not genuine, then it seems that he held this in the early dialogues as well and *his* Socrates does have at least some of the metaphysical 'baggage' that Vlastos and Penner wish to deny him.

I will not here rehearse the arguments for and against the authenticity of this dialogue. I believe it is authentic, but if it is not, then some early Academic evidently saw the point about the insufficiency of the pragmatic interpretation of the Socratic paradoxes. More important for my argument is that the claim that the person is identical with the soul or, in other words, that the person is *not* the composite of soul and body that is the human being, is a claim that is much more apt to be confirmed in a non-question-begging manner if the soul can exist separate from the body and if I have some reason to believe that I am identical with this separated soul.[81] That is, of course, exactly what *Phaedo* tries to show. So much is agreed by all. But not only do Penner and Vlastos have to insist on the inauthenticity of *Alcibiades* I because otherwise their case is severely damaged, but they are also then committed to making *Phaedo* a middle dialogue, that is, a dialogue that expresses the philosophy of Plato and not the philosophy of Socrates. As we have already seen, separating *Phaedo* from *Euthyphro*, *Apology*, and *Crito* in this way is problematic and in fact indicated only by the antecedent determination to separate Socratic intellectualism from Plato's philosophy.

In the case of Penner, it is all the more problematic because he (like Vlastos) does recognize *Gorgias* as an early Socratic dialogue in which Socratic philosophy is present. But in *Gorgias*, though we do not have a proof for the immortality of the soul, we do have an extensive myth about the disposition of the soul in the afterlife, a myth that assumes that this disposition refers to *us*.[82] So Penner is reduced to holding that Plato has inserted this myth in spite of the Socratic philosophy that he is otherwise representing in that dialogue. This seems to me unlikely. It may well be the case that the historical Socrates was diffident or agnostic about the immortality of the soul.[83] But we are here concerned with whether the Socrates of the early dialogues is just the historical Socrates. The above considerations suggest that he is not.

---

80. See *Lg.* 959B3–4, with 721B7–8, 773E5ff.; *Phd.* 76C11, 92B5, 95C5–6; *Tim.* 90C2–3.

81. Brickhouse and Smith (2010, chap. 4), while criticizing Penner's rigorous intellectualism, yet acknowledge (107) that their own position is a form of intellectualism, agreeing that Socrates holds that wrongdoing is to be avoided at all costs because it harms the soul, indeed, that it harms the soul necessarily. But unless the soul is the self, one might well make a prudential decision to bear a certain amount of 'soul harm,' particularly in extremis.

82. See *Gorg.* 493A1–C3. Cf. Cooper 1999, 29–75, for a related argument that *Gorgias* is a 'transitional' dialogue, transitional between the dialogues of Socratic intellectualism and the innovations in moral psychology in *Republic*.

83. See *Ap.* 40C–41D.

Christopher Rowe

The last Socraticist I will consider is Christopher Rowe, whose 2007 book, *Plato and the Art of Philosophical Writing*, takes a radically new approach in opposition to the position that the dialogues somewhere contain the philosophy of Socrates and somewhere else contain the philosophy of Plato.[84] Rowe wants to argue that *all* the dialogues are Socratic, that is, that Plato is in every dialogue representing Socratic philosophy.[85] What appears to most as a change of mind on Plato's part is actually only a change of strategy.[86] Hence, his view is a very unusual sort of unitarianism as opposed to developmentalism: the unitarianism of Socraticism rather than of Platonism as traditionally understood.

Thus, Rowe's Plato embraces the truth of the Socratic paradox that no one does wrong willingly, the unity of the virtues, and the claims that virtue is knowledge and that we always and only desire our own good.[87] Like Penner, Rowe believes that a doctrine of the unity of soul and hence of the impossibility of ἀκρασία is intended by Socrates to provide the necessary support for these claims. For this reason, to abandon this unity in favor of the partitioning of the soul is (as it is for Penner) to abandon Socrates' philosophy. For Rowe, however, Plato is to be understood not to take partitioning seriously, that is, it is not a necessary consequence of embodiment.[88] In fact, the embodied soul only appears to have three parts; in reality or in its essence it is a unity.[89] If people choose to act on their appetites, then we can characterize this within a tripartite framework, but it is not necessary for people so to act.

Rowe's position that in *Republic* the soul is truly a unity would be easier to understand and endorse if by 'true soul' he meant the soul when separate from the body. For in *Republic* 10 and in *Timaeus* Plato seems to hold just that.[90] In fact, though, Rowe maintains that tripartition is not the burden of the philosophical adept in their embodied state. It is not the burden of the virtuous since virtue is knowledge, and with this knowledge, it is not possible for one to be overpowered by one's appetites. One who is virtuous has, potentially, the appetites or passions that ordinary people have, but these are completely within the control of his knowledge of what is good for himself.

---

84. Rowe 2007. Peterson (2011) outbids Rowe in the market for Socratic purity by arguing that not only is Socrates innocent of metaphysics and of 'doctrine' generally, but that Plato is, too.

85. Rowe 2007, viii.

86. Ibid., 13.

87. Ibid., 26.

88. Ibid., 166–67.

89. Ibid., 170–71. This claim seems to contradict explicitly *Rep.* 612A4–6: νῦν δὲ τὰ ἐν τῷ ἀνθρωπίνῳ βίῳ πάθη τε καὶ εἴδη, ὡς ἐγῷμαι, ἐπιεικῶς αὐτῆς διεληλύθαμεν. (We have, I think, given now a rather good account of the states and forms of it [the soul] in human life.)

90. *Rep.* 611B9–612A6; *Tim.* 41C–D, 69C5–6, 69E1, 90A.

So he will never act contrary to what he knows is good, which is supposedly the phenomenon that leads to the postulation of a partitioned soul.

For this interpretation to work, Rowe has to assume that Plato, in presenting his moral psychology in *Republic*, is making a distinction between knowledge and belief such that it is only the former that is impervious to appetite and hence to actions that appear to be acratic. Leontius does act against his belief that corpse-gazing is bad for him because he embraces another (false) belief that his appetite for corpse-gazing ought to be satisfied. By contrast, someone who *knew* that corpse-gazing was bad for him would never even recognize in himself such an appetite.

Here is the problem with this interpretation. Leontius's belief that corpse-gazing is bad for himself could not, if true, differ from the belief of a virtuous man that corpse-gazing is bad for himself. Even if the virtuous man can be said to know the reasons for this, that is, have a true moral theory about why it is wrong for him to do it, the psychological states of this person and Leontius do not or at least need not differ in this regard at the moment of decision.[91] Where they differ is in the fact that the virtuous person has no appetite for corpse-gazing, whereas Leontius does. Rowe interprets this to mean that in his case what is about to be overpowered when he gazes is "[his] own particular belief about what it is best for him to do."[92] If that is so, then how are we to understand Leontius's belief that corpse-gazing is wrong for him? Was not *that* the belief he held about what is best for him to do? Either Leontius is or is not acting against what he thinks is the best thing for him to do. If he is, then his appetite for corpse-gazing is not to be identified with his belief that this is the best thing for him to do; if he is not, then he is not an acratic. In short, his appetite for corpse-gazing cannot be characterized or constituted by his belief that corpse-gazing is best for him. Consequently, Rowe either has to describe Leontius in such a way that he is really not an acratic—in which case Plato's explicit analysis of his state of mind and his action is pointless—or else he has to show that knowledge as opposed to belief makes a substantive difference to the psychology of action. But since for Rowe, Plato wants to maintain that knowledge just is a form of belief, it is difficult to see how he can do this.[93]

On Rowe's behalf, it must be said that the apparent denial of the possibility of ἀκρασία in *Protagoras* and the apparent recognition of the phenomenon in *Republic* poses a problem for any unitarian, whether Socraticist or Platonist. For the latter, it is open to maintain that Plato changed his mind at the same time as he held to his fundamental principles, namely, the identity of the person with the rational soul and the desire of every person

---

91. See below for Rowe's discounting of the difference between knowledge and belief in *Republic* and *Theaetetus*.

92. Rowe 2007, 173.

93. See ibid., 134, where it is clear that Rowe thinks that *if* we had knowledge of Forms before birth, then that knowledge would be part of our 'belief set.'

for the good. For the former, however, any dialogue after (or other than) *Protagoras* must be interpreted such that ἀκρασία is utterly trivialized in order to maintain the appropriate interpretation of the claim that virtue is knowledge and no one does wrong willingly. More than this, ἐγκράτεια, or continence, must also be trivialized or turned into something mysterious, since if one knows (or strongly believes) that something is bad for one, it will on Rowe's interpretation not be possible for one even to be tempted to do the opposite in the sense in which we would ordinarily say that a continent person was tempted but did not give in. The inevitable elimination of continence (or its conflation with virtue) along with incontinence (or its conflation with vice) might strike one as exactly right. That is probably what the early Stoics thought. But then Rowe's task, like that of any interpreter of Plato, is to determine what Plato held, not what Plato should have held or would have held had he taken the apposite Stoic counsel.

Rowe's relentless discounting of Platonic metaphysics and epistemology on behalf of the thesis that Plato is thoroughly Socratic in all the dialogues in which Socrates appears as the principal interlocutor is implausible on many fronts.[94] But it is particularly damaging to his Socraticism in regard to knowledge (ἐπιστήμη) and the Forms. For Rowe wants to argue that the core of Socratic doctrine is that virtue is knowledge, and that this knowledge or wisdom is about what is good and bad for us. To have knowledge is to grasp the truth about such things.[95] That, for Rowe, is equivalent to 'seeing' the Forms of Justice, Good, Beauty, etc. In *Republic*, what differentiates the 'lovers of sights and sounds' from true philosophers is not that the former have mere belief about sensibles whereas the latter have knowledge of separate Forms, but that the former have false belief about Forms whereas the latter have (more or less) true beliefs about Forms.[96] In fact, anyone who is making a universal judgment

---

94. Ibid., 255–56. See 200–201: "[In the *Republic*, book 5] Socrates does not set out to give an exposition of epistemology or metaphysics, and if we read it as such we are liable to convict him of saying things he doesn't want to say at all." One wonders how we are to determine "what Socrates wants to say" other than by what he in fact does say. Does it not make more sense, at least, to take what he does say as a starting point for determining what he wants to say?

95. Ibid., 209.

96. Ibid., 213. Cf. Fine (1990) for a similar view. In Gerson 2003, 148–73, I have tried to show that there is no textual basis in *Republic* for this view. One might adduce *Rep.* 505B5–6, where it is said that the many believe the Good to be pleasure, as evidence that it is possible to have δόξα of Forms. But this passage (and others) cannot mean that the many are referring to the Idea of the Good and then making a propositional claim about it. For, surely, Plato would deny that one could have a vision of the Good, a vision that is available only to philosophers, and then go on to make false statements about it. As much can be said for claims like those of Stemmer (1985, 86) that the false answers to the 'what is X' question in the early dialogues proves that there can be false belief about Forms. To suppose that there can be false beliefs about Forms is to conflate false belief with ignorance, something that is inconsistent with the Divided Line's separation of these. Someone who believes that the Good is pleasure would be no different from someone who was ignorant of—that is, had no cognitive contact with—the Good. In order to separate false belief from ignorance, one would have to stipulate that the

is referring to Forms. Rowe allows that the separation of Forms and the radical distinction of knowledge and belief would make Platonism substantially different from Socraticism, but in fact Plato does not subscribe to this.

It is clear why Rowe's Socratic unitarianism would be undermined by ascribing to Plato the view that Forms are separate and that knowledge of them is discontinuous with belief about sensibles. For the knowledge that is to be virtue is for Rowe a true belief about what our good consists in doing at any particular moment. But such a belief could not have as its object a Form much less a separate Form. That is apparently why Rowe goes on to suggest that the knowledge is of an 'Aristotelian universal.'[97] Perhaps Rowe can draw some support for this claim from Aristotle's criticism of Forms to the effect that Forms are supposed to function as universals as well as separate particulars.[98] And yet the dilemma facing Rowe is that if this Form-as-universal is supposed to be the object of the knowledge that is virtue, how will this amount to a true belief about what to do in a particular circumstance or what is good or bad for the individual at this moment?[99] But if it does not amount to this belief, then it is also far from obvious why knowledge of it—knowledge, say, of what justice is—will motivate someone to act in the way that Rowe thinks one must act. For this knowledge of what justice is will not amount to the knowledge that justice is good for me here and now. And if it does not, then it is false that virtue just is this knowledge of a universal.

What Rowe requires is an objective link between all the virtues, understood to be necessarily expressions of the Good and one's own good. That is, he needs a metaphysical link between universal goodness and the goodness that is the core of his interpretation of Socrates' psychological egoism. But Rowe's Socrates *and* Rowe's Plato eschew such metaphysical excess. Granted, it is not decisive to insist that Aristotle and other members of the Old Academy present a radically different picture.[100] Still, as I have argued, on Rowe's view Plato spent most of his career making claims he did

---

one holding the false belief was actually referring to the subject to which the attribution of the predicate was equivalent to the false belief. But the only way to refer to an immaterial Form is to know it. It is not clear that even the mathematicians in the Divided Line are referring to Forms when they hypothesize their existence. If, though, they are, their mode of cognition, διάνοια, must be distinct from δόξα. Cf. *Phd.* 84A8, where the philosopher's vision of that which is true and divine is a vision of "that which is not an object of belief" (ἀδόξαστον).

97. Rowe 2007, 251.
98. See *Meta.* Z 13, 1038b35–1039a3; Z 16, 1040b26–30; M 9, 1086a32–35.
99. For Aristotle, the φρόνιμος is able to see the application of the universal principle to the particular circumstance. But a universal principle is certainly not a Form.
100. See Rowe 2007, 48, "But there is no reason why we should follow Aristotelian doxography here....Aristotle's 'authority' amounts to nothing." This unequivocal rejection of the entire body of Aristotle's testimony seems to spring more from a refusal to accept what this testimony tells us about Plato's philosophy than from a reasoned examination of its import and value.

not believe in support of an ethical position that would be defensible only if those claims were true. The hypothesis that there is a fully articulated Socratic philosophy in the dialogues distinct from and even opposed to Platonic philosophy has very little to recommend it. I think that the extant historical evidence enables us to do better than this.

CHAPTER 3

Reading the Dialogues Platonically

If we are going to give ownership of all the doctrines in the dialogues to Plato—the elements of UP and the positive responses to them—then we are going to have to face the question of whether Plato's thought 'developed' in any way.[1] We have already seen that he may have changed his mind about the possibility of ἀκρασία. He also may have changed his mind about the relation between the philosopher and the statesman, the nature of pleasure, the need for a *superordinate* Idea of the Good, the extent of the realm of Forms—indeed, whether separate Forms exist at all—the relation of Forms to numbers, the 'part' of the soul that is immortal (as opposed to the entire soul), the nature of the correct philosophical method, the relation of the soul to the body, and the nature of emotions. This list is not intended to be exhaustive. Given Plato's preferred way of communicating his philosophical views, there is an almost irresistible tendency to try to sort out these hypothetical changes in his views along something like a developmental trajectory. That is, since we have to work so hard in ferreting out the position being maintained, it would help considerably if we could discover that that position was a revision or repudiation of an earlier version.

Another reason for the allure of developmentalism is that at one level it seems obviously true. It can hardly be supposed that whenever Plato first created a dialogue with the character Socrates, he already had in mind all the detailed claims that flow through the entire corpus. Moreover, with the founding of the Academy in 387 or thereabouts, one must suppose that the regular opportunity to discuss his views with others presented Plato with

---

1. See Press 1996 for a valuable survey of modern opinion on the relationship between the dialogues and Plato's thought, that is, Platonism.

questions and problems that he was naturally inclined to consider.[2] It is not unreasonable that, prodded by such challenges, ideas occurred to him that had not occurred before. It hardly needs to be added that with the arrival of Aristotle and his association with Plato over the last twenty years or so of the master's life, Plato was, shall we say, inspired, to put it in the most neutral manner, to come at some of his central concerns in ways that could not be found in works written earlier.

It will be noted that all of the above putative 'developments' can be accounted for within the ambit of UP. Even a reconsideration of the range of Forms or the exact meaning of 'separation' need not entail a wavering of commitment to UP. In fact, if the arguments of the last chapter are thought to be at least somewhat plausible, there is not a shred of evidence that Plato ever 'developed' regarding his fundamental oppositions or 'antis.'[3] This is the unanimous opinion of the Platonists of antiquity.

When, though, we do compile a list of issues on which Plato's precise views are not incontrovertibly clear, we can begin to see the origin of the various versions of Platonism. For example, the nature of the soul, the relations existing among the entities within the intelligible realm, and the nature of cognition are not unequivocally determinable from axioms derived from UP. Some versions of Platonism are constructed by giving greater weight to an argument in one dialogue than to one in another. The authority accorded to Plato for having 'revealed' the best, that is, most complete and most defensible, version of Platonism does not preclude the opting for some specific claims that do actually contradict what Plato says in one dialogue if not contradicting what he says in another.

In the light of deep puzzlement about how to arrive at a non-question-begging developmental picture of Plato's thought, many scholars have striven to construct a chronology of the dialogues based on some criterion other than philosophical.[4] The preferred method is stylometric analysis. This involves an attempt to discover significant, albeit subtle, shifts in Plato's style of Greek composition, shifts that, owing to their subtlety, are likely to be largely unconscious. The method has been much refined over the last century since its inception, particularly with the invention of computer-assisted analysis. The results are neither surprising nor particularly enlightening.

---

2. See Nails 2002, 248, who argues that the actual date of Plato's birth was not 427 but 424/3. Coupled with Plato's claim in the *Seventh Letter* that he first visited Syracuse at about forty years of age, and the remark in D.L. 3.20 that the Academy was founded after Plato returned from Sicily, that would make its founding around 383 instead of 387. The view of Ryle (1966, 222–25) that there is no evidence that the Academy was founded earlier than 370 depends on rejecting both the chronology of the *Seventh Letter* and that of Diogenes Laertius. According to Ryle's chronology, *Euthydemus, Meno, Gorgias,* and the unfinished *Thrasymachus* [*Republic* 1] must have preceded the founding of the Academy.

3. See Fronterotta 2001, 2007.

4. See Campbell 1867 and 1896 for pioneering studies. More recently, see Ledger 1989, Brandwood 1990, Kahn 2002.

That is, even assuming their reliability, they do not begin to settle the larger philosophical issues motivating developmentalism.[5]

Developmentalism of various sorts is to be distinguished from unitarianism, the view that there is no change in doctrine across the dialogues. Just as there are, of course, many versions of developmentalism, so there are many versions of unitarianism.[6] The unitarianism of those who hold that the dialogues are the sole locus of Plato's philosophy is substantially different from the unitarianism of those who hold that the so-called unwritten teachings are the locus of Plato's philosophy and the dialogues serve only a protreptic function in relation to these. I will deal with the unitarianism of those who hold that there are no doctrines in the dialogues in the section below titled "Plato the Artist, Plato the Philosopher," and the proponents of the unwritten teachings in "Plato's Self-Testimony."

Plato and Developmentalism

Here I address developmentalism generally. None of the versions of this view with which I am familiar suggest that Plato developed out of or into a commitment to UP, although the version that Socraticists tend to embrace yields an 'early' Plato whose philosophical commitments are obscure. All versions of developmentalism try to divide the dialogues into early, middle, and late phases. Since we have nothing like a certain chronology for the dialogues, a hypothetical chronology is made to follow by an immediate inference from a developmental ordering. Thus, for instance, if the tripartitioning of the soul is supposed to be a development out of a unified psychology, then *Republic* is supposed to have been written later than *Phaedo* or *Protagoras*. Since *Phaedrus* seems to assume a tripartite soul (albeit in a myth), it is supposed to have been written later than *Republic*. Since *Timaeus* explicitly mentions the immortal *part* of the tripartite soul, it must, too, not only assume tripartition, but be later than *Republic*, which does not unambiguously affirm the immortality of only one part of the tripartite soul.

With respect to Forms, developmentalists generally hold, partly on the basis of Aristotle's testimony, that Plato separated the Forms, whereas Socrates did not. So dialogues are 'early' if they contain explicit or implicit reference to supposedly unseparated Forms, but 'middle' if they discuss separate Forms. Thus, the dialogues without separate Forms seem to coincide with the aporetic dialogues, which, for the Socraticists, represent Socratic philosophy, but for other developmentalists represent the early phase of Plato's development.[7]

---

5. See the magisterial *Studies in Platonic Chronology*, reprinted in Thesleff 2009, whose skepticism about the chronological ordering of the dialogues based on an exhaustive survey of over one hundred years of attempts is a salutary counterpoint to the blithe assumptions of the 'early-middle-late' chronologists.
6. See Shorey 1904, 1933; Cherniss 1936; Kahn 1996.
7. See Beversluis 2006, 88.

For developmentalists, *Parmenides* represents something of a watershed. In this dialogue, the hypothesis of Forms is attacked, albeit by Parmenides himself and his disciple Zeno. Socrates—a very young Socrates—is cast as the defender of the hypothesis. In one version of developmentalism, these Eleatic attacks are for Plato decisive, and subsequent to *Parmenides*, he abandoned the hypothesis of separate Forms in favor of some other realistic theory of universals, perhaps something that is supposedly akin to an Aristotelian theory.[8] In another version, *Parmenides* does not mark Plato's abandonment of the theory of Forms, but rather its modification. The modification is supposedly a response to irrefutable Eleatic criticisms, though it is not always noted that Parmenides himself is made to say that unless his objections can be met, then discourse is completely destroyed.[9] What a theory of Forms would be that is not a theory of separate Forms is not anywhere clearly articulated.

The principal stumbling block for the first version is *Timaeus*, traditionally thought to be a late dialogue, containing unambiguously an assertion of the existence of separate Forms. The bold hypothesis of G. E. L. Owen to redate *Timaeus* to the 'middle' period instead of the 'late' period and hence to remove the impediment to the hypothesis of an abandonment of separate Forms in the latter has not been widely accepted.[10] The main reason brought against Owen's hypothetical redating of *Timaeus* is that the hypothesis of Form seems to be operating, even if not prominently, in other dialogues that Owen himself agrees are to be dated later than *Parmenides*, including *Sophist, Statesman,* and *Philebus*.[11]

The principal stumbling block to the second version is the difficulty in explaining exactly what modifications to the hypothesis of separate Forms are supposed to answer the objections to that hypothesis in the first part of *Parmenides*. This difficulty is no doubt exacerbated by the obvious fact that the 'exercise' that is supposedly going to lay down the principles for answering the objection consists of the second part of *Parmenides*, perhaps the most obscure part of the Platonic corpus. How this exercise will yield the principles for modifying the hypothesis that the young Socrates defends in the first part of the dialogue has never been satisfactorily explained. For example, a standard diagnosis of the problem raised by Parmenides in the

---

8. See Owen 1953.

9. *Parm.* 135B6–C3: Σώκρατες, αὖ μὴ ἐάσει εἴδη τῶν ὄντων εἶναι, εἰς πάντα τὰ νυνδὴ καὶ ἄλλα τοιαῦτα ἀποβλέψας, μηδέ τι ὁριεῖται εἶδος ἑνὸς ἑκάστου, οὐδὲ ὅποι τρέψει τὴν διάνοιαν ἕξει, μὴ ἐῶν ἰδέαν τῶν ὄντων ἑκάστου τὴν αὐτὴν ἀεὶ εἶναι, καὶ οὕτως τὴν τοῦ διαλέγεσθαι δύναμιν παντάπασι διαφθερεῖ. τοῦ τοιούτου μὲν οὖν μοι δοκεῖς καὶ μᾶλλον ᾐσθῆσθαι. (Socrates, if, considering all these difficulties and others, too, one will not allow Forms of these things, nor some Form defined in every case, he will not have anywhere to turn his thinking, so long as he will not allow that there is an Idea of each of these things that is eternally self-identical; if he does this, he will destroy altogether the power of discourse. But you seem to me to be more than aware of this.) Cf. *Soph.* 259E4–6.

10. See Owen 1953, and the response of Cherniss 1957.

11. See Ross 1951, chaps. 6 and 7, for a convenient collection of the passages in these dialogues in which Forms appear.

so-called Third Man Argument is that it assumes that Socrates is committed to the self-predication of Forms. Thus, the Form of Largeness must be itself large, making it apt for including with other large things thus requiring another Form of Largeness "over and above them."[12] A nondevelopmental view, or a unitarian, will want to say that self-predication was no part of the character of Forms in the first place, in which case Plato does not need to alter his account to exclude this assumption. A developmentalist will want to say that self-predication follows from separation, in which case the solution to the problem is to recast the account of Forms minus the offending metaphysical claim. Forms then become something like universals; whereas it is perhaps the case that a separately existing Form of Largeness must be paradigmatically large, it makes no sense to say that the universal largeness is large. The problem here is, once again, *Timaeus*, which seems committed to separation, as well as the other dialogues mentioned above in which there is not a shred of evidence that separation is abandoned in favor of a realistic theory of universals.

Regarding the apparent conflicts or tensions or even contradictions in the dialogues thought to be fodder for a developmentalist story, I think the evidence is inconclusive. One part of the reason for this may well be the nature of the dialogue. For the most part, as, for example, in *Sophist*, Socrates only adduces the metaphysical apparatus immediately required to solve the problem posed in the dialogue, in this case, how, given that the sophist is a purveyor of falsity or nonbeing, can he really have a métier after all? How, in short, is it possible for nonbeing to be the something that is supposedly the sophist's stock-in-trade? There is, in fact, a good deal of metaphysical apparatus needed to solve this problem, though not every possible consideration regarding Forms, including the superordinate Idea of the Good. So the question of whether at the time of writing *Sophist* Plato was still committed to this Idea and to all that he said about Forms in *Republic* (including the maximally wide-ranging criterion for positing Forms in the first place) cannot be answered definitively. It is reasonable to think that Plato did not express everything he in fact believed at the time of writing each dialogue; it is equally reasonable to think that at the least Plato wrote some dialogues believing that some things he had said previously were said incautiously, precipitously, or without sufficient precision.

The prospects for developmentalism providing us with illuminating results regarding the ultimate version of Platonism embraced by Plato himself are, therefore, dim. This is not, of course, to say that developmentalism is necessarily false. I wish to argue, however, that what is called for is another approach to dealing with the evidence that inspires developmentalism.

12. See, e.g., Vlastos 1954.

Let us begin with the consideration that there is no evidence that Plato wrote any of his dialogues prior to the founding of the Academy.[13] This in itself is not a particularly important point, though if true it does suggest that all of his writings were those of a decidedly mature thinker, at least forty years of age. My main point, however, is that on the hypothesis of a post-387–383 dating for all of the dialogues, we might speculate that they are all in one sense the product of his discussions with colleagues and students of philosophy.[14] With the arrival of Aristotle at the Academy about twenty

---

13. See Taylor 2002, 77, summarizing what he takes to be the "present paradigm" for understanding Socrates and Plato, "Plato's *immediate* reaction to Socrates' death was to compose a series of works (*Apology, Crito, Gorgias, Euthyphro,* and *Meno*) linked by their content more or less *immediately* to Socrates' trial and its aftermath" (my italics). Note that Taylor simply omits *Phaedo*, which, one would think, is no less immediately linked to Socrates' trial and death than are the others listed. It was perhaps Schleiermacher (1836, 16, 44) who first made the groundless claim that a number of Plato's dialogues (including *Phaedrus, Protagoras,* and *Parmenides*) are "youthful" and were written "in early manhood." Cf. Burnet 1928, 48: "I have tried to show that what are known as the 'Socratic dialogues' of Plato were written in the years just after the death of Socrates—I cannot believe that any of them were written before that—and that his chief purpose in them was to give as complete and faithful a picture as he could of his master's personality and teaching." Burnet is followed by, among many others, Guthrie 1975, 67. There is an ancient tradition that after the death of Socrates in 399, Plato went to Tarentum in southern Italy, where he met the Pythagorean Archytas of Tarentum. See Cicero, *Rep.* 1.10.16, *De fin.* 5.29.87. D.L. 3.6 has him also traveling to Megara, Cyrene, and Egypt, as well as to Italy, where he supposedly met the Pythagoreans Philolaus and Eurytus. See Huffman 2005, 32–42, for a judicious consideration of the evidence supporting a visit to Tarentum—or at least to southern Italy—early after the death of Socrates and conflicting evidence suggesting that the first visit to the Pythagoreans occurred shortly before the founding of the Academy. The issue here is whether Plato's well-documented interest in fourth-century Pythagoreanism antedates or postdates the 'early' dialogues. See Kennedy 2011, who presents a detailed case for the Pythagorean architecture of all Platonic dialogues, including those that have been thought to be 'Socratic' and, therefore, 'early.' See 247–49, where Kennedy argues that the Pythagorean allegorical structure found in later dialogues is equally present in *Apology* and *Euthyphro*. Rejecting the identification of early dialogues with Socratic philosophy and later dialogues with Platonic philosophy, Kennedy concludes (249): "If instead of a distinction between early and late, we have only a distinction between elementary and advanced, the simpler 'Socratic' dialogues are merely evidence that, as has been suggested, Plato varied the degree to which he revealed the complexities of his philosophy."

14. See Kahn 1981, 307, who agrees that there is no evidence for dating any of the dialogues in the 390s, though for some reason he goes on to date tentatively *Ion, Apology, Crito,* and *Hippias Minor* during this period. See also Kahn 1992, 239, who seems to assume that the early dialogues were written in the period 399–387. On the basis of this assumption, Kahn argues against Vlastos that it is implausible that during this twelve-year period Plato's views did not change, meaning that during this period they changed from being purely 'Socratic' to being at least in part 'Platonic.' I see no grounds for Kahn's and Vlastos's shared assumption that during this twelve-year period, Plato was writing dialogues, whether these be Socratic or Platonic. Allen (2010, 13) argues that some Platonic dialogues must have been written before 383 to 'justify' the opening of the Academy. She then goes on to list a host of dialogues (166, n. 13) as "generally thought to have been written by the opening of the school." These dialogues include *Apology, Crito, Euthyphro, Protagoras, Charmides, Ion, Laches, Hippias Minor, Euthydemus, Gorgias, Hippias Major, Lysis, Menexenus, Meno, Cratylus, Phaedo, Symposium,* and *Republic* 1. There is no evidence for the pre-Academic dating of even one of these dialogues, let alone all of them. The idea that Plato had to be seen as having intellectual stature by means of

years later, the hypothesis of dialogues reflecting discussions becomes more concrete. For in Aristotle's own works, beginning with his dialogues, onward through his 'esoteric' writings, produced while Plato was still alive, and then for the last twenty-five years or so of his own life, there is also abundant evidence that he is reflecting ongoing Academic discussions. In this regard, the parallels between Plato's dialogues that are probably late and the earliest of Aristotle's writings are particularly striking.

We need to keep in mind that it was in Plato's Academy that a technical vocabulary for the expression of versions of Platonism based UP was being formulated. The vocabulary for making distinctions and formulating arguments regarding being, cognition, causality, emotions, conation, argument, etc., was actually being constructed in the discussions that were occurring daily in the Academy. Some of the results of these discussions are found in the dialogues; some are found in Aristotle's works, including those that are probably early. Sometimes we find Plato shifting his vocabulary, for example, his alteration in the use of the words for desire or appetite, ἐπιθυμία, from *Symposium* to *Republic,* or his shift *within Republic* regarding the use of the term ἐπιστήμη. In *Philebus* we discover a settled vocabulary about how to talk about the emotions, a vocabulary that is taken up by Aristotle in his *Rhetoric*. In Plato's various accounts of causality, we find a shifting vocabulary that is finally fixed in Aristotle's *Physics.* Plato in *Timaeus* and elsewhere uses metaphor to discuss what Aristotle eventually expresses in the technical language of ὕλη, or matter. Aristotle's accounts of the types of desire in his *Nicomachean Ethics* reflect distinctions that are found in the dialogues, though not formally so. Discussions regarding the technical vocabulary of logic begin to get their airing in the second part of *Parmenides* and then are later formalized by Aristotle, beginning with his *Prior Analytics,* and extending to *Physics* and book Delta of *Metaphysics* containing a philosophical compendium of technical vocabulary. The extremely difficult problem of the relation between the various modes of cognition and the noncognitive properties of organic life are treated by Plato mostly metaphorically and with a loose vocabulary and then expressed formally only by Aristotle in *De anima:* "intellect [νοῦς] is a genus different from soul [ψυχή]." Plato strives in *Laws* to articulate a vocabulary for different kinds of motion (κίνησις), wishing to distinguish the 'motion' of thought from any other kind, though he is still willing to call that 'motion.' Aristotle invents an entirely new word—ἐνέργεια—for the 'motion' of thought.

This list can be easily extended. What we need to keep in mind is that Plato is quite obviously looser in his terminology than is Aristotle, and that this looseness sometimes leads the reader to conclude that Plato is asserting

---

multiple publications in order to justify his school is entirely gratuitous. The entire hypothesis of an 'early' dating is, it seems to me, driven by an antecedently determined groundless theory about Platonic development. If we do not accept that theory, the hypothesis that the dialogues are all intra-Academic exercises is at least as plausible as the alternative.

something different from what he asserts elsewhere, whereas in fact he is saying the same thing in different words.[15] And the justification for this—if it needs one—is that Plato is in the process of inventing the distinctions and arguments that are being used to express what he takes to be the most solid edifice that can be built on the foundation of UP. It is entirely plausible that amid the Academic discussions, and especially as a result of Aristotle's critical scrutiny, Plato did alter his view on a number of particular issues and, even more likely, on how to express a particular position. What we need to keep in mind alongside a discussion of these changes is Plato's unwavering continued commitment to UP, a commitment shared unequivocally by Aristotle. This fluidity in the expression of his thinking at the time of writing one dialogue or another should not be taken as equivalent to an abandonment of systematization altogether. On the contrary, the differing responses to metaphysical, epistemological, and psychological questions found in the dialogues are all undertaken with a systematic goal in mind. This system will, as we will see, be a construction on the basis of the claims composing UP. Accordingly, rather than thinking of later Platonists as systematizing Plato—a view common among scholars of Platonism[16]—we should think of them (and Plato) as systematizing UP.

My main contention is the denial of the claim that a pre-Academic set of dialogues needs to be postulated in order to distinguish the 'Socratic' Plato from Plato himself. If we set aside the fictitious 'Socratic' Plato, an alternative hypothesis regarding the composition of the dialogues that fits the evidence better is that all of them or most of them were intra-Academic exercises. I do think the indirect evidence for this is stronger than any indirect evidence for pre-Academic compositions. But the only good reason for preferring my hypothesis over the contrary must be its superiority in accounting for the dialogues themselves, including its answer to the obviously important question of why Plato wrote dialogues in the first place. What I propose is that all the dialogues are in a sense occasional pieces, responding to ongoing discussions in the Academy.[17] They are all efforts to express, not only Plato's

---

15. See D.L. 3.63–64, who says that Plato used a variety of 'terms' (ὀνόμασι) in order to make his system not 'transparent' (εὐσύνοπτον) to the unlearned. This view, common enough in antiquity, assumes that the dialogues represent Platonism rather than constitute it. The shifting vocabulary of the dialogues reveals the ongoing intra-Academic project of formulating a canonical vocabulary for the discussion of philosophical issues. The best record we have of this vocabulary is found in the works of Aristotle.

16. See, e.g., Dillon 2003, 98, 154.

17. I do not in this book intend to make this case for each and every dialogue. But I do not think I have to do so. If some dialogues were intended to appeal directly to the public or if some were written primarily in fond memory of Socrates or if some were written prior to the founding of the Academy, this does not undermine the thesis that UP is the matrix out of which the positive construct that is Platonism arises. Cf. Steinthal 1998, 59, who characterizes the dialogues all as responding to *"hic et nunc."* See Thesleff 2009, 310–29, who argues that, with the exception of a proto-*Republic* book 1 and *Apology*, all the dialogues are intra-Academic exercises. He thinks (264) that these two works were composed around 392. Ryle (1966, 200–203) argues that most of the dialogues are "dramatized documentaries" or

thinking about one issue or another at a specific time, but also the thinking of other members of the Academy. The latter sometimes make anonymous appearances as Socrates' interlocutors expressing objections and philosophical positions that were 'on the table' in the Academy.[18] In no sense, then, are the dialogues the exclusive vehicle for the expression of Platonism.[19] As we will see presently, Plato tells us as much himself. On this hypothesis, it is inconceivable that it would have occurred to Plato that anyone would take any one dialogue as 'self-contained,' that is, as exempt from being illuminated by what is said elsewhere. Every single one of these occasional pieces has to be referred to the fluid or ongoing construction of Platonism, the positive side of UP. For this reason, the dichotomy developmentalism/unitarianism is a false one. Plato's Platonism and the Platonism of all his followers was continuously developing on the unchanging foundation that is UP.[20]

The question of why Socrates is the principal interlocutor in almost all the dialogues is harder to answer. We should, I think, only be inclined to the view that there are no dialogues whose unique purpose is to memorialize Socrates or to express his putatively distinctive (non-Platonic) philosophy.[21]

"Moot-memoranda" of actual discussions. Ryle, however, thinks that "the eristic dialogues" (basically, the so-called Socratic dialogues) were pre-Academic, and so the provenance of the discussions they record is obscure. Sayre (1995, 21–27) agrees that the dialogues are records of "regular conversations," but he takes these to have been between Plato and Socrates. This seems implausible, especially for the more technical dialogues. Moreover, what grounds are there for identifying Plato with *any* of the interlocutors of the Socrates in the dialogues?

18. The fact that Plato does not mention any of his own contemporary philosophers in his dialogues (with the exception of Phaedo in *Phaedo*) supports my interpretation of the reason for selecting Socrates as his central figure. If Plato wanted to discuss his own contemporaries, that is, those philosophers who were working during the time of the early Academy, then Socrates would obviously be dramatically impossible.

19. That Plato's unwritten teachings or doctrines are distinct from but continuous with that which is contained in his dialogues or exoterica is an important part of the interpretation of the Tübingen School. See Gaiser 2004. The supposed 'lecture on the Good' is an exception since it is 'exoteric' because it is nontechnical but 'esoteric' because it is unwritten. Gaiser (2004, 296) is emphatic that the term 'esoteric' refers only to 'intra-Academic' teachings, and does not indicate doctrine intended only for a cult or religious or elite group. He further insists (297) that the unwritten teachings take philosophical priority over the written works. According to my interpretation, the distinction between written and oral transmission of doctrine needs to be largely effaced or at least downplayed, though no doubt there was much technical material that did not find explicit expression in the dialogues. That which underlies the putative distinction between oral and written transmission is the commitment to a positive construct out of UP, variously communicated. The quest for the best systematic account of reality is far more important than the mode of communication of results. Cf. Mann 2006, 374–79, who tends to agree on the effacement of the distinction between the Platonism of the dialogues and the Platonism of the Academy, orally transmitted.

20. There is perhaps a nice parallelism between the negative side of UP and Socratic elenchus in the dialogues. All of the claims that UP stands against are defeated by refutative arguments of Socrates.

21. Cf. Schofield 2000, 37, who asserts, "Nearly the entire output of the most powerful and fertile thinker in the entire tradition of Western philosophy is conceived as a homage to Socrates and in re-creation of *his* philosophizing." This hypothesis assumes that the dialogues in which Socrates is the principal interlocutor belong to a genre of Σωκρατικοί λόγοι, whose

My hypothesis is that Socrates' central role in the dialogues—and his actual presence in all the dialogues except *Laws*—is explained by Plato's wish to have his Platonism encounter all the actual historical proponents of the views whose contradictories constitute UP. With a little judicious artistry, Plato could bring them all into discussion with Socrates.[22] Perhaps the unique status of *Laws* in this regard is owing to the fact that there really were no giants of practical political philosophy that Plato cared to confront. This hypothesis does not, of course, preclude a secondary aim of memorializing the life of an authentic Platonic hero. But the heroism is to be located for Plato as much in Socrates' personal integrity and independence of mind as in his ethics. In any case, nowhere do the paradoxes of Socratic ethics appear in the dialogues without the explicit or implicit metaphysical apparatus Plato acquired, probably from Pythagoreans, and then in his own Academy.

The above hypothesis seems more than merely speculative if we consider that Socrates is the principal interlocutor in dialogues that are, according to all Socraticists, expressive of Platonic philosophy, for example, *Theaetetus* and *Philebus*. It does, indeed, seem odd that if it were Plato's intention to make Socrates the principal interlocutor in the early dialogues in order to have him argue for his own distinctive philosophy, he would not use another principal interlocutor when he wished to propound his own philosophy. The hypothesis that the dialogues should be ordered according as Plato developed from an expounder of Socratic philosophy to a proponent of his own is in fact less supported by the evidence than the hypothesis according

---

central motivation is apparently the commemorating of Socrates. But this hypothesis runs up against the testimony of Aristotle and the dialogues themselves wherein even the proponents of the hypothesis concede that not all dialogues in which Socrates is the principal interlocutor are dedicated to the "re-creation of *his* philosophizing." Hence, it is arbitrary to classify some dialogues as 'Socratic' and some as not. According to Boys-Stones and Rowe (2013, vii) there are some two hundred known works by those who were in some sense followers of Socrates. No doubt many of these were written in the decade after the death of Socrates and before the founding of the Academy. I do not mean to exclude the very real possibility that part of the reason for Plato making Socrates his principal interlocutor was to produce a memorial to Socrates superior to all those that had come before. So D.L. 3.48, who thinks Plato succeeded in this. See Long 1998, 119, who argues that "Plato, up to and including the composition of the *Theaetetus*, never stops rewriting the *Apology* [that is, writing an *hommage* to Socrates]. With the *Theaetetus* Plato completes that task, lets his former Socrates go, and moves on." His "moving on" is occasioned (121) by "a gradual but profound change in [his] conception of philosophy and the philosopher." This position seems to me to be pure fantasy. Sedley (2004, 8) argues that in *Theaetetus* Plato develops a picture of Socrates as the "midwife of Platonism." For Sedley, as for Vlastos, this "midwife" is innocent of metaphysics. *Theaetetus* represents Plato's "break" with Socrates.

22. Socrates appears in *Timaeus*, albeit as a secondary character. His appearance is, however, important for linking *Timaeus* with *Republic*, the discussion that *Timaeus* says occurred on the "previous day." But if Socrates appears in *Timaeus*, then the principal interlocutor cannot be the obvious choice for an eminent Pythagorean philosopher known to Plato, namely, Archytas of Tarentum, who lived too late for the probable dramatic date of *Republic*.

to which the character Socrates is always a stand-in for the author. This, of course, does not mean that Plato's thought did not develop, but it did not develop in the way that proponents of Socratic philosophy in the dialogues claim.

Plato the Artist, Plato the Philosopher

All interpreters of Plato agree that he is more than a philosopher. He is a literary artist as well. All agree that, apart from the *Letters*, he chose to express himself in the form of dramatic dialogues, some of these more intensely or completely 'dialogic' than others.[23] Assuming that *Laws* is his last work (and, of course, that it is authentic), he wrote dialogues to the end. Most of these dialogues make Socrates the principal interlocutor. Owing to the nature of these dialogues, their author does not explicitly intrude into the text. This is no more or less the case than for any other author of any literary work. These banal facts have left interpreters and disciples with one obvious question: How, if at all, can the philosophy of their author be extracted from them? Most ancient interpreters, including Aristotle, seem to have simply assumed that in the dialogues Socrates and, in a few cases, other leading interlocutors were representatives of Plato's views, and therefore that the dialogues were a perfectly appropriate place to look for these. It is not that they were impervious to the literary qualities of the dialogues; it is just that these provide no more than a colorful background for the expression of philosophy.[24] If Socrates is located by the author of the dialogues in the agora, or in the countryside, or at the gymnasium, or at a private party, these locations simply offer a "setting" for argument.

In addition to the basic literary form of Plato's writings, there are literary forms within the dialogues, including myths and rhetorical displays. Although these could be subjected to independent analysis according to

---

23. See Schleiermacher 1836, who is the true originator of the idea that the philosophy is inseparable from the literary form of the dialogues. Thesleff (2009, 199–210) distinguishes five types of dialogue techniques in the Platonic corpus: question and reply, specifically, elenchus; conversation; narrative; dialogue approximating monologue; speech or continuous exposition. Thesleff uses these distinctions, along with much else, to try to determine both an absolute and a relative chronology for the dialogues. He has drawn up a table (201) showing how the various techniques are interwoven in each of the dialogues. I will not take up the many complex issues canvassed by Thesleff, especially that of the likelihood of there being multiple versions of individual dialogues.

24. This requires some qualification, especially for later Platonists. For example, in the *Anonymous Prologue to Plato's Philosophy*, written probably by a disciple of Olympiodorus in the second half of the sixth century, the author (chaps. 15–16) claims that each dialogue is a "sort of universe," comprising, like our universe, a material component, a formal component, a principle that combines these, soul, intellect, and the divine. It is perhaps the case that the penchant for integrating literary and philosophical interpretations of the dialogues followed from the growing presentation of Platonism *through* the dialogues, which began most likely with Iamblichus.

their own literary criteria, in antiquity they were generally brought within the ambit of the supposed aim, or σκοπός, of the dialogue.[25] A myth, for example, was somehow to serve this aim. The nature of the aim was, of course, open to interpretation; there was no suggestion that Plato's actual intention or aim was revealed otherwise than through the dialogue itself.

At the extreme opposite of the view that the dialogues are a vehicle for Plato's philosophy is the view that the literary nature of the dialogues precludes the ascription of philosophical positions to their author.[26] This view does not deny that there are arguments and claims made in the dialogues—how, after all, could it?—but it does deny that Plato intends for us to attribute them to him. Specifically, the literary integrity of the dialogues precludes the justifiability of going outside the boundaries of a particular dialogue in the sense of making inferences about the philosophy contained therein. It is a crucial feature of this view that fidelity to literary integrity not only precludes making inferences from one dialogue to the philosophical position of their author, but it also precludes the use of one dialogue to interpret the philosophy of another.[27] This point is crucial because it is agreed by all parties to this dispute that no single dialogue—not *Republic*, or *Timaeus*, or *Parmenides*, or any other—completely expresses Plato's views on any single significant subject much less his overall philosophical position. Not even 'dogmatists' of the strictest observance deny that the literary form of Plato's writings guides the composition in a way that precludes anything like a comprehensive exposition and defense of a philosophical system. Socrates' interlocutors are often not philosophers—or at least not skillful philosophers—and so not likely to appreciate the intricacies of philosophical argument given at length; even when his interlocutors are philosophers, they and Socrates are always focused on the solution to particular problems, a constraint that, were it not observed, would turn the dialogue into something very different.

---

25. From D.L. 3.57–61 we learn that Thrasyllus, when editing the dialogues into tetralogies, gave each dialogue a double title, one for the principal interlocutor and one for the 'subject' (πρᾶγμα) of the work. He then classifies the dialogue according to its 'type,' that is, 'ethical,' 'political,' 'tentative,' 'logical,' 'maieutic,' 'refutative,' and 'critical.' Of course, the so-called Socratic dialogues do not align with any one or more of these categories. Sextus Empiricus, *PH* 1.221, attempts to divide the dialogues into those that are 'dogmatic' and those that are 'dubitative,' but since Socrates appears as the principal interlocutor in what Sextus considers to be both types of dialogues, he has to rely on a distinction between those dialogues in which Socrates is speaking 'playfully' (παίζων) and those in which he is speaking 'seriously' (σπουδάζων). It is only in the latter case that Plato is 'dogmatizing through Socrates.'

26. See Press 2007.

27. See Tejera 1984 for a particularly rigorous effort to limit the analysis of one dialogue to material from that dialogue alone. Tejera, however (93–100), must ultimately rely on "interdialogic" evidence for his interpretation, which is, principally, that Socratic irony blocks the representation of doctrine. For example, *Republic* is taken to be "an ironic attack on Spartansim, militarism, and Pythagoreanizing oligarchism" (238).

Let us briefly consider two examples. The first is from *Phaedo*. In the course of his 'autobiography,' Socrates offers his 'simple hypothesis' that it is, say, the Form of Largeness or the Form of Beauty or the Form of Twoness that explains the fact that something is large or beautiful or two, not the material out of which these are constructed.[28] He then adds that, when asked to give an account of one of these hypotheses, that is, examining its consequences, one would adduce another hypothesis until one arrived at "something adequate" (τι ἱκανόν).[29] Many scholars have supposed that this "something adequate" is another hypothesis of the sort that each Form is supposed to be.[30] It is, indeed, difficult to see how hypothesizing another 'simple' Form would be adequate for answering the objections that are supposed to arise from the consequences of the original hypothesis that may be 'discordant' (διαφωνεῖ) with one another. And yet we have in *Republic* Forms hypothesized by mathematicians and a claim that these hypotheses are *inadequate*.[31] By contrast, dialecticians use these hypotheses as real hypotheses, that is, as "stepping stones" or a "launching point" until they reach something "unhypothetical" (ἀνυπόθετον), that is, the first principle of all, the Idea of the Good.[32] Given that this unhypothetical first principle of all is, among other things, the source of the "knowability" (τὸ γιγνώσκεσθαι) of Forms, the obvious question is why one would be forbidden from using the *Republic* passage—that, too, speaks about Forms as hypotheses and appeals to an unhypothetical principle of all to supply what is missing from these hypotheses—to interpret the otherwise unintelligible passage in *Phaedo*. The *only* reason that is given for this extraordinary restriction is that it would violate the integrity of the literary composition. But, then, unless we are given another reason why violation of this integrity for philosophical purposes is illicit, the reasoning seems circular. I am aware of no such additional reason ever being adduced.

---

28. See *Phd.* 100C9ff.

29. See *Phd.* 101D5-E1. On this passage, see, e.g, Gallop 1975, 187-92. At 100B6, τὸ ἀγαθόν is given as one among other Forms that are hypothesized. This suggests that τὸ ἱκανόν is here indicating a placeholder, so to speak, for whatever provides an adequate explanation. In *Republic,* the adequate explanation is designated as *unhypothetical* and it is identified with the Idea of the Good. It is not possible to know if the 'promotion' of the Good into a first principle of all represents a change in Plato's thinking or whether listing the Good among the other Forms is simply loose talk where all the elements of the 'really real' are lumped together.

30. See Gallop 1975, 187-92, for references. Gallop himself can make no sense of this claim, though he denies there is evidence for any other interpretation.

31. See *Rep.* 510B2ff.

32. See *Rep.* 511B6, 510B7. *Rep.*532B1 with 533C9 seem to make virtually certain that the reference to an unhypothetical first principle is in fact a reference to the Idea of the Good. See Baltzly 1996 and Bailey 2006, who both assume that for Plato there may be multiple unhypothetical principles and that these are propositions, like the principle of noncontradiction. But there is no talk about propositions in these passages, and the uniqueness of the first principle is clear. It is the cause of the existence and being and knowability of Forms. Cf. Sayre 1988, 99-101.

The second example comes from *Timaeus*. Timaeus introduces his discussion of the receptacle of becoming and its contents with the caveat that his account at this time will be limited. That is, he is not going to speak about a "first principle or principles of all" (τὴν περὶ ἁπάντων εἴτε ἀρχην εἴτε ἀρχάς) of all things owing to the difficulty of giving an account of these according to their present method of exposition.[33] Considering that *Timaeus* is dramatically situated the day after the discussion of *Republic*, one would have thought it fairly obvious that the reference to a "first principle of all" is a reference to the Idea of the Good, so designated in *Republic*. But what about "principles" in the plural? *Republic* mentions no such first principles. And yet Aristotle does, claiming that Plato "reduced" Forms to the One and the Great and the Small or the Indefinite Dyad.[34] If, in fact, the *Timaeus* passage is alluding to the possibility that the Idea of the Good may itself need to be conceptualized as the One and along with it the Indefinite Dyad needs to be included as a first principle, not only would the arbitrary limitations on interpretation imposed by the literary theory be breached, but more important, the interpretation of *Timaeus* itself would be enormously enriched. For that dialogue tells us that the Demiurge brought intelligibility to the cosmos by using "shapes and numbers" (εἴδεσι τε καὶ ἀριθμοῖς).[35] Assuming that the One and the Indefinite Dyad are in the background, the origin of the shapes and numbers is readily understandable. Without this background, the passage makes little sense, and is for that reason usually simply ignored. For if these shapes and numbers are only *some* of the Forms—which is presumably what one would want to argue if one thought that the mathematical reduction of Forms was an Aristotelian fiction—then the Demiurge is not, contrary to what is said in the text, "ungrudging" in his desire that the cosmos should be maximally endowed with intelligibility.

In *Phaedo* and *Timaeus*, then, we have two dialogues whose relation to things said in *Republic* and, indeed, to things said by Aristotle about Plato would appear obvious unless one were in the grips of a theory the

---

33. See *Tim.* 48C2–6. Cf. 53D4–7.
34. See Aristotle, *Meta.* A 6, 987b18–25. In the light of this specific reference to Plato, we should not hesitate to include Plato among those who are criticized in *Meta.* N 4–5, particularly for identifying the Good with the One as a principle of all. At 5, 1092a5–11, it seems clear that one of the targets is Speusippus and the other, given A 6, 987b18–22, must be Plato. So, too, Λ 10, 1075a34–b1, where the contrast seems again to be between Speusippus and Plato, the latter holding that "Good is a principle," as is the One. Cf. *EE* A 8, 1218a15–32: διὰτὸ εἶναι τὸ ἕν αὐτὸ τἀγαθόν (20–21). See Brunschwig 1970, for a comprehensive argument showing that, contrary to claims made by some that the target of Aristotle's criticism is Xenocrates or Pythagoreans, it is in all likelihood Plato. In fact, Aristotle is probably making reference to his own *On the Good* containing testimony about Plato's unwritten teachings.
35. *Tim.* 53B5. See Taylor 1928, 358, on why these εἴδη are not nonquantitative Forms, but rather the geometrical shapes that are measured by the accompanying numbers. If, however, one takes the εἴδη as Forms in general, it is entirely unclear what the ἀριθμοί are supposed to be.

motivations for which are perhaps more obscure than these relations. By contrast, if *Republic* helps explain what is said in *Phaedo* and is itself helped to be explained by what is said in *Timaeus* and in Aristotle's testimony, then Platonism must be detached from the dialogues, not, of course, insofar as these are a witness to it, but only insofar as these are supposed to contain it exclusively. And according to the literary interpretation, even this jejune result is unavailable, since on its showing, 'dialogic' Platonism gets shattered into as many authentic dialogues as one cares to postulate.

The resolve to take the literary form of Plato's works seriously is completely empty, of course, if it does not show us how either that form absolutely precludes philosophical analysis or somehow shapes it. The view that the literary form precludes ascription of the philosophy in the dialogues to Plato is equally empty unless it can give some plausible account of what (presumably literary) function that philosophy serves. To say that the function is protreptic will hardly do. For no one, including no one in antiquity, denied that the dialogues have a protreptic function; what they most firmly did deny, however, is that the presentation of philosophical argument was not itself serving such a function.[36] Accordingly, focus on the protreptic function of the dialogue is vacuous unless this is combined with the claim that the author is intentionally distancing himself from the philosophical claims made therein. Then, the philosophy becomes, as it were, orphaned, attributable to no one in particular. On this view, there is no more reason to ascribe to Plato any element of UP rather than the opposite of that element. Plato may as well have been a materialist as an antimaterialist; he may have actually agreed with Protagoras that man is the measure of all things rather than opposed him. It seems to me that Aristotle's testimony, if nothing else, gives the lie to this interpretation. For nowhere are we led to believe that Plato does not subscribe to the views put into the mouth of Socrates. On the contrary, Aristotle repeatedly refers to things said by the literary Socrates as claims made by Plato. In short, Aristotle does not treat Plato as a sophist. The suggestion that he was one seems to be completely gratuitous.

More promising perhaps is the view that the literary form of Plato's writings must merely shape our view of the philosophy contained therein. As reasonable as this hypothesis might seem, no one who holds it has to my knowledge ever shown how exactly it is to yield tangible results. That Socrates responds to his interlocutors in a particular way or that his interlocutors respond to him in a particular way does not seem to be the sort of thing that would in itself make us hesitate to take an argument offered on its own terms. On this view, the Socrates of the dialogues is a literary character, and as such he is all and only what the author wants him to be. If he says he is ignorant, then that is what the author wants to convey to the reader.

---

36. Compare Thomas Aquinas's *Summa contra Gentiles*, an explicitly protreptic work filled with argument. Indeed, the arguments are supposed by Aquinas to *be* the protreptic.

Socrates' famous irony is never expressed in relation to the elements of UP; it is always expressed in relation to the pretensions of his interlocutors or in relation to his own perceived inadequacies, which include his ignorance about the very specific things he claims to be ignorant of.[37]

That Plato had a generally low opinion of many of the people represented in his dialogues hardly needs defending. And this includes, of course, the self-proclaimed intellectual elite of Athenian society. The multifarious ways in which Socrates ridicules and dismisses their unreflective claims certainly enhance our conviction that they are, indeed, unreflective and indefensible. This hardly amounts to a basis for undermining our confidence in Plato's commitment to UP or, indeed, to any of the elements of the edifice built on that foundation.

What *would* undermine that confidence would be the inability to adduce the contents of one dialogue on behalf of the interpretation of another.[38] If the Socrates who is a literary character in, say, *Meno*, is fundamentally different from the Socrates who is a literary character in *Phaedo*, then we cannot use the latter to illuminate the philosophical claims made in the former. It is, I agree, difficult to separate those cases in which a later dialogue contains Plato's rethinking of an issue from those that contain his further explication of a position held earlier. In the first case, one would suppose that the later dialogue cannot be used to interpret the earlier; in the second case, there would be no such restriction. But the literary interpretation of the dialogues, insisting on the integrity of each work, does not permit interdialogue interpretation. When reading *Phaedo*, we must arbitrarily burden ourselves with a sort of hermeneutical Alzheimer's disease. A resolve to limit oneself to the experience of each dialogue in

---

37. See Tarrant 2000, 26, who argues that the presence of 'Socratic irony' in the dialogues is a central problem for those who wish to see Socrates as essentially a spokesman for Plato himself. This problem, however, disappears if we take the dialogues in the way I have suggested. That is, the irony of the dialogues need not indicate more than an artistic representation of a fragment of an intra-Academic discussion. Moreover, the doctrine of the essential incommunicability of philosophical knowledge may well invite the representation of an ironic or aporetic or ignorant Socrates. So, Nightingale 1995, 168. Nightingale offers an insightful explanation for the literary character of the dialogues, namely, that Plato intends to demarcate philosophy by the encounter of philosophers, especially Socrates, with nonphilosophers within other genres of discourse, like poetry and drama. Nightingale concludes (193), "Plato also marked the boundaries of philosophy by scripting intertextual encounters with traditional genres of poetry and rhetoric."

38. Blondell (2002, 5–6) emphasizes the "primacy of the individual dialogue," allowing at the same time the location of the "events" in the dialogue in a "web of spatial, temporal, and cultural contexts." In her treatment of individual dialogues, Blondell rarely allows herself an appeal to distinctions and arguments in other dialogues. Gonzalez (1995) argues that because for Plato knowledge is nonpropositional, there cannot be doctrine in the dialogues. To extract doctrine from the dialogue would be to betray this claim. I agree with Gonzalez on the nonpropositional nature of the highest form of cognition for Plato. But from this it does not follow that there is no doctrine in the dialogues in the sense of 'beliefs' (δόξαι) that Plato takes to be true.

its entirety without any dissonance caused by adducing 'alien' doctrine from elsewhere no doubt has a certain austere charm. If, however, this approach takes seriously the doctrine in the target dialogue, what is the possible justification for excluding help in its interpretation coming from other dialogues? The response that drawing on such help undermines the appreciation of the literary work is of consequence only if there is doctrine in one dialogue supposedly insulated from critical analysis resting on doctrines from another. Even if the doctrine in one dialogue is inseparable from the literary form of its presentation, it is a non sequitur to go on to claim that for this reason doctrines from another dialogue cannot be adduced on behalf of its interpretation. For to make the doctrine inseparable from the form of its delivery is to make the delivery part of the doctrine. But then *this* doctrine ought to be apt for illumination provided from elsewhere. For example, if it is held that in a dialogue wherein the subject of knowledge is considered, the real doctrine being conveyed is not the nature of knowledge but the nature of the communication of knowledge, then what is said elsewhere about this ought to be relevant to its interpretation. Again, if it is held that the doctrine that no one does wrong willingly is shown in the unmovable character of Socrates, then the doctrine of how knowledge affects behavior can be illuminated from elsewhere, too.

There is no argument that I am aware of that shows that there is something philosophically mistaken in using *Republic* to help understand *Symposium*. If *Republic* is so usable, then the literary interpretation of the dialogues is substantially false if that interpretation entails the illicitness of such use. No one expects Shakespeare's Hamlet to appear onstage in *King Lear* to comment on the king's behavior. Yet Plato's Socrates on numerous occasions makes reference to previous discussions or to issues that were discussed elsewhere.[39] The "elsewhere" need not necessarily be in other dialogues. What, though, could be the motive for denying the use of what is said in one dialogue to interpret another, unless one starts with the assumption that there is no doctrine to interpret in the first place?[40]

---

39. See Scott 2007, xi–xii, who thinks that the dialogues are in fact more like the plays of Shakespeare than like philosophical treatises. This seems to me clearly to be a false dichotomy. Nor (xiv) does it follow from Socrates' self-proclaimed ignorance that we should not take him to be a spokesman for Plato. Socrates' ignorance regarding the definitions of Forms—which is really the only sort of ignorance he consistently claims—certainly does not preclude his expression of argument or his expression of his commitment to the truth of the conclusions of arguments.

40. See McCabe 2000, 8–13, who is among the minority of those arguing for the relevance of the literary form to the philosophy and who also insists on the licitness of adducing doctrines in one dialogue to help interpret those in another. McCabe also maintains that the Socrates of the dialogues is entirely a literary creation, not to be taken as an accurate representation of the historical figure. The particular relevance for which McCabe argues is based on the patent fictions of the dialogue that are supposed to inspire the readers to search for the philosophical position behind the dialogue. This strikes me as an entirely innocuous claim.

For example, at the beginning of *Timaeus* an explicit reference is made to the discussions on the "previous day" that are contained in *Republic*. Most scholars assume that *Timaeus* was written some considerable time after *Republic*. Whether or not this is the case, the reference to *Republic* is a clear invitation to the reader to consider at least the political claims in that dialogue as relevant. Consider also the passage in *Phaedo* that 'introduces' Forms as entities familiar to the interlocutors.[41] Or Parmenides' attribution to the young Socrates of a theory of Forms discoverable in *Phaedo* and *Republic*.[42] Or *Theaetetus*, where Socrates lays down criteria for knowledge—that it must be of what is and infallible—that are intelligible only by adducing their appearance in the context of *Republic*.[43] Or *Philebus*, which introduces Forms in the language of *Parmenides*.[44] Finally, consider the example of *Symposium* and *Republic*. In the former, Diotima claims in her discourse on the mysteries of love that love of the beautiful is nothing but desire for the good. Other dialogues, including, for example, *Meno*, have Socrates make the claim that all desire the good.[45] *Republic* provides an ontological foundation for this desire and, according to Platonists, an explanation of how Beauty and Good are related. It is one thing to argue that this interpretation is false; it is another to argue that it is not in principle possible even to use *Republic* in this way owing to the literary integrity of *Symposium*.

I do not take these cross-references to indicate a particular pedagogical ordering of the dialogues. Far more important is that they indicate that there is a philosophical position of their author that makes its appearance in various ways throughout the dialogues. The more confident one is that material from one dialogue can be used to help interpret another, the more one is committed to the assumption that Plato has a comprehensive philosophical position across or behind the dialogues. The unchanging anchor of this position is, in my view, UP; the positive construct on its foundation always appears to us as a work in progress.

---

41. See *Phd.* 65Dff. At 76D8, Socrates refers to the Forms as "those things that we are always babbling about" (ἃ θρυλοῦμεν ἀεί). The "always" seems to me to be a problem for the strict literary view. For the passage is talking about *separate* Forms, which are supposedly introduced in *Phaedo*. If the "always" is a dramatic reference, then *Republic* precedes, say, *Euthyphro*, where the Forms are supposedly not separate. If we must read the "always" strictly within the confines of *Phaedo*, the word has no apparent meaning. It is a dramatic grace note. This is, of course, possible. But there is a clear and obvious interdialogic (and intra-Academic) meaning for the reference; the refusal to recognize this seems quite inexplicable.

42. See *Parm.* 130Eff. Unlike the historical Socrates, according to Aristotle's evidence, the young Socrates of *Parmenides* affirms separate Forms. What, in *Parmenides*, is attributed to the "young" Socrates is said in *Symposium* to be the doctrine of Diotima, who delivered it to Socrates long after his youth.

43. See *Tht.* 152C5–6 and *Rep.* 477 B10–11 and 477E6–7.

44. See *Phil.* 15A4–7 and *Parm.* 132A1. Annas (2006, 34–41) makes a similar antidevelopmentalist point regarding *Euthydemus* and *Theaeteteus* in relation to *Republic*.

45. *Meno* 77B2–78B6. Cf. *Euthyd.* 278D–E; *Gorg.* 468B; *Protag.* 358C–D; *Symp.* 205D.

Taking this together with the Aristotelian evidence, one will, I believe, arrive at the conclusion that the dialogues contain iterations of this positive construct.[46]

Developmentalism is true—almost too obviously true. Every dialogue contains evidence of development within the Academy regarding the elements of the positive construct. These developments concern technical terminology, conceptual distinctions, methodological experiments, and specific arguments addressing one or more concrete problems. There are perhaps substantive developments, too, for example, concerning matters like the unity of the virtues, the possibility of incontinence, the embodied and disembodied partitioning of the soul, and the exact nature of knowledge and its intelligible objects. Unitarianism is as true as developmentalism. But the unity is that of UP, not a unity in any of the areas just mentioned. Platonism was always open to development within this unified framework.

Plato's Self-Testimony

There are two passages in the Platonic corpus that are potentially of vital importance for judging all the issues discussed above. These are the passages in *Phaedrus* (274B6–278E3) and in the *Seventh Letter* (340B1–345C3) in which Plato seems to speak, albeit in the first case through the mouth of Socrates, about his own attitude toward writing. The two passages need to be interpreted together.

In the first passage, a number of points are made regarding the value and nature of writing.[47]

1. Writing does not increase wisdom; it only provides memoranda (ὑπομνήματα) for oneself. It is inferior to the oral transmission of wisdom.
2. Writing cannot enter into dialogue with readers; it cannot defend itself. Rather, it is more like drawing or painting, although actually even more misleading.

---

46. See Burnyeat 1990, 60–61, who contrasts two readings of *Theaetetus*, Reading A and Reading B. According to the former, "we determine [*Theaetetus*'s] meaning from the horizons of expectation established in earlier works of the same author." According to Reading B, "we read Part 1 of the *Theaetetus* in its own terms, as a self-sufficient critique of empiricism." Notice that Burnyeat does not in this passage even allow that the other parts of *Theaetetus* are relevant to determining the meaning of part 1. But if these parts are relevant, the explicitly aporetic conclusion of the dialogue raises the inevitable question of what the dialogue is supposed to teach us other than that knowledge is not sense perception or true belief or true belief plus a λόγος. Reading A allows us to appeal to other dialogues to discover what this is; Reading B does not do this, though it appeals to independently derived information that Plato rejects Protagorean relativism and extreme Heraclitean flux theory.

47. See Reale 1997, 51–62 on how the *Phaedrus* passage challenges the 'Schleiermacher paradigm.'

3. Writing is not serious. To write is analogous to planting a "garden of Adonis."[48]
4. It requires philosophy to control writing as appropriate for a particular audience.

Reading this passage, it is difficult to resist the conclusion that Plato is referring to his own writings, that is, to the dialogues. The idea that the criticisms of writing here refer only to the writings of *others* is, absent any supporting evidence, without merit. So, taking these criticisms seriously, how should we revise our view of the dialogues, if at all?

The claim that writing is inferior to speech for the transmission of wisdom seems to be in line with what is at least one plausible raison d'être for the founding of the Academy, namely, philosophical discussion and research. None of the above points, with the possible exception of the third, are even particularly Platonic in their basic import. Certainly, there is no suggestion that the inferiority of writing to speech entails the irrelevance of writing to the wisdom supposedly transmitted orally. Indeed, the claim that writing can serve as ὑπομνήματα seems to require their direct relevance; writing would hardly serve as an aid to memory if what was written bore no resemblance to what was being remembered.[49]

The statement of the superiority of oral transmission to writing is taken (along with the passage from the *Seventh Letter*) as a major confirmation for the claim of the so-called Tübingen School that the core of Plato's philosophy is to be found in what Aristotle refers to as his "unwritten teachings" (ἄγραφα δόγματα).[50] According to this interpretation, the unwritten

---

48. See Baudy 1986, for the meaning of "Adonis garden." The idea, as explained by Szlezák 1999, 42–44, is the use of a small amount of surplus seed retained after the summer harvest for a rapid flowering in clay pots or baskets during the festival of Adonis. After exposure to the sun, the plants wilted and were thrown into the sea in the ritual lament for Adonis. The principal point of the analogy is that the philosopher, like the wise farmer, will not plant his seed in such gardens for they are bound soon to wither. Allen (2010, 24–29) argues that even planting in a "garden of Adonis" has generative results. She takes this, without any evidence, as indicating that Plato intends to convey the message that writing has a positive role in "teaching the unlearned and less able" (28).

49. Cf. Frede 2006 for a different interpretation of the *Phaedrus* passage. Frede thinks that the dialogues are "memoranda" because each is adjusted to the capacity of the interlocutors. This hardly accounts for dialogues such as *Parmenides* and *Sophist*. Nor does it begin to explain the use of the term ὑπομνήματα here. See 275A5, D1; 276D3; 278A1.

50. See *Phys.* Δ 2, 209b11–17. In this passage, Aristotle distinguishes Plato's account of the receptacle in *Timaeus* from the account of it in Plato's "unwritten teachings." In the latter (see 209b33–210a2), Aristotle says that Plato identified the receptacle with the Great and the Small (or the Indefinite Dyad), whereas in *Timaeus* he identified it with space (and matter). This is perhaps evidence too slight to make the obvious inference that when Aristotle refers *only* to a dialogue for Plato's view, we may assume that nothing in his unwritten teachings contradicts this. Great controversy surrounds the question of the reference of these "unwritten teachings." In antiquity, they were identified with lectures by Plato on the Good. See Simplicius, *In Phys.* 151.6–19, 545.23–25 Diels, who says that Aristotle, Speusippus, and Xenocrates all gave accounts of the lecture; and Philoponus, *In Phys.* 521.9–15 Vitelli, who makes the identification

teachings focus on the reduction of Forms to two ultimate principles, the One and the Indefinite Dyad. I will have much more to say about these in the context of Aristotle's testimony in the next chapter. The Tübingen School maintains that the unwritten teachings are alluded to in numerous passages in the dialogues.[51] Although it is not possible to say whether all the dialogues were written by an author who unambiguously embraced these teachings, the above hypothesis that the dialogues were written no earlier than 387 does suggest that if we are to attribute such teachings to Plato, then there is no dialogue from which those teachings may be assumed to be entirely absent.[52]

Nevertheless, if the unwritten teachings focus on the reduction of Forms to first principles, that still leaves as part of the *written* teachings the derivation of Forms from a first principle, as in *Republic;* the relations among the Forms, as in *Phaedo, Parmenides,* and *Sophist;* and the relation between Forms, intellect, soul, and the sensible world, as in *Timaeus.* In other words, the unwritten teachings do not seem to indicate a sort of parallel doctrine, but the last step in an array of doctrines displayed throughout the dialogues.[53] Even on the assumption of unwritten teachings, there is nothing in the *Phaedrus* passage to lead us to think that the dialogues are, as it were, misdirecting the reader. We have no reason to doubt the conclusion that both the dialogues and the unwritten teachings belong to Plato's constructive metaphysical response to UP.[54]

---

explicit. On the historicity of Plato's lectures on the Good, see Cherniss 1945, 15, who argued that the so-called unwritten teachings referred merely to a single popular lecture by Plato. See Richard 1986, 70–82, for the evidential grounds for rejecting Cherniss's interpretation of the *Physics* passage. On the foundational arguments of the Tübingen School, see especially Krämer 1959; Gaiser 1968; Findlay 1974; Szlezák 1985; Krämer 1986; Richard 1986; Reale 1997. Also, see the valuable survey of De Vogel 1988. For some critical observations on the Tübingen School, see Brisson 1993; Mann 2006.

51. See Gaiser 1963, 446–557, for the direct and indirect testimonies; and Krämer 1990, 199–202, for the principal texts in the dialogues that scholars claimed were alluding to the unwritten teachings: *Protag.* 356E8–357C1; *Meno* 76E–77B1; *Phd.* 107B4–10; *Rep.* 506D2–507A2, 509C1–11; *Parm.* 136D4–E3; *Soph.* 254B7–D3; *Sts.* 284A1–E4; *Tim.* 48C2–E1, 53C4–D7; *Lg.* 894A1–5. See Erler 2007, 406–29, for a valuable survey of the issues surrounding the unwritten teachings and a comprehensive list of the testimonia.

52. See Ferber 2007, 29–32, who agrees that the critique of writing does not invalidate the testimony of the dialogues. He agrees further that as ὑπομνήματα, the dialogues must have a reference to intra-Academic discussions.

53. See Kahn 1996, 59–65, and passim, who argues for an "ingressive interpretation" of the dialogues. According to this interpretation, all the dialogues prior to *Republic* look forward or anticipate that dialogue. Kahn does not consider that this interpretative approach can, by the same logic, extend beyond *Republic* such that that dialogue, too, "looks beyond" to what I take to be a projected complete Platonic system. Nor indeed, does Kahn consider the possibility that *all* the dialogues are expressions of a "single philosophical view" (42) that in fact resides primarily outside the dialogues themselves. Following Kahn is Altman 2010. See Besnier 1996, 128–29, who argues against a "radicale séparation entre les dialogues et ces discussions internes [to the Academy]."

54. Gaiser (1963; 2nd ed. 1968, 586–89), in an addendum to the second edition of his work, offers a summarizing statement of his position: (a) the dialogues simply cannot be understood on their own; (b) the dialogues have in some ways a priority in our interpretations;

Still, the *Phaedrus* passage, if it is self-referring, makes an unambiguous claim about the relative worth of writing. Platonists and philosophers in antiquity generally had no difficulty in making a distinction between philosophy and philosophical writing, including the writing of Plato.[55] Philosophy as a way of life (βίος), including the oral transmission of wisdom through the practice of dialectic, was unquestionably thought to be superior to the written expression of the constitutive principles of that way of life in λόγοι. Accordingly, for Platonists, since Aristotle's testimony regarding the philosophy of Plato was assumed to be substantially accurate, there was no suggestion that the dialogues held a sort of exclusive canonical status for the expression of that philosophy. In a way, Aristotle's testimony held for them an advantage over the dialogues because that testimony had a systematic purpose lacking in them when considered individually.[56]

The passage from the *Seventh Letter* presents somewhat different problems, in part because of doubts about its authenticity and in part because, if authentic, the discovery of its full import requires a context that is unavailable to us.[57] Like the *Phaedrus* passage, the *Letter* speaks about the weakness of writing in relation to oral teaching and about the dangers of writing for the philosophically inept.[58] There is, however, one line that has been thought to invalidate the doctrinal bona fides of the dialogues altogether. Plato says at 341C4–5 that he has never written a σύγγραμμα that expresses

---

and (c) the dialogues nevertheless do illuminate and are illuminated by the oral tradition. The reason for (a) is that the oral tradition preserves answers to questions that are explicitly left open in the dialogues. Hence, the motivation for (b) and (c).

55. Cf. Hadot 1995, 62–64, on the subordination of the written expression of philosophy to philosophy itself. Also, Hadot 2002, 64, "I think we can say that although Plato and the other teachers at the Academy disagreed on points of doctrine, they nevertheless all accepted, to various degrees, the choice of the way or form of life which Plato had proposed."

56. See Krämer 1964b, 75–77, on the implications of *Phaedrus* and the *Seventh Letter* for the systematic understanding of Plato's philosophy.

57. See von Fritz 1971, for a defense of the authenticity of the *Seventh Letter*. Von Fritz, however (1966, 147), thinks that since the entirety of what we know of Plato's philosophy is contained in the dialogues, the authenticity of the *Seventh Letter* should not encourage us to attribute any "unwritten teachings" to Plato. See Erler 2007, 314–18, for a survey of opinion on authenticity and for an analysis of the content of the letter. Also, see Huffman 2005, 42–43, and Knab 2006, 2–6, for brief surveys of the state of the question today. If the letter is not authentic, it is almost certainly of Academic provenance, a fact that supports the identification of Platonism as a collaborative Academic project. Tarrant (1983) argues that the bulk of the letter is authentic, but the so-called philosophical digression, 340B1–345D, is a very late addition, inserted sometime between the first century BCE and the latter part of the second century CE at Alexandria. He believes that this section reflects the Platonism of the time of its composition. His principal argument is that the letter, apparently without the digression, is referred to by numerous Platonists—especially Plutarch—before the middle of the second century, whereas afterward it appears to be playing a greater role. As Gaiser (2004, 304–5) points out, if the letter is inauthentic, its author nevertheless seems to confirm the existence of unwritten teachings.

58. Sayre (1988, 95–97) makes the important point that the 'philosophical digression' of 342A–344D (esp. 343D5–9) considers all λόγοι, not just written words, as imperfect vehicles for the wisdom the soul seeks. This does not, however, amount to a contradiction of the *Phaedrus* on the inferiority of the written to the spoken word.

his own views. Certainly, the feeble efforts of the tyrant Dionysius to reveal Platonic philosophy are not to be taken seriously.

It has been argued by Thomas Szlezák, among others, that the term σύγγραμμα should be taken to refer to any sort of writing in prose, as opposed to poetry.[59] If this is the case, then Plato seems to be saying that even his own dialogues do not express his views. The older understanding of this term is that it refers to a treatise or systematic statement, in which case it would exclude the dialogues. On the one hand, it is difficult even to understand what it would mean for Plato to claim that nothing in the dialogues expresses his own views, even the 'meta' view that there is value in writing philosophical dialogues. On the other, why would he claim that no systematic treatise could express exactly what is in the dialogues? After all, that is what scholars have been trying to do for quite a long time.

At 344C1–E2, Plato writes:

> For this reason anyone who is seriously studying high matters will be the last to write about them and thus expose his thought to the envy and criticism of men. What I have said comes, in short, to this: whenever we see a book, whether the laws of a legislator or a composition [συγγράμματα] on any other subject, we can be sure that if the author is really serious, this book does not contain his best thoughts; they are stored away with the fairest of his possessions. And if he has committed these serious thoughts to writing, it is because men, not gods, have taken his wits away.
>
> To anyone who has followed this discourse and digression it will be clear that if Dionysius or anyone else—whether more or less able than he—has written concerning the first and highest principles of nature, he has not properly heard or understood anything of what he has written about; otherwise he would have respected these principles as I do, and would not have dared to give them this discordant and unseemly publicity. Nor can he have written them down for the sake of remembrance [ὑπομνημάτων]; for there is no danger of their being forgotten if the soul has once grasped them, since they are contained in the briefest of formulas. (trans. Glenn Morrow)[60]

Several points deserve emphasis. First, this passage explicates Plato's previous remark (341C4–5) that there has never been a composition by

---

59. See Szlezák 1979a, 360–63. Cf. Gaiser 2004, 306, n. 9. Cf. *Lg.* 858C10.

60. The *Second Letter*, whose authenticity has been doubted even more strenuously than that of the *Seventh Letter*, contains the following claim by its author (314C1–4): διὰ ταῦτα οὐδὲ πώποτ' ἐγὼ περὶ τούτων γέγραφα, οὐδ' ἔστιν σύγγραμμα Πλάτωνος οὐδὲν οὐδ' ἔσται, τὰ δὲ νῦν λεγόμενα Σωκράτους ἐστὶν καλοῦ καὶ νέου γεγονότος. (This is why I have never written on these matters [the principles, see 312E–313A] nor is there a composition by Plato on them nor will there ever be; those that are now said to be so are those of a renovated and beautified Socrates.) See Morrow 1962, 109–18, whose argument against the authenticity of the letter depends strongly on the *authenticity* of the *Seventh Letter*, on which the *Second Letter* is supposedly dependent, and who argues that since there are no references to the 'first principles' in the dialogues, this letter makes no sense if it attributes these to Socrates in the dialogues. But Morrow thinks this because he supposes that the words περὶ τούτων would have to be understood as referring unqualifiedly to these specific first principles (the One and the Indefinite Dyad)

him on the matter with which he is seriously concerned.[61] The suspicion or disdain that Plato shows here for writing is, in contrast to *Phaedrus*, focused on the 'most serious matters' (344C1–3), the first principles of nature. In a previous passage (341B–E), Plato expresses the same view as *Phaedrus* regarding the weakness of writing in comparison with the oral transmission of wisdom. But here he implies that Dionysius could not have written his treatise for the sake of 'remembrance' since the first principles are few and can be easily memorized. This remark seems to provide some context for the similar one in *Phaedrus*. That is, the rationale for writing as an aid to memory is that what needs to be remembered is more than a few concise principles. This is certainly what the written dialogues do in their representation or re-creation of substantive discussions in the Academy. Among other things, they reinforce the lesson of the explanatory inadequacies of all non-Platonic philosophical positions.

That the teachings on first principles are not found explicitly in the dialogues but rather in Aristotle's testimony in regard to Plato's philosophy in general supports the authenticity of the remarks in the *Seventh Letter* and the *Phaedrus* passage.[62] Still, one might maintain that the more we take the unwritten teachings seriously, the less seriously should we take the putative teachings in the dialogues, and vice versa. In fact, as we will see in the next chapter, the unwritten teachings (so far as these are known) do actually appear in the dialogues, though not as a principal subject of investigation. On the hypothesis that the dialogues represent the ongoing discussions in the Academy, this is hardly surprising.

---

throughout the passage. It seems, though, that while the words can easily be supplied in the following clauses, they can quite naturally be understood 'indexically'; that is, that the first principles that are discussed in the dialogues, presumably, the Forms along with the Idea of the Good, are not in fact the absolutely first principles that he, Plato, is exploring. The "Socrates renovated and beautified" refers to Plato's views apart from or before his embrace of the reductivist first principles of all. Even *Philebus* fits into this picture because the absolutely first principles are not explicitly mentioned.

61. The words "the matters regarding which I am seriously concerned" (ὅσοι...περὶ ὧν ἐγὼ σπουδάζω) are perhaps most plausibly taken as referring to the project of the positive construct on the basis of UP.

62. See Gonzalez 1995, who maintains that the *Seventh Letter* supports the view that a putative expression of doctrine in the dialogues would be about ultimate principles, the nature of which cannot be expressed. See also along the same lines Schefer 2001, esp. chap. 2. Schefer thinks that the unwritten teachings are unwritten because they refer to an inexpressible mystical, religious experience, the culmination of philosophy. This is certainly not Aristotle's view of the matter. It is perhaps worth adding that some of Aristotle's own works had their origin as ὑπομνήματα either *from* or *for* lectures. Kraut (1992, 22–23) argues that since Aristotle does not give "special weight" to the explicitly mentioned unwritten doctrines, we need not "downgrade" the dialogues or "attach priority to the unwritten opinion of Plato precisely because it was unwritten." Kraut's view seems to ignore such things as Aristotle's testimony about the reduction of Forms to Numbers and the superordinate status of the Good, identified as the One. Acknowledging the accuracy of this testimony, as Kraut does, does not amount to giving priority to the unwritten opinions except in the sense that these deal with first principles, as the dialogues for the most part do not.

CHAPTER 4

Aristotle on Plato and Platonism

Our best source for our knowledge of Plato's Platonism—apart from the dialogues—is without question the works of Aristotle. In these writings there are extensive reports of Platonic doctrine as well as detailed criticism of these. Aristotle, as we have all been instructed, came to Athens and Plato's Academy as a seventeen-year-old in 364 and remained there until Plato's death in 347. Traditionally, Platonists and Plato scholars have supposed that the Aristotelian testimony is based on both a reading of the dialogues as well as daily, or at least regular, discussion with Plato himself. Although Aristotle frequently refers to the dialogues in his discussion of Platonic doctrine, he never does so as if this were something different from what he learned orally.[1] The one apparent exception to this, discussed in

---

1. Kahn (1996, 81–82) argues that most of what Aristotle has to say about Plato's philosophy comes from his reading of the dialogues. He thinks that the assumption that Aristotle conversed with Plato about his philosophy "seems entirely gratuitous." I believe Kahn adheres so strongly to this implausible view because he also assumes that Plato's philosophy is just what is found in the dialogues. Penner (2002, 204, n. 2) shares my deep skepticism about the plausibility of Kahn's view. Given Plato's written expression of his reservations about writing in *Phaedrus*, the claim that Aristotle did not or could not corroborate his reading of the dialogues with oral discussion seems unjustified. In addition, the founding of Aristotle's own Lyceum apart from the Academy seems to indicate that the Academy had *some* purpose, namely, and minimally, the discussion of philosophy. It does seem gratuitous to assume that this discussion did not include Plato's philosophy. And Aristotle was evidently a participant in such discussions for almost twenty years. Schofield (2000, 55) concedes that the 'late' dialogues "reflect discussion within the Academy." Why not the 'early' dialogues, too? For other apparent references to oral transmissions by Plato, see, e.g., *Meta.* A 9, 992a20–22 (Plato called a point the principle of a line); Δ 11, 1019a1–4 (Plato introduced a new sense of 'prior'); Λ 3, 1070a18–19 (Plato said that there are as many Forms as there are things that exist by nature); N 8, 1083a31–33 (Plato made claims about the nature of number); *EN* A 1, 2.1095a32–33 (Plato

the last chapter, is in reality no exception at all. Aristotle contrasts the manner (τρόπος) in which Plato speaks about the receptacle in *Timaeus* and in the unwritten teachings.² Whether or not these unwritten teachings extend beyond what was contained in Plato's public lectures on the Good, there is no suggestion by Aristotle that there is a contradiction between these. In fact, Aristotle never makes a distinction between the doctrines found in the dialogues and the doctrines he ascribes to Plato similar to the apparent distinction he makes between the historical Socrates and the Socrates of the dialogues.³ Nor is Aristotle alert to anything like development in Plato's thought.⁴ Granted that he met Plato when Plato was around sixty years old

---

raised the problem about whether we should argue to or from principles); *GC* B 3, 330b16–17 (Plato's way of dividing elements). These passages, of course, are in addition to those in which Aristotle refers to the identification of the Good with the One and to the mathematization of the Forms not mentioned in the dialogues. See Ross 1951, 142–53, for a discussion of these passages. In this regard, it should be mentioned that Aristotle's testimony about the views of the historical Socrates at *Meta.* N 4, 1078b17–34 sharply differs from the views of Socrates of the dialogues. Is it not most natural to assume that Aristotle got this information about the historical Socrates from Plato?

2. Aristotle, *Phys.* Δ 2, 209b13–14, refers to Plato's unwritten teachings (ἀγράφοις δόγμασιν). The earliest reference to a lecture or lectures on the Good is in Aristoxenus, *Harm. Elem.* 2.30–31 (= *De bono*, p.111 Ross). It should be noted that Aristoxenus says specifically that he got his information from Aristotle. Cherniss (1944, 166–68 with n. 95) takes the fact that all later testimony about the unwritten teachings goes back to Aristotle as grounds for rejecting it. See Krämer 1964b, 73–74, with notes, on the important question of whether Plato gave one or more lectures on this subject. Krämer rejects the idea that there was only one lecture if we identify the lecture with Plato's unwritten teachings. Whether there were one or more public lectures we simply do not know. A passage in *Magna moralia* should also be considered here, even if this work is not genuine. See A 1, 1182a27–30: τὴν γὰρ ἀρετὴν κατέμιξεν εἰς τὴν πραγματείαν τὴν ὑπὲρ τἀγαθοῦ, οὐ δὴ ὀρθῶς. οὐ γὰρ οἰκεῖον (For he incorrectly mixed in virtue with the treatment of the Good, for that is inappropriate). This πραγματεία would seem to be a reference to a technical lecture on the Good such as the one Aristoxenus mentions; otherwise, it would be bizarre for Aristotle—or the author of this work, if a student of Aristotle—to criticize Plato for connecting the study of good with virtue. This is confirmed by the next line: ὑπὲρ γὰρ τῶν ὄντων καὶ ἀληθείας λέγοντα οὐκ ἔδει ὑπὲρ ἀρετῆς φράζειν· οὐδὲν γὰρ τούτῳ κἀκείνῳ κοινόν (for when speaking about being and truth, he should not have spoken about virtue, for the two have nothing in common).

3. There is one text that by its uniqueness actually supports this point. At *GC* A 9, 335b10, Aristotle says that *the* Socrates of *Phd.* 101C2–9 (i.e., the character Socrates) argues for a distinction between Forms and participants and claims that the Forms are responsible for the being of each thing that participates in it. This is the claim that Aristotle attributes to Plato in *Meta.* A 6, 987b9–10. It seems that the reference to the Socrates of the dialogue is made to distinguish him from the Socrates of history. The Socrates of the dialogues is just Plato, whose views are expressed, according to Aristotle, either orally or in these dialogues or in both. In the present case, Aristotle criticizes the Socrates of the dialogue for implying that Forms are responsible for generation and destruction. Perhaps the reference to *this* Socrates indicates that Aristotle knew perfectly well that Plato did not hold this view, but that from the dialogue alone one might make this inference. See Sharma 2009, 151–56, for some good discussion of this.

4. As Burnet (1914, 313) pointed out almost a century ago, "One thing, at any rate, seems clear. Aristotle knows of but one Platonic Philosophy, that which identified Forms with numbers. He never indicates that this system has taken the place of an earlier Platonism in which the Forms were not identified with numbers, or that he knew of any change or

and had probably already written most of his dialogues, his evident deep familiarity with these works as well as those written while he and Plato were together never leads him to distinguish anything like early, middle, and late stages of Plato's thought or even between a 'pre-Aristotle' and an 'Aristotle-inspired' Plato.

The sketch of Aristotle as a reliable and trenchant reporter of a unified Platonism reflected both in the dialogues and in oral discussion has been put into question at various times, but no more so than in the writings of Harold Cherniss.[5] Cherniss's principal argument is that Aristotle is not a reliable witness to Platonic doctrine, which, according to Cherniss, is found exclusively in the dialogues. Whether intentionally or not, Aristotle, he argues, gets Plato wrong. On this view, if there is a version or form of Platonism orally transmitted, either this is identical with that found in the dialogues, in which case Aristotle got it wrong on both counts, or it is something different from that found in the dialogues, in which case we must remain completely ignorant of what this is.[6] Cherniss, though, agrees with one thing Aristotle apparently assumed, namely, that there is no substantial development in the dialogues. Cherniss's Plato holds to a constant doctrine, though it is one quite different from that which Aristotle criticized.[7]

We should be careful here to distinguish between Cherniss's criticism of Aristotle and the criticisms of Aristotle made in defense of Platonism in antiquity. The latter generally assumed that Aristotle's testimony regarding what Plato taught was accurate, even if Aristotle misunderstood the implications of these teachings or even if he criticized them unjustly. Thus, for example, whereas Platonists assumed that Aristotle was correct in supposing that Plato identified the Good with the One, Cherniss denies this. Accordingly, Cherniss believes that a defense of Plato does not require a defense of this identification; Platonists in antiquity thought otherwise. In fact, a great deal of Platonic doctrine from the Old Academy up through the latest versions of Platonism is shaped with a view to responding to Aristotle's criticisms. The difficulty of producing an adequate response is, no doubt, part of the explanation for the variety of responses.

---

modification introduced by Plato into his philosophy in his old age. That is only a modern speculation." Cf. Steinthal 1998, 67.

5. See esp. Cherniss 1944, 1945.

6. Cherniss rejects unequivocally the existence of unwritten teachings and even of a number of lectures on the Good, as opposed to a single lecture, which, he maintains, did no more than summarize the doctrines in the dialogues. For an extended and detailed response to Cherniss, see Krämer 1959. Also see Findlay 1974, appendix 2, 455–73. The basic position of Cherniss is an application of the fundamental interpretive stance of the man who deserves to be known as the founder of modern Platonic scholarship, F. Schleiermacher. See Tigerstedt 1974, 5–6, who shows that acceptance of Schleiermacher's thesis by later scholars was the principal fulcrum used for isolating Platonism as revealed in the unwritten teachings and in Aristotle's testimony from a version of Platonism exclusively derived from the dialogues. On Schleiermacher's argument that the dialogues have a pedagogical progression of ideas, with *Phaedrus* as the first and programmatic dialogue, see Lamm 2000, 232–37.

7. See Cherniss 1936, 1957. Cherniss's unitarianism is in line with that of Shorey 1904.

Another alternative presents itself: Aristotle is an accurate reporter of Plato's views, but if these views developed, he might appear to be inaccurate only if one tried to match the reports with the "wrong" dialogues. That is, if, say, Plato's identification of the Good with the One occurred only late in his career, then we should expect that any report regarding Platonic doctrine that is based on dialogues earlier than those in which the later view is reflected would appear inaccurate. Thus, according to the conclusions reached by Léon Robin in his 1908 book *La théorie platonicienne des idées et des nombres d'aprés Aristote,* Aristotle's testimony reveals a doctrine that looks, perhaps surprisingly, 'Neoplatonic.'[8] If this doctrine cannot be found in some dialogues, that is because Plato's thought developed into such a position. Accordingly, in a later book, Robin argued that Aristotle's testimony applies only to "late dialogues, those written after *Parmenides,* namely, *Sophist, Statesman,* and *Philebus.*"[9]

As we have already seen, with developmentalism of any sort we are in exceedingly murky waters. Apart from the fact that Aristotle nowhere indicates 'phases' of Platonic doctrine, it is virtually impossible according to this position to determine whether Plato's alluding to a first principle of all in a dialogue prior to *Parmenides* represents a phase of his development before he identified the Good with the One or whether it represents simply his disinclination (for whatever reason) to reveal that identity at that time. Given the dramatic exigencies of any dialogue, and the fact that all of them are directed to the solution of one concrete problem each or to answering one specific question, it is intrinsically plausible that Plato never thought that he had to adduce or even mention on any single occasion *all* the metaphysical and epistemological apparatus that he was in fact prepared to deploy. And yet, it is also not implausible that Academic discussion as well as Plato's own extra-Academic contacts—especially with Pythagoreans in Italy and in Sicily and probably in Athens as well—inspired him to further reflection on his fundamental position. We need not minimize Plato's dominant doctrinal role in the Academy when he was alive in order to suppose the research-oriented nature of that institution. If Academic research in metaphysics is somewhat odder an idea than is Peripatetic research in the biological sciences, it was still research. And who is to say that the results of that research were not embraced by Plato and recorded in some of his dialogues?

This is where it seems to me especially useful to keep the UP hypothesis in mind. Both the developmentalist and the unitarian accounts of Plato's philosophy cohere with his commitment to UP. That is why it is possible to make a case for each. I think we can go further. The developmentalist is correct inasmuch as Plato's entire career was an ongoing attempt to construct

---

8. See Robin 1908, 598–600.
9. See Robin 1935 for the conclusions drawn from the earlier book, which aims to reconstruct Platonic doctrine solely from Aristotle's testimony.

the most defensible positive response to UP.¹⁰ The unitarian is correct inasmuch as Plato never wavered in his commitment to UP. Aristotle's testimony regarding Plato's philosophy seems to assume the truths contained in the last two sentences. This is as much as to say that the contrast between developmentalism and unitarianism is based on a misunderstanding. There is, it seems, development *within* a unitarian position.¹¹

Out of UP came versions of what later came to be called 'Platonism.' The Platonists regarded Plato's version as the best of these. Hence, it would have been natural for them to privilege that version with the name 'Platonism' if they had been so inclined to label it. Aristotle, not surprisingly, writes of Plato's positive construction synoptically, that is, almost never focusing on a single dialogue or dialogues, and trying to examine the core of his comprehensive and unified response to UP. For this reason, Aristotle's use of the dialogues as evidence for that positive response is constantly controlled by his access to the ongoing discussions in the Academy.¹² The result is a picture that is in some ways substantially at odds with a picture that uses the dialogues exclusively or even a picture (like that of Robin) that excludes the dialogues to focus on Aristotle's testimony. For us, the best approach seems to be to use the dialogues and Aristotle's testimony, especially in regard to the unwritten teachings, to track Plato's construction of a comprehensive philosophy based on UP. In doing this, I do not discount the likelihood that 'triangulating' the results of oral discussions and the dialogues is a delicate matter. Given that the criticisms of Plato found in the first book of *Metaphysics* were written perhaps fifteen or so years after Plato died, it would be no easy task to give an accurate account of the basic philosophical positions that were partially expressed in the dialogues and continually refined in the dynamic of Academic discussions.

I believe we will find it illuminating to view Aristotle's testimony about Platonism and, indeed, Aristotle's entire philosophical enterprise as being

10. See Nails 1995, 223–26, who applies the idea of continuous development to either a theory, or the theory, of Forms in the dialogues. On the basis of the Aristotelian evidence alone, it is impossible to accept the claim that there was a single and complete theory of Forms, developed out of some sort of Socratic theory of universals, and then subject to an array of criticisms in *Parmenides,* and finally abandoned or altered in a specific way in the later dialogues.

11. One may compare in this regard the development of Augustine's theology within his basic Christian commitment. Indeed, one may go further and compare his development within his basic commitment to UP. By contrast, Kant's development from a precritical philosophy to a critical philosophy or Wittgenstein's development from the philosopher of the *Tractatus* to the philosopher of the *Philosophical Investigations* are not within a framework like that of UP.

12. See Vlastos 1973, 397–98, who concludes a scathing review of H. J. Krämer's *Arete bei Platon und Aristoteles* and a rejection of the idea of Plato's unwritten teachings with the suggestion that the 'discrepancies' between Aristotle's testimony and what we find in the dialogues can plausibly be attributed to the fact that much Academic speculation or research was in fact conducted orally. In this book I am trying to take this reasonable assumption one step further in arguing that the speculation was rooted in UP and the search for a positive construct out of it. I am not sure there is a great distance between 'speculation' and 'unwritten teachings' in general, but the weight of evidence from the dialogues themselves as well as from the indirect testimony suggests something more formal or systematic than mere speculation.

aimed at identifying and repairing problems in the Platonic positive construction out of UP.¹³ In addition, as we will see, part of that task involves the creation of a technical philosophical vocabulary to express the distinctions and insights obtained through ongoing Academic work.

Aristotle and Ur-Platonism

Aristotle's extensive criticisms of Plato's philosophy are variously judged to be devastating or misguided. Those who hold the first view typically go on to construct an interpretation of Aristotle's own philosophy crucial elements of which are claims that are the contradictories of the claims of Plato that Aristotle has rejected. Thus, for example, a rejection of separate Forms is supposed to commit Aristotle to the unqualified immanence of Forms. Or the rejection of the immortality of the soul is supposed to mark Aristotle's commitment to the soul's mortality owing to its inseparability from the body. Those who hold the second view typically maintain that Aristotle's polemical aims led him to give a distortive picture of the doctrines found in the dialogues. Thus, for example, when Aristotle says in *Metaphysics Alpha* that "Plato uses only two causes, the cause of the whatness and the cause according to matter," this is supposedly at odds with the final causality of the Idea of the Good and the efficient causality of the Demiurge.¹⁴

Both interpretations share the assumption that Aristotle's treatment of Plato in his own works is presented from the perspective of a φιλόσοφος, not a φιλόλογος. Either Aristotle has seen from his own superior philosophical position the flaws in Plato's thinking or just because he is an independent thinker with his own agenda he was not particularly interested in scrupulous scholarship. I want to argue that the polemical use of Aristotle either against Plato or on Plato's behalf has the unfortunate result that it occludes or inhibits the correct understanding of Platonism. For example, one might reject Aristotle's testimony about Plato's identification of the Good with the One merely because such an identification is thought to be absurd or indefensible. Or, desiring to endorse Aristotle's apparent rejection of Plato's arguments for the immortality of the soul, one misses the Platonic view that Aristotle completely embraced, namely, the immortality of intellect.¹⁵

---

13. We thus have an explanation for Aristotle's otherwise puzzling use of the first-person plural in his *Metaphysics* in referring to views of Plato. See Ross 1924, 1:190–91, for citations, though Ross seems to share the view of Jaeger according to which the use of the plural indicates Aristotle's 'early' Platonic phase. I suggest rather that this use indicates a shared commitment to UP.

14. See *Meta.* A 6, 988a7–10. Cf. Λ 6, 1071b14–16.

15. See Irwin 1988, 11, who says, "There is no evidence that Aristotle was ever a disciple of Plato (in the sense of accepting all the main philosophical doctrines discoverable from Plato's dialogues), or that his later works are less Platonic than his earlier." He adds, "A more plausible picture of Aristotle's development suggests that his earlier philosophical views are the product of his criticisms of Plato, resulting from actual debate in the Academy; further

I have argued in a previous book that the view of Platonists in antiquity that the philosophies of Plato and Aristotle are in harmony has much to be said for it.[16] The harmonists were not blind to Aristotle's extensive criticisms of Plato's philosophy. But in their responses to these criticisms they assumed that they depended on something like a commitment by Aristotle to what I am calling UP.[17] Thus, because Aristotle was an antinominalist, his rejection of one or more theories of Forms did not mean that he was not committed to explaining the qualified or compromised identity of things with their properties.[18] How, after all, can 'Socrates is pale' be true if, as is surely the case, 'Socrates is Socrates' is also true? Again, just because Aristotle was explicitly an antimechanist, his rejection of one or more of the causal roles supposedly performed by Forms did not mean that he was not committed to the inadequacies of a 'bottom-up' account of nature or of cognition.[19] A similar commitment to antimaterialism, antirelativism, and antiskepticism is evident throughout Aristotle's writings.[20] So when he proceeds to argue for his own superior metaphysical or epistemological explanations, he was taken to be offering another version of Platonism. My point here is not that ancient Platonists had a particularly capacious tolerance for the use of the term 'Platonist,' but that their understanding of what Platonism is was more accurate precisely because they saw it as arising out of UP. A better understanding of what we find in the dialogues is to be had if we assume that what

---

reflection on Plato led him, in later works, to form a more sympathetic view of some of Plato's views and doctrines." The putative tension in Aristotle's development that Irwin alludes to, rejects, and then tentatively tries to account for in this passage seems to me to be resolved by the hypothesis that Aristotle, like Plato, was *always* an adherent of UP, though, again like Plato, he was continually striving to construct the most coherent edifice possible on that foundation.

16. See Gerson 2005.

17. Mann (2006, 380–85) wants to distinguish two ways of understanding the claim that Aristotle was a Platonist. According to the first, 'Platonism' refers to certain doctrines; according to the second, it refers to certain 'concerns,' 'methods,' or 'standards' of philosophical investigation. Mann holds that Aristotle was not a Platonist according to the first way, but that he was according to the second. This is a demonstrably false dichotomy unless one understands 'doctrines' narrowly as referring exclusively to those matters wherein Aristotle specifically does contradict Plato. Mann himself goes on to allow that Aristotle's disagreements with Plato are "scarcely intelligible...except against the background of Plato's philosophy." I fail to see why this philosophy should be thought to exclude doctrine.

18. See Aristotle's criticism of Antisthenes, *Meta.* Δ 29, 1024b24–1025a5.

19. See Aristotle's criticism of Empedocles and Democritus (*Phys.* B 2, 194a18–27), namely, that they focused only on matter and not form in their causal explanations, and his criticism (B 4, 195b36–196b5) of those (probably including Democritus) who say that all things happen by chance.

20. In each case, Aristotle expresses his opposition to the views of his predecessors, in particular those who were materialists, relativists, and skeptics. Those named include the Atomists, Protagoras, Anaxagoras, Empedocles, and Megarians. There are no doubt many other unnamed opponents to whom Aristotle alludes when expressing his commitment to UP. See Hussey 2012, 22, for some compatible remarks—aimed in part against the conclusions of Cherniss regarding Aristotle's treatment of Pre-Socratic philosophers—about Aristotle's assumption that his predecessors' contributions should be evaluated in the light of a 'teleology of truth.'

we find there is constructed on the basis of a commitment to UP. I think the same thing is true for the works of Aristotle. If nothing else, such an assumption should militate against the truly bizarre tendency among scholars to simply ignore the plain text of Aristotle on so many crucial points.

The claim that Aristotle was in fact committed to UP seems to me beyond question, even if we were to insist that his commitment to the negative elements of UP might be firmer than his commitment to a positive unified construct based on those elements. This commitment bridges the exoterica, or dialogues, and the esoterica, or treatises, supposed by Jaeger and others to divide Aristotle's 'Platonic phase' from his 'anti-Platonic phase.'[21] Indeed, Aristotle's criticisms of Parmenides, Protagoras, Empedocles, and Anaxagoras are substantially those of Plato. His criticism of Democritus—whose apparent lack of appearance anywhere in the dialogues remains a mystery—is in accord with UP.[22] We must add, of course, Aristotle's extensive criticisms of Pythagoreanism along with his claim that Plato was in certain respects following Pythagoras. But this criticism in no way negates or presupposes a lack of commitment to UP on Aristotle's part, but only to a 'Pythagoreanizing' philosophy built on it.[23]

Even more explicitly than in Plato, for Aristotle the inadequacies of the positions the contradictories of which together constitute UP are explanatory in nature. Like Plato and the Pre-Socratics, Aristotle, too, assumes a reductivist approach to this explanatory framework. It is not much of an oversimplification to claim that the fourfold explanatory schema in *Physics* is the central building block of Aristotle's positive construction out of UP. It is this schema, understood as arising out of UP, that leads Aristotle to the postulation of the primacy of hylomorphic substance (οὐσία) in nature.

So much is relatively uncontentious. Considerable difficulties arise, however, when we consider the specific nature of the explanatory framework. For those committed to UP generally, and for Aristotle in particular, this framework is hierarchical. The core idea is this. If B explains A, that is, provides a necessary and sufficient condition for A, then B cannot be in need of the same sort of explanation as A. If it does need the same sort of explanation, then B is at best an instrumental cause or explanation for A. Let us call that which is in need of an explanation 'heteroexplicable' and

---

21. See Jaeger 1948, 34, who avers that "it is certain that the dialogues contradict the treatises." As Jaeger goes on to argue, the contradiction is between the Platonism of the dialogues and the anti-Platonism of the treatises. For further references, see Gerson 2005, chap. 2.

22. See Furley 1989, who argues that the fundamental division in ancient cosmological theory is between atomists and Aristotelians, though he aligns Aristotle with Plato and the Stoics. According to Furley, the fundamental distinction is between what I have called a 'top-down' and a 'bottom-up' approach to scientific explanation. My disagreement with Furley rests on what is bound to be an equivocal understanding of explanation in a Stoic materialist world and among the Platonists.

23. Jaeger (1948, 97) says that the Pythagorean basis of Platonism was "the official view of the Academy," though he offers no evidence for this claim.

that which is in need of no explanation outside of itself 'autoexplicable.'[24] Within a particular explanatory framework, heteroexplicable items are not irrelevant; often, depending on the aims of the explanation or the questions asked, they are adequate. Indicating B when inquiring into the parent of A does not amount to a failure to explain. But the aim of comprehensiveness or completeness for Aristotle precludes definitive adequacy for a heteroexplicable B like a parent. As Aristotle in *Metaphysics Alpha Elatton* asserts and then proceeds to prove:

> But clearly there is a beginning, and the causes of things are not infinite, either as a series or in kind.[25]

The principal task of *Metaphysics* as set out by Aristotle is to demonstrate that there is an ultimate cause or explanation for everything and that this ultimate cause is indeed autoexplicable. So a divine science, a science of principles and causes, a science of being qua being, must find in the ultimate cause of the being of everything else (that is, everything that is heteroexplicable) an autoexplicable 'beginning,' or ἀρχή. A property of the autoexplicable in relation to the heteroexplicable is that it is ontologically prior, meaning that the autoexplicable can exist without the heteroexplicable but not vice versa. Aristotle says that this sense of 'priority' was used by Plato.[26] The fact that Aristotle rejects Forms as autoexplicable agents must be seen against the background of UP according to which Aristotle unqualifiedly affirms autoexplicability as a desideratum of a science of wisdom.

There is another passage in *Alpha Elatton* that expands on the notion of ontological priority within an explanatory framework:

> Now we do not understand a truth without its cause; also, of things to which the same predicate belongs, the one to which it belongs in the highest degree

---

24. I am using this term in the first instance as a gloss on the term ἀνυπόθετον in *Rep.* 510B7, 511B6, which is used in reference to the Idea of the Good. As 'unhypothetical,' it is an ἀρχή of all things. Autoexplicability is what being an unqualified ἀρχή entails. That which is 'hypothetical' is only relatively an ἀρχή and so only relatively autoexplicable, that is, it is autoexplicable in relation only to the sort of thing it is adduced to explain. Thus, an essence, or οὐσία, is relatively autoexplicable. There is no reason other than itself why it is what it is, but its existence is not thereby explained.

25. *Meta.* α 2, 994a1–2: Ἀλλὰ μὴν ὅτι γ' ἔστιν ἀρχή τις καὶ οὐκ ἄπειρα τὰ αἴτια τῶν ὄντων οὔτ' εἰς εὐθυωρίαν οὔτε κατ' εἶδος, δῆλον.

26. See *Meta.* Δ 11, 1019a1–4: τὰ μὲν δὴ οὕτω λέγεται πρότερα καὶ ὕστερα, τὰ δὲ κατὰ φύσιν καὶ οὐσίαν, ὅσα ἐνδέχεται εἶναι ἄνευ ἄλλων, ἐκεῖνα δὲ ἄνευ ἐκείνων μή· ᾗ διαιρέσει ἐχρήσατο Πλάτων (objects are, then, called 'prior' and 'posterior' in this way, but others are so called according to nature or substance, when such things can exist without others, but not conversely—a distinction employed by Plato). There is no such use of the term πρότερα in the dialogues. It is likely that, as Ross (1924, 1:317) notes, Aristotle is here referring to oral discussion within the Academy.

is that in virtue of which it belongs also to the other. For example, fire is the hottest of whatever is truly called 'hot,' for fire is the cause of hotness in the others. So, therefore, that is most true which is the cause of truth in whatever is posterior to it. Accordingly, the principles of eternal things are of necessity always the most true; for they are true not merely sometimes, nor is there anything which is the cause of their being, but they are the cause of the being of other things; accordingly, as each thing is related to its being, so is it related to its truth.[27]

The first point to be noted in regard to this portentous passage is the connection with book Alpha's claim that the science of wisdom that Aristotle is seeking aims for understanding ultimate causes and principles.[28] That is why it is a science of the divine.[29] Our passage adds three crucial claims: (1) ultimate causes do not have a cause of their being; that is, they are autoexplicable; and (2) the autoexplicable cause of the heteroexplicable gives to the latter its predicate name, but itself possesses that predicate 'in the highest degree'; (3) truth is 'gradable' according to (2).[30] Leaving aside for the moment the rather vague reference in 'principles of eternal things,' what is most remarkable for my purposes is the conclusion Aristotle draws from the assumption of UP coupled with the exigencies of ultimate explanation. If the heteroexplicable ultimately requires the autoexplicable, the latter must be different in kind from the former. Thus, as Aristotle will famously argue, the ultimate explanation for the motion of anything movable will be that which is unqualifiedly immovable.[31] But that which is unqualifiedly immovable cannot be a material body because all material bodies are movable, at least in place.[32] So that which is the ultimate cause of that which is movable must be without magnitude.[33] Whether Aristotle's commitment to the antimaterialism of UP is the *result* of his argument regarding the immateriality of the ultimate cause of motion or whether it is the cause is irrelevant. In fact, I think both are the consequence of

---

27. *Meta.* α 1, 993b23–31: οὐκ ἴσμεν δὲ τὸ ἀληθὲς ἄνευ τῆς αἰτίας· ἕκαστον δὲ μάλιστα αὐτὸ τῶν ἄλλων καθ' ὃ καὶ τοῖς ἄλλοις ὑπάρχει τὸ συνώνυμον (οἷον τὸ πῦρ θερμότατον· καὶ γὰρ τοῖς ἄλλοις τὸ αἴτιον τοῦτο τῆς θερμότητος)· ὥστε καὶ ἀληθέστατον τὸ τοῖς ὑστέροις αἴτιον τοῦ ἀληθέσιν εἶναι. διὸ τὰς τῶν ἀεὶ ὄντων ἀρχὰς ἀναγκαῖον ἀεὶ εἶναι ἀληθεστάτας (οὐ γάρ ποτε ἀληθεῖς, οὐδ' ἐκείναις αἴτιόν τί ἐστι τοῦ εἶναι, ἀλλ' ἐκεῖναι τοῖς ἄλλοις), ὥσθ' ἕκαστον ὡς ἔχει τοῦ εἶναι, οὕτω καὶ τῆς ἀληθείας. Cf. Ν 5, 1092a11–16, which criticizes Speusippus for inverting the ontological hierarchy. Jaeger in his edition of *Metaphysics* reads ἀληθέστερον in line 27 instead of ἀληθέστατον. But there is no ms. support for Jaeger's reading and the latter fits better with μάλιστα in line 24.

28. See *Meta.* Α 1, 982a1–3, with b7–10.

29. *Meta.* Α 2, 983a5–10.

30. Cf. the gradations implicit in *Rep.* 515D3 on the intelligibles as "things that are more" (μᾶλλον ὄντα) and *Soph.* 248E7–249A1 on τὸ παντελῶς ὄν.

31. See *Meta.* Λ 6, 1071b3–22.

32. All bodies are in place. Place is an accidental attribute of a body. Therefore, all bodies are movable in place, even though they are never necessarily in motion at any time.

33. See *Phys.* Θ 10, 266a10–b24.

his and Plato's general commitment to the explanatory framework set out by the Pre-Socratics. I think this because that explanatory framework is essentially the framework of all science, at least in the tradition of realism. What sets Plato and all the versions of Platonism—including that upheld by Aristotle—apart from this is the importation of this framework into a purely philosophical context.[34]

The 'principles of eternal things' are the autoexplicable causes of their being. These eternal things include presumably the eternal sensible mentioned in *Lambda*, namely, the Moon, Sun, and other heavenly bodies.[35] But the point being made about these is general and would also include Forms and Mathematical Objects if these exist. Aristotle is perhaps purposefully vague about how the heavenly bodies are the cause of being of 'other things.' But elsewhere in *Metaphysics* he identifies 'the cause of being' of a substance (οὐσία) with the form of that substance.[36] For this reason, the form is itself called 'substance.' If this is indeed the meaning in our passage, then the eternal, autoexplicable causes of the being of things not eternal are their forms, only here these forms are separate. The gradation of predication arises from the autoexplicable/heteroexplicable distinction. In Aristotle's example, fire is said to be hottest because fire alone is hot just because it is fire, whereas everything else is hot because there is fire in it.[37]

Aristotle's commitment to UP combined with his search for ultimate explanations impels him to the idea of 'derivative' synonymy.[38] That is, though two things might have the synonymous predicate, one of these (the cause or principle) possesses that predicate in the highest degree

---

34. Two watershed texts in this regard are *Phd.* 95E7–102A2, Socrates' 'autobiography,' in which he recounts the discovery of a 'second sailing' toward explanation; and *Tim.* 46C7–47E2, in which true causes are distinguished from 'accessory causes.' I discuss these passages below.

35. See *Meta.* Λ 1, 1069a30–31. On the grammatical problems in this sentence, see Frede and Charles 2000, 78–80, though the reference to the heavenly bodies seems secure. Cf. Z 2, 1028b12; H 2, 1042a10.

36. Cf. Δ 8, 1017b14–16; H 2, 1043a3; H 3, 1043b13. The form is the cause of the 'to be' of a substance because the 'to be' is always to be something or other, that is, some kind of thing. So, naturally, the form is the cause of this.

37. One might compare the argument in *Phd.* 105B8–C2: εἰ γὰρ ἔροιό με ᾧ ἂν τί ἐν τῷ σώματι ἐγγένηται θερμὸν ἔσται, οὐ τὴν ἀσφαλῆ σοι ἐρῶ ἀπόκρισιν ἐκείνην τὴν ἀμαθῆ, ὅτι ᾧ ἂν θερμότης, ἀλλὰ κομψοτέραν ἐκ τῶν νῦν, ὅτι ᾧ ἂν πῦρ· (If you were to ask me owing to what being present will that body be hot, I will not give the safe and crude reply that it is hotness, but I will give a fancier reply based on what is being said now, that it is owing to fire.) Proponents of a profound Aristotelian-Platonic divide need to explain why Aristotle's words in the above text "fire is the hottest of whatever is truly called 'hot,' for fire is the cause of hotness in the others" are thought to be claiming anything substantially different from what is claimed in the passage from Plato's *Phaedo*.

38. We must distinguish derivative synonymy from πρὸς ἕν equivocity such as is found in the use of the word 'healthy' for bodies and, say, climate. In the latter, there is no synonymy at all. Whether πρὸς ἕν equivocity is a development within Aristotle's own thought from derivative synonymy will be discussed below.

while the other (that which is caused) possesses it derivatively. This idea of derivative synonymy is especially intriguing because it is also found in Aristotle's *On the Ideas* in the so-called Argument from Relatives, an argument that Aristotle *criticizes:*

> In cases in which something identical is predicated of a plurality not homonymously, but so as to reveal some one nature, it is true of them either (a) because they are fully what is signified by that which is predicated, as when we call Socrates and Plato man; or (b) because they are likenesses of the true ones, as when we predicate man of pictured men (for in their case we reveal the likenesses of man, signifying some identical nature in all of them); or (c) because one of them is the paradigm, the others likenesses, as if we were to call Socrates and the likeness of him men.[39]

The first obvious question here is whether in fact the relation between Socrates and a picture of Socrates is the same as the relation between the hotness of fire and the hotness of a bowl of soup. The answer seems to be obviously no, since the soup is really hot whereas the picture of Socrates is not really a man. Plato, of course, can readily agree that the picture of a man is not a man. What he wants to claim, rather, is that an instance of a Form is derivatively synonymous with the Form.[40] So the equality in equal sticks is equality, but it is not really real equality, that is, it is not autoexplicable equality.[41] Moreover, an account of autoexplicable Equality, unlike

---

39. Alexander of Aphrodisias, *In Meta*. 82.11–83.7: ἐφ' ὧν ταὐτόν τι πλειόνων κατηγορεῖται μὴ ὁμωνύμως, ἀλλ' ὡς μίαν τινὰ δηλοῦν φύσιν, ἤτοι τῷ κυρίως τὸ ὑπὸ τοῦ κατηγορουμένου σημαινόμενον εἶναι ταῦτα ἀληθεύεται κατ' αὐτῶν, ὡς ὅταν ἄνθρωπον λέγωμεν Σωκράτην καὶ Πλάτωνα, ἢ τῷ εἰκόνας αὐτὰ εἶναι τῶν ἀληθινῶν, ὡς ἐπὶ τῶν γεγραμμένων ὅταν τὸν ἄνθρωπον κατηγορῶμεν (δηλοῦμεν γὰρ ἐπ' ἐκείνων τὰς τῶν ἀνθρώπων εἰκόνας τὴν αὐτήν τινα φύσιν ἐπὶ πάντων σημαίνοντες), ἢ ὡς τὸ μὲν αὐτῶν ὂν τὸ παράδειγμα, τὰ δὲ εἰκόνας, ὡς εἰ ἀνθρώπους Σωκράτη τε καὶ τὰς εἰκόνας αὐτοῦ λέγοιμεν. On the argument, see Fine 1993, 51; chaps. 10–13.

40. Graded synonymy is to be distinguished from ungraded synonymy, which implies an absence of ontological priority. The latter is what leads to the regress arguments of *Parmenides*. The failure to make this distinction and therefore to suppose this to be a problem for Plato (but not for Aristotle) can be found in Burge 1971, Annas 1982, and Sedley 1998, among others. Cf. *Rep.* 515D3, where in the Allegory of the Cave, things outside the cave have "more being" (μᾶλλον ὄντα) than things in the cave. *That* is graded synonymy.

41. Cf. the entire Recollection Argument at *Phd.* 72E3–78B3. The phrase αὐτὸ ὅ ἔστι that Plato regularly uses to characterize Forms is an emblem of autoexplicability. Cf. 75D2, etc., and Alexander's text at 83.15–18: ἔστι τι αὐτόισον καὶ κυρίως, πρὸς ὃ τὰ ἐνθάδε ὡς εἰκόνες γίνεταί τε καὶ λέγεται ἴσα, τοῦτο δέ ἐστιν ἰδέα, παράδειγμα [καὶ εἰκὼν] τοῖς πρὸς αὐτὸ γινομένοις (there is something which is the equal itself, that is, primarily equal, in relation to which, as likenesses, things here come to be and are said to be equal. And this is an Idea, a paradigm of the things that come to be in relation to it). The words καὶ εἰκὼν that appear after παραδείγμα in the mss. are deleted by most editors. Against Fine 1993, 150, I take the words αὐτόισον καὶ κυρίως as indicating that (relative) autoexplicability is understood by Aristotle to entail primacy, that is, having a predicate in the highest degree, just like the hotness in fire in relation to the hotness in the soup.

an account of the equality of equal sticks and stones, will be explanatorily adequate or complete.[42]

One naturally supposes that there is a difference between the graded synonymy that Aristotle proposes in *Metaphysics* and the graded synonymy of the theory of Forms that Aristotle is here reported by Alexander as criticizing. The objections that Alexander reports Aristotle as making to the Argument for Forms from Relatives are (1) a Form is a substance and no relative—for example, Equality—is a substance (83.22–26); (2) the Form of Equality will be equal to another Form of Equality, thus undercutting the uniqueness of Forms (83.26–28); (3) according to the argument, there will have to be a Form of Inequality that will have to be unequal to another such Form (83.28–30); (4) if Forms are paradigms, they will be relative to that of which they are paradigms, in which case all Forms are relatives, in which case they will be posterior to those sensible substances to which they are relative (86.13–23).

It is to be noted especially that all of these objections follow from taking Forms to be substances, or οὐσίαι. This is supposed to be disastrous for Forms of Relatives, like Equality. The sense in which a Form is supposed to be an οὐσία is then presumably different from the sense in which the 'cause of the being' of noneternal things is an οὐσία.[43] The former is said to be a substance in the sense of an individual; the latter is a substance in the sense of the form of that individual. Plato does consider Forms to be οὐσίαι, but it is far from certain that he does so in the former sense.[44] If the form of a substance is separate from that substance, it does not follow that that form becomes *another* individual substance. In short, in this case Aristotle's complaint regards not the separation of the autoexplicable cause of the being of 'other things,' but rather the manner in which its separation is to be understood.

There are good grounds for maintaining that in the dialogues, though Plato makes Forms completely independent of the sensible world, he did not ever represent the Forms as being completely independent of each other or of a divine intellect or of the superordinate Idea of the Good.[45] If this is the case, what were Aristotle's grounds for taking them to be so? The most reasonable explanation seems to be that Aristotle held that whatever

---

42. Cf. *Phd.* 96E6–97B3.
43. See *Meta.* Δ 18, 1022a14–15: Τὸ καθ' ὃ λέγεται πολλαχῶς, ἕνα μὲν τρόπον τὸ εἶδος καὶ ἡ οὐσία ἑκάστου πράγματος. (The phrase "that in virtue of which" is spoken of in many ways, one of these being the form or the substance of each thing.) Cf. 26–27; Z 6, 1031a18: καὶ τὸ τί ἦν εἶναι λέγεται εἶναι ἡ ἑκάστου οὐσία (and the "what is was to be" is said to be the substance of each thing.)
44. Cf. *Rep.* 509B9.
45. See Gerson 2005, chap. 7. For the alternative view, see Nehemas and Woodruff 1995, xliii: "Another feature of the middle theory of Forms is that it is not at all clear that it allows the Forms to be related to one another. Each Form is complete in itself, its nature is independent of *everything else*" (emphasis added).

Plato might say or write, he is forced perhaps in spite of himself to make Forms into individuals. The 'force' here is, of course, relative to the explanatory role that Forms are supposed to play. If sameness in difference or genuine predication is possible, then separate Forms must exist, where their separation entails that they are individuals in the self-defeating sense. By contrast, Aristotle must argue for a way of accounting for sameness in difference or genuine predication without positing separate individual Forms. The account must preserve the ontological priority of the *explanans* to the *explanandum*.[46] In other words, Aristotle must find a way to posit a principle and cause that does what Forms do even if that principle or cause is not an unqualifiedly separate Form. That later Platonists assumed that the Unmoved Mover was supposed to do this job, eternally thinking all that is intelligible, namely, those principles and causes of the intelligible properties of sensible substances, is interesting but not the main point.[47] The main point is that Aristotle's antinominalism, one element of UP, led him to the positing of an eternal immaterial principle and cause, thereby confirming his commitment to antimaterialism, another element of UP.

The claim that antinominalism commits one to a version of Platonism may seem extreme. One might want to argue that the phenomenon of sameness in difference or the truth of predicative judgments is a sort of brute fact in no need of an explanation. In that case, it does not need a Platonic explanation. But this is not *Aristotle's* approach. In book Zeta of *Metaphysics* Aristotle hypothesizes that the age-old question 'What is being?' is just the question 'What is substance?'[48] He proceeds to examine sensible substances, and by the end of the third chapter, he dismisses the substance that is a composite of matter and form as 'posterior.'[49] So the being of a sensible composite is heteroexplicable, not autoexplicable. It is very difficult to maintain the practically unintelligible conclusion that the composite is ontologically posterior to its own form; rather, its posteriority seems to be to the autoexplicable eternal principles and causes in

---

46. See *Meta.* Θ 8, 1050b6–1051a3.

47. Cf. Simplicius, *In Phys.* 1359.6-8: τὴν ὅλην φυσικὴν καὶ σωματικὴν σύστασιν ἐξηρτημένην ἔδειξε [Aristotle] τῆς ὑπὲρ φύσιν ἀσωμάτου καὶ ἀσχέτου νοερᾶς ἀγαθότητος τῷ Πλάτωνι κἀνταῦθα συνακολουθῶν. (Aristotle showed that the entire physical or bodily order was dependent on nonbodily and limitless intellectual goodness above nature, in this following Plato.) Also, 1360.24–31. Sedley (2010, 313–22) thinks that the Unmoved Mover is disanalogous to the Demiurge because the former is "eternally detached and self-focused" whereas the latter is "partly engaged in world management." But the intellectual activity (ἐνέργεια νοῦ) of the Unmoved Mover is not at all obviously different from the intellectual motion (κίνησις νοῦ) of the Demiurge. Indeed, at *Meta.* Λ 6, 1071b17, Aristotle rejects separate Forms as eternal causes because they are incapable of causing changes owing to their not being active (ἐνέργῃσει). Cf. Berti 2010, 376, on the efficient causality of the Unmoved Mover.

48. *Meta.* Z 1, 1028b2–4.

49. *Meta.* Z 3, 1029a30–32.

Alpha Elatton discussed above.⁵⁰ Aristotle does add that the form of the composite or the composite itself are substance to a higher degree than the matter of the composite, and by inference that the form is substance to a higher degree than the composite owing to its including matter.⁵¹ But that the form of the composite is the absolutely primary referent of 'being' or 'substance' is undermined by the fact that unless the form of the composite is an actuality over and above the actuality that is the composite, then the form of the composite is not prior in actuality to the composite. If, though, the form of the composite *is* an actuality over and above the actuality that is the composite, then the composite, contrary to Aristotle's claim, consists of two actualities.⁵²

From all this two conclusions follow. First, it is compositeness that, portentously, makes possible the phenomenon of predication or sameness in difference. It is the form that is predicated of the matter and the attributes that are predicated of the composite.⁵³ Compositeness is not the explanation for predication, but rather that which itself needs to be explained. This leads to the second point. The search for the primary referent of 'being' cannot stop at composites or sensible substances because these are heteroexplicable. To give the cause or principle for the being of the composite is at the same time to give the explanation not merely for the possibility of predication, but for the reality of predication. So we should be in no doubt that the positive construction of Aristotle's entire metaphysical project is at least in part a consequence of his antinominalism. Moreover, his antinominalism and his commitment to ultimate explanations make him both an antimaterialist and an antimechanist since nothing with matter could be an ultimate *explanans* for the being of things with matter.

Aristotle's antirelativism is on display in *Metaphysics* Gamma where he criticizes Protagoras's doctrine that man is the measure of all things, of what is that it is and of what is not that it is not.⁵⁴ He claims that the (epistemological) relativist position is the same as the position according to which contradictions can be true. But then later in the chapter he claims that both of these positions arise from supposing that only sensibles exist.⁵⁵

---

50. See, e.g., Wedin 2000 for a heroic defense of the idea that it is the form of the composite that is unqualifiedly prior to the composite in the manner demanded by the science of being qua being.

51. *Meta.* Z 3, 1029a27–30.

52. At *Meta.* Θ 8, 1049b23–25, Aristotle says that this individual man exists now in actuality (ἐνέργειᾳ). This seems not to be an identification of the individual man with actuality, for the man's being is more than his actuality; it includes his potencies. Later in the chapter, 1050b2, Aristotle adds that the οὐσία or εἶδος is actuality. I interpret this line to mean that the οὐσία or εἶδος provides the actuality to the man. In any case, there cannot be two actualities, the man and his essence or form.

53. *Meta.* Z 3, 1029a20–26.

54. *Meta.* Γ 5. The source is Plato's *Theaetetus* 161C3. Cf. Sextus Empiricus, *M.* 7.60.

55. *Meta.* Γ 5, 1010a1–3: —αἴτιον δὲ τῆς δόξης τούτοις ὅτι περὶ τῶν ὄντων μὲν τὴν ἀλήθειαν ἐσκόπουν, τὰ δ' ὄντα ὑπέλαβον εἶναι τὰ αἰσθητὰ μόνον· (The reason for their

It is reasonably clear here that Aristotle's grounds for rejecting relativism include his antimaterialism. However, the mere assertion that immaterial entities exist would not even begin to show that relativism is false, at least for the cognition of sensibles. In fact, Aristotle does explicitly link this assertion and the reason for rejecting relativism when he says that Protagoras and others were led to this view because among sensibles, the nature of the indeterminate (ἡ τοῦ ἀορίστου φύσις) exists to the greatest extent.[56] So, because things appear differently under different circumstances and at different times, they inferred that things are just as they appear, and if they appear at times in contradictory ways, the law of noncontradiction must be false. If only sensibles exist, then relativism might seem true. But if there are immaterial entities that are eternally stable, then it is at least possible that there is a relative stability among sensibles.[57] This is what Aristotle proceeds to argue. In any case, it will be false that man is the measure of *all* things by means of sense perception.

If things are in reality other than or more than the way they appear to sense perception, then it is false that the relativist attains the truth about things in general.[58] If, in addition, the relativist must maintain that having the truth about things amounts to having true beliefs based on sense perception, then it is false that true belief is knowledge.[59] If sense perception does not attain the truth about things, then a true belief representing the sense perception does not either.[60] So at least the argument for skepticism from relativism does not succeed. One could go on in this vein throughout the Aristotelian corpus, showing the connection between the positive claims made there and their basis in UP. That would, however, be the topic for another book.

It is sometimes claimed that Aristotle is not a systematic philosopher and even that this is the reason that Peripatetic philosophy was overwhelmed in later ancient philosophy by Platonism.[61] It seems to me more accurate and certainly more fruitful to think of Aristotle as being engaged, like Plato, in producing a positive construct on the basis of the UP that they shared. It is true, I think, that the systematization that later Platonists sought was

---

belief about things is that, though they were seeking the truth, they supposed that only sensibles exist.) Cf. 1009a36–38, where Aristotle affirms his belief that things other than sensible exist.

56. *Meta.* Γ 5, 1010a3–4.

57. *Meta.* Γ 5, 1010a15–1010b1.

58. This is the import of the argument in Plato's *Tht.* 184E–186B, refuting Protagoras.

59. As Plato argues at *Tht.* 187A–201C.

60. Cf. *Meta* Γ 5, 1009b12–15, where Aristotle says that the relativists maintain the identity of φρόνησις and αἴσθησις, where it is clear that Aristotle is using φρόνησις as a synonym for ἐπιστήμη or γνῶσις in general. Cf. *Meta.* N 4, 1078b15; *DC* Γ 1, 298b23.

61. See Wehrli 1967, 10:95–97, who argues that Aristotle's followers could not resolve the "tension" between his Platonic exoteric works and his anti-Platonic esoteric works. See also Ackrill 1981, 1–2, who, though attributing to Aristotle a "systematic and comprehensive philosophy," argues that the primary focus should be on his "arguments and ideas and analyses."

focused mainly on Plato's version, not Aristotle's, though as the collaborative construction of Platonism proceeded, Aristotle's philosophy came to be recognized more and more as a 'contributing cause' in the ongoing project.[62]

Aristotle's Testimony on the Mathematization of Forms

The criticisms Aristotle levels against Plato are all made against the background of their shared commitment to UP. If adherence to UP is what makes someone a Platonist, then Aristotle is a Platonist of a somewhat dissident cast.[63] It is probably also true that many of the criticisms are directed against one or more versions of Platonism regardless of whether or not Plato himself endorsed them. Finally, we should not be surprised to discover that the version of Platonism ultimately defended by Plato and the version defended by Aristotle will overlap to a considerable extent. As we have already seen, the uniqueness of the first principle of all, its property of being the ultimate good of everything, and the identification of the real person with the intellect are highly contentious positions shared by Plato and Aristotle, despite the nuanced differences in the consequences drawn from these positions.

Aristotle locates Plato's positive construction on the basis of UP as a type of Pythagoreanism.[64] That is, he takes it to be a system in which the

---

62. Thomas Aquinas is the stellar example of a philosopher who seeks to create a positive construct out of UP on the basis of authentically Aristotelian materials alone. See, however, Little 1949, who argues that Aquinas was forced to have recourse to "Platonic participation" to complete his systematic construct.

63. Cf. Krämer 1959, 13, who at the beginning of his book explains his project this way: "Die Darstellung erkennt in Platon und Aristoteles zwei Spielformen desselben Platonismus."

64. See *Meta*. A 6, 987a29–31: Μετὰ δὲ τὰς εἰρημένας φιλοσοφίας ἡ Πλάτωνος ἐπεγένετο πραγματεία, τὰ μὲν πολλὰ τούτοις ἀκολουθοῦσα, τὰ δὲ καὶ ἴδια παρὰ τὴν τῶν Ἰταλικῶν ἔχουσα φιλοσοφίαν. (After the philosophies named, the system of philosophy of Plato arose, which followed these in many respects, but also had peculiarities of its own distinguishing it from the philosophy of the Italians.) See Huffman 2008, 284–91, who questions the standard reading (cf. Cherniss 1944, 177, n. 100) of this passage, according to which the τούτοις refers to Pythagoreans, and the final clause qualifying this by saying that Plato had several distinctive features of his philosophy compared with the Italians (i.e., Pythagoreans). Huffman argues that the referent of τούτοις is much more likely to be the philosophies of all the Pre-Socratic philosophers and that the last clause merely contrasts the way Plato differs from these with the way the Pythagoreans do. Huffman's reading is a possible one, but as he himself suggests, its plausibility is directly tied to when we take Plato's unquestioned Pythagorean tendencies to begin. Huffman is disinclined to see these earlier than the late dialogue *Philebus*. He thinks that Aristotle's testimony about Plato's attraction to Heraclitean thinking as a young man suffices to account for his early metaphysical views. On my hypothesis, even assuming it is true that Plato was led to posit Forms in the light of Heraclitean arguments early on, his Pythagorean attachment preceded the writing of all the dialogues. Meinwald (2002) follows Huffman in finding Plato's Pythagoreanism no earlier than *Philebus*. But see *Men*. 81A–B; *Phd*. 61D; *Gorg*. 493A–B; *Rep*. 530D–E—all of which show an awareness of and interest in Pythagorean doctrine and all of which are ordinarily taken to have been written earlier than *Philebus*. Huffman and Meinwald have to assume that in these dialogues Plato was actually distancing himself

principles of all things are in some sense mathematical. Specifically, there is a hierarchical derivation of substance of all things from the One itself (αὐτὸ τὸ ἕν) and the Indefinite itself (αὐτὸ τὸ ἄπειρον).⁶⁵ Perhaps the most difficult part of Aristotle's account of Plato's philosophy is his statement of the mathematization of Forms. First, Aristotle claims that Plato introduced Mathematical Objects between the Forms and sensibles.⁶⁶ These Mathematical Objects or Intermediaries are required to account for the eternal truths of mathematics, which is something that unique Forms of Numbers supposedly cannot do. I will have a bit more to say about these Mathematical Objects below. For now we need to turn to the most consequential part of this account.⁶⁷

> Since the Forms are the causes of all other things, he thought that the elements of Forms are the elements of all things. As matter, the Great and the Small are the principles; as substance, it is the One. For from the Great and the Small and by participation in the One come the Forms and these are Numbers.⁶⁸

There is considerable additional evidence in *Metaphysics* that Aristotle believes that Plato held that Forms are Numbers in some sense.⁶⁹

---

from Pythagorean doctrines, whereas in *Philebus* and, presumably, *Timaeus* (20A) Plato came to embrace them. This seems most implausible given Aristotle's testimony. The bold hypothesis of Kennedy 2011 that *all* of Plato's dialogues have a precise Pythagorean "musical structure" would, if confirmed, settle the matter. According to Kennedy (248–49), even *Apology* has this compositional structure. Since so many scholars take *Apology* as the anchor for their differentiation of Socratic and Platonic philosophy, evidence that that dialogue is composed as a kind of Pythagorean allegory would deliver a resounding blow to the Socraticist position.

65. See *Meta.* 1.5.987a17–18. Previously, at 986a20–21, Aristotle says that for Pythagoreans number comes from the One, which at least suggests that the dualism of first principles is itself reducible to a monism. Cf. [Plato?] *Epin.* 991D–992A; Hermodorus, ap. Simpl. *In Phys.* 247.30–248.18 Diels; Theophrastus, *Meta.* 6a22–b23.

66. *Meta.* A 6, 987b14–18.

67. See Annas 1976; Mueller 1984; Franklin 2012.

68. *Meta.* A 6, 987b18–22: ἐπεὶ δ' αἴτια τὰ εἴδη τοῖς ἄλλοις, τἀκείνων στοιχεῖα πάντων ᾠήθη τῶν ὄντων εἶναι στοιχεῖα. ὡς μὲν οὖν ὕλην τὸ μέγα καὶ τὸ μικρὸν εἶναι ἀρχάς, ὡς δ' οὐσίαν τὸ ἕν· ἐξ ἐκείνων γὰρ κατὰ μέθεξιν τοῦ ἑνὸς [τὰ εἴδη] εἶναι τοὺς ἀριθμούς. Ross (1924), ad loc., argues for omitting τὰ εἴδη. In this case, the decision on the correct text is going to depend entirely on substantive philosophical considerations regarding what Plato's doctrine is likely to have been, at least in Aristotle's eyes. Cf. A 5, 987a13–19.

69. Cf.A 8, 990a29–32; Z 7, 11.1036b13–25; Λ 8, 1073a18–19; M 6, 1080b11–14; M 7, 1081a5–7; M 8,1083a18; M 8, 1084a7–8; M 9, 1086a11–13; N 2, 1090a4–6; N 3, 1090a16. On the second and the last two passages especially, see Saffrey 1955, 24–33. It is worth noting that at M 4, 1078b9–12 (repeating the substance of A 6, 987a32–b1), Aristotle distinguishes a nonmathematical version of the theory of Forms from a mathematical one. The words ὡς ὑπέλαβον ἐξ ἀρχῆς οἱ πρῶτοι τὰς ἰδέας φήσαντες εἶναι ('in the way that those who first said that there were Ideas conceived of them to be at the beginning) suggest a nonmathematical version eventually being 'reduced' to a mathematical one. This is perhaps how the positive construction of Platonism developed. We do not know, however, when the development occurred or, indeed, whether or not it occurred prior to any dialogues, and existed in oral form alongside the written expression of Platonism in the dialogues.

The evidence is all the more impressive given that Aristotle in several passages explicitly distinguishes the view of Plato from those of other members of the Academy. The problem is, of course, what this is supposed to mean. Many scholars have suggested that Aristotle intends to say (or that, despite what he intends to say, Plato means) that there are Forms that are Numbers, the so-called Form-Numbers, but that these are in addition to other Forms that are not Numbers, for example, a Form of Justice.[70] If this were true, it would not explain the nature of Aristotle's criticism of this view. For one would have thought that his general criticism of separate Forms would suffice for a subclass of Forms, namely, Form-Numbers. In fact, nowhere does Aristotle suggest that Form-Numbers, for Plato, are among the Forms; he simply states the identity of the two.

Among Plato's writings, the identification of Forms and Numbers does find some ambiguous support. In *Timaeus*, the Demiurge is said to import intelligibility and perfection into the precosmic chaos by imposing 'shapes and numbers' (εἴδεσι τε καὶ ἀριθμοῖς) on things.[71] Here it is not entirely obvious how shapes are supposed to be related to numbers, although there is no suggestion that the cosmos would be deprived of any part of the intelligible model were it to lack an instance of a Form that is other than mathematical. And yet the Demiurge performs his creative task by using as a model the "Living Animal" that has in it "all intelligible living animals" (τὰ νοητὰ ζῷα πάντα).[72] It is certainly not obvious how what are presumably the Forms of all the Living Animals could be numbers or even shapes. Similarly, at the beginning of *Philebus*, the question is raised regarding the existence of imperishable "monads" (μονάδες) such as Man, Ox, Beauty, and Good.[73] If these imperishable Monads are Forms, are we supposed to take them to be Numbers in some sense? In the *Seventh Letter*, Plato describes "things knowable," that is, the Forms, as including Colors, Good, Beautiful, Just, Body (whether artificial or natural), Fire, Water, all Living Beings, all Characters in Soul, all Actions and Affections.[74] Moreover, these are mentioned in *addition to* Straight Line and Circle.

This evidence is ambiguous because the claim that a Form, say, a Character in Soul, exists, is to say nothing about whether such a Form is in fact in some sense a Number. Of course, the possibility exists that Plato's putative reduction of Forms to Numbers postdates these dialogues or even came about parallel to these in his unwritten teachings.[75] The prospects for

---

70. E.g., Cherniss 1945, 59; Annas 1976, 13–19, 61–68.

71. *Tim.* 53B5. That these εἴδη are shapes and not nonmathematical Forms is clear from 53C5, 54D4–5, 55D8.

72. *Tim.* 30C2–D1.

73. *Phil.* 15A4–B2.

74. *Seventh Ep.* 342D2–E2.

75. See Robin 1908, 58, who, in concluding his exhaustive study of Aristotle's account of Plato's theory of Forms, says, "La doctrine des Nombres idéaux et des Figures idéales se lie de la façon la plus étroite à la pure théorie des Idées. Elle ne s'y juxtapose pas simplement, elle

attaining clarity, much less certainty, on these matters are not very good. In any case, one overriding question does remain, for which a plausible answer might still be found. That question is, broadly, what does mathematics have to do with the nature of Forms at all?

The appropriate context for beginning to answer this question is the first part of Aristotle's above testimony, namely, that Forms have 'elements' and that these elements are the One and the Great and the Small. Consider this text a bit further on.

> It is evident from what has been said that he [Plato] uses only two causes, the cause of the whatness and the cause according to matter (for the Forms are cause of the whatness of the other things, and the cause of the whatness of the Forms is the One). It is also evident what the underlying matter is, in virtue of which the Forms are predicated of the sensible things, and the One is predicated of the Forms; this is the Dyad, or the Great and the Small.[76]

That the Dyad here (elsewhere called 'the Indefinite Dyad') is identical with the 'Unlimited' in *Philebus* and the principles of Excess and Deficiency in *Statesman*, and the One with the 'Limit' is something that no one in antiquity ever doubted.[77] There is in fact no reason for us to doubt it either.[78] But the difficult question is why Plato thought—or, if one insists, why Aristotle thought that Plato thought—that the Forms had principles or 'elements.' This question just involves an elaboration of the question

---

en continue l'évolution naturelle dans la pensée du philosophe, elle l'achève, elle en comble les lacunes et elle répond à des nécessités auxquelles la théorie des Idées n'avait pu satisfaire."

76. *Meta.* A 6, 988a8–14: φανερὸν δ' ἐκ τῶν εἰρημένων ὅτι δυοῖν αἰτίαιν μόνον κέχρηται, τῇ τε τοῦ τί ἐστι καὶ τῇ κατὰ τὴν ὕλην (τὰ γὰρ εἴδη τοῦ τί ἐστιν αἴτια τοῖς ἄλλοις, τοῖς δ' εἴδεσι τὸ ἕν), καὶ τίς ἡ ὕλη ἡ ὑποκειμένη καθ' ἧς τὰ εἴδη μὲν ἐπὶ τῶν αἰσθητῶν τὸ δ' ἓν ἐν τοῖς εἴδεσι λέγεται, ὅτι αὕτη δυάς ἐστι, τὸ μέγα καὶ τὸ μικρόν. Cf. N 4, 1091b13–15. For a convenient digest of other passages in Aristotle regarding the One and the Great and the Small, as well as testimony in Alexander of Aphrodisias and the Platonic commentators on Aristotle, see Krämer 1990, 203–17.

77. See *Meta.* N 7, 1081a22, etc., where whoever is the subject of Aristotle's criticism, it is clear that 'Dyad' is a shortened form of 'Indefinite Dyad.' At A 6, 987b25–26, Aristotle says that Plato differed from the Pythagoreans in making the Indefinite a duality. See *Phil.* 16C1–17A5, 23C–27C on the Unlimited and the Limit. I take it that even if we suppose that in *Philebus* the Unlimited refers to a principle of sensibles, we may suppose that it is an instantiation of the first principle of the Indefinite Dyad. Sayre (2005, 133–55) has a good discussion of the issues and defense of the identification of the Unlimited and the Limit with the Indefinite Dyad and the One. See also Sayre 2006, 139–70, who provides what I take to be conclusive evidence regarding the equivalencies of the various expressions for the Indefinite Dyad in antiquity.

78. Cherniss 1944 is not in my opinion able to counter the truly overwhelming evidence for the identification. See also Cherniss 1945 for his attack on Aristotle's testimony. Jonathan Barnes 1995, in his review of a French translation of *The Riddle of the Early Academy,* expresses what is now perhaps the predominant view, namely, that not only is Cherniss's theory about the Aristotelian evidence "patently false"; it is also "uninterestingly false." See Ferber 1989, 162–68, for a sympathetic assessment of the Aristotelian evidence, though he inclines to the view that Form-Numbers are not identical with Forms *tout court;* rather, they are one kind of Form.

that arises directly from *Republic* regarding the reason for the positing of a superordinate Idea of the Good. This seems to me a question the answer to which is necessary if we are going to answer the previous question about the mathematization of the Forms.[79]

One general consideration that will not take us very far is that Plato was in principle committed to the reductivist tendency found in all Pre-Socratic philosophy and, indeed, in all theoretical natural science. This is the tendency to reduce the number of fundamental principles of explanation to the absolute minimum. This is evident in the Milesian positing of a single ἀρχή of all. It is hardly surprising that Plato—apart from any other considerations—would have been unhappy with the postulation of a large, perhaps infinitely large, number of explanatory principles in the universe. The reduction of these to the fewest possible would have probably seemed to him to be a compelling desideratum. But this explains neither the mathematical dimension of the question nor the manner in which this reduction is to be accomplished.

Another way to pose our question is to ask why, given that there must be a unique first principle of all, this principle must be identified as the One, the principle of number. In order to answer this question, we need to look closely at the way in which Plato thinks about cognition generally, and the nature of its intelligible objects in particular. I am here focusing on the cognitional correlate of the metaphysical one-over-many principle. That the Form is a one-over-many is clear. The statement of this in *Parmenides* is one of the rare programmatic passages in the entire corpus. Parmenides is trying to draw Socrates out on his reason for positing Forms in the first place:

> I suppose you think that each Form is one for the following reason: whenever some number of things seem to you to be large, probably there seems to you to be one identical Idea when you look at them, on the basis of which you think that Largeness is one.[80]

I am particularly concerned here with the cognitive side of this claim. The positing of the explanatory entity that is the Form is the result of an act of cognition wherein the observer 'sees' a unity or 'one' in some 'many.'[81]

---

79. See *Tht.* 202E1, where Socrates recounts his 'dream' that all things are made of 'elements' (στοιχεῖα). The originator of the theory contained in the dream is the subject of much dispute. But given that Socrates goes on (202B5–6) to elaborate the theory as holding that "elements are inexplicable and unknowable, but perceivable," the source is more likely to be Antisthenes than it is Pythagoras. See Burnyeat 1990, 164–73, on Antisthenes and the doctrine of 'elements.'

80. *Parm.* 132A1–4: Οἶμαί σε ἐκ τοῦ τοιοῦδε ἓν ἕκαστον εἶδος οἴεσθαι εἶναι· ὅταν πόλλ' ἄττα μεγάλα σοι δόξῃ εἶναι, μία τις ἴσως δοκεῖ ἰδέα ἡ αὐυτὴ εἶναι ἐπὶ πάντα ἰδόντι, ὅθεν ἓν τὸ μέγα ἡγῇ εἶναι. Cf. esp. *Rep.* 596A6.

81. Cf. *Phil.* 17D7–E3: ὅταν γὰρ αὐτά τε λάβῃς οὕτω, τότε ἐγένου σοφός, ὅταν τε ἄλλο τῶν ἓν ὁτιοῦν ταύτῃ σκοπούμενος ἕλῃς, οὕτως ἔμφρων περὶ τοῦτο γέγονας· (For when you grasp them in this way, then you are wise, and when in your examinations, you get hold of any other

The many (πολλά) are certainly numerically many, but they also may and usually do manifest 'manyness' in countless other phenomenological respects. The combination of numerical distinctness and some sort of qualitative distinctness makes the cognition of a self-identical Idea a portentously sophisticated act.[82] It is important that we understand the word αὐτή as self-identical, that is, as an attribute of one thing, *not* many things. The claim that a 'many' are self-identical is, therefore, prima facie self-contradictory. But what Parmenides actually takes Socrates to be maintaining is not that the many are self-identical in a way that contradicts their numerical and qualitative distinctness, but that despite their 'manyness' they are in a way one, that is, that there is a self-identical 'idea' or character that can be predicated of each. We may leave aside for the moment the further inference that only if there is a Form 'over and above' or separate from these can this be possible. Here we need to consider the cognitive act of 'seeing' a self-identical unity within or among a many.

For Plato, this 'seeing' is the essence of human cognition.[83] To see that two (or more) things are in fact one is what unites belief, understanding, judgment, knowledge, and so on.[84] We can call this knowledge by acquaintance if we like, though if knowledge is to be understood as what Plato means by ἐπιστήμη, then the implication that there are types of knowledge other than knowledge by acquaintance is false. More important, the acquaintance or direct cognition is *always* distinct from the expression of this in words or thoughts, to oneself or to someone else. My 'seeing' that many things called 'large' are correctly so called because there is one self-identical character in which they all share is distinct from my thinking this to myself because my thinking this is, according to Plato, a type of internal conversation in language. Representing what I cognize is always distinct from the cognitional act. This is so even if my access to my own cognition is no less through representation than is my expression of my cognition. Thus, thinking with

---

one in this way you will be expert in regard to this.) The word αὐτά is a reference to "the many and the one" in the previous line.

82. Often Plato (and Aristotle) uses ἰδέα as synonymous with εἶδος. Here, though, the context seems to demand something like a distinction between the cognitive 'one' that is constitutive of the judgment and the ontological 'one' that is hypothesized to account for the unity in difference.

83. The use of 'seeing' for higher cognition is not so much a metaphor drawn from sense perception as it is the primary referent of 'seeing,' whereas perceptual seeing is a defective form. See, e.g., *Rep.* 534C6–8: ἡ νόησις...ἰδεῖν. Cf. 511A1–2; 525A2: τὴν τοῦ ὄντος θέαν; 527E8–D3: μόνῳ γὰρ αὐτῷ ἀλήθεια ὁρᾶται. What sets sense perception apart from all other forms of cognition for Plato is that it has an irreducible material or physical component.

84. Cf. Aristotle, *Meta.* E 4, 1027b24–25, on thinking as a 'unifying' activity (ἕν τι γίγνεσθαι). See Gerson 2009, chap. 3, for further discussion of this in Plato, and passim for this feature of ancient epistemology more widely.

images, including the images that are words, is not identical with pure thinking even if for human beings there is no thinking without images.[85]

If all cognition is the seeing of a unity behind a many, then how is it possible to cognize Forms themselves other than in relation to the 'manys' they are supposed to explain? It would seem that either it is false that all cognition requires a one and a many or else Forms are not themselves cognizable. Against this background, Plato's assertion in *Republic* that it is the Idea of the Good that makes Forms cognizable takes on considerable significance.[86] And yet, that there be such a superordinate unity above the many Forms hardly seems to solve the problem in any but a superficial manner. For if the Idea of the Good is not an οὐσία, that is, if it has no nature or essence, then the seeing of this unity behind the diversity of Forms can only mean seeing that they are all somehow identical in the sense that there is a self-identical Good or One in which they all share. How is *that* supposed to help us to cognize, say, the Form of Justice?

Before I answer this question, we should be clear that in the subsequent discussion of the Divided Line, there is no doubt that cognition of Forms requires ascending to an 'unhypothetical' first principle, namely, the Good.[87] Without this ascent, there is no cognition of Forms because the only possible cognition of Forms is knowledge of them. This ascent, we are told, requires grasping (ἁψάμενος) the Idea of the Good. And this would appear to be a sort of cognition.[88] But even if this is so, it is fundamentally different from any cognition that requires that its objects have an οὐσία. As we will see, cognition or quasi-cognition of the first principle of all remains a deep puzzle within the Platonic tradition. Yet perhaps we can begin to see the reasoning leading to the identification of this principle as the One, not for the superficial reason that it is unique (as are, after all, each of the Forms), but because One is the principle of number. And if the Forms are in some sense Numbers, what unifies them as a principle would be, accordingly, the One.

---

85. Aristotle's insistence that there is no thinking without images (see *DA* Γ 7, 431a16-17, 432a9; *De Mem.* 449b31-450a1) is, I assume, a Platonic point. Thinking for Plato is λόγος in the soul, and λόγος is or contains images. The paradigm or principle of thinking is ἐπιστήμη, which is nonimagistic. For that reason it is the prerogative of the separate intellect, not its embodied manifestation.

86. See *Rep.* 509B6-10: Καὶ τοῖς γιγνωσκομένοις τοίνυν μὴ μόνον τὸ γιγνώσκεσθαι φάναι ὑπὸ τοῦ ἀγαθοῦ παρεῖναι, ἀλλὰ καὶ τὸ εἶναί τε καὶ τὴν οὐσίαν ὑπ' ἐκείνου αὐτοῖς προσεῖναι, οὐκ οὐσίας ὄντος τοῦ ἀγαθοῦ, ἀλλ' ἔτι ἐπέκεινα τῆς οὐσίας πρεσβείᾳ καὶ δυνάμει ὑπερέχοντος. (Then, not only do we say that the objects of knowledge owe their being knowable to the Good, but their being and essence are present to them owing to it; the Good, though it is not essence, is beyond essence exceeding it in seniority and in power.) The fact that the Good is 'beyond essence' is not contradicted by 534B8-C1, where dialectic is tasked with "separating apart the Idea of the Good, distinguishing it in an account from everything else" (διορίσασθαι τῷ λόγῳ ἀπὸ τῶν ἄλλων πάντων ἀφελὼν τὴν τοῦ ἀγαθοῦ ἰδέαν). A λόγος of the Good need not be a λόγος τῆς οὐσίας. See lines B3-4 immediately before this passage. The Good is to be distinguished from any οὐσία.

87. See *Rep.* 511B3-C2.

88. Cf. the claim that the study of the Good is the greatest μάθημα at 505A2.

With the above context, we may return to the implications of the description of how the Demiurge brings intelligibility to the precosmic chaos. The principal direct implication is that the intelligibility that our present cosmos possesses is entirely owing to the 'shapes and numbers' that the Demiurge has imposed. Therefore, the reality of the present sensible world includes more than what is intelligible to us. This begins at the elemental level of earth, air, fire, and water, and continues for all things constructed out of these elements. The nonintelligible aspect of reality includes the receptacle (ὑποδοχή) and sensible qualities.[89] The former, which is described as having the characteristics of both extension and unqualified matter, is only cognizable by a sort of bastard reasoning (λογισμῷ νόθῳ).[90] The latter are (in part) the basis for the beliefs that we have of the sensible world.[91] The reason we are able to have such cognition as belief at all about sensibles is that these are images of the intelligibles imposed by the Demiurge; only these intelligibles are the objects of intellection (νόησις).[92] Presumably, it is possible to have beliefs about sensibles as such, for example, that fire is hot or that water is wet. But if by 'hot' or 'wet' we mean to refer to the phenomenological aspect of the experience of fire or water, we are not referring to anything that is, strictly speaking, intelligible.[93]

According to this interpretation, the primary identities found among sensibles and in virtue of which 'ones over and above' are to be posited are the five regular solids and the triangles (and their 'grades,' or relative magnitudes) out of which they are constructed. As Plato explains, these are the 'building blocks' of the cosmos. The natural organic and inorganic compounds made out of these elements are not merely aggregates of regular bodies, but aggregates according to formulas provided by the Demiurge. These formulas will consist of proportions of the elements. In order to 'make' an organism of a certain sort, a certain proportion of elements or compounds out of elements is to be aggregated. As the *Philebus* passage introducing the principles of Limit and Unlimited explains, the construction of substances and qualities occurs according to the imposition of the former on the latter. We are evidently to suppose that the Unlimited refers in general to that which in the precosmic chaos was represented by the uninformed receptacle (which includes the precosmic elements).[94] In some sense, the proportions imported by the Demiurge have to be ideals, that is, Forms. Out of all the infinitely possible proportions available to the

---

89. *Tim.* 49A–50A.
90. *Tim.* 52B2.
91. *Tim.* 52A4–7.
92. *Tim.* 52A4. The images have the same name as the intelligible. Cf. *Parm.* 132D1–4.
93. It is tempting to understand Plato here making the same point that Aristotle makes in his *Physics* (A 8, 191a7–8) when he claims that matter is knowable only by analogy. This is so because matter is potency and only form or actuality is cognizable. The potency of sensibles for producing a certain experience in us is as such unintelligible.
94. Contra: Cherniss 1945, 18, who argues that Limit and Unlimited refer only to phenomena in the realm of becoming.

Demiurge, he chooses those that are contained in the perfect Living Animal, since he wants the world to be as good as possible.⁹⁵

The question of what it means to hold that Forms are Numbers may be answered if we do not suppose that Aristotle intends to present Plato as saying that all Forms are ideal integers, but rather that Forms—in addition to the Forms that *are* ideal Integers—like, for instance, the Form for Bird, are the ideal proportions of elements making up that animal.⁹⁶ In order to apply this understanding to the imposition of geometrical shapes on the receptacle, we only need to add that geometrical shapes are analyzable into the principle of Unlimited and the principle of Limit or Number: the Indefinite Dyad is the former and the One is the latter.⁹⁷

In *Statesman*, the passage in which the two sorts of measurement (ἡ μετρική) are distinguished clarifies this considerably:

> VISITOR: About length and brevity, and excess and deficiency in general, I suppose the art of measurement relates to all of these.
> YOUNG SOCRATES: Yes.
> VISITOR: Then let's divide it into two parts; that's what we need towards our present objective.
> YOUNG SOCRATES: Please tell me how we should divide it.
> VISITOR: This way: one part will relate to the association of greatness and smallness with each other, the other the being necessary for generation.

---

95. See Cherniss 1944, 565–80, and 1945, 18, for an argument why *Timaeus* does not support Aristotle's testimony. Contra Cherniss is Krämer 1964a, 204–8; Findlay 1974, 455–73. See Aristotle, *DA* A 2, 404b16–21, where he reports (from his early work *On Philosophy*) that the Living Animal was composed of "One itself, primary Length, primary Breadth, and primary Depth." See Saffrey 1955, 7–46, for an extensive argument that supports the attribution of this passage to *On Philosophy* and, more important, that the passage in *On Philosophy* contains reliable testimony about Plato's unwritten teachings. According to the testimony of Sextus Empiricus, *M.* 10.276, Plato distinguished between the One as first principle (πρώτη μόνας) and one as the first number (τὸ ἐν τοῖς ἀριθμοῖς ἕν). The point is of some importance for Aristotle adds at *Meta.* 14.3.1090b20–24 that "Lines are generated from Two, Planes from (perhaps) Three, and Solids from Four or other Numbers (for it makes no difference)." This explains both the core idea in the reduction of geometry to arithmetic and the puzzling claim made by Aristotle that Platonists seemed to limit the generation of Form-Numbers to the Decad (cf. *Meta.* Λ 8, 1073a20–21; N 8, 1083b26–1084a13, 1084a29–32). The corresponding manifestations of the Indefinite Dyad are as follows: (for number) the Many and the Few (N 1, 1087b16); (for lines) the Long and the Short; (for planes) the Broad and the Narrow; and (for solids) the Shallow and Deep (A 9, 992a10–15). Cf. Syrianus, *In Meta.* 147.29–148.7, who argues that the Decad contains the articulated principles of all the Forms in the cosmos. That is, even if Forms are Numbers, they are not limited to ten.

96. On the use of ἀριθμοί for proportions or fractions as well as integers, see Töplitz 1929; Huffman 1993, 173–74. Cf. *Rep.* 500C5 and Aristotle, *DA* Γ 7, 431a23; *Meta.* A 9, 991b18–21. See also Findlay 1974, 54–80.

97. See Huffman 1993, 10 and 76, on the Pythagorean Philolaus's influence on Plato's thinking about mathematics as underlying the intelligibility of nature. In frr. 2 and 3 (93–113), Philolaus sets out the basic idea of the first principles of Limit and Unlimited as underlying number.

YOUNG SOCRATES: What do you mean?
VISITOR: Does it seem to you that by its nature the greater has to be said to be greater than nothing other than the less, and the less in its turn less than the greater, and nothing else?
YOUNG SOCRATES: It does.
VISITOR: What about this: shan't we also say that there really is such a thing as what exceeds what is in due measure, and everything of that sort, in what we say or indeed in what we do? Isn't it just in that respect that those of us who are bad and those who are good most differ?
YOUNG SOCRATES: It seems so.
VISITOR: In that case we must lay it down that the Great and the Small exist and are objects of judgment in these twin ways. It is not as we said just before, that we must suppose them to exist only in relation to each other, but rather as we have now said, that we should speak of their existing in one way in relation to each other, and in another in relation to what is in due measure. Would you like to know why?
YOUNG SOCRATES: Of course.
VISITOR: If someone will admit the existence of the greater and everything of the sort in relation to nothing other than the less, it will never be in relation to what is in due measure—you agree?
YOUNG SOCRATES: That's so.
VISITOR: Well, with this account of things we shall destroy—shan't we?—both the various sorts of expertise themselves and their products, and in particular we shall make the one we're looking for now, statesmanship, disappear, and the one we said was weaving. For I imagine all such sorts of expertise guard against exceeding due measure or falling short of it, not as something nonexistent but as something which is and is troublesome in relation to what they do. It is by preserving measure in this way that they produce all the good and fine things they do produce. (trans. Rowe, with some alterations)[98]

98. *Sts.* 283C11–284B2: {ΞΕ.} Μήκους τε πέρι καὶ βραχύτητος καὶ πάσης ὑπεροχῆς τε καὶ ἐλλείψεως· ἡ γάρ που μετρητικὴ περὶ πάντ' ἐστὶ ταῦτα. {ΝΕ. ΣΩ.} Ναί. {ΞΕ.} Διέλωμεν τοίνυν αὐτὴν δύο μέρη· δεῖ γὰρ δὴ πρὸς ὃ νῦν σπεύδομεν. {ΝΕ. ΣΩ.} Λέγοις ἂν τὴν διαίρεσιν ὅπῃ. {ΞΕ.} Τῇδε· τὸ μὲν κατὰ τὴν πρὸς ἄλληλα μεγέθους καὶ σμικρότητος κοινωνίαν, τὸ δὲ [τὸ] κατὰ τὴν τῆς γενέσεως ἀναγκαίαν οὐσίαν. {ΝΕ. ΣΩ.} Πῶς λέγεις; {ΞΕ.} Ἆρ' οὐ κατὰ φύσιν δοκεῖ σοι τὸ μεῖζον μηδενὸς ἑτέρου δεῖν μεῖζον λέγειν ἢ τοῦ ἐλάττονος, καὶ τοὔλαττον αὖ τοῦ μείζονος ἔλαττον, ἄλλου δὲ μηδενός; {ΝΕ. ΣΩ.} Ἔμοιγε. {ΞΕ.} Τί δέ; τὸ τὴν τοῦ μετρίου φύσιν ὑπερβάλλον καὶ ὑπερβαλλόμενον ὑπ' αὐτῆς ἐν λόγοις εἴτε καὶ ἐν ἔργοις ἆρ' οὐκ αὖ λέξομεν ὡς ὄντως γιγνόμενον, ἐν ᾧ καὶ διαφέρουσι μάλιστα ἡμῶν οἵ τε κακοὶ καὶ [οἱ] ἀγαθοί; {ΝΕ. ΣΩ.} φαίνεται. {ΞΕ.} Διττὰς ἄρα ταύτας οὐσίας καὶ κρίσεις τοῦ μεγάλου καὶ τοῦ σμικροῦ θετέον, ἀλλ' οὐχ ὡς ἔφαμεν ἄρτι πρὸς ἄλληλα μόνον δεῖν, ἀλλ' ὥσπερ νῦν εἴρηται μᾶλλον τὴν μὲν πρὸς ἄλληλα λεκτέον, τὴν δ' αὖ πρὸς τὸ μέτριον· οὗ δὲ ἕνεκα, μαθεῖν ἆρ' ἂν βουλοίμεθα; {ΝΕ. ΣΩ.} Τί μήν; {ΞΕ.} Εἰ πρὸς μηδὲν ἕτερον τὴν τοῦ μείζονος ἐάσει τις

As the Visitor then explains:

> It is clear that we should divide the art of measurement, cutting it into two just the way we said, positing as one part of it all those sorts of expertise that measure the number, lengths, depths, breadths, and speeds of things in relation to what is opposed to them, and as the other, all those that measure in relation to what is in due measure, what is fitting, the right moment, what is as it ought to be—everything that removes itself from the extremes to the middle. (trans. Rowe)[99]

A number of points in this most revealing passage require special attention. First, in the last passage, the art of measurement covers numbers, geometrical magnitudes (length, depth, and breadth), and the measure of magnitude in motion (speed and slowness). Statesmanship is one example of this art of measurement. There is no suggestion that the art of measurement according to an ideal measure is anything other than a mathematical art. But it is not specifically an arithmetic art; rather, it is mathematical in the generic sense, that is, an art of quantity or universal mathematics. It seems also to be the case that the statesman, or any other practitioner of an art of measurement, must look to an ideal measure in order to bring about an image of this in the sensible world.[100] He does this by imposing the due measure on that which is describable in terms of excess and deficiency, namely, a continuum unlimited in principle.[101] This is just what the Unlimited is supposed to be in *Philebus* and what the receptacle is in *Timaeus*. Any quantitative imposition on a continuum will produce a 'mixture' of Unlimited and Limit, but only one such imposition will produce the one that is beautiful or fitting or right. Insofar as virtues are for Plato a priori expressed in axiological terms, there seems little reason to deny that here Plato is affirming the mathematical nature of these ideals, too.

The imposition is of a ratio, that is, a ratio composed of the two 'poles' of the continuum that is being limited. The Form itself is the ideal Ratio,

---

φύσιν ἢ πρὸς τοὔλαττον, οὐκ ἔσται ποτὲ πρὸς τὸ μέτριον· ἢ γάρ; {ΝΕ. ΣΩ.} Οὕτως. {ΞΕ.} Οὐκοῦν τὰς τέχνας τε αὐτὰς καὶ τἆργα αὐτῶν σύμπαντα διολοῦμεν τούτῳ τῷ λόγῳ, καὶ δὴ καὶ τὴν ζητουμένην νῦν πολιτικὴν καὶ τὴν ῥηθεῖσαν ὑφαντικὴν ἀφανιοῦμεν; ἅπασαι γὰρ αἱ τοιαῦταί που τὸ τοῦ μετρίου πλέον καὶ ἔλαττον οὐχ ὡς οὐκ ὂν ἀλλ'ὡς ὂν χαλεπὸν περὶ τὰς πράξεις παραφυλάττουσι, καὶ τούτῳ δὴ τῷ τρόπῳ τὸ μέτρον σῴζουσαι πάντα ἀγαθὰ καὶ καλὰ ἀπεργάζονται.

99. *Sts.* 284E2–8: Δῆλον ὅτι διαιροῖμεν ἂν τὴν μετρητικήν, καθάπερ ἐρρήθη, ταύτῃ δίχα τέμνοντες, ἓν μὲν τιθέντες αὐτῆς μόριον συμπάσας τέχνας ὁπόσαι τὸν ἀριθμὸν καὶ μήκη καὶ βάθη καὶ πλάτη καὶ ταχυτῆτας πρὸς τοὐναντίον μετροῦσιν, τὸ δὲ ἕτερον, ὁπόσαι πρὸς τὸ μέτριον καὶ τὸ πρέπον καὶ τὸν καιρὸν καὶ τὸ δέον καὶ πάνθ' ὁπόσα εἰς τὸ μέσον ἀπῳκίσθη τῶν ἐσχάτων.

100. Any "knowledge-based practice" (πράξεις ἐπιστήμονα), 284C2.

101. At *Sts.* 285B6–C2, the expression used is ὑπεροχή καὶ ἔλλειψις, which I take to be a variant of ὑπερβολή καὶ ἔλλειψις.

relative to a particular continuum. That is, the Form is not, say, the ratio m/n, or the formula or proportion m/n: o/p: q/r, but the ratio or formula or proportion of certain contraries on a continuum.[102] The imposition of an ideal ratio may be either absolute or relative, that is, relative to a certain time or place. The Demiurge imposed the absolute ideal measure on the structure of the cosmos and its parts.[103] The production of virtuous dispositions and virtuous behavior would seem to be of relative ideal measure. Crucially, it is always the work of a mind, divine or human, to impose an ideal Ratio or formula on a continuum.

Returning now to the cognitive dimension of the mathematical project, knowing will on this interpretation be the seeing of an ideal ratio present in many things that are not only numerically but also phenomenologically diverse. To what extent this is possible for embodied individuals is not made clear. If the Form is an ideal ratio of contraries on a continuum, it may well be that Plato came to see the diversity of instances of Forms differently from the way they are represented in, for example, *Symposium*. There the one Form Beauty is supposed to be present in some bodies, souls, institutions, laws, sciences, etc. But Plato may have come to see this as imprecise; rather, the term 'beautiful' would have a primary, ideal referent and derivative references, causally related to the primary.

If each Form is an ideal ratio, and if, as *Republic* tells us, the Idea of the Good is that which provides being and essence to the Forms and makes them knowable, this would be because the Idea of the Good is the second-order property that is instantiated whenever a Form or ideal ratio is instantiated. The reason why each and every Form 'brings with it' the Good is that the Good is what each Form is in the sense in which a cause is or contains its effects. The reason why the Good is aptly called the One is that each Form is a unity, that is, it makes one each of the things it informs. The reason why one must 'ascend' to the Good or the One in order to know any Form is that knowing the Form necessitates seeing it as a unity.[104] But this is evidently true for all ratios, not just ideal ones, that is, all the infinite ratios possible among the Mathematical Objects. To see the ideal among all these is to see the one and only one way that goodness can be instantiated in a given continuum. This does indeed seem to be the prerogative of a divine

---

102. Cf. *Tim.* 73B–C.

103. *Sts.* 283D8–9: κατὰ τὴν τῆς γενέσεως ἀναγκαίαν οὐσίαν seems to be an allusion to this sort of absolute measure.

104. See *Phil.* 15B1–2 on Forms as μονάδες. This claim should be considered with *Parm.* 135B5–C2, wherein Parmenides argues that if Forms do not exist or are totally separate, then thought (διάνοια) and the capacity for rational conversation (ἡ δύναμις τοῦ διαλέγεσθαι) will be destroyed. See Aristotle, *Meta.* Δ 6, 1016b20–21: ἀρχὴ οὖν τοῦ γνωστοῦ περὶ ἕκαστον τὸ ἕν (the principle, then, of the knowability for each thing is that which is one). The fact that the Good is the ultimate ἀρχή, that it is the cause of the knowability of Forms, and that the μέγιστον μάθημα is of the Good in *Rep.* 504E8 and 505A3, seems to provide textual support for Aristotle's claim about the identity of Good and One.

intellect, who comprehends the array of Forms the instantiations of which constitute the best of all possible worlds.

Aristotle's Criticism of the Mathematicization of Forms

As we have already seen, Aristotle's criticisms of Plato generally rest on a shared set of principles, which I have labeled UP. In particular, his criticisms of the mathematization of the Forms and the reduction to the principles of the One and the Indefinite Dyad have a precise context. That context includes Aristotle's argument for a unique, absolutely simple first principle of all; his argument for a principle of matter for the composition of everything other than this unique first principle; and an account of cognition according to which the paradigm of cognition is the identification of the intellect with intelligibles.[105] What Aristotle does reject is the unqualified identification of intelligibility with mathematical structure.

For Aristotle, quantity is an attribute of substance. Therefore, to know the quantitative properties of a species of substance or the quantitative accidents of a particular substance is not equivalent to knowing substance itself. So even if we opt for a capacious interpretation of the knowledge possessed by the Unmoved Mover, maintaining that he knows all that is knowable or intelligible, he cannot be said to know formulas or ratios for these will not be equivalent to the knowledge of the essences of substances.

If one states the issue in this way, it is evident that the basis for the criticism of the mathematization of Forms is the assumption that there exist substances with essences and that these essences are not reducible to geometrical structures represented arithmetically. As Aristotle insists in *De anima*, the natural scientist must include matter in his accounts because the essence of things that exist by nature is not without matter. By contrast, the mathematician considers these things only by abstraction in their quantitative aspect, and the first philosopher considers only things that are completely separate from matter.[106] If natural substances have essences, then these would seem not to be the subject of mathematics or of a mathematical science.[107]

---

105. *Meta.* Λ 7, 1072b20–21; Λ 9, 1074b33–35; Λ 9, 1075a4–5. What the Unmoved Mover does eternally, we do only from time to time (7, 1072b24–25), that is, cognitively identify with intelligibles. When Aristotle says in *DA* Γ 4, 429a27–29, presumably about Plato, that "those who say that the soul is the place of forms speak well, except that it is not the whole soul but only the thinking part," he is acknowledging the fundamental point. This is particularly the case since he adds, "and that is not actually but potentially the forms." It is clear that Aristotle is here referring to the hylomorphic composite of soul and body, not to the separate intellect, which Aristotle says "we are especially" (*EN* I 4, 1166a22–23; I 8, 1169a2; K 7, 1178a2–8). My focus here is not on the obvious agreement between Plato and Aristotle on the ideal identity of the intellect and intelligibles but on the underlying reason for this remarkable agreement.

106. See *DA* A 1, 403b7–16. Cf. *Meta.* E 1 for a fuller discussion of the distinction among the theoretical sciences.

107. With the exception, of course, of 'mixed' sciences like optics and mechanics, where the quantitative properties of certain kinds of bodies are part of the science.

And yet Plato, as we know, distinguishes the work of mathematicians from the work of dialecticians in *Republic*, making the former inferior to the latter.[108] So the dispute turns not on conflicting views about the nature of ordinary mathematics, but on the different mathematical character of dialectic. Moreover, as we recall, the Demiurge has a role in matching a ratio or formula with various sorts of unlimited contraries or continua that cannot be eliminated from composites. So the natural scientist for Aristotle only aims, so to speak, to know what the Demiurge knows, whether or not the essence of things that exist by nature are separable from those things.

One of Aristotle's most penetrating objections to the general mathematizing project is as follows:

> Again, if the Forms are Numbers, how will they be causes? Is it in view of this that the things themselves are other numbers, for example, that the one man is this number, Socrates is that number, and Callias is another? Why then are the Numbers causes of the latter? If the former are eternal but the latter are not, this difference, too, would not account for it at all. On the other hand, if it is in view of this that the things about us are ratios of numbers, like a harmony, clearly there is still some one thing in each of the numbers which form that ratio. If this thing then is the matter, it is evident that the Numbers themselves will be certain ratios of something to something else. I mean, for example, that if Callias is a numerical ratio of fire and earth and water and air, his Idea, too, will be a Number of certain underlying things; and Man Himself, whether it is a Number of a sort or not, will still be a numerical ratio and not just a Number. Because of this, then, none of these will be just a Number. (trans. Apostle)[109]

There are several difficulties being canvassed here. First, if the Form is to be a cause of that which is present in its participants, and the Form is a Number in the sense of an ideal ratio or array of ratios, then the Form must not be *just* the ratio, for then the Form would be constructed of comparable or commensurable numbers. But the Form-Numbers are supposed to be unique and not made of commensurable units. Then, however, the Form will have to be a ratio of certain kinds of, say, elements; for example, a certain amount of fire in proportion to a certain amount of earth, etc. These will differ, then, in their units. The problem with this is that the

---

108. See *Rep.* 510Cff.
109. *Meta.* A 9, 991b9–21: —ἔτι εἴπερ εἰσὶν ἀριθμοὶ τὰ εἴδη, πῶς αἴτιοι ἔσονται; πότερον ὅτι ἕτεροι ἀριθμοί εἰσι τὰ ὄντα, οἷον ὁδὶ μὲν <ὁ> ἀριθμὸς ἄνθρωπος ὁδὶ δὲ Σωκράτης ὁδὶ δὲ Καλλίας; τί οὖν ἐκεῖνοι τούτοις αἴτιοί εἰσιν; οὐδὲ γὰρ εἰ οἱ μὲν ἀΐδιοι οἱ δὲ μή, οὐδὲν διοίσει. εἰ δ' ὅτι λόγοι ἀριθμῶν τἀνταῦθα, οἷον ἡ συμφωνία, δῆλον ὅτι ἐστὶν ἕν γέ τι ὧν εἰσὶ λόγοι. εἰ δή τι τοῦτο, ἡ ὕλη, φανερὸν ὅτι καὶ αὐτοὶ οἱ ἀριθμοὶ λόγοι τινὲς ἔσονται ἑτέρου πρὸς ἕτερον. λέγω δ' οἷον, εἰ ἔστιν ὁ Καλλίας λόγος ἐν ἀριθμοῖς πυρὸς καὶ γῆς καὶ ὕδατος καὶ ἀέρος, καὶ ἄλλων τινῶν ὑποκειμένων ἔσται καὶ ἡ ἰδέα ἀριθμός· καὶ αὐτοάνθρωπος, εἴτ' ἀριθμός τις ὢν εἴτε μή, ὅμως ἔσται λόγος ἐν ἀριθμοῖς τινῶν καὶ οὐκ ἀριθμός, οὐδ' ἔσται τις διὰ ταῦτα ἀριθμός.

Forms as Numbers are supposed to be generated from the operation of the One on the Indefinite Dyad. Precisely because the Indefinite Dyad is undifferentiated in principle, the results of the generation should be combinable units of Numbers, not the noncombinable units of Numbers that the Forms are supposed to contain.[110]

It is possible that Plato posited a distinction between combinable (συμβλητοί) and noncombinable (ἀσύμβλητοι) numbers to address Aristotle's criticism.[111] The evidence is distressingly sparse that Plato proceeded in this way. It seems to me that the more fundamental issue is what precisely it is for something to be intelligible. For both Plato and Aristotle, *all* the intelligibility in composites is owing to their form even though composite cannot exist without matter or some principle of unlimitedness or indeterminateness. Given the priority of form to matter that all Platonists embrace, and the conclusion that some sort of intellect is inseparable from whatever we call what is intelligible, our question becomes what does the Demiurge or the Unmoved Mover eternally contemplate?[112] The answer that he is contemplating a celestial encyclopedia (with pictures?) is no more facetious than is the answer that he is contemplating a complete list of the mathematical formulas for everything that could possibly exist. A more fruitful way of posing the question is to ask how we are to represent what it is that the Demiurge or the Unmoved Mover are eternally contemplating. It should by now be clear that neither for Plato nor for Aristotle can the answer to this question be in terms of the deliverances of sense perception, that is, in terms of physical descriptions of the dynamic and static attributes of things that we perceive. To proceed in this way is to apply a concept of understanding to ancient Platonism that is wholly anachronistic.

If intelligibility is owing entirely to form, is form in any sense nonmathematical? Aristotle says in *Metaphysics* in the course of his discussion of form that it is like the arrangement of letters in a syllable or flesh in relation to

---

110. Cf. *Meta.* N 7, 1080b37–N 8, 1083a17, and Annas 1976, 162–65, on the dilemma posed for Plato regarding the combinability of the units making up Form-Numbers.

111. See Annas 1976, 17–18, 165–67. The derivation of all numbers from the One Being at *Parm.* 143B8–144A4 is not helpful. The 'units' derived are specifically different and so would appear to be noncombinable, but Parmenides says that they may be combined ('both,' 'couple,' 'added,' etc.) to form odd and even numbers. Blyth (2000) argues that the way numbers are generated in *Parm.* 143A–144A suggests that the Ideal Numbers are ordinals, not cardinals. That is, the ideal numbers represent the ordering of the logical generation from the One operating on the Indefinite Dyad. So on this interpretation the ideal numbers are noncombinable; instances of the combinable cardinals are members of classes each of which is a noncombinable ideal number. These instances are the Mathematical Objects.

112. See Miller 2004, 143–49, who denies that the Forms are derived from the One and the Indefinite Dyad. Hence, the mathematization of Forms applies only to the Intermediates. Miller thinks that the variety of Forms could not be accounted for if they are Numbers derived from the two first principles. In this regard, I think he does not sufficiently take into account the role that a divine intellect is supposed to play.

the fire and earth out of which it is made.¹¹³ Is the arrangement or ordering of the elements understandable as nonmathematical? My aim here is not to try to give a definitive answer to this question, but to suggest that it is a question that is being addressed by Platonists within the framework provided by UP. It is not surprising that Platonists should provide different and even conflicting answers precisely because the answers will amount to different ways of representing what is necessarily beyond our grasp, namely, the divine intellect, whether we dub that Demiurge or Unmoved Mover. For Plato, the impetus to reduction to a unique first principle seemed inevitably to suggest that the nature of the order was mathematical; for Aristotle, a similar reduction to a first principle apparently did not. Aristotle's complaint that those in the Academy were obsessed with mathematics may well have been met by a retort to the effect that the only nonbodily order that Aristotle himself explicitly recognized and was able to describe was in fact that of mathematics. Why is that? For Plato, it seems that the answer is that cognition is paradigmatically the seeing of an order or orderly arrangement and that order is essentially a mathematical concept.¹¹⁴

Aristotle's testimony regarding the reduction of Form to Numbers and these to the first principles of the One and the Indefinite Dyad is unlikely to reveal definitive answers to questions of how Plato thought this reduction was to work. More important, in my view, is that this testimony regarding reduction reveals the fundamental impetus moving the positive construct out of UP. The principal desideratum is a *unified* metaphysical framework. Because the unified framework must aim at an autoexplicable starting point, the absolute simplicity of the first principle is necessary. Simplicity requires incompositeness and uniqueness, which are mutually entailing properties. Hence, inevitably, the metaphysical framework will be hierarchical, 'gradable,' as it were, in terms of relative simplicity or complexity. That the first principle of all is labeled 'One' is, in this context, hardly surprising. That it is alternatively labeled 'Good' is no more surprising given that its explanatory role with respect to the being of everything else is just a more technical expression of its fecundity. As we will see in the next part of the book, the multifarious difficulties attendant on this breathtaking complex research project consisting of a unified construct out of UP are everywhere in evidence among self-declared followers of Plato.

In this part of the book, I have tried to put up a principled resistance to what I take to be certain widespread misconceptions about how to read Plato. I have tried to show that in the dialogues Plato sets himself against many, if not most, of the philosophical positions of his predecessors. It is on

---

113. *Meta.* Z 17, 1041b11–33. It may be, as some editors have thought, that the words at 1041b8, τοῦτο δ' ἐστὶ τὸ εἶδος, are a gloss, in which case, nowhere else in this chapter does Aristotle explicitly say that the οὐσία of each thing and the αἴτιον πρῶτον of its being (27–28) is form. But elsewhere Aristotle says as much. See Z 7, 1031b1–2; Z 10, 1035b14–16, b32.

114. Cf. Adams 2007, 52, for an interesting contemporary mathematical account of intelligibility that he labels "broadly Pythagorean and Platonic."

the basis of his rejection of these positions that he embarked on the project of constructing a positive, integrated alternative. This positive construct is discernible and even at times evident in the dialogues when we remove some of the unnecessary and unsupported assumptions about what Plato is doing in them. There is no evidence that in some of these dialogues Plato is devoted to displaying the philosophy of someone other than himself. There is no evidence for maintaining that each dialogue was philosophically self-contained despite the literary unity that each possesses. The prima facie plausibility of using the contents of one dialogue to help understand what is being maintained in another should lead us to conclude that Platonism is recorded in the dialogues but not identical with them. Consequently, the reasons that have sometimes been offered for ignoring the testimony of Aristotle regarding the nature of Plato's philosophy are considerably weakened. Aristotle was from the start always thinking about the ongoing project that is Platonism even if it is the case that his access to this was principally via the dialogues. In the next part of the book, I aim to provide what can be really no more than a sampling of the contributions of those devoted to the Platonic project.

PART 2

The Continuing Creation of Platonism

CHAPTER 5

The Old Academy

I propose to consider in this chapter the Old Academy after Plato as continuators of the project he began. That is, I take it that they, like Aristotle himself, are adherents of UP and that the work apparently left undone by Plato at his death was the focus of their efforts. Apparently, this work included the matters on which Plato in his *Seventh Letter* said he was intently working at least late in his life, namely, the first principles of all, the One and the Indefinite Dyad, and the construction of the intelligible world out of them. Naturally, these are not the only "loose ends" of the Platonic enterprise. It would not be surprising if Aristotle's criticisms and his own research led to substantial differences as to how to complete the job. These would have been evident well before Plato's death in 347. We cannot be certain of the reason or reasons why Speusippus, Plato's nephew, was chosen over Aristotle to succeed Plato as the head of the Academy.[1] He retained the headship until his death in 339. Although he was a prolific writer, nothing but fragments remains of his thirty or so works. For my purposes, the main reason for considering Speusippus is that, apart from Aristotle, he is the first philosopher we know of to take up the project of explaining the nature of the first principle of all.

---

1. The reason may have been, as Debra Nails notes in private correspondence, that a non-Athenian like Aristotle would not have been allowed to own the property on which the Academy rested. No doubt, the fact that Speusippus was some twenty years older than Aristotle would have also been a consideration.

Speusippus and First Principles

I begin with the juxtaposition of a passage from Aristotle's *Metaphysics* and a testimony about Speusippus recorded by Diogenes Laertius. Aristotle, in various places, distinguishes three views among his colleagues in the Academy: (1) Plato's view that both Forms and Mathematical Numbers exist; (2) Speusippus's view that Mathematical Numbers exist *instead* of Forms; and (3) Xenocrates' view that Forms *are* Mathematical Numbers. Here is the passage:

> All these and other difficulties, then, make it evident that Numbers and Magnitudes cannot exist separately. What is more, the disagreement among the leading thinkers concerning Numbers is a sign that it is the falsity of the alleged facts which brings about this confusion in their positions. For those who posit only the Mathematical Objects as existing apart from sensible things, perceiving the difficulties about the Forms and their fictitiousness, abandoned the Numbers as Ideas and posited Mathematical Numbers. Those who wished to posit the Forms and at the same time the Numbers, not seeing how, if one posits the identical principles, Mathematical Numbers can exist in addition to the Numbers as Ideas, posited both the Ideas and Mathematical Numbers as being the identical Numbers in formula, although the Mathematical Numbers are in fact done away with; for they put forward hypotheses which are peculiar to themselves but not mathematical. The first thinker, who posited the existence of the Forms as Numbers and also the Mathematical Objects, separated the two for good reason. Thus, it turns out that all of these thinkers are right in some respect, but on the whole they are not right. And they themselves admit that their statements are not identical but contrary to each other. The cause of this is the fact that their hypotheses and principles are false.[2]

Before dealing with some of the many difficulties raised by this passage, let me set beside it the line in Diogenes Laertius's biography of Speusippus in which he claims baldly that "he [Speusippus] adhered to Plato's teachings."[3] What is striking in this rather offhand remark is that Diogenes

---

2. See *Meta.* N 3, 9.1085b34–1086a16: πάντα δὴ ταῦτα καὶ ἄλλα τοιαῦτα φανερὸν ποιεῖ ὅτι ἀδύνατον εἶναι τὸν ἀριθμὸν καὶ τὰ μεγέθη χωριστά, ἔτι δὲ τὸ διαφωνεῖν τοὺς τρόπους περὶ τῶν ἀριθμῶν σημεῖον ὅτι τὰ πράγματα αὐτὰ οὐκ ὄντα ἀληθῆ παρέχει τὴν ταραχὴν αὐτοῖς. οἱ μὲν γὰρ τὰ μαθηματικὰ μόνον ποιοῦντες παρὰ τὰ αἰσθητά, ὁρῶντες τὴν περὶ τὰ εἴδη δυσχέρειαν καὶ πλάσιν, ἀπέστησαν ἀπὸ τοῦ εἰδητικοῦ ἀριθμοῦ καὶ τὸν μαθηματικὸν ἐποίησαν· οἱ δὲ τὰ εἴδη βουλόμενοι ἅμα καὶ ἀριθμοὺς ποιεῖν, οὐχ ὁρῶντες δέ, εἰ τὰς ἀρχάς τις ταύτας θήσεται, πῶς ἔσται ὁ μαθηματικὸς ἀριθμὸς παρὰ τὸν εἰδητικόν, τὸν αὐτὸν εἰδητικὸν καὶ μαθηματικὸν ἐποίησαν ἀριθμὸν τῷ λόγῳ, ἐπεὶ ἔργῳ γε ἀνῄρηται ὁ μαθηματικός (ἰδίας γὰρ καὶ οὐ μαθηματικὰς ὑποθέσεις λέγουσιν)· ὁ δὲ πρῶτος θέμενος τὰ εἴδη εἶναι καὶ ἀριθμοὺς τὰ εἴδη καὶ τὰ μαθηματικὰ εἶναι εὐλόγως ἐχώρισεν· ὥστε πάντας συμβαίνει κατὰ μέν τι λέγειν ὀρθῶς, ὅλως δ' οὐκ ὀρθῶς. καὶ αὐτοὶ δὲ ὁμολογοῦσιν οὐ ταὐτὰ λέγοντες ἀλλὰ τὰ ἐναντία. αἴτιον δ' ὅτι αἱ ὑποθέσεις καὶ αἱ ἀρχαὶ ψευδεῖς.

3. D.L. 4.1.7–8: καὶ ἔμεινε μὲν ἐπὶ τῶν αὐτῶν Πλάτωνι δογμάτων. Brittain (2011, 526) thinks that the view of Plato's philosophy as systematic is not earlier than the first century BCE.

should make it despite Aristotle's claim that Speusippus perceived "the difficulties about the Forms and their fictitiousness."[4] Of course, it is possible that Diogenes never actually read the works of Speusippus (or, indeed, that he never got very far into Aristotle's *Metaphysics*) and made his remark on the assumption that Plato's successor in the Academy would naturally embrace his teachings. Still, it is hard to fathom why he would make the remark unless he was at least repeating a received opinion. Perhaps one tentative conclusion that one may draw from the juxtaposition of these passages is that embracing Forms, apart from Mathematicals, was not in antiquity thought to be a necessary condition for adherence to Plato's "teachings."[5]

Diogenes' remark is further illuminated by another passage in Aristotle's *Metaphysics* in which Speusippus is criticized for the way he conceives of the One, the first principle of all:

> Nor has anyone[6] the right belief if he likens the principles of all that exists to those of animals and plants (where generation always proceeds from the indefinite and the incomplete to the more complete) and says, because of this, that it is the same also for the first principles, and consequently that the One itself is not even a being. For even in animals and plants generation of the incomplete proceeds from principles which are complete, for it is a man that begets a man, and it is not the seed that is first.[7]

So Speusippus evidently takes the One to be the first principle of all and also takes it to be in some sense 'beyond being' or 'beyond essence,'

He adds that it was probably not until the second century CE that the idea of systematically interpreting Plato's texts arose. The only reason Brittain gives for this view is that the advent of the Hellenistic philosophical schools checked the development of a specifically Platonic philosophy within the Academy. This interpretation seems gratuitous and ignores the possibility that the Old Academy accepted the Platonic 'system' though its members disputed the nature of the first principles. Indeed, Aristotle, *Meta.* Λ 6, 072b13–14, follows Plato precisely in arguing for a first principle of all "upon which heavens and nature depend." Thus, Aristotle counts as a systematizer of Platonism.

4. One might object that Aristotle does not explicitly refer to Speusippus here. Yet in the light of *Meta.* Λ 10, 1075b37–1076a3; M 1, 1076a20–21; M 6, 1080b14; and the one reference to Speusippus by name, at Z 2, 1028b21–24, most scholars have supposed that Aristotle means to include Speusippus among those who rejected Forms in favor of Mathematicals, in contrast to Xenocrates. How rejecting Forms in favor of Mathematicals differs from *identifying* them, as Aristotle says Xenocrates did, is a problem I will address below.

5. Tarán (1981, 335) thinks that because for Speusippus goodness is in completion and that completion is a temporal notion that applies to plants and animals but not to numbers, that mathematical principles are not supposed to apply to living things. But this does not follow. See Dancy 1991, 161, n. 140, who points out that the testimony in the passage from Iamblichus cited below in n. 17, has Speusippus claiming that the Decad, arising from the One, is complete.

6. See Λ 7, 1072b30–34, where Speusippus is identified (along with Pythagoreans) as holding this doctrine.

7. See *Meta* M 5,1092a11–17: οὐκ ὀρθῶς δ' ὑπολαμβάνει οὐδ' εἴ τις παρεικάζει τὰς τοῦ ὅλου ἀρχὰς τῇ τῶν ζῴων καὶ φυτῶν, ὅτι ἐξ ἀορίστων ἀτελῶν τε ἀεὶ τὰ τελειότερα, διὸ καὶ

the position that Aristotle claims Plato holds as well. It would seem that Speusippus's adherence to this principle counts more for his Platonic bona fides than does his aversion to Forms.

But with Speusippus's adherence to the absolute priority of the One goes his disinclination to identify it with the Good, for he is said to hold that goodness and beauty are in the outcome of a procession of the first principle not in that principle itself.

> Those who suppose, like the Pythagoreans and Speusippus, that the most beautiful and the best are not in the first principle, because the principles are causes of plants and of living things, whereas the beautiful and the complete are in the things that come from these, do not think correctly. For the seed is from other prior and complete things, and the first is not a seed, but the complete thing is. For example, one could say that a man is prior to the seed, not the man who comes from the seed, but the man from whom the seed comes.[8]

The point that Aristotle claims that Speusippus is making here is illuminated by one of the other few references to Speusippus by Aristotle, this time in his *Nicomachean Ethics*:

> The Pythagoreans seem to have spoken more persuasively about the Good [than Plato] when they place the One in the column of goods. Speusippus, too, seems to have followed closely their line of thought.[9]

By placing the One in the column of 'goods' (that is, finite, odd, one, right, male, rest, straightness, light, goodness, and square), which is opposed to the other column of 'bads' (infinite, even, many, left, female, motion, curvature, darkness, badness, and oblong), Pythagoreans and Speusippus in

---

ἐπὶ τῶν πρώτων οὕτως ἔχειν φησίν, ὥστε μηδὲ ὄν τι εἶναι τὸ ἓν αὐτό. εἰσὶ γὰρ καὶ ἐνταῦθα τέλειαι αἱ ἀρχαὶ ἐξ ὧν ταῦτα· ἄνθρωπος γὰρ ἄνθρωπον γεννᾷ, καὶ οὐκ ἔστι τὸ σπέρμα πρῶτον. But see Merlan 1953, 95–96, for evidence from Theophrastus that Aristotle did not necessarily regard the seed as inferior to that which comes from it. If the seed is undeveloped, though not inferior, Speusippus may be claiming that what the first principle is fully or completely is evident only in what is derived from it. This insight will be applied by later Platonists to the contemplation of the One by Intellect, which sees everything that the One is by seeing all that is intelligible. Cf. Plotinus, *Enn.* III 8, 7; IV 8, 6; V 9, 6, for the One as 'seed.'

8. *Meta.* Λ 7, 1072b30–1073a3 (= Fr. 53 Isnarde Parente [IP]): ὅσοι δὲ ὑπολαμβάνουσιν, ὥσπερ οἱ Πυθαγόρειοι καὶ Σπεύσιππος τὸ κάλλιστον καὶ ἄριστον μὴ ἐν ἀρχῇ εἶναι, διὰ τὸ καὶ τῶν φυτῶν καὶ τῶν ζῴων τὰς ἀρχὰς αἴτια μὲν εἶναι τὸ δὲ καλὸν καὶ τέλειον ἐν τοῖς ἐκ τούτων, οὐκ ὀρθῶς οἴονται. τὸ γὰρ σπέρμα ἐξ ἑτέρων ἐστὶ προτέρων τελείων, καὶ τὸ πρῶτον οὐ σπέρμα ἐστὶν ἀλλὰ τὸ τέλειον· οἷον πρότερον ἄνθρωπον ἄν φαίη τις εἶναι τοῦ σπέρματος, οὐ τὸν ἐκ τούτου γενόμενον ἀλλ' ἕτερον ἐξ οὗ τὸ σπέρμα. As Dillon (2010b, 68) notes, Iamblichus assumed that Speusippus is following the rule that a principle cannot have the properties it is a principle of. See below, n. 17. So the principle of goodness cannot be good. This is certainly one way of construing the genitive in 'the Idea of the Good.'

9. See *EN* A 4, 1096b5–7 (= Fr. 63 IP): πιθανώτερον δ' ἐοίκασιν οἱ Πυθαγόρειοι λέγειν περὶ αὐτοῦ, τιθέντες ἐν τῇ τῶν ἀγαθῶν συστοιχίᾳ τὸ ἕν· οἷς δὴ καὶ Σπεύσιππος ἐπακολουθῆσαι δοκεῖ.

effect maintained that there are different kinds of goods as well as different kinds of ones; that is, the Good is not one thing. Therefore, it is not a unique principle of all. Therefore, as in the first passage, goodness may be found in the fruition of a plant or in the maturity of an animal.[10] Accordingly, the 'badness' in the table of opposites would be found in the failure of a plant or animal to achieve its own nature.[11]

To fill out the basic picture, we need to add a valuable bit of testimony from Proclus in his *Commentary on Plato's Parmenides* regarding the view of Speusippus (here explicitly mentioned by name in the line preceding this passage):

> For they[12] held that the One is higher than being and is the source of being; and they delivered it even from the status of a principle. For they held that, given the One in itself conceived as separated and alone without the other things, with no additional element, nothing else would come into existence. And so they introduced the Indefinite Dyad as the principle of beings. (bk. VII, p. 38.32–40.7 Klibansky = fr. 48 Tarán (1981) = fr. 62 IP)[13]

So Speusippus, supposedly loyal to the teachings of Plato, rejected Forms in favor of Mathematical Objects, yet retained what was for Plato the reduction of Forms to the One and to the Indefinite Dyad.[14] As we proceed to analyze this result, the hypothesis that I am going to follow is that Speusippus's 'innovations' amount to a revised version of the first principles of Plato's Platonism that he derived ultimately from UP.

The obvious assumption in accounting for Speusippus's rejection of Forms and substitution of the Mathematicals is that, given Plato's own assimilation of Forms to Numbers, and his derivation of these from the One and the Indefinite Dyad, Speusippus thought that the positing of Forms was otiose.[15] The 'difficulties' that Aristotle reports that Speusippus had with Forms

---

10. I take it that Aristotle's point is that however the Pythagoreans characterize the first principle of all, oneness and goodness are diverse and so not properly jointly identifiable with that principle. For Plato and Pythagoreans, One as a principle is neither odd nor even; the one in the column of 'goods' is the unit, opposed to the many.

11. See Iamblichus, *De communi mathematica scientia* 4.106–7 Festa/Klein (= fr. 72 IP): κακίαν γενέσθαι οὐ προηγουμένως, ἐκ δὲ τοῦ ἐκ πίπτειν καὶ μὴ κατακρατεῖν τινα τοῦ κατὰ φύσιν. See Merlan 1953, 86–103, and Dillon 2003, 41, n. 28, for the defense of this work as containing evidence for the view of Speusippus against Tarán 1981, 86–107.

12. Here Proclus is evidently quoting Speusippus. "They" refers to the "ancients" whom Speusippus claims to be following.

13. Preserved only in the Latin translation of William of Moerbeke. Proclus, explicitly quoting from Speusippus, assumes that he is following Plato's claim in *Republic* that the Good is above being because it is the source of being to the Forms. Aristotle may be taking Speusippus tendentiously to mean that the One is nothing (μὴ ὄν) rather than that it is above οὐσία, but there is no conclusive reason for supposing so.

14. See Ross 1951, 279–94; Richard 1986, 211–17.

15. See Dillon 2003, 48–49, 51–52, who argues that Speusippus did not necessarily give up the Forms; "rather, he restructured and rationalized them." Perhaps this is equally the case for Plato.

presumably included the problem raised in book Alpha of *Metaphysics* that if the One's initial 'acting' on the Indefinite Dyad makes that which has the cardinality of 'two' in some sense, then 'two' must have already existed prior to the acting.[16] And why should this 'two' be identified as a Form-Number as opposed to a Mathematical? After all, its units, like those of Mathematicals, are all equal or comparable, whereas the 'units' of the Form-Numbers are not. If this is, indeed, the basis for Speusippus's reasoning, we must suppose that he thought that in the One and Indefinite Dyad could be found somehow the ideal paradigms of intelligibility that the Forms were posited by Plato as being. Yet quite apart from Proclus's somewhat puzzling distinction between the One as the 'source of being' and the Indefinite Dyad as the 'principle of beings,' it is far from obvious how this is supposed to work.[17]

At this point in the consideration of Speusippus's philosophy, scholars typically throw in the towel, either dismissing Speusippus as hopelessly incompetent or trying to eke out some intelligible picture of the rationale for his views, including his apparent dissent from Plato. The dearth of evidence perhaps makes this approach understandable, if not inevitable. I would like to suggest that we can see even in the few bits of testimony a deeper issue than whether Form-Numbers or Mathematicals are to be posited. Indeed, I want to show that the issue of the articulation of the structure of the intelligible world is at the heart of Platonism and that the extreme difficulty in presenting a coherent account of that structure is the main reason for the variety of positions within Platonism regarding first principles.

Let us recall that Forms are explanatory entities, that the Idea of the Good or the One is posited as the ultimate explanatory entity, and that the Indefinite Dyad is evidently introduced because it was thought that the One or the Good was not sufficient for explanatory purposes. Forms explain the possibility of identity in difference. They are the 'ones' whose separation is required to explain how two or more things—different at least by being more than one—can yet be identical. The One or the Good seems to have a more complicated explanatory role. We have already seen that it is supposed to explain the knowability of Forms. It is also said to explain their essence and existence. If anything is clear in all this, it is that the One is

---

16. See *Meta.* A 9, 991b27–992a1.
17. Cf. Iamblichus, *De comuni mathematica scientia* 4.15–23 Festa/Klein (= fr. 72IP): Τῶν δὴ ἀριθμῶν τῶν μαθηματικῶν δύο τὰς πρωτίστας καὶ ἀνωτάτω ὑποθετέον ἀρχάς, τὸ ἕν (ὅπερ δὴ οὐδὲ ὂν πω δεῖ καλεῖν, διὰ τὸ ἁπλοῦν εἶναι καὶ διὰ τὸ ἀρχὴν μὲν ὑπάρχειν τῶν ὄντων, τὴν δὲ ἀρχὴν μηδέπω εἶναι τοιαύτην οἷα ἐκεῖνα ὧν ἐστιν ἀρχή), καὶ ἄλλην πάλιν ἀρχὴν τὴν τοῦ πλήθους, ἣν καὶ διαίρεσιν οἷόν τ' εἶναι καθ' αὑτὸ παρέχεσθαι, καὶ διὰ τοῦτο ὑγρᾷ τινι παντάπασι καὶ εὐπλαδεῖ ὕλῃ, προσηκόντως εἰς δύναμιν παραδεικνύντες, ἀποφαίνοιμεν ἂν ὁμοίαν εἶναι· (Among Mathematical Numbers, we must hypothesize the two highest and primary principles, the One (which we should not even call a being owing to its simplicity and to its being a principle of beings; a principle not yet being like those things of which it is a principle) and another principle, that of the Multiplicity, which is able by itself to provide the division [into beings] and which we may call a fluid and in every way pliant matter if we are to represent its nature in the most suitable manner.) My translation is adapted from Dillon's, 43.

supposed to be the autoexplicable principle of all things. Everything beside the One is heteroexplicable.

Let us focus for the moment on the fact that the Good or the One is the explanation for the 'to be' of Forms.[18] For Plato, the exigencies of explanation require that the Good is 'above essence' (ἐπέκεινα τῆς οὐσίας). Speusippus adds the logical consequence of this that the One must be (a) 'simple' and (b) 'unlike anything of which it is the principle.' The problem thus becomes: How can the One thus described be an explanation or principle for anything? Plato's assumption that the Good is essentially self-diffusive scarcely solves anything. To suppose that what is 'diffused' is goodness and that goodness is a property of being seems to indicate that being is 'diffused' from the Good as well.[19] If that is the case, what does the simplicity of the first principle amount to? Aristotle's proposal that the first principle of all—shown by Aristotle to be as perfectly simple as the One—serves its explanatory role by being a final cause only if final causal explanation is indeed ultimate explanation. On the one hand, Aristotle himself seems to deny this when he posits an explanation for the 'to be' of noneternal things.[20] This is not what a final cause does. On the other hand, Aristotle, in his rejection of separate Forms, seems to opt for the strategy of saying that the composite identity of things with properties is not a case of the heteroexplicable, requiring, of course, an autoexplicable principle. The very idea of explanation is thus brought critically to the fore within the framework of UP.[21]

It is important to stress that it is not compositeness as such that generates the explanatory path. It is only the compositeness of a whole, as opposed to that of a sum—to use the language of *Theaetetus*—that produces

---

18. Recall Aristotle, *Meta.* α 1, 993b28–31 on the explanation for the 'to be' of all things that the gods provide.

19. See *Rep.* 508B6–7, referring to the Sun, which is analogous to the Good: Οὐκοῦν καὶ τὴν δύναμιν ἣ ἔχει [τὰ ὄμμα] ἐκ τούτου [τοῦ ἡλίου] ταμιευομένην ὥσπερ ἐρίππυτον κέκτηται; (So, does it not receive the power it has from the sun, just like an infusion from an overflowing treasury?)

20. Cf. *Meta.* E 1, 1025b3–18, where Aristotle distinguishes the science of causes and principles of things qua things from the special sciences, especially line 10, where Aristotle says that the special sciences οὐδὲ τοῦ τί ἐστιν οὐθένα λόγον ποιοῦνται. It would be surprising if this meant that the special sciences say nothing about the essence of the things they study; as Aristotle says, they arrive at this by sense perception or by hypothesis. The remark seems to mean rather that these sciences do not investigate the cause or principle of the οὐσία of what they study. This is exactly the position of mathematics in Plato's Divided Line in relation to dialectic. The special sciences do not account for the being of anything with an essence. That is what the Idea of the Good is supposed to do.

21. See Dancy 1991, 94–96, who denies the relevance of the *Republic* passage to the interpretation of Speusippus. Dancy thinks this because he holds that the status of the Idea of the Good does not mean that it is beyond being in the sense of nonexistent. I think he is right about this, but I think he is wrong in thinking that Speusippus thinks otherwise.

the problems.[22] Specifically, it is the compositeness of the whole that is constituted by the 'what' or οὐσία of something and the 'that' or εἶναι of that thing.[23] For a Platonist, to deny that this sort of compositeness is heteroexplicable is tantamount to nothing less than the abandonment of philosophy. Such a denial would require one to say that this composite is not contingent, where 'contingency' entails heteroexplicability. A denial of the contingency of the composite entails an assertion of its necessity or autoexplicability. It might be supposed that if the οὐσία of something is autoexplicable, so, too, would be the εἶναι. Thus, there are two brute facts: what something is and that something of that sort exists. The brute-fact party is the antiphilosophy party. Either it pronounces everything a brute fact that really is the apotheosis of antiphilosophy or else it tries to limit 'bruteness' to a faction of the party, in which case it must allow some sort of heteroexplicable or contingent facts.[24] It is difficult to see why the existence of things could be nonarbitrarily excluded from among these.

At any rate, Platonists, including Speusippus, took the import of the argument in *Parmenides* to indicate that οὐσία 'alone' is not autoexplicable because οὐσία alone does not exist.[25] Whatever has οὐσία must *also* have εἶναι, hence, the compositeness. It seems obvious that the only possible ultimate or non-question-begging explanation for such compositeness is that which is incomposite, that in which οὐσία and εἶναι are indistinct. But exactly how this is supposed to explain is left mostly, though not entirely, unspoken.

Again, in the second hypothesis of *Parmenides*, the composite of οὐσία and εἶναι is, owing to the fact that the whole that it is is indefinitely divisible, 'unlimited in multiplicity' (ἄπειρον τὸ πλῆθος).[26] This is evidently the Indefinite Dyad to which, along with the One, Plato reduced Forms, according to Aristotle. This is what Speusippus calls simply 'Multiplicity.' But

---

22. See *Tht.* 204A–B. Cf. *Parm.* 142D4–5: ἆρα οὐκ ἀνάγκη τὸ μὲν ὅλον ἓν ὂν εἶναι αὐτό, τούτου δὲ γίγνεσθαι μόρια τό τε ἓν καὶ τὸ εἶναι; —Ἀνάγκη. (Is it not necessary that the whole be itself one being, and the parts of this be "one" and "to be"? —It is necessary.)

23. See *Parm.* 142B5–8: ἓν εἰ ἔστιν, ἆρα οἷόν τε αὐτὸ εἶναι μέν, οὐσίας δὲ μὴ μετέχειν; {—} Οὐχ οἷόν τε. {—} Οὐκοῦν καὶ ἡ οὐσία τοῦ ἑνὸς εἴη ἂν οὐ ταὐτὸν οὖσα τῷ ἑνί· (If it is one, is it possible for it to be but not to partake of essence? —It is not possible. —So the essence of the one would not be identical with the one.) Cf. *Soph.* 244B–245E, where the core of the argument against Parmenides' One is that if it has being, that is, if it is one being, it is therefore complex and so not absolutely one or simple. The Idea of the Good in *Republic* is above οὐσία because as a first principle of all, it cannot have even the minimal complexity of 'one being.' See Krämer 1969, 8–10, on the origin of the Idea of the Good as One in Plato's reflections on Eleaticism.

24. I am assuming that to maintain that everything is a brute fact is equivalent to maintaining that everything is autoexplicable.

25. This is a generalization of the conclusion of the first hypothesis of the second part of *Parmenides*. One major strand of Platonic interpretation has it that the first hypothesis refers to the uniquely autoexplicable One. But it is precisely because the One is 'beyond οὐσία' that the point about οὐσία alone not being autoexplicable stands.

26. 143A2. Cf. *Phil.* 17E3 for the phrase, and Sayre 2005, 127.

if this is correct, then the One and the Indefinite Dyad are arrayed in two separate hypotheses of the dialogue; they are not coordinate principles.[27] Only the One of the first hypothesis is absolutely simple. So Aristotle is at least somewhat misleading when he refers to the reduction of Forms. He could have more accurately characterized the generation or reduction in two hierarchical stages, not one. Thus the generation of Forms from the One and the Indefinite Dyad is a generation logically posterior to the generation of the Indefinite Dyad itself.[28]

This still leaves us with the question of what it means to say that the absolutely simple One is the autoexplicable principle for the οὐσία and εἶναι of all (heteroexplicable) else? As Proclus tells us in the passage cited above, Speusippus understood that the One "conceived as separate and alone" would produce nothing. The rather obscure phrase "conceived as separate and alone" reveals the crux of the problem.[29] If the One is indeed so conceived, in what sense could it be the autoexplicable principle of everything else? But what would it mean to conceive it *not* as separate and alone? Presumably, that would mean to conceive it with the Indefinite Dyad. How to do so without making it a coordinate principle, and hence without compromising the uniqueness of the One as a first principle, is, alas, obscure.[30]

---

27. Thereby making the Indefinite Dyad to be derived from the One, as implied in the testimony above in Proclus and Aristotle, *Meta.* N 1, 1087b4–12. Cf. Halfwassen 2002a for a nuanced argument that the One-Being of the second hypothesis of *Parmenides* was understood at least by Platonists from Speusippus onward as derived from the absolutely simple One of the first hypothesis. The key point is that the One-Being is or represents the principles of One and Indefinite Dyad that are the principles of Forms. The One 'beyond being' of the first hypothesis, the ultimate principle, is to be distinguished from the principle of number, the Monad or One.

28. Cf. Halfwassen 1992, 265–402. We do not have to commit ourselves to the Platonic interpretation of *Parmenides* according to which hypothesis one refers to the One and hypothesis two refers to Intellect, and hypothesis three refers to Soul in order to achieve this result. We could simply suppose that the logical distinctions that are made in one and two provide the framework for the Platonic hypostases; they are not direct references to them. I think that this is fact the case, but if so, it does not by itself invalidate the later Platonic understanding of Plato's Platonism. See Halfwassen 1993 for an argument that Speusippus originated the interpretation of *Parmenides* according to which there is a hierarchical ordering of the hypotheses of the second part. Also, Horn 1995; Bechtle 1999, 113–17; Dillon 2010b.

29. Dillon (2003, 56, n. 63) suggests that the phrase refers to *Parm.* 143A6–8, where the One that has being is considered apart from the being it has. This may be correct, in which case the role of the One as first principle becomes even more obscure.

30. It is presumably in recognition of this difficulty that Speusippus wanted to insist that, since the Indefinite Dyad cannot be supposed to be evil, the One is not good. See Iamblichus, *De communi mathematica scientia* 4.32–49 Festa/Klein. Cf. Aristotle, *Meta.* M 4, 1091b30–35; *EE* A 8, 1218a15–32. But this need not mean that the One is not the principle of good (and hence, properly called 'Good'), according to the axiom that Speusippus himself accepts, namely, that a principle must be unlike that of which it is a principle. The reason for denying that the One is good is to be taken in the same sense in which, according to Proclus, Speusippus denied (or should have denied?) that the One is a principle.

Naturally, the problems increase in complexity and acuteness when we wish to consider the nature of the products of the One and the Indefinite Dyad. For it is necessary to find ultimately 'in' the One or the Idea of the Good not only the array of intelligible structures—whether mathematized or not—but also that which accounts for cognition and that which accounts for life. Speusippus is reported by Aëtius as holding that "[god] is Intellect, which is not identical with the One or the Good but has its own nature."[31] No doubt, this is, as Dillon notes, a reference to Plato's Demiurge.[32] But this continues to leave unexplained the plurality of principles consisting of the One, Indefinite Dyad, Forms or Mathematicals, and Demiurge. To this list, of course, we must at some point add Soul.

The Aristotelian strategy is to 'collapse' these principles, or at least the sense in which they function as principles, into one, the Unmoved Mover. This strategy requires that the burden of the first principle of all be lessened. First, the Unmoved Mover is not needed to explain matter, which is an eternal autoexplicable principle. It is not its eternity, however, that is supposed to relieve it of the need for an explanation. It is that matter does not exist on its own; it has no οὐσία and no εἶναι that need to be explained. It is purely a function of that which does have these. Second, the status of soul remains a problem, for though soul is a principle of nature and so within the context of natural science does not require an explanation for its existence, Aristotle admits that all nature depends on the supernatural or intelligible.[33] Finally, the issue of Mathematicals and/or Forms or Form-Numbers is avoided by making the Unmoved Mover cognitively identical with all that which is intelligible—whatever that might be. As Aristotle acknowledges, all this depends entirely on the assumption that the Unmoved Mover is incomposite or absolutely simple. That is, there must be no real distinction between the οὐσία and the εἶναι of the Unmoved Mover. This seems to be an especially difficult position to maintain given that the Unmoved Mover has a very distinctive οὐσία, namely, thinking (νόησις). It is this activity (ἐνέργεια) that, says Aristotle, must exist (εἶναι).[34]

---

31. Aëtius, *Placita* 1.7.20 Diels = fr. 58 Tarán: τὸν νοῦν οὔτε τῷ ἀγαθῷ τὸν αὐτόν, ἰδιοφυῆ δέ. The context is a chapter in which the author is listing the identity of the divine in various philosophers.

32. See Dillon 2003, 63, and *Tim.* 47E4.

33. *Meta.* Λ 7, 1072b13–14: ἐκ τοιαύτης ἄρα ἀρχῆς ἤρτηται ὁ οὐρανὸς καὶ φύσις. The nature of this dependence is, of course, controversial. Is it merely final causality as the object of love? Or is it more? At *De motu an.* 4, 699b32–700a6; *De gen. et corr.* B 10, 336b30–32; and *Gen. an.* B 1, 731b24–732a1, the causality certainly looks like more than final. Also, cf. *De mun.* 6.397b16–398a6, on the authenticity of which see Gerson 2005, 50, n. 11. I cannot explore this issue further here, though the more 'active' the Unmoved Mover appears to be, the more it looks like Plato's Demiurge, understood as having a role subordinate to the first principle of all.

34. *Meta.* Λ 6, 1071b19–20: δεῖ ἄρα εἶναι ἀρχὴν τοιαύτην ἧς ἡ οὐσία ἐνέργεια (there must, therefore, be such a principle the substance of which is activity).

What we evidently have before us is an intra-Academic dispute that can be characterized generally as a dispute about the nature of philosophical explanation. In particular, it is a dispute that turns on responses to the following dilemma: if the existence of the cosmos and all its parts is to be explained by a necessary and sufficient cause, that cause must exist. But its existence must either be distinct from its essence or not. If it is, then how does the *explanans* differ from the *explananda*? If it is not, then what does the explanation amount to? To say that the first principle of all—whether we call this 'the One' or 'the Good'—is the cause of the οὐσία and εἶναι of anything is hardly perspicuous. The problem is actually no different for an Unmoved Mover conceived as being absolutely simple. Yet to say that the first principle of all is itself composite is to exclude it from being a cause of the εἶναι of anything as opposed to being that which itself is in need of an explanation for its εἶναι. For Aristotle, it is, explicitly, at any rate, only a final cause.

The profound difficulty of the dilemma invites the renunciation of efforts to discover an *explanans* for the εἶναι of anything as being fundamentally misguided. An explanation for the becoming of something, or its γένεσις, suffices. Such renunciation and shifting of attention comes at a cost. That cost is that the existence of composites or wholes is reduced to a brute fact. Why should this be thought of as a 'cost'? Because if the existence of composites is a brute fact, then a science of being qua being or 'first philosophy' is unnecessary. For the Stoic or Epicurean or Pyrrhonist, this is certainly an acceptable or even welcome cost. For the Platonist, it is not. For the Platonist, first philosophy is the linchpin of UP. To put it in other terms, Platonism grows in plausibility as an articulation of UP to the extent that it arrives at a satisfactory first philosophy; to cut this off is to make UP at best question-begging and at worst unsustainable. To put this in other terms, one of the principal justifications for maintaining UP is that there is something like a correct or defensible systematic first philosophy. Without this, the claims that constitute UP seem less impressive. This is so because the need to posit immaterial entities seems real only if they are a necessary part of a systematic explanatory framework, that is, first philosophy. If it should be necessary to situate the Good or the One at the 'top' of this framework, and it is further necessary to posit the Indefinite Dyad as a principle of extensive magnitude, we then have the basis for the rejection of relativism, nominalism, and mechanism. Particularly important in this regard, it seems, is the intuition that the intelligibility of things that is constitutive of the explanatory framework is in some sense mathematical. For if what things are is ultimately found in formulas or ratios, we have the most straightforward path from messy nature up to first principles, that is, the first principles of number.

Speusippean Knowledge

Speusippus rejected separate Forms and substituted for these Mathematicals. Yet he maintained Plato's distinction between that which is an object of

144   CHAPTER 5

knowledge (ἐπιστήμη) and that which is otherwise cognitively available.³⁵ As we have seen, it is a fundamental tenet of UP that those who maintain the impossibility of knowledge are mistaken. For Plato, the basic argument for this negative tenet is a sort of transcendental one, namely, that if we did not possess knowledge, then other modes of cognition would not be possible. But we do have, for example, beliefs, including true beliefs. So these would not be possible unless we possess knowledge; therefore, we possess knowledge. This argument is part of the argument for the immortality of the soul in *Phaedo*, the so-called Recollection Argument.³⁶ I say "part of the argument" because the complete argument aims to show not only that we possess knowledge but that this knowledge could not have been acquired while embodied; it must have been acquired prior to our embodiment. Hence, the soul existed separately from the body. It does this by claiming not merely that we possess true beliefs, but that we possess true beliefs that we could not have acquired empirically, so to speak. We are capable of believing truly that sticks and stones, though they be equal, are defective in their equality in relation to the Form of Equality. We could not make this judgment if we did not already know the standard in comparison with the sensible equals are defective.

Let us leave aside for the moment the putative defectiveness of the sensible equals and all matters pertaining to the soul and its separability in order to concentrate on the nature of the knowledge that we supposedly possess. As I will argue, all versions of Platonism, including those of Aristotle and Speusippus, are distinguished by their consideration of Plato's positive response to this tenet of UP.

It is in *Republic* where we find Plato's most extensive account of the nature of ἐπιστήμη. The first crucial facet of that account is found within the context of the distinction of philosophers from their counterfeits, lovers of sights and sounds.³⁷ The former seek ἐπιστήμη whereas the latter are content with δόξα, or belief. The hallmark of the power of knowledge is that it is inerrant (ἀναμάρτητον), while belief is not.³⁸ The objects of

---

35. I infer this from Aristotle's claim in *Meta*. N 3, 1090a25–28 that those who posit the Mathematicals as first (i.e., Speusippus and perhaps others) maintained that there was no ἐπιστήμη of those things they hypothesized (as consisting of numbers and magnitudes), that is, of sensibles. The plural ἐπιστῆμαι usually means areas of cognition in which ἐπιστήμη is possible. It seems reasonable to infer that Speusippus is maintaining the basic Platonic distinction between the realm of the intelligible and the realm of the sensible and claiming that only the former is an object of ἐπιστήμη. Aristotle himself maintained that there is no ἐπιστήμη of "things that can be otherwise," i.e., of particular sensibles. See *EN* Z 3, 1139b19–24; *Post. An.* A 8,75b24, A 33, 88b30–37.

36. *Phd.* 72E3–78B3.

37. The argument is made in three stages: (a) 476A9–D7; (b) 476D8–478E6; (c) 478E7–480A13. In (a), Plato distinguishes philosophers and lovers of sights and sounds by the objects of their love; in (b), he tries to establish the difference between the modes of cognition belonging to each, belief and knowledge; in (c), he seeks to explain in greater detail the sorts of objects distinguished in (a).

38. *Rep.* 477E6–7. It is clear from the argument that 'inerrancy' is not a property of true as opposed to false belief. It is the power (δύναμις) of knowledge, as opposed to belief *simpliciter*,

knowledge are Forms, or 'that which is,' in contrast to the objects of belief, or 'that which is and is not at the same time.'³⁹ That there is a deep connection between inerrancy and the kind of things that can be cognized inerrantly is clear enough.⁴⁰ The implications of this connection are considerable.

The explication of what it means to pursue ἐπιστήμη as opposed to δόξα is advanced in the famous triptych of the Sun, the Divided Line, and the Cave. In the first analogy, the Idea of the Good is compared with the Sun:

> Therefore, you should say that not only do the objects of cognition owe their being cognized to the Good, but their existence and essence are present to them owing to it, although the Good is not an essence, but something above essence, exceeding it in rank and power.⁴¹

Among the many questions that arise in regard to this portentous passage, we need to focus here on why the Good is said to be necessary somehow for the cognition of Forms. As we discover in the Divided Line, it is only by somehow grasping (ἁψάμενος) the Good that knowledge of Forms is possible.⁴² And as Plato tells us a bit later, it is *only* at the top portion of the Divided Line, where the philosopher or dialectician operates, that ἐπιστήμη, strictly speaking, is possible.⁴³

If we try to connect the conclusion of the Recollection Argument with the passages from *Republic*, it is reasonable to suppose that Plato distinguishes the ἐπιστήμη that the soul possesses prior to embodiment from the ἐπιστήμη that the philosopher is seeking, and is able to find only if she somehow 'grasps' the unhypothetical first principle of all that is knowable. A distinction that looks very much like this one is made explicitly in *Theaetetus*, where Socrates suggests that there is a distinction between possessing (κεκτῆσθαι) and having (ἔχειν) knowledge.⁴⁴ This is presented as the distinction between an item of knowledge being in the mind, though not present to consciousness, as we would say, and our bringing it into consciousness. Though the definition of knowledge as true belief is

---

that is inerrant. At 478B1-2 we have the consequence: οὐκ ἐγχωρεῖ γνωστὸν καὶ δοξαστὸν ταὐτὸν εἶναι (it follows that it is not possible for the identical thing to be both knowable and believable).

39. *Rep.* 478D5-8, 479E1-5.

40. Cf. *Tht.* 152C5-6, where the two criteria of knowledge to be met by any definition (in the first instance as sense perception) are (a) that it be inerrant, and (b) that its objects be "that which is": Αἴσθησις ἄρα τοῦ ὄντος ἀεί ἐστιν καὶ ἀψευδὲς ὡς ἐπιστήμη οὖσα. That the words τοῦ ὄντος refer to intelligibles as opposed to sensibles ("that which is and is not") will develop dialectically throughout the dialogue. Of course, if the oddly placed ἀεί goes with τοῦ ὄντος, this would be obvious.

41. *Rep.* 509B6-10: Καὶ τοῖς γιγνωσκομένοις τοίνυν μὴ μόνον τὸ γιγνώσκεσθαι φάναι ὑπὸ τοῦ ἀγαθοῦ παρεῖναι, ἀλλὰ καὶ τὸ εἶναί τε καὶ τὴν οὐσίαν ὑπ' ἐκείνου αὐτοῖς προσεῖναι, οὐκ οὐσίας ὄντος τοῦ ἀγαθοῦ, ἀλλ' ἔτι ἐπέκεινα τῆς οὐσίας πρεσβείᾳ καὶ δυνάμει ὑπερέχοντος.

42. REP. 511B7.

43. *Rep.* 533E4-534A2. Cf. *Tim.* 51D3-E6.

44. See *Tht.* 196D-199C, especially 197B8-9. The context is Socrates' examination of Theaetetus's definition of knowledge as true belief.

rejected, and hence the above distinction, when applied to beliefs, is not to be taken as a distinction between two ways of knowing, the distinction still stands as an important one. Plato now has the language to say that when the philosopher comes to know, she 'has' what she has always possessed.

Independent of the inerrancy criterion of knowledge, it should be obvious that the knowledge that the disembodied soul possesses is not to be identified as something like an encyclopedic knowledge of all the propositional truths knowable. As countless scholars have pointed out, if this were the case, the acquisition of that knowledge, far from explaining how we embodied animals can know, would be equally opaque. If, though, we add the inerrancy criterion, the radical distinction between knowledge and belief in *Republic*, and the rejection of the definition of knowledge as true belief in *Theaetetus*, it appears likely that knowledge for Plato is not of propositions, and knowledge itself is not a propositional attitude. For if it were, it would be possible to have different propositional attitudes in regard to the same proposition, i.e., knowledge and belief, counter to Plato's explicit claim that their objects are different. Moreover, as Plato argues, and as philosophers, generally, assume, the fact that someone believes a proposition to be true does not entail that the proposition is true. But if knowledge is to be inerrant, and it is to be a propositional attitude, whatever it is that would turn mere belief into knowledge would have to leave intact the fact that if one knows the proposition, then this *does* entail that the proposition is true. In other words, the knowledge could not be a belief at all. And it could not be possible to say, "I know but I could be mistaken." For all these reasons, and in fact many more, there is no sound basis for thinking that Plato held knowledge to be other than immediate and nonpropositional.

Let us next note that knowledge is viewed by all Platonists as the pinnacle of cognition.[45] It is what philosophers seek; indeed, the desire for it is what distinguishes philosophers from everyone else. If knowledge is inerrant, it does not just happen to be so. It is necessarily so. This is because the only mode of cognition that attains that which is really real inerrantly is what, for Plato, knowledge is. Or, to put it slightly differently, the only way of attaining the really real is to attain it inerrantly. For to attain it otherwise, say, by a belief, one first has to refer to or designate that which is the object of belief. But for intelligibles, one could do this only by grasping them. One cannot believe something about Forms unless one already knows them.[46] And if one knows them, what would the belief amount to, since beliefs are only of 'what is and is not at the same time (ἅμα)'? If the ne plus ultra of cognition must then only be of intelligible reality, or of Forms, and if the

---

45. Sometimes, as for Aristotle, the term used for the highest mode of cognition is νόησις (the activity of νοῦς) instead of ἐπιστήμη. See Gerson 2009, chap. 4, for some of the terminological issues.

46. Even a belief that Forms exist or even that the Idea of the Good exists is not a belief *about* Forms. Vogt (2012, 64) argues that Plato "must find room for the deficient application of belief to intelligible objects." There is, however, no textual warrant for this claim.

only way to cognize intelligible reality is by knowing it, then a commitment to the elements of UP has, to say the least, extraordinarily broad implications. To maintain that skepticism about what is assumed to be the highest mode of cognition is false means quite a lot when the analysis of this mode of cognition yields the above two criteria. And when it is further assumed that knowledge will require grasping of what is ultimately autoexplicable ('unhypothetical' in *Republic*), the connection with the antinominalism, antimechanism, antimaterialism, and antirelativism of UP begins to emerge. I mean that these elements begin to appear to be mutually supporting pillars of the Platonic edifice.

Let us now return to the issue of how the Good is supposed to make Forms knowable. Most of what is written on this passage in *Republic*, when the specific claim about the Good is noted at all, generally evades the issue. No doubt, in some sense the Idea of the Good makes knowledge of Forms a desirable thing. No doubt, it also makes Forms, such as those of the virtues, good. But the text is quite specific in claiming that the Idea of the Good makes the Forms cognizable, which in this context, as explained above, means knowable. And that is something else. I submit that this claim is and will always remain utterly opaque unless we explicate it in terms of Aristotle's testimony about the reduction of Forms to the One and the Indefinite Dyad.[47] Regardless of the details of how this works, it is only if the Forms are themselves derived from and thus ultimately explicable by the autoexplicable Good that it makes sense to claim that the Good is what makes them knowable. As we have seen, to possess the ne plus ultra of cognition is to see a unity behind or over some 'many.' It is also to grasp the autoexplicable as cause of the heteroexplicable. To have knowledge of Forms, or of Form-Numbers, is to grasp what they are expressions of, namely, the operation of the One on the Indefinite Dyad.

I readily concede that the Indefinite Dyad makes no appearance in this passage in *Republic* and that the identification of the Good with the One is only marginally more secure on the basis of the text alone.[48] So set aside the Indefinite Dyad and consider only the Good as Plato presents it. It is not its goodness that makes Forms knowable; that is, if anything, what makes them desirable. Consider the oddness involved in claiming that to know, say, Justice, one must have a vision of its goodness. Would not one first have to know Justice *before* knowing any of its properties? And if grasping that Justice is good is a prerequisite for knowing Justice, it is, of course, also

---

47. See Szlezák 2003, 128, on the necessity for adducing the identification of the Good with the One in order to make sense of the characteristics of the former in *Republic*.

48. I mean that, independent of Aristotle's testimony, the role of unity as an ideal in *Republic* does lend some support to the accuracy of that testimony. See Vegetti 2003, 278–79, who denies the accuracy of Aristotle's testimony on the grounds that the Good is 'above' οὐσία and 'oneness' seems to be an οὐσία. But if oneness were an οὐσία, that would presumably be a quantitative essence, whereas in fact one is a principle of number and not a number itself.

a prerequisite for knowing, say, Beauty or Triangularity.[49] Apart from the hopelessness of the claim that one must know that Triangularity is good before one can know Triangularity, how is grasping this unique principle supposed to help us in dialectic? Is it not rather the case that whatever we call this first principle, if it is to be the explanation for the knowability of Forms, must function in some way like the way that the One is said by Aristotle to function? Only, I believe, if the Good is in fact the One as principle of number does the claim have a chance of making any sense. As for the Indefinite Dyad, we may recall that Speusippus called this 'Multiplicity.' We may also recall that he is reported as holding that god is Intellect and different from the One. The relation between Intellect and Multiplicity or the Indefinite Dyad comes to be thematized in later Platonism. It is only speculation, but it seems to me not implausible that Speusippus should have connected Intellect and Multiplicity in some way.[50] If this is so, he was actively engaged in working out the Platonic project. I will develop this theme later in the book.

Returning to the role of the Good/One, it is, as our passage tells us, not only the explanation for the knowability of Forms, but the cause of their existence and essence. Once again, if the Idea of the Good is meant to indicate a property of the Forms, is there any sense at all in saying that this property is the cause of the existence and essence of each Form? On the contrary, what makes the One also the Good is that it is this cause. It is the cause of the Form-Numbers, not as a unit, but as what these Form-Numbers are virtually.

The major epistemological problem facing this view is that if knowing Forms requires 'grasping' the Good/One as a first principle, then how is it possible to know one Form without knowing them all? Since the Good/One is absolutely simple and 'beyond οὐσία,' grasping it in relation to one Form cannot be different from grasping it in relation to another. It cannot, for example, be a matter of grasping one 'aspect' of it for one Form and another 'aspect' for another. It appears that there is a sort of holism embedded in Plato's epistemology.[51] And yet this holism is at least in tension with the description of the dialectical descent from the Good/One:

> Having grasped this principle [the Good/One], it goes back, holding that which follows from it, it proceeds in this way to a conclusion, making no use of

---

49. It is true that we read at *Rep.* 505A2-4: ἐπεὶ ὅτι γε ἡ τοῦ ἀγαθοῦ ἰδέα μέγιστον μάθημα, πολλάκις ἀκήκοας, ᾗ δὴ καὶ δίκαια καὶ τἆλλα προσχρησάμενα χρήσιμα καὶ ὠφέλιμα γίγνεται (that the investigation of the Idea of the Good is the greatest study you have heard many times, and that just things and others become useful and beneficial by their relation to it). But the Idea of the Good is the explanation for the existence, essence, and knowability of *all* the Forms, not just those that represent virtues or values. That the 'greatest study' is of the Good does not imply that it has an οὐσία.

50. Cf. Halfwassen 1993, 357–72.

51. See *Phdr.* 247D5–E2: ἐν δὲ τῇ περιόδῳ καθορᾷ μὲν αὐτὴν δικαιοσύνην, καθορᾷ δὲ σωφροσύνην, καθορᾷ δὲ ἐπιστήμην, οὐχ ᾗ γένεσις πρόσεστιν, οὐδ' ἥ ἐστίν που ἑτέρα ἐν ἑτέρῳ οὖσα ὧν ἡμεῖς νῦν ὄντων καλοῦμεν, ἀλλὰ τὴν ἐν τῷ ὅ ἐστιν ὂν ὄντως ἐπιστήμην οὖσαν· (In the circumambulation, [the soul] sees Justice itself and it sees Self-Control, and it

sensibles at all, but only of Forms themselves, going through Forms to Forms, and ending in Forms.[52]

How does one "go through" Forms without knowing them already? And if one knows them already, what need is there to go through them? If we are to make any sense of this passage, we must first of all distinguish the dialectical ascent and descent, which are both constituted by λόγος, or reasoning, from any grasping itself.[53] What the philosopher actually practices when engaged in dialectic is a discursive representation of what is knowable to himself and to others. He operates in the interstice between 'possessing' the knowable and 'having' it. The grasping is, from top to bottom, as it were, comprehensive or complete. There is no grasping any Form without grasping them all.

Let us be clear that the cognition of, say, what a triangle is or what a line is, is specifically excluded from the realm of knowledge by Plato.[54] Grasping a Form is not to be confused with what mathematicians do when they hypothesize geometrical or arithmetic intelligible entities. They regard these as things they know (εἰδότες), but they really are not known by them. So there is no possibility of taking knowledge to be cognition of the propositions that are definitions in geometry and arithmetic. What knowing is must be the simultaneous grasping of the array of products of the One operating on the Indefinite Dyad.

The peculiar status of the Decad (numbers up to ten) and the Pythagorean Tetraktys (1-2-3-4, the sum of which is the Decad) in Plato and Platonism is probably relevant here.[55] The scrap of evidence that Speusippus identified

---

sees Knowledge—not the knowledge that occurs with becoming, and not the knowledge that varies as it knows different things which we consider real here below, but the knowledge of what really is.) I take it that the 'knowledge' here below is knowledge only in a loose sense, a sense corrected in *Republic*. Real knowledge is in some sense holistic, because though different Forms are known, the knowledge is not different (ἑτέρα) for each. I doubt that this means that whereas there are different kinds of knowledge here below (e.g., astronomy, mathematics, biology), there is only one kind in the intelligible realm. For whatever would make these sciences different would presumably also make the knowledge of, say, the virtues different from the knowledge of the mathematical Forms. Rather, it seems that the knowledge of all the Forms is supposed to be one, that is, in knowing each Form, we know one and the same thing. Understood thus, the description of dialectic in the Divided Line in *Republic* provides an explication of the *Phaedrus* passage.

52. *Rep.* 511B7–C2: ἁψάμενος αὐτῆς, πάλιν αὖ ἐχόμενος τῶν ἐκείνης ἐχομένων, οὕτως ἐπὶ τελευτὴν καταβαίνῃ, αἰσθητῷ παντάπασιν οὐδενὶ προσχρώμενος, ἀλλ' εἴδεσιν αὐτοῖς δι' αὐτῶν εἰς αὐτά, καὶ τελευτᾷ εἰς εἴδη.

53. The verbs of motion—ἰών, ἐχόμενος, καταβαίνῃ, τελευτᾷ—stand in contrast to the actual grasping, which is the achievement.

54. *Rep.* 510C1–D3.

55. For Aristotle's testimony that Plato posited numbers only up to ten, see *Phys.* Γ 6, 206b32. Cf. *Meta.* Λ 8, 1073a19–21; Λ 8, 1084a10–13; M 8, 1084a29–31. See Findlay 1978, 40, for an interpretation of the relevant passages according to which 1+2+3+4 = 10 refers to the Tetraktys consisting of integer (1), line (2), surface (3), plane (4), serially derived by projection or 'fluxion.'

the Decad with the Living Animal in *Timaeus* is revealing.⁵⁶ For it seems that Plato associates the elements of the cosmos with 'shapes or magnitudes and numbers.' Speusippus, apparently explicating this insight, held that one is the principle of number, two of lines, three of planes, and four of solids. That is, the Tetraktys is the principle of the shapes or magnitudes and numbers that the Demiurge imposes on the receptacle. Presumably, the ideal ratios of numbers that the Demiurge employs to construct the classes of entities in the cosmos are the 'result' of the Demiurge's eternally achieving the Good by knowing what it is virtually.⁵⁷ Thus, the comprehensiveness of knowledge consists in grasping the array of Forms as owing their existence, essence, and knowability to the One, that is, as grasping the reductive unity of the Tetraktys.

In Speusippus, this comprehensiveness appears as the claim that the knowledge of any species requires the knowledge of how it differs from every other species. Aristotle explains this view thus:

> Now he who is to form a definition or divide [a genus] need not know all things. Yet some assert that it is impossible to know the differences between a thing and each of the others without the knowledge of all things and that one cannot know each thing without [knowing] its differentiae; for, according to them, a thing is identical with another thing from which it does not differ, but it is distinct from a thing from which it differs.⁵⁸

The argument Aristotle attributes to Speusippus is that to know A, one must know how it differs from that with which A is not identical, which is everything that is not A. But to know how A differs from any B is to know how B differs from A, since difference is a reciprocal relation.⁵⁹ Aristotle, then, objects that a differentia (διάφορα) is not the same thing as difference (ἑτερότης).⁶⁰ If, for example, 'rational' is the differentia of human, one does not have to know the differentia of fish, though one knows that fish are different from humans.

---

56. See Ps.-Iamblichus, *Theologoumena Arithmeticae*, fr. 28 Tarán, especially lines 11–14. Cf. Plato, *Tim.* 30C–31B, 39E–40A. Dancy (1991, 106–7) points out that the properties of the Decad that make it 'perfect' (it has as many odds as evens; it has as many primes and incomposites as secondaries and composites; it has in it as many multiples as submultiples) require that one be considered a number. This reinforces the interpretation according to which the One is not a number or the principle of number, that is, the unit.

57. Cf. *Rep.* 500C4–5 on the Forms: κόσμῳ δὲ πάντα καὶ κατὰ λόγον ἔχοντα. The words κατὰ λόγον indicate proportion and the word κόσμῳ indicates an ideal proportion. See Krämer 1964a, 198–99.

58. See *Post. An.* B 13, 97a6–11 = fr. 63a Tarán: οὐδὲν δὲ δεῖ τὸν ὁριζόμενον καὶ διαιρούμενον ἅπαντα εἰδέναι τὰ ὄντα. καίτοι ἀδύνατόν φασί τινες εἶναι τὰς διαφορὰς εἰδέναι τὰς πρὸς ἕκαστον μὴ εἰδότα ἕκαστον· ἄνευ δὲ τῶν διαφορῶν οὐκ εἶναι ἕκαστον εἰδέναι· οὗ γὰρ μὴ διαφέρει, ταὐτὸν εἶναι τούτῳ, οὗ δὲ διαφέρει, ἕτερον τούτου. See Tarán 1981 on the attribution of this view to Speusippus.

59. Cf. Plato, *Parm.* 143B1–2, 147E3–148A3; *Soph.* 254D14–15.

60. Cf. *Meta.* I 3, 1054b23.

This reply seems decisive, but it ignores the claims that knowledge is only of intelligibles and intelligibles are postulated to be mathematical in nature. So let us consider a mathematical example. Is it the case that to know the differentia of a triangle one must know the differentia of every other plane figure? To put it in other terms, can one know what a triangle is and know that a square is different from a triangle without knowing what a square is? Suppose one answers in the affirmative. Then the obvious response of Speusippus is to deny that one then knows that the square is different. That is, he would deny that one *knows* it, not merely believes it. What is the plausibility of this? One can be taught to identify a square or name it on sight; similarly, one can be taught to distinguish a triangle from a square. But this has nothing to do with knowledge. Recall that for Plato, even mathematicians do not have knowledge of triangles and squares. The mode of cognition they possess, which Plato calls διάνοια, is not knowledge. Knowing a square could not be identical with correctly identifying it, even if doing so is a cognitive achievement of some sort

Notice that I used the phrase "know what triangularity is," which, as we have already seen, makes knowledge seem to be a propositional attitude. But it is not that for Plato and very likely not for Speusippus. Knowing triangularity is more like acquaintance with it. This, however, seems to make the holistic doctrine even more implausible: Why should having acquaintance with triangularity be impossible unless one has acquaintance with all other plane figures? The answer is, I believe, that the acquaintance is with the Good/One as the unity behind the diversity of geometrical figures and numbers, and with the Indefinite Dyad as the principle of extensive magnitude. In terms of the second hypothesis of the second part of *Parmenides*, the one being is unlimited in multitude. And on the Platonic assumption that the first hypothesis gives us the first principle of all, it is from the latter operating on the former that the diversity of intelligible reality is derived. Knowing any one aspect of this requires being acquainted with the derivation. It does not mean knowing all the properties of triangles or squares; that is the purview of the mathematician.

In *Theaetetus*, epistemological holism seems to emerge in Socrates' examination of Theaetetus's definition of knowledge as true belief plus an account. In the second version of what an account is, Theaetetus claims that knowledge is the enumeration of the elementary parts of something.[61] Socrates argues that an enumeration of the elements of a complex cannot amount to knowledge because knowing the putative elements requires knowing them as they appear in any complex. The example Socrates gives is rather odd. One cannot be said to know the first syllable of the names 'Theaetetus' and 'Theodorus' if one thinks that in the first case it is 'The' but in the second case 'Te.' Many scholars have supposed that the example is inept because it is, of course, possible to cognize in some sense that 'The' is the

---

61. *Tht.* 206E–208B.

first syllable of 'Theaetetus' but not cognize in some sense that it is also the first syllable of 'Theodorus.'[62] But the point is that this would not be knowledge; it would be a case of getting the right answer or true belief, which has already been eliminated as a candidate for knowledge. The point of the argument seems to be rather that if one *could* have knowledge of the syllable 'The,' that would amount to seeing or grasping it wherever it appears.[63] This is, I take it, analogous to the claim that knowing Triangularity is grasping the One as virtually that.

Holism is, I am claiming, a property of ἐπιστήμη, as this analysis of *Theaetetus* shows. That is, given the tenet of UP that knowledge is possible, that 'knowledge' stands for a real human state, and that it is not merely a word or a concept, an analysis of knowledge proceeds according to the criteria that knowledge be of what is and that it be inerrant or infallible. The criteria are defining criteria and are mutually implicative. That is, it is not possible to have cognition of what is that is not infallible and it is not possible to have infallible cognition that is not of what is. The incorrigibility of sense perception is not infallibility; the propositional attitudes that have as objects propositions purportedly 'about' what is do not amount to cognition of what is.

Join this analysis to the explicit account of the role of the Idea of the Good in relation to all the Forms and to Aristotle's testimony that this Idea is the One. Consequent on this is the reduction of Forms to Numbers. The ne plus ultra of cognition is ἐπιστήμη and it is of 'what is,' namely, the Forms, but only in relation to the One. Within this framework, the alternative to holism is that one could possibly 'know' the elements of the three-sided plane figure without knowing the elements of the four-sided plane figure, five-sided plane figure, etc. But since the 'generation' of the geometrical Forms consists in an iteration of the application of the One to the Indefinite Dyad, such putatively 'partial knowledge' would suggest a failure to grasp what *any* iteration of that application amounts to.[64]

---

62. Cf. McDowell 1973, 252; Burnyeat 1990, 209–18.

63. 'Appears' here would indicate visual or auditory appearance. So if you knew the syllable 'The' and then heard 'Theodorus' being spoken, you would grasp what is in fact the first syllable as 'The.' There is an extremely important clue here to help explain why Plato would ever use ἐπιστήμη of anything in the sensible world given that ἐπιστήμη is of Forms. One who has the latter, could, in a sense, be said to have knowledge of the presence of instances of Forms. Thus, if one knew the Form of Piety, one could know that a particular action had this property, but one could know this only hypothetically—if *this* is pious, then it has the properties of Piety. In this case there would be an immediate inference from what Aristotle in the Square of Opposition calls a universal 'A' proposition to a particular 'I' proposition.

64. In *Seventh Ep.*, 344D9–E2, Plato is questioning the motives of anyone—especially Dionysios—who purports to write a treatise on Plato's first principles. There is no good motive for having done so, because οὔτε γὰρ ὑπομνημάτων χάριν ἔγραψεν—οὐδὲν γὰρ δεινὸν μή τις αὐτὸ ἐπιλάθηται, ἐὰν ἅπαξ τῇ ψυχῇ περιλάβῃ· πάντων γὰρ ἐν βραχυτάτοις κεῖται (nor can he have written them down for the sake of remembrance; for there is no danger of their being forgotten if the soul has grasped them altogether since they are contained in the shortest formula). The word ἅπαξ ("altogether" or "at once") does not here indicate a time at which the cognition occurred, but should be taken with περιλάβῃ, indicating a comprehensive or holistic cognitive event. If this *Letter* is genuine, these words seem to support the present

Speusippus's epistemological holism was evidently applied or supposed to be applicable to biological classifications, where it is implausible in the extreme.[65] It may be, as Dillon argues, that Speusippus is in fact presenting a *reductio* argument for the impossibility of ἐπιστήμη of sensible reality.[66] It seems to me more likely that Speusippus is addressing an issue that continually occupied Plato, namely, what sort of cognition can we have of the sensible realm given that knowledge is infallible cognition only of that which is intelligible. To say, as Plato repeatedly does, that the sort of cognition we can have is called δόξα is not so much to answer the question as to label a response to it. For it is not δόξα simpliciter that we aspire to possess, of course, but *true* δόξα, or at the very least, rational or well-grounded δόξα. That is what philosophers, educated in Plato's ideal system, purport to be able to bring to and use to justify their political rule. But since, for Plato, the essences of biological entities are separate from them, which is to say that these entities themselves do not as such have essences, the acute problem is how to attain a rational classificatory schema, or what it would even mean to attain a true one. The profound skeptical challenge to Platonism consists in the claim that if Plato is right in his analysis of knowledge, then there is in fact no such thing as a rational classificatory schema; indeed, there is no such thing as rational belief. As later Platonists will contend, if, after all, belief can be justified and a classificatory schema can be found that does not rely on arbitrary assumptions, then these will most likely be found in the works of Aristotle. Thus was Aristotle put in the service of Platonism.[67]

The holism, traces of which are found in the dialogues and in the fragments of Speusippus, is perhaps the inevitable result of an attempt to construct a unified metaphysical system along with a consideration of what knowledge must be if it is different from mere belief. To make knowledge, the ne plus ultra of cognition, a potentially encyclopedic grasp of propositions is to undermine the highly unified structure that is being posited. To do *that* is to threaten to destroy the system's explanatory adequacy, which is as much as to concede to the materialists, mechanists, relativists, and nominalists that their alternative explanations (or renunciation of explanations) are more or less capable of being legitimated.

---

interpretation. If it is a forgery, it demonstrates the holistic line of argument taken by early Platonists. The holism is the necessity for grasping the unity of intelligible reality, the starting point for the positive construct out of UP.

65. See Aristotle, *PA* A 2, 642b5–644a11 = fr. 67 Tarán. Tarán (1981, 397) identifies the unnamed proponent of dichotomous division as Speusippus. But as Lennox (2001, 152–53) argues, the criticisms Aristotle makes apply equally well to Plato's later dialogues.

66. See Dillon 2003, 80.

67. See Simplicius, *In Cat.* 6.19–32, for the later Platonic distinction between the starting points of Plato and Aristotle and the latter's universally acknowledged preeminence in matters pertaining to nature.

Xenocrates

According to Diogenes Laertius, Xenocrates, the successor to Speusippus as head of the Old Academy, wrote over seventy works, comprising in total about a quarter of a million *lines*, none of which survive, even in fragmentary form. He served for some twenty-five years in his position—whatever that means exactly—until he died in 314/313. Simplicius refers to a work of his on the life of Plato (not mentioned by Diogenes), and calls him the "most authentic" (γνησιώτατος) of Plato's disciples.[68] Judging from the titles of his works, he wrote on the full range of philosophical topics canvassed in the dialogues. According to Sextus Empiricus, he was the first to explicitly divide the study of philosophy into physics, ethics, and logic, a division followed within Hellenistic philosophy generally.[69] This division suggests to some that Xenocrates was the first systematizer of Platonism.[70] Most of what we know in regard to his philosophical positions is owing to critics or expositors of Academic philosophy who, like Aristotle and Plutarch, sometimes distinguish the view of Xenocrates from those of Plato or Speusippus. We have a slightly better idea of what his position was on physics, including first principles, than on any other topic. It is with this that we will be concerned.

Aëtius preserves for us a doxographical report that is the starting point for any consideration of his version of Platonism:

> Xenocrates, son of Agathenor, of Chalcedon, [believes] the Monad and the Dyad are gods, the former as male having the position of father, ruling in heaven, which he termed "Zeus" and "odd" and "intellect," which is for him the primary god; the latter as female, in the manner of mother of the gods, ruling over the realm below heaven, which is for him the soul of the universe.[71]

The testimony is difficult on many counts, as scholars have long recognized.[72] It seems to make of the second principle, the Dyad, or "the mother of the gods," the soul of the universe as well. But as we learn from Plutarch, Xenocrates held that soul is the secondary *product* of the Monad and the Dyad

---

68. Simplicius, *In Arist. DC* 12.23 = fr. 265 Isnardi Parente (IP) (1982). D.L. (5.1.6) uses the same honorific term for Aristotle. Cf. Ps.-Galen, *Hist. Phil.* 3.18 = *Dox. Gr.* 599.16f. referring to Xenocrates: τῶν Πλατωνικῶν δογμάτων ἐξηγητήν.

69. See Sextus, *M.* 7.16 = fr. 82 IP.

70. See, e.g., Dillon 2003, 98. Dillon (2010a, 128) speculates that the suggestion, originally made by Alline (1915, 50–56), that Xenocrates produced the first "edition" of all the works of Plato, is "an entirely probable conjecture."

71. Aëtius 1.7.30, p.304 (Diels) = fr. 213IP: Ξενοκράτης Ἀγαθήνορος Καλχηδόνιος τὴν μονάδα καὶ τὴν δυάδα θεούς, τὴν μὲν ὡς ἄρρενα πατρὸς ἔχουσαν τάξιν ἐν οὐρανῷ βασιλεύουσαν, ἥντινα προσαγορεύει καὶ Ζῆνα καὶ περιττὸν καὶ νοῦν, ὅστις ἐστὶν αὐτῷ πρῶτος θεός· τὴν δ' ὡς θήλειαν, μητρὸς θεῶν δίκην, τῆς ὑπὸ τὸν οὐρανὸν λήξεως ἡγουμένην, ἥτις ἐστὶν αὐτῷ ψυχὴ τοῦ παντός.

72. See Krämer 1964a; 2nd ed. 1967, 21–45, 119–26; Baltes 1988, 223–46; Dillon 2003, 102ff. Dillon is particularly skeptical about the accuracy of the testimony.

plus a 'mixture' of self-sameness or identity and difference. The primary product is number.[73] It is not certain whether the report of Aëtius is garbled or even whether Xenocrates himself made conflicting claims in regard to the first principles. For our purposes, what is central is the identification of the first principles of nature with the Monad and the Dyad, and Xenocrates' further identification of the former with Intellect. In addition, as Plutarch testifies, these two principles produce number. Whether the Dyad is supposed by Xenocrates to be a soul or whether it is the principle of soul is a further matter, perhaps beyond determination on the basis of the texts alone.

The identification of the first principle as intellect and 'first god' and 'father' naturally recalls *Timaeus*, where the Demiurge is explicitly called 'father,' is apparently the first 'god,' and is implicitly referred to as Intellect.[74] But even if we accept the Aristotelian evidence that for Platonists the first principles of all are the One and the Indefinite Dyad and that 'Monad' is another name for 'One,' it is far from obvious that the One is identical with the Demiurge. If, moreover, the One is the Idea of the Good, and the Good, as *Republic* tells us, is 'beyond' the Forms, how can it be the case that the Demiurge is both identical with the One *and* apparently identical with Forms?[75] Supposing that Xenocrates wishes to be a competent 'exegete' of Platonic doctrines, whence the confusion?[76]

Leaving aside for a moment the mathematical dimension of all this, the fourfold functionality of the principles of Demiurge, or a divine intellect, Forms, and One or Good and soul is, we recall, collapsed by Aristotle into the unique, absolutely simple Unmoved Mover.[77] The re-expansion of these

---

73. See Plutarch, *De proc. an. in Tim.* I, 1012E–F = fr. 188 (IP).

74. For 'father,' see *Tim.* 28C3, 37C7, 41A7; for 'first' or 'primary god,' see esp. 30D3, 69B3; for Intellect, see 39E7, 48A1. Cf. *Crat.* 396A7f. See below, chap. 7, on this question, much disputed within Middle Platonism.

75. See *Tim.* 29E1–3 and 30C2–D1, which, taken together, seem to imply that the Demiurge is at least cognitively identical with the 'Living Animal' that in some sense 'contains' all the Forms. Also, 36E5–37A2, where the Demiurge is apparently the 'best,' that is, the maker of the soul of the universe and other intelligibles (τῶν νοητῶν ἀεί τε ὄντων ὑπὸ τοῦ ἀρίστου). The Demiurge wanted to make the world "near to resembling himself" (παραπλήσια ἑαυτῷ) and so he made the world "to be the same as" (ὁμοιῶσαι) the Living Animal. Cf. Krämer 1964a, 379; Perl 1998; Ferrari 2003a. Cherniss (1944, 603–10) argues that the intellect of the Demiurge must be *in* a soul and that soul is necessarily subordinate to the Forms. But even if the Demiurge is or has a soul in some sense because it is alive, it seems clear enough that it cannot be identified with the soul of the universe it creates. See Halfwassen 2000, 43–44.

76. See Baltes 1999, 194, n. 7, for a helpful survey of the ancient Platonic tradition revealing the confusion. Aëtius 1.7.20, claims that Speusippus rejects the identification of Intellect with the One and the Good.

77. See Krämer 1964; 2nd ed. 1967, 188–91, for an illuminating comparison between the Xenocratean Monad and the Aristotelian Unmoved Mover. Theophrastus, *Meta.* 4b18ff., explores the problems with a first principle of all that operates only as an object of desire. One of the central difficulties is that a unique final cause does not seem to be able to explain all the various circular motions of the heavens. Another is that imitation of the Unmoved Mover should not produce motion but rather rest.

by all Platonists after Aristotle into the puzzling configurations seen in Xenocrates and others is at once indicative of a recognition of the ineliminability of the functions and of the difficulty of relating them. The locus of Plato's doctrine of principles or the unwritten teachings may be situated precisely within or among these desiderata.[78]

The difficulty of whether Intellect is identical with the absolutely first principle or derived somehow from it is mirrored by the difficulty of whether Intellect itself is or has a soul or whether the principle Soul is derived from it. On the one hand, the Demiurge of *Timaeus* makes the soul of the universe, which suggests that Soul is derived; yet the Demiurge, if identical with the Living Animal, would seem to have a soul.[79] Aristotle's argument for the absolute simplicity of the first principle must have been taken as confirmation of the argument in the first hypothesis of the second part of *Parmenides* as interpreted by Speusippus and later Platonists.[80] Given such simplicity, one does not know quite what to do with a multiplicity of Forms, and a divine Intellect that makes a cosmos according to the complex pattern of intelligible reality. And yet, to *subordinate* Intellect or the Demiurge or Zeus (!) to a 'higher' principle seems impossible or, perhaps more cogently, counterproductive. Either Intellect is an ultimate explanation or it is not; if it is not, exactly what explanatory role does it serve?[81]

The positing of Intellect is quite obviously a linchpin in the entire enterprise.[82] I would suggest, however, that we possess sufficient evidence—from Aristotle, Speusippus, and even, indirectly, from Xenocrates himself—to indicate that the motive for positing the principles of One and Indefinite

---

78. See Thiel 2006, 228–30, who shows that Xenocrates' construction of a version of Platonism is based on both the dialogues and the oral tradition.

79. See *Phil.* 30C9–10: Σοφία μὴν καὶ νοῦς ἄνευ ψυχῆς οὐκ ἄν ποτε γενοίσθην (Wisdom and intellect could never come to be without soul), with 28D–E. Cf. *Soph.* 248E6–249A2. The identical issue surrounds the Unmoved Mover, which is pure intellection yet seems to have a life. See *Meta.* Λ 7, 1076b26–27: ἡ γὰρ νοῦ ἐνέργεια ζωή, ἐκεῖνος [the Unmoved Mover] δὲ ἐνέργεια (the activity of intellect is life, and the Unmoved Mover is that activity).

80. See the seminal article by Miller (1995) on the presence of the elements of Aristotle's account of Plato's unwritten teachings in the second part of *Parmenides*.

81. Plato's *Second Ep.* reveals an important aspect of the problem, *especially* if it is spurious. For in this letter, 312E1–4, the author, expressing his (Plato's or his imitator's) view of the basic principles of the universe, says: περὶ τὸν πάντων βασιλέα πάντ' ἐστὶ καὶ ἐκείνου ἕνεκα πάντα, καὶ ἐκεῖνο αἴτιον ἁπάντων τῶν καλῶν· δεύτερον δὲ πέρι τὰ δεύτερα, καὶ τρίτον πέρι τὰ τρίτα (upon the king of all do all things turn; all things are on account of him and he is the cause of all things beautiful. And things of the second order turn upon the second principle, and things of the third upon the third.) Is the 'king of all' the Demiurge (Intellect) or is it the One?

82. Cf. Baltes (1999, 235–41), who, referring mainly to Middle Platonic material, holds that "the central dogmas" of Platonism center on the soul rather than on intellect. Among these are free choice, the eternity of the world, reincarnation, gradation of reality, and the location of Forms in the intelligible world. I will argue in chap. 7 that the Middle Platonic teachings about soul are a specification or application of the larger Platonic issues hitherto canvassed.

Dyad or Monad and Dyad is in Plato not separable from reflection on the nature of intellect.

The account of both human and divine intellect in *Republic*, *Timaeus*, and *Philebus* moves back and forth from its practical or productive to its contemplative or theoretical role.[83] In its former role, it orders or produces according to the intelligible pattern it contemplates in its latter role. No one in the Platonic tradition supposes that this contemplation is a representation or reproduction of the intelligible pattern. On the contrary, contemplator and objects of contemplation are cognitively identical. Paradigmatically, intelligible and intellect are inseparable, as Aristotle so clearly saw. In a Platonic hierarchical framework, the hypothesis that representations or images of intelligibles will also be found inseparable from representations or images of intellect easily follows. That which possesses intelligible structure such as nonhuman animals and plants, though apparently bereft of intellect, still manifests the intellectual goal-directed activity of the principle Intellect.

Plato's account of intellect in relation to soul is more complex. Part of the reason for this is no doubt that throughout the dialogues we can witness a gradual clarification of the concepts for indicating cognitive powers and faculties in relation to other life functions. In *Phaedo*, the Recollection Argument implies that the principal or perhaps sole activity of the disembodied soul is knowledge (ἐπιστήμη).[84] Insofar as 'soul' (ψυχή) is the common term for that which produces life activities in general, it would seem to follow that knowing is such an activity and therefore cannot exist outside of or apart from soul. Yet in *Timaeus*, though the Demiurge engages in life activity including thought and willing, and evidently has or is an intellect, it is said to produce the soul of the universe. So it is not clear if its life activity is to be attributed to something strictly other than soul, or if it possesses or is a soul of a different sort. The matter is not resolved in *Laws* where 'intellectual motion' (κίνησις νοῦ) seems to be distinguished from and superior to all 'psychic motion.'[85] I take it that Aristotle's blunt statement in *De anima* that "intellect is a *genos* different from soul" represents the final Academic determination of the terminological issue.[86]

Yet for proponents of UP (including Aristotle), this hardly settles the philosophical issue. As a subject of modes of cognition other than intellection, like sense perception, imagination, belief, and so on, it is not at all clear how one with a soul is able to access the life of that which belongs to another *genos*. This difficulty is, principally, what underlies the obscurity of

---

83. On the fecundity of the analogy between human and divine souls in the Platonic tradition, see Gersh 1986, 77ff., 84ff.

84. See *Phd.* 72E3–78B3.

85. See *Lg.* 897D3 and *Tim.* 89A1–3. Cf. Baltes 1999, 200.

86. See *DA* B 2, 413b25–26: ἀλλ' ἔοικε [νοῦς] ψυχῆς γένος ἕτερον εἶναι. Cf. B 3, 415a11–12. This generically different νοῦς, which is said to be possibly immortal *because* of its difference, is to be distinguished from "the so-called intellect" (ὁ καλούμενος νοῦς) at Γ 4, 429a22–24, which is a faculty of the soul.

De anima 3.5. Again, from a Platonic perspective, the conceptual tools are available for *grading* intellectual activity and other types of activity, including psychic activity, so that intellection is the paradigmatic life and activity and other modes of cognition are inferior versions of this. This approach is in fact much more explicit in Aristotle than it is in Plato; and later Platonists showed no hesitation in employing the Aristotelian version of the gradation to represent the Platonic position.[87]

What does this account of intellect have to do with the positing of the principles of the One and the Indefinite Dyad? First, the irreducible functionalities of both One and Indefinite Dyad—analogous to the functionality of form and matter for Aristotle, at least in the sublunary context—have to be deployed in accounting for the eternal contemplation by Intellect of a plurality of intelligible objects. This is so because Intellect could not be cognitively identical with a plurality of monadic objects if it were not apt for their reception. If there were not within Intellect a principle other than a principle of unity, its cognitive identification with these objects would make *them* identical with *it*, thereby negating their plurality. At the same time, without a principle that functions as does the One, each intelligible object could not be the one thing that Intellect achieves cognitively, that is, the 'one' over and above the 'many' that Intellect 'sees.' So whether One and Indefinite Dyad are above Intellect or whether the first is and the second is not or whether Intellect is identical with the first and the second is subordinated to the first, where, as a result, intellection really occurs, is a matter for dispute.[88] As we will see, the particular configuration of Intellect and Soul as principles and their relation to the One and the Indefinite Dyad will be determined for each philosopher according to additional considerations.

Second, as we have seen, the reduction of Forms to the One and the Indefinite Dyad is a mathematical hypothesis, specifically the hypothesis that intelligibility is a mathematical concept.[89] To make Zeus the Monad and Rhea the Dyad is at once to signal some sort of priority for the former and

---

87. See *EN* K 7, 1177b26–1178a4. Cf. I 4, 1166a22–23; I 8, 1169a2 on the 'intellect' as being 'really' what we are. It should be noted that the obscurity of the relation of intellect to soul is evident in the various positions regarding the immortality of the soul: Is it the entire soul that is immortal or only the rational part? Both Xenocrates and Speusippus seem to have maintained that the entire soul is in some sense immortal. See Damascius, *In Phd.* 1177, p. 124.13ff. Norvin (= fr. 211IP). This commentary is transmitted under the name of Olympiodorus.

88. See Dillon 2003, 105, for the last mentioned possibility. On this schema, there is an implicit division of labor between contemplative intellection and practical intellection, the latter being the activity of the soul of the universe. See also Krämer 1964a, 119–26.

89. Cf. Philolaus, fr. 4 Huffman (*ap.* Stobaeus, *Ecl.*1.2.7b = 1.188.5 Wachsmuth): Καὶ πάντα γα μὰν τὰ γιγνωσκόμενα ἀριθμὸν ἔχοντι. Οὐ γὰρ οἷον τε οὐδὲν οὔτε νοηθῆμεν οὔτε γνωσθῆμεν ἄνευ τούτου. (And indeed all the things that are cognized have number. For it is not possible for anything to be thought or cognized without this.) See Huffman 1993, 172–76, for the interpretation of this fragment, and the important evidence that 'number' includes ratios.

to claim that intellection is ultimately of Mathematical Objects, whether these be Numbers or ideal ratios of numbers.[90] It seems to me that the most plausible hypothesis that accounts for the confusion is that discussion about these matters was ongoing in the Academy up until Plato's death and that he never published (for whatever reasons) a definitive statement of his own position. What does seem clear, though, is that no one in the Academy who was interested in following Plato had the slightest inclination to abandon the One and the Indefinite Dyad or the hypostasizing of the functionality of a principle of Intellect and a principle of Soul.

Aristotle's testimony that Xenocrates claimed that Forms and Numbers have one nature (μίαν φύσιν) must be understood in this context.[91] In Aristotle's own usage, two principles can be one in reality, yet their λόγοι are plural.[92] What Xenocrates is perhaps claiming is that Forms and Numbers are identical in the divine Intellect, yet the λόγοι of Forms differ from those of Numbers when in Soul or at least when imposed on the sensible universe. So, for example, let us suppose that the Form of Humanity is identical in 'nature' with an ideal mathematical ratio or formula, whereas the λόγος of this ratio will differ from the λόγος of Humanity expressed in phenomenal terms. So it is both true that the Form of Humanity is a Number (ideal ratio of numbers) and that an account of Humanity could be given in, say, biological terms. If this is even approximately correct, Xenocrates is offering a remarkably sophisticated interpretation of Plato because that interpretation takes into account Aristotle's argument in *Metaphysics* that if there were a Form of Humanity, its λόγος would have to include the matter, meaning, roughly, that that λόγος would need to be given in phenomenal terms.[93] Humanity, as Aristotle himself would define it, is also a mathematical formula, but only in the way that the color red is a number of wavelengths of light.

One salient feature of this interpretation is that Soul becomes in a sense the place of Forms, which are in reality the Numbers with which Intellect is cognitively identical.[94] As we will see in the seventh chapter, the puzzling

---

90. Zeus should be paired with Hera, not Rhea, though Rhea is the mother of the gods, including Zeus. Dillon (2003, 104) speculates that Xenocrates, following Orphic tradition, has simply assimilated Hera to Rhea.

91. See above, n. 1, and cf. *Meta.* N 1, 1076a21.

92. See *Meta.* Δ 9, 1018a4–9 and Γ 2, 1003b22–24: εἰ δὴ τὸ ὂν καὶ τὸ ἕν ταὐτὸν καὶ μία φύσις τῷ ἀκολουθεῖν ἀλλήλοις ὥσπερ ἀρχὴ καὶ αἴτιον, ἀλλ' οὐχ ὡς ἑνὶ λόγῳ (if, in fact, being and unity are identical or one nature in the sense that they follow each other like principle and cause, but not as being one in formula).

93. See *Meta.* Z 14, 16.

94. Cf. Aristotle, *DA* Γ 3, 429a27–28, who says that those who hold that "the soul is the place of Forms" speak well, though Aristotle goes on to dispute their mode of existence in the soul. Contrary to Hicks 1907, 482, ad loc., Plato does not maintain that the soul is the place of Forms in the sense in which Socrates suggests at *Parm.* 132B–133C that Forms are just 'thoughts' (νοήματα) and so in the soul. That suggestion is decisively refuted by Parmenides. If Plato's view is indeed that the soul is the place of Forms, it is the World Soul, not the

tendency of some Middle Platonists to make Forms thoughts or concepts in a divine mind is really a consequence of a variant of the view that conflates Intellect and Soul.[95]

Thus, we seem to have some rationale for the famous definition of a Form that Proclus attributes to Xenocrates: "the paradigmatic cause of things that are continuously being constituted according to nature."[96] The natural understanding of this definition, followed consistently throughout the Platonic tradition, is that it excludes Forms of artifacts since artifacts are not constituted according to nature. If the words "according to nature" have their usual Platonic meaning, then biological monstrosities are excluded as well.[97] If we approach the intelligible world from the bottom up, so to speak, we arrive first at 'enmattered forms' (τὰ ἔνυλα εἴδη), which are instantiations of the instantiations of Forms in the World Soul. These Forms themselves are identical in their nature with the Numbers or ideal ratios with which Intellect is cognitively identical.

According to Aristotle, "by far the most unreasonable doctrine concerning the soul is that it is a number which moves itself" (ἀριθμόν κινοῦνθ' ἑαυτόν).[98] There is ample evidence that this was the position at least of Xenocrates. That he arrived at this position from his exegesis of *Timaeus* is reasonably certain. There we learn that the Demiurge made soul by combining Indivisible Being with Divisible Being and Indivisible Identity and Difference with Divisible Identity and Difference.[99] The World Soul is made first, with the highest degree of purity; the human soul after with a lesser degree of purity.[100] According to Xenocrates' exegesis of this passage,

---

individual human soul, that is at issue. But then this is only the case if these Forms are identical in nature with the intelligible aspect of Intellect or the Demiurge. See Merlan, 1953, 3rd ed. 1968, chaps. 1 and 2 on the identification of soul and mathematicals.

95. Krämer (1964a; 2nd ed. 1967, 121) believes that Xenocrates is the first philosopher to makes Forms immanent in the mind of the divine being. I think this is correct only in the sense that Xenocrates is making explicit what is in both Plato and Aristotle; he is in no way original in this respect.

96. See Proclus, *In Parm.* 888.18–19 = fr. 94 IP: αἰτίαν παραδειγματικὴν τῶν κατὰ φύσιν ἀεὶ συνεστώτων. Cf. the definition of Forms cited by D.L. (3.77): αἰτίας τινὰς καὶ ἀρχὰς τοῦ τοιαῦτ' εἶναι τὰ φύσει συνεστῶτα, οἷάπερ ἐστίν αὐτά (the Ideas are certain causes or principles of the nature of such things as are constituted by nature).

97. See, e.g., *Crat.* 393C2. Cf. 387A–B, where the use of an artifact (for cutting) can be natural or unnatural, depending on whether the right one is used. I take it that this does not mean that the artifact is constituted according to nature, but that it is natural to use a saw for cutting, not, say, a hammer. So the functioning or purpose of an artifact can be according to nature, but not the artifact itself. Therefore, there could be a Form of Cutting, but not a Form of Saw. If there are Forms for purposes or functions (of the things that are constituted according to nature), there can be Forms for excellence in fulfillment of purposes or functions. Hence, the Xenocratean definition, on its traditional interpretation, does not threaten in the slightest Forms for the virtues.

98. *DA* A 4, 408b32–33. Cf. A 2, 404b27–28 and frr. 164–187 (IP). At *Phdr.* 245E6–246A2 Plato defines the soul as τὸ αὐτὸ ἑαυτὸ κινοῦν.

99. *Tim.* 35A–C.

100. Ibid., 41D4–7.

THE OLD ACADEMY   *161*

Indivisible Being is equivalent to the Monad and Divisible Being to the Indefinite Dyad.[101] Hence, soul, the product of these, is number or ratio.[102] And, according to *Laws* 10, soul is defined as 'self-moving motion.'[103] It is not, I think, so far-fetched to suppose that Xenocrates took Plato to account for the nature of soul by the addition of the mixtures of Indivisible and Divisible Identity and Difference.[104] The former is the principle of rest; the latter the principle of its contrary.

Aristotle's complaint that that which has principles of identity and difference within it is not necessarily in motion is, strictly speaking, well taken.[105] But Xenocrates here is evidently following *both* Plato and Aristotle in taking the fundamental motion that is psychic motion to be circular, that is, around a fixed point.[106] The World Soul is thus paradigmatically self-identical and different in its motion, that is, it traverses a circular path. These properties are the condition for its cognition.[107] For Plato, this motion is an 'image' of intellectual motion; for Aristotle, this motion imitates the activity of the Unmoved Mover.[108]

The little we know about the thought of those in the Old Academy makes it likely that their central 'research project' revolved around getting right the first principles of all.[109] Viewed thus, Aristotle belongs among these philosophers both in his positive contribution to the problem and in his objections to the solutions of Plato and his immediate successors, Speusippus and Xenocrates. It seems equally clear to me, at any rate, that this is a dispute among proponents of UP. Aristotle's remark that "to judge

101. See Plutarch, *De proc. an. in Tim.* I, 1012E–F = fr. 188 IP.
102. Cf. Aristotle, *DA* 2.1.412b15–17: οὐ γὰρ τοιούτου σώματος τὸ τί ἦν εἶναι καὶ ὁ λόγος ἡ ψυχή, ἀλλὰ φυσικοῦ τοιουδί, ἔχοντος ἀρχὴν κινήσεως καὶ στάσεως ἐν ἑαυτῷ (the soul is the essence and the ratio [or formula] not of such a body [an artifact], but of such a natural body having a principle of motion and rest in itself). The English translations of and commentaries on this canonical definition of soul usually do not make perspicuous that λόγος is the term for ratio. See, e.g., Polansky 2007, 163–70, who simply transliterates λόγος without comment.
103. *Lg.* 895E10–896A2: τὴν δυναμένην αὐτὴν αὐτὴν κινεῖν κίνησιν.
104. I think Dillon (2003, 122) is mistaken to conflate psychic motion with intellectual motion here.
105. See *Phys.* Γ 2, 201b19–21 and *Meta.* N 8, 1084a34–35.
106. See *Tim.* 36C3; *Lg.* 898A3–6; *Meta.* Λ 6, 1071b10–11. The circular motion is the motion of the outermost sphere of the heavens. If this sphere moves in its desire to emulate the Unmoved Mover, it would seem to be ensouled. Its soul causes the circular motion.
107. See *Tim.* 37A2–C5.
108. See *Lg.* 897E4–6; *Meta.* Λ 7, 1072a19ff. Cf. Θ 8, 1050b28–29.
109. This does not seem to be the case for Xenocrates' successor as head of the Academy, Polemo, who served in this role for some forty years. D.L. (4.18) says that Polemo eschewed "dialectical speculations" (διαλεκτικοῖς θεωρήμασι) in favor of focusing on "facts" (τοῖς πράγμασι), a claim that evidently did not stop Polemo from producing ethical theory. Nevertheless, Dillon (2003, 177) is probably correct in maintaining that Polemo is "an important bridge figure between Platonism and Stoicism." Such a "bridge," hypothetically, would point to the abandonment of UP and the commitment to a positive construct on its foundation.

from observations, nature does not seem to be a series of episodes, like a bad tragedy," may or may not be a criticism specifically of Speusippus.[110] But as the last line of book Lambda of the *Metaphysics*—a quotation from Homer—indicates, Aristotle undoubtedly accepted as legitimate the task of producing a systematic construct on the basis of UP. He also accepts the task of a *reduction* of principles to the absolute minimum. One or two or three principles? Inevitably, if the answer is "more than one," problems arise whether we say that the second (or second and third) are irreducible to the first or we say that they are somehow reducible, and yet still deserve somehow to be called principles.

Reductivism is the bane of a top-down metaphysics perhaps even more than for its polar opposite.[111] For the materialist need not even countenance the existence of more than one principle expressible in, say, the language of quantum mechanics. The Platonist, however, argues against a reduction of being and intellection to material terms. Hence, the problems about the Demiurge or the Unmoved Mover in relation to the first principle of all—whatever that might be. How are we to reduce that which appears to be irreducible? Mathematics probably seemed to be a promising tool of reduction in its potential for 'commensurating' all that is intelligible in any way. Naturally, further questions about the nature of knowledge are going to be determined at least in part by how this principle or these principles are to be conceived, given that wisdom is supposed to be knowledge of them.

---

110. See *Meta.* N 3, 1090b19–20. Cf. Λ 10, 1075b37–1076a1. Speusippus is not mentioned by name in either passage, but it is generally held that he is the target.

111. There is a striking pronouncement of the Platonic position that a top-down metaphysics is "more likely" (εὐλογώτερον) than its opposite in Theophrastus, *Meta.* 4a9–17. Theophrastus identifies the "principles" (ἀρχάς) with "eternal things" (τὰ ἀΐδια) and affirms their "priority" (πρότερα). Cf. Aristotle, *Meta.* Θ 8, 1050b6–7: τὰ μὲν γὰρ ἀΐδια πρότερα τῇ οὐσίᾳ τῶν φθαρτῶν (for eternal things are prior in substance to destructible things).

CHAPTER 6

The Academic Skeptics

As we saw in the first chapter, one of the elements of UP is antiskepticism. Aristotle's testimony strongly suggests that Plato was, for virtually his entire career, wedded to the view that knowledge (ἐπιστήμη) is possible and that it is not of sensible but rather of 'separate' intelligible entities. It seems a straightforward matter to characterize the Skeptics' position as the contradictory of the claim that knowledge is possible. But in fact many things that both Plato and Skeptics actually say about knowledge should give us pause. First, in *Phaedo* Socrates claims that "if it is not possible to know anything purely while we are embodied, either nowhere is knowledge possessed or it is only for the dead."[1] It is, I think, a serious mistake to take 'know purely' to imply that there is a type of knowledge that is 'impure.' This is the case not merely because it would contradict Aristotle's testimony. More important, if, as Plato himself argues in *Republic*, knowledge is of Forms, a putative 'impure' knowledge of Forms would be something other than ἐπιστήμη. Not only is there not a single word in the entire Platonic corpus to suggest that there is a mode or cognition of Forms other than ἐπιστήμη (or its equivalent νόησις), but the argument in *Theaetetus* that true belief cannot be knowledge—even if true belief is 'supplemented' by some sort of λόγος—is sufficiently broad in its scope that there is no room left over for a mode of

---

1. *Phd.* 66E4–6: εἰ γὰρ μὴ οἷόν τε μετὰ τοῦ σώματος μηδὲν καθαρῶς γνῶναι, δυοῖν θάτερον, ἢ οὐδαμοῦ ἔστιν κτήσασθαι τὸ εἰδέναι ἢ τελευτήσασιν. Cf. D7–E2, 65E1–4, 67A2–6. In the context of the passage, it is clear that the words used here for 'knowledge' (γνῶναι, εἰδέναι) are being used for the 'highest' form of cognition, knowledge or wisdom (σοφία).

cognition of Forms that is not ἐπιστήμη and not belief.[2] The words "know purely," then, should be understood as suggesting that the ne plus ultra of cognition alone is not available to embodied individuals.[3]

And yet, not too much after this passage we have the Recollection Argument for the immortality of the soul, an argument the principle conclusion of which is that we do in some sense have ἐπιστήμη; for if we did not, we could not make the judgments about the relevant deficiency of instances of Forms in the sensible world. It seems evident that the ἐπιστήμη we perhaps cannot possess while embodied is different in some way from the ἐπιστήμη we must possess if we are to be able to make judgments like "these equal things are deficiently equal." The relevant distinction is made in *Theaetetus*. This is the distinction between "possessing" (κεκτῆσθαι) knowledge and "having" (τὸ ἔχειν) it.[4] This is a distinction between the presence in the knower of that which is knowable ('possessing') and the awareness of the presence ('having'). Deploying this distinction in the argument in *Phaedo*, we would say that we must 'possess' knowledge in order to make judgments about the deficiencies of sensibles, whereas 'having' knowledge is definitely problematic for embodied individuals.

If Plato's antiskepticism regards only the *having* of knowledge, it remains an open question as to whether he concedes the Skeptics' claim with regard to the impossibility of *possessing* knowledge. The account in *Republic* of the education of the rulers culminating in knowledge via a vision of the Idea of the Good at fifty years of age only slightly mitigates the pessimism of *Phaedo*.[5] At most, this knowledge is possible only for the elite few and then only near the end of their lives.

For many scholars, the temptation to discount Plato's epistemic rigorism is considerable. One way of doing this is to insist that ἐπιστήμη or a *kind* of ἐπιστήμη is possible for sensibles as well as for intelligibles.[6] Apart from the fact that there is virtually nothing in the texts of Plato

---

2. See Gerson 2009, 44–55. The mode of cognition that Plato calls διάνοια ('understanding' or 'thought') in *Republic* is clearly not the required *tertium quid*. It is not a kind of ἐπιστήμη. Cf. 533C7–E2.

3. Cicero, *De nat. deo.* 1.11, refers to Socrates as the originator of the idea of refraining from judgment and Arcesilaus as having revived it (*repetita*). This implicitly drives a wedge between Socrates and Plato, but only if we identify Socrates not with the historical figure, but, rather arbitrarily, with the figure in the 'aporetic' dialogues alone. Shields (1994, 343–45) argues that Arcesilaus, "by extending certain Socratic practices" in what Shields assumes to be the early dialogues, can be understood not to have completely misunderstood Plato. I do not agree that Arcesilaus's possible Platonic bona fides requires accepting an arbitrarily selected group of dialogues ('early') as containing a distinctly skeptical position.

4. See *Tht.* 197B–D. Aristotle employs basically the same distinction, using his invented term ἐνέργεια. He makes a distinction between first and second 'actuality' in cognition.

5. See *Rep.* 540Aff. It is clear from the text of the analogy of the Divided Line (511B–D, esp. C8–D2) that it is only by seeing the Idea of the Good that the philosopher is able to have knowledge of Forms.

6. See Fine 2003, where this position is developed in many papers, especially in one devoted to knowledge and belief in Plato's *Republic*. See also Burnyeat 1990.

to support this interpretation, to make of Plato a proponent of what we might call 'empirical knowledge' is, I believe, to ally him with Stoic epistemology in a way that makes the Academic skeptical opposition to that incomprehensible. Another way of doing this is to stipulate that knowledge is (or should be) for Plato something other than a mode of cognition whose sole objects are Forms. So we can just call rational belief (δόξα) 'knowledge' if it meets some arbitrarily concocted criterion or even if it does not. Whether the inclination to do this arises from a rejection of Plato's view on how we possess knowledge or whether it arises from a rejection of the difficulty or impossibility of embodied persons having knowledge is irrelevant. In either case, the view that when in *Theaetetus* Plato seeks to define ἐπιστήμη he is in fact searching for a stipulative definition of the word ἐπιστήμη or offering an analysis of the concept of ἐπιστήμη as opposed to dialectically constructing a definition of the real thing that ἐπιστήμη is seems to me frankly unbelievable. More to the present point, it makes nonsense of the construction of Platonism within the Academy including its skeptical 'phase,' as we will see presently.

With respect to UP, there is a latent tension between the element of antiskepticism and the positive claim that the objects of knowledge are other than sensibles. The fact that the highest mode of cognition is reserved for intelligibles is owing to the instability or relative unintelligibility of the sensible world. Then, an appropriate mode of cognition for the latter is thrown into question, at least insofar as that cognition is supposed to attain truth.[7] If the attainment of truth is possible for this mode of cognition, why is it not knowledge or a kind of knowledge? If it is not possible, what is it that the inferior mode does attain? Underlying this question is more than a terminological issue. For the hierarchical metaphysics and epistemology of Platonism is not purchased at the cost of the dismissal of the sensible world as completely unintelligible and of a mode of cognition for it that is conducive, if not to the attainment of embodied knowledge, at least to our psychological and ethical advancement. Plato's rejection of the extreme nominalism of the Eleatics brought with it a sort of commitment to the rehabilitation of the intelligibility of the sensible world. But this commitment is fraught with difficulties.

What Is Academic Skepticism?

The bestowal of the honorific "founder of skepticism" was probably given to Pyrrho of Elis (c. 360–c. 270) by Aenesidemus, the first-century BCE

---

7. See *Tht.* 186C9–10: Οὗ δὲ ἀληθείας τις ἀτυχήσει, ποτὲ τούτου ἐπιστήμων ἔσται; (If someone cannot hit upon the truth of something, will he then have knowledge of it?) It does not follow logically from this claim that if one *does* hit upon the truth, then one has knowledge. For it seems that one may hit upon the truth adventitiously, as it were, without knowing it. But to assume that this is what Plato meant to allow is to gainsay his hierarchical metaphysics such that truth—whether in the intelligible or sensible realms—is one thing. As I will argue, this view constitutes a misreading of Plato's Platonism because it undermines the possibility of a consistent positive construct on the basis of UP.

Academic Skeptic.⁸ It is not impossible that the supposed founder of Academic skepticism, Arcesilaus (316/5–241/40), knew of Pyrrho, though we have no indication of this. Sextus Empiricus, at any rate, is quite emphatic that, while Arcesilaus shares the true skeptical 'approach' (ἀγωγή), his successors, Carneades (214–129/8) and Clitomachus (187/6–110/09), do not.⁹ The question I wish to pose is what insight if any the skepticism of Arcesilaus and (pace Sextus) Carneades provide for our understanding of Platonism. It would, of course, be a mistake to suppose that the very flexible label 'Academic' need indicate anything but the most tenuous tie to Plato. Indeed, a standard scholarly view is that the Academic Skeptics represent a wholesale abandonment of Platonism and that only with Antiochus is Platonism reunited with the Academy. Still, it is worth pursuing the question of whether a skeptical 'procedure' or a skeptical approach to knowledge has a Platonic provenance.¹⁰

First, it is certain that Academic skepticism is aimed squarely at a Stoic account of knowledge. Here is Sextus Empiricus's admirably lucid presentation of that account followed by Arcesilaus's criticism:

> For they [the Stoics] hold that three things are linked to each other: knowledge, belief, and, placed between these, grasping. Of these knowledge is sure and stable grasping unalterable by reasoning; belief is weak and false assent; and grasping is what is between these, assent to a graspable presentation. According to the Stoics, a graspable presentation is true and such that there could not be a false one just like it. They say that knowledge is present only in the wise, belief is present only in base men, but that grasping is common to both groups, and that this is the criterion of truth.¹¹

Here is how Arcesilaus apparently responded to this account:

> These being the Stoics' views, Arcesilaus countered them by showing that grasping is in no respect a criterion midway between knowledge and belief.

---

8. Two of Aenesidemus's works are *Pyrrhonian Discourses* and *Outline Introduction to Pyrrhonian Matters*. See Photius, *Bib.* 212. But see D.L. 9.70, where the medical doctor Theodosius is said in his book *Skeptical Chapter* to deny that Pyrrhonism should be identified as skepticism for the fittingly skeptical reason that we cannot know what it was that Pyrrho taught.

9. See Sextus, *PH* 1.220–35.

10. See Krämer 1972, 14–107, who finds a number of elements in the later works of Plato and in the works of the members of the Old Academy apt for skeptical interpretation. See Sedley 1996, 98, on the anonymous commentary on Plato's *Theaetetus* that argues that the members of the New Academy "virtually all endorsed dogmatic Platonism." Sedley (84) concurs with Tarrant in dating this commentary to the late first century BCE.

11. Sextus, *M.* 7.151.1–153.1: τρία γὰρ εἶναί φασιν ἐκεῖνοι τὰ συζυγοῦντα ἀλλήλοις, ἐπιστήμην καὶ δόξαν καὶ τὴν ἐν μεθορίῳ τούτων τεταγμένην κατάληψιν, ὧν ἐπιστήμην μὲν εἶναι τὴν ἀσφαλῆ καὶ βεβαίαν καὶ ἀμετάθετον ὑπὸ λόγου κατάληψιν, δόξαν δὲ τὴν ἀσθενῆ καὶ ψευδῆ συγκατάθεσιν, κατάληψιν δὲ τὴν μεταξὺ τούτων, ἥτις ἐστὶ καταληπτικῆς φαντασίας συγκατάθεσις· καταληπτικὴ δὲ φαντασία κατὰ τούτους ἐτύγχανεν ἡ ἀληθὴς καὶ τοιαύτη οἵα οὐκ ἂν γένοιτο ψευδής. ὧν τὴν <μὲν> ἐπιστήμην ἐν μόνοις ὑφίστασθαι λέγουσι τοῖς σοφοῖς, τὴν δὲ δόξαν ἐν μόνοις τοῖς φαύλοις, τὴν δὲ κατάληψιν κοινὴν ἀμφοτέρων

For that which they call grasping and assent to a graspable presentation occurs either in a wise man or in a base man. But if it occurs in a wise man, it is knowledge, and if in a base man, it is belief, and there is nothing else left besides these two but a name.[12]

The difference between the Stoic account of knowledge that is criticized here and the Platonic account jumps out in the first line. For the Stoics, knowledge, grasping, and belief are "linked" (συζυγοῦσα). The link is provided by the "graspable presentation" that is available to both wise man and fool. This is a mode of cognition that arises primarily from sense perception.[13] What differentiates the wise man from his opposite is that the former has "sure and stable grasping unalterable by reasoning," whereas the latter has weak belief and gives false assent. Thus, there is both knowledge and belief about the same presentations to sense perception. For Plato, however, knowledge and belief are discontinuous; there is no knowledge of that of which there is belief and vice versa. Further, for the Stoics what differentiates the wise and the base men is the false assent that the latter gives to his presentations. This is not equivalent to an assent to a false proposition; false assent is possible to a true proposition. What makes the assent false is that it is unjustified. By contrast, the wise man never gives assent to a proposition that is unjustified. That is why he and he alone has knowledge. So it seems fairly clear that for the Stoic, knowledge is true justified belief or, what amounts to the same thing, a mode of cognition in relation to a true proposition that differs from belief only in that it is "unalterable by reasoning." Even if, as we have already seen, the passage in Plato's *Meno* in which knowledge and belief are joined might be rather implausibly interpreted along these lines, the account in *Republic* and *Theaetetus* effectively eliminates this possibility. Knowledge is not for Plato justified belief because knowledge does not have *any* sorts of propositions as its objects, but rather the Forms themselves.[14]

The astute criticism of Arcesilaus aims to show that there is in fact no middle ground between a mere belief and knowledge. The putative 'grasping' is

---

εἶναι, καὶ ταύτην κριτήριον ἀληθείας καθεστάναι. Cf. Stobaeus, 2.73.19 = *SVF* 1.68–9; Cicero, *Acad.* 1.41 = *SVF* 1.60. The term μεθόριος does not indicate a third possibility (either knowledge or belief or something between these) but rather the 'boundary' between knowledge and belief, that is, something that they both share. See Gerson 2009, 100–111, for an account of Stoic epistemology.

12. Sextus, *M.* 7.153.1–154.1: ταῦτα δὴ λεγόντων τῶν ἀπὸ τῆς Στοᾶς ὁ Ἀρκεσίλαος ἀντικαθίστατο, δεικνὺς ὅτι οὐδέ ἐστι μεταξὺ ἐπιστήμης καὶ δόξης κριτήριον ἡ κατάληψις. αὕτη γὰρ ἣν φασι κατάληψιν καὶ καταληπτικῆς φαντασίας συγκατάθεσιν, ἤτοι ἐν σοφῷ ἢ ἐν φαύλῳ γίνεται. ἀλλ' ἐάν τε ἐν σοφῷ γένηται, ἐπιστήμη ἐστίν, ἐάν τε ἐν φαύλῳ, δόξα, καὶ οὐδὲν ἄλλο παρὰ ταῦτα ἢ μόνον ὄνομα μετείληπται.

13. There can also be presentations from incorporeal and nonevident corporeals like god. See D.L. 7.49–52 = *SVF* 2.52 (in part).

14. Scott (1995, 215) claims that in *Meno*, although Socrates argues for recollection, there is no commitment to the theory of Forms "or to the other assumptions that support the argument in the *Phaedo*." I take this claim to be contradicted by Aristotle's testimony.

either knowledge *or* belief. If it is mere belief it is unjustified, even if the belief is true. If it is knowledge, then a justification is otiose since knowledge is, as defined by the Stoics, unalterable by reasoning. If a so-called justified belief is had by someone, that belief is in fact knowledge; if what one has is not knowledge, it is unjustified. For this reason, the attack on the possibility of knowledge is a fortiori an attack on the possibility of rational or justified belief. A would-be defender of the Stoic account of knowledge is not in a position to concede the impossibility of knowledge as defined by Stoics and instead move to defend rational belief as an almost-as-good alternative. The core skeptical strategy is not to show the impossibility of a rarified form of cognition, thereby leaving something else in its stead. Rather, that strategy eliminates the possibility of rational belief by eliminating the possibility of knowledge. But this conclusion is entirely rooted in the Stoic account that defines knowledge and belief as two forms of the grasping of one and the same proposition. Even a true belief—true because, according to the criterion of truth, the presentation is grasped—is not rational because it is not knowledge.

It is evident that the Stoics' vulnerability to the Academic critique turns on their insistence that knowledge is "unalterable by reasoning," that is, that it is in some sense infallible or incorrigible.[15] A desire to be faithful to Plato, who also held that knowledge is in some sense infallible (ἀναμάρτητον, ἀψευδής), can hardly be the reason for the Stoics' claim. It is more likely that the Stoics in fact reasoned that the ne plus ultra of cognitive achievement must be infallible. For the idea that knowledge is fallible ("I know but I may be mistaken") conflates knowledge with belief. And even if one adds that what one knows must be true, knowledge will not differ from a true belief, which, in turn, does not differ from a lucky guess. But if knowledge is conflated with a lucky guess or an adventitious true belief, then one does not know that one knows. And if this is the case, the knowledge as the supreme achievement of the philosopher becomes something hollow, to say the least. But a true belief differs from a lucky guess only if the former is justified or based on sufficient evidence. Either the putative justification guarantees the truth of the belief, in which case there is knowledge, or else it does not. So suppose a justified true belief is knowledge. It is not enough, however, that there exists some justification for the belief, and that the justification entails that the belief is true. One must also *know* that the justification or evidence does this. But, then, one must either have justification or evidence for the evidence or else the evidence must be self-evident. That is, one must know that one knows that the evidence entails what it is evidence for.[16] On this analysis, one cannot know unless one knows that one

---

15. Aristotle, *Top.* E 2, 130b15–16; E 4, 133b28ff.; E 4, 134b16–17; Z 8, 146b1–2, gives "ὑπόληψις incontrovertible by λόγος" as a definition of knowledge. It is not clear whether this was the accepted Academic definition or not. But in any case, it was certainly open to the Stoics to reject it in favor of something more modest had they wished to do so.

16. Cf. Cicero, *Acad.* 2.145 = *SVF* 1.66. In this passage, Cicero quotes the Stoics as maintaining that the one who grasps (but only believes) is like one who 'grasps' something with the

knows. That is, knowing *is* knowing that one knows. So there is no knowing without evidence (including the limiting case of self-evidence) or else one knows that the evidence entails what it is evidence for. But without entailing evidence, there is mere belief, as the Stoics saw, not a justified belief, which would just be knowledge. Stated otherwise, there is only justification when there is knowledge; without justification there is only belief. Worse, the belief is without justification, which is as much as to say that it is irrational. There is literally no more reason to believe a proposition than the opposite.

The Stoics agree that there is a mode of cognition that is better than ungrounded belief. This is knowledge. There is no middle ground between ungrounded belief and knowledge. So the stakes are high in defending against the attack on the possibility of knowledge.[17] This defense amounts to showing that it is possible to be in a mental state that is "unalterable by reasoning." Obviously, one cannot hope to attain such a state merely by cultivating a preternatural stubbornness. Since the state of knowing is one in which the knower assents to the truth of a proposition, a proposition that represents the (graspable) presentation, the knower must maintain that no reasoning could alter the inference that is made from the presentation to the assent to the proposition.[18] After all, what makes belief the métier of the fool is that his assent *is* alterable by reasoning, whether cogent or not.[19] Yet the claim that the graspable presentation is, for the knower, such that there could not be a false one like it, must be an inference. For otherwise there would be no difference between the assent of the sage and the assent of the fool to the same graspable presentation. The sage's mental state is "unalterable by reasoning" because he is convinced that his presentation is sufficient evidence for assent to the proposition representing that presentation.

As Skeptics argued, however, there can be no presentation that is absolutely indistinguishable from one that in fact does not entail the truth of a proposition representing it for the simple reason that the presentation is false:

> Among presentations, some are true and some are false. A false presentation is not graspable [*percipi non potest*]. But every true presentation is such that a

---

fist, whereas the one who knows is like one who grasps that fist with the other fist. This seems to me best interpreted as a claim that knowing entails and is entailed by knowing that one knows.

17. The Stoics generally conceded that there were no living sages, that is, no one who actually had knowledge. Although the existence of such a sage would show that knowledge is possible, the actual nonexistence of one would not entail that knowledge is not possible.

18. On assent being to a proposition, see Stobaeus 2.88.4 = *SVF* 3.171: "Propositions are the objects of acts of assent." Perhaps assent to the proposition is extensionally equivalent to assent to the graspable presentation.

19. Cf. *Tim.* 51E4, where true belief is distinguished from knowledge (here, νοῦς) by the fact that the former is overturnable by persuasion (μεταπειστόν) whereas the latter is not. The fact that the Stoics adhere to a Platonic distinction in the face of Academic criticism is not without significance. One might have guessed that an embrace of materialism would have led Stoics to abandon the claim that knowledge is infallible precisely because infallibility would be applicable to cognition of immaterial entities only by immaterial entities.

false one of the same sort can occur. And where presentations are such that there is no difference between them, it cannot occur that some of them are graspable and some are not. Therefore, no presentation is graspable.[20]

This is the so-called argument from illusion. Its true provenance is, once again, Stoic epistemology. The force of the argument is usually represented as consisting in the observation that the phenomenology of illusions is indistinguishable from that of veridical perception. So the straight stick in the water looks like a bent stick, which is indistinguishable from what a bent stick really looks like. I do not believe, however, that this is here the central focus. In reply to this argument, the Stoics are said to have added that the graspable presentation must be one that could not come from something that does not exist. So a true presentation is stipulated to be different in some way from a false one. The straight stick that looks bent must presumably be different from the one that is really bent. The point could not be that straight sticks and bent sticks are in reality different; no Skeptic need deny this. The point must be that they are phenomenally different. But this will not do. For the Stoic is committed to an inference from a proposition regarding the way things appear (the graspable presentation) to the truth of a proposition regarding how things really are. It is irrelevant that it is true that things appear a certain way to the knower. Yet it is also question-begging and destructive of the inference to claim that the way things appear is the way they are, for then there is no inference to a proposition about the way they are. In order to create 'inferential space,' there must be some criterion according to which the graspable presentation could, but does not necessarily, provide a basis for the truth of the proposition representing this. The argument from illusion is not an argument about whether we are or are not sharp enough to tell illusions from reality; rather, it is an argument that seeks to show that a claim to knowledge, as the Stoics have it, must have a justificatory or evidentiary basis. Such a basis could exist only if the justification or the evidence entails what it is evidence for. But entailment is a logical relation, not a psychological one. That the Stoic sage is more circumspect in his assent than is the fool is beside the point. The problem is that there is no legitimate inference from the way things appear to the way things are even if there is a trivially true inference from the way things epistemically appear, that is, truth-preserving appearance, to the way they are. And this is so because there is no legitimate inference from the way things appear to the truth of a proposition that they are appearing epistemically. If, though, the sage forgoes justification, his claim to know does not differ in weight from the claim of one who merely believes. But if the sage accepts a justificatory burden, in what sense is his mental state "unalterable by reasoning"?

So Arcesilaus urges suspension of judgment regarding *all* presentations. That is, for any p, no belief that p is the case is more rational than a belief

20. Cicero, *Acad.* 2.40; cf. Sextus, M. 7.402–10.

that not-p. In this conclusion, it is not inapposite to compare the sort of argument that Socrates makes in, say, *Euthyphro,* namely, that if we do not know what the Form of Piety is, we cannot give a λόγος of it, and if we cannot give a λόγος of it, then we are in no position to claim with any justification whatsoever that a deed is pious or not. The only basis for such a claim would be that we could see that the deed bore the hallmark of Piety. But this assumes that we know Piety.[21] The point is easily generalizable for any claim about any property in the sensible world whose intelligibility rests ultimately on a separate Form. Plato, like the Academic Skeptic, is not only opposed to the idea that there is such a thing as empirical knowledge, but he is also opposed to the idea that there is such a thing as rational belief unless there is nonempirical knowledge. It is only such knowledge that makes rational belief possible or intelligible. This is the case because only knowledge could provide the justification or the evidence for the belief. In Platonic terms, if Euthyphro is to believe rationally that it is true that prosecuting his father is pious, his justification for this claim is that he knows Piety.

But the rational belief, of course, regards an object that is not the object of knowledge, but only that which participates or imitates the knowable. I am not claiming that Arcesilaus's attack on the Stoic account of knowledge is made from the vantage point of a Platonic account of knowledge, particularly a Platonic account that assigns the possession of knowledge to a disembodied soul. What I do wish to claim is that the logic of the Skeptic attack on the rationality of belief (the major Skeptic claim), given the impossibility of knowledge as the Stoics conceive of it, is identical to the Platonic attack on the rationality of belief absent at least the possession of knowledge. That Plato believes that knowledge is possible and that he believes that he has proven in the Recollection Argument that without knowledge one cannot make certain judgments about the sensible world that in fact are made leaves open the possibility that Arcesilaus's attack on Stoic knowledge is compatible with the acceptance of Plato's claims.[22]

---

21. So *Eu.* 11A6–B1. Cf. *Men.* 71B1–8, where knowledge of the Form of Virtue is necessary both for knowledge of its properties—like teachability—and for 'knowing' whether something instantiates it.

22. It is difficult to know quite what to make of the consistent ancient evidence that Arcesilaus regarded himself as a disciple of Plato. See D.L. 4.33; Sextus, *PH* 1.232; Plutarch, *Adv. Col.* 1121F–1122A. The difficulty is principally whether Arcesilaus's supposed adherence to Plato refers to an aporetic or dialectical method (cf. Cicero, *Acad.* 1.46) or to substantive doctrines. It seems not implausible that Arcesilaus would be correct in claiming a sort of fidelity to Plato insofar as he held that there is no ἐπιστήμη of the sensible world. That there might be more to his fidelity to Plato than this is suggested by Cicero, *Acad.* 2.60, which may or may not be the passage Augustine is thinking of at *C. Acad.* 3.43. Gigon (1944, 1972) stresses the Stoics as primary Academic targets in support of his argument endorsing the texts that claim that the Academic Skeptics did not reject Plato's "esoteric teaching." Glucker (1978, 296–306), criticizing Gigon, identifies this supposed "esoteric teaching" with the theory of Forms, and rightly complains that this theory is hardly concealed in the dialogues. But the esotericism perhaps has more to do with the positive construct of UP, including the important addition

Skepticism, Rationalism, and Platonism

Sextus reports that Arcesilaus was alive to the criticism that a Skeptic who withheld assent to all propositional claims could not conduct ordinary life without contradicting himself. For in acting, the Skeptic—implicitly or not—must assent to *some* propositions, namely, those the presumed truth of which makes his behavior rational. Arcesilaus is reported to have held

> that he who suspends judgment about everything regulates choices and avoidances and, generally, actions by reasonableness, and proceeding according to this criterion, will act correctly. For happiness arises because of prudence, and prudence resides in correct actions, and a correct action is that which, having been done, has a reasonable defense. Therefore, he who adheres to reasonableness will act correctly and will be happy.[23]

It was a commonplace even in antiquity that Arcesilaus's acknowledgment of the possibility of reasonable behavior undercut his principled skepticism. It seems likely that Aenesidemus's effort to revive a pure, uncompromised 'Pyrrhonian' skepticism was aimed precisely at such apparent backsliding.[24] We ought to realize, though, that the proposed skeptical criterion of action is not a criterion of truth. A course of action is not rendered less reasonable just because it fails to achieve its goal. That which is reasonable could not be a criterion of truth since 'the reasonable' is not used to justify a claim to truth as if it were a kind of evidence. If this is so, in what sense is 'the reasonable' a criterion?

In order to answer this question, it will be useful to have before us the famous passage from Plato's *Timaeus* in which the principal interlocutor, Timaeus, declares that physical science can only be a "likely story" (εἰκός μῦθος):

> Again, these things being so, our world must necessarily be a likeness of something. Now in every matter it is of great moment to start at the right point in accordance with the nature of the subject. Concerning a likeness, then, and its model we must make this distinction: an account is akin to that of which it is an account: an account of that which is stable and secure and discoverable by thought will itself be stable and incontrovertible (and insofar as this is possible and it belongs to an account to be irrefutable and unchangeable

---

that Plato could well be interpreted to have held that at least occurrent ἐπιστήμη is not available to embodied individuals.

23. Sextus, *M*. 7.158.5–12: ὅτι ὁ περὶ πάντων ἐπέχων κανονιεῖ τὰς αἱρέσεις καὶ φυγὰς καὶ κοινῶς τὰς πράξεις τῷ εὐλόγῳ, κατὰ τοῦτό τε προερχόμενος τὸ κριτήριον κατορθώσει· τὴν μὲν γὰρ εὐδαιμονίαν περιγίνεσθαι διὰ τῆς φρονήσεως, τὴν δὲ φρόνησιν κεῖσθαι ἐν τοῖς κατορθώμασιν, τὸ δὲ κατόρθωμα εἶναι ὅπερ πραχθὲν εὔλογον ἔχει τὴν ἀπολογίαν. ὁ προσέχων οὖν τῷ εὐλόγῳ κατορθώσει καὶ εὐδαιμονήσει. The "reasonable defense" is an obvious reaction to the Stoic doctrine of κατορθώματα, which, supposedly based on knowledge, have such a defense.

24. See Burnyeat 1980, 27–31.

one ought not to fall short of this); while an account of that which is made in the image of the other but is only a likeness, will itself be only likely, standing to accounts of the former kind in a proportion: as being is to becoming so is truth to persuasion. If, then, Socrates, in many respects concerning many things—the gods and the generation of the universe—we prove unable to give accounts that are in every way consistent with themselves and exact, you shouldn't be surprised. If we can provide accounts no less likely than others, we must be content, remembering that I who speak and you my judges are only human, and consequently it is fitting that we should, in these matters, accept the likely story and look for nothing further. (trans. Cornford, slightly altered)[25]

This passage in a way provides a gloss on the Divided Line in *Republic*. There we learn that what is believed stands to what is known as the image stands to what is imaged.[26] Here, what we learn is that "a likely story" is all that we will attain in regard to the things that become, that is, the objects of physics.

What is particularly interesting about this passage for the current discussion is the use of the word "truth" (ἀλήθεια). There is no doubt that this is the ontological use of the term, that is, a property of being in relation to an intellect.[27] At the same time, Plato can qualify the noun δόξα with the adjective ἀληθής, using the term to indicate a semantic property of propositions and derivatively a mode of cognition, δόξα, in relation to these.[28] Beliefs can be true, but belief does not attain the truth, we might say, because belief has the realm of becoming, not being, for its objects. The distinction between the ontological and semantic notions of truth does not undercut the dependence of the latter on the former, according to Plato. True belief is possible because of the eternal truth that the objects of true belief are likenesses or images of.[29] So the fact that only a 'likely story' regarding physics

---

25. *Tim.* 29B1–D3: τούτων δὲ ὑπαρχόντων αὖ πᾶσα ἀνάγκη τόνδε τὸν κόσμον εἰκόνα τινὸς εἶναι. μέγιστον δὴ παντὸς ἄρξασθαι κατὰ φύσιν ἀρχήν. ὧδε οὖν περί τε εἰκόνος καὶ περὶ τοῦ παραδείγματος αὐτῆς διοριστέον, ὡς ἄρα τοὺς λόγους, ὧνπέρ εἰσιν ἐξηγηταί, τούτων αὐτῶν καὶ συγγενεῖς ὄντας· τοῦ μὲν οὖν μονίμου καὶ βεβαίου καὶ μετὰ νοῦ καταφανοῦς μονίμους καὶ ἀμεταπτώτους—καθ' ὅσον οἷόν τε καὶ ἀνελέγκτοις προσήκει λόγοις εἶναι καὶ ἀνικήτοις, τούτου δεῖ μηδὲν ἐλλείπειν—τοὺς δὲ τοῦ πρὸς μὲν ἐκεῖνο ἀπεικασθέντος, ὄντος δὲ εἰκόνος εἰκότας ἀνὰ λόγον τε ἐκείνων ὄντας· ὅτιπερ πρὸς γένεσιν οὐσία, τοῦτο πρὸς πίστιν ἀλήθεια. ἐὰν οὖν, ὦ Σώκρατες, πολλὰ πολλῶν πέρι, θεῶν καὶ τῆς τοῦ παντὸς γενέσεως, μὴ δυνατοὶ γιγνώμεθα πάντῃ πάντως αὐτοὺς ἑαυτοῖς ὁμολογουμένους λόγους καὶ ἀπηκριβωμένους ἀποδοῦναι, μὴ θαυμάσῃς· ἀλλ' ἐὰν ἄρα μηδενὸς ἧττον παρεχώμεθα εἰκότας, ἀγαπᾶν χρή, μεμνημένους ὡς ὁ λέγων ἐγὼ ὑμεῖς τε οἱ κριταὶ φύσιν ἀνθρωπίνην ἔχομεν, ὥστε περὶ τούτων τὸν εἰκότα μῦθον ἀποδεχομένους πρέπει τούτου μηδὲν ἔτι πέρα ζητεῖν.
26. *Rep.* 510A9. Here δόξα encompasses both πίστις and εἰκασία. But see *Tim.* 52A5, where δόξα (with αἴσθησις) seems equivalent to πίστις in 29C3.
27. Cf. *Rep.* 508E1, where it is the Idea of the Good that gives 'truth' to the Forms.
28. See *Tim.* 37B9, 51D6; Johansen 2004, 48–68.
29. Cf. *Parm.* 135B5–C2, where Parmenides warns Socrates that if the problems with Forms cannot be resolved, thus relegating them to the realm of the impossible, then the ability to have intelligent conversation (τοῦ διαλέγεσθαι δύναμιν) will be completely destroyed. Kahn (1996, 297) takes the ability to refer to philosophical dialectic, not to ordinary conversation.

is possible does not mean that there are no true propositions in that story or that they do not differ from false ones. But the only possible justification for the claim that a belief is true is the knowledge of Forms or the existence of ontological truth.[30]

Returning to Arcesilaus, the claim made by the Skeptic is that there is a criterion of reasonable action, but embracing this presumes no claim to have a justification for any beliefs related to the action.[31] What, then, does the 'reasonable defense' of the action imply? Unfortunately, Sextus does not record any answer by Arcesilaus to this question. We may speculate, however, that a reasonable defense of an action would consist in or would at least include a statement that happiness was thus obtained. That is, the defense is pragmatic. It is reasonable to act one way or another because in so acting one attains the absence of anxiety or contentment that is, for the Skeptic, the substance of happiness. Since happiness thus conceived is a state of the soul, as opposed to, say, an activity, as it is according to Aristotle, the Skeptic's 'reasonable defense' amounts only to a report on his own subjectivity or 'what seems to him.' If this is what Arcesilaus means, he is cleverly exploiting the ambiguity of the meaning of 'appearances' (τὰ φαινόμενα) between an epistemic and a nonepistemic sense. To state that "I seem to be content" in the former sense implies a justification consisting in a reason for saying that the appearance is epistemic. In the latter sense, nothing like this is implied. Arcesilaus renounces any interest in whether his appearances are (semantically) true. By contrast, one who took his appearances as epistemic would be open to the same objections that are raised against Protagoras in *Theaetetus*. Arcesilaus's skepticism implies a rejection of a dogmatic relativism along with the dogmatism of Stoicism. At the same time, it leaves Plato's account of knowledge untouched.[32]

The illustrious successor to Arcesilaus, Carneades, offers a valuable chapter in the history of those struggling to come to terms with Platonic epistemology.[33] Sextus tells us that Carneades was no Skeptic, despite any claims

---

But if for Plato dialectic is about Forms, the consequence of giving up Forms is, of course, that the philosophical study of them will be impossible. It seems implausible that Parmenides is saying what is trivially true; rather, he is best taken to be making the extremely portentous and controversial claim that without Forms ordinary conversation turns into nonsensical noise.

30. See *Tim.* 28A2, 28C1, 52A7, where δόξα is acquired μετ' αἰσθήσεως. There is no suggestion here that sense perception provides the justification for, as opposed to the source of, belief. Indeed, at 28A3, sense perception is characterized as ἄλογος. How could this ever be the justification for anything?

31. Sextus, *M.* 7.150, says that Arcesilaus did not define a criterion "in the proper sense" (προηγουμένως). I take it that this is intended to imply that a criterion of action is not a criterion in the proper sense because it is not a criterion of truth.

32. See Glucker 1978, 296–306, for some acute observations about the tantalizingly ambiguous evidence regarding the existence of 'an esoteric Platonism' within the skeptical Academy.

33. Carneades was actually about a hundred years younger than Arcesilaus. We are informed that between the Academic headship of Arcesilaus and that of Carneades there were a number of heads of lesser distinction including Lacydes, Telecles, Evander, and Hegesinus.

to the contrary.³⁴ Sextus reports that Carneades, like Arcesilaus, rejected a criterion of truth. But like Arcesilaus, he offered a criterion

> for the conduct of life and for the attainment of happiness... introducing the persuasive presentation [πιθανὴν φαντασίαν], and the presentation that is at the same time persuasive, uncontroverted [ἀπερίσπαστον] and thoroughly tested [διεξωδευμένην].³⁵

Apart from Carneades' substitution of τὸ πιθανόν for Arcesilaus's τὸ εὔλογον, why does Sextus think that Carneades' criterion is a betrayal of skepticism? The answer to this question is revealed in Sextus's observation that Carneades takes the persuasive presentation to be an "apparently true" one (ἡ φαινομένη ἀληθὴς φαντασία).³⁶ As such, he goes beyond Arcesilaus in implicitly claiming to be able to distinguish epistemic and nonepistemic appearances. But practically the whole point of skepticism is the principled rejection of this possibility. That Carneades has abandoned the skeptical stance is evident in his grading of presentations according to whether they are merely persuasive or also uncontroverted, and finally, thoroughly tested. The gradation implies an endpoint or ideal such that when it is reached, the apparently true will coincide with the true.³⁷ In short, the apparently true presentation will be an epistemic appearance. The Skeptic must insist that there cannot be such presentations in principle, which is exactly what Carneades denies with his refined standards of empirical confirmation. For the Skeptic, *any and all* appearances are nonentailing, that is, there is no entailment from a proposition that represents an appearance to a proposition that represents the truth. Yet this is exactly what Carneades implies when he states that "for the most part" our appearances are "truth revealing" (ἀληθευούσῃ).³⁸

It is of no use for Carneades to counter the skeptical argument by conceding that the persuasive presentation is not a criterion of knowledge, but only

---

Virtually nothing is known about these philosophers, including whether or not they embraced a form of skepticism.

34. See Sextus, *PH* 1.226–32, who, for this reason, distinguished the 'Middle Academy' of Arcesilaus from the 'New Academy' of Carneades.

35. *M.* 7.166.

36. *M.* 7.174.

37. See Tarrant 1985, 13–21, whose ingenious thesis it is that Carneades was arguing for the coincidence of the seeming true with the true for universal judgments, not particular ones. These universal judgments required the possession of 'common notions' or concepts that, on Tarrant's view, were a sort of simulacrum for Platonic Forms.

38. Sextus, *M.* 7.175. It may be objected on Carneades' behalf that the presentation that is 'truth revealing' is not a proposition and so is not supposed to entail another proposition representing the truth. But the claim that the apparently bent stick really is bent is first a claim about how things appear to someone. Given this, there must be *some* inference to the claim that things are as they appear. The only way to avoid the inferential claim is to identify the appearance with reality, which is presumably what a consistent Protagoras would have done. But, of course, that amounts to a form of dogmatism, too, because it is a claim about how things really are.

of rational belief. For as we have already seen, rational belief requires that knowledge be at least possible, knowledge the proximity to which makes a belief rational. This proximity has nothing to do with truth and everything to do with evidence or justification. But alas, as Plato himself insists, δόξα has no part in justification.[39] A belief may well be true but it is not thereby rendered rational. Nor is its rationality sequentially fortifiable by being arrived at according to the application of Carneadean evidentiary criteria.

As with Arcesilaus, we can only guess at Carneades' view of Plato's account of knowledge. His rejection of Stoic epistemology in favor of a calculus of rational belief is not obviously incompatible with the Platonic position if we imagine that our 'possession' of knowledge is itself the underlying criterion for the rationalization of belief.[40] Such rationalized belief seems not at all unlike what physics is supposed to be in *Timaeus*. This is admittedly speculative. Yet the Academic argument against the Stoic criterion of knowledge should have resulted in the unqualified rejection of rational belief, as it apparently does for Arcesilaus. Did Carneades think that such radical skepticism was avoidable given that Platonic knowledge is a human endowment?[41]

One fairly slight piece of evidence in favor of this interpretation is that the Academic Philo of Larissa (158–84 BCE), pupil of Clitomachus, explicitly capitulated on the matter of whether knowledge must be infallible. The little evidence we have for Philo's view suggests that he summarily dismissed the Stoic criterion of truth as a 'graspable presentation,' that is, as one that (a) comes from what is; and (b) is stamped and impressed (in us) in accordance with what is; and (c) in such a way that it could not come from what is not.[42] The third clause, said by Sextus to have been added precisely to guard against skeptical arguments, is what Philo attacked. Such an attack is what a Skeptic like Sextus would endorse doing. Yet Philo's innovation seems to have been to argue that the elimination of (c) does not erase knowledge altogether but only *infallible* knowledge.[43] Thus, an appearance can be epistemic even if it might not have been. The fact that any presentation may be false does not entail that we never attain knowledge from our presentations. The idea of fallible knowledge ("I know but I may be mistaken") really is a departure from anything authentically Platonic. Insofar

---

39. See *Tim.* 51D5–E4, where δόξα—*true* δόξα—is ἄλογον.

40. That Carneades was primarily focused on rebutting Stoic epistemology seems clear from his well-known quip (quoted by Diogenes Laertius, 4.62), "If it was not for Chrysippus, I would not be." And yet Sextus, *M.* 7.159, says that Carneades aimed his arguments against the criterion of truth of all of his predecessors, including, it would seem, Plato.

41. Cf. Cicero, *TD* 1.57, for the claim (certainly not Stoic, but perhaps intended as Academic) that our embodied conceptualization would not be possible if we did not possess previous disembodied cognition of Forms. Also, see Karamanolis 2006, 48, n. 11, who cites *Acad.* 1.13, 2.11–12, 18, and Sextus, *PH* 1.235, as suggesting that the Academics did not "denounce" knowledge in the non-Stoic sense.

42. See Sextus, *M.* 7.248.1–4: καταληπτικὴ δέ ἐστιν ἡ ἀπὸ ὑπάρχοντος καὶ κατ' αὐτὸ τὸ ὑπάρχον ἐναπομεμαγμένη καὶ ἐναπεσφραγισμένη, ὁποία οὐκ ἂν γένοιτο ἀπὸ μὴ ὑπάρχοντος. Cf. D.L. 7.46; Cicero, *Acad.* 2.18.

43. See Barnes 1989, 71–74; Brittain 2001, chap. 3.

as this view is an innovation, we may infer that it was not one that Carneades or Arcesilaus shared. As we will see in the next chapter, it was this innovative deviation from Platonism by Philo that inspired Antiochus of Ascalon to attempt a reinvigoration of the authentic Platonic position.

The Stoics, the principal target of Academic skepticism, adhered to the Platonic claim that knowledge is irreversible by reasoning. The Academics did not challenge this view before Philo of Larissa. The dispute between Arcesilaus and Carneades regarding the existence of a criterion of truth reveals not their rejection of the possibility of knowledge, but their rejection of the possibility of knowledge of the sensible world. This, of course, was the only knowledge that the Stoics thought possible. In their denial of the latter possibility, the Academic Skeptics displayed their Platonic bona fides. It is not until Sextus Empiricus or perhaps his unknown source or perhaps even Aenesidemus that a more comprehensive challenge to the possibility of infallible knowledge *tout court* was mounted.[44] This challenge is aimed at the heart of Platonism far more than anything attributable to the Academy. The reason for this is that Sextus saw that the claim to the possibility of infallible knowledge depended on the existence of an immaterial intellect. If there were no such thing, the putative knowledge of intelligible reality could only be some sort of representation. But just as the Academic Skeptics had no difficulty in showing against the Stoics that representations of sensible reality could not be infallible, so the self-described Pyrrhonians had no difficulty in showing that if intellect is material, then all one could conceivably aspire to would be a representation of immaterial reality, and as such infallibility was impossible.

The proponent of UP cannot forego the possibility of infallible cognition, at least for the Demiurge. The triad of Idea of the Good-Forms-Intellect is, as we have already seen, the core of the positive construct built on the foundation of UP. If the Demiurge cognized only representations of Forms—whatever these might be—he would, among other things, not eternally 'attain' the *ontological* truth that the Idea of the Good provides to the Forms. This state of affairs would import an adventitiousness or, better, haphazardness into the generation of the cosmos that is unthinkable given the comprehensive worldview of *Timaeus*. More fundamentally, it would place a limitation on the goodness of the first principle of all. That is, the Good could not give ontological truth to the Demiurge, but only to the Forms. As a result, the Demiurge's desire to make the cosmos like the Forms would be hollow. For the supposed intelligibility imposed on the receptacle would not amount to images of Forms, but only images of the Demiurge's representations of Forms, thus making the Demiurge more like the earthly craftsman than the maker of heaven and earth.[45]

---

44. See Gerson 2009, 129–33.

45. The debilitating result of having only representations of Forms in the intellect and not the Forms themselves only intensifies if Forms are Numbers and their representations are only images of these.

As Academic skepticism shows, adherence to the idea that the ne plus ultra of cognition is infallible reveals a new problem about the possibility of rational belief, a problem that the doctrine of ἀνάμνησις is supposed to solve. If we do already know the Forms, then we have the basis at least for a justification for our claims about sensibles. But in order to prove that ἀνάμνησις in the relevant sense exists, one must demonstrate the immortality of the soul. This is the burden of the Recollection Argument in *Phaedo*. Further, the idea that being a knower is, so to speak, our natural or true state, and that it is the state of the disembodied soul, underlies the ethical dimension of Platonism. Philosophy is a preparation for death, as Socrates says in *Phaedo,* because the state of an accomplished or successful lover of wisdom is the state to which we aspire, or ought to aspire. This is exactly the case also for the exhortation to assimilate oneself to the divine in *Theaetetus*.[46] This exhortation was to become emblematic of Plato's ethics for later Platonism. Thus, the immortality and immateriality of the soul and its capacity for the highest form of cognition, that which is possessed by the Demiurge, is a critical part of the Platonic construct. The antiskepticism and the antimaterialism of UP, whatever its precise origin as a challenge to one or another of Plato's predecessors may have been, was the starting point for the distinctive epistemology at the heart of Platonism.[47]

The shared conviction of Stoics and Academic Skeptics that knowledge must be infallible also reveals the core problem in the attempts to hive off a 'nondogmatic' Socratic philosophy from Platonism. 'Prudential judgment' or 'elenctic knowledge' or even rational belief, taken to be the main idea in Socrates' intellectualism, is, as Arcesilaus shows, hollow because there is no justification short of complete and 'unoverturnable' justification. Each and every one of Socrates' claims regarding what he firmly believes or even knows is controvertible. Either Socrates gives no reason for his beliefs—beliefs like "one must absolutely never do wrong"—or his reasons are never conclusive, such as his reasons for thinking that it would be wrong for him to escape from prison. Yet the reasonableness of these claims, if indeed it be such, is restored when we set this putative *Socratic* intellectualism within the Platonic context. For Plato wants to maintain that recollection or even the midwifery of Socrates in *Theaetetus* presupposes the possession of knowledge, that is, infallible knowledge of Forms, on the basis of which rational λόγοι about the sensible world, including human life, may be produced.

---

46. See *Tht.* 176A8–B3: διὸ καὶ πειρᾶσθαι χρὴ ἐνθένδε ἐκεῖσε φεύγειν ὅτι τάχιστα. Φυγὴ δὲ ὁμοίωσις θεῷ κατὰ τὸ δυνατόν· ὁμοίωσις δὲ δίκαιον καὶ ὅσιον μετὰ φρονήσεως γενέσθαι. (For this reason, it is necessary to try to flee from here to there as quickly as possible. This flight is the assimilation to the divine as much as possible. And this assimilation is to become just and pious with accompanying wisdom.)

47. See *Tim.* 52C–E, where antimaterialism follows from the distinction of knowledge and true belief, since knowledge must be exclusively of immaterial entities.

CHAPTER 7

Platonism in the 'Middle'

The term 'Middle Platonism,' like the term 'Neoplatonism' is an artifact of the predilection for periodization among historians of ancient philosophy.[1] The former is typically used to refer to the Platonic doctrines found first in Antiochus of Ascalon (c. 130–c. 68 BCE) especially after his break with his mentor Philo of Larissa in the so-called *Sosus* affair around 87.[2] Middle Platonism, by default as it were, is said to end with Plotinus (204/5–270 CE) and the onset of Neoplatonism. Once the *termini* and the personages are fixed, the qualifications usually commence: Antiochus was perhaps more of a Stoic than a Platonist, the 'later' phase of Middle Platonism includes something that may be termed 'Neopythagoreanism,' and those termed 'Middle Platonists' certainly differed among themselves in regard to particular doctrines. Attempts to delineate the 'nature' of Middle Platonism are repeatedly undercut by the essential arbitrariness of the historical label.[3] The approach taken in this book is to explore the doctrines

---

1. See Ferrari 2010, 83, on what is apparently the first use of the term '*der mitteler Platonismus*' by Karl Praechter (1909), possibly in imitation of the term '*der mitteler Stoicizmus*' introduced some twenty years earlier by Schmekel.
2. See Glucker 1978, 13–15. The events are recounted in Cicero's *Academica*, book 2, otherwise known as *Lucullus*, 11–12 (= *Acad.* 2.11–12). See Barnes 1989, 68–69, who is skeptical about the claim that the publication of Philo's *Roman Books* was the occasion for Antiochus's break with the Academy. See Göransson 1995 for an argument against the claim that Antiochus was the founder of a Platonic school.
3. This is not to say, of course, that stellar work on individual philosophers in this period has not been done by Dillon, Glucker, Tarrant, and many others. See Tarrant 1993 for an attempt to isolate one form of Platonism in this period, namely, 'Thrasyllan.' Also, Tarrant 2007, 323, 330, who argues that the primary legacy of Antiochus is to have established Platonism as

of the soi-disants followers of Plato (whether 'Platonists' or 'Academics') assuming their common commitment to UP.[4] I maintain that this approach has the advantage of offering a satisfactory explanation for most of the differences in doctrine among Plato's followers. This explanation is that a commitment to UP is underdetermined for one 'version' of Platonism rather than another.[5] For example, the rejection of skepticism is one element of UP. But it is possible to derive from UP various views about the nature of the objects of knowledge in relation to the first principle of all and also in relation to the objects of other modes of cognition.

To take a different example, the assumption of the falsity of relativism in ethics, though not, of course, entailing one particular view about the nature of objective morality, does seem to entail objectivity. If this objectivity is in regard to what is good for a human being or what is a good life, it is difficult to distinguish this objectivity from universality if we are committed to rejecting relativism. For the view that what is objectively good for A (that is, independent of what A thinks is good for A) is only equivocally said to be good for B is highly implausible. Hence, some sort of ἔργον argument—moving the objectivity up to the level of species in the direction of universality—such as we find in book 1 of *Republic* and in book 1 of Aristotle's *Nicomachean Ethics,* seems viable. A Platonist will commit to such an argument. But Plato's own commitment to antimaterialism, to knowledge and Forms, the objects of knowledge, leads him to conclude that immaterial souls exist separately from the body. And further, he concludes that we are identical with our souls, in which case we are not unequivocally identical with the soul-body composite that is a human being. So to tie the nature of happiness or virtue to the ἔργον argument, which is an argument about the function of a human being, is to leave rather unclear the nature of what

---

a set of doctrines rather than a collection of dialogues. I have been arguing, on the contrary, that Platonism was always the former.

4. See Annas 1999 for a defense of a 'Middle Platonic' approach to the reading of the dialogues. This defense focuses largely on the ethics and assumes that Platonism and what is found in the dialogues are identical. There is one chapter in the book that attempts to connect the metaphysics with the ethics (chap. 5), but there (112) Annas argues that metaphysics has to be seen in the "context of ethics." I think it is actually the other way around.

5. See Cicero, *Acad.* 2.15, where Antiochus is said to claim that Plato "left a complete system" (*reliquit perfectissiman disciplimnam*) that was followed by Peripatetics and Academics. Since he adds that Stoics, too, differed from this system only in words rather than in substantial beliefs, it seems that the 'system' does not rest on UP, but only a positive construction more or less detached from that basis. Antiochus's error, I believe, was in thinking that Stoic materialism did not amount to a fundamental difference in *sententiis* with the Platonists. Cf. 1.17. Cicero, *De fin.* 3.74, refers to the *admirabilis composito disciplinae incredibilisque ordo* of Stoic doctrine, something that many Middle Platonists no doubt wished to emulate. See Bonazzi 2012, especially on his argument that Antiochus's position was of the "subordinated integration" of Stoicism into Platonism. Annas (1999, 115) makes the eminently reasonable suggestion that Stoics and Platonists can agree on ethics while disagreeing on metaphysics even if, one might add, Platonists or Stoics argue that their ethics follows from or otherwise depends on their metaphysics.

is good for *us*. That is, what is good for a human being may or may not be identical with what is good for me.

Antiochus of Ascalon

As discussed in chapter 1, an expression of Platonism is for both Platonists and their opponents measured by the coherence of the various elements of the positive construct made from the matrix of UP. Just as the materialism and the nominalism of the Stoics were held to be mutually entailing, so, too, were the antinominalism and the antimaterialism of the Platonists.[6] From the perspective of the neo-Pyrrhonian Skeptics, Stoicism and Platonism were simply different types of dogmatism. They both insisted on the possibility of knowledge, a claim that was itself taken to be a claim to knowledge. The challenge for the dogmatists (and here we should include Academic Skeptics such as Carneades) was to discover an account of knowledge consistent with the Platonic or Stoic principles they embraced. Among the philosophers to be dealt with in this chapter, it seems clear that Skeptics and Stoics presented different sorts of challenges to Platonism. Philo of Larissa wanted to deny that knowledge had the property of infallibility. The Stoics acknowledged the infallibility of knowledge, but wanted to do so within a materialist framework.

Based on Cicero's evidence, the motivation for the '*Sosus* Affair' was Philo of Larissa's having published *Roman Books*, in which he argued that there was no difference between the Old Academy of Plato and the New Academy of Arcesilaus and his followers.[7] In particular, he argued that both Plato and the philosophers of the New Academy maintained the possibility of knowledge. What the latter had opposed was the Stoic criterion of κατάληψις, or the graspable presentation.[8] That is, there was no such thing as a 'graspable' presentation, one that could not come from something other than that from which it comes. Such a presentation was supposed to be self-evident, meaning that if one had it one could not fail properly to assent to its truth. As we saw in the last chapter, Skeptics disputed the existence of such presentations, arguing that there could be illusory presentations that were indistinguishable from those that were real. It was Philo's innovation to maintain that this possibility of error or illusion did not preclude the possibility of knowledge. Under certain circumstances, it was possible to have knowledge, though this does not eliminate the possibility that on occasion I do not know what I think I know because I am having an illusory or otherwise misleading experience.

---

    6. On the Platonist understanding of Stoic nominalism, see Syrianus, *In Meta.* 104.17–23 (= *SVF* 2.361), who claims that the Stoics take "particulars" (τὰ καθ' ἕκαστα) as the sole reality.
    7. On the details of the affair, which occurred in 87 BCE, see Cicero, *Acad.* 2.11–12; on the claim about Philo, see *Acad.* 1.13.
    8. Cicero, *Acad.* 2.18; Sextus, *PH* 1.235; Numenius, fr. 28.6–12 Des Places.

Antiochus in his *Sosus* rejected Philo's claim that the Old and New Academies were in agreement on knowledge. He maintained that Philo, in rejecting the Stoic criterion, had also thereby rejected the Platonic criterion, namely, that knowledge be infallible. The issue between Philo and Antiochus—apart from the matter of the historical accuracy of Philo's account of Academic unanimity—is whether knowledge must be infallible. Antiochus insisted that infallibility is a property of knowledge, and Philo insisted that it is not.[9] As Jonathan Barnes put it, Antiochus argued that if it was merely logically possible that my experience was illusory, then I could not be said to possess knowledge, whereas Philo maintained in effect that admitting this logical possibility did not entail the epistemic possibility that I might in fact be mistaken on every particular occasion.[10] Antiochus (and Pyrrhonian Skeptics) would no doubt want to insist that a distinction between logical and epistemic possibility in this context is specious. If it is logically possible that my putative evidence does not entail what it is taken to be evidence for, then it is not evidence at all.[11] Barnes, on behalf of Philo, claims in effect that there is such a thing as nonentailing evidence, evidence that makes me justified in claiming to know but that does not *guarantee* that I know.

I believe that Barnes is assuming that if there is no infallible knowledge, then it makes perfectly good sense to argue that knowledge is justified true belief, that is, belief that (logically) may be false, but in fact is not. Plato, Aristotle, the Stoics, and the Academic and Pyrrhonian Skeptics all concur in maintaining that infallibility is a property of knowledge, with dogmatists of all stripes arguing that knowledge is possible for us and the Skeptics arguing that just because knowledge must be infallible, it is not possible. Antiochus defends the dogmatic position; Philo stands alone in claiming

---

9. Cicero, *Acad.* 2.23, 33. See Brittain 2012, 105, "Antiochus' epistemology is profoundly—as well as explicitly—Stoic." Brittain goes on to argue that this means that "Antiochus was not a Platonist" (106, n. 7).

10. See Barnes 1989, 84–85.

11. Cicero, *Acad.* 2.34, 36. Brittain (2006, xxxv) argues that Antiochus "may have thought that we assent to cataleptic impressions because we *infer* from this phenomenal 'sign' or feature that they are true." Brittain adds in a note that "the orthodox interpretation does not make the 'clarity and distinctness' of a cataleptic impression, in virtue of which it 'can't be false', something that is in principle available to the perceiver (although it may be to experts or to the Stoic sage, with practice)." However, it is only the Stoic sage who possesses knowledge. Cf. 22, n. 47, where Brittain adds that Antiochus adopted an Academic misinterpretation of the Stoic criterion. For "on the Stoic view, the [cataleptic] impression is a natural and automatic criterion of truth; we do not infer the truth of its content from a 'sign.'" If there is no 'sign' or evidence on the basis of which we infer that which we claim to know, then the Stoic criterion amounts to the claim that the sage is by definition one who knows. But the whole point in offering a criterion of truth for the Stoics is to distinguish the presentations of the sage from those of everyone else. So the presentation is for the 'fool' no evidence for what he claims to know; the same presentation then must be evidence for the sage's claim to know. If Brittain's interpretation of the Stoic view is correct, then it is the case either that for the sage there is no logical possibility of error or, if there is such a possibility, then the sage must infer that which he claims to know.

that infallibility is not a property of knowledge.[12] His only argument for this view seems to be that if knowledge were infallible, then there would be no such thing as knowledge of sensibles. So wishing to take a position according to which something like empirical knowledge is possible, he denies that knowledge is infallible. He does not opt for the qualified skeptical conclusion that empirical knowledge is impossible *because* knowledge is infallible. Why, though, is Philo not content to agree that infallibility is a property of knowledge, for which reason empirical knowledge is not possible, but that nevertheless justified true belief about the empirical realm is possible? Why does he apparently insist that fallible, though justified, true belief *is* knowledge? Presumably, the answer to this question is based on the Skeptics' insight that if the knowledge that is infallible is not attainable by us, then justified true belief is a chimera. Philo's innovative strategy is to redefine knowledge such that it coincides with justified true belief. This strategy must fail unless there is, as Barnes suggests, genuine evidence that does not entail that for which it is supposedly evidence. But the idea of nonentailing evidence is completely obscure, as Sextus Empiricus and presumably his sources so clearly saw. Certainly, Philo's predilection for counting certain presentations as nonentailing evidence is strictly irrelevant to whether they in fact are such.

Philo's position, constructed to avoid the radical skeptical conclusion, actually plays nicely into the Skeptics' hands. Presumably, what enraged Antiochus was Philo's suggestion that his position was in fact that of the Old Academy. In effect, while Philo is claiming that he is faithful to the Old Academy in acknowledging the possibility of knowledge, Antiochus is rejecting Philo's claim on the grounds that he is equivocating on the meaning of 'knowledge.' And yet Philo's claim to be in harmony with Plato and the Old Academy is no less puzzling than Antiochus's counterclaim that it was Zeno, founder of Stoicism, who 'corrected' Plato in his account of knowledge.[13] This correction appears to be that Zeno claimed that (infallible) knowledge was available through the senses, albeit to the sage alone.[14]

---

12. See Cicero, *Acad.* 1.17; cf. 2.15 for Antiochus's view that Academics and Peripatetics are in philosophical harmony with Plato. This notorious remark may refer either merely to the view that knowledge is infallible (something that Skeptics are more than happy to concede) or it may refer to something like UP. In the latter case, the remark is especially provocative depending on which of the Academics Antiochus means.

13. See Cicero, *Acad.* 1.43, 2.69. Sextus, *PH* 1.235, says that Antiochus transferred the Stoa into the Academy, and tried to show that Stoic dogmas were present in Plato. Karamanolis (2006, 56) says that "the prime example of the unity of the 'ancients' for Antiochus is their unanimous construal of Plato's philosophy as being doctrinal in nature." In this book I am arguing that it is illuminating to see 'behind' the doctrinal nature of Plato's philosophy the substructure that is UP and that disputes among Platonists arise principally from their questions regarding the cogency and comprehensiveness of Plato's doctrines as the ideal positive construct on the basis of UP.

14. See Cicero, *Acad.* 1.42. At 2.113, he points out that for the Old Academics, it was possible for the wise man to have opinions, but for the Stoics it was not. These opinions are

Presumably, this counts as a correction to Plato and not a rejection of him in favor of a new systematic position because Zeno retained the property of infallibility, even though he 'corrected' Plato on the sources of knowledge. In addition, as a materialist, Zeno could not have agreed with Plato that the objects of knowledge are Forms. Then why does Antiochus suppose otherwise? Should we dismiss him as a syncretist who, for whatever reasons, irenic or otherwise, wished to build something like a dogmatic alliance?[15]

There is one passage in Cicero's *Academica*, however, that should give us pause. Varro, in presenting Antiochus's historical account of Academics and Peripatetics who followed Plato, says that these philosophers held that mind (*mens*) alone is able to discern "what was simple, uniform, and self-identical."[16] What this simple object is, is exactly what Plato called ἰδέα, but which, Varro says, can be properly called by the Latin *species*. By contrast, the senses were unable to cognize things people supposed were available to perception. The ever-changing sensible realm was in fact the realm of opinion; knowledge (*scientia*) resided only in the soul's concepts (*notiones*) and in acts of reasoning (*rationes*). It is clear enough that the members of the Old Academy and Aristotle did in fact agree with Plato that there was no knowledge of that of which there was belief or opinion, and this despite the fact that Aristotle, Antiochus concedes, "undermined" (*labefactavit*) the Ideas.[17] It seems that it is the separateness or transcendence of Forms

---

uncertain in their provenance. But if the opinions that the Academic wise man possesses are based on his knowledge of Forms, Antiochus's conflation of the Academic and Stoic view does not seem particularly egregious. See Tarrant 2006, 11–16.

15. Praechter (1909, 536) simply assumes the '*Eklektizismus*' of the 'Middle Platonists' from which, he claims, only Epicurean elements are missing. See Barnes 1989, 79–81, for the case that Antiochus was a syncretist rather than an eclectic. See Karamanolis 2006, 80–81, who argues that Antiochus was neither a syncretist nor an eclectic, but a Platonist, striving for consistency with the help of the testimonies of Academics, Aristotle, and the Stoics. Sedley (2012b) claims that Antiochus' "interest is in re-aligning himself with the mainstream tradition of the Academy as a school, not with the thought of Plato in particular." I believe that the core of this 'mainstream tradition' is a commitment to UP. In this particular debate, I would suggest instead that Antiochus was exploring the extent to which Stoicism could be incorporated into that Academic tradition. Indicative of that exploration was perhaps the hypothesis that Stoic materialism was not an impediment to *any* version of Platonism.

16. See Cicero, *Acad.* 1.30: simplex et unius modi et tale quale esset. Cf. Plato, *Symp.* 211B1–2.

17. Cicero, *Acad.* 1.33. See Barnes 1989, 95–96, arguing against Dillon (1977, 93) and Donini (1982, 95, n. 4), that it is doubtful that Antiochus had any allegiance to a theory of Forms even though he recognized the role of such a theory in the history of Platonism. Considering Antiochus's recognition that Aristotle did not "undermine" the necessity of stable objects for the possibility of knowledge, what Antiochus probably meant by Aristotle's undermining Ideas was that he raised problems—perhaps insurmountable—with the claim that each Idea was absolutely separate and independent of anything else, including a divine mind. Cf. Bonazzi 2012, 317, n. 32, who suggests that *labefactavit* means "weaken" not "undermine." As we have seen, Plato himself undermines a presumption of the unqualified separateness of each object of knowledge. Boys-Stones (2012, 224–28) argues that Antiochus understood Aristotle to have undermined the Ideas by making them unstable entities. This would

that Antiochus thinks needs "correcting."[18] Accepting this correction, the epistemological position shared by Academics, Peripatetics, and Stoics remains standing.[19] Philo, Antiochus concluded, misread their shared insight when he wrongly claimed Plato as an adherent of the position he advanced in his *Roman Books*.

As we will see later in this chapter, the 'conceptualizing' of knowledge is virtually a Middle Platonic commonplace. Such a move needs to be distinguished from another, one that is decisively rejected by Plato, namely, that the Forms just are concepts.[20] Despite the multiple problems with this approach, at least as an interpretation of Plato's response to UP, it has its attractions. The principal one is that it seems to rescue knowledge from the danger of being the exclusive preserve of the pre- and postembodied person. The embodied mind that uses concepts and acts of reasoning is on this view able to attain knowledge of the nature of things. In particular, ethical knowledge becomes possible.[21]

The claim that "knowledge resides only in the soul's concepts and acts of reasoning" neatly avoids the matter of the objects of knowledge. As Aristotle tells us, at least one reason for Plato's positing of Forms was that these separately existing, immaterial, and immutable entities are the only things that could be the objects of knowledge. So how could Antiochus suppose that there was a Platonic warrant for holding that knowledge—infallible knowledge—is of the *species* that are in sensibles?

We recall that *Theaetetus* makes the distinction between "possessing" (κεκτῆσθαι) knowledge and "having" (ἔχειν) knowledge, and implies that knowledge is primarily the latter. This is the distinction that Aristotle expresses in terms of first and second actuality. If we read this dialogue dialectically, then the distinction only need imply that *if* the distinction between possessing and having something were to be applied to knowledge, then knowledge would be primarily the latter. If Antiochus reads Plato's dialogue

---

presumably be the result of denying their transcendence and situating them within the sensible realm.

18. See Boys-Stones 2012, 222–23. Boys-Stones cites *SVF* 1.65, 2.360, 365 and Syrianus, *In Meta.* 105.19–106.13, as evidence that ἰδέα is being used here in the Stoic sense of 'concept.' As Boys-Stones notes, however, a predilection for a materialist metaphysics is not necessarily incompatible even with the claim that Ideas are thoughts in a divine mind when the divine mind is conceived of in Stoic fashion. See also Dillon 1977, 93–96; Sharples 1989, 233.

19. See *Acad.* 1.14 and 2.16 on what is apparently Antiochus's desire to separate the dialectical stance of Socrates from Platonism. Such an attempt is a hallmark of the beginning of a positive construction out of UP.

20. See *Parm.* 132B3ff., where Socrates suggests that a Form is a νόημα existing only ἐν ψυχαῖς. Parmenides has little difficulty in showing Socrates that a Form, in order to do the job it is meant to do, must not be 'in souls' but rather 'in nature.' Karamanolis (2006, 65) thinks that Antiochus equated Stoic concepts (ἔννοιαι) with immanent Forms, that is, the instances of Forms in sensibles. This seems to me to be mistaken because concepts are distinct from that of which they are concepts, even if the latter are 'immanent' in sensibles.

21. See Cicero, *Acad.* 2.23. See Helmig 2012 for a richly detailed study of 'concept formation' in the Platonic tradition.

in the assertoric mode, so to speak, then he would take the distinction to imply that there is the knowledge that the soul possesses prior to embodiment and the knowledge that is acquired here below, no doubt at least in part via sense perception. The Stoic 'correction' of the Platonic position would amount to the intention to focus on the knowledge acquired or reacquired when embodied. It may well be that Zeno's view was in fact intended as a correction in a much stronger sense, namely, a rejection of the Platonic assumption regarding what the possession of knowledge must be, namely, the immaterial soul being cognitively identical with an immaterial entity. It is not so difficult to see, however, that Antiochus was not entirely unjustified in finding a convergence in the Stoic and Platonic accounts of the 'having' of knowledge as opposed to the more exotic claim of 'possessing' it prior to embodiment.[22]

For Plato, the existence of knowledge, established by a transcendental argument that shows that if we did not possess knowledge, we could not make the judgments we do about sensibles, presents the following deep problem. If human beings possess knowledge, then it is the disembodied soul or intellect that has it. But my ability to 'access' this knowledge when I judge, for example, that sensible equals are deficiently equal, means that I have it, too, or at least that I am identical with that which has it. So am I the intellect or am I the human being? Analogously, I am the subject of bodily states and also the subject of the judgments in regard to these. How can I be both? Plato certainly does want to insist that I am primarily the intellect or 'the human being inside the human being' and only in a derivative way the manifest human being, and so I am more the subject of judgments than I am the subject of bodily states.[23] All Platonists struggle with the problem of the relation between the real self and the embodied avatar.

Plato's rejection of skepticism and consequent account of knowledge is supposed to cohere with his antimaterialism. In *Phaedo* it is evident that these are inseparable. As far as we know, Antiochus did not see—or if he saw, he did not accept—this inseparability.[24] He opted for 'having' knowledge in the Stoic mode without 'possessing' it in the Platonic. And he thereby avoided the above problem of the relation between the embodied and disembodied self.[25]

22. On the knowledge of Plato's *Theaetetus* in the Skeptical Academy, see Annas 1992, and among Middle Platonists, see Sedley 1996. For Antiochus, perhaps the knowledge that we 'have' was supposed to include as objects the particular facts or states of affairs directly implied by universal knowledge. See *SVF* 3 Antipater 56, where Clement of Alexandria quotes Antipater as maintaining that, in addition to holding that virtue is sufficient for happiness, Plato was in harmony (σύμφωνα) with the Stoics on many other doctrines (δόγματα).

23. See *Rep.* 589A7: τοῦ ἀνθρώπου ὁ ἐντὸς ἄνθρωπος.

24. Cf. his rejection of the immateriality of the mind or soul at Cicero, *De fin.* 4.36. Dillon (1977, 84) perhaps goes too far in inferring from Antiochus's rejection of the immateriality of the mind the rejection of the existence of any immaterial entities whatsoever.

25. See Boys-Stones 2012, 223, who argues that Antiochus is a materialist, citing *Acad.* 1.24 as evidence. But this passage refers only to the Stoicizing account of nature. It says nothing about that which is strictly supernatural or immaterial.

We do not have any evidence, though, as to whether Antiochus had a cogent response to the multiple skeptical attacks on the Stoic account of knowledge. Antiochus's motive for insisting on the possibility of infallible knowledge in the Stoic mode seems to be his belief that knowledge of the "criterion of truth" (*iudicium veri*) and of the "moral end" (*finem bonorum*) were the two greatest philosophical tasks.[26] It was not enough to have a true belief about these matters or even to have a rational true belief; one must have no "doubts" (*dubia*) whatsoever.[27] Hence, Skeptics ought to at least concede that they have no doubts regarding the truth of the proposition that nothing is knowable. If they make this concession, then they reveal their inconsistency. If they do not, then they actually have no real doctrine at all. Antiochus seems to have seriously missed the point here. One may fail to have doubts regarding all sorts of matters in which one has no right not to have doubts, or at least no rational basis for being doubt free. If Antiochus has no doubts regarding the end or goal of human life, that is, if he is confident that he does or can know what this end is, he has not even begun to answer the skeptical objection to the alleged justification of this position. If, by contrast, Antiochus means to suggest that having no doubts is equivalent to being in an infallible mental state, it is difficult to see how the graspable presentation (as much a presentation for the fool as it is for the sage) provides this.

Antiochus's apparent effort to connect his two "greatest philosophical tasks" reveals him engaged in a tentative *re*construction of Platonism on the foundation of UP. His effort to recruit the Stoics for this task shows him questioning the indispensability of the element of antimaterialism in the foundation.

Plutarch of Chaeronea

In the vast writings of Plutarch, we see, perhaps for the first time, a number of the principles employed in the construction of Platonism on the basis of UP: (a) the amalgamation of Platonic and Pre-Socratic (especially Pythagorean) doctrines; (b) the use of Aristotle for the elucidation of

---

26. Cicero, *Acad.* 2.29.
27. See Tarrant 1985, 97–102, who argues that at Sextus, *M.* 7.141–45, Antiochus is the source for an interpretation of *Tim.* 28A according to which Plato held that reason was "comprehensive" (περιληπτικός) and was employed both for the cognition of Forms and for deriving intelligible content from sense perception. The latter 'doxastic' reason assisted 'epistemic' reason. Although it is no doubt true that reason is for Plato involved with the beliefs that arise from sense perception, Antiochus needs more than a faculty to 'bridge' the Platonic and Stoic positions. He needs a mental state that is capable of grasping infallibly. See Sedley 2012b, 93–97, on how, assuming this passage is a report of Antiochus's epistemology, he misreads Plato's *Timaeus* to make the Platonic περιληπτικόν for intelligibles into the Stoic καταληπτικόν for sensibles. Contra Tarrant: Brittain 2012, 108–13.

Platonic doctrines; and (c) the effort to show that a consistent Platonic account of issues arising in contemporary debates could be given.[28]

The strategy behind (a), that of bolstering Plato's authority by showing that what he said is an expression of ancient wisdom, has a significant impact, as we will see, on (c).[29] This happened in a fairly straightforward manner. If, for example, what Plato was saying was actually what Pythagoras was saying, then Pythagoreanism could be used to support an interpretation of the unspoken or unwritten implications of what we find in the dialogues. Those who rejected elements of UP were claimed to be outside the mainstream of the wisdom tradition. Thus, a *systematic* articulation of Platonism acquired a reinvigorated legitimacy. In addition, and incidentally for my purposes, the systematic expression of Platonism could be employed to interpret Plato's predecessors, especially the Pre-Socratics.[30]

This last point is connected with (b) above. The interpretation of the Pre-Socratics through a systematized Platonism is supplemented by the use of Aristotle's interpretation of Plato. For example, Plutarch understands Parmenides in the second part of his poem as offering an account of the sensible world according to which, in Platonic terms, the sensible world is only available to belief (δόξα), not intellect (νοῦς).[31] As we learn a page later, what is available to intellect is the world of Platonic Forms. Aristotle, too, took the second part of Parmenides' poem to be offering an account of "appearances" (τὰ φαινόμενα), which, as Plutarch well knew, was one way that Plato refers

---

28. As Dillon (1988) points out, the idea that Plutarch was in any sense 'heretical' in his construction of Platonism presumes a notion of 'orthodoxy' for which there is no solid evidence. Dillon goes on to show in this article that Plutarch—judging both from his extant works and the titles of his lost works—was eager to show an underlying unity in the Platonic tradition. I would suggest that this, admittedly rather loose, unity consisted in adherence to UP. Plutarch's commitment to UP is most evident in his various attacks on Stoics and Epicureans. For antimechanism, see also, e.g., *De def. or.*, 435F–436E; for antinominalism, see *Adv. Col.* 1115A–1116E; for antimaterialism, see *De E.*, 392A–393A, *De Is.*351Dff.; for antirelativism, see *Adv. Col.* 1108F–1109B. Plutarch's antiskepticism is complicated by his efforts to take seriously and integrate into his Platonism the accounts in the dialogues of Socratic ignorance and aporetic method. See Opsomer 1998, 127, 186; Karamanolis 2006, 85–86; Shiffman 2010. As Karamanolis suggests, Plutarch devoted "considerable energy" to a defense of Academic skepticism. I understand this as commitment to a zetetic approach to anti-Platonic dogmatic claims on the foundation of the elements of UP.

29. Cf. *De Is.* 354E with *De E.* 393C–D. In the first passage, we read that "the wisest of the Greeks," Solon, Thales, Plato, Eudoxus, and Pythagoras, all agreed on, broadly speaking, their conception of the supreme deity. Pythagoras, it is said, acquired his wisdom from Egyptian priests. In the second passage, the account of the unicity of the supreme deity is supported by his various names, e.g., 'Apollo,' which is taken to mean 'ἀ-πολλά' (cf. *De Is.* 381F). Also, *De Is.* 360E, 363Dff., where the philosophical interpretation of Greek myth is elucidated by 'Egyptians.' Schefer (2001, 214–27) argues that the mystical experience that is the culmination of philosophy for Plato is in fact union with Apollo. She thus recurs in essence to the Middle Platonic interpretation.

30. See Mansfeld 1992, 278–300.

31. See *Adv. Col.* 1114C–E.

to the sensible world.³² An even more portentous example of Plutarch's use of Aristotle to interpret Plato, to which we will return in a bit, is his identification of the receptacle in Plato's *Timaeus* with matter.³³ Aristotle, in his *Physics,* says that Plato identified matter and space because he identified the receptacle and space.³⁴ It is not just that the identification, nowhere explicitly stated in *Timaeus,* assumes the correctness of Aristotle's interpretation, but that his interpretation allows Plutarch to bring to bear the larger Aristotelian account of matter to make a variety of systematic Platonic claims.

It is hardly surprising that self-declared followers of Plato should appeal to *Timaeus* as the starting point for an explication and defense of Platonic cosmology against contemporary opponents. The importance of this dialogue was bound to grow in the face of non-Greek cosmologies entwined with eastern religions. There are, however, numerous fundamental lacunae in this dialogue itself regarding issues that had to be settled in order to arrive at anything like a satisfactory account of the universe. Two of the most prominent of these are the absence in *Timaeus* of any explicit reference to a single superordinate Idea of the Good and the dialogue's silence regarding the presence of evil in the world. Clearly the two omissions are related; if, somehow, the Idea of the Good is integratable with the cosmology of *Timaeus* as the first principle of all, as it is in *Republic,* the very possibility of evil in the world becomes problematic. That is, if the Good explains the being of everything, either directly or indirectly, how can we suppose that the Good is to explain evil?³⁵ As Plutarch reasons,

> For, if nothing naturally comes to be without a cause, and if the Good cannot provide a cause for what is evil, then it is necessary that nature must have in itself the origin and principle of evil just as it has that of good.³⁶

It seems that Plutarch cannot mean that nature is itself literally the principle of good for, as he says elsewhere, the first principle of all is god, and

---

32. See Aristotle, *Meta.* A 5, 986b31–34. Parmenides was, says Aristotle, "compelled to follow appearances" (ἀναγκαζόμενος δ' ἀκολουθεῖν τοῖς φαινομένοις).

33. See *De Is.* 372F; *Proc. An.* 1023A. At 1015C–D, he interprets Plato, *Sts.* 273C6–D1, as indirectly identifying the receptacle with matter. As Sorabji (1988, 33) notes, the identification of the receptacle with matter "was practically universal in antiquity."

34. See Aristotle, *Phys.* Δ 2, 209b11–17. Aristotle adds that what Plato says in *Timaeus* about the receptacle differs from what he says in his "so-called unwritten teachings," although Aristotle does not say in what respect. Most Platonists, at any rate, supposed that when in his *Metaphysics* Aristotle says that for Plato the underlying matter of sensibles is to be identified with the Indefinite Dyad or the Great and the Small, he is reporting the description of the receptacle delivered in the unwritten teachings. See *Meta.* A 6, 988a12–14.

35. See *Rep.* 379B15–16: Οὐκ ἄρα πάντων γε αἴτιον τὸ ἀγαθόν, ἀλλὰ τῶν μὲν εὖ ἐχόντων αἴτιον, τῶν δὲ κακῶν ἀναίτιον. (The Good is not, then, the cause of all things; it is the cause of all things that are good, whereas it is not responsible for evils.) Cf. C5–6.

36. *De Is.* 369D2–5: εἰ γὰρ οὐδὲν ἀναιτίως πέφυκε γίνεσθαι, αἰτίαν δὲ κακοῦ τἀγαθὸν οὐκ ἂν παράσχοι, δεῖ γένεσιν ἰδίαν καὶ ἀρχὴν ὥσπερ ἀγαθοῦ καὶ κακοῦ τὴν φύσιν ἔχειν.

god is separate from nature, and god is supremely good.[37] In fact, later in *De Iside et Osiride* Plutarch explicitly says that the receptacle (matter)

> has an innate love for and longs for and pursues that which is first and most authoritative of all things, that which is identical with the Good. But the part that comes from evil she flees and rejects and, being both space and matter, inclines always toward the better part and provides to it [i.e., form] an opportunity to impregnate and to generate from her with effluences and likenesses in which she rejoices and is glad that she is filled up with these creatures. For becoming is the image of essence in matter and that which becomes is an imitation of being.[38]

Nature is, then, composed of form and matter and the goodness in nature is owing to its form, longing for the Good. What is the source of evil? Not, apparently, matter itself, which Plutarch elsewhere explicitly denies to be evil. As Plutarch argues, matter is "without quality" (ἄποιον) and "neutral" (ἀδιάφορον), for which reason Plato could not have supposed it to be a principle of evil.[39] But this still seems to leave the problem of whether the Good is responsible for evil over and above its responsibility for good owing to the Forms that somehow come from it. Furthermore, there is the slightly embarrassing problem that nowhere in *Timaeus* does Plato discuss cosmological evil, though he does have at the end of the dialogue a few words to say about moral evil.[40]

The deeper problem is this. In his summary of the foundations of cosmology, Timaeus says that there are three principles "even before the heavens

---

37. *De def. or.* 423D. At *Plat. Quaest.* 1000E, addressing *Tim.* 28C3–4, Plutarch asks, "Why did Plato call the highest god [τὸν ἀνωτάτω θεός] father and maker of all things [τῶν πάντων]?" The *Timaeus* passage actually says "of this all" (τοῦδε τοῦ παντός), meaning the cosmos, not "all things," which would include the receptacle and its contents. The combination of "the highest god" and "all things" seems to assume a conflation of Demiurge and Good. As Ferrari (2006, 54–56) shows, in *Plat. Quaest.* 1000E–1001B, Plutarch considers a number of answers to the question, Why did Plato call god "maker *and* father"? Plutarch's answer is that god is ποιητής with respect to the body of the universe and πατήρ with respect to the soul. In the former respect, he is efficient cause; in the latter, constitutive or formal cause. Cf. *De sera* 559D.

38. *De Is.* 372E9–73A1: ἔχει δὲ σύμφυτον ἔρωτα τοῦ πρώτου καὶ κυριωτάτου πάντων, ὃ τἀγαθῷ ταὐτόν ἐστι, κἀκεῖνο ποθεῖ καὶ διώκει· τὴν δ' ἐκ τοῦ κακοῦ φεύγει καὶ διωθεῖται μοῖραν, ἀμφοῖν μὲν οὖσα χώρα καὶ ὕλη, ῥέπουσα δ' ἀεὶ πρὸς τὸ βέλτιον καὶ παρέχουσα γεννᾶν ἐξ ἑαυτῆς ἐκείνῳ καὶ κατασπείρειν εἰς ἑαυτὴν ἀπορροὰς καὶ ὁμοιότητας, αἷς χαίρει καὶ γέγηθε κυϊσκομένη καὶ ὑποπιμπλαμένη τῶν γενέσεων. εἰκὼν γάρ ἐστιν οὐσίας <ἡ> ἐν ὕλῃ γένεσις καὶ μίμημα τοῦ ὄντος τὸ γινόμενον. Cf. Aristotle, *Phys* A 9, 192a22–25.

39. See *De proc. an.* 1014F–1015D. At *De Is.* 371A Plutarch adds that evil is "innate" (ἐμπεφυκυῖαν) in the soul of the world and in its body, that is, its animate body. So evil is related to corporeality if not to matter itself, and so perhaps we can say that matter is a condition for the presence of evil. Cf. *De Is.* 375B; *De def. or.* 414D.

40. See *Tim.* 86B–87B. See Krämer 1964a, 92–101, and Hager 1987, 97–108, for the evidence that Plutarch derived his interpretation of the Platonic principle of evil from Xenocrates. Specifically, the dualism of Plutarch is an axiological extension of the principles of the One and the Indefinite Dyad. See Opsomer 2007a, 393–94, who argues against Krämer on the use of Plutarch as a source for our understanding of Xenocrates or the unwritten teachings of Plato.

came to be": being, space, and becoming.⁴¹ If we accept the identification of space and matter, as does Plutarch, it seems that the Good, found, if anywhere, in the realm of 'being,' is not responsible for matter and so, if matter is evil, is not responsible for evil. Apparently the only drawback to this interpretation is that the first principle of all is shorn of omnipotence.⁴² This hardly seems implausible if the first principle is the Demiurge or a divine intellect whose causal 'reach' would not unreasonably stop just short of being able to affect that which is absolutely without intelligibility, namely, matter.⁴³ If, however, the Demiurge, as putative first principle of all, is not just good but the Good, then one who holds this is apparently contradicting Plato in *Republic* when Socrates says that "it is right to believe both of these [knowledge and truth] to be goodlike, but wrong to think that either of them is the Good, for the state of the Good is yet more honored."⁴⁴ So if, as *Republic* explicitly says, the Idea of the Good is "beyond οὐσία," and hence beyond knowledge and truth, what are the grounds for denying its omnipotence? For to say that something is not omnipotent is to say that it has a limitation of some sort; a limitation must be owing to something's nature, that is, because it is *this* sort of thing, it cannot do *that*. But the Good does not have a distinct nature or essence or οὐσία. If, then, the Good is omnipotent, why is there evil?

There is another problem in the interpretation of *Timaeus*, one that is in fact faced squarely by Plutarch. This is that in *Timaeus* the receptacle is said to possess a disorderly motion, evidently independently of any operation by the Demiurge on it.⁴⁵ But we already know from *Phaedrus* that all motion occurs owing to soul.⁴⁶ So perhaps the obvious inference is that there is a soul that causes the disorderly motion in the receptacle. But this soul must be different from the soul of the universe or any other soul generated by the Demiurge since it is, if it exists, present in the receptacle prior to his intervention.

Plutarch insists that evil is owing not to matter itself but to the cause of its disorderly motion:

> For while Plato calls matter mother and nurse, the cause of evil is the motive power of matter and becomes divisible in bodies, the disorderly and irrational

---

41. *Tim.* 52D2–3. See Opsomer 2004, 152, who shows that Plutarch thinks that "becoming" refers to the motion of the precosmic soul.

42. He is apparently not thereby deprived of omniscience, according to Plutarch. See *De Is.* 351E.

43. See *De Is.* 369A9–B1: ἀδύνατον γὰρ ἢ φλαῦρον ὁτοῦν, ὅπου πάντων, ἢ χρηστόν, ὅπου μηδενὸς ὁ θεὸς αἴτιος, ἐγγενέσθαι (for it is impossible that anything bad should happen wherever god is the cause of everything or anything useful should happen wherever god is the cause of nothing). I take it that this claim intentionally leaves open the possibility that something bad could happen where god is *not* the cause, namely, in the receptacle prior to his imposition.

44. *Rep.* 509A2–5: οὕτω καὶ ἐνταῦθα ἀγαθοειδῆ μὲν νομίζειν ταῦτ' ἀμφότερα ὀρθόν, ἀγαθὸν δὲ ἡγεῖσθαι ὁπότερον αὐτῶν οὐκ ὀρθόν, ἀλλ' ἔτι μειζόνως τιμητέον τὴν τοῦ ἀγαθοῦ ἕξιν.

45. See *Tim.* 30A4–5, 52D4–53A2, 69B2–5.

46. See *Phdr.* 245C5–9; cf. *Lg.* 896A5–B1.

but not nonliving motion, which in the *Laws* [896E4–6], as has been said, he called a soul, contrary and opposed to that which is beneficent. For soul is the cause and principle of motion, whereas intellect is the principle of order and harmony in motion.⁴⁷

I set aside the tantalizing suggestions of, for example, Zoroastrian or generally "oriental" ideas of dualism as motivating Plutarch.⁴⁸ Plutarch argues for his position on the basis of Platonic texts and general Platonic principles. He is, clearly enough, motivated by the desire to arrive at a Platonic solution to a problem of far-reaching significance.

The texts Plutarch is working with are the three passages in *Timaeus* referring to disorderly motion, the *Laws* passage supposedly affirming the existence of an evil soul, and the myth in *Statesman* in which a world bereft of guidance by the divine goes astray.⁴⁹ The postulation of an evil World Soul seemed to Plutarch the most plausible way to make consistent what is said in all these texts. He does not consider either the possibility that Plato means to limit the causality of soul to *cosmic* motion or that cosmic evil is somehow to be explained away as a side effect of cosmic generation. The first alternative has been a favorite of scholars.⁵⁰ The second alternative requires a substantial reconstruction of the nature of the first principle of all and how it operates on everything else.

Yet another impediment to this reconstruction is that a literal reading of the generation of the cosmos in *Timaeus* seems to make that generation

---

47. *De proc. an.* 1015D11–E6: ὁ γὰρ Πλάτων μητέρα μὲν καὶ τιθήνην καλεῖ τὴν ὕλην, αἰτίαν δὲ κακοῦ τὴν κινητικὴν τῆς ὕλης καὶ περὶ τὰ σώματα γιγνομένην μεριστὴν ἄτακτον καὶ ἄλογον οὐκ ἄψυχον δὲ κίνησιν, ἣν ἐν Νόμοις ὥσπερ εἴρηται ψυχὴν ἐναντίαν καὶ ἀντίπαλον τῇ ἀγαθουργῷ προσεῖπε. ψυχὴ γὰρ αἰτία κινήσεως καὶ ἀρχή, νοῦσ δὲ τάξεως καὶ συμφωνίας περὶ κίνησιν. Cf. *De Is.* 370F.

48. See Bianchi 1986; Froidefond 1987, 211–30; Mansfeld 1992, 274–90; Opsomer 2007a, on the putative sources and the elements of Plutarch's dualism. See Donini 1986 on Plutarch's use of Aristotle in reinforcing his interpretation of Plato.

49. *Sts.* 273B–E. *Lg.* 896E4–6: Μίαν ἢ πλείους; πλείους· ἐγὼ ὑπὲρ σφῶν ἀπο κρινοῦμαι. δυοῖν μέν γέ που ἔλαττον μηδὲν τιθῶμεν, τῆς τε εὐεργέτιδος καὶ τῆς τἀναντία δυναμένης ἐξεργάζεσθαι. (One soul or more than one? I'll answer for you both: more than one. At any rate, we must not posit less than two; one as capable of effecting good deeds and one as capable of effecting their opposite.) The passage goes on to contrast the good and evil kinds of soul. See Carone 1994, for a useful discussion of the *Laws* passage, its basic harmony with earlier works, especially *Timaeus*, and an argument against any 'Manichean dualism' in it. Carone (286–88) argues that evil is indeed produced by soul, but not a cosmic entity different from the World Soul.

50. See Vlastos 1939 for an interpretation along the lines of the first alternative. I refer to the reprint (1965, 397), where Vlastos argues that soul causes only cosmic motion. In a footnote to the reprint of the original article, however (396, n. 4), Vlastos says that he "no longer believes Ackrill (1997) that the primordial motion in the *Timaeus* can be 'reconciled' on these terms with the uncompromising doctrine of *Laws* 896A–B and *Phdr.* 245C–E that the soul is the 'source' of all motion."

temporal.⁵¹ Proclus suggests that the reason for this interpretation is that Plutarch did not wish to saddle the Demiurge with either the existence of matter or the existence of the disorderly motion therein.⁵² If the receptacle existed *prior to* the cosmos, then the Demiurge is not its creator, and so it follows that the generation of the cosmos is in time, that is, *after* the original 'state.' And if the disorderly motion is the result of an evil soul, the all-good Demiurge can hardly be responsible for that.

Plutarch assumes that the Demiurge is an intellect (νοῦς).⁵³ But Plutarch thinks that for Plato there is no intellect without soul.⁵⁴ So it follows that the Demiurge has a soul.⁵⁵ And yet Plutarch also acknowledges that intellect is 'higher' than soul.⁵⁶ The point here is not that we could not stipulate that the soul of the Demiurge is 'higher' than the intellect of the soul of the universe, or even that Plutarch is left to explain how the evil soul has an intellect, but that Plutarch is saddling himself with the task of making the Demiurge the first principle of all.⁵⁷ As such, the Demiurge's necessary limitations are evident.

If the Demiurge is the first principle of all, then all he has to "work with" are the contents of the Living Animal. The contents of the receptacle are, accordingly, completely out of his control. These provide the elements of "necessity" (ἀνάγκη) with which the divine intellect must contend. This is perfectly in line with Plato's account of what the Demiurge does. And yet Plato also says that the receptacle (as matter, presumably, not space), prior to the imposition of shapes and numbers on it by the Demiurge, "partakes in some very puzzling way in the intelligible."⁵⁸

51. See *Tim.* 30A3–6. For Plutarch's interpretation, see *Proc. An.* 1014B–1016C, perhaps following Aristotle, *Phys.* 8.1.251b17–28; *De Ca.* 1.10.280a28–32, 3.2.300b16–18. Plotinus, *Enn.* III 5, 9.24–28, gives the rationale, accepted by most later Platonists, for expressing in a temporal sequence via myth nontemporal ontological priority and posteriority. Proclus, *In Tim.* 2.276.30–277.32, surveys the range of Platonic opinion, and follows Plotinus. See Baltes 1976, 1:1, for the most extensive treatment of the early interpretations of the temporal generation of the universe in Plato.

52. See Proclus, *In Tim.* 381.26–382.14.

53. See *Tim.* 47E4; cf. 46E4, 48A5. See *De proc. an.* 1016C, 1023D, 1024A–C, 1026E; *De Is.* 371A–B, 376C, 377E–F; *De fac.* 944E.

54. See *Tim.* 30B3, 46D5–6; cf. *Phil.* 30C9–10; *Soph.* 249A4–6. On the first *Timaeus* passage, see *Plat. Quaest.* 1002F. Plutarch's words φησὶν οὐκ ἂν γενέσθαι ψυχὴν ἄνευ σώματος οὐδὲ νοῦν ἄνευ ψυχῆς (Plato says that soul could not come to be without body nor intellect without soul) may perhaps be taken to allow for the possibility of an intellect, namely, that of the Demiurge, that does not have a soul because it does not "come to be." The problem of the soul of the Demiurge is, I think, fictitious. The motion of the Demiurge is not psychic motion, strictly speaking, but only the "intellection motion" of thought (κίνησις νοῦ).

55. See *De Is.* 377F1: οὐ γὰρ ἄνουν οὐδ' ἀνθρώπος ὁ θεὸς ὑποχείριον.

56. *De fac.* 943A4–6: νοῦς γὰρ ψυχῆς, ὅσῳ ψυχὴ σώματος, ἄμεινόν ἐστι καὶ θειότερον. See for the Platonic source *Phdr.* 247C7–9. See Schoppe 1994, 158–65, for a discussion of the texts and Plutarch's problem here.

57. At *De Is.* 370F, Plutarch seems to imply that the evil soul is ἄλογον, which in the context must mean that it is without intellect.

58. *Tim.* 51A7–B1: μεταλαμβάνον δὲ ἀπορώτατά πῃ τοῦ νοητοῦ. Cf. 50C5 and 53B2, where the contents of the receptacle are said to be "traces" (ἴχνη) of their own nature.

If the intelligible are what the Demiurge looks to when he puts order into the cosmos, how can the receptacle partake in it prior to that imposition of order, no matter how puzzlingly? Either the Demiurge is more powerful than Plutarch supposes him to be on his interpretation, owing to the fact that participation in the Living Animal is 'outside' of time or eternal, or else participation in the intelligible is not explained completely by the Demiurge. And yet if the Demiurge is the first principle of all, there is no other *explanans* available.

It is fairly obvious that Plutarch has no real solution to this problem. In this regard, he is hardly exceptional among the so-called Middle Platonists. Of paramount importance for my account is the reason for his failure to offer a solution. Plutarch assumes that the Demiurge is the first principle of all. This is reasonable enough if one takes *Timaeus* as an authoritative expression of the principles of Platonism and also if one takes Aristotle's Unmoved Mover both as expressing an interpretation of the Demiurge *and* as the first principle of all.[59] It is important to see that Aristotle's interpretation of creation in *Timaeus* as in time (shared by Plutarch) and his own denial of this position does not solve the problem. At least it does not solve the problem for a Platonist or for any philosopher who aims for a maximally consistent positive construct based on UP. Either the first principle is ontologically prior or it is not. If the latter, we cannot have the hierarchy that, as we have seen, is integral to Platonism. If the former, then we have to posit a first principle that has the power of universal causality.

Plutarch is also seemingly on solid Platonic grounds in identifying the Demiurge as himself intelligible.[60] Whether or not this makes the Forms thoughts in the mind of the Demiurge, the prior problem is how that which is 'among the intelligibles' could ever be the cause of the existence of matter or anything else. If Plutarch did in fact deny that Forms are divine thoughts,

---

59. See Karamanolis 2006, 88, 96–97, 115, on Plutarch's commitment to the harmonization of Plato and Aristotle generally despite Plutarch's acknowledgment of their differences. The claim that Plutarch identified the Demiurge and Unmoved Mover has been challenged by Ferrari 1999 and Opsomer 2005b. See Aristotle, *Top.* E 6, 136b7, on god as the "intelligible living animal" (τὸ ζῷον νοητόν), a text that supports the claim that the Unmoved Mover is doing the job of the Demiurge if, as argued above, the Demiurge is cognitively identical with the Living Animal.

60. See *Tim.* 37A1–2 and *Plat. Quaest.* 1002B10: ὁ γὰρ θεός ἐν τοῖς νοητοῖς. Cf. *De proc. an.* 1016B; *De Is.* 373F. Cf. Aristotle, *Meta.* Λ 7, 1072a26 for the Unmoved Mover as 'intelligible.' But Plutarch seems to deny that the Demiurge is, like the Unmoved Mover, a self-thinker. See *De def. or.* 426D: οὐχὶ κενὸν ἄπειρον ἔξω βλέπων οὐδ' ἑαυτόν ἄλλο δ' οὐδὲν (ὡς ᾠήθησαν ἔνιοι) νοῶν. He does this no doubt in order to preserve divine providence. Jan Opsomer suggests to me that Plutarch conceived of two orders of causality, the temporal and the non-temporal, with the first order headed by the Demiurge and the second by the One or Good. It is only in the first order that providence obtains. This would explain why Plutarch takes the generation of the cosmos in *Timaeus* as temporal.

as some have argued, their multiplicity at least compromises the primacy of the Demiurge as a unique first principle of all.[61]

It will not do to insist that only the existence of things other than the first principle requires no explanation. For the necessary uniqueness of the first principle (on which Plato, Aristotle, and other Platonists all agree) means that everything else exists by being one kind of thing or another. So to explain the being-one-kind-of-thing-rather-than-another without explaining the existence of that kind of thing would seem to be impossible. In order to see this point, one need only ask the question of *what* it is that we are claiming is in need of no explanation. It is never simply existence, but rather the existence of some kind of thing.

Alcinous

The only complete extant work aimed at anything like a comprehensive expression of Platonism from the period of Middle Platonism is the Διδασκαλικὸς τῶν Πλάτωνος δογμαάτων (*Handbook of Plato's Teachings*) by the philosopher once thought to be Albinus, but now apparently restored to his real name, Alcinous.[62] What the term διδασκαλικός meant to the author of this work is revealed at its end, when he announces the conclusion of his εἰσαγωγὴ εἰς Πλάτωνος δογματοποιίαν (introduction to the study of the doctrines of Plato).[63]

The work, though relatively modest in size, is impressively comprehensive in scope, attempting an exposition of a Platonic account of the nature of philosophy itself, philosophical method, knowledge and cognition

---

61. See Ferrari 1995, chap. 9, who evinces skepticism regarding the Middle Platonic commonplace that Forms are divine thoughts. Ferrari (242–43) argues that *Quaest. conv.* 719A, which seems to claim explicitly that Forms are god's thoughts (Forms are said to be ἐν αὐτῷ... καὶ σὺν αὐτῷ καὶ περὶ αὐτόν), is not Plutarch's position but that of his interlocutor. In this regard, Ferrari compares *De sera* 550D, where Plutarch says that the Forms are merely περὶ τὸ θεῖον. He argues that Plutarch posits an autonomous status for Forms in relation to the Demiurge. But this autonomous status would not, it seems, necessarily preclude their being 'internal' to the Demiurge. We find what is perhaps a similar view in the Middle Platonist Atticus, fr. 28.2 Des Places: οὔτε γὰρ αἱ ἰδέαι κεχωρισμέναι τοῦ νοῦ καθ' αὐτάς ὑφεστήκασιν, ἀλλ' ὁ νοῦς εἰς ἑαυτὸν ἐπεστραμμένος ὁρᾷ τὰ εἴδη πάντα (the Ideas do not exist on their own separated from Intellect, but Intellect sees all the Forms when it is turned toward itself) (= Proclus, *In Tim.* 1.394.2–4).

62. For the scholarly question, which goes back to the nineteenth century, see Whittaker 1990, vii–xii; Dillon 1993, ix–xiii. If Alcinous is in fact not identical with Albinus (fl. ca. 150 CE), pupil of Gaius and teacher of Galen, then we have very little to go on to establish his *floruit*. We know that in several places Alcinous relies heavily on a work by Arius Didymus, court philosopher of Augustus, which fixes a *terminus post quem* of probably sometime in the Christian era. Since, as Whittaker notes, there is no hint of 'Neoplatonism' in this work, and since it seems in many regards like a work of 'Middle Platonism,' it would appear that a *terminus ante quem* of 200 CE is likely.

63. See *Didask.* 189.28–29 Whittaker (= 36.1 Dillon). I will refer to the numbering in Whittaker's critical edition (originally that found in Hermann's 1853 edition) and Dillon's translation. The term δογματοποιίαν is rare. It does, I think, suggest something like a construction, systematic or otherwise, rather than a mere digest.

generally, the architecture of the universe and its generation, the construction of bodies, the soul, gods, human nature, immortality, the virtues, assimilation to divinity, the emotions, friendship and love, and politics.[64] It is difficult to assess the originality of the work since we possess so little of anything resembling an epitome of Platonism prior to Alcinous, though judging from the absence of any reference to it among later Platonists, it is not likely to have been considerable.[65] Perhaps the most striking feature of this work is that along with three hundred or so references to most of Plato's dialogues, there are about half that number of references to the works of Aristotle, employed by Alcinous to expose *Platonic* teachings. Although Aristotle is nowhere in the *Handbook* mentioned by name, Alcinous, like Plutarch, frequently helps himself to terminology, distinctions, and arguments found in the Aristotelian corpus. We need not suppose that Alcinous was unaware of Aristotle's opposition to Plato's teaching on a number of fundamental matters; it is just that this opposition is evidently not thought to be sufficiently basic to undermine Aristotle's constructive support for the larger Platonic project.[66]

Alcinous, also perhaps like Plutarch, seems to conflate the Idea of the Good as first principle of all with the Demiurge of *Timaeus* and with Aristotle's Unmoved Mover.[67] He writes in chapter 10:

> Since the primary intellect is the finest of things, it follows that the object of its intelligizing must also be supremely fine. But there is nothing finer than this intellect. Therefore, it must be everlastingly engaged in thinking of itself and its own thoughts, and this activity of it is the existing Idea. The primary god, then, is eternal, ineffable, 'self-perfect' (that is, deficient in no respect), 'ever-perfect' (that is, always perfect), and 'all-perfect' (that is, perfect in all respects); divinity, essentiality, truth, commensurability, <beauty>, good. I am not listing these terms as being distinct from one another, but on the assumption that one single thing is being denoted by all of them. He is the Good, because he benefits all things according to their capacities, being the cause of all good. He is the Beautiful, because he himself by his own nature is perfect and commensurable; Truth, because he is the origin of all truth, as the sun is of all light; he is Father through being the cause of all things and bestowing order on the heavenly intellect and the soul of the world in accordance with himself and his own thoughts. By his own will he has filled all things with himself, rousing up the soul of the world and turning it towards himself, as being

---

64. As Tarrant (1993, 208) points out, Alcinous evidently had at his disposal the complete Platonic corpus, probably owing to the compilation of Thrasyllus.

65. See Loenen 1957, who argues for the originality and consistency of Alcinous's interpretation of Plato without, it seems to me, a great deal of evidence.

66. The unswerving fidelity of Alcinous to UP and to the project of a positive construction on its basis is easy to document: (1) antinominalism, chap. 9; (2) antimaterialism, chap. 9; (3) antimechanism, chap. 10; (4) antirelativism, chap. 27; (5) antiskepticism, chap. 4.

67. Cf. Armstrong 1960, 403–5; Opsomer 2005a, 79–83.

the cause of its intellect. It is this latter that, set in order by the Father, itself imposes order on all of nature in this world. (trans. Dillon)[68]

That Alcinous takes the *Republic*'s Idea of the Good and the *Timaeus*'s Demiurge to be identical is obvious. That he also identifies these with the Unmoved Mover seems to follow from the previous section where the 'primary god' is described as the 'object of desire' (τὸ ὀρεκτόν) that moves by being loved.[69]

There are many notable features in this passage. Let us begin with the unspoken principle employed, namely, that there is a unique or 'primary' god. That primacy entails uniqueness, I take it, is entailed by the methodological principle, universally accepted among Platonists, that explanatory adequacy demands reduction to a unique *explanans*. That is, if there were more than a single or primary first principle, the multiplicity itself would be in need of an explanation. Aristotle argued that the first principle must be unqualifiedly actual, whereas if there were a plurality of first principles, none of these could be such owing to the necessary compositeness of each.[70] Plotinus, as we will see, will add a further argument.

---

68. *Didask.* 164.29–165.4 Whitaker (= 10.3 Dillon): Ἐπεὶ δὲ ὁ πρῶτος νοῦς κάλλιστος, δεῖ καὶ κάλλιστον αὐτῷ νοητὸν ὑποκεῖσθαι, οὐδὲν δὲ αὐτοῦ κάλλιον· ἑαυτὸν ἂν οὖν καὶ τὰ ἑαυτοῦ νοήματα ἀεὶ νοοίη, καὶ αὕτη ἡ ἐνέργεια αὐτοῦ ἰδέα ὑπάρχει. Καὶ μὴν ὁ πρῶτος θεὸς ἀίδιός ἐστιν, ἄρρητος, αὐτοτελὴς τουτέστιν ἀπροσδεής, ἀειτελὴς τουτέστιν ἀεὶ τέλειος, παντελὴς τουτέστι πάντη τέλειος· θειότης, οὐσιότης, ἀλήθεια, συμμετρία, ἀγαθόν. Λέγω δὲ οὐχ ὡς χωρίζων ταῦτα, ἀλλ' ὡς κατὰ πάντα ἑνὸς νοουμένου. Καὶ ἀγαθὸν μέν ἐστι, διότι πάντα εἰς δύναμιν εὐεργετεῖ, παντὸς ἀγαθοῦ αἴτιος ὤν· καλὸν δέ, ὅτι αὐτὸς τῇ ἑαυτοῦ φύσει τέλεόν ἐστι καὶ σύμμετρον· ἀλήθεια δέ, διότι πάσης ἀληθείας ἀρχὴ ὑπάρχει, ὡς ὁ ἥλιος παντὸς φωτός· πατὴρ δέ ἐστι τῷ αἴτιος εἶναι πάντων καὶ κοσμεῖ τὸν οὐράνιον νοῦν καὶ τὴν ψυχὴν τοῦ κόσμου πρὸς ἑαυτὸν καὶ πρὸς τὰς ἑαυτοῦ νοήσεις. Κατὰ γὰρ τὴν ἑαυτοῦ βούλησιν ἐμπέπληκε πάντα ἑαυτοῦ, τὴν ψυχὴν τοῦ κόσμου ἐπεγείρας καὶ εἰς ἑαυτὸν ἐπιστρέψας, τοῦ νοῦ αὐτῆς αἴτιος ὑπάρχων· ὃς κοσμηθεὶς ὑπὸ τοῦ πατρὸς διακοσμεῖ σύμπασαν φύσιν ἐν τῷδε τῷ κόσμῳ. Cf. *Meta.* Λ 9, 1074b15–35; Λ 7, 1072b18–21. On this text, see Mansfeld 1972; Donini 1988.

69. *Didask.* 164.25 Whittaker (= 10.2 Dillon). Cf. *Meta.* Λ 7, 1072a26–b4. Theophrastus, in a fragment of his Φυσικῶν δόξαι (or Φυσικαὶ δόξαι) (fr. 48 Wimmer = fr. 230 Fortenbaugh-Huby-Sharples-Gupta), says that Plato posited two principles of nature: matter and that which is αἴτιον καὶ κινοῦν, the latter being then identified with the Good. Perhaps this implies that the Good is identified with the Demiurge, the obvious moving cause. And yet the two principles referred to at *Tim.* 48C2–6 *not* to be discussed in the dialogue evidently do not include the Demiurge. It is hardly surprising that Alcinous should be confused by the evidence. See Dörrie and Baltes 1996, 4:439–48, for a survey of the Middle Platonic discussion that possibly is taking into account Theophrastus's testimony.

70. See *Meta.* Λ 8, 1074a31–38. The argument here is for the uniqueness of the universe, but this conclusion is reached by showing the necessary uniqueness of the first mover. The derivation of the uniqueness of the first principle of all based on its unqualified actuality seems to contradict *De Int.* 13.23a23–26, where "the primary substances" (αἱ πρῶται οὐσίαι) are said to be "without δύναμις". Presumably, the extension of the term δύναμις beyond the sensible realm into the intelligible realm, noted at the beginning of *Meta.* Θ 1, 1045b27–1046a4, accounts for the discrepancy between the earlier and the later work.

Assuming that there must be at least one and no more than one first principle, Alcinous draws on *Timaeus, Philebus,* and Aristotle's *Metaphysics* to give an account of its nature. Why does Alcinous accept—seemingly against the very texts he cites—that, for example, the Demiurge is the Good and the Good has will and the Unmoved Mover bestows order on the heavenly intellect? I believe we can begin to discern Alcinous's reasoning in the first line after our passage, where the perfection of the first principle is emphasized: 'self-perfect' (that is, deficient in no respect); 'ever-perfect' (that is, always perfect); and 'all-perfect' (that is, perfect in all respects). The first principle of all must be perfect, as Aristotle argued against Pythagoreans and Speusippus, because the perfect cannot arise, that is, be caused by, the imperfect.[71] So a universal and unique cause of all properties or perfections must itself be unqualifiedly perfect. Is will, that is, rational will (βούλησις), a perfection? It is, evidently, for Plato's Demiurge.[72] So insofar as the Demiurge can be said to be the first principle of all, that principle must have will.

Why, then, does this first principle, being good and, as Plato says, "ungrudging" (ἀφθόνος),[73] not endow all possible perfections on everything that he makes? To answer this question, Alcinous appeals to the principle that the first god "benefits things according to their capacity."[74] To argue that, say, cats do not have rational will because they do not possess the capacity for receiving it, puts the question back one step. Why do they not have this capacity? Presumably, the seemingly circular response is that they do not have it because the Form of Cat does not have it and so anything instantiating that Form will lack rational will. The circularity is removed or at least mitigated, however, if we stipulate that if cats had rational wills, then cats would be human beings. So if there are to be animals other than human beings—a possibility shown to be actual by the existence of such animals—then there will be animals without the relevant capacity.[75]

This rationale for making the Demiurge the first principle runs up against the explicit denial in *Republic* that truth and knowledge are the Good, rather than merely 'goodlike' (ἀγαθοειδῆ).[76] Alcinous says that god is the Good because he is the source of all good. This is the same sort of reasoning he uses for identifying the Demiurge with truth. In addition,

---

71. See *Meta.* Λ 7, 1072b35–1073a2. Cf. α 1, 993b26–31.

72. See *Tim.* 29E3, 30A2. The Demiurge has *good* will because he is good. He has will because he is the cause of creatures with will. Cf. 30D1–31A1.

73. See *Tim.* 29E1–3.

74. See Dodds (1933; 2nd ed. 1963, 273–74), who supplies numerous citations for this principle within the Platonic tradition, though none earlier than Philo of Alexandria. See also Whittaker 1990, 104, who adds references to Proclus, *In. Tim.* 1.375, to which *PT* 1.83.12–85.5 should be added.

75. See *Tim.* 37D1–2: καθάπερ οὖν αὐτὸ τυγχάνει ζῷον ἀΐδιον ὄν, καὶ τόδε τὸ πᾶν οὕτως εἰς δύναμιν ἐπεχείρησε τοιοῦτον ἀποτελεῖν. (So, then, just as it [the paradigm] is an eternal Living Animal, the Demiurge tried to make the cosmos in this way like it as much as possible.) The cosmos, that is, is to be a temporalized copy of the eternal Living Animal.

76. *Rep.* 509A3.

insofar as we take truth to be a name for the Forms, and insofar as these are cognitively identical with the Demiurge, it is even more difficult to maintain that the Good and the Demiurge are identical if the Good is explicitly held to be 'above' the Forms.[77] No doubt, Alcinous will be relying on a passage from *Philebus* where Socrates says,

> So, if we are not able to capture that which is good in one idea, let us get at it with three, with beauty and commensurability and truth, and say that we would be most correct to treat these as in a way one and responsible for what is in the mixture [of the elements of the good life], and that it is owing to this being god that it becomes so.[78]

Emphasizing at the beginning of the passage that different ways of indicating the first principle of all do not imply multiplicity or complexity in it, Alcinous can appeal to the *Philebus* passage to support a conflation of the locus of truth (i.e., the Demiurge) and the Idea of the Good.[79] The important term οἷον ("in a way") will, then, be glossed as the claim that if A causes B, then A is "in a way" B. So the first principle of all, as cause of all, is in a way all things.

This resolution of the tension caused by conflating the Demiurge and the Idea of the Good still leaves us with the Unmoved Mover. The real problem here is not, I believe, in concocting an interpretation of the argument of Aristotle's *Metaphysics* according to which the Unmoved Mover acts in some way not only as a final cause but also as an efficient cause.[80] Such a view is not groundless. The problem is rather with the fact that the Unmoved Mover, like the Demiurge, is an intellect, or, if we like, intellection. Actually, there are two facets of this problem. First, if the first principle is an intellect, it is, as Aristotle says, intelligible to itself. But to say that the Good is intelligible is, it seems, to make it into an essence, or οὐσία, whereas Plato has Socrates say explicitly that the Good is 'above' essence. Second, if the first principle is doing the work of the Demiurge, contemplating the Living Animal that contains all the Forms of living things, then in addition to the duality of thinker and object of thought this creates, there is the multiplicity of the many objects of thinking.[81] These objects or Forms are, then, thoughts in the divine intellect.[82]

---

77. See Baltes 1997, 12–15, for an abundance of references to the Middle Platonists who make this identification.

78. Plato, *Phil.* 65A1–5: Οὐκοῦν εἰ μὴ μιᾷ δυνάμεθα ἰδέᾳ τὸ ἀγαθὸν θηρεῦσαι, σὺν τρισὶ λαβόντες, κάλλει καὶ συμμετρίᾳ καὶ ἀληθείᾳ, λέγωμεν ὡς τοῦτο οἷον ἓν ὀρθότατ' ἂν αἰτιασαίμεθ' ἂν τῶν ἐν τῇ συμμείξει, καὶ διὰ τοῦτο ὡς ἀγαθὸν ὂν τοιαύτην αὐτὴν γεγονέναι.

79. He can also appeal to the fact that in *Lg.* 904A Plato refers to the Demiurge as "king" (βασιλεύς), whereas in *Rep.* 509D, it is the Idea of the Good that is taken to be king. Cf. *Second Ep.* 312E1–4.

80. Contra Witt 1937, 122–44. See Gerson 2005, 200–204.

81. Cf. *Didask.* 166.40ff. Whittaker (= 12.1 Dillon).

82. See *Didask.* 153.6 Whittaker (= 3.2 Dillon); cf. 163.14–15 (= 9.1); 163.30–31 (= 9.2); 164.29–30 (= 10.3); 169.39–40 (= 14.3). Alcinous uses the terms νοήσεις and νοήματα for the Ideas. This seems to involve a direct contradiction of the claim in *Parm.*132B3–7 that a

There is no doubt that all parties to this dispute would agree that the putative *explanans* of everything must itself not be among the *explananda*. One drastic way out is to hold that plurality as such is not among the things needing to be explained. In that case, the plurality that seems unavoidable in an intellectual first principle would be no problem at all. Apart from the Atomists, I am not aware of any philosophers in antiquity who took this approach. It is reasonably clear that all Platonists follow Plato in maintaining that no plurality is without a causal explanation that is ultimately the first principle of all. The reasoning is that any plurality—even a minimal plurality of two things—requires minimal complexity in each, that is, there must be a distinction between each individual being and the kind of thing it is.[83] In *Republic* we learn that both 'components,' being or existence and essence, are explained by the Idea of the Good, the first principle of all.[84] We will return to this important issue, but for the moment we may suppose that Alcinous is not tempted to allow an unaccountable plurality in the first principle.[85]

How, then, to account for the apparent plurality in the first principle? Alcinous, remarkably, seems to adduce the first hypothesis of the second

---

Form is not a νόημα. The argument that Parmenides provides—an argument that Plato seems to believe is decisive—is that a Form is an ontological entity, whose hypothesized role in explaining identity in difference could not be filled if a Form were a thought. Rather, a Form is the object of thinking, τὸ νοούμενον or τὸ νοητόν. The point is of considerable importance in deciding whether multiplicity is irremovable from a divine intellect thereby making it unsuitable as a first principle of all. Cf. Plotinus, *Enn.* V 9, 7.14–16, where the Platonic point is explicitly affirmed. That Alcinous's view is a Middle Platonic commonplace may be inferred from the testimony of Aëtius, *De placitis reliquiae* 288.2–6 Diels: ὁ δὲ θεὸς νοῦς ἐστι τοῦ κόσμου, ἡ δὲ ὕλη τὸ ὑποκείμενον γενέσει καὶ φθορᾷ, ἰδέα δὲ οὐσία ἀσώματος ἐν τοῖς νοήμασι καὶ ταῖς φαντασίαις τοῦ θεοῦ. (God is the intellect of the cosmos, matter is that which underlies generation and corruption, and the Idea is an immaterial substance in the thoughts and impressions of God.)

83. So *Parm.* 142B5–7. Cf. *Crat.* 423E1–5.

84. *Rep.* 509B7–8: ἀλλὰ καὶ τὸ εἶναί τε καὶ τὴν οὐσίαν ὑπ' ἐκείνου [the Good] αὐτοῖς προσεῖναι. Given this passage, it seems that the criticism of pluralists in *Soph.* 243D–244B, namely, that they do not explain what 'real' means when they say, for example, that the hot and the cold are real or have εἶναι, can be adumbrated as maintaining that the reason why pluralists need to give an explanation for their claim that hot and cold are real is that 'realness' and 'hotness' or 'coldness' indicate two facts about each of these. But there is an additional fact, namely, that each is a unity or one, albeit a qualified unity. And a qualified unity, like any imperfect representation, is only explained by a perfect or unqualified unity. See *Didask.* 165.27–34 Whittaker (= 10.5 Dillon), where this is perhaps what Alcinous is alluding to in appealing to the ascent to the Good in *Symp.* 210A–D.

85. See *Didask* 169.32–35 Whittaker (= 14.3 Dillon), where Alcinous claims that the world is both generated and everlasting. Proclus, *In Tim.* 1.219.2–13, who is recounting Albinus's (i.e., Alcinous's) position, gives the reason for the causal dependence of that which does not come to be in time as its being "from multiple and dissimilar parts," that is, from its complexity. Proclus claims further, *In Tim.* 1.277.8–10, that Crantor, a younger associate of Polemo, argued that in *Timaeus* the cosmos is generated just in the sense that it is heteroexplicable (ὡς ἀπ' αἰτίας ἄλλης παραγόμενον). No temporal generation is thereby implied.

part of Plato's *Parmenides* on behalf of the claim that first principle is, owing to its absolute simplicity, above qualification in any way:

> God is ineffable and graspable only by the intellect, as we have said, since he is neither genus, nor species, nor differentia, nor does he possess any attributes, neither bad (for it is improper to utter such a thought), nor good (for he would be thus by participation in something, to wit, goodness), nor indifferent (for neither is this in accordance with the concept we have of him), nor yet qualified (for he is not endowed with quality, nor is his peculiar perfection due to qualification) nor unqualified (for he is not deprived of any quality which might accrue to him). Further, he is not a part of anything, nor is he in the position of being a whole which has parts, nor is he identical with anything nor different from anything; for no attribute is proper to him, in virtue of which he could be distinguished from other things. Also, he neither moves anything, nor is he himself moved. (trans. Dillon, slightly modified)[86]

As Dillon points out in his commentary, this passage is important evidence for the metaphysical interpretation of the second part of Plato's *Parmenides*, an interpretation that, as we have seen, can already be found in the Old Academy.[87] Alcinous denies that the first principle can be qualified in any way. For this reason, neither of any pair of contraries can be attributed to it. We will return to the general topic of negative theology within the Platonic tradition. For now, the principal point concerns the reason for the denial of properties. It would seem that Alcinous is following *Parmenides* 139B4–E6 in denying that the first principle is "identical with anything or different from anything." As Plato argues in this passage, the hypothesized one is neither identical with nor different from *itself*. By contrast, in the second hypothesis, the complexity of the one hypothesized is a necessary condition for its existence. A consequence of this complexity is that this one *is* both identical with and different from itself.[88]

Alcinous is thus led to hold that the first principle is absolutely simple and yet it is also an intellect that seems to endow it with irreducible complexity.[89] He does not bother to add, for example, that the first principle neither is nor is not thinking, which would seem to be a claim parallel to

---

86. *Didask.* 165.5–16 Whittaker (= 10.4 Dillon): Ἄρρητος δ' ἐστὶ καὶ νῷ μόνῳ ληπτός, ὡς εἴρηται, ἐπεὶ οὔτε γένος ἐστὶν οὔτε εἶδος οὔτε διαφορά, ἀλλ' οὐδὲ συμβέβηκέ τι αὐτῷ, οὔτε κακόν (οὐ γὰρ θέμις τοῦτο εἰπεῖν), οὔτε ἀγαθόν (κατὰ μετοχὴν γάρ τινος ἔσται οὗτος καὶ μάλιστα ἀγαθότητος), οὔτε ἀδιάφορον (οὐδὲ γὰρ τοῦτο κατὰ τὴν ἔννοιαν αὐτοῦ), οὔτε ποιόν (οὐ γὰρ ποιωθέν ἐστι καὶ ὑπὸ ποιότητος τοιοῦτον ἀποτετελεσμένον), οὔτε ἄποιον (οὐ γὰρ ἐστέρηται τοῦ ποιὸν εἶναι ἐπιβάλλοντός τινος αὐτῷ ποιοῦ)· οὔτε μέρος τινός, οὔτε ὡς ὅλον ἔχον τινὰ μέρη, οὔτε ὥστε ταὐτόν τινι εἶναι ἢ ἕτερον· οὐδὲν γὰρ αὐτῷ συμβέβηκε, καθ' ὃ δύναται τῶν ἄλλων χωρισθῆναι· οὔτε κινεῖ οὔτε κινεῖται.
87. See Dodds 1928; Whittaker 1969, 96ff.; Dillon 1993, 107–9.
88. See *Parm.* 143A4–B8. See Whittaker 1969, 99–100.
89. Cf. *Didask.* 165.34–166.7 Whittaker (= 10.7 Dillon), where Alcinous argues that god is partless because he is absolutely 'prior.' If this indicates causal priority, then Alcinous is expressing the core Platonic position. But Alcinous also seems to assume that if god is incorporeal,

that of the denial of any other pair of contraries to it. The denial of thinking follows from the denial of any properties; but this does not mean that the first principle cannot be identical with thinking, that is, as its being. This is Aristotle's argument.[90] Yet it seems that what thinking is requires the complexity consequent upon the plurality of intelligible objects. Further, though this is a point that Alcinous apparently does not notice, if the primal god is acting demiurgically in bestowing order on nature by using the Forms, it would seem that the divine mind is cognizable just insofar as we can know the essence of things. That it is 'graspable by the intellect' seems to suggest as much, unless this grasping is supposed to indicate something else.[91]

There is a tantalizing passage at the beginning of the chapter that on the surface at least suggests a distinction between a primary intellect and something that has a prior existence to it:

> Since intellect is superior to soul, and superior to potential intellect there is actualized intellect, which cognizes everything simultaneously and eternally, and finer than this again is the cause of this and whatever it is that has an existence still prior to these, this it is that would be the primal god, being the cause of the eternal activity of the intellect of the whole heaven. It acts on this while remaining itself unmoved, as does the sun on vision, when this is directed towards it, and as the object of desire moves desire, while remaining motionless itself. In just this way will this intellect move the intellect of the whole heaven. (trans. Dillon)[92]

This primal god is said to be both an intellect and prior to the intellect possessed by the soul of the universe.[93] The question of why intellect generates intellect (or soul with intellect) and not something inferior to itself leaps out at us. More important, if the actual or agent intellect cognizes all that

---

then he is simple because 'parts' refer to the extensive parts of a body. He seems to think that absolute causal priority coincides with immateriality or incorporeality.

90. Perhaps Alcinous is alluding to the Aristotelian argument that the Unmoved Mover must be not a νοῦς but rather νόησις when he says that god is either νοῦς or νοερόν. See 163.32–33 Whittaker (= 9.3 Dillon). As Dillon (99) notes, the distinction is hardly perspicuous, though if Alcinous is taking νοερόν as a kind of synonym for νόησις, the motive to protect the absolute simplicity of the first principle would be evident.

91. See Whittaker 1990, 105 ad loc. Whittaker's references to *Phdr.* 247C7–8 and *Tim.* 28A1–2 do not solve the problem for Alcinous, for in these passages Plato is talking about cognition of Forms, not of a simple first principle.

92. *Didask.* 164.18–27 Whitaker (= 10.2 Dillon): Ἐπεὶ δὲ ψυχῆς νοῦς ἀμείνων, νοῦ δὲ τοῦ ἐν δυνάμει ὁ κατ' ἐνέργειαν πάντα νοῶν καὶ ἅμα καὶ ἀεί, τούτου δὲ καλλίων ὁ αἴτιος τούτου καὶ ὅπερ ἂν ἔτι ἀνωτέρω τούτων ὑφέστηκεν, οὗτος ἂν εἴη ὁ πρῶτος θεός, αἴτιος ὑπάρχων τοῦ ἀεὶ ἐνεργεῖν τῷ νῷ τοῦ σύμπαντος οὐρανοῦ. Ἐνεργεῖ δὲ ἀκίνητος, αὐτὸς ὢν εἰς τοῦτον, ὡς καὶ ὁ ἥλιος εἰς τὴν ὅρασιν, ὅταν αὐτῷ προσβλέπῃ, καὶ ὡς τὸ ὀρεκτὸν κινεῖ τὴν ὄρεξιν ἀκίνητον ὑπάρχον· οὕτω γε δὴ καὶ οὗτος ὁ νοῦς κινήσει τὸν νοῦν τοῦ σύμπαντος οὐρανοῦ. Cf. Aristotle, *On Philosophy*, fr. 16 Ross.

93. Cf. Plato, *Phil.* 22C6, where θεῖον νοῦν is taken by some to indicate that the first principle of all, the Good, is an intellect.

is intelligible eternally, how does it differ from the primal god? As we saw, the primal intellect, if it is identical with the primary god, is eternally engaged in the activity of thinking its own thoughts.[94] If, indeed, the primary god is an intellect, then why does Alcinous use the words in referring to it "whatever it is that has an existence still prior to these"?[95] And why is it ineffable?

One possible explanation for this ambivalence is that Alcinous has in mind throughout his exposition the pregnant aside in *Timaeus:*

> We are not now to speak of the first principle or principles of all things—or whatever is the right term—if only because of the difficulty of explaining what we think by our present method of exposition.[96]

Alcinous is certainly not unaware of Aristotle's account of Plato's first principle or principles (the One and the Indefinite Dyad), or of the superordinate position of the Idea of the Good in *Republic*.[97] The *Didaskalikos* is, after

---

94. See above, n. 56.
95. Cf. Simplicius, *In De caelo* 485.19–23: ὅτι γὰρ ἐννοεῖ τι καὶ ὑπὲρ τὸν νοῦν καὶ τὴν οὐσίαν ὁ Ἀριστοτέλης, δῆλός ἐστι πρὸς τοῖς πέρασι τοῦ Περὶ εὐχῆς βιβλίου σαφῶς εἰπών, ὅτι ὁ θεὸς ἢ νοῦς ἐστιν ἢ καὶ ἐπέκεινά τι τοῦ νοῦ (that Aristotle thought that there is something above intellect or substance is clear from the end of his book *On Prayer* where he says clearly that god is either intellect or something beyond intellect). See Szlezák 1979b, 212–13, on the various interpretations that have been given to this phrase and in particular the reasons for rejecting the suggestion that ἢ...ἢ καί cannot indicate exclusive alternatives. See Menn 1992, 552, n. 13, who mentions the importance of this fragment, though he takes the words "god is either intellect or something beyond intellect" as referring to two views of different philosophers (Aristotle and Plato) rather than to two alternatives about which Aristotle is himself unsure. This seems to me to be a rather implausible reading of the phrase. Usually when Aristotle is expressing the views of different thinkers he will oppose the different groups in a way like this: οἱ μὲν λέγουσιν...οἱ δὲ λέγουσιν, *vel sim.* We have also already seen that Xenocrates (chap. 4, n. 62) calls the primal god an intellect. On Alcinous's extensive use of Xenocrates, see Witt 1937, 14–20. Krämer (1964a; 2nd ed., 1967, 110–11) argues for a direct connection between the theology of Xenocrates and Alcinous and against the "Verschmelzung von platonischer Ideenlehre und aristotelischer Nus-Theologie."
96. *Tim.* 48C2–6: τὴν μὲν περὶ ἁπάντων εἴτε ἀρχὴν εἴτε ἀρχὰς εἴτε ὅπῃ δοκεῖ τούτων πέρι τὸ νῦν οὐ ῥητέον, δι' ἄλλο μὲν οὐδέν, διὰ δὲ τὸ χαλεπὸν εἶναι κατὰ τὸν παρόντα τρόπον τῆς διεξόδου δηλῶσαι τὰ δοκοῦντα.
97. Cf. *Didask.* 179.34–42 Whittaker (= 27.1 Dillon): Ἑξῆς δ' ἐπὶ κεφαλαίων περὶ τῶν ἠθικῶς τῷ ἀνδρὶ εἰρημένων ῥητέον. Τὸ μὲν δὴ τιμιώτατον καὶ μέγιστον ἀγαθὸν οὔτε εὑρεῖν ᾤετο εἶναι ῥᾴδιον οὔτε εὑρόντας ἀσφαλὲς εἰς πάντας ἐκφέρειν· πάνυ γοῦν ὀλίγοις τῶν γνωρίμων καὶ τοῖς γε προσκριθεῖσι τῆς περὶ τοῦ ἀγαθοῦ ἀκροάσεως μετέδωκε· τὸ μέντοι ἡμέτερον ἀγαθόν, εἴ τις ἀκριβῶς αὐτοῦ τὰ συγγράμματα ἀναλάβοι, ἐτίθετο ἐν τῇ ἐπιστήμῃ καὶ θεωρίᾳ τοῦ πρώτου ἀγαθοῦ, ὅπερ θεόν τε καὶ νοῦν τὸν πρῶτον προσαγορεῦσαι ἄν τις. (We must next deal summarily with the ethical doctrines of Plato. The most valuable and greatest good he considered to be neither easy to discover, nor, when discovered, to be such as to be safely revealed to all. Certainly he only imparted his views on the Good to a very small group of associates and to those he had chosen to hear his lecture on the Good. However, if one examines his works with care, one will see that he placed the good for us in the knowledge and contemplation of the primal Good, which one may term god and the primal intellect. [trans.

all, an introductory work, and the above passage could understandably be taken as providing an honorable excuse for refraining from this most difficult topic, apart from Alcinous's rather curious use of the first hypothesis of the second part of *Parmenides*. Nevertheless, it is one thing to decline to discuss an obscure topic in an introductory work; it is another to take the simplified route of conflating the Demiurge and the Unmoved Mover with the first principle.[98]

What we may call for now the "tension" in Alcinous's interpretation of Plato's first principle as, on the one hand, an intellect thinking all the Forms, and, on the other, an ineffable and simple cause is evident in his summary account of Platonic ethics. This account, like that of virtually all later Platonists, takes as the first principle of ethics or, rather, the primary injunction, to "assimilate oneself to the divine."[99] The explicit means of the assimilation in the *Theaetetus* text is "to become just and pious with wisdom."[100] Alcinous seems to understand the injunction to be based on the Platonic claims that virtue is sufficient for happiness and that virtue is knowledge.

> If one examines his [Plato's] works with care, one will see that he placed the good for us in the knowledge and contemplation of the primal good, which one may term god and the primal intellect. (trans. Dillon)[101]

> Happiness, he considered not to be found in human goods, but in the divine and blessed ones. For this reason he asserted that truly philosophical souls

---

Dillon, slightly modified]) See Dillon 1993, 166–67, who, while questioning whether this passage is in fact a reference to Plato's lecture on the Good, also refers to a parallel in Proclus, *In Parm.* 688.1off. Steel, which seems to support the story that only a hardcore of Platonic adepts stayed to hear the entire lecture. The story is found in Aristoxenus, *Harm.* 2.20.16–31.3 Macran (= Aristotle, *On the Good*, Ross 1955, 111). The most remarkable feature of this passage from Alcinous is the explicit identification of the Good with an intellect.

98. See Aëtius, *ap.* Stobaeus, 1.37.6–15 Wachsmuth: Πλάτων δὲ τὸ ἕν, τὸ μονοφυὲς, τὸ μοναδικόν, τὸ ὄντως ὄν, τἀγαθόν. πάντα δὲ τὰ τοιαῦτα τῶν ὀνομάτων εἰς τὸν νοῦν σπεύδει. νοῦς οὖν ὁ θεός, χωριστὸν εἶδος·τὸ δὲ χωριστὸν ἀκουέσθω τὸ ἀμιγὲς πάσης ὕλης καὶ μηδενὶ τῶν σωματικῶν συμπεπλεγμένον, μηδὲ τῷ παθητῷ τῆς φύσεως συμπαθές. (For Plato [god is] the One, uniform, unitary, really real, and the Good. All of these names Plato applies to Intellect. God is, then, Intellect, a separate Form. Understand that being separate means being unmixed with all matter and unconnected with any bodily entities, and not experiencing anything of the things that natural things experience.) This was no doubt a commonplace among many Platonists. See Fronterotta 2008 on the configurations produced by Plutarch, Alcinous, and Plotinus for the Demiurge, Unmoved Mover, and the first principle of all, especially with an aim of preserving providence.

99. See Plato, *Tht.* 176A–B; *Rep.* 613A–B; *Phd.* 82A–C; *Phdr.* 248A; *Lg.* 716C. See Lavecchia 2006 for a thorough study of these texts; for a brief survey of the course of this idea in Platonism, see 294–96.

100. *Tht.* 176B2–3.

101. *Didask.* 179.41–42 Whittaker (= 27.1 Dillon): τὸ μέντοι ἡμέτερον ἀγαθόν, εἴ τις ἀκριβῶς αὐτοῦ τὰ συγγράμματα ἀναλάβοι, ἐτίθετο ἐν τῇ ἐπιστήμῃ καὶ θεωρίᾳ τοῦ πρώτου ἀγαθοῦ, ὅπερ θεόν τε καὶ νοῦν τὸν πρῶτον προσαγορεύσαι ἄν τις.

are filled with great and marvelous things and that after the dissolution of the body...they would become capable of grasping the nature of all that is rational. (trans. Dillon)[102]

The two passages taken together reveal the problem. If the knowledge or wisdom that constitutes the assimilation to the divine is to be knowledge of the nature of the good, then it is one thing if this good is the Demiurge or Unmoved Mover and the knowledge is of the 'thoughts,' that is, the Forms in his intellect. It is quite another if this good is an ineffable first principle, subject of the negative theology of the first hypothesis of the second part of *Parmenides*. How, in this case, could our good consist in the knowledge of that which is unknowable?

One might suppose that this problem is Plato's as much as it is Alcinous's. Supposing that Plato did in fact wish to make the Idea of the Good a superordinate first principle 'beyond essence,' how would knowing the Forms amount to knowing this principle? Indeed, how could this principle be known if it is above essence; though it provides 'knowability' to the Forms, it is itself evidently not knowable. And yet knowing what, say, the Form of Justice is, seems not only distinct from knowing that justice is good, but also prior to that. If this is so, what more does one know when one knows that justice is good?

The process of assimilation includes the acquisition of some sort of knowledge and the actual practice of the virtues based on this knowledge. But the goal of these is a distinct achievement, the result of the assimilation process. One actually becomes divine as a result of the theoretical achievement of knowledge and the practical application of it. If this result is only achievable postmortem, as Plato seems to think, the point remains the same.[103] If this is so, there is a considerable difference between identifying the good with the Demiurge/Unmoved Mover and identifying it with a superordinate, superintelligible first principle. In the former case, it is difficult to see how the assimilation is distinct from the knowledge and from the practices of virtue; in the latter, one is at least in a position to raise the question about the transformative result of the intellectual and moral exercises. That is, exactly how do knowledge and virtue make one the same as god?

---

102. *Didask.* 180.16–28 Whittaker (= 27.3 Dillon): Τὴν δὲ εὐδαιμονίαν οὐκ ἐν τοῖς ἀνθρωπίνοις ἡγεῖτο εἶναι τοῖς ἀγαθοῖς ἀλλ' ἐν τοῖς θείοις τε καὶ μακαρίοις· ὅθεν δὴ καὶ μεγάλων τε καὶ θαυμασίων τὰς τῷ ὄντι φιλοσόφους ψυχὰς ἔφασκεν ἀναμέστους καὶ μετὰ τὴν τοῦ σώματος διάλυσιν συνεστίους θεοῖς γινομένας καὶ συμπεριπολούσας καὶ τὸ τῆς ἀληθείας πεδίον θεωμένας, ἐπείπερ καὶ ἐν τῷ ζῆν ἐφίεντο τῆς ἐπιστήμης αὐτοῦ καὶ τὴν ἐπιτήδευσιν αὐτοῦ προετίμων, ἀφ' ἧς ὥσπερ τι ὄμμα ψυχῆς ἐκκαθηραμένους καὶ ἀναζωπυρήσαντας ἀπολλύμενόν τε καὶ ἀποτυφλούμενον κρεῖττον ὂν σώζεσθαι μυρίων ὀμμάτων, δυνατοὺς γίνεσθαι ἐπορέξασθαι τῆς τοῦ λογικοῦ παντὸς φύσεως.

103. At *Didask.* 178.1–12 (= 25.3 Dillon) Alcinous references the Recollection Argument from *Phaedo* that the immortality of the soul is shown from our preembodied knowledge of Forms. Alcinous does not contradict Plato in maintaining that embodied ἐπιστήμη is possible, though this passage provides the grounds for a response to radical skepticism. For some general remarks on assimilation in Middle Platonism, see Tarrant 1993, 144–47.

Many scholars have uncritically supposed that Plato maintained that acquiring philosophical knowledge of the virtues makes one a 'better' person and that *that* is what assimilation to the divine means. Apart from the dubious assumption that the practice of the virtues is not possible without the knowledge or that the knowledge guarantees the practice, it is hard to see why becoming a wise and virtuous human being is thought to make one the same as the divine. Gods are not virtuous; they are beyond virtue.[104] The divide between the human and the divine is actually unquestioned by Plato. On the other hand, the process of assimilation is taken by him to be the recovery of that which we already are. One of the primary characteristics of the divine that divides it from us is immortality. When in *Timaeus*, we are exhorted to embrace the philosophical life, this is in order to achieve immortality.[105] The immortality that is an achievement is evidently not the immortality that is an endowment. The latter, as argued for in *Phaedo*, belongs to philosophers and nonphilosophers alike. The achievement is rather the active identification with what we are really, namely, immortal souls.[106]

The issue might seem to be precisely whether Plato means to assert that assimilation to divinity is assimilation to the Good or One as first principle or to the life of the Demiurge as second principle. What I do not think Plato can mean is what Alcinous takes to be the case, namely, that assimilation is to the Demiurge as first principle and thereby identical with the Good. The acquisition or recovery of knowledge and the practice of virtue are means to immortalization because they lead to our recognition that our identity is an intellectual one. As is stressed in *Republic*, the highest cognitive achievement is found in seeing the connection between the Good and the Forms.[107] So assimilation to divinity consists in the recognition of the unity of the Forms as produced by the Good. This is, presumably, what the Demiurge does eternally. Since knowing is an identification of knower and known, the assimilation becomes a recognition that the Good is one. It is also, on Aristotle's evidence, a recognition that the Good is the One, that the One is virtually what I am really or ideally.[108]

The reason why the practice of true virtue, as opposed to mere behavior with ulterior motives, is constitutive of assimilation is that in the practice of true virtue, for Plato, reason rules. And reason is impersonal in the sense that one who acts on the basis of reason excludes as a decisive motive

---

104. This is the position that the Stoics rejected in holding that divine and human virtue were identical. See *SVF* 1.529, 564; 3.149, 245–52. But it is a position shared by Aristotle. See *EN* 7.1.1145a25–27.

105. See *Tim.* 41C–D, 90C. Cf. Aristotle, *EN* K 7, 1177b33.

106. See Sedley 1997.

107. See *Rep.* 511B3–C2.

108. See *Rep.* 509B8–9, where the use of the term δύναμις in the representation of the Good cannot mean that it has potency, that is, that it is lacking or unfilled in any way. To say that it means "power" also cannot be right if power indicates an active potency. The claim that the Good is virtually all things is reinforced by its identification with the One.

idiosyncratic or personal appetites or emotions. One who is just, say, for the right reason is one who identifies his own good with the Good simpliciter just as one who arrives at what he believes is the correct answer to a mathematical question by reasoning arrives at the correct answer simpliciter. So, as one becomes virtuous, one "becomes one out of many."[109]

On this analysis, assimilation to the Demiurge and the Unmoved Mover is assimilation to that which imitates the One or Good by knowing the first principle of all in the only way it can be known, that is, by knowing all that is knowable, namely, all the Forms. To conflate the Demiurge or Unmoved Mover with the Good is, at best, to avoid the identification of the Good with the One, since, as we have seen, although Demiurge and Unmoved Mover are in a way each one, they are each not unqualifiedly one. This is certainly the case for someone like Alcinous who does take the Unmoved Mover to be the Demiurge as opposed to one who wishes to argue that the Unmoved Mover is actually unlike the Demiurge because it *is* perfectly one whereas the Demiurge is not. "Assimilation to divinity" is emblematic of Platonic ethics for virtually all Platonists in the way that, for example, the "Golden Rule" is emblematic of Judeo-Christian ethics for many. This being the case, it is important that the nature of the assimilation be understood correctly. And this, I contend, is not done if Plato's metaphysical hierarchy is not articulated properly.

Alcinous, in a way, recognizes the main point when he argues that assimilation to the divine is not assimilation to god 'above the heavens' but to god 'in the heavens.'[110] The former does not possess virtue; only the latter does. The latter is, evidently, the intellect of the World Soul.[111] So Alcinous has grasped that imitation is not of the first principle, but since he identifies the first principle with the Demiurge and the Unmoved Mover, he misses what I maintain is the intended meaning of the Platonic exhortation. Alcinous, like Plutarch, struggles to conceive of the Platonic first principle of all in a way that preserves both its metaphysical primacy and its ultimate explanatory role in uniting the elements of UP.

---

109. See *Rep.* 443E1: ἕνα γενόμενον ἐκ πολλῶν (having become one from many). Cf. 554D9–10 and *Phd.* 83A7–8, where philosophy exhorts the soul αὐτὴν δὲ εἰς αὑτὴν συλλέγεσθαι καὶ ἀθροίζεσθαι ('to collect and gather itself together'). Superficially, "becoming one out of many" is just the rule of reason in the soul. But it is the identification of the self with the rational part of the soul that characterizes the philosopher and sets him apart from one in whom reason rules for the sake of the composite human being with which he identifies *himself.*
110. See *Didask.* 181.44–45 Whittaker (= 28.3 Dillon).
111. See Dillon 1993, 106–7.

CHAPTER 8

Numenius of Apamea

Numenius of Apamea, the Syrian city on the bank of the Orontes, probably flourished in the second century of the Christian era. Even this scrap of biographical knowledge is tenuous. It is based on a famous reference in Clement of Alexandria's *Stromates* where he quotes Numenius as asking the question, "What is Plato other than Moses speaking Attic Greek?"[1] Since Clement wrote this work about the turn of the second century, the dating is really only a terminus ad quem, though there are no earlier references to him of which we are aware. If Proclus's account of the opinions of Platonists follows chronological order, one of his references to Numenius is followed by a reference to Atticus, a Platonist who flourished around 180 CE. So a floruit for Numenius in the middle of the second century is not unlikely. There is really very little else that we know about his life or about those with whom he studied. One of the most tantalizing bits of information we have about him is the remark in Porphyry's *Life of Plotinus* that Plotinus had been accused by some from Greece—that is, from Athens—of "plagiarizing" (ὑποβάλλεσθαι) Numenius.[2] Whatever truth there is in this charge, it should certainly encourage us in the hypothesis that Numenius had some substantial role to play in the development of Platonism.[3]

---

1. This is found in book 1, chap. 22 of the *Stromates* of Clement. Throughout this chapter I will use the collection of the fragments of Numenius by Des Places. See fr. 8.14: τί γάρ ἐστι Πλάτων ἢ Μωσῆς ἀττικίζων. I will return to the significance of this below.

2. See Porphyry, *Life of Plotinus* 17.1–2.

3. This remark by Porphyry also indicates that some one hundred years after Numenius, philosophers in Athens were taking note of the leading philosopher in Rome and making judgments about him in relation to an earlier philosopher of Apamea. The philosophers

Some philosophers after Numenius referred to him as a Platonist; some referred to him as a Pythagorean.[4] The contemporary scholarly classifications of him as a neo-Pythagorean or a proto-Neoplatonist seem to indicate not much more than ignorance about his sources.[5] There is one important fragment of his work *On the Good* in which Numenius offers what he takes to be a Platonic account of the incorporeality of being, adding that if his own views are taken not to agree with those of Plato, then he would insist that they agree with those of Pythagoras.[6] But in implicitly taking Plato to be a Pythagorean, Numenius is doing nothing more than following Aristotle.[7]

As H. J. Krämer has argued, many of the Pythagorean features of Numenius's philosophy seem to have an Old Academic source, especially in the works of Xenocrates.[8] And in an extremely influential early paper, E. R. Dodds sought to discover the source of the so-called Neoplatonic interpretation of Plato in the Pythagoreanism of Numenius, and a century earlier in Moderatus.[9]

The work of Numenius for which we have the largest number of fragments is, fortunately, also his most important for my thesis. This is a work titled *On the Good*, portions of which are preserved for us verbatim in Eusebius's *Preparatio evangelica*. In this work, evidently written in six books, Numenius offers his understanding of Plato's Idea of the Good. Nothing in the fragments we possess suggests that he is thinking of Plato's public lecture on the Good, but then there is also nothing to indicate that he thought that such a lecture contained anything other than what could be gotten from the dialogues, the letters, and Aristotle's testimony.

---

whom we tend to think of as islands of thought in antiquity were probably connected with each other at a level of communication we can scarcely imagine.

4. Platonist: Porphyry, Iamblichus, Proclus; Pythagorean: Nemesius, the Christian Origen, Calcidius. Both Platonist and Pythagorean: Longinus. For a salutary skepticism regarding the attribution of 'neo-Pythagoreanism' to Numenius, see Centrone 2000, 168.

5. See Tarrant 1993, 148–77, on the 'neo-Pythagorean' Moderatus (first century CE) as a source for Numenius. Tarrant is keen to show that a metaphysical hierarchy is a well-established feature of interpretations of Plato's *Parmenides* long before Plotinus. Along similar lines see De Vogel 1953, 43–50. See Bechtle 2000 on a relatively new line of investigation of pre-Plotinian 'Neoplatonism.' It is worth noting that Moderatus and Alcinous can hardly be supposed to be dependent on Antiochus; rather, their Platonism surely has sources in the undocumented period after the Old Academy and before the first century BCE. Presumably, these sources are to be found in and among the rather misleadingly called 'neo-Pythagoreans.'

6. Fr. 7.4–7 Des Places.

7. *Meta.* A 6, 987a29–31, where Aristotle says that Plato followed the Italians (i.e., Pythagoreans) in many respects, but added some distinctive doctrines of his own.

8. See Krämer 1964a, 63–92.

9. See Dodds 1928. Numenius, in his work *On the Divergence of Academics from Plato*, fr. 24.5–12 Des Places, says that Speusippus and Xenocrates and Polemo "maintained for the most part the identical character of Plato's teachings" (τὸ ἦθος διετείνετο στῶν δογμάτων σχεδὸν δὴ ταὐτόν), though he adds that they did "detach themselves from Plato on many issues and tortured the sense of others" (εἴς γε τἆλλα πολλαχῇ παραλύοντες, τὰ δὲ στρεβλοῦντες). I take this to indicate (a) fidelity to UP, and (b) diversity in the positive construct out of it.

On the Good

We may start with one of the more remarkable features of Numenius's approach to Plato. I have already mentioned his apparent belief that Plato was essentially a Pythagorean and at least in harmony with the Old Testament, in the person of Moses. In the first fragment we have of this work, Numenius remarks on the agreement of Brahmins, Jews, Magi [Zoroastrians], and Egyptians with Plato.[10] The ultimate harmony among the ancients is a hoary Platonic trope, though Numenius's large claim regarding agreement is, I believe, unprecedented, at least in the surviving testimonies regarding Platonism. As tempting as it is to speculate on the supposed extent of this doctrinal harmony, we really only need to presume that Numenius is referring to the fact that the Good is the unique principle of all. Although this will require a qualification, one that renders Zoroastrian dualism as apt for inclusion in the above list, it is apparently Numenius's starting point. In the light of his attempt to make what looks like an appeal to virtually the entirety of ancient wisdom as he knew it, it seems safe to say that Numenius embraced the Idea of the Good as the starting point for the positive construction on the basis of UP. Here, though, UP is taken not to be a position with a uniquely Pythagorean provenance.

In the first book of *On the Good*, we find the identification of the *Republic*'s Idea of the Good as the first principle of all. The immaterial realm in which the Good dwells is

> something ineffable and indescribable, absolutely alone and divine, there where the Good spends its time and revels in its glories, being itself at peace, benevolent, at rest, the gracious commander ensconced upon essence.[11]

Though this passage is evidently a sort of meditation on *Republic* 509B9, there are important additions made. The Good is alive and active, perhaps an allusion to the passages in *Republic* where the Good is "the most radiant part of that which is" (τοῦ ὄντος τὸ φανότατον) and "the happiest of that which is" (τὸ εὐδαιμονέστατον τοῦ ὄντος).[12] Numenius uses the Stoic term τὸ ἡγεμονικόν, the leading part of the soul in an animal and the mind in an individual human being, for the Good in relation to οὐσία. Here one sees more of a reference to Aristotle's Unmoved Mover, who in *Metaphysics* is said to be a "military leader" (στρατηγός) rather than to the Good of *Republic*.[13] As we will see presently, Numenius is in

---

10. Fr. 1a Des Places.
11. Fr. 2.13–16 Des Places: ἀλλά τις ἄφατος καὶ ἀδιήγητος ἀτεχνῶς ἐρημία θεσπέσιος, ἔνθα τοῦ ἀγαθοῦ ἤθη διατριβαί τε καὶ ἀγλαΐαι, αὐτὸ δὲ ἐν εἰρήνῃ, ἐν εὐμενείᾳ, τὸ ἤρεμον, τὸ ἡγεμονικὸν ἵλεω ἐποχούμενον ἐπὶ τῇ οὐσίᾳ.
12. *Rep.* 518C9, 526E3–4.
13. See *Meta.* Λ 10, 1075a14. Cf. Karamanolis 2006, 143.

line with the predominant position of the philosophers discussed in the previous chapter in eliding the Good with the Aristotelian first principle of all.

At the end of the fragment, the study (τὸ μάθημα) of the Good is said to be the study of "what being is" (τί ἐστι τὸ ὄν).[14] Again, we have an Aristotelian question ("what is being?"), but not with the Aristotelian answer that being is substance or essence (οὐσία); rather, we have the beginning of the Platonic answer that being is "ensconced upon essence or substance" (ἐποχούμενον ἐπὶ τῇ οὐσίᾳ).[15] But somewhat surprisingly, and much later in the work in book 6, Numenius describes the Good as "the first intellect and being itself" (τὸν πρῶτον νοῦν, αὐτοόν).[16] Leaving aside for the moment the identification of the Good as an intellect, let us focus for now on what Numenius wants to say about being itself that is, nevertheless, in some sense beyond οὐσία. There is an important bit of testimony in Proclus's *Commentary on Timaeus* in which he lists Numenius among those who affirm "participation among intelligibles, not only among sensibles."[17] What this appears to mean according to Proclus is that the Forms participate in the Good, whereas sensibles participate in the Forms. As Numenius himself says in another fragment from book 6, the Good is the Idea in which the Demiurge, being good, partakes.[18] It is insufficient to say that the participation of Forms in the Good is simply that which makes each of them itself good. For following Plato, Numenius says that the Good is the cause of the being of the Forms, not merely the cause of the fact that they possess the property of being good.[19]

Numenius says not only that the first principle is αὐτοόν, but that it is ὁ ὤν, "he who is," evidently—by referencing the book of Exodus—giving a reason why he thinks that Plato is Moses speaking Attic Greek.[20] So we must infer that the Forms get their being by participation in that which is being itself and whose 'name' is being. Moreover, this first principle is absolutely simple (ἁπλοῦς), that is, indivisible (μὴ διαίρετος).[21] Accordingly,

---

14. Fr. 2.23 Des Places.
15. Fr. 2.16 Des Places.
16. Fr. 17.4 Des Places. Cf. Alcinous, *Didask.* 164.27 Whittaker (= 10.3 Dillon), and for the identification of the first principle as being itself, Plutarch, *De Is.* 352A, 372F, 373A, 375C, and Aëtius (*Plac.* 17.31). Krämer (1964a, 109) traces this back to what he calls the "Xenocratean tradition."
17. Fr. 46c Des Places (= *In Tim.* 3.33.33–34).
18. Fr. 20.5–6 Des Places: μετουσίᾳ τοῦ πρώτου τε καὶ μόνου.
19. Fr. 16.3 Des Places: ἀρκεῖ τὸ ἀγαθὸν οὐσίας εἶναι ἀρχή.
20. Fr. 13.4 Des Places. See Exodus 3:14 in the Hellenistic Greek translation, where God calls himself ὁ ὤν. Some scholars have questioned the text of the fragment, though for no other reason than that they find it exceedingly odd that a Greek philosopher should characterize Plato's first principle of all with language drawn from the Old Testament. See, for the controversy, Des Places, p. 108, ad loc.; Whittaker 1967; Dillon 1977, 368; Whittaker 1978; Tarrant 1979; Burnyeat 2005.
21. See Fr. 11.12–13 Des Places.

Numenius says, Plato claimed that the Good is the One.[22] The problem this leaves us with is how participation in this first principle thus characterized is supposed by Numenius to account for the being of each Form, that is, for one Form having one οὐσία and one Form having another.

One element of Numenius's response to this problem is found in a difficult text regarding the creative power of the Demiurge and the absence of such power in the Good:

> For if it is necessary that the first not act demiurgically, then it is necessary to believe that the first god is the father of the god that does act demiurgically. If, then, we were examining the demiurgic god, in saying that it must exist prior, it must be able to make eminently, the course of the argument itself would have been reasonable. But if the argument is not about the Demiurge, but we are examining the first, it would be impious to say these things; so, let us consider them unsaid, since I think the argument takes another trail.[23]

On the one hand, it is fairly clear that in this passage Numenius is denying that the Good is eminently all things, because the Good is not a creator.[24] Indeed, as Numenius tells us a few lines later, the Good is also inactive (ἀργός), which certainly shows that it is unlike the second god, the Demiurge, who actually orders the cosmos.[25] So, presumably, eminence is a function of creative ability. That which creates or produces must be the paradigm of all that is produced. And yet the Good, it seems, is at least the paradigm of goodness; it is eminently what the Demiurge is by participation. More generally, since the Good is an intellect eternally contemplating intelligibles, which are supposed not to compromise its simplicity, one would assume that these intelligibles are not different from the Good itself.

---

22. Fr. 19.13 Des Places. Numenius says that Plato asserted this as the result of a syllogism (ἐκ συλλογισμοῦ). Since there is no such syllogism in the dialogues, it is tempting to suppose that Numenius is referring directly to the account of Plato's lecture on the Good in Aristoxenus. Cf. Merlan 1967, 102–3. It is also worth noting that Numenius wrote a treatise titled *On the Secrets of Plato* (Περὶ τῶν παρὰ Πλάτωνι ἀπορρήτων) in which he claims that Plato refrained from writing on theology because he feared the wrath of Athenians. See fr. 23. No doubt, θεολογία would not be the term that Plato would have used for an account of first principles, but that does not mean that Numenius would not have used it. At any rate, what this fragment shows is that Numenius did not find it odd that Plato's thoughts on the most important matters were not written.

23. Fr. 12.1–10 Des Places: Καὶ γὰρ οὔτε δημιουργεῖν ἐστι χρεὼν τὸν πρῶτον καὶ τοῦ δημιουργοῦντος δὲ θεοῦ χρὴ εἶναι νομίζεσθαι πατέρα τὸν πρῶτον θεόν. Εἰ μὲν οὖν περὶ τοῦ δημιουργικοῦ ζητοῖμεν, φάσκοντες δεῖν τὸν πρότερον ὑπάρξαντα οὕτως ἄν ποιεῖν ἔχειν διαφερόντως, ἐοικυῖα ἡ πρόσοδος αὕτη γεγονυῖα ἂν εἴη τοῦ λόγου· εἰ δὲ περὶ τοῦ δημιουργοῦ μὴ ἔστιν ὁ λόγος, ζητοῦμεν δὲ περὶ τοῦ πρώτου, ἀφοσιοῦμαί τε τὰ λεχθέντα καὶ ἔστω μὲν ἐκεῖνα ἄρρητα, μέτειμι δὲ ἐλεῖν τὸν λόγον, ἑτέρωθεν θηράσας. See Frede 1987, 1064–65 on this passage.

24. Even though, as we see in fr. 15.9, the Good is that "from which the order of the *cosmos* proceeds" (ἀφ᾿ ἧς ἥ τε τάξις τοῦ κόσμου).

25. In fact, the Demiurge is also a "lawgiver" (νομοθέτης, fr. 13.6) and "commanding" (ἡγεμονεῖν, 14), which is in contrast to the commanding of the Good in fr. 2, quoted above.

Why, then, is the Good not eminently all those intelligible that the Demiurge must employ in producing the ordered universe? But, again, this eminence cannot compromise its simplicity. In other words, absolutely simple being should not be eminently the multiplicity of οὐσίαι. So the being that the Good or One is is the paradigmatic cause of the being that every Form possesses, as a being that is limited by being *this* οὐσία and by not being all the rest.[26]

Readers familiar with the metaphysics of Thomas Aquinas will see immediately the striking similarity between what Numenius is claiming and Aquinas's characterization of the first principle of all as *ipsum esse*, the actuality of all essence. But Aquinas says that God is both eminently and virtually all things, meaning that *esse* is essentially active and that this active 'power' is what produces all that there is according to the paradigms that God is eminently. One would think that Numenius eschews any productive power for an inactive first principle. And yet in the passage in which he references the book of Exodus, he says that "he who is sows the seed of every soul in all things that partake of it."[27] The image of a seed is perhaps Stoic, and suggests virtuality. Numenius's claim is all the more fascinating when we compare it with what Plotinus says. For Plotinus denies that the One is eminently all things, insisting rather that it is only virtually all things (δύναμις πάντων).[28] He does this because eminence implies multiplicity, whereas virtuality does not. The explanation of why Plotinus thinks this is so I must leave to the next chapter.

Moreover, Numenius enriches the causal role of the first principle when he claims that it uses the second instrumentally.

> Numenius orders the first according to the category "that which is the Living Animal" and says that this first thinks in utilization of the second, whereas the second is categorized according to "intellect" and this by its demiurgic activity utilizes the third, which is categorized according to "discursive thinking."[29]

I assume that the words "that which is the Living Animal" is a reference to Plato's *Timaeus*, where we are told that the Demiurge looks to the "Living

---

26. Cf. Opsomer 2005a, 68–69, who observes that Numenius takes the transcendence of the Good to refer only to its eminence, that is, its being the paradigm of being.

27. Fr. 13.4–6 Des Places: Ὁ μέν γε ὢν σπέρμα πάσης ψυχῆς σπείρει εἰς τὰ μεταλαγχάνοντα αὐτοῦ χρήματα σύμπαντα.

28. See III 8, 10.1; V 1, 7.9–10; V 4, 1.23–26, 36; V 3, 15.33; V 4, 2.38; VI 9, 5.35–38. See below, 235–37.

29. Fr. 22.1–5 Des Places: Νουμήνιος δὲ τὸν μὲν πρῶτον κατὰ τὸ "ὅ ἐστι ζῷον" τάττει καὶ φησιν ἐν προσχρήσει τοῦ δευτέρου νοεῖν, τὸν δὲ δεύτερον κατὰ τὸν νοῦν καὶ τοῦτον αὖ ἐν προσχρήσει τοῦ τρίτου δημιουργεῖν, τὸν δὲ τρίτον κατὰ τὸν διανοούμενον. On the difficulties in this fragment, see Holzhausen 1992. The idea of the "utilization" (πρόσχρησις) of something lower by something higher is evidently inspired by Plato's references to the soul's use of the body. See *Alc.* 129C–E; *Phd.* 79C2–4; and esp. *Tim.* 28A6–B2, where the Demiurge

Animal" in creating the cosmos.³⁰ Specifically, this Living Animal contains all the Ideas that the Demiurge discerned in it. Numenius, remarkably, identifies the first principle with this Living Animal rather than with the Demiurge himself or with a separate generic Form. As a result of this, the Forms have a sort of twofold existence, in the Good and in the Demiurge, the latter being reflections or images of the former.³¹

Turning to the utilization of the second principle by the first, this instrumentality guarantees the causal role of the Good according to the principle that the effect must somehow be contained in the cause.³² The undiminished and inexhaustible giving of the Good seems to endow it with an infinite power, which is, after all, one way of describing virtuality. It seems that this instrumentality cannot be transitive such that the instrumentality of the third by the second entails the instrumentality of the third by the first. For in that case, there would be no distinction between the causal roles of the Good and the Demiurge in relation to the cosmos.

One hesitates, though, to take the image of the seed and its sowing and the instrumental use of the Demiurge as indicating virtuality. The reason for this is that Numenius is quite clear that the positing of a first principle of all is not intended to preclude dualism.³³ There is a very useful statement of Numenius's position in Calcidius's *Commentary on Plato's "Timaeus"*:

> Let us now consider the Pythagorean doctrine. Numenius, who was of the Pythagorean school, in order to refute Stoic doctrine, had recourse to Pythagorean doctrine, which he claimed was in line with Plato's. He said that it should be understood that Pythagoras had given the name "Monad" to god and the name "Dyad" to matter. This Dyad, according to him, was indeterminate and ungenerated, but when a limit was imposed on it that was its generation, that is, prior to adorned and endowed with form and order, it is without birth or generation, but once it is adorned and illuminated by the demiurgic god it is generated, and so, because the generation would be a posterior occurrence, that unadorned and ungenerated principle must be judged the equivalent of the god to which it is ordered. But certain Pythagoreans have not correctly gotten the force of this view, saying that that indeterminate and unlimited Dyad is produced by the unique Monad when this Monad removes itself from

---

utilizes the living paradigm as a model for the intelligible content of the sensible world. Cf. *Tim.* 46C, 68E.

30. See *Tim.* 39E8.

31. See fr. 16.10–11 Des Places: Ὁ γὰρ δεύτερος διττὸς ὢν αὐτοποιεῖ τήν τε ἰδέαν ἑαυτοῦ καὶ τὸν κόσμον, δημιουργὸς ὤν, ἔπειτα θεωρητικὸς ὅλως. (For the second, being double, makes by itself its own Idea and the cosmos, being the maker; afterward he is entirely contemplative.) These words seem to indicate that the Demiurge's ἰδέα is different from the paradigm that he contemplates.

32. Cf. fr. 14.6–7 Des Places: τὰ δὲ θεῖά ἐστιν οἷα μεταδοθέντα ἐνθένδ' ἐκεῖθι γεγενημένα ἔνθεν τε οὐκ ἀπελήλυθε (but divine gifts are such that, having been shared, once they come to be here, they have not left there).

33. See Krämer 1964a, 77, n. 198; Baltes 1975, 255; Dillon 1977, 373–74; Frede 1987, 1051–52.

its own nature as Monad and mutates into the state of a Dyad. This cannot be right, for it would mean that the Monad would disappear and the Dyad, which did not exist, would come to exist, and god would be transformed into matter and the Monad transformed into an indeterminate and unlimited Dyad. This is an opinion not even worthy of men of poor culture.[34]

The passage is patently dualistic. Most remarkably, later in the passage, Numenius is said to identify the Dyad, prior to being ordered, with chance (*fortuna*).[35] For this reason, Numenius cannot consistently maintain that the Good or the One is virtually all things. It has nothing to do with the being of the Indefinite Dyad as such. Because the Indefinite Dyad is beyond the "reach" of the Good, it is the principle of evil.[36] If, though, the Good is just virtually all the Forms or all that which is intelligible and good, this would compromise its position as beyond οὐσία. For the Good would then turn out to be limited in the precise sense that it is impotent with regard to the being of the Indefinite Dyad; that being is owing to chance. Since the hallmark of οὐσία is limitation—limitation in regard to the kinds of things that it is not owing to the kind of thing it is—the Good or the One is not beyond οὐσία.[37] Indeed, Numenius maintains this explicitly when he is reported as saying that "the Good itself is the Demiurge of essence, connatural with essence."[38] This is exactly why the Good must be an intellect.[39]

---

34. Fr. 52.1–14 Des Places: Nunc iam Pythagoricorum dogma recenseatur. Numenius ex Pythagorae magisterio Stoicorum hoc de initiis dogma refellens Pythagorae dogmate, cui concinere dicit dogma platonicum, ait Pythagoram deum quidem singularitatis nomine nominasse, silvam vero duitatis; quam duitatem indeterminatam quidem minime genitam, limitatan vero generatam esse dicere, hoc est, antequam exornaretus quidem formamque et ordionem nancisceretur, sine ortu et generatione, exornatam vero atque illustratam a digestore deo esse generatam, atque ita, quia generationis sit fortuna posterior, inornatum illud minime generatum aequaevum, deo, a quo est ordinatum, intellegi debeat. See Petty 2012, 210–18, for discussion of the entire passage and for the evidence that this is a literal translation of Numenius rather than a paraphrase.

35. See fr. 52.96–99. Baltes 1975, 256.

36. See fr. 52.33–44. Numenius, fr. 52.64–75, like Plutarch, interpreted *Lg.* 896E4–6 and 897D1 as positing two soul principles, one evil and one good. The evil soul principle is responsible for the motion in the universe other than that infused by the good soul and is also responsible for psychic motions in us other than those of the rational part of the soul. See O'Brien 1999, 23–24, "Numenius' resurrection of Empedocles' god of evil of course entirely subverts the teleology of the *Timaeus*." As O'Brien notes, Plato's correction of Empedocles is recapitulated in Plotinus's correction of Numenius.

37. See fr. 4a.11–12 Des Places: Οὔκουν τὴν αὐτὴν οὔτε τὰ σώματα εἶναι ὄν. (Therefore, I say that neither matter itself nor bodies are being.) This cannot mean that matter or the Indefinite Dyad is nothing; it must mean that matter does not possess οὐσία, that is, it does not possess the being of something that partakes of οὐσία. Thus, it is the counter image of the One. See fr. 3 Des Places, where the utter lack of determination of the Indefinite Dyad *presumes* its being.

38. Fr. 16.9–10 Des Places: ὁ τῆς οὐσίας δημιουργὸς αὐτοάγαθον, σύμφυτον τῇ οὐσίᾳ.

39. Fr. 16.1–4 Des Places: Εἰ δ' ἔστι μὲν νοητὸν ἡ οὐσία καὶ ἡ ἰδέα, ταύτης δ' ὡμολογήθη πρεσβύτερον καὶ αἴτιον εἶναι ὁ νοῦς, αὐτὸς οὗτος μόνος εὕρηται ὢν τὸ ἀγαθόν. (If essence

There seems to be little doubt that this dualism rests primarily on an interpretation of Plato's *Timaeus*.[40] As that dialogue tells us, there are three principles of this universe: Forms, their copies, and space. But even before the ordered universe came into being, there was being, space, and becoming.[41] Assuming that Numenius is, rightly or wrongly, following the tradition that makes space equal to matter, and the tradition that identifies matter with the Indefinite Dyad, he does seem justified in claiming that his dualism is rooted in *Timaeus* itself. And yet, as we have already seen, the above threefold division follows the text in which it is said that "the first principle or principles of all things will not be adduced in the exposition that is to follow."[42] We do not know how Numenius took this passage, but it seems clear that if the first principle of all is to provide the explanation for the being of the Indefinite Dyad, then prescinding from that principle, the Indefinite Dyad will appear as uncaused by anything other than chance. It is not the case that Numenius ignores the first principle of all or even that he identifies it with the Demiurge of *Timaeus*.[43] He seems to reason, though, that if the first principle is the Good, then it cannot be the principle of evil, which it would seem to be if one eschewed all forms of dualism. Accordingly, if the Good or One is an intellect eternally contemplating Forms in a way that does not compromise its absolute simplicity, then it is exonerated from having anything to do with evil, at least insofar as evil is identified or produced in something beyond the Good's explanatory reach.[44]

If the Good is not virtually all things, it must somehow be eminently all things; otherwise, it would not be a principle of the being of anything with essence. Numenius follows the tradition going back to Parmenides, according to which the combination of a unique first principle with the exigency of identifying a principle for all that which is intelligible requires that the first principle be an intellect. If Forms or intelligibles were to exist

---

and the Idea are intelligible, and Intellect is agreed to be superior and the cause of these, this Intellect alone has been found to be the Good.)

40. See Baltes 1975, 255–57. Also, Staab 2009, 76–81.

41. *Tim.* 51E–52D. Cf. 48B3–4.

42. *Tim.* 48C2–6. Cf. 53C4–D7.

43. As Baltes (1975, 263) notes, Numenius probably treats *Tim.* 28C3–5, where Plato says that the "father and maker is hard to find," as referring to the "unknowable" Good or One, not to the Demiurge. This would suggest that he takes 48C2–6 to refer to this principle. At fr. 21.1, it is the first principle that is said to be "father." At fr. 16, the "maker" (ποιητής) is distinct from the "father" (πατήρ). See above, chap. 7, n. 32, for Plutarch's use of this passage.

44. Eudorus of Alexandria (fl. ca. 25 BCE), according to Simplicius, *In Phys.* 181.7–30, appears to have argued that the second principles (limit and its opposite) are derived from the first, evidently called "the supreme god" (ὁ ὑπεράνω θεός). Whether Numenius is arguing against such a derivation is not clear from the scanty evidence. See Bonazzi 2005. Staab (2009, 67–70) argues that Eudorus in fact distinguished a first principle of all called ἕν from the ἕν that is paired with the δύας (i.e., Indefinite Dyad), as secondary principles of number. By contrast, Atticus (fl. 175–80 CE), like Plutarch, seems to conflate the Good with the Demiurge. See Proclus, *In Tim.* 1.305.6–9. It may well be that, as Dillon suggests (1977, 127), Eudorus is relying on an interpretation of *Phil.* 26E–30E where a divine intellect or Zeus presides over the principles of limit and unlimited. See Whittaker 1969, 97–98.

outside an intellect, one would presumably have an infinity of principles. An intellect that somehow thinks all that which is intelligible 'together' may be posited as being somehow absolutely simple, assuming there is not another absolutely simple first principle prior to it. In that case the multiplicity in intellect remains unproblematic.

For Numenius, the principal differences between the intellect that the Good is and the intellect that the Demiurge is is that the former is immobile and concerned solely with intelligibles, whereas the latter is in motion and concerned both with intelligibles and sensibles.[45] The extravagance of intellects needs to be seen as an expression of the fundamental Platonic principles to which Numenius is attempting to adhere. The second intellect is required in order to endow the Indefinite Dyad with form. In doing this, it moves itself. If the first intellect were to do this, its simplicity would be compromised. And yet the immobility of the first intellect is also said to be an "innate motion" (κίνησιν σύμφυτον).[46] This way of characterizing the first principle seems ambiguous. It may refer to the way the Unmoved Mover moves as the object of desire, as Alcinous characterizes the motion of the first principle.[47] But it may also refer, as Krämer notes, to the motion of intellect in Plato's *Sophist*.[48] As we have seen, Aristotle found it unduly paradoxical to call that which is perfect a motion, and so he coined the word ἐνέργεια for the 'motion' of the first principle. Numenius, as we have seen, denied that the first principle is active; indeed, it is ἀνενέργητον. We do not know if, like Plotinus, he distinguished between ἐνέργεια (actuality) and τὸ ἐνεργεῖν (activity), asserting that the One is the first but does not have the second.[49] In any case, it is in order to observe the constraint of a system with an absolutely simple causal principle, the Good or the One, at the top of a hierarchy of principles, that Numenius makes this principle an intellect.

Proclus tells us in his commentary on *Timaeus* that

> Numenius proclaimed three gods: the first he calls "Father," the second he calls "Maker," and the third he calls "Product" for, according to him, the cosmos is the third god. So, according to him, the Demiurge is double, the first god and the second, while the thing made is the third.[50]

---

45. Fr. 15.3–5 Des Places: Δηλονότι ὁ μὲν πρῶτος θεὸς ἔσται ἑστώς, ὁ δὲ δεύτερος ἔμπαλίν ἐστι κινούμενος· ὁ μὲν οὖν πρῶτος περὶ τὰ νοητά, ὁ δὲ δεύτερος περὶ τὰ νοητὰ καὶ αἰσθητά (It is clear that the first god will be motionless, while the second god, by contrast, is in motion. The first is concerned with the intelligibles, while the second is concerned with intelligibles and with sensibles.)
46. Fr. 15.8–9 Des Places.
47. See *Didask.* 164.25 (= Dillon 10.2).
48. See *Soph.* 245E8ff., and Krämer 1964a, 70, n. 173.
49. See *Enn.* V 6, 6.4. Cf. III 8, 11.9. The text at VI 8, 40.24 is more difficult, but seems to use ἐνέργεια as the noun for τὸ ἐνεργεῖν, yet the activity is distinguishable from the actuality that the One is.
50. Fr. 21.1–5 Des Places: Νουμήνιος μὲν γὰρ τρεῖς ἀνυμνήσας θεοὺς πατέρα μὲν καλεῖ τὸν πρῶτον, ποιητὴν δὲ τὸν δεύτερον, ποίημα δὲ τὸν τρίτον· ὁ γὰρ κόσμος κατ' αὐτὸν ὁ τρίτος ἐστὶ θεός· ὥστε ὁ κατ' αὐτὸν δημιουργὸς διττός, ὅ τε πρῶτος θεὸς καὶ ὁ δεύτερος, τὸ δὲ

Evidently, apart from *Timaeus,* Numenius is here referencing the Platonic *Second Epistle,* where the doctrine of the three principles is mysteriously mentioned.[51] This threefold schema, eventually taken as a given in later Platonism, requires some detailed attention.

Let us begin by noticing that Numenius takes the Demiurge to be double, both the 'father' and the 'maker.'[52] We have already seen that differentiating the first and second principles is problematic if each is an intellect. The doubleness or duality of the Demiurge is a result, I think, of Numenius's being unable to conceive of how the work required by father and maker, or their explanatory roles, could be performed by only one principle. And yet, to conceive of either of these principles as other than an intellect seemed impossible. An analogous problem arises for the second and third gods:

> The first god, existing in itself, is simple because of the fact that, wholly being self-contained, it is never divided. However, the god that is second and third is one, but associated with matter, which is dual, and though it unifies it, it is split apart by it, which itself has an appetitive character and is flowing. Not being attached to the intelligible (for it would then be in itself), because it is looking at matter, it comes to occupy itself with this and overlook itself. And it seizes upon that which is sensible and tends to it and leads it to its own character, being desirous of matter.[53]

The claim that the second and third are one seems stronger than the claim that the first and second are double, for these are only generically the same, so to speak. As we saw in fr. 22, the second and the third are distinguished in that it is only the latter that is engaged in discursive thinking exclusively, while the second orders the cosmos and then withdraws into contemplation. It seems fairly clear that the third is taken by Numenius to

---

δημιουργούμενον ὁ τρίτος. Cf. fr. 22. It is not entirely unlikely that Proclus has here garbled Numenius's doctrine. See Petty 2012, 173–74, for references to the skeptical scholarship.

51. *Second Ep.* 312E1–4: ὧδε γὰρ ἔχει. περὶ τὸν πάντων βασιλέα πάντ' ἐστὶ καὶ ἐκείνου ἕνεκα πάντα, καὶ ἐκεῖνο αἴτιον ἁπάντων τῶν καλῶν· δεύτερον δὲ περὶ τὰ δεύτερα, καὶ τρίτον περὶ τὰ τρίτα. (For it is like this: upon the king of all do all things turn; he is the goal of all things and the cause of all goods. Things of the second order turn upon the second principle, and those of the third order upon the third.) Cf. *Tim.* 24B8: εὐδαίμονα θεόν. Frede (1987, 1056) suggests that Numenius might well be the first to have used the *Second Ep.* in this way.

52. Krämer (1964a; 2nd ed. 1967, 63–83), in the course of a very rich survey of Platonic versions of the three principles contemporary with Numenius, argues that for Numenius, the Demiurge is equivalent to the third principle, the soul of the world or cosmos (75). As Baltes (1975, 265) shows, this interpretation cannot stand in the light of fr. 20, where the Demiurge is identified with the second god.

53. Fr. 11.11–20 Des Places: Ὁ θεὸς ὁ μὲν πρῶτος ἐν ἑαυτοῦ ὤν ἐστιν ἁπλοῦς, διὰ τὸ ἑαυτῷ συγγιγνόμενος διόλου μή ποτε εἶναι διαιρετός· ὁ θεὸς μέντοι ὁ δεύτερος καὶ τρίτος ἐστὶν εἷς· συμφερόμενος δὲ τῇ ὕλῃ δυάδι οὔσῃ ἑνοῖ μὲν αὐτήν, σχίζεται δὲ ὑπ' αὐτῆς, ἐπιθυμητικὸν ἦθος ἐχούσης καὶ ῥεούσης. Τῷ οὖν μὴ εἶναι πρὸς τῷ νοητῷ (ἦν γὰρ ἄν πρὸς ἑαυτῷ) διὰ τὸ τὴν ὕλην βλέπειν, ταύτης ἐπιμελούμενος ἀπερίοπτος ἑαυτοῦ γίγνεται. Καὶ ἅπτεται τοῦ αἰσθητοῦ καὶ περιέπει ἀνάγει τε ἔτι εἰς τὸ ἴδιον ἦθος ἐπορεξάμενος τῆς ὕλης.

be the discursive intellect of the World Soul, which, again, must be different from the second because their differing work cannot be combined. If this is so, then why are the second and third said to be one?

The answer to this question seems to lie in the claim that matter is unified by the 'one' god but that god is split apart by matter.⁵⁴ The splitting is probably the embodiment of the World Soul, which leaves separate the demiurgic intellect. As embodied, this World Soul engages in discursive reasoning in its directing of nature. If this soul were ever disembodied (an impossibility, according to Plato, it would seem),⁵⁵ it would again be one with the intellect that the Demiurge is.⁵⁶

On this interpretation, discursive intellection is, in general, how the intuitive intellection of a disembodied intellect operated when embodied. This is a position that is more or less implied by Plato's claims regarding the identity and immortality of the human person. The argument in *Phaedo* for immortality tries to show that the embodied person is identical with a disembodied intellect, that which knew the Forms prior to embodiment. How can the person, the subject of nonintellectual psychic states and bodily states, be identical with the pure intellect?⁵⁷ The answer seems to be that just as an immaterial Form may be manifested variously in bodies, so, too, may an intellect. For example, in the account or definition of the Form of

---

54. See fr. 4b.31–34 Des Places: Οὕτως οὖν καὶ τῇ ψυχῇ καθ' ἑαυτὴν μὲν πρόσεστι τὸ ἀδιάστατον, κατὰ συμβεβηκὸς δὲ τῷ ἐν ᾧ ἐστι τριχῇ διαστάτῳ ὄντι συνθεωρεῖται καὶ αὐτὴ τριχῇ διαστατή. (In this way, then, in the soul itself there is present lack of dimensionality, but when considered in that which it is, which is three-dimensional, it is accidentally itself in three dimensions.) The idea of accidental three-dimensionality is difficult. I take it that Numenius is using Aristotelian terminology to make a Platonic point, namely, that when soul is present in a body, it is present in a (Platonically) diminished way, that is, as an image of its disembodied self. No doubt, *Tim.* 37A–B is relevant here as well. In this passage the World Soul is placed within the world's body and has contact with its bodily existence. Also, see 69Dff., where the parts of the human soul are 'dispersed' in the human body.

55. See *Tim.* 41A, where it is said that the handiwork of the Demiurge is indissoluble, except where he consents.

56. See Frede 1987, 1058, who explains the oneness of the second and third gods by the fact that the third is essentially that which the second is, in the way, I suppose, that the essence of an instantiated Form is identical with the essence of the Form itself. I am not sure that Frede's solution is really different from mine. See 1073, where his interpretation is more clearly the same as my own. See Simplicius, *In Phys.* 230.36–231.7, for Porphyry's account of Moderatus's three Ones. Moderatus's interpretation of the second part of *Parmenides* is probably different from that of Numenius but strikingly similar in finding in that dialogue the framework for the positive construct out of UP. See Petty 2012, 145–51, for some additional useful comments on Middle Platonic conceptions of a 'second' god.

57. See fr. 46 Des Places, where Olympiodorus reports the very different views among Platonists, including Numenius, on whether the whole soul in all its parts is immortal or whether less than all of the parts are immortal. The minimalist view, that only the rational part of the soul is immortal, is held by Porphyry and Proclus. According to Olympiodorus, Numenius held that the immortality extends from the rational part of the soul down to the sentient part of the soul (τῆς ἐμψύχου ἕξεως). Numenius is probably relying on an interpretation of *Phdr.* 245C5: ψυχὴ πᾶσα ἀθάνατος. On this interpretation, the words are taken to mean "all parts of the soul are immortal" rather than "all soul has an immortal part."

Beauty, there would be no mention of the bodies that manifest physical beauty and without which the latter could not manifest beauty. Being a subject of discursive reasoning and other psychic states and activities is the way that a disembodied intellect is manifested when embodied.

A fundamental ambiguity in Plato's argument in *Phaedo* will be a source of much puzzlement when later Platonists reflect on it. According to that argument, soul is both life and the bearer of life, that is, a property of an entity and an entity itself.[58] If this can be shown to be true, it is possible to maintain that soul makes me, the human being, alive, but that I am identical with an entity that lives even when I, the human being, am not alive. But I, when the human being is dead, am apparently solely an intellect. So intellect has life, but brings life to me in the form of a human soul, a soul that is manifested by its attachment to a body, and so with 'additional' characteristics, those pertaining to embodiment. Applying this argument to the Demiurge in *Timaeus*, we can infer that the intellect that he is is alive even though he does not have a soul. When he creates the World Soul, he is, in a way, manifesting himself in the world's body.

Plato would have avoided much confusion if he had adapted Aristotle's clear distinction between intellect (νοῦς) and soul (ψυχή).[59] Instead, Plato calls intellect 'the highest part of the soul' or 'the rational part of the soul' or 'the immortal part of the soul.'[60] It is not irrelevant to add, however, that Aristotle, too, succumbs to the ambiguity when he says, in referring to the Unmoved Mover, that "life belongs to [him], for the actuality of intellect is life, and he is actuality."[61] For both Plato and Aristotle, and regardless of the vocabulary, it is difficult to explain how intellect that is able to exist disembodied is related to embodied intellection *and* to other psychic activities. This is especially difficult to explain when the disembodied intellect is supposed to be the intellect of the person who is embodied.

According to the testimony of Proclus, Numenius held that the soul is composed of the Monad and the Indefinite Dyad.[62] In holding this, Numenius is applying the general principle from Plato's *Philebus* that "all things that are always said to be are composed of a one and a many, having by nature a limit and an unlimited in them."[63] According to Iamblichus,

> Numenius appears to prefer a unification and undifferentiated identity of the soul and its principles.[64]

---

58. Cf. Alexander Polyhistor *ap.* D.L. 8.28, where Pythagoras is reported as holding that "soul differs from life" (διαφέρειν τε ψυχὴν ζωῆς).

59. See *DA* B 2, 413b24–27. Cf. B 3, 415a11–12.

60. See *Tim.* 90A–C.

61. *Meta.* Λ 7, 1072b26–27: καὶ ζωὴ δέ γε ὑπάρχει· ἡ γὰρ νοῦ ἐνέργεια ζωή, ἐκεῖνος δὲ ἡ ἐνέργεια. Life without soul would seem to be equivalent to Plato's "intellectual motion" (κίνησις νοῦ).

62. Fr. 39 Des Places.

63. Plato, *Phil.* 16C9–10: ὡς ἐξ ἑνὸς μὲν καὶ πολλῶν ὄντων τῶν ἀεὶ λεγομένων εἶναι, πέρας δὲ καὶ ἀπειρίαν ἐν αὐτοῖς σύμφυτον ἐχόντων.

64. Fr. 42 Des Places: Ἕνωσιν μὲν οὖν καὶ ταυτότητα ἀδιάκριτον τῆς ψυχῆς πρὸς τὰς ἑαυτῆς ἀρχὰς πρεσβεύειν φαίνεται Νουμήνιος.

If the unity here is the unity that Numenius speaks of in fr. 11, it is not easy to see what to make of Iamblichus's assertion that this is an undifferentiated identity, especially in the light of the 'splitting apart' of the second and third gods. Presumably, the act of unification is a result of the separation of the soul from the body, an act that it would seem the second and third gods cannot perform.[65] What we see Numenius doing here is hypothesizing a systematic metaphysical structure on the basis of *Timaeus* using the Platonic doctrines that he sees in the other dialogues and in the testimony of the tradition. For Numenius, the systematic structure is unequivocally Pythagorean in its basic components.[66]

The apparent insistence by Numenius on there being three gods or principles is reflected in the different function of each. Psychic functioning, especially cognitive psychic functioning, requires a body. By contrast, the pure or essential functioning of intellect not only does not require a body, but is not possible in a body. This functioning is that of cognizing being, which is incorporeal.[67] We do not possess any material from Numenius *On the Good* in which he explains why it is that the cognition of being is possible only for that which is incorporeal. It is likely, however, that Numenius would give the same reason for this as Plato and Aristotle and, indeed, the entire tradition, namely, that cognition of being is a kind of identification with it. If intellect were bodily it could not achieve this identification. It could operate only via representations of that which is cognizable. But Numenius also says that soul is incorporeal, too.[68] Soul is one with intellect in the sense that, separated from the body, it reverts to its unique intellectual function. When present in the body, it is capable only of being an image or imitation of that. Thus, διανοεῖν (discursive thinking) is an imitation of νοῦς (intellect).[69]

Discursive reasoning is, for Numenius, the tool for managing a bodily existence. It is practical in the sense that it is reasoning about the achievement or satisfaction of desire; without desire, discursive reasoning would be entirely otiose. As Numenius says, the embodied soul (here, in particular, the World Soul) has an "appetitive character" (ἐπιθυμητικὸν ἦθος).[70]

---

65. Aristotle, DA Γ 5, 430a22–23, says that when our intellect is separated from us, "it is what it is alone." Conversely, when our intellect is associated with the human composite, it is other than what it is alone. I interpret this to mean that it manifests itself in a way other than what it is when it is separated. In other words, embodied intellection is 'one' with disembodied intellection, though they are different in λόγος, as Aristotle would put it.

66. See fr. 24.68–73 Des Places, which comes from Numenius's *On the Divergence of Academics from Plato*. There Numenius expresses a hope to recover the "torn apart limbs" of Plato. I take it that these "limbs" are the elements of a systematic philosophical position. Among those who were responsible for the violence to the Pythagorean Plato were the Stoics and the Academic Skeptics.

67. Fr. 6 Des Places.

68. Fr. 4b Des Places.

69. See fr. 16.16–17 Des Places, where the cosmos is an imitation of the Demiurge. Presumably, part of the imitative nature is found in the discursive reasoning of the World Soul.

70. Fr. 11.16 Des Places.

Consequently, the principle of soul is not reducible to the principle of intellect. That is, the paradigm of practical or discursive reasoning is not reducible to the paradigm of theoretical or intuitive thinking. The principle of discursive reasoning is, more accurately, the principle of embodied rational desire. No doubt, it is also the principle of embodied nonrational desire, though none of the extant fragments consider this. It would be a fair, though minor objection, to Numenius, to point out that the Demiurge of *Timaeus* does manifest some sort of desire in wanting the universe to be like himself and like the Living Animal on whom it is modeled. But this sort of desire is not embodied.[71] The Demiurge desires the Good, like everything else. It attains the Good, that is, it is good by eternally contemplating, which is what embodied rational animals strive to attain intermittently.[72] The faculty of judgment is what enables it to see how best to instantiate the Living Animal in the preexistent chaos. Since this is a sort of practical activity, there is an impulse present. Its desire is for the Good. And this desire is, presumably, fundamentally different from the ἐπιθυμία that is present in its embodied manifestation, the soul. The practical activity of the Demiurge is not continuous. He creates and then retires to contemplate. Indeed, it is not likely to be temporal either.[73] For the fact that the Demiurge creates and then contemplates must be put alongside the claim that he derives his faculty of judgment from his contemplating.

What is remarkable about the Demiurge's activity is that it is dual. If the Good is just a contemplator and the World Soul is just a discursive reasoner, then it must have seemed to Numenius that a *tertium quid* was needed, a principle that would 'mediate' between the completely uninvolved first principle and the embodied and so created soul. But this, of course, leaves us with the problem of how the Demiurge is a principle at all, for a principle is a unified starting point. This does not mean that a principle cannot itself be complex. If, though, the principle is complex, it is not a principle qua complex. That is, its complexity does not pertain to its nature as a principle, even if it should be the case that its complexity is a necessary condition for its being a principle. In the case of the Demiurge,

---

71. See fr. 18.13 Des Places, where the second god receives its "impulse" (τὸ ὁρμητικόν) from its "desire" (ἔφεσις) as it receives its "faculty of judgment" (τὸ κριτικόν) from its "contemplating" (θεωρία). The faculty of judgment is what enables it to see how best to instantiate the Living Animal in the preexistent chaos. Since this is a sort of practical activity, there is an impulse present. Its desire is for the Good. And this desire is, presumably, fundamentally different from the ἐπιθυμία that is present in its embodied manifestation, the soul. The practical activity of the Demiurge is not continuous. He creates and then retires to contemplate.

72. Cf. *Tim.* 29A2–3: εἰ μὲν δὴ καλός ἐστιν ὅδε ὁ κόσμος ὅ τε δημιουργὸς ἀγαθός, δῆλον ὡς τὸ ἀΐδιον ἔβλεπεν (if this cosmos is beautiful and its maker good, it is clear that he looked to the eternal).

73. See fr. 16.11–12 Des Places: ἔπειτα θεωρητικὸς ὅλως (afterward he is entirely contemplative). I agree with Des Places 1971, who rejects Dodds's suggestion that 'afterward' (ἔπειτα) indicates a temporal succession. The temporal succession of practical activity by contemplation is a human imitation of the divine atemporal state.

its complexity consists in its engaging in a properly demiurgic activity, that of creating order in the universe, and its theoretical activity, that of contemplating all that is intelligible and thereby achieving the Good. Perhaps it is the case that the Demiurge is taken to be essentially a maker or creator and his contemplative activity is merely a sort of grace note, so to speak. The word ὅλως is against this, as is the priority of contemplation to judgment in him. In fact, the dearth of evidence makes it impossible to know even if Numenius perceived this to be a problem, and if so, how he solved it.

Numenius's provocative speculations on the ontological status of the Good and the Demiurge reveal the central conundrum for the cohort of Platonists who sought to articulate the foundation for a consistent positive construct on the basis of UP. Numenius seems to be in no doubt that clarity with regard to first principles is essential for meeting the challenges of the anti-Platonists. For after all, the Platonic position on particular philosophical questions will always have recourse, ultimately, to these principles in order to provide non-question-begging responses to these challenges. And yet the fragmentary evidence suggests that consistency was elusive for Numenius. Evidently, he could not see clearly how to reconcile the simplicity of the first principle of all with a causal role without making it some sort of intellect and thereby undermining the very consistency he sought. The tantalizing description of the first principle as 'He who is' does not guide him to a resolution. When Proclus lauded Plotinus as the great exegete of the Platonic revelation, he was no doubt in part comparing him implicitly to Numenius and to earlier Platonists. It is to Plotinus's 'renovations' that we now turn.

Part 3

Plotinus

"Exegete of the Platonic Revelation"

CHAPTER 9

Platonism as a System

Proclus, in his *Platonic Theology*, avers that Plotinus is the greatest exegete (ἐξηγητής) "of the Platonic revelation" (τῆς Πλατωνικῆς ἐποπτείας).[1] The coupling of the term 'exegete' with the term 'revelation' indicates that Proclus is talking about more than a commentary on the dialogues or an explication de texte. As Plotinus himself says in the course of his presentation of the three fundamental 'hypostases' of Platonism:

> These statements of ours are not recent or new, but rather were made a long time ago, though not explicitly. The things we are saying now are exegeses of those, relying on the writings of Plato himself as evidence that these are ancient views.[2]

Plotinus, like Numenius, has no doubt that the principles of the Platonic system have been grasped by others long before Plato. But Plotinus, like Proclus, is certain that Plato has revealed these in an incomparable way. This passage tells us three things: Plotinus does not consider himself an innovator

---

1. Proclus, *PT* 1.1.16ff. Saffrey-Westerink. In second rank of exegetes are Plotinus's disciples Porphyry and Amelius; in the third rank are Iamblichus, Theodore of Asine, and unnamed others. In modern times, at the polar opposite to Proclus's evaluation of the accuracy of Plotinus's exegetical prowess, is the far more frequently made assessment of Shorey 1938, 36, who held that generally "Neo-Platonic ideas are persistently and mistakenly attributed to Plato himself." This is done according to a "pseudodialectical exegesis" (39).
2. Plotinus, *Enn.* V 1, 8.10–14: Καὶ εἶναι τοὺς λόγους τούσδε μὴ καινοὺς μηδὲ νῦν, ἀλλὰ πάλαι μὲν εἰρῆσθαι μὴ ἀναπεπταμένως, τοὺς δὲ νῦν λόγους ἐξηγητὰς ἐκείνων γεγονέναι μαρτυρίοις πιστωσαμένους τὰς δόξας ταύτας παλαιὰς εἶναι τοῖς αὐτοῦ τοῦ Πλάτωνος γράμμασιν.

or an original philosopher; the exegete is tasked with making explicit what is only implicit; and Plato, too, is not original, at least in his expression of fundamental metaphysical principles. Among the ancients that Plotinus goes on to claim dimly saw the truth are Parmenides, Pythagoras, Anaxagoras, Heraclitus, and Empedocles. Of Aristotle's unequivocal commitment to this "chorus," Plotinus is in some doubt. Those especially who regard Plotinus as an innovator, perhaps *malgré lui-même*, will hardly be persuaded by the inclusion of Pre-Socratics among those who were 'Platonists' before Plato.

In this regard, one may perhaps contrast Aristotle's survey of his predecessors' treatment of causality and his conclusion that, although all of these have touched on the four causes in some sense, none of them have done so in an adequate manner.[3] Neither Aristotle nor Plotinus seems to have any difficulty in attributing to their predecessors views that are only 'implicit' in the texts. The reason for this is clear: both assumed that their predecessors, like themselves, were focused on the truth, which serves as the criterion for exegesis. If, for example, the four causes are the logically necessary and sufficient framework for scientific explanation, then anything that the Pre-Socratics say that shows that they were, however dimly or partially, aware of this, can be attributed to their approach to wisdom. As for Plotinus, it is not that he does not have what he regards as textual support for his claim that his system is identical to Plato's. We have already referred in a number of places to some of these texts as they were cited by earlier Platonists. But the deeper point is that his focus, like Aristotle's, is on the truth. And again, like Aristotle, he believes the truth is attainable independently of the exegesis of any of one's predecessors. As Plotinus says, there are numerous arguments one could employ to show the existence of a first principle of all. His citation of Platonic texts is always in support of the conclusion, never as a substitute for independent arguments for that conclusion. I suppose that this is at least part of what Proclus means when he speaks of the 'Platonic revelation.' On the matters for which Plato does argue, namely, for particular consequences of his fundamental principles, Plotinus is usually either silent or else he offers an interpretation that he believes to be most consistent with fundamentals. Often enough, Plotinus is dealing with matters that have arisen over the course of philosophy in the six hundred years or so between Plato and himself and on which Plato does not speak directly. In such cases, Plotinus will defend a position that he thinks anyone committed to the fundamental principles must take.[4]

We can also observe in Plotinus's appeal to 'ancient wisdom' and in his use of the Platonic material that UP is a deep underlying assumption. As we will see presently, the postulation of the three basic principles or

---

3. See *Meta.* A 7, 988a18ff.

4. Dörrie and Baltes (1993, 3:155–61) list the names of more than 160 "*berühmten*" Platonists almost exclusively from the 'Middle Platonic' period. Another 180 or so are added in the period after Plotinus and before the end of antiquity. Many of these are to us just names, but undoubtedly many are also authors of works known to Plotinus. As we learn from Porphyry's *Life of Plotinus*, he was immersed in the contemporary philosophical literature.

hypostases of Plotinus's Platonism can be inferred immediately from the conjunction of the tenets of UP. Thus, if materialism, mechanism, nominalism, relativism, and skepticism are false, then the ultimate explanations of the phenomena that are implicitly affirmed in the face of the falsity of these positions—the existence of immaterial entities, of life as not supervenient on bodies, of intelligible reality, of universal truths, and of knowledge—will have a conclusion in the three hypostases. Without the One or Good, Intellect, and Soul, suitably arrayed hierarchically in terms of explanatory scope, there can be no explanation for, say, the existence of rationality, virtue, love, or evil.[5] For a particularly vexed question, such as the relation between an immaterial person and his living body, Plotinus will bring to bear all three hypostases. That is, we need to understand how Soul is related to Intellect, how Intellect is related to the One, and, conversely, how the One employs Intellect and Soul, in order to give an adequate account of what a human being is. In the remainder of this chapter, I am going to offer an explication of the Plotinian system independently of its putative Platonic basis. In the following two chapters, I will turn to Plotinus as an exegete of Plato and to his reasons for believing that he is faithful to the master's vision.

The First Principle of All

The term 'hypostasis' (ὑπόστασις) is not a particularly felicitous one in representing the principles of Plotinus's system. Plotinus will frequently use the term to refer to the existence, that is, roughly, extramental existence, of things like love, time, motion, numbers, and so on.[6] Generally, he does not suppose that there is any question about the existence of such items, but rather that the accounts of their existence, by non-Platonists especially, are defective. By contrast, the claim that there are three fundamental hypostases or existents is, of course, controversial. Porphyry gives as a title to the treatise V 1 "On the Three Primary Hypostases," which nicely indicates their privileged status as principles. But it is the claim that these three must exist in a hierarchical arrangement that is most important and controversial. Their status as categories of understanding or of explanation is secondary.

So we need to begin with the proof of the existence of a first principle of all, variously, though diffidently, called by Plotinus 'the Good' or 'the One.'[7] In V 4, 1, Plotinus argues as follows:

> If there is something after the First, it is necessary that that which comes from that does so either immediately or else it has its ascent back to it through

---

5. See O'Meara 1975, 105–8, 116–19.
6. On love, see III 5, 3.1; on time, see III 7, 13.49; on motion, see VI 6, 16.41; on numbers, see VI 6, 5.17.
7. The diffidence follows from Plotinus's insistence that since the first principle has no predicates, a genuine name for it would be misleading at best. See III 8, 10.29–35; V 4, 1.5–13; VI 9, 5.38–46. See Meijer 1992, 181–92, on the problem of naming the One and various strategies for "approaching" it, including negation and analogy.

intermediaries, and that there be an ordering of things second and third,[8] with the second ascending to the first and the third to the second. For there must be some simple prior to everything, and this is different from everything after it, being by itself, not mixed with the things that come from it, all the while being able to be present to other things, having what those other things have in a different manner, being truly one, and not with its being different from its oneness, in which case it would be false that it is one,[9] and of which there is no "account or knowledge" of it;[10] it is in fact said to be "beyond essence"[11]—for if it is not simple, beyond all combination and composition and not truly one, it would not be a principle—most self-sufficient by being simple, and first of all. For that which is not first[12] needs that which is prior to it, and that which is not simple is in need of the simples in it in order that it should be made out of them.

That which is like this must be unique. For if there were something other like this, both of these would be one. For we are not speaking about two bodies or saying that the One is the first body. For a body is not simple, and a body is generated, and it is not a principle; "the principle is ungenerable,"[13] not being bodily, but truly one, that would be the First. If, therefore, there would be something different after the First, that would no longer be simple. That, therefore, will be a one-many.[14]

Let us begin by noting that Plotinus is here giving an argument for what he takes to be the existence of the Idea of the Good from *Republic*. In addition, he assumes that the Idea of the Good is identical with the One, whose being and oneness are not distinct. This is the One of the first hypothesis of the second part of *Parmenides*. I leave until next chapter the

8. See Plato (?), *Second Ep.* 312E3-4.
9. See Plato, *Parm.* 142B5-C2.
10. See ibid., 142A3-4.
11. See Plato, *Rep.* 509B9. See Charrue 1978, 246-47, for discussion of the roughly thirty places in the *Enneads* in which the phrase "beyond essence" is cited and commented on by Plotinus. As Charrue notes, one of Plotinus's key interpretative moves is to argue that whatever is "beyond essence" is also "beyond intellect" as well.
12. Reading τὸ γάρ τοι μὴ with Igal, instead of the reading of the majority of mss., τὸ γὰρ τὸ μή.
13. See Plato, *Phdr.* 245D3.
14. V 4, 1.1–21: Εἴ τι ἔστι μετὰ τὸ πρῶτον, ἀνάγκη ἐξ ἐκείνου εἶναι ἢ εὐθὺς ἢ τὴν ἀναγωγὴν ἐπ' ἐκεῖνο διὰ τῶν μεταξὺ ἔχειν, καὶ τάξιν εἶναι δευτέρων καὶ τρίτων, τοῦ μὲν ἐπὶ τὸ πρῶτον τοῦ δευτέρου ἀναγομένου, τοῦ δὲ τρίτου ἐπὶ τὸ δεύτερον. Δεῖ μὲν γάρ τι πρὸ πάντων εἶναι—ἁπλοῦν τοῦτο—καὶ πάντων ἕτερον τῶν μετ' αὐτό, ἐφ' ἑαυτοῦ ὄν, οὐ μεμιγμένον τοῖς ἀπ' αὐτοῦ, καὶ πάλιν ἕτερον τρόπον τοῖς ἄλλοις παρεῖναι δυνάμενον, ὂν ὄντως ἕν, οὐχ ἕτερον ὄν, εἶτα ἕν, καθ' οὗ ψεῦδος καὶ τὸ ἕν εἶναι, οὗ μὴ λόγος μηδὲ ἐπιστήμη, ὃ δὴ καὶ ἐπέκεινα λέγεται εἶναι οὐσίας—εἰ γὰρ μὴ ἁπλοῦν ἔσται συμβάσεως ἔξω πάσης καὶ συνθέσεως καὶ ὄντως ἕν, οὐκ ἂν ἀρχὴ εἴη—αὐταρκέστατόν τε τῷ ἁπλοῦν εἶναι καὶ πρῶτον ἁπάντων· τὸ γὰρ <τοι> μὴ πρῶτον ἐνδεὲς τοῦ πρὸ αὐτοῦ, τό τε μὴ ἁπλοῦν τῶν ἐν αὐτῷ ἁπλῶν δεόμενον, ἵν' ᾖ ἐξ ἐκείνων. Τὸ δὴ τοιοῦτον ἓν μόνον δεῖ εἶναι· ἄλλο γὰρ εἰ εἴη τοιοῦτον, ἓν ἂν εἴη τὰ ἄμφω. Οὐ γὰρ δὴ σώματα λέγομεν δύο, ἢ τὸ ἓν πρῶτον σῶμα. Οὐδὲν γὰρ ἁπλοῦν σῶμα, γινόμενόν τε τὸ σῶμα, ἀλλ' οὐκ ἀρχή· ἡ δὲ ἀρχὴ ἀγένητος· μὴ σωματικὴ δὲ οὖσα, ἀλλ' ὄντως μία, ἐκεῖνο ἂν εἴη τὸ πρῶτον. Εἰ ἄρα ἕτερόν τι μετὰ τὸ πρῶτον εἴη, οὐκ ἂν ἔτι ἁπλοῦν εἴη· ἓν ἄρα πολλὰ ἔσται. Cf. V 3, 11.27 on the absolute simplicity of the One; and Plato, *Parm.* 144E5.

interpretative basis for this identification.[15] Here, we need to concentrate the argument that is being advanced. Plotinus argues for two conclusions: (1) the existence of every composite or complex entity requires an unqualifiedly simple entity as its *explanans;* (2) there is at most one such entity.[16]

Let us next focus on the reasoning leading to the assertion of (2). This is essentially a reductio ad absurdum proof.[17] If there were more than one absolutely simple entity, each would be one, yet different from the other.[18] That wherein they would supposedly differ would, therefore, be distinct from each entity itself. Suppose that the second 'One,' call it B, had a property f, namely, the property in virtue of which it was different from the first One, which we may call A. So we seem committed to the truth of 'B is f.' But this proposition purports to supply us with two pieces of information: B exists and it is f.[19] If, though, this is the case, then there is a minimal complexity in B, the complexity consisting of the existent B and its property f. Even if B were a 'bare particular,' this complexity would be unavoidable. This is precisely what Plotinus denies of the One, which is "beyond all combination and composition." Stated in Platonic terms, if B exists it must have some οὐσία or nature that is really distinct from it, the existing thing.[20] If B were not really distinct from its οὐσία, it would be indistinguishable from A, counter to the original hypothesis.

If, then, there can be no more than one absolutely simple entity, we ask next why he thinks that there must be at least one such entity. In the above passage, Plotinus just seems to assume that this entity exists. But there is an argument for this conclusion at the beginning of the treatise VI 9. The treatise begins with the assertion "all beings are beings by that which is

---

15. Many scholars have supposed that if Plotinus's interpretation of the first hypothesis in the second part of *Parmenides* is implausible, then his One cannot be identified with the Idea of the Good, and that, further, this somehow undermines Aristotle's testimony about the identification of the Good with the One. See, e.g., Cornford 1939, 131–34; Armstrong 1940, 116; Rist 1964, 43; Allen 1983, 189–95, et al. Plotinus, however, typically adduces passages from *Parmenides* in support of his own arguments and in the light of his interpretation of all the dialogues, the Aristotelian testimony, and the oral tradition. I do not think that his interpretation of *Parmenides* has for Plotinus a unique or even crucial role to play.

16. At V 5, 3.23–24 Plotinus identifies the external actuality of the One as the ὑπόστασιν οὐσίας (the existence of essence). This seems to be a fairly clear affirmation of Plotinus's existentialist metaphysics. Of course, like the Idea of the Good for Plato, the One is the cause of both the existence of essence and of essence itself.

17. This is a slightly revised version of the analysis in Gerson 2008 103–5.

18. It is important that this proof be understood as a reductio, starting from a premise that Plotinus does not accept and in fact thinks impossible. The counterfactual condition in which there was something other than the One that was absolutely simple and hence an 'additional' one, does not imply that the One is numerable or that it is a 'unit' of some sort.

19. In this case, we need not, of course, worry about a true proposition without existential import since our hypothesis is that B exists.

20. I am for now leaving it ambiguous as to whether that which is distinct from the οὐσία of B is the existence of B or the existent B itself.

one."[21] That is, the unity of a composite—the minimal unity arising from the minimal complexity of the existent and its οὐσία—is not owing either to the existent or to the οὐσία that it has. The examples that Plotinus gives here of a complex unity are an army, a chorus, and a flock of animals. But it would be a mistake to focus on the artificiality of these examples; none of these exist by nature. His point is that these composites would not exist if they were not unified as an army or chorus or flock and the unified whole would not exist without the parts. Yet the unity of the whole is not self-explanatory.[22] To put this intuitively, consider a set of sheep, say all the sheep in New Zealand. They do not become a flock until they are 'unified' and caused to be such. Nothing in any of the individuals provides this unity. It follows that since there can be no more than one absolutely simple in the universe, anything—whether its unity is that of an individual soldier or that of an army, say—we can think of with any nature or property is a whole as opposed to a mere sum.[23]

The point is generalizable. The One is necessary to explain the existence or being of any composite whatsoever, including the minimal composite of an entity with an οὐσία.[24] The οὐσία that such a minimal being has could not constitute its identity, for that identity is the identity of a composite, not of the οὐσία alone.[25] Nor, of course, could the existent itself explain its existence, for the existent has no logical or causal priority to its οὐσία,

---

21. See VI 9, 1.1: Πάντα τὰ ὄντα τῷ ἑνί ἐστιν ὄντα. See Meijer 1992, 94–106, who provides an extensive argument that τὸ ἕν is probably to be understood here as unity in general and is not a direct reference to the One. So Fronterotta in Brisson and Pradeau 2002–10, vol. 2, ad loc. This appears to be how Proclus understood the claim. See *ET* Prop. 1. Supporting this interpretation are claims such as are found in V 5, 6.26–37 and VI 9, 5.29–33, 38–40 to the effect that 'one' is not a predicate or name of the One. Cf. *Parm.* 141E10–11: Οὐδ' ἄρα οὕτως [τὸ ἕν] ἔστιν ὥστε ἓν εἶναι· εἴη γὰρ ἤδη ἂν καὶ οὐσίας μετέχον. (Therefore, the One is thus not one so as to make it one being; for it would then straightaway be and also partake in essence.) The central point is that, though the One is ultimately the cause of the being of that which is one, it is not the One's oneness that is the cause, as if the One were paradigmatically one. That the One cannot be one does not mean that it does not exist.

22. Cf. Aristotle, *Meta.* Z 17, 1041b11–33, who argues that a composite is unified by form, which is not an element in the composite. Plotinus is generalizing Aristotle's argument: the cause of the unified composite is other than it. Plotinus will elsewhere argue that the unifying cause cannot be form, basically because if it were, the form would have to exist, in which case its own unity would require an explanation.

23. I leave aside any discussion of the criteria for wholeness that for Plotinus will vary according to whether the putative whole exists by nature or not. In any case, if the argument for the need for the explanation of the being of a minimally complex individual whose wholeness consists entirely of its existence and its essence works, that argument is a fortiori applicable to anything more complex.

24. See V 3, 15.11–13; V 3, 15.28; V 3, 17.10–14; VI 7, 23.19–25. Plotinus, V 1, 8.22–28, cites *Soph.* 245A8–9, Plato's criticism of Parmenides for positing a One that is in fact not absolutely simple because it contains parts. In the text, these parts seem to be extended, but in *Parm.* 141E10–11 the One would have parts just because it partakes of οὐσία.

25. Take an οὐσία, say, horse. Horse cannot be identical with an existing horse, or else there could be only one of them. So the unity possessed by an existing horse is not owing to the οὐσία in which it partakes. We may observe that this argument depends on the truth of the antinominalistic element of UP.

that is, its existence is always existence as something having this οὐσία. If it were to explain its own existence as an entity with this οὐσία, there would be something about it that would make it an *explanans*. But there is nothing about this existent, that is, no property in it, that does not belong to its οὐσία. Consequently, nothing that is composite or whose unity is over and above its being and its essence could be autoexplicable. And since we have already shown that there can be no more than one absolutely simple principle, the proof that there must be *some* autoexplicable principle to explain all the heteroexplicable composites is a proof of the existence of an absolutely simple autoexplicable principle.[26] That is, the One is self-caused (αἴτιον ἑαυτοῦ).[27]

It is, of course, open for one to object that any assumption of heteroexplicability begs the question. Even if there is no more than one absolutely simple entity, in which case everything else must be composite, at least minimally so, this does not entail the heteroexplicability of these composites. Perhaps they are just *in*explicable. But maintaining this position is, one would think, rather costly. As a blanket assertion, it simply abolishes explanations, at least for the existence of anything. It abolishes the distinction between necessary and contingent existence, since a contingent existent would seem, by definition, to be contingent on something that explains its existence. If one foregoes the autoexplicability of the first principle, then one must as a consequence forego the heteroexplicability of everything else, which is as much as to say that everything becomes inexplicable.[28]

At this point, the Plotinian task is to show that this absolutely simple first principle of all really does explain the existence of everything else.[29] Perhaps the most puzzling claim that Plotinus repeatedly makes in this regard is that the One is "the power of all things" (δύναμις τῶν πάντων).[30] Plotinus explicitly denies that this means that the One is potency, as is matter.[31] For matter is passive, whereas the sense in which the One is δύναμις is the

---

26. See III 1, 1.1–8.
27. VI 8, 14.41–42. This is the first appearance of this phrase in the history of philosophy so far as we know. It is a good example, I think, of Plotinus trying to make explicit what is implicit in Plato's writings. See Beierwaltes 1999 on the One as *causa sui*.
28. See V 8, 7.45. This is essentially the Aristotelian argument of *Metaphysics* Alpha Elatton that lines of explanation must terminate. Either A is autoexplicable or if A is explained by B, then there must be some X that explains A and is itself autoexplicable, whether this be B or something else. Cf. *Phys.* A 5, 188a27–28: δεῖ γὰρ τὰς ἀρχὰς μήτε ἐξ ἀλλήλων εἶναι μήτε ἐξ ἄλλων, καὶ ἐκ τούτων πάντα (for the principles must neither come from each other nor from other things, and everything comes from them).
29. See Beierwaltes 1985, for a magisterial study of how, especially in late Platonism, the very idea of metaphysics is indissolubly bound to *Denken des Einen*.
30. See V 5, 3.15.33. Cf. III 8, 10.1; V 1, 7.9–10; V 3, 16.2–3; V 4, 1.24–25, 36; V 4, 2.38; V 5, 12.38–39; VI 7, 32.31; VI 7, 40.13–14; VI 9, 5.36–37.
31. Krämer 1964a, 340, argues that the One is the pure potency of all things and holds its consequences amorphously and latently in itself. This seems to me an impossible interpretation for that which is perfect and absolutely simple.

opposite of passivity.³² This clarification has led many to suppose that Plotinus is claiming that the One is the *active* potency of all things, following the distinction Aristotle makes in book Theta of his *Metaphysics*.³³ Perhaps this interpretation is reinforced by Plotinus's evident reference to *Republic* where the Idea of the Good is said to be "beyond οὐσία by exceeding it in seniority and in power [δυναμέι]."³⁴ There are, I believe, insurmountable objections to this interpretation. First, for Aristotle, active or agent potency is potency nevertheless, distinct from actuality (ἐνέργεια).³⁵ But as we will see in a moment, the primary 'operational' property of the One is that it is ἐνέργεια. Like Aristotle's Unmoved Mover, in which even a distinction between thinker and thinking is rejected because this would imply potency in it, so in the One there is no complexity or compositeness at all because this would undermine the requisite simplicity of the first principle of all.³⁶ If the One has or is an active potency, then there is an actuality of it outside of it or other than it. Then it would obviously be incomplete, something Plotinus unequivocally denies.³⁷ Second, if the One is an active potency, then it is the active potency of all things, as the text maintains. Its actuality would be those things. If this were so, the One's explanatory role—that which it is postulated to fulfill in the first place—would be obliterated, since in actualizing its potency it would just be those things whose existence needs explaining. How, we may ask, is the power to be all things an explanation of these things? But if the putative active power is the power to make all things, then we are not elucidating the explanatory role of the One when we say this, for it is not the possibility of the existence of all things that is in need of an explanation but their actual existence. Finally, if the actuality of the One's active potency is in something other than it or is outside of it, then a real relation between the One and this other thing would be erected or, perhaps, presupposed. But the One is not really related to anything; if it were, it would have to have the complexity of an entity that stands in relation to something different from or other than it.³⁸

---

32. See V 3,15.33–35.

33. See *Meta.* Θ 1, 1046a16–19: πάλιν δ' αὗται δυνάμεις λέγονται ἢ τοῦ μόνον ποιῆσαι ἢ παθεῖν ἢ τοῦ καλῶς, ὥστε καὶ ἐν τοῖς τούτων λόγοις ἐνυπάρχουσί πως οἱ τῶν προτέρων δυνάμεων λόγοι (again, these are said to be potencies either by merely acting or being acted upon, or by acting or being acted upon well, so that even in the accounts of the latter the accounts of the former potencies are somehow present).

34. *Rep.* 509B9–10.

35. See *Meta.* Θ 6, 1048a30–32: ἔστι δὴ ἐνέργεια τὸ πρᾶγμα μὴ οὕτως ὥσπερ λέγομεν δυνάμει (now actuality is the existence of the thing, but not in the way we say it is in potency).

36. See *Meta.* Λ 9, 1074b28–35.

37. See V 6, 2.13; V 1, 6.38. The One is perfect (τέλειον) because it is self-sufficient (αὐτάρκης). Further, *because* the One is perfect, it produces. Its perfection is not achieved as the result of any production.

38. See VI 8, 8.12–13: Δεῖ δὲ ὅλως πρὸς οὐδὲν αὐτὸν λέγειν. (We should say that it [the One] is altogether related to nothing.) Cf. Proclus, *In Parm.* 1135.17–21; *In Tim.* 1.304.6–9, who clearly grasped this crucial point.

What, then, is Plotinus claiming when he calls the One δύναμις τῶν πάντων? As we saw in the last chapter, Numenius, in trying to explain the causality of the first principle, says that it would be impious to say that it is eminently all things, that is, that it is the paradigm of all the Forms. This is the role of the Demiurge, who makes all things according to the model with which he is cognitively identical. But the Good is 'he who is,' which, I am supposing, Plotinus glosses as δύναμις τῶν πάντων. To be absolutely simple and 'being itself' (αὐτοόν) is to be virtually all things in the sense in which 'white' light is virtually all the colors of the spectrum and a function is virtually its domain and range.[39] The One is virtually all things because all things exist by participating in an οὐσία, which is really distinct from themselves. The One is above οὐσία, but yet the postulated cause of all the composites with οὐσία.[40] It is virtually all of them in the sense that it is what the cause of composites of εἶναι and οὐσία would have to be if it is to have the nature to explain the being of such things.[41]

The identification of the One, cause of the being of all things, with the Idea of the Good entails a causal role for the latter. That is, the goodness and the being of everything are distinct only insofar as this goodness and being belong to that which has οὐσία, which is various. It is not the case that being is univocally attributable to everything, but goodness is not. Being and goodness are both equivocal in their attribution. Goodness is the One insofar as it is an ultimate end or goal of desire. That the Good is unlimited in its causal power may be glossed by the principle *bonum est*

---

39. That the One or Good is virtually all things is an interpretation to be firmly distinguished from that according to which it is the Form of all the 'formal' properties of the Forms, that is, all the properties they have qua Forms. For this view, see Santas 2002; Ferrari 2003b, 305–17, and 2007a, 192–94. On this interpretation, the δύναμις of the Good refers to its causal power, that is, the power to produce the general attributes of Forms qua Forms. Ferrari thinks this causality is efficient and argues that Santas thinks it is purely formal. But the absolute simplicity of the first principle would be compromised if it were, for example, the paradigm of both the distinct properties of eternality and immateriality. For this reason alone, the One or Good cannot be eminently anything. Ferrari's comparison (2003b, 318–22) of the Good with Aristotle, *Meta.* α 1, 993b23–31, according to which fire is eminently hot because it is the cause of hotness in hot things, is inapt. If the Good had any predicates, it could not be absolutely simple. See Fronterotta 2006, 431–36, who also points out the inaptness of Ferrari's comparison, though Fronterotta appears to think that the Good, as participatable, is eminently all its effects.

40. See VI 8, 13.6–7 and 14.39, where the ἐνέργειαι of the One are said to be οἷον ("in a way") its οὐσία and that it is οἷον the παράδειγμα of all things. The qualification 'in a way' indicates that the One cannot be really or literally a paradigm of anything. The real paradigms are the Forms. Cf. V 5, 6.17–20, which focuses on the analogy between the One and Forms, on the one hand, and Forms and sensibles, on the other. The One is 'in a way' the 'Form' of 'Forms' but only qua cause; it itself transcends intelligibility, which is why it is not really a paradigm.

41. Aubry (2006, 223) misconstrues my previous account of virtuality as potentiality of some sort, citing V 3, 15.32–35 and V 3, 12.26–33 as evidence that Plotinus eliminates all potentiality from the One. Aubry, however, reverts to an interpretation of the δύναμις of the One as "puissance active" (229) or "puissance productrice" (234).

diffusivum sui.⁴² In Plotinus, this principle is expressed in terms of the 'two activities.' Soul is the "activity external to the essence of Intellect" (ἐνέργεια ἐκ τῆς οὐσίας), as Intellect is the external activity of the One. This is distinct from the "internal activity of the essence" of each principle (ἐνέργεια τῆς οὐσίας).⁴³ Of course, the One does not have an essence, nor does it, properly speaking, have an activity, though it can be said to *be* activity.⁴⁴ Because the One is perfect activity, it is diffusive of itself. The goodness of anything is precisely what is diffused. One may say, accordingly, that to be good is to be caused to be by the One.

The proof that goodness is essentially self-diffusive relies on the self-evident multiplicity of intelligible forms in the universe. That the knowledge of intelligible reality necessarily produces true virtue is one expression of the necessary production of intelligible form from the Good. The Good must love itself if in the achievement of its desire it necessarily produces. Since it necessarily produces, and since production is the work of love of the Good, the perfect self-possession of the Good that is present in the first principle of all must result from its self-love.⁴⁵ The self-love of the first principle is expressed by Plotinus as a sort of gloss on the fact that the first principle is autoexplicable. Anything other than the first principle is, accordingly, heteroexplicable.⁴⁶ Whatever has its causality outside of it is, then, the product or work of the self-love of the One. Since love is always for the Good, the products of the One's self-love are not loved by it.⁴⁷ But at the same time, production by the One ensures that whatever is capable of desire loves the One or the Good.

The self-causality of the One is also, remarkably, described as "[making] itself from nothing."⁴⁸ Since there are no real distinctions whatsoever within the One, its being and its activity are indistinguishable. Its being is the activity of self-love. What, then, is the difference between the making that belongs to the One's 'self-making' and the making that results in the One's products? Stated otherwise, how can the self-making of the absolutely simple first principle of all result in something *other than* that first principle? The answer is that what is not the One is also not made from nothing; nor is it identical with the One. The One is virtually what everything else is.

---

42. See Kremer 1987; Miller 2007, 338.
43. See V 1, 6.30–39; V 3, 7.23–24; V 9, 8.13–15; VI 8, 18.51–52.
44. See VI 8, 20.9–15.
45. VI 8, 15.1–2. I will return to this passage below.
46. Cf. Iamblichus, *De communi mathematica scientia*, chap. 4.16–19: τὸ ἕν ὅπερ δὴ οὐδὲ ὂν πω δεῖ καλεῖν, διὰ τὸ ἁπλοῦν εἶναι καὶ διὰ τὸ ἀρχὴν μὲν ὑπάρχειν τῶν ὄντων, τὴν δὲ ἀρχὴν μηδέπω εἶναι τοιαύτην οἷα ἐκεῖνα ὧν ἐστιν ἀρχή (one should say that the One is somehow non-being because it is simple and because, since the principle of all things exists, that principle must never be such as is that of which it is a principle).
47. V 5, 12.40–49.
48. VI 8, 7.53–54: αὐτὸ αὑτὸ ποιεῖ, καὶ ἑαυτῷ καὶ οὐδενός. Cf. 15.9.

It is worth emphasizing at this point that whatever Plotinus does in fact mean by attributing δύναμις to the One, he is saying what he says as an explication of the central idea of Platonism, one that he believes Plato embraces, even if it is obscurely expressed in the dialogues. In the next chapter, we will look more closely at Plotinus's reasons for attributing to Plato the view that I am attributing to Plotinus.

Intellect

If the absolutely simple first principle of all is virtually all things in the above sense, it cannot be eminently all things, too. For if it were, its simplicity would be destroyed. That is, it cannot be the multitude of οὐσίαι that constitute the paradigms of all intelligible reality.[49] Like Numenius and many others, Plotinus takes the Demiurge to fulfill this role.[50] That the Demiurge so conceived must exist as distinct from the One follows from (1) an argument that Forms must exist and (2) an argument that these Forms, though each is a distinct οὐσία, must be somehow the same. Let us leave (1) aside for the moment and concentrate on (2). When I say that the Forms must be the same, I mean that they must be various expressions of a unity such that it makes it possible to explain the existence of necessarily true predicative judgments. For example, that horses are animals and not plants or that four is half of eight are, for Plotinus, unquestioned necessary truths. To assume that there are Forms of horse and animal and four and eight and one-half is not sufficient to make these propositions true. Roughly, we could say that what makes them true is that horse is one of the things that animal is, and that half of eight is one of the things that four is. But, of course, the nexus of Forms providing the basis for necessarily true propositions is infinite. It is the Demiurge or Intellect that is supposed to be that which unifies all the

---

49. See V 1, 7.21–22, where Plotinus argues that if the One were identical with all οὐσίαι, it would be something like the 'sum' of them all (τῶν πάντων).

50. See V 1, 8.5: δημιουργὸς γὰρ ὁ νοῦς αὐτῷ [Plato]. Plotinus takes the 'Living Animal' in *Timaeus*, which contains all intelligibles within it as parts, as cognitively identical with the Demiurge. See III 9,1.12–13: ἓν εἶναι ἄμφω [νοῦς and εἴδη], διαιρούμενα δὲ τῇ νοήσει (both [Intellect and Forms] are one, though distinguished in thought). He is all the Forms he is thinking because in thinking the thinker becomes identical with the objects of thought. The two passages in *Timaeus* he reads together are 29E3 and 30D2. See Halfwassen 2000, 51–62. Pépin (1956, 48) may well be correct that the *Timaeus* passages are not the direct source of Plotinus's identification of Intellect and Forms. It is possible that, based on independent arguments such as those found in V 5, he was led to interpret the *Timaeus* passages in the way he does. If, indeed, the Demiurge and the Living Animal are thus identified, Aristotle's otherwise puzzling remark at *Meta*. A 6, 999a7, namely, that Plato introduced only two causes, the material and the formal, becomes clearer. For the Demiurge, who seems to be both an efficient and a final cause, is then apparently being 'conflated' with the formal cause. Thus, efficient and final causality are, in a way, 'reducible' to formal causality as Aristotle himself recognizes. See *Phys.* B 7, 198a24–25: ἔρχεται δὲ τὰ τρία [τὸ εἶδος, τὸ κινῆσαν, τὸ οὗ ἕνεκα] εἰς [τὸ] ἓν πολλάκις. (the three causes [form, moving, and final] often amount to one).

Forms such that there is an ontological basis for the kind of identification that Plotinus thinks is presumed in the assertion of necessary truths.

To speak of a kind or, worse, a degree of identity makes little sense in a contemporary context in which identity is a purely formal notion. But for Plotinus, the One, which is virtually all things, and uniquely self-identical, is the source of all identities.[51] Everything that exists is one, but nothing is absolutely or perfectly one except the One. Hence, for him, a distinction between a predicative judgment and an identity statement rests on an ambiguity that, taken in one way, offers a false dichotomy. On the one hand, to say what something is, is to state its identity; on the other, to say that something is just what it is and nothing else is not to preclude its possessing a compositional, and hence compromised, identity. What Plotinus is doing is, in effect, drawing out some of the consequences of antinominalism. Thus, a proposition stating what a Form is or what its properties are is an identity statement of a particular sort. And yet metaphysically graded identity does not preclude formal identity, that which one claims when one asserts that each Form is "itself by itself what it is." We must be clear that, for Plotinus, to maintain that the elephant is a mammal is not to claim that being a mammal is a property of the Form of Elephant any more than to say that Justice is a virtue is to claim that Justice is virtuous.[52] If this is the case, whence the necessary metaphysical identity that explains the necessity of necessarily true propositions?

Intellect (νοῦς) fulfills this role. As Plotinus says,

> It is, then, perhaps foolish to seek to discover if Intellect is among real things even if some would contend that it is not.[53] It is better to ask if Intellect is such as we say it is, and if it is something separate, and if this is the real beings, that is, if the nature of Forms is there.[54]

---

51. Strictly speaking, Plotinus follows Plato, *Parm.* 140E3–4, in maintaining that the One is not self-identical, because self-identity implies the possession of οὐσία, although in a sense its existence (ὑπόστασις) is ταὐτόν with its will (βούλησις) and its 'sort of' (οἷον) οὐσία. See VI 8, 13.6–8, 55–59.

52. See I 2, 6.14–18: Κἀκεῖ μὲν οὐκ ἀρετή, ἐν δὲ ψυχῇ ἀρετή. Ἐκεῖ οὖν τί; Ἐνέργεια αὐτοῦ καὶ ὅ ἐστιν· ἐνταῦθα δὲ τὸ ἐν ἄλλῳ ἐκεῖθεν ἀρετή. Οὐδὲ γὰρ αὐτοδικαιοσύνη καὶ ἑκάστη ἀρετή, ἀλλ' οἷον παράδειγμα· τὸ δὲ ἀπ' αὐτῆς ἐν ψυχῇ ἀρετή. (And in the intelligible world, there is not virtue; virtue is in the soul. What, then, is in the intelligible world? Its own activity, that is, what it really is. But here, when virtue comes from the intelligible world, it is in another. For neither justice in itself nor each other virtue in itself is a virtue, but rather a paradigm. That which comes from it when in the soul is a virtue.)

53. Perhaps an allusion to Epicureans and Stoics whose materialism prevents them from recognizing the sort of immaterial entity that intellect must be.

54. V 9, 3.4–8: Ἴσως μὲν οὖν γελοῖον ζητεῖν, εἰ νοῦς ἐστιν ἐν τοῖς οὖσι· τάχα δ' ἄν τινες καὶ περὶ τούτου διαμφισβητοῖεν. Μᾶλλον δέ, εἰ τοιοῦτος, οἷόν φαμεν, καὶ εἰ χωριστός τις, καὶ εἰ οὗτος τὰ ὄντα καὶ ἡ τῶν εἰδῶν φύσις ἐνταῦθα.

Intellect is metaphysically identical with all the Forms.[55] That is why Plotinus dubs it a "one-many."[56] But this is not quite adequate to the task, for Intellect could just be the one entity that, say, contemplates all the Forms, in which case, their identity is, so to speak, extrinsic. They would only be one in the sense that they are being contemplated by one entity. Plotinus, like Aristotle, however, is firm in holding that the highest mode of cognition, that which Intellect exercises, consists in an identification of the subject and the object.[57] As Plotinus puts it, "Whenever something thinks itself, this is thinking in the primary sense."[58] So the qualified identity that Intellect possesses is the identity of all intelligibles.[59]

Necessarily true propositions represent Intellect, but they do so not by stating a supposed fact, like a contingent state of affairs made up of what the subject and the predicate "stand for." Necessarily true propositions represent that actual states of affairs produced by Intellect or, in Platonic language, the Demiurge.[60] Thus, if, *per impossibile*, the Demiurge did not produce this orderly universe, a copy or image of the Living Animal, it would still be the case that what would make 'the elephant is a mammal' true would exist, but the proposition would have no referential meaning. That is, there would be no elephants to refer to in claiming for them mammality. And to say that the proposition is 'true of Intellect' is exceedingly feeble since it is the identical Intellect of which it is also 'true' that 'the whale is a mammal.' All that one could say in this counterfactual circumstance is that Intellect's identity is that of the fullness of intelligible reality, a reality that is accessible to us as embodied intellects principally via our sensible experience.[61] Thus, for Plotinus it follows that whereas the One is virtually

---

55. See V 3, 5.22–23: καὶ τὸν νοῦν ταὐτὸν εἶναι τῷ νοητῷ· καὶ γάρ, εἰ μὴ ταὐτόν, οὐκ ἀλήθεια ἔσται (intellect must be identical with the intelligible; if it is not identical, there will be no truth). Cf. Aristotle, *Meta.* Λ 9, 1075a4–5: ἡ νόησις τῷ νοουμένῳ μία.

56. IV 8, 3.10; V 1, 8.26; V 3, 15.11, 22; VI 2, 2.2; VI 2, 10.11; VI 2, 15.14; VI 2, 21.7, 46–47; VI 2, 22.10; VI 5, 6.1–2; VI 6, 8.22; VI 6, 6.13; VI 7, 8.17–18; VI 7, 14.11–12; VI 7, 39.11–14.

57. See Aristotle, *DA* Γ 4, 429b5–9; Γ 5, 430a19–20; Γ 7, 431a1–2, b17.

58. V 3, 13.13–14: ὅταν αὐτό τι ἑαυτὸ νοῇ, ὃ δὴ καὶ κυρίως ἐστὶ νοεῖν. Cf. V 3, 5.22–23, 42–43; II 9, 1.50–52: Ὥστε ἐν τῷ πρώτως νοεῖν ἔχοι ἂν καὶ τὸ νοεῖν ὅτι νοεῖ ὡς ἓν ὄν· καὶ οὐδὲ τῇ ἐπινοίᾳ ἐκεῖ διπλοῦν. (So that in it [Intellect] as primary thinking, it would have the thinking that it is thinking as one being and so it is not double there even in thought.) Cf. III 8, 6.15–17, which makes the same point with the important addition that "identification with the object cognized" (εἰς ἓν τῷ γνωσθέντι ἔρχεται) is a process or activity, indicating that identification is not equivalent to identity understood as a formal property.

59. See Emilsson 2007, 141–70, for a comprehensive discussion of the identity of Intellect and all intelligibles; and Szlezák 1979b and O'Meara 1993, 32–37, on the roots of Plotinus's account of intellect in Plato and Aristotle.

60. See I 3, 5.17–19, where Plotinus distinguishes between knowing the truth and having cognition of (necessary) propositions. Intellect does not know the latter since knowledge is not of propositions; it knows the truth that the latter express by being identical with it. The truth is ontological, which is prior to semantic truth.

61. Plotinus's preferred way to express the claims made in this paragraph is to argue that the being of, say, a particular living thing in its identitative complexity is, ultimately, a λόγος of

all things, Intellect is eminently all things. That is why it is a 'one-many.' It is both, paradoxically, minimally complex and maximally complex since it is cognitively identical with all possible Forms. It is the eternal guarantor of the necessarily complex intelligible realm.[62]

The 'division of labor' between One and Intellect does not preclude a hierarchical ordering. In fact, Intellect is an instrument of the One, and Soul (the third hypostasis) is an instrument of Intellect and thereby an instrument of the One.[63]

> Since Soul depends on Intellect and Intellect on the Good, in this way all things depend on the Good through intermediaries, some of these being close and some of these beings neighbors of those things which are close, and sensibles at the farthest distance being dependent on Soul.[64]

In what respect do all things depend on the One?

> What, then, are "all things"? In fact they are those things of which the One is the principle. But how is the One the principle of all things? Is it because by making each of them to be one it preserves them? In fact, it is also because it made them exist. But how did it do this? In fact it was by having them prior to their existence. But has it not been said that in this way it will be a multiplicity? So, therefore, we must say that it had them, in a way, so as not to be distinct, whereas the things in the second principle are distinguished by reason, for this is at once actuality, whereas the One is virtually the totality.[65]

If the One is virtually all things and Intellect is eminently all things, then the straightforward, though highly misleading, deduction would be that οὐσία depends on Intellect and εἶναι depends on the One. This, however, cannot be the division of labor. For the One is virtually all οὐσίαι. And as

---

a Form, meaning what the Form is when found at a 'lower level' of reality. Cf. III 2, 2.15–18. But this is as much as to say that it is a λόγος of Intellect.

62. Plotinus follows Plato's description of Forms as "uniform" (μονοειδές, *Symp.* 211B1) and "units" (μονάδες, *Phil.* 15B1; *Parm.* 132A1–4). And yet the identity of each Form is necessarily complex. Each is what it is, ultimately, in relation to all the other Forms.

63. We recall that Numenius explicitly deploys a hierarchy that operates instrumentally. See fr. 15 Des Places and Des Places's note, 110, n. 3. It should be added, however, that for Numenius the instrumentality is occasioned by the fact that the Good or One is ἀργός (fr. 12 Des Places), whereas for Plotinus the first principle of all is limitlessly active.

64. VI 7, 42.21–24: 'Ἀνηρτημένης δὲ ψυχῆς εἰς νοῦν καὶ νοῦ εἰς τἀγαθόν, οὕτω πάντα εἰς ἐκεῖνον διὰ μέσων, τῶν μὲν πλησίον, τῶν δὲ τοῖς πλησίον γειτονούντων, ἐσχάτην δ' ἀπόστασιν τῶν αἰσθητῶν ἐχόντων εἰς ψυχὴν ἀνηρτημένων. Cf. IV 3, 12.30–32; III 2, 2.15–18. Cf. Proclus, *ET* Prop. 57.8–16, which formalizes the point. Dodds (1933; 2nd ed., 1963, 231) thus seems to me mistaken in maintaining that this is a "post-Plotinian development."

65. V 3, 15.26–33: Τίνα οὖν πάντα; "Ἡ ὧν ἀρχὴ ἐκεῖνο. Πῶς δὲ ἐκεῖνο ἀρχὴ τῶν πάντων; Ἆρα, ὅτι αὐτὰ σῴζει ἓν ἕκαστον αὐτῶν ποιήσασα εἶναι; "Ἡ καὶ ὅτι ὑπέστησεν αὐτά. Πῶς δή; "Ἡ τῷ πρότερον ἔχειν αὐτά. Ἀλλ' εἴρηται, ὅτι πλῆθος οὕτως ἔσται. Ἀλλ' ἆρα οὕτως εἶχεν ὡς μὴ διακεκριμένα· τὰ δ' ἐν τῷ δευτέρῳ διεκέκριτο τῷ λόγῳ. Ἐνέργεια γὰρ ἤδη· τὸ δὲ δύναμις πάντων. Cf. II 4, 5.25–26; III 8, 10.1–2; IV 8, 6.1–6; V 3, 17.10–14; V 5, 4.4–7; VI 7, 23.19–25; VI 7, 42.11; VI 9, 1.1–2.

the canonical passage from *Republic* has it, "the Good is that which provides εἶναι and οὐσία to the things that are knowable." So we are left to conclude that the One is virtually not just all the essences with which Intellect is cognitively identical, but that it is virtually all that is. It is virtually the being or existence as well as the essence of everything.

The instrumentality of Intellect is crucial here. For it is often supposed that the causality in Plotinus's metaphysical hierarchy is a *per accidens* series, in which the One causes Intellect, and Intellect causes Soul.[66] Thus is emanation construed, something like the segmented unfolding of entities inchoately contained in the first. But apart from how we analyze instrumentality, this cannot be the case because if the One were to cease its productive activity with Intellect, it would be limited in a very specific way: it would not have the power to produce anything else. But since the One is infinite in power and unlimited, it is false to claim that there could be any limitation whatsoever in its productive activity.[67] Whatever has being must ultimately depend on the One.[68] The term "ultimately," of course, presumes intermediacy or instrumentality.[69]

If the One is the *per se* cause of everything, that is because it is virtually everything. But it is not, therefore, eminently everything. That there are in this sensible realm elephants and whales and virtuous people requires that there be eternal paradigms of these. Such paradigms exist unequivocally, but their eternal existence is eternally caused by the One, which is virtually all of them. As we have seen, this multiplicity of Forms is what Intellect is. Anything that partakes of a Form has some sort of being ultimately caused by

66. See Gerson 1993 for further discussion on *per accidens* and *per se* causality in Plotinus's creation metaphysics.
67. See V 5, 9.1–18, a particularly lucid explanation of this principle. Also, V 8, 9.24–25. At V 5, 11.1–2, Plotinus says, "Further, this [the One] is unlimited by being not more than one, and it has nothing in relation to which something that comes from it will have a limit." (Καὶ τὸ ἄπειρον τούτῳ τῷ μὴ πλέον ἑνὸς εἶναι μηδὲ ἔχειν πρὸς ὅ ὁριεῖ τι τῶν ἑαυτοῦ.) Plotinus here seems to reject the theories found within the Platonic tradition according to which the One imposes limit on the Indefinite Dyad, thereby producing the Forms or Numbers. But the One could not be a principle of limitation. The One produces the Indefinite Dyad, which is just Intellect in its logically first phase. Limitation is produced then by Intellect itself when it turns to the One. The denial of the One as a principle of limit follows from Plotinus's rejection of dualism of any sort, especially that which makes the Indefinite Dyad an irreducibly first principle of unlimitedness, thereby requiring the One to be a coordinate principle of limit.
68. See I 7, 2 and VI 5, 4.13–20, where the converse of the instrumental hierarchy is explicitly expressed: things partake of the One by variously partaking of Soul, and through Soul, Intellect, and through Intellect, the One. Apart from Intellect, however, the partaking is always in an image of the One, not directly of the One itself.
69. Cf. V 1, 7.1–4, where Intellect is said to be the same as the One, though inferior to it. So, too, Soul is the same as Intellect, though inferior to it. Therefore, Soul is the same as the One, though inferior to it. Accordingly, if Intellect is implicated in the generation of that which is the same as it, namely, Soul, so is the One. Cf. V 2, 1.14: Οὗτος οὖν [Intellect] ὢν οἷον ἐκεῖνος [the One] τὰ ὅμοια ποιεῖ. But the One cannot *directly* produce anything other than that which is "closest" to itself. Intellect is the instrumental cause of that which Intellect alone cannot produce, that is, the being of Soul as a unity. At VI 7, 23.19–20, the instrumentality of Intellect in the production of Soul seems to be indicated, though it is admittedly odd that Plotinus uses the genitive here, ἐκ τούτου [that is, Intellect].

the One with the instrumentality of Intellect. But anything that so partakes is diminished in reality in relation to that paradigm. The most important consequence of this—one that will loom large in Plotinus's interpretation of a number of Platonic texts—is that a 'return' to the One amounts to a 'reconnection' with Intellect in some way. This achievement of unity or the unification of the person happens via an active identification with Intellect, something that needs to be explored in the next chapter.

Soul

The activity of Intellect is thinking or intellection (νόησις). Plotinus follows Aristotle precisely in identifying intellect as the paradigm of life.[70] So, on the one hand, the One is the ultimate cause of life, but on the other, Intellect is the instrumental or 'relatively ultimate' cause of life. How, then, is life supposed to be related to soul (ψυχή)? Just as the paradigmatic cause of being must be distinct from that of which it is the paradigm, so the paradigmatic cause of life must be distinct from it.[71] The activity of Intellect is participated in in two ways: by psychical activity and by nonpsychical, though intelligible being. Soul is the principle of psychical activity. Its causal 'scope' is narrower than that of Intellect, whose scope includes all that is in any way intelligible. And the causal scope of Intellect is narrower than the causal scope of the One, whose scope includes all being.

Soul is the principle of embodied life, whether this be the life of an individual living thing or the life of the universe.

> Soul is another principle that should be added to real things. Not just the soul of the universe, but also that of each individual, as a nontrivial principle, to weave all things together, not itself coming to be like other things from seeds, but being a principal cause of activity.[72]

---

70. See Aristotle, *Meta.* Λ 7, 1072b26–28: καὶ ζωὴ δέ γε ὑπάρχει· ἡ γὰρ νοῦ ἐνέργεια ζωή, ἐκεῖνος δὲ ἡ ἐνέργεια· ἐνέργεια δὲ ἡ καθ' αὑτὴν ἐκείνου ζωὴ ἀρίστη καὶ ἀΐδιος (and life belongs to [the Unmoved Mover]. For the actuality of intellect is life, and it is activity. And the activity is in virtue of itself the best life and eternal). Cf. VI 9, 9.17: τὸ δὲ ἐκεῖ ζῆν ἐνέργεια μὲν νοῦ. The word ἐκεῖ is Plotinus's normal term for the realm of Intellect and the One.

71. See I 4, 3.33–40: Ὅτι δ' ἡ τελεία ζωὴ καὶ ἡ ἀληθινὴ καὶ ὄντως ἐν ἐκείνῃ τῇ νοερᾷ φύσει, καὶ ὅτι αἱ ἄλλαι ἀτελεῖς καὶ ἰνδάλματα ζωῆς καὶ οὐ τελείως οὐδὲ καθαρῶς καὶ οὐ μᾶλλον ζωαὶ ἢ τοὐναντίον, πολλάκις μὲν εἴρηται· καὶ νῦν δὲ λελέχθω συντόμως ὡς, ἕως ἂν πάντα τὰ ζῶντα ἐκ μιᾶς ἀρχῆς ᾖ, μὴ ἐπίσης δὲ τὰ ἄλλα ζῇ, ἀνάγκη τὴν ἀρχὴν τὴν πρώτην ζωὴν καὶ τὴν τελειοτάτην εἶναι. (It has been said many times that the perfect life and the true and real life is in that intellectual nature and that the other sorts of life are imperfect and reflections of life and do not exist perfectly or purely, and are no more lives than the opposite of this. And now let it be said summarily that so long as all living beings are from one source and they do not have life in the same way that it does, it is necessary that the source is the primary life, that is, the most perfect life.)

72. III 1, 8.4–8: Ψυχὴν δὴ δεῖ ἀρχὴν οὖσαν ἄλλην ἐπεισφέροντας εἰς τὰ ὄντα, οὐ μόνον τὴν τοῦ παντός, ἀλλὰ καὶ τὴν ἑκάστου μετὰ ταύτης, ὡς ἀρχῆς οὐ σμικρᾶς οὔσης, πλέκειν τὰ πάντα, οὐ γινομένης καὶ αὐτῆς, ὥσπερ τὰ ἄλλα, ἐκ σπερμάτων, ἀλλὰ πρωτουργοῦ αἰτίας

That Soul is not from "seeds" means that it is not itself supervenient or epiphenomenal; it is the starting point for the explanation of a particular kind of phenomenon. What is this?

Soul is the principle of the motions that originate in desire for the Good.⁷³ Plotinus takes the phrase "desire for the Good" to be ambiguous. It means either a desire directly for the Good or a desire for that which is good, that is some kind of thing that is good and so a manifestation of the Good. It is only Intellect that eternally and directly possesses that which it desires.⁷⁴ Soul is the principle of the desires of embodied living things that pursue the Good via particular goods.⁷⁵ Only embodied animals with intellects can aspire to have the kind of direct experience of the Good that Intellect has.

For the moment, let us focus on the two types of activity in relation to Intellect and Soul. The external activity is an image or representation of the internal.⁷⁶ Soul is not just a product of Intellect, but inferior to it in the manner of a Platonic image.⁷⁷ So psychic activity images intellectual activity. For individual human souls, the imaging constitutes the life of embodied persons, who live rational lives.⁷⁸ That is, they operate according to discursive reasoning applied to the satisfaction of rational desires. For individual nonhuman souls, the imaging operates differently.

Nature, Plotinus tells is, is the lowest part of the soul of the universe.

> For nature is an image of intelligence, and since it is the limit of soul, has the limit of λόγος, which shines in it, just as in a thick lump of wax, a stamp

---

οὔσης. Our souls and the soul of the universe are "sisters." Cf. II 9, 18.16; IV 3, 6.13. On the distinction between the hypostasis Soul and the soul of the universe or World Soul, see IV 9, 4.15–20; IV 9, 1.10–13; IV 3, 2.50–59.

73. See I 7, 1.13–19; III 5, 9.40–41. Cf. Plato, *Lg.* 892aff. for the priority of soul to body in cosmic explanations.

74. IV 4, 16.26–27.

75. Often Plotinus uses the term ἔφεσις for the individual soul's desire for the Good and the term ὄρεξις for the soul's desire for the goods relative to an embodied living being. See, e.g., I 4, 6.17–21. In this same passage, Plotinus distinguishes between "will" (βούλησις) in the principal sense (κυρίως) and "will" when the term is used for cases where, for example, we want some bodily good to be present or some bodily ill to be absent. The former sense is roughly equivalent to ἔφεσις and the latter to ὄρεξις.

76. IV 5, 7.15–17; V 4, 2.27–30.

77. The Platonic provenance of the production of soul by an intellect is, of course, *Tim.* 35A, 41D, where the Demiurge makes the World Soul and then the immortal part of individual souls. To this passage, we then must add the identification of the Demiurge with Intellect, which seems to follow from 47E4, a reference to the "things crafted by intellect" (τὰ διὰ νοῦ δεδημιουργημένα).

78. 'Rational' here is ambiguous between (1) the nonnormative rationality that is constitutive of any ὄρεξις of a human being even just insofar as the state of desiring has to be conceptually categorized in order for there to be action; and (2) the normative rationality belonging to ἔφεσις. With (2), a human being is cable of making normative judgments in regard to his own ὀρέξεις, that is, judging whether the apparent good that is desired really is a good.

impresses itself through to the surface of the other side, and is clear on the upper side, but only leaves a weak trace below.[79]

The λόγος that nature is or has produces "nonrandomized movement" (κίνησις τίς οὐκ εἰκῇ).[80] The motion produced by nature is bodily, as distinct from the "motion of intellect" (κίνησις νοῦ) belonging to Intellect and the higher part of the embodied soul.[81] The variety of nonrandomized bodily motions are expressions of Soul-Intellect-One analogous to the way that a solid geometrical shape is an expression of a plane geometrical figure, which in turn is a 'projection' of an algebraic formula, which in turn is an expression of the principle of number. This analogy, however, is defective in that it does not consider the property of conscious desire in Soul. The digestive system in an animal, say, or a tropism in a plant are nonconscious expressions of the desire for the only true object of desire, namely, the Good.[82]

The hierarchy of instrumental causality is evident in the way Plotinus represents the operation of nature. Plato employs instrumental causality in explaining how the sensible world acquires intelligibility: beautiful things are beautiful by means of beauty; large things are large and small things are small by means of largeness and smallness.[83] Since Forms do not in themselves operate as efficient causes, *some* instrumentality must come into this picture. The correct way to represent the precise configuration of instrumentality, including the World Soul, the Demiurge, and, ultimately, the Idea of the Good or the One, is, of course, the principal interpretative battleground among Platonists. If the Demiurge wanted to make a horse, then the horse must 'already' exist eternally. I take it that this 'wanting to make' is to be analyzed according to the hierarchy of wanting in the One, Intellect, and Soul. Ultimately, it is because of what the One 'wants' that the World Soul wants to provide the horse with a suitable body. Intellect alone cannot explain why an animal looks the way it does. Intellect can explain only what is unequivocally intelligible, whereas the 'look' of an animal is owing in part to its embodiment. Soul alone cannot explain why the animal looks the way it does because the way it looks follows from the exigencies

---

79. IV 4, 13.3–7: ἴνδαλμα γὰρ φρονήσεως ἡ φύσις καὶ ψυχῆς ἔσχατον ὂν ἔσχατον καὶ τὸν ἐν αὐτῇ ἐλλαμπόμενον λόγον ἔχει, οἷον εἰ ἐν κηρῷ βαθεῖ διικνοῖτο εἰς ἔσχατον ἐπὶ θάτερα ἐν τῇ ἐπιφανείᾳ τύπος, ἐναργοῦς μὲν ὄντος τοῦ ἄνω, ἴχνους δὲ ἀσθενοῦς ὄντος τοῦ κάτω.
80. III 2, 16.19–20.
81. V 2, 2.9–11.
82. Cf. III 2, 3.33–37; III 3, 2.3–6; and Plotinus's dependence here on Aristotle, *Meta.* Λ 7, 1072b13–14 and 10, 1075a18–22.
83. See *Euthyd.* 301A1–4; *Phd.* 100D–E. I take τῷ καλῷ, μεγέθει, and σμικρότητι as instrumental datives. Cf. VI 6, 14.27–30, where Plotinus appeals to the *Phaedo* passage in his explanation of the causality of number.

of its eternal nature. Soul, then, becomes the necessary instrument of Intellect, which in turn is the necessary instrument of the One.[84]

Nature is perhaps best described as the expression of Soul that determines matter, that is, determines the anatomy or shape of living things and the fundamental reproductive or nutritive properties.[85] According to nature, living things grow and reproduce in kind. If one were to remove in thought the ultimate 'shape' of the living thing, one would arrive at matter.

Matter

The antimaterialist Platonist maintains that things other than bodies and their properties exist. Further, he maintains that bodies and the matter of which they are composed are ontologically posterior in the hierarchy of being. So he is perhaps particularly obliged to explain the place of matter in the universe. Although the word ὕλη is not used as a technical term in Plato's dialogues, later Platonists had no doubt that Plato did have a view about what Aristotle called 'material causality.'[86] Aristotle himself is confident that when in *Timaeus* Plato is speaking of the 'receptacle of becoming,' he means matter or a material principle.[87] Plotinus's primary problem is not with Aristotle's interpretation, but with accounting for matter given the refined role of the One or the Idea of the Good as 'virtually all things.' For if the Good is in any sense the explanation for matter, then matter, like everything else the Good produces, bears a trace of goodness. Later Platonists, like Proclus, did not shrink from this implication, arguing, rather, that matter cannot be

---

84. Thus, Plotinus answers Aristotle's objection to Forms at *Meta.* A 9, 991a8–11 (cf. M 5, 1079b12–15; *GC* B 9, 335b18–21), to the effect that if Forms are eternal then their causal effects should be continuous. Forms cannot, it seems, explain change. Plotinus's answer is that Soul is, in its aspect as nature, the instrumental cause of Intellect and Forms. See VI 5, 12.1; VI 5, 9.1–13. A good discussion of this point can be found in Lee 1982, 95–101.

85. See I 1, 8.15–23; III 4, 1; IV 4, 13.19–22; IV 4, 14.9–11, which makes clear that the shape is distinct from nature itself. In identifying nature, broadly speaking, as that which explains nutrition and reproduction, Plotinus is following Aristotle, *DA* B 4, 415a23–b7.

86. There are two passages in Plato where the word ὕλη does seem to be used in other than its ordinary use for 'wood.' These are *Tim.* 69A6, where the word is used metaphorically for the 'building blocks' of his cosmology, namely, the principles of reason and necessity; and *Phil.* 54C2, where 'raw materials' may be the correct sense. In the latter passage, we may be witnessing the technical meaning in the process of being created. Plutarch, *De def. or.*, 414F4–415A1, claims that Plato discovered the idea of matter, though the actual term was introduced later.

87. See *Phys.* Δ 2, 209b11–16. Cf. *GC* B 1, 329a23. So, too, Theophrastus, fr. 48 Wimmer, who seems to be referring to intra-Academic discussions, not to any dialogue. See Gerson 2005, 102–17, for further discussion of how the Platonic tradition uses Aristotle's interpretation of Plato's account of material causality. For a recent defense of Aristotle's account of the receptacle as matter, see Ferrari 2007b. Also, see Reale 1997, 369–90, esp. 385–86. That the receptacle appears as a principle (51E–52D) must be balanced by the reference to the untreated 'principle or principles' at 42C2–6. Thus, the fact that the receptacle is independent of the Demiurge does not mean that it is independent of the first principle of all, the One.

evil.⁸⁸ Plotinus, however, has argued for a linear hierarchy of being. That is, the Good is one terminus on this 'line'; its opposite is the other.⁸⁹ An embodied human being, finding himself somewhere on this line, either moves in the direction of the Good or in the opposite direction.⁹⁰ Since the Good is virtually all that is, and as we have seen, all that is partakes of οὐσία, it is by identification with intelligible being that the Good is approached and by the loss of intelligible being that someone distances himself from it. For Plotinus, that matter is to be identified with the terminus opposite to the Good, or evil, is a conclusion of an argument, not the premise. The premise is that the hierarchy of intelligible being comes to an end with nature.⁹¹ Beyond that is a principle of unintelligibility. And that is what matter is supposed to be. There can be nothing 'after' matter. So, since the Good is one terminus of the hierarchy, evil is the other terminus and this can be nothing else but matter.⁹² But the problem still remains: How can the Good or the One be its cause?

In order to understand this, we need to focus first on a distinction Plotinus makes between "A generates B" and "A is the cause or principle of B." This is in effect a distinction between an instrumental and an ultimate cause. Thus, Intellect in some sense generates Soul.⁹³ It is also the case that it is even possible to say that the One in a sense generates Intellect.⁹⁴ So it might seem rather straightforwardly that the lower part of Soul, that is, nature, would be the generator of matter. The principal, and indeed, perhaps the only text supporting this claim is in the treatise on evil.

---

88. See *ET* Props. 57, 72; *In Parm.* 1064.7-10; *In Tim.* 1.356.5-7; 384.19-385.13, for the generation of matter ultimately from the One. Cf. *Rep.* 379C5-7, where responsibility for evils is disallowed for divinity. See Narbonne 2007 for the evidence that, though Proclus denies that matter is evil, he does not attribute to Plotinus the view that matter is not generated ultimately from the One. Also, Opsomer 2001; 2007b, 169, n. 20.

89. See I 8, 7.19-20 where matter is said to be the ultimate limit (τὸ ἔσχατον) in the descent from the One. It is the limit in the sense that is comes 'after' the least intelligible product of the hierarchy, which is, in fact, the physical shape or form of a body. It is also said in this passage that there is nothing further generated after, implying that matter itself is generated.

90. See V 1, 1.7: τὴν ἐναντίαν δραμοῦσαι (running in the opposite direction), a metaphorical description of human beings who separate themselves from the Good.

91. That there cannot be an indefinite diminution of intelligible being such that we would never arrive at the absolutely unintelligible, that is, at matter, follows from (1) that derivation is always from a higher to a lower, and (2) that the kinds of being derived must be finite in number because the One is uniquely unlimited or infinite. See V 1, 6.38-39: τὸ δὲ ἀεὶ τέλειον ἀεὶ ἀΐδιον γεννᾷ. καὶ ἔλαττον δὲ ἑαυτοῦ γεννᾷ (that which is eternally perfect generates an everlasting reality, and it generates something inferior to itself). See O'Meara 2005 for an analysis of the argument. Cf. Opsomer 2007b, 167-68.

92. See I 8, 6.36-41, where Plotinus argues against Aristotle that, in a sense, substance does have a contrary. That is, what stands 'furthest apart' from the first principle of all—which is in a sense substance—its contrary. On matter as explicitly identified with evil, see I 8, 7.21-23; VI 7, 28.12.

93. See V 1, 3.15-16; V 1, 7.42.

94. See V 2, 1.7.

And this is the fall of the soul: to come in this way into matter and to be weakened, because all of its powers are not present in the activity, matter preventing their presence by occupying the region that soul inhabits and in a way makes it "contract itself"[95] and what it seized in a way by theft it makes evil, until soul would be able to lift itself up again. Matter, then, is the cause of weakness in the soul and the cause of vice. Therefore, it is prior evil, that is, the first evil. For even if the already affected soul itself generated matter, and if it associated with it and became evil, matter is the cause of that by its presence. For soul would not have come to be in it if it were not by the presence of matter that soul came to be generated.[96]

The ambiguity in the words "for even if the already affected soul itself generated matter" need mean nothing more than that Plotinus is considering a possibility that soul generated matter. It is difficult to take these words, as O'Brien does, and in the absence of any other passage that unambiguously says that soul generated matter, to indicate Plotinus's own view. On the other hand, that matter is generated is beyond doubt; that is, it is not a principle coextensive with the One. If that were the case, Plotinus would seem to be contradicting the monism that he constantly affirms. It is clear in the cases of Intellect and Soul that their generation is not ex nihilo. But Plotinus is also insistent that matter, though it is generated, exists always and necessarily.[97] The reason for this, which is especially relevant to the question with which we are now dealing, is that the 'divine principles'—that is, One, Intellect, and Soul—operate necessarily. So, if matter exists owing

---

95. See Plato, *Symp.* 206D6.
96. I 8, 14.44-54: Καὶ τοῦτό ἐστι πτῶμα τῆς ψυχῆς τὸ οὕτως ἐλθεῖν εἰς ὕλην καὶ ἀσθενεῖν, ὅτι πᾶσαι αἱ δυνάμεις οὐ πάρεισιν εἰς ἐνέργειαν κωλυούσης ὕλης παρεῖναι τῷ τὸν τόπον ὃν κατέχει αὐτὴ καταλαβεῖν καὶ οἷον συσπειραθῆναι ποιῆσαι ἐκείνην, ὃ δ' ἔλαβεν οἷον κλέψασα ποιῆσαι κακὸν εἶναι, ἕως ἂν δυνηθῇ ἀναδραμεῖν. Ὕλη τοίνυν καὶ ἀσθενείας ψυχῇ αἰτία καὶ κακίας αἰτία. Πρότερον ἄρα κακὴ αὕτη καὶ πρῶτον κακόν· καὶ γὰρ εἰ αὐτὴ ἡ ψυχὴ τὴν ὕλην ἐγέννησε παθοῦσα, καὶ εἰ ἐκοινώνησεν αὐτῇ καὶ ἐγένετο κακή, ἡ ὕλη αἰτία παροῦσα· οὐ γὰρ ἂν ἐγένετο εἰς αὐτὴν μὴ τῇ παρουσίᾳ αὐτῆς τὴν γένεσιν λαβοῦσα. Cf. III 9, 3.7-16; III 3, 4.1; V 1, 7.47-48; V 2, 2.29-31. Although these texts do not explicitly say that matter is thus generated, the language employed perhaps creates a presumption that this is the case. For example, in III 4, 1, the product of nature is that which is totally unlimited (παντελῆ ἀοριστίαν, 11-12, 13), no longer a form (οὐ ἔτι εἶδος, l.11), and a receptacle (ὑποδοχή, 15). See O'Brien 1971, 1991, and 1996, who argues at great length for the generation of matter by the vegetative part of soul or nature. Against this view, Phillips (2009) argues that the direct product of nature is not matter but rather the "trace-soul" (ψυχῆς τι ἴχνος). This is a sort of image of soul that is inseparable from the body, unlike the 'higher' soul. According to Phillips, the descriptions of the product of nature in the passage from III 4, 1 above are all intended to apply to the trace-soul, not to matter. O'Brien (2011) replies to Phillips. See Narbonne 2006 and 2007, 130-41, who argues against O'Brien, that the generation of matter by soul is impossible. Narbonne bases his argument principally on the following texts: II 9, 2.31-44; I 6, 5.31-34; IV 7, 10.11-12; I 8, 5.17; I 8, 8.20; I 8, 14.24. All of these passages seem to affirm that evil is something external to the soul. And, indeed, if matter is straightforwardly identical with evil, then soul generates evil if it generates matter.
97. See Plato, *Symp.* 206D6.

to prior principles, it necessarily exists. There was no time when it did not exist after which it did. This is true despite the fact that it was generated. So the causality of Intellect and the One and the part of Soul that is not nature, far from being set aside by the generation of matter, is implicated. The phrase 'A generates B' indicates that A, owing to its own nature, causes B to receive whatever of A it is able to receive. Thus, Intellect can receive the One only as essence, or οὐσία; Soul can receive Intellect only as the image of essence contained in the different kinds of embodied souls. Soul, as nature, is the last vestige of intelligible reality. This vestige has a kind of indefiniteness *within* sensible form that is different from the total indefiniteness that is matter.[98] It is the former that is given to body. This is the bodily shape referred to above. But for there to be a receiver of bodily shape, there must be that which is without shape altogether. And that is matter, which is unqualified privation of all form.[99]

To say that matter is generated is to conceive of it as the condition for the possibility of embodied life.[100] The proof that there must be such a condition

---

98. See II 9, 3.12–21: Οὐ τοίνυν ἐγένετο, ἀλλ' ἐγίνετο καὶ γενήσεται, ὅσα γενητὰ λέγεται· οὐδὲ φθαρήσεται, ἀλλ' ἢ ὅσα ἔχει εἰς ἅ· ὃ δὲ μὴ ἔχει εἰς ὅ, οὐδὲ φθαρήσεται. Εἰ δέ τις εἰς ὕλην λέγοι, διὰ τί οὐ καὶ τὴν ὕλην; Εἰ δὲ καὶ τὴν ὕλην φήσει, τίς ἦν ἀνάγκη, φήσομεν, γενέσθαι; Εἰ δὲ ἀναγκαῖον εἶναι φήσουσι παρακολουθεῖν, καὶ νῦν ἀνάγκη. Εἰ δὲ μόνη καταλειφθήσεται, οὐ πανταχοῦ, ἀλλ' ἔν τινι τόπῳ ἀφωρισμένῳ τὰ θεῖα ἔσται καὶ οἷον ἀποτετειχισμένα· εἰ δὲ οὐχ οἷόν τε, ἐλλαμφθήσεται. (Things that are said to have come into being did not just come into being, but always did and always will come into being. Nor will things be decomposed, apart from those things that have something to be decomposed into; but what does not have anything into which it can be decomposed, will not do so. If someone says that things will be decomposed into matter, why is this not the case for matter, too? But if he will say that this is so for matter, we will say, what necessity was there for it to come to be? But if they will say that it is necessary for it to follow from [other principles], it is necessary now. But if matter is left alone, the divine principles will not be everywhere, but limited to being in one place, and in a way they will be walled off from it. But if this is not possible, it will be illuminated by them.) By contrast, the general Middle Platonic position was that matter is not generated, but an independent principle. See Narbonne 2007, 123, n. 1, for references to the Middle Platonic authors who denied that matter is generated in any sense.

99. See III 4, 1.12–17: Εἰ μὲν γὰρ κἂν τοῖς προτέροις ἡ ἀοριστία, ἀλλ' ἐν εἴδει· οὐ γὰρ πάντῃ ἀόριστον, ἀλλ' ὡς πρὸς τὴν τελείωσιν αὐτοῦ· τὸ δὲ νῦν πάντῃ. Τελειούμενον δὲ γίνεται σῶμα μορφὴν λαβὸν τὴν τῇ δυνάμει πρόσφορον, ὑποδοχὴ τοῦ γεννήσαντος καὶ ἐκθρέψαντος· καὶ μόνον τοῦτο ἐν σώματι ἔσχατον τῶν ἄνω ἐν ἐσχάτῳ τοῦ κάτω. (Even if there is unlimitedness in the things before it [soul], it is unlimitedness in form; for it is not absolutely unlimited, but is so in relation to the completion of it. What we are concerned with now is absolutely unlimited. When it is completed it becomes a body, receiving the shape appropriate to its potentiality, a receptacle for that which produced it and nourished it; and only this shape in the body is the ultimate representation of the things from above in the ultimate things below.) See Narbonne 2006, 57–60, with n. 33, who rightly claims that the words "when it is completed it becomes a body" cannot refer to matter. They must refer to the elements. But this does not show that matter itself is not generated.

100. See II 4, 16.3–4: Διὸ καὶ μὴ ὂν οὕτω τι ὂν καὶ στερήσει ταὐτόν, εἰ ἡ στέρησις ἀντίθεσις πρὸς τὰ ἐν λόγῳ ὄντα. (For this reason, though it is non-being, it has some being in this way, and is identical with privation, assuming privation is the opposite of the things that are in an expressed principle.) Cf. Plato, *Parm.* 158C5–6, on the "nature" (φύσις) that is in itself other than form. Plotinus is specifically opposing Aristotle, *Phys.* A 9, 192a3–8, who distinguishes

is simply that embodied life exists and, without matter, it could not. Since the operations of the three principles are eternal and necessary, anything that does exist, insofar as it is dependent on these principles, must exist. The insistence on distinguishing matter from body follows from the Aristotelian argument that all body, insofar as it is capable of change of any sort, is a composite of matter and form. But this account hardly completes the explanation of the being of the sensible world or of matter in particular. As Plotinus puts it,

> How, then, does a plurality come from a one? It is because the One is everywhere. For there is nowhere it is not. It, then, fills all things. Then, it is already many, or rather, it is all things. If it were only everywhere, it would be all things. But since it is also nowhere, all things come to be owing to it, because it is everywhere, but are other than it because it is nowhere.[101]

The One or Good is thus the explanation of the being of everything that is, even the absolute formless 'nonbeing' of matter. It does this by being virtually all things. 'Generation' is just the name of the instrumental causality for the diffusion of the Good. So the existence of matter is, ultimately, a condition for the possibility of the unlimited diffusion of the Good. And why must the diffusion be unlimited? This must be so simply because the Good is beyond limitation. If its diffusion were to cease short of the existence of a material world that we know is a possibility, this would indicate a defect in the Good, and this is impossible.

> Again, if we say that that nature [the One] is unlimited—for it is indeed not limited—what would this mean other than that it will not be defective? But if it is not defective, does that mean that it is present to each thing? If it were not able to be present, it will be defective and there will be somewhere that it is not.[102]

---

matter and privation, arguing that Platonists fail to do this in positing the Indefinite Dyad, which serves as matter, though it is evidently indistinct from privation as a principle of change.

101. III 9, 4.1–6: Πῶς οὖν ἐξ ἑνὸς πλῆθος; Ὅτι πανταχοῦ· οὐ γάρ ἐστιν ὅπου οὔ. Πάντα οὖν πληροῖ· πολλὰ οὖν, μᾶλλον δὲ πάντα ἤδη. Αὐτὸ μὲν γὰρ εἰ μόνον πανταχοῦ, αὐτὸ ἂν ἦν τὰ πάντα· ἐπεὶ δὲ καὶ οὐδαμοῦ, τὰ πάντα γίνεται μὲν δι' αὐτόν, ὅτι πανταχοῦ ἐκεῖνος, ἕτερα δὲ αὐτοῦ, ὅτι αὐτὸς οὐδαμοῦ. Cf. III 6, 14.1–2: Μὴ οὔσης οὐδὲν ὑπέστη ἄν; Ἦ οὐδὲ εἴδωλον κατόπτρου μὴ ὄντος ἤ τινος τοιούτου. (If matter did not exist, would nothing have come to exist? No, and there would be no image if there were no mirror or some such thing.) Cf. I 8, 7.1–7, where Plotinus argues that matter as underlying subject is a necessary condition for the presence of any good thing, that is, anything put into order by the Demiurge. Also, VI 3, 7.4–5. Proclus, *De mal. subst.* 34.1–6, argues, too, that matter is a necessary product of the One, but that in itself it is neither good nor evil. My view is that Plotinus's argument is not as different from Proclus's as the latter believes. Opsomer (2001, 169, n. 20, and 2007b) defends the difference between the views of Plotinus and Proclus, arguing from O'Brien's position that for Plotinus nature generates matter, whereas for Proclus matter is generated by the One. See *In Tim.* 1.385.1–5.

102. VI 5, 4.13–17: Πάλιν δέ, εἰ ἄπειρον λέγομεν ἐκείνην τὴν φύσιν—οὐ γὰρ δὴ πεπερασμένην—τί ἂν ἄλλο εἴη, ἢ ὅτι οὐκ ἐπιλείψει; Εἰ δὲ μὴ ἐπιλείψει, ὅτι πάρεστιν ἑκάστῳ. Εἰ γὰρ μὴ δύναιτο παρεῖναι, ἐπιλείψει τε καὶ ἔσται ὅπου οὔ.

Admittedly, it is odd, if not paradoxical, to say that the Good or One is present to the sort of nonbeing that is unqualified privation. But the privation is of Form, and so the nonbeing is not absolute nothingness, but rather the admittedly peculiar nonbeing of that which is, though it is no sort of thing.

Plotinus acknowledges that we do approach somewhat closer to paradox when we consider how that which does not participate in form in any way can, after all, participate in being.

> Since it is not possible for that which is in any way apart from being not to participate in being—for it is the very nature of being to produce beings—and since that which is totally nonbeing cannot combine with being, a marvelous thing occurs, that is, how that which does not participate participates, and how it has in a way something from its neighbor even though by its own nature it is incapable of being stuck to it.[103]

Here, matter is clearly distinguished from absolute nonbeing.[104] The sort of being of which it partakes does not turn it into anything other than what it is. That is, insofar as it is pure potency and privation, the presence of form to it does not actualize it. Matter is, in Plotinus's vivid phrase "a decorated corpse" (νεκρὸν κεκοσμημένον).[105] The manner in which matter participates by not participating is by being unqualified privation of form. It can receive the form that produces body, but it is not actualized by this at all. Presumably, it has the being of a receptacle, which means both that it has a kind of being and that it is other than the being of anything that it could conceivably receive. What it receives are the traces of nature that comprise the intelligible shapes or forms of bodies. Because matter has a kind of being, it has a kind of compositeness, consisting of itself and what we might as well call the quasi-οὐσία that privation is. Matter must have this compositeness for two reasons. First, the One is uniquely simple. Second, if matter were not composite, it could not be divisible, that is, it could not be the matter of a plurality of bodies.

There is another difficult passage, which actually seems to embrace the paradox that matter, which is evil, does partake of the Good.

---

103. III 6, 14.18–23: Ἐπεὶ γὰρ οὐχ οἷόν τε τοῦ ὄντος πάντη μὴ μετέχειν ὅ τι περ ὁπωσοῦν ἔξω ὂν αὐτοῦ ἐστιν—αὕτη γὰρ ὄντος φύσις <εἰς> τὰ ὄντα ποιεῖν—τὸ δὲ πάντη μὴ ὂν ἄμικτον τῷ ὄντι, θαῦμα τὸ χρῆμα γίγνεται, πῶς μὴ μετέχον μετέχει, καὶ πῶς οἷον παρὰ τῆς γειτνιάσεως ἔχει τι καίπερ τῇ αὐτοῦ φύσει μὲν οἷον κολλᾶσθαι ἀδυνατοῦν.

104. Cf. VI 9, 11.35–38, where absolute nonbeing (τὸ παντελὲς μὴ ὄν) is distinguished from the nonbeing (τὸ μὴ ὄν) that is evil or matter. Also, I 8, 3.6–7; I 8.15.1–3, where "the necessity of the existence" (τὴν ἀνάγκην τῆς ὑποστάσεως) of matter is affirmed. Cf. Plato, *Soph.* 238C8–10, 258A11–B3, on the distinction between absolute and relative nonbeing. Cf. O'Brien 1996, 181; 2012, 40–45.

105. See II 4, 5.18. Cf. III 3, 8.24–34, where the "corpse" is not matter itself but matter along with its visible form or shape, i.e., the "adorned corpse."

The nature of matter, then, either existed forever, and it was not possible for it, since it existed, not to partake of that which grants to all things as much of the Good as each is able to have; or else, the generation of it followed by necessity from the causes prior to it, and as such it did not have to be separate for the reason that that which gave it being in a way as a gracious gift stood still before coming to it owing to a lack of power.[106]

The puzzles in this passage are numerous. If the first alternative ("it existed forever") applies to matter, then it seems to partake of the Good. But if one wants to deny this, then presumably one would want to deny that the words "existed forever" do not apply to it, since it seems to be implied that *because* it existed forever it partakes of the Good.[107] If we can somehow get over this, and we embrace the second alternative ("the generation of it followed from prior causes"), it still seems that matter is in some way not separate, presumably from the Good. Further, if it followed necessarily from the causes prior to it, this hardly counts as a denial of its existing forever; indeed, it seems to be an implicit claim to such existence. If matter is not separate from its causes, it does then seem somehow to participate in the Good without "really" participating.

And yet, in one of Plotinus's latest treatises where the problem of matter and evil is most extensively discussed we read,

> But when something is absolutely deficient—which is what matter is—this is really evil, having no share of good.[108] For matter does not even have being, which would have allowed it to partake of good to this extent; rather we say

---

106. IV 8, 6.18–23: Εἴτ' οὖν ἦν ἀεὶ ἡ τῆς ὕλης φύσις, οὐχ οἷόν τε ἦν αὐτὴν μὴ μετασχεῖν οὖσαν τοῦ πᾶσι τὸ ἀγαθὸν καθόσον δύναται ἕκαστον χορηγοῦντος· εἴτ' ἠκολούθησεν ἐξ ἀνάγκης ἡ γένεσις αὐτῆς τοῖς πρὸ αὐτῆς αἰτίοις, οὐδ' ὣς ἔδει χωρὶς εἶναι, ἀδυναμίᾳ πρὶν εἰς αὐτὴν ἐλθεῖν στάντος τοῦ καὶ τὸ εἶναι οἷον ἐν χάριτι δόντος. See III 6, 11.37–38: ἀλλ' ὅτι μὲν ἀναγκαῖόν ἐστι μεταλαμβάνειν ἀμηγέπη μεταλαμβάνει ἕως ἂν ᾖ (but because it is necessary for it to participate, it participates in some way as long as it is). The subject of the phrase is matter. Plotinus goes on to say (41–43) that if matter really participated, it would not be absolute evil and it would be altered by the Good. O'Brien (1981, 110–11) argues that because matter does not participate "really," it does not participate. It seems more accurate to say, based on the text, that matter participates in a unique manner, that is, without its participation causing it to be identified with or actualized by form in any manner. Cf. II 4, 13.22–24; II 5, 5.20–22, where matter is said to be "incapable of being informed" (μορφοῦσθαι μὴ δυνάμενον).

107. See O'Brien 1981, 114–15, who argues that the first alternative refers to intelligible matter and only the second to sensible matter. But it seems that the reason for holding this, namely, that participation in the Good should be barred for sensible matter though not for intelligible matter, is gainsaid in the second alternative.

108. Note that at line 21 in the above passage the second alternative has matter coming into being as a necessary consequence of its causes. The plural, I take it, indicates the hierarchical pattern of instrumental causality. Cf. II 9, 12.44: ὥστε ἐπὶ τὰ πρῶτα ἡ αἰτία (so that the causality goes back to the first principles). The principles here are said to be the cause of "darkness" (τὸ σκότος, 40), evidently equivalent to matter. But it is not clear that Plotinus is himself drawing this conclusion or maintaining that it follows for the Gnostics from their own account of the generation of matter by soul.

that it has being in name only, so that the true way to speak of it is as nonbeing. Deficiency, then, is not being good, but evil is absolute deficiency.[109]

Putting these two passages together, it seems that matter as such is thought by Plotinus to have nothing of the Good in it, yet not to be separate from its causes, which includes, ultimately, the Good.[110]

The resolution of this problem is, I believe, as follows. Matter, as we have seen, is a necessary condition for the possibility of a sensible world that imitates the intelligible world. In this imitation, there is all manner of derived goodness. Matter is not separate from its causes just in the sense that it is this necessary condition. Matter, though, is evil when it is pursued as an end.[111] Since everything desires that which is good, to pursue the opposite is, as it were, to be oriented in the most perverse way possible. It is to do more (or less) than to take the apparent good as the Good itself. For, according to Plotinus, apparent goods will have a measure of the Good in them insofar as they have any semblance of an intelligible nature. In fact, it is not obvious that the successful pursuit of evil as such is anything other than a theoretical possibility for Plotinus.[112] What is, however, all too real is vice (κακία). The distinction between evil and vice is, says Plotinus, the distinction between that which is unqualified privation of form or measure and that which is a particular sort of lack of measure, such as injustice.[113] By contrast, virtue is not the Good, but *a* good, which enables us to dominate matter.[114] The reason why injustice, for example, is a vice is that it constitutes an orientation in the sensible world in the 'direction' of evil, that is, away from the Good. It does this by one directing one's desires to the body as if its good were the Good. The goods of the body do appear to be the

---

109. I 8, 5.8–13: Ἀλλ' ὅταν παντελῶς ἐλλείπῃ, ὅπερ ἐστὶν ἡ ὕλη, τοῦτο τὸ ὄντως κακὸν μηδεμίαν ἔχον ἀγαθοῦ μοῖραν. Οὐδὲ γὰρ τὸ εἶναι ἔχει ἡ ὕλη, ἵνα ἀγαθοῦ ταύτῃ μετεῖχεν, ἀλλ' ὁμώνυμον αὐτῇ τὸ εἶναι, ὡς ἀληθὲς εἶναι λέγειν αὐτὸ μὴ εἶναι. Ἡ οὖν ἔλλειψις ἔχει μὲν τὸ μὴ ἀγαθὸν εἶναι, ἡ δὲ παντελὴς τὸ κακόν·

110. Cf. Plato, *Phil.* 20D1, 54C10, 60B4.

111. But see I 8, 6.33–34: ἥτις ἐστὶ κακοῦ φύσις καὶ ἀρχή· ἀρχαὶ γὰρ ἄμφω, ἡ μὲν κακῶν, ἡ δὲ ἀγαθῶν (it [matter] is the nature and principle of evil; for both [matter and the Good] are principles, the one of evils and the other of goods). Speaking of matter as the principle of evils sounds like an admission of dualism. But if matter is caused to be, it is not a principle like the One, but like other principles (Intellect, Soul) whose qualified status as principles do not compromise Plotinus's monism. Proclus, *De mal. subst.*, chaps. 31–33, argues that it is necessary to sever matter from evil, while retaining the dependence of matter on the Good. See Hager 1987, 34–60, for an account similar to mine of how Plotinus recognizes the existence of evil while remaining a monist. Also Rist 1965.

112. Schaefer (2004) has a similar argument, though he goes too far, I think, in maintaining that matter is not evil. According to Schaefer (277–84), matter is not intrinsically evil; it is evil only in its effects. But it seems fairly clear from the texts both that Plotinus identifies matter with evil and that matter would not have evil effects if it were not the principle of evil.

113. Cf. O'Brien 1971, 145: "But in Plotinus' philosophy, where everything, even the quasi non-existence of matter, depends ultimately on the One, we might well suppose that there is no room for what is intrinsically evil."

114. See I 8, 5.14–17.

Good because body is not without intelligible form. But to take the goods of the body merely as apparent goods without deception would be not to desire them other than as images of the intelligible reality that they imitate.[115]

This interpretation is supported by the claim made by Plotinus that certain gods and certain men, though having bodies, are not inclined to evil.[116] It is not the presence of matter alone that produces any vice. So to call matter 'evil' is to indicate matter operating in a certain condition or circumstance. This circumstance is the embodied life of a soul that has a certain weakness.[117] At least part of the explanation of the weakness is the occlusion of personal identity owing to embodiment. Thus, a person on being embodied discovers embodied desires, or ὀρέξεις. He does not merely discover them; he discovers the self that is their subject. But no subject of bodily desires can be the true self, that which is identical with a disembodied intellect.[118] The difficulty of discerning one's true self amid its pretenders is the weakness embodied humans experience. Without a firm sense of one's true self-identity, the nonnormative use of reason as servant of one's desires competes often quite effectively with the normative use of reason that, when operating properly, judges desires according to whether or not they instantiate the Good.[119] Those fortunate gods and men not inclined

---

115. See I 8, 6.19–20. Cf. I 8, 13.5–7.

116. See I 8, 8.1–28 and I 8, 9, where Plotinus contrasts an accurate and a deceptive appraisal of form in bodies. For bodily evils like sickness or ugliness, see I 8, 4.1–2; I 8, 14.10–13; V 9, 10. Cf. IV 4, 44.30–32: τὸ γὰρ οὐκ ἀγαθὸν ὡς ἀγαθὸν διώκειν ἐλχθέντα τῷ ἐκείνου εἴδει ἀλόγοις ὁρμαῖς, τοῦτό ἐστιν ἀγομένου ὅπου μὴ ἤθελεν οὐκ εἰδότος (pursuing what is not good as good, having been attracted by the appearance of it through irrational impulses, belongs to someone who is being led, in ignorance, where he does not want to go).

117. See I 8, 5.30–34. See O'Brien 1971, 129–30, on the textual difficulties in this passage.

118. See IV 8, 4.1–24. Cf. V 1, 1.1–17, where birth itself for most people is the occasion for regarding matter as attractive and so in fact evil. The cause of the descent into bodies is called by Plotinus "daring" (τόλμα) and "primary otherness" (πρώτη ἑτερότης, 5). Whether this weakness is intellectual or moral and why Plotinus thinks that some persons have this weakness and others do not are questions that cannot be treated here.

119. See IV 7, 13. Cf. Rep. 612A3–6. See also VI 4, 15.32–40: Τοῦτο δὲ καὶ ἀνθρώπου κακία αὐξοντος δῆμον ἐν αὑτῷ ἡδονῶν καὶ ἐπιθυμιῶν καὶ φόβων κρατησάντων συνδόντος ἑαυτὸν τοῦ τοιούτου ἀνθρώπου δήμῳ τῷ τοιούτῳ· ὃς δ' ἂν τοῦτον τὸν ὄχλον δουλώσηται καὶ ἀναδράμῃ εἰς ἐκεῖνον, ὅς ποτε ἦν, κατ' ἐκεῖνόν τε ζῇ καὶ ἔστιν ἐκεῖνος διδοὺς τῷ σώματι, ὅσα δίδωσιν ὡς ἑτέρῳ ὄντι ἑαυτοῦ· ἄλλος δέ τις ὁτὲ μὲν οὕτως, ὁτὲ δὲ ἄλλως ζῇ, μικτός τις ἐξ ἀγαθοῦ ἑαυτοῦ καὶ κακοῦ ἑτέρου γεγενημένος. (This is also the vice of humans; he, too, has a populace of pleasures and appetites and fears which gain control when a human being of this sort gives himself over to a populace of this sort. But whoever subdues a mob of this sort and runs back to the being he once was, lives according to that and is that and gives to the body such things as belong to something other than himself. Someone else at one time lives this way and at another lives another way, having become something mixed from his own good and the evil of the other). This passage is essentially a commentary on *Lg.* 689A5–E3. Cf. *Phdr.* 256B2–3. The words "lives according to that and is that" indicate that the embodied intellect is only ideally identical with the disembodied undescended intellect. To live according to that undescended intellect is to strive for the ideal. But the ideal would be vacuous or arbitrary if that ideal were not really what each of us is.

to evil are evidently so well aware of their own true identities that they can scarcely desire other than that which their intellects tell them is really good.

In this chapter, I have tried to provide a sketch of the Plotinian system without much attention to its foundation in the Platonism of Plato. Even those who regard Plotinus as something of an eccentric innovator must concede that he did not consider himself to have innovated at all except in the special sense of having applied Platonic principles to the solution of particular contemporary problems. He may also in a way be said to have innovated in his particular articulation of the metaphysics principles underlying Platonism. In the next two chapters of this book, I would like to develop the case that Plotinus was correct to see himself as faithful heir to a tradition going back to Plato and perhaps even beyond to Pythagoras. The key claim on which this case rests is that the philosophy of Plato is itself based on UP in the precise sense that it aims to be a positive construct in response to UP that is maximally consistent and complete. Of course, consistency alone is a minimal criterion of success and completeness here is an open-ended concept. Nevertheless, both consistency and completeness are held by Plato to be attainable only within the correct metaphysical structure. Plato's response to all his opponents is, ultimately, a metaphysical one. It is his hierarchical metaphysics that guides his research and shapes his solutions to the full range of philosophical problems of his day, including practical ones. In his embrace and articulation of these principles Plotinus was—so I will argue—no innovator.

CHAPTER 10

Plotinus as Interpreter of Plato (1)

In this chapter I am primarily concerned with the justness of Proclus's reverence for Plotinus as an expositor of Platonism. Proclus no doubt thought his view was uncontroversial. The situation looks to many scholars entirely different today. At the extreme, Plotinus's version of Platonism is taken to be a travesty of the true Platonism of the dialogues. A more moderate position would perhaps allow a core of authenticity in Plotinus's Platonism while insisting that the consequences Plotinus draws from this core are remote or at least different from anything Plato could reasonably be thought to have held.

My working hypothesis throughout this book is that what we find in the dialogues is an expression of one positive, continuously refined, construct out of UP. Actually, as I have argued, the positive construct is properly located within the ongoing work of the Academy under Plato's leadership and the dialogues represent in effect occasional dramatized summaries of provisional results in the course of that work. I conjecture that were we to possess an accurate relative chronology of the composition of the dialogues, their function in this regard would be evident.[1] Aristotle's testimony is indispensable for connecting the positive Academic construct to the corpus of writings. In addition, Aristotle's own work, both within the Academy and then in his own Lyceum, represents an alternative positive construct out of UP. Exactly the same thing can be said for other members of the

---

1. The categorization of the dialogues into early, middle, and late periods invites us to ignore or at least undervalue both the doctrinal differences among dialogues within the putative periods and the unifying substructure that is, I contend, UP.

Old Academy, especially Speusippus and Xenocrates. Various central elements of Plato's positive construct are also discernible in the New Academy and among the so-called Middle Platonists. Much of this material—and no doubt much else not extant today—was available to Plotinus and, judging from Porphyry's account of Plotinus's seminars, was the subject of intense discussion. Nevertheless, Plotinus's access to texts, his apparent reliance on a long tradition of the oral transmission of Platonic doctrine, and his manifest bona fides are certainly not sufficient to guarantee the accuracy of his systematic account.[2]

As Porphyry tells us in his biography of Plotinus, Plotinus was the student of Ammonius Saccas, who, according to Plotinus, was content to transmit Platonism to his disciples orally.[3] Plotinus came to Rome with the intention of doing the identical thing. Only the appearance of the writings of his fellow students Erennius and Origen incited him to write himself during the last sixteen or seventeen years of his life. The story seems to suggest that Plotinus, like Ammonius, thought that the appropriate way to transmit Platonism was orally. It does not seem to me to be implausible that Plotinus thought this because he believed, rightly or wrongly, that Plato himself thought that this was the appropriate way to transmit truth. After all, Plotinus reasonably took the passages in *Phaedrus* and the *Seventh Letter* to confirm this. The point of this is not that Plotinus privileged the oral doctrine over the dialogues. He certainly thought that they were of a piece and mutually illuminating. The point is rather that Plotinus did not think that a systematization of Plato's Platonism was a novelty or even a translation of an inspired way of thinking into a formal mode. There is no reason to believe that Plotinus regarded his own work as, say, analogous to a systematic theology constructed out of a scriptural narrative. As far as we know, he thought that the system was articulated by Plato, not for the first time, but most profoundly and persuasively.[4] And by 'system,' of course, I mean fundamental metaphysical principles, certainly not all the possible consequences that can be drawn from these.

It is not particularly difficult to locate the textual basis in Plato's dialogues for the three fundamental principles of Plotinus's version of Platonism.[5] As we saw in the last chapter, the primary provenance of the Good is

2. See V 1, 9.30–32, where Plotinus seems to implicitly identify Plato as a Pythagorean and among those who transmitted his teachings orally. Cf. V 1, 8.1–10.

3. See Porphyry, *Life of Plotinus* 3.32–34.

4. See Charrue 1978, 259–66, for a balanced and largely favorable assessment of the accuracy of Plotinus's representation of the Platonism of Plato. Plotinus's fidelity to the teachings of Plato does not, of course, exclude the fact that there is undoubtedly considerable originality in Plotinus, especially in his responses to criticisms of Platonism and to the treatment of philosophical issues relevant to the third century CE.

5. The second part of Plato's *Parmenides* was, of course, a central text in late Platonic systematic constructs, though its interpretation is and evidently always has been controversial. Plotinus's use of this material is more cautious than that of his successors. See Vorwerk 2010. The work by Halfwassen and others to locate the ontological interpretation of the second part

Republic, where the superordinate Idea of the Good is found. Its identification with the One is confirmed by Aristotle's testimony. That identification of Intellect with the Demiurge and Soul as the principle of the soul of the universe and individual souls derives from *Timaeus*. The identification of nature with the lowest part of the World Soul and matter with the receptacle follows somewhat less directly. Aristotle says that the receptacle is identical with matter as *he*, Aristotle, understands that. Theophrastus follows Aristotle in testifying that this is what Plato taught as a result of his investigations of nature. Plotinus, too, accepts that it is Plato's authentic teaching. That nature and matter are the final steps of the procession from the One are claims that must be seen as following from the integrated hierarchical metaphysics that Plotinus embraces. A good place to start to test Plotinus's systematic version of Platonism is just here, where there is not an obvious proof text for Plotinus to rely on.

Matter in the Platonic System

As we saw in the previous chapter, Plotinus accepts Aristotle's interpretation of space or the receptacle in *Timaeus* as equivalent to matter roughly as he, Aristotle, conceives of it. The specific question faced by Plotinus is whether matter (or space or the receptacle) has an independent existence, that is, independent of the One and the Demiurge and Soul. In *Timaeus*, it seems that the receptacle is indestructible and everlasting.[6] It is also clear that the receptacle exists independently of the order imposed on it by the Demiurge.[7] So in what sense, if any, can Plato have thought, like Plotinus, that all things depend on the first principle of all?

We may also recall that Aristotle not only says that Plato identified the Good and the One, but that he claimed that there was a second principle, the Indefinite Dyad or the Great and the Small, and that together with the One, these generated the Forms. Specifically, the Indefinite Dyad was

---

of the dialogue in the Old Academy itself and not in the early second-century philosopher Moderatus of Gades, as does Dodds 1928, is potentially a valuable bit of progress. This work suggests that *Parmenides* should be elevated to the status of primary evidence rather than marginal. Cf. Miller 1995. See Hubler 2010 for an important criticism of Dodds's hypothesis on the role of Moderatus.

6. See *Tim.* 52A8–B1. Cf. 52D3–4: ὄν τε καὶ χώραν καὶ γένεσιν εἶναι, τρία τριχῇ, καὶ πρὶν οὐρανὸν γενέσθαι. (there are being, space, and becoming—three distinct things—even before the heavens came to be). See Miller 2003, chaps. 2 and 5, who argues persuasively that the 'third kind' includes both the receptacle and space (or place) and that these are distinct entities. That is, the identification of the receptacle with matter and space (or place) by Aristotle is mistaken. If this is so, it would still be the case (and perhaps even more so) that the receptacle is matter. See also Sattler 2012, 177–78, who rejects the identification of the receptacle with matter.

7. See *Tim.* 48B3–52D4, where the condition of the receptacle is described prior to the imposition on it by the Demiurge of shapes and numbers (53B5).

matter to the One.⁸ Simplicius, in his commentary on Aristotle's *Physics*, adds the important point that in his lecture *On the Good* Plato used the Indefinite Dyad as a material principle both in the sensible world and in the intelligible world.⁹ With the addition of the Indefinite Dyad, we may seem to have actually exacerbated the problem: there now seem to be two principles independent of the One, the Indefinite Dyad in the intelligible and its counterpart in the sensible world. Let us suppose that the Demiurge is not the direct cause of the receptacle. Neither does it appear to be the cause of the Indefinite Dyad, especially insofar as we think that the Demiurge is cognitionally identical with Forms and that the Indefinite Dyad is a principle of Forms, along with the One. So either we are left with a proliferation of independent principles or these are somehow unified in the order of causality.

In Plotinus's account of Plato's Platonism, the identification of Demiurge and Forms implies their derivation from the One or the Idea of the Good, according to Aristotle's testimony. This derivation, of course, is nontemporal.[10] The interpretative choice at this point is to maintain that the Demiurge, that is, Intellect, is derived independently of the Indefinite Dyad or not. But given the identity of Intellect and Forms, the former possibility seems unintelligible. In fact, Plotinus argues that the Indefinite Dyad *is* Intellect as 'product' of the One, and that Intellect is just the Indefinite Dyad 'actualized' by its reversion to the One.[11] Since all things desire the Good, anything derived from the Good desires it. Intellect desires the Good and achieves the object of its desire in the only way that something can come to be identified with that which is other than it.[12] That is, it thinks all the Forms, that which the Good is virtually.[13]

With respect to the Indefinite Dyad as matter in the sensible world or the receptacle, even though matter is pure privation, it is not absolute nonbeing.[14] It is a necessary condition for the possibility of the instantiation of the intelligible world. Although *Timaeus* presents the receptacle as existing

---

8. See *Meta.* A 6, 987b18ff. As such, it is a principle of evil, A 6, 988a7–17.
9. Simplicius, *In Phys.* 453.22–30. Cf. 151.6–19.
10. See Proclus, *In Tim.* 1.277.8–10, for this Old Academic idea of nontemporal generation. Proclus says that this is the view of Crantor (c. 336–276/5). So, too, does Plutarch, *De gen. an.* 1012F–1013B.
11. See V 1, 5–7. See Atkinson 1985, ad loc., for many valuable comments on the text and the arguments here. Also, O'Meara 1993, 60–65.
12. See V 6, 5.9–10: ἡ γὰρ ἔφεσις [for the Good] τὴν νόησιν ἐγέννησε καὶ συνυπέστησεν αὐτῇ (the desire for the Good generates thinking and causes it to exist along with that desire). See VI 5, 1.1–14 on the desire for the Good as the desire for unity or oneness. Cf. VI 2, 11.20–29; VI 5, 1.19–20.
13. See VI 9, 5.33–34 where the One is "better known" by means of οὐσία. At VI 2, 22.1, Plotinus says that Plato speaks "riddlingly" (ᾐνιγμένως) of the way in which Intellect sees the Forms in the Living Being, meaning that he must be interpreted at this point in the argument.
14. See II 4, 16.3: Διὸ καὶ μὴ ὂν οὕτω τι ὂν καὶ στερήσει ταὐτόν. (For this reason, though it is in this way nonbeing, it has some sort of being and is identical with privation.)

prior to the generation of the heavens, it also says that "the first principle or principles of all things" are to be left out of the discussion.[15] Accordingly, that the receptacle is independent of the Demiurge does not imply that it is independent of the One. On the contrary, Plato's positing of a unique causal first principle seems to imply that everything, including the Indefinite Dyad, is derived from it. The manner of this derivation in regard to the Indefinite Dyad as matter in the sensible world is left unexplained in the dialogue, although the explicit exclusion of discussion of the first principle at least suggests that it could have been.

Faced with the problem of the generation of matter in Platonism, Plotinus has no more evidence from the dialogues than do we. Aiming for the most coherent systematic expression of Platonism possible, to leave the receptacle as fundamentally independent of the One would, Plotinus believes, contradict the unlimited power of the One. Since Plato says that the Good is "beyond οὐσία," there could be no limitation in its activity other than the impossible or self-contradictory. But the existence of matter, along with everything else in the universe, guarantees its possibility, that is, *ab esse ad posse*. If the One were not the ultimate cause of the existence of sensible matter, the One would be limited in the sense that it was not in its nature to produce matter or that it was a task it was not up to. For this to be the case, it would have to have a nature that was capable of doing some things and not others. But this is as much as to say that it has an οὐσία that limits it in this way. Finally, Plotinus has argued that the One must be uniquely self-caused. So the hypothesis that matter should be uncaused by anything else because it is self-caused fails. Fidelity to Platonism, it seems, demands an integrated metaphysical hierarchy with the One or the Idea of the Good at the top and matter at the bottom.[16]

---

15. *Tim.* 48C2–6.
16. See De Vogel 1953, 52–64; 1954; and Steel 1989. See II 9, 3.11–12: Ἀνάγκη τοίνυν ἐφεξῆς εἶναι πάντα ἀλλήλοις καὶ ἀεί, γενητὰ δὲ τὰ ἕτερα τῷ παρ' ἄλλων εἶναι. (Necessarily, then, all things must exist always in a dependent order; those other than the One are generated by being derived from principles other than themselves.) Cf. Vlastos 1939, who attempts to give a coherent explanation of the disorderly motion of the receptacle prior to creation. Vlastos says (repr., 1965, 390) that what Plato offers is a "makeshift." The "traces" in the receptacle are literally a contradiction of the idea that all mathematical ordering of the cosmos must be owing to the Demiurge. Vlastos's insistence that Plato must be understood to mean that γένεσις must have a "precise, inalienable order of its own" prevents him from seeing how Plato could give a coherent cosmological account. Cherniss (1944, 423–31, with notes) concedes that it is inconsistent to say that the creation of the universe in *Timaeus* is literal and that the receptacle always existed. It is for this reason that he thinks that Plato did not take the creation of the universe literally. But Cherniss accepts a false dichotomy: either literal creation in time or no creation. Plotinus takes the creation account literally, but he does not think that the creation is in time. See IV 8, 4.40–42. See Baltes 1996, who provides a compelling argument for nontemporal creation in *Timaeus* He concludes (94) that the dependence of the cosmos on the Demiurge is ontological, not temporal. Cf. VI 1, 26.1ff., for Plotinus's criticism of Stoic materialistic ontology based on the Aristotelian principle of the absolute priority of actuality to potency.

260   CHAPTER 10

As we have seen, however, the logic of the hierarchy requires that the One is the unmediated cause only of Intellect; for everything else, it causes with the instrumentality first of Intellect, and then of Intellect and Soul. It would seem that nature, the lowest part of soul, is thought by Plotinus to generate the receptacle, that is, matter. So, we read,

> For even if there is unlimitedness in the things prior to it [matter], it is unlimitedness in form; for it is not completely unlimited but only in relation to its perfection. But now we are concerned with total unlimitedness. When it is completed, it becomes a body, receiving shape that is appropriate to its potentiality, a receptacle for that which generated it and brought it to maturity. And this alone in body is the ultimate stage of that which is above in the last of that which is below.[17]

It seems quite clear here that there are two stages of the generation of the universe. In the first, matter is somehow generated, and in the second, the Demiurge imposes order on that matter that already exists. In fact, if the Platonic system is to include an integrated hierarchy, something like this must be the case. For in *Timaeus*—and, again, assuming that the receptacle is equivalent to matter—the description of the receptacle prior to the imposition of order by the Demiurge includes both 'traces' of the nature of the elements and a disorderly motion.[18] That is, the matter there is qualified both by these traces and by its motion; it is not unqualified matter. But it is in a condition that one would expect to find when some god is absent from it. Thus, if matter is generated ultimately by the One, its generation is distinct from the imposition of order by the Demiurge or Intellect. How can this be, if the One causes things to be only with the instrumentality of the Demiurge?

As we saw in the last chapter, the involvement of Intellect in the generation of everything that is below Intellect does not entail that intellection is a property of all living and nonliving things.[19] We can express this important point in the following way. The realm of the possible includes many existents that do not have intellects or do not have life. The cognitive identity

---

17. III 4, 1.12–17: Εἰ μὲν γὰρ κἂν τοῖς προτέροις ἡ ἀοριστία, ἀλλ' ἐν εἴδει· οὐ γὰρ πάντῃ ἀόριστον, ἀλλ' ὡς πρὸς τὴν τελείωσιν αὐτοῦ· τὸ δὲ νῦν πάντῃ. Τελειούμενον δὲ γίνεται σῶμα μορφὴν λαβὸν τὴν τῇ δυνάμει πρόσφορον, ὑποδοχὴ τοῦ γεννήσαντος καὶ ἐκθρέψαντος· καὶ μόνον τοῦτο ἐν σώματι ἔσχατον τῶν ἄνω ἐν ἐσχάτῳ τοῦ κάτω.

18. See *Tim.* 52D2–53C3.

19. In his treatise "On Nature and Contemplation" Plotinus does argue that all living things in some sense contemplate. For example, in III 8, 8.12–16, we learn that in the case of things with only sense perception or other psychic powers but not with intellect, they are thinking in the sense that their psychic activity is a λόγος of the thinking of Intellect. This is also the case for nonliving things, e.g., the elements. Cf. III 8, 2.25–27. Also, cf. Proclus, *In Tim.* 1.383.1–22 and 1.388.1–15, where the two stages of generation are clearly expressed and where the distinction between participation in Intellect and participation in Forms is explained.

of Intellect and the Forms of all that which is possible does not entail that the instantiation of all possibilities owing to the diffusion of goodness will make only things with intellect. This is so because *any* instantiation of the intelligible realm entails defective intelligibility and so defective intellect. The defective versions of Forms will include both the 'weak' intellection of nonhuman living things and the even weaker intellection of nonliving things. Matter is generated last in the sensible realm in the sense that it is completely unintelligible but first in the sense that it is a condition for the possibility of the instantiation of anything in that realm.

The generation of matter or the receptacle of becoming is the result of the One's overflowing production of all that is possible. This result outstrips the instantiation of things with intellect. It outstrips the instantiation of living things. It even outstrips the instantiation of nature, the lowest part of Soul. But nature still produces. It produces a "sort of form that is not true form."[20] It is this 'sort of form' that is responsible for the disorderly motion of the receptacle and constitutes the 'traces' of the elements found there. The subsequent activity of the Demiurge or Intellect ends with the imposition of order on this disorderly motion, an order that also transforms the 'traces' into the genuine elements. This imposition of order requires the instrumentality of Soul in the production of the ensouled bodies of living things.[21] Since the receptacle has its own disorderly motion, and since all motion is accounted for by Soul, the ultimate product of nature is a "trace of soul" (ψυχῆς τι ἴχνος).[22] It is the trace of soul that makes the protoelements suitable for being constructed as the bodies of the living and nonliving things that make up the sensible realm.

If matter or the receptacle is not generated or dependent for its being on something else, then an integrated metaphysical hierarchy is not part of Platonism. Doubtless, the consequent of this statement is appealing to some. But the antecedent is difficult to maintain if only in the light of the postulation of a superordinate Idea of the Good and of Aristotle's testimony that this principle is identical with the One. Plotinus's account of the metaphysical hierarchy depends entirely on taking seriously (a) the evidence of the dialogues and (b) the testimony of Aristotle. I suspect that a widespread emphasis on (a) to the exclusion of (b) among modern scholars is rooted in the assumption that Platonism is just what is found in the dialogues. Taken in its strongest form, this assumption is that Platonism is just the *sum* of what is found in the dialogues. For to allow that the dialogues can be used to interpret each other is already to concede that Platonism is more

---

20. See I 8, 4.2: εἶδος τι οὐκ ἀληθινόν. See Phillips 2009, 132–33, for a discussion of this point with further references to Proclus and other Platonists.

21. Cf. *Tim.* 69B–D. At VI 4, 15.1–6 Plotinus says that the reception of Soul varies analogous to the reception of speech by other living things. That is, some living things only hear sounds; humans can receive meaning.

22. See *Phdr.* 245C and *Lg.* 896B on soul as the source of all motion. For the "trace of soul," see II 3, 9.22; III 8, 2.27–34; IV 4, 18–20, and VI 4, 15, and Phillips 2009, 122–31.

than that mere sum. But this assumption is, at the very least, gratuitous. Moreover, it is an assumption that frequently leads to ignoring or distorting the dialogic evidence itself.

On Plotinus's account—perhaps we should say reconstruction—of the generation of all things from the One, dead matter is the conclusion of the One's overflowing. The 'adornment' that this corpse receives are the shapes and numbers imposed by the Demiurge. But these shapes and numbers never transform matter in the sense that it becomes actual, that is, intelligible in any way. This is why Plotinus insists, against Aristotle, that the principle of matter is not distinct from the principle of privation.[23] This does not mean that Plotinus denies that something can have a potency for the acquisition of a property that is the contrary of a property it possesses. In this case, the potency that is had is distinct from the specific privation. Thus, a potency that Socrates has to stand when he is seated is not identical with his not standing. This is clearly so since if it were not, then his potency for standing would be identical with his potency for reclining. But this is absurd, for the account of each is different. The conflation of potency with privation pertains rather to unqualified or prime matter, which is identical with 'prime' privation.[24] That Aristotle is perhaps ambivalent about the existence of prime matter reveals to Plotinus the weak point in Aristotle's doctrine of sensible substance. For if there is prime matter, substantial form does not transform or actualize it into anything. If it were otherwise, then prime matter would *have* a potency instead of being pure potency. To object that prime matter just is the potency for the generation and destruction of any sensible substances solves nothing. For in that case, prime matter is a potency had by sensible substances. But all potencies for Aristotle are functionally related to the forms of the sensible substances. So, for example, Socrates has a potency for death. If this is so, prime matter does not underlie the substantial change that is Socrates' death. In any case, Socrates' potency for death is the potency for the death of a human being as opposed to, say, a plant. If, however, we make prime matter really an underlying subject, the metaphysical primacy of the sensible substance is compromised.

Plotinus thinks that Aristotelian sensible substances fit badly into the metaphysical hierarchy of Platonism. He thinks they cannot be accommodated within the framework according to which the intelligible realm is prior to the sensible realm and constitutive of its explanation. In the next

23. See Aristotle, *Phys.* A 9, 192a27ff.

24. On the absence of any affect in matter, see III 6, 9.18–19. See Scharle 2009, who argues that Aristotle has a synchronic justification for postulating prime matter separate from any diachronic justification. The latter depends essentially on there being substantial changes that must, like all changes, have an underlying subject. The difficulties with this view are well known. Plotinus rejects Aristotelian sensible substances and so *this* possible justification for prime matter. But the synchronic one, according to which the elements are necessarily metaphysically composed of a nature and that which has a nature, namely, matter, is perhaps consonant with Plotinus's own Platonic commitment.

section, I consider Plotinus's systematic account of Plato's view of becoming, an account that is at the same time a criticism of Aristotelian sensible substances.

Substance and Becoming

In *Republic*, Socrates explains the distinction between philosophers and "philodoxers." These, he says, are distinguished by their modes of cognition, which in turn are distinguished by the sorts of objects on which these modes are directed. Philosophers aim for knowledge (ἐπιστήμη) of that which is. Therefore, philodoxers must have a different sort of object.

> So, if something should appear to be and not to be at the same time, would it not be intermediate between what purely is and what altogether is not, and what is directed to it would be something intermediate between knowledge and ignorance?[25]

The mode of cognition employed by the philodoxer is belief (δόξα). He is in love with things that "are and are not at the same time." How are we to interpret the phrase "are and are not at the same time"? The objects of belief are and are not at the same time; the objects of knowledge alone are "what purely is." As we learn in *Timaeus*, the relation between that which purely is and that which is and is not is the relation of a paradigm to its image or imitation.[26] The Platonic commonplace that sensibles or the realm of becoming are composed of images of the Forms is brought into sharper focus by Aristotle's claim that sensible substances are somehow basic in the universe and that the essence of these cannot be separated from them. For example, the essence of Socrates cannot be separate from Socrates. Yet, if Plato is right, this is exactly what must be the case, for the essence of Socrates, the Form of Humanity, must be separate from Socrates and that in virtue of which we call him a man must be only an image of that essence.[27] If the essence of Socrates is found in the Form of Humanity and not in Socrates himself, then what we have come to call Aristotelian essentialism is false. Socrates—*this* particular individual—will have only a sort of accidental relation to his own putative essence.

---

25. *Rep.* 478D5–9: εἴ τι φανείη οἷον ἅμα ὄν τε καὶ μὴ ὄν, τὸ τοιοῦτον μεταξὺ κεῖσθαι τοῦ εἰλικρινῶς ὄντος τε καὶ τοῦ πάντως μὴ ὄντος, καὶ οὔτε ἐπιστήμην οὔτε ἄγνοιαν ἐπ' αὐτῷ ἔσεσθαι, ἀλλὰ τὸ μεταξὺ αὖ φανὲν ἀγνοίας καὶ ἐπιστήμης. Silverman (2002, 70) reads the passage as if "appearing to be and not to be at the same time" is not the reason for a diminished ontological status; rather, if something was not and will not be x, then it *might* just appear to be both at the same time. But if this is so, we cannot explain the clear inference in the passage.
26. See *Tim.* 51B–52D.
27. See *Meta.* Z 4, 1029b13–14; Z 13, 1038b14–15; Z 17, 1041b7–9.

Plotinus has no quarrel with Aristotle's inference from "the Form of Humanity is separate from Socrates" to "Socrates has only an accidental relation to humanity." Plotinus thinks, however, that Forms are separate and that the sensible realm is made up of images of Forms. So the absurdity is to be located not in the separation of Forms, but in the claim that a sensible individual like Socrates is identical with that separate essence.

> And the account of Humanity is what is the "something," whereas that which is its product in the nature of body, since it is an image of Form, is rather a "such and such." In a way, it is as if the visible Socrates is a man, and his image in a drawing, consisting of colors in artistic media, were called Socrates. In the same way, then, since there is an account according to which Socrates is, the perceptible Socrates should not rightly be called Socrates, but rather colors and shapes that are imitations of that which is found in the account. And this account [in the perceptible Socrates] in relation to the truest account of Humanity has the identical relation [as the image in relation to the perceptible Socrates].[28]

Plotinus could not be firmer in his conviction that the Platonist must embrace the necessity of that which Aristotle deems to be an absurdity. On the contrary, if Socrates were identical with the essence of Socrates, not only would it be impossible for anyone else to have the identical essence, but Socrates' putative accidental attributes could be no part of his identity. The Peripatetic will reply that this is precisely why they are *accidental* attributes. But this cannot be quite right. For Socrates' accidental attributes are an actualization of him; they constitute what Socrates has or is at any particular time and place. If this were not so, then the actuality of any attribute would be distinct from the actuality of Socrates when he possessed that attribute. And if that were so, then the so-called predicative use of 'is' as in 'Socrates is pale' could not indicate Socrates' identity at all.[29]

Plotinus insists, following Plato, that Forms are explanatory entities. As such, Forms must be distinct in some way from that which they explain. If this were not so, then the attributes possessed by anything would be, in the terms used previously, not heteroexplicable but autoexplicable. But

---

28. VI 3, 15.27–37: καὶ ὁ μὲν λόγος εἶναι οἷον πυρὸς τὸ "τί" σημαίνων μᾶλλον, ἣν δὲ μορφὴν ἐργάζεται, ποιὸν μᾶλλον· καὶ ὁ λόγος ὁ τοῦ ἀνθρώπου τὸ "τί" εἶναι, τὸ δ' ἀποτελεσθὲν ἐν σώματος φύσει εἴδωλον ὂν τοῦ λόγου ποιόν τι μᾶλλον εἶναι. Οἷον εἰ ἀνθρώπου ὄντος τοῦ Σωκράτους τοῦ ὁρωμένου ἡ εἰκὼν αὐτοῦ ἡ ἐν γραφῇ χρώματα καὶ φάρμακα ὄντα Σωκράτης λέγοιτο· οὕτως οὖν καὶ λόγου ὄντος, καθ' ὃν Σωκράτης, τὸν αἰσθητὸν Σωκράτη <λέγομεν Σωκράτη>· ἀλλὰ χρώματα καὶ σχήματα ἐκείνων τῶν ἐν τῷ λόγῳ μιμήματα εἶναι· καὶ τὸν λόγον δὲ τοῦτον πρὸς τὸν ἀληθέστατον ἤδη λόγον τὸν ἀνθρώπου τὸ αὐτὸ πεπονθότα εἶναι.

29. Indeed, talk of a predicative use of 'is,' that is, a semantic use, does not even begin to address the ontological issue. The idea that identity is only formal identity, as in "Socrates is Socrates," does not contribute to the understanding of the ontological commitment in affirming "Socrates is a man" or "Socrates is pale."

as we have seen, the One is uniquely autoexplicable. Plato does claim that it is owing to the "presence" (παρουσία) of the Form or owing to "association" (κοινωνία) with it that things bear the Form's name.[30] But this presence cannot be the identity both of the Form and that which is 'in' the sensible. For one thing, just as with an Aristotelian essence, if it were uniquely present in one thing it could not be present in another. But for present purposes, more important is the fact that the nonidentity of Form and instance requires the inferiority of the latter, the inferiority of image to paradigm that in *Republic* is described as the 'being and nonbeing' of the former in relation to the 'being' of the latter. So Plotinus reasons that if the essence of something is a Form, then the essence—which is in any case not identical with its instance—must be separate from the thing whose essence it is. The way to describe this is to say that, for example, Socrates participates in Humanity; he is in no way identical with it.

> Then, why will Literacy have less [substantiality] in relation to a particular case of literacy or Knowledge in relation to a particular bit of knowledge? For Literacy is not posterior to the particular literacy, but rather it is because Literacy exists that that which is in you exists; since that which is in you is particular by being in you, but in itself is identical with that which is universal. And Socrates did not give being human to the nonhuman but Humanity gave being human to Socrates; the particular human is so by participation in Humanity. Since what could Socrates be except "a man of a particular kind" and what could the "of a particular kind" do toward being more of a substance? But if it is because "Humanity is only a Form" whereas Socrates is "form in matter," then Socrates is less man than is the Form. For the account in matter is inferior. If, though, the man is not the Form itself, but the form in matter, why will the Form have less [substantiality] than the form in matter, given that it is itself the account of something that is in a certain matter?[31]

The ontological or substantial priority of a Form to an instance of it is evident in this passage. As Aristotle himself points out, this is a sort of priority introduced by Plato.[32] And, as Aristotle argues in his own account of substantiality,

---

30. *Phd.* 100D5-6.
31. VI 3, 9.23-36: Ἔπειτα τί ἔλαττον ἔχει ἡ γραμματικὴ πρὸς τινὰ γραμματικὴν καὶ ὅλως ἐπιστήμη πρὸς τινὰ ἐπιστήμην; Οὐ γὰρ ἡ γραμματικὴ ὕστερον τῆς τινος γραμματικῆς, ἀλλὰ μᾶλλον οὔσης γραμματικῆς καὶ ἡ ἐν σοί· ἐπεὶ καὶ ἡ ἐν σοί τίς ἐστι τῷ ἐν σοί, αὐτὴ δὲ ταὐτὸν τῇ καθόλου. Καὶ ὁ Σωκράτης οὐκ αὐτὸς ἔδωκε τῷ μὴ ἀνθρώπῳ τὸ εἶναι ἀνθρώπῳ, ἀλλ' ὁ ἄνθρωπος τῷ Σωκράτει· μεταλήψει γὰρ ἀνθρώπου ὁ τὶς ἄνθρωπος. Ἔπειτα ὁ Σωκράτης τί ἂν εἴη ἢ ἄνθρωπος τοιόσδε, τὸ δὲ "τοιόσδε" τί ἂν ἐργάζοιτο πρὸς τὸ μᾶλλον οὐσίαν εἶναι; Εἰ δ' ὅτι τὸ μὲν "εἶδος μόνον ὁ ἄνθρωπος", τὸ δὲ "εἶδος ἐν ὕλῃ", ἧττον ἄνθρωπος κατὰ τοῦτο ἂν εἴη· ἐν ὕλῃ γὰρ ὁ λόγος χείρων. Εἰ δὲ καὶ ὁ ἄνθρωπος οὐ καθ' αὐτὸ εἶδος, ἀλλ' ἐν ὕλῃ, τί ἔλαττον ἕξει τοῦ ἐν ὕλῃ, καὶ αὐτὸς λόγος τοῦ ἔν τινι ὕλῃ;
32. See *Meta.* Δ 5, 11.1019a1-4.

actuality is prior in substance to potentiality in the more dominant sense; for eternal things are prior in substance to destructible things, but nothing that exists potentially is eternal.[33]

Now, it might be argued that in accepting the general principle of the ontological priority of the actual to the potential or the eternal to the destructible, Aristotle is not in any way committed to the ontological priority of, say, a Form of Humanity to the individual man. Still, his commitment to UP—in particular, to antinominalism—leaves open the question of how humanity as such is related ontologically to the humanity of Socrates.[34]

In the second book of his *Metaphysics*, Aristotle addresses this question in a manner remarkably similar to the above passage from Plotinus.[35] Let us focus first on what I have elsewhere called 'graded synonymy' in both passages.[36] Plotinus says that "that which is in you is particular by being in you, but in itself is identical with that which is universal." He then adds that Humanity is the cause of humanity in Socrates and that the latter is therefore less of a man than is Humanity. Aristotle says that the eternal fire (in the Sun) is the hottest among hot things, including the things that are caused to be hot by the Sun's fire. Such causes are 'truest' because (a) they are not true at one time and not at another; and (b) nothing is the cause of their being; rather, they are the cause of the being of other things. It is perhaps possible to interpret (a) as making a semantic point, namely, that propositions about eternal beings are always true and so, in a sense, more true than propositions about contingent states of affairs. But this is not the case for (b), which claims that the cause (if it is itself without a cause) is truer than that which is caused and has the 'same predicate' as the cause.

So Plotinus claims that the Form of Humanity is 'superior' to the humanity in Socrates, and Aristotle claims that the hotness in the Sun is superior to the hotness in other hot things. But Aristotle also claims that it is absurd to separate Humanity from Socrates' humanity because in that case the Form would be more of a man than is Socrates. The comparison seems tendentious because there are two different types of causality here exposed: the Sun is the efficient cause of the hotness in other things whereas the Form of Humanity is supposed to be the paradigmatic cause of Socrates' humanity. When Aristotle makes his claim about the Sun and its hotness, he need not thereby withdraw his claim about the separation of the Form of Humanity on pain of self-contradiction. It is, of course, true that the Sun is a cause different from the manner in which the Form of Humanity is supposed to be a cause. But it is not the case that Aristotle has thereby ignored paradigmatic causality. It is the hotness of the Sun that is hot in the highest degree *because*

---

33. *Meta.* Θ 8, 1050b6–8: ἀλλὰ μὴν καὶ κυριωτέρως· τὰ μὲν γὰρ ἀΐδια πρότερα τῇ οὐσίᾳ τῶν φθαρτῶν, ἔστι δ' οὐθὲν δυνάμει ἀΐδιον. Cf. M 2, 1077b1–9.

34. Cf. Code 1985, 102, "A particular like Socrates is not, according to the hylomorphic analysis of *Metaphysics Z*, a primary substance, and he is not identical with his essence."

35. *Meta.* α 2, 1.993b23–31. See above, 105–6, for the full text.

36. See Gerson 2005, 180–83.

the Sun is the cause of the hotness in other things. That is, paradigmatic causality results from efficient causality, but only when the efficient cause is the first in a causal line. The Sun is hottest because there is no cause of its hotness. Plotinus, of course, thinks that the Platonist is committed to holding that paradigmatic causality results from efficient causality in the identical manner. The crucial difference, as we have already seen, is that Plotinus wants to separate the ultimate efficient cause of the being of everything from the paradigmatic cause that is Intellect and the Forms. By contrast, Aristotle makes no such separation.

We may set aside the obvious fact that Aristotle's Unmoved Mover is a final cause just as is the One qua Good. The pertinent question here is whether it is also an efficient cause in some sense and a paradigmatic cause.[37] I doubt that it makes any sense to maintain that it is one and not the other. I mean that if it is an efficient cause without being a paradigmatic cause, then the obscurity of its supposed efficient causal activity is obvious; if it is a paradigmatic cause without being an efficient cause, then it is perhaps even more obscure how the science of being qua being is supposed to depend on the universality of the first, that is, on the being that the Unmoved Mover is deriving to the being of all other things. My intention is not here to settle the question of the causality of the Unmoved Mover beyond final causality. Rather, I wish to suggest that this *is* a question that Aristotle cannot avoid given his manifest commitment to producing a coherent positive structure on the basis of UP. And I take the identification of the primary referent of the science of being as pure immaterial actuality and the derivative nature of all other types of being as testifying to that commitment. This is exactly why an account of Aristotle's antinominalism aimed at making unproblematic the 'graded synonymy' of paradigmatic causality is superficial.

Aristotle concedes that there are cases in which something and its essence are identical, for example, curvature and the essence of curvature.[38] He adds, however, that

---

37. See Berti 1983 and 2003. The later article has a useful survey of literature on the causality of the Unmoved Mover. Berti concludes that the causality of the Unmoved Mover is solely efficient causality; it is only *similar* to a final cause in the sense that it is unmoved. Berti adds (2003, 297) that it was the Platonists, not Aristotle or the Peripatetics, who took the desire for the Unmoved Mover to be equivalent to an imitation of it. But this seems to be in conflict with *Meta*. H 8, 1050b28–29: μιμεῖται δὲ τὰ ἄφθαρτα καὶ τὰ ἐν μεταβολῇ ὄντα, οἷον γῆ καὶ πῦρ (indestructible things are imitated by changing things such as earth and fire). It seems reasonable to suppose that the Platonic interpretation of the Unmoved Mover as an object of imitation is based on the assumption that Aristotle was—incorrectly—taking the Unmoved Mover to be the first principle of all. It is, after all, the good of all things. Cf. Berti 2009 and 2010, 371–82, who further questions the final causality of the Unmoved Mover, arguing that it is an end only for itself. Platonists take the legitimate tendency to see the Unmoved Mover as an efficient cause as arising from its postulated role as supplanting the One, Intellect, and the Forms.

38. See *Meta*. Z 11, 1037a33–b2. Jaeger brackets the words καμπυλότης καὶ καμπυλότητι εἶναι, (curvature and the essence of curvature) as a gloss drawn from *Cat*. 3b11ff. But see the examples at Z 6, 1031a31–b9.

things that exist as matter or that include matter are not identical with their essence, nor are they one accidentally, such as is Socrates and his musicality; for these are identical accidentally.[39]

So Socrates is not identical with humanity, the essence of Socrates. Presumably, though, if we were to then separate the essence of Socrates as Plotinus believes Platonists must do, we will be led to an absurd conclusion. If, then, Socrates and the essence of Socrates are not identical but they are not separate, how are they related? Not, presumably, merely accidentally, in the way that Socrates and his musicality are. One might propose that Socrates is an actualization of humanity, but this would seem to make his humanity in potency to him. In any case, a form cannot be in potency to anything because form just is actuality.[40] As an antinominalist, Aristotle also cannot say that humanity is posterior to the man Socrates, as if it were a *post rem* universal. So the question remains as to whether there is an antinominalist account of Socrates' humanity that does not result in the separation of a Form of Humanity from Socrates.

Plotinus believes that the Platonic answer to this question is no. When he says, provocatively, that "Socrates is less man than is the Form," he is not, I think, suggesting that the Form of Humanity is a particular man with all that that would entail. Socrates is less man because his humanity is inseparable from matter. The λόγος of Socrates' humanity must include all that is particular, that is, all that is unique to him; the λόγος of Humanity is different. Stated otherwise, the reality of Socrates is distinct from the Form of Humanity. And because that reality includes his matter, it is less than the reality of that which is unqualifiedly immaterial or intelligible.[41]

There is another important consideration in Plotinus' systematic defense and reconstruction of the Platonic position in response to Aristotle's criticisms. Aristotle says that the question what is being is just the question what is substance (οὐσία).[42] Aristotle's answer to this question is that being or substance is a πρὸς ἕν equivocal the primary referent of which is the Unmoved Mover. Plotinus accepts the conclusion that the being of everything that is not primary is derived from the primary. But, following Plato, he

---

39. *Meta.* Z 11, 1037b4–7: ὅσα δὲ ὡς ὕλη ἢ ὡς συνειλημμένα τῇ ὕλῃ, οὐ ταὐτό, οὐδ' <εἰ> κατὰ συμβεβηκὸς ἕν, οἷον Σωκράτης καὶ τὸ μουσικόν· ταῦτα γὰρ ταὐτὰ κατὰ συμβεβηκός. Cf. H 2, 1043b2–3. Ross and Jaeger add <εἰ> between οὐδ' and κατά, which seems unnecessary.

40. Aristotle does not in fact say explicitly that form and actuality are identical. Nevertheless, he says, for example, that soul is the first actuality of a body and that soul is the form of a body. That there are second actualities of a living thing does not mean that the form alone is in potency to these, but that the composite, owing to its matter, has a potency for further actualization. Cf. *Meta.* H 6, 1045a31–33, where it is the essence of a sphere that causes it to be actually a sphere. Also, Θ 6, where actuality and form seem to be used synonymously.

41. For Plotinus, strictly speaking, matter does not 'infect' the forms of sensibles. It is not matter as such that makes Socrates less man than the Form, but his particular qualified body, which, of course, requires matter as a condition for its existence.

42. See *Meta.* Z 1, 1028b2–4.

denies that the primary is substance. The One or Good is above substance, and all beings have their being owing to the One. So the separation of Forms entails the priority of intelligible substance to sensible substance—as it does for Aristotle—but it does not entail that the being of all things is derived ultimately from such intelligible substance. What this means is that the primary cause of the being of sensibles is not separated from those things, though the intelligible substance in which sensibles participate is. As we saw in the last chapter, this is clear in the case of matter that has a kind of being but no intelligibility whatsoever. The One outstrips the 'reach' of intelligible substance only in this case. Because Plotinus denies the identity of being and substance, he does not think that the Platonist has to embrace the absurdity of claiming that because the paradigm of Humanity must be separate from the humanity of its participants, Socrates is bereft of his being.

Plotinus's alternative to the Aristotelian account of sensible substance is to say that it is a conglomeration (συμφόρησις) of qualities (ποιοτητῶν) and matter.[43] Plotinus is not, as some suppose, describing the receptacle prior to the imposition of order by the Demiurge, but rather the nature of sensibles in the fully informed cosmos. The fundamental point is that no essence or Form identifies a sensible individual, that is, no sensible individual is unqualifiedly a self-identical 'this something.' As Plato says in *Philebus*, everything that exists now is composed of an indeterminate and a determinate principle.[44] The latter is, as we saw in the passage above, an 'imitation' of a Form or Forms; the former is the matter, a condition of instantiation. Insofar as the putative substance has matter, it does not have a determinate identity, which is what it would need to be a 'this something.' All of the essentiality of the sensible is owing to participation, not to its own necessarily indeterminate identity.

Why could we not say, then, that Socrates' essence is to be an imitation of Humanity? He would then be, so to speak, a perfectly imperfect human, in contrast to the paradigm. Such an essence would have more in common with John Locke's 'nominal essences' than with anything that Aristotle would accept.[45] A nominal essence, according to Locke is the "abstract idea to which a name is annexed." So, in Locke's famous example, 'gold' is the name for that which is of a certain color, weight, malleability, etc. For Locke, the 'real essence' is "the constitution of the insensible parts of that body, on which those qualities and all other properties of gold depend." For Plotinus, the

---

43. See VI 3, 8.20. Cf. VI 3, 15.24–38; II 7, 3.4–5. Cf. II 6, 1.48–49: οὐδὲν γὰρ αὐτῶν οὐσίαν εἶναι, ἀλλ' αὐτῆς πάθη (for none of them [sensibles] is substance; rather, they are affections of substance). The second half of this sentence sounds like it contradicts the first. In fact, what Plotinus means is that the 'affections' constitute what is only called substance by 'homonymy' (ὁμωνύμως). Cf. VI 3, 2.1–4.

44. See *Phil.* 16C–17A, which seems more relevant to Plotinus's understanding of the sensible world than *Tim.* 49D–E, where the indeterminacy of the elements is precosmic.

45. See John Locke, *Essay on Human Understanding*, 3.6.2.

'real essence' must be separate because it is the paradigmatic cause of the 'conglomerate' that consists of the 'nominal essence.' Any attempt to construct the real essence out of the nominal essence is bound to fail because the latter is inseparable from matter.[46]

Essentialism regarding sensible substances, as Aristotle well knew, was a condition for the possibility of the sciences of things that exist in nature.[47] Plotinus accepts this implication, following Plato's claim in *Republic* that there is only science (ἐπιστήμη) of intelligibles and his claim in *Timaeus* that physical theory concerns what comes to be and is perceptible.[48] The rejection of Aristotelian essentialism in thus taken by Plotinus to follow from the basic ontological hierarchy of Platonism. If the essence of Socrates were not separate from Socrates, then the priority of paradigm to image could not serve to explain the being of anything. Dialectic would not be an ontological method, but merely a logical one.[49]

Plotinus's defense of Plato against Aristotle's attack based on his own version of essentialism assumes that Platonism is a *system* and that this system has the resources to counter that attack. Equally worthy of emphasis, I believe, is that Plotinus also assumes that Aristotle shares the general principles underlying that system. Aristotle, however, though committed to UP, misconceived some of the exigencies of the correct positive construct. This led him to some faulty conclusions, among which was essentialism about the natural world.

Categories in the Intelligible World

Plotinus's rejection of Aristotelian essentialism entails the denial of the cogency of the distinction between essence and accident attributes. So Aristotle's categorical schema, based on the fundamental distinction between that which is 'said of' individual substances (essentially) and that which is

---

46. See VI 2, 22.11–13: Ὅλως δὲ οὐκ ἔστι τὸ ἓν ἀριθμῷ λαβεῖν καὶ ἄτομον· ὅ τι γὰρ ἂν λάβῃς, εἶδος· ἄνευ γὰρ ὕλης. (In general, it is not possible to grasp that which is numerically one, and an individual for that which you would be grasping would be form, and that is without matter.)

47. See *Meta.* Z 6, 1031b6–7: ἐπιστήμη τε γὰρ ἑκάστου ἔστιν ὅταν τὸ τί ἦν ἐκείνῳ εἶναι γνῶμεν (for there is science of each thing when we know its essence).

48. *Rep.* 511B3–C2 and *Tim.* 28B4–C1, 29C3. See I 3, 6.1–5, where Plotinus describes the theorizing about nature as dependent on dialectic, that is, a Platonic science of Forms, though distinct from it. The 'science' of nature 'borrows' (κομίζεται) from dialectic and is closer to it than are the crafts to arithmetic. Cf. *Rep.* 522C1–6. If by means of dialectic we could know the Form of a type of animal, we could then, presumably, have true beliefs regarding the collocation of the qualities of instances of that animal type here below. But cf. *Phil.* 62B5ff., where a list of ἐπιστῆμαί seems to include τέχναί. I believe that the use of ἐπιστήμη in the plural indicates areas of human inquiry in which ἐπιστήμη is possible, not that a τέχνη is itself ἐπιστήμη.

49. See I 3, 4, where, referring explicitly to dialectic in Plato, he says that it is dialectic that "distinguishes the Forms, and the essence of each thing [τὸ τί ἐστι]" (13), leaving the so-called logical business (λογικὴν πραγματείαν) of propositions and syllogisms to another art (18–20).

'present in' individual substances (accidentally) is undermined. Plotinus, however, does not deny a categorical schema for the intelligible world. There are here, of course, no accidental attributes. There are, though, as Plotinus reads Plato's *Sophist*, "greatest kinds" (μέγιστα γένη) among the Forms that serve as the fundamental categories of real οὐσία.⁵⁰ The kinds are Motion (κίνησις), Rest (στάσις), Being (ὄν), Identity (ταὐτόν), and Difference (θάτερον). The deduction of the five greatest kinds in *Sophist* is on behalf of the search for the reality of the sort of nonbeing that is the sophist's stock-in-trade. It turns out that difference is another name for that type of nonbeing. Hence, the sophist's products, false propositions and beliefs, although being different from truth, have some reality after all because they are instances of one of the greatest kinds.

Since, as we have seen, Plotinus identifies his Intellect with the Demiurge and argues that it is cognitively identical with all the Forms, the greatest kinds must be fundamental categories both of intellection and of the intelligible nature. This is not particularly difficult to show, at least in a fairly superficial manner. For in *Timaeus* the Demiurge constructs the World Soul out of two types of identity and difference and being (οὐσία), namely, the indivisible and divisible types.⁵¹ The indivisible types are evidently that which belong in some manner to the Demiurge himself; the divisible type belonging to the realm of becoming. And as for motion and rest, we learn from an earlier passage in *Sophist* that there can be no intellection without them.⁵²

Plotinus takes the five greatest kinds as the fundamental properties of Intellect.⁵³ More precisely, they are the fundamental properties of Intellect and the Forms with which Intellect is cognitively identical.⁵⁴ How accurately is Plotinus representing Plato's intentions in his deductions of the greatest kinds? We have already seen Plotinus's justification for taking the Demiurge or Intellect and the Forms to be a 'one-many,' the initial 'product' of the One or Good. The distinction between Intellect and Forms

---

50. See *Soph.* 254B7ff.
51. See *Tim.* 35A1–6.
52. See *Soph.* 249B5–10. According to Plotinus, the correct interpretation of the conclusion of the passage, 249C10–D4, is that the words τὸ ὄν τὸ καὶ τὸ πᾶν consists of ὅσα ἀκίνητα καὶ κεκινημένα means that primary being, τὸ παντελῶς ὄν, includes such things that are both in motion and at rest. That is, the Forms and Intellect itself are in motion insofar as they are identical with the activity (ἐνέργεια) of Intellect, but are at rest insofar as they do not change. Other interpretations of this passage tend to ignore the fact that this passage is supposed to correct both the Friends of the Forms and their Eleatic allies and the proponents of Heracliteanism. See Gerson 2006 for more evidence in support of Plotinus's interpretation.
53. See VI 2, 7.1–24; VI 2, 8; III 7, 3.7–11. See Hadot 1960, 111, "Les genres de l'être du *Sophiste* (254–5): être, movement, repos, identité, et altérité, apparaissent comme les different aspects sous lesquels notre intelligence morcelante saisit la vue unique de l'intelligence. Mais c'est bien parce que la réalité intelligible est doué de vie et de pensée que cette multiplicité de points de vue est possible."
54. See VI 2, 8.14; VI 2, 19.20; VI 2, 21.39–40; VI 7, 36.12; VI 7, 39.5; VI 8, 9.30–31.

must be real, not merely conceptual.[55] This follows from the unique simplicity of the One. The distinction is, according to Plotinus's reading of the second hypothesis of the second part of *Parmenides,* a distinction between Intellect and its οὐσία.[56] Following Plato, this means that Intellect and its οὐσία are not unqualifiedly identical. They must somehow be different. Plotinus's reason for taking motion at this level of generality is that the cognitive identification of Intellect and Forms is an activity, the activity of thinking. Plotinus simply assumes that the Aristotelian term ἐνέργεια as applied above all to the Unmoved Mover is synonymous with Plato's term κίνησις νοῦ.[57] But this is the sort of motion that, like Aristotle's ἐνέργεια νοῦ, is completely stable. That is, there is no alteration or imperfection in it. So, given the legitimacy of the systematizing task Plotinus has set before himself, it does not seem unreasonable for him to understand the greatest kinds in this way.[58]

One of the reasons for resisting this interpretation is that it seems absurd to foist on Plato the idea of Being as a genus and the seemingly contradictory companion claim that Motion and Rest are not species of this genus.

> Now, there are many species of Being, and there is a genus of Being. But Motion is not classed under Being nor over Being, but is alongside Being. It is found in Being but not as inhering in a subject. For it is an activity of Being and neither is without the other except in our conception of them. And the two natures are one. For Being is in actuality not in potency.[59]

It is perhaps inadequate, though true, to insist that Motion and Rest could not be greatest kinds if they were species of Being. And it is also true that the greatest kind Being could not be equivalent to 'thatness' as opposed to 'whatness,' either for Plato or for Plotinus. For the One or Good is 'above' οὐσία. Indeed, it is also 'above' τὸ εἶναι, but only in the sense of the εἶναι that follows from partaking in οὐσία. Only the Good or the One has an

---

55. See II 9, 1.40–41, where Plotinus criticizes his opponents who say that the distinction between the thinking of Intellect and Intellect's thinking that it is thinking is merely "conceptual" (ἐπινοίᾳ). If they were right, then a multiplicity of intelligibles would be impossible, that is, there would be no real distinctions within the intelligible realm. The distinction among intelligibles *within* Intellect is a distinction within that which is, nevertheless, one being (ἓν ὄν). Because Forms are really distinct, Intellect, being identical with each, is really distinct from that which thinks the array of intelligibles. And because Intellect is not primary in the order of being, it is not—indeed, cannot be—absolutely simple.

56. See *Parm.* 142B5–6.

57. See VI 2, 7.6 for κίνησις as πρωτὴ ζωή, a gloss on Aristotle's description of the ἐνέργεια νοῦ of the Unmoved Mover as ζωή, indeed the best life. See *Meta.* Λ 7, 1072b26–28.

58. But see Brisson 1997 and Santa Cruz 1997, who think Plotinus has significantly falsified Plato's meaning.

59. VI 2, 7.16–20: Ὄντος μὲν δὴ εἴδη πολλὰ καὶ γένος· κίνησις δὲ οὔτε ὑπὸ τὸ ὂν τακτέα οὔτ' ἐπὶ τῷ ὄντι, ἀλλὰ μετὰ τοῦ ὄντος, εὑρεθεῖσα ἐν αὐτῷ οὐχ ὡς ἐν ὑποκειμένῳ· ἐνέργεια γὰρ αὐτοῦ καὶ οὐδέτερον ἄνευ τοῦ ἑτέρου ἢ ἐπινοίᾳ, καὶ αἱ δύο φύσεις μία· καὶ γὰρ ἐνεργείᾳ τὸ ὄν, οὐ δυνάμει.

οὐσία that is absolutely identical with its εἶναι, which is to say that it does not *have* an οὐσία at all.

The key to Plotinus's understanding of the matter is the claim that Motion and Being are not without the other except in our conception of them. We can conceive of something having being without being in motion, even the motion of intellect. We can even conceive of something in motion, that is, matter, that is, in a way, bereft of being. What the intelligible realm is supposed to do, according to Plotinus's understanding of Platonism, is explain, among other things, the diminished intelligibility of things of which we have conceptions. What, for example, is the nature of the being without motion? In our conceptions, we can distinguish the activity of Intellect from the array of essences with which it is actually cognitively identical.[60] And so we can conceive of the images of intelligibility here below without conceiving of them as thinking, though if Intellect were not eternally thinking them, they would not be distinguishable, even in thought.[61]

In *Sophist*, we learn that the kinds Motion and Rest are contrary, that Being 'blends' with each of these, but they do not blend with each other.[62] Plotinus acknowledges these distinctions.[63] But the question that Plotinus asks, and those who believe that Plotinus is deviating from Plato neglect to ask, is what is the ontological claim being made when one says that two of the kinds (Motion and Rest) are unmixed with each other (ἀμείκτω πρὸς ἀλλήλω)? The claim is not that the two kinds are distinct; this is also true for Being, which is distinct from Motion and Rest, but nevertheless blends with each. It is certainly true that from the absence of blending we can deduce that if something is at rest, then in the respect that it is at rest, it is not in motion, and vice versa. But this is only to avoid the question, since this follows *because* of the absence of blending of the kinds; it does not constitute that absence of blending. If this were not so, then the entire point of separating Forms in order for them to be explanatory entities would be lost.

---

60. On the holism of Intellect, see Emilsson (2007, 199–207).

61. See Silverman (2002, 294), "They are the greatest kinds also because they are required for metaphysical (and all other types of) inquiry and because they allow the postulated Forms and particulars to play the sorts of roles required of them by Plato's special metaphysical theory. They are formal conditions on Formhood and, therefore, derivatively apply to particulars, souls, and everything else in a fashion appropriate to each."

62. See *Soph.* 252D6–10, 254D4–10. At 256B6 the Eleatic Stranger says that there is nothing outrageous if in fact Motion did partake of Rest in some way and therefore was stable. Heindorf, followed by Cornford (1934, 286–87, n. 3), conjectured a lacuna after this claim, though the reply by Theaetetus is "absolutely correct, so long as we agree that some kinds blend and some do not." Heindorf filled the lacuna with words to the effect that Motion does not partake of Rest at all, though it does partake of Identity and Difference. Thus, according to Heindorf, Theaetetus's reply does not confirm that Motion does partake of Rest in some way. But this elaborate reversal of the text as received is not necessary on Plotinus's interpretation. The most recent OCT edition of the text (2003) rejects the conjectured lacuna.

63. See VI 2, 7.31–32; VI 2, 8.43–49.

The way Plotinus answers this question, and so the way he interprets Plato, is to focus on the claim that Intellect is a "one-many" (ἓν πολλά).⁶⁴ This term of art, like Aristotle's "what it was to be" (τὸ τι ἦν εἶναι), is used to make a very specific claim, namely, that Intellect could not be the first principle of all. And yet Intellect is the locus of being. The oneness of Intellect is the oneness of a multiplicity. So being is necessarily and irreducibly complex.⁶⁵ This makes sense only if the first principle of all is, as Plato says, above being. The multiplicity is manifested among the objects of Intellect's thinking and in the duality of Intellect and these objects.⁶⁶ As object of thinking, Being, which we may understand here as essence, is a genus, the genus of all that which is intelligible. The duality entails difference; the oneness entails identity. The activity of Intellect is its intellectual motion. Rest is the one-many as the static array of Forms. So it can be true that Motion and Rest do not 'mix'; otherwise, there would not be a multiplicity in Intellect. And it can be true that Being mixes with each, because the Being that Intellect is is the Being of the one-many.

Some scholars have underestimated the difficulty of making sense of Plato's greatest kinds in any other way.⁶⁷ To make of Being a distinct kind and not to identify it as essence as opposed to existence is to court serious confusion. For in concluding the deduction of the five kinds, the Eleatic Stranger says that

> each one is different from the rest, not by virtue of its own nature, but because it partakes of the Idea of Difference.⁶⁸

From this it follows that Being is different from the other kinds not by virtue of its own nature, but by virtue of its partaking of Difference. To make any sense of this, we have to make a distinction between the subject that partakes ('nature of Being'), which by itself does not make Being different from the other kinds, and the difference Being has from the other kinds

---

64. See V 3, 13.9–11; V 3, 15.22; VI 2, 15.11–13.
65. See V 3, 13.25: τὸ γὰρ ὂν πολύ ἐστιν.
66. See, e.g., III 8, 9.5: καὶ οὗτος νοῦς καὶ νοητὸν ἅμα, ὥστε δύο ἅμα (and this is Intellect and intelligible at the same time, so that it is at the same time two); VI 9, 2.36–37: Καὶ εἰ μὲν αὐτὸς τὸ νοοῦν καὶ τὸ νοούμενον, διπλοῦς ἔσται καὶ οὐχ ἁπλοῦς οὐδὲ τὸ ἕν. (And if Intellect is itself that which thinks and that which is thought, it will be double and not simple, and so not one.) Both of these passages are aimed at Aristotle, *Meta.* Λ 9, 1074b15–1075a12. See O'Meara 1993, 49–53. Nyvlt (2012, 127–28, n. 82; 215–26) argues that Plotinus is wrong to insist on the complexity of Intellect as Aristotle understands it for the complexity is only "formal," by which I take it Nyvlt means "conceptual." Of course, conceptual distinctions can be made for the One, that which is absolutely simple, e.g., that it is the ultimate explanation for A and also for B. But the complexity within Intellect or the Unmoved Mover is internal, not external owing to things that are differently related to the One.
67. See Griswold 1977, who thinks that the account is so internally inconsistent that it could not even be Plato's.
68. *Soph.* 255E4–6: ἓν ἕκαστον γὰρ ἕτερον εἶναι τῶν ἄλλων οὐ διὰ τὴν αὑτοῦ φύσιν, ἀλλὰ διὰ τὸ μετέχειν τῆς ἰδέας τῆς θατέρου.

by virtue of its partaking of the Idea of Difference. So Being has difference 'over and above' its own nature, making it complex in some sense. It cannot be irreducibly simple, which it would be if 'Being' just indicated 'existence.'

An analogous problem arises for the kind Difference. For Difference is, too, different from the other kinds not by virtue of its own nature, but by virtue of its partaking of the Idea of Difference.[69] So what should we suppose that the nature of difference is other than the Form of Difference? Plotinus supposes that the subject is Intellect.[70] It is different from the Forms, its intelligible objects, by virtue of its partaking in Difference. The nature of Difference ("its own nature"), that which partakes, is identical with Intellect. This goes, too, for the other greatest kinds; Intellect is the one subject characterized by the Ideas of the five greatest kinds.

The gulf that separates Plotinus's interpretation of the five greatest kinds from those of modern scholars is owing to Plotinus's insistence on situating the interpretation of any passage in the dialogues dealing with Forms within the general system of principles. In particular, for him it is not possible to understand what Plato says about Being, Identity and Difference, Motion and Rest without considering the Intellect or Demiurge who is cognitively identical with all that is intelligible and without considering the One or Idea of the Good, which is the true first principle of all, which is 'beyond being' yet provides existence and being to all the Forms.[71] Those who in my view have unjustly dismissed or ignored Plotinus's interpretation flounder in their own interpretations precisely because they refuse to acknowledge

---

69. At *Soph.* 255D9–E1, the nature of Difference is said to be a Form (εἶδος), like the others. Vlastos (1973, 340, n. 13) refuses to accept that the account of how each kind is different from each other applies to Difference.

70. See V 3, 15.37–40: Εἴρηται μὲν οὖν, ὅτι, εἴ τι ἐκ τοῦ ἑνός, ἄλλο δεῖ παρ' αὐτό· ἄλλο δὲ ὂν οὐχ ἕν· τοῦτο γὰρ ἦν ἐκεῖνο. Εἰ δὲ μὴ ἕν, δύο δέ, ἀνάγκη ἤδη καὶ πλῆθος εἶναι· καὶ γὰρ ἕτερον καὶ ταὐτὸν ἤδη καὶ ποιὸν καὶ τὰ ἄλλα. (It has been said that if something comes from the One, it must be other than it; being other than it, it is not one. Otherwise, it would be that. But if it is not one, but two, it is necessarily already many. For it is already different and identical and qualified and the rest.) Aristotle, *Meta.* A 6, 987b33, says that the nature of difference is for Plato the Indefinite Dyad. Cf. *Parm.* 158C5–6, 158D5–6. If Plotinus is following Aristotle's account, then the Indefinite Dyad is that which accounts for the difference between Intellect and intelligibles. There could not be anything other than the One unless that were complex in some way. Intellect is minimally complex and the Indefinite Dyad is a condition for this complexity. See the next section.

71. See Baltes 1997, 5–9, who provides the substantial evidence that the Idea of the Good is not 'beyond being' in the sense that it is nothing or nonexistent. Plotinus scrupulously aims to reflect his understanding of the Idea of the Good in making the One beyond being only in the sense that it does not have οὐσία and therefore does not have the being of a composite. I disagree with Baltes, however, when he concludes (8) that the Idea of the Good "does not transcend the realm of being, but …it still belongs to it." The transcendence of a first principle is axiomatic. See Abbate 2003, 628–39, who shows that Plotinus speaks of the One both as ἐπέκεινα τῆς οὐσίας and as ἐπέκεινα τοῦ ὄντος (or ἐπέκεινα ὄντος) indifferently, even though when discussing, in particular, the being of Intellect, and following Plato, he does distinguish between εἶναι and οὐσία in it.

a systematic framework for them. This seems indefensible given that the systematic framework is both sketched in various dialogues and confirmed by the testimony of Aristotle and the indirect tradition.

The One and the Indefinite Dyad

As we saw in the chapter on Aristotle's testimony and in the chapter on the Old Academy, there was substantial agreement that Plato identified the Idea of Good with the One and that he posited a second principle, the Indefinite Dyad, on which the One worked to produce Forms and Numbers. And though we found speculation on the relation between Forms and Numbers, including their identity, we found nothing like a comprehensive and self-consistent interpretation of the supposed connection between the first principles and the Demiurge. Omitting the Demiurge is perhaps one reason for the unclarity in regard to Forms and Numbers. In contrast to the tentative remarks found among the Platonists in the Old and Middle Academies, Plotinus has a fairly straightforward account of how Intellect is related to the One and *therefore* of the ontological status of the Forms.

Here is the core of that account:

> If, then, Intellect itself were that which is generating, that which is generated must be inferior to Intellect, though as close as possible to Intellect and the same as it. But since that which generates is above Intellect, that which is generated is necessarily Intellect. Why is it not Intellect, the actuality of which is thinking? But thinking sees the object of thinking and turns toward this and is in a way completed by this; it is itself indefinite like sight, and made definite by the object of thinking. For this reason, it is said that "from the Indefinite Dyad and from the One" come the Forms or Numbers.[72] For this is Intellect. For this reason, Intellect is not simple, but multiple, revealing itself as a composition, although an intelligible one, and consequently seeing many things. It is, then, itself intelligible, but also thinking. For this reason, it is already two. But it is also an intelligible other than the One owing to the fact that it comes after the One.[73]

In this passage, Plotinus identifies the Indefinite Dyad as Intellect considered in abstraction from the fullness of its being, that is, purely in relation

---

72. See Aristotle, *Meta*. A 6, 987b21–22 and M 7, 1081a13–15.

73. See V 4, 2.1–12: Εἰ μὲν οὖν αὐτὸ νοῦς ἦν τὸ γεννῶν, νοῦ ἐνδεέστερον, προσεχέστερον δὲ νῷ καὶ ὅμοιον δεῖ εἶναι· ἐπεὶ δὲ ἐπέκεινα νοῦ τὸ γεννῶν, νοῦν εἶναι ἀνάγκη. Διὰ τί δὲ οὐ νοῦς, οὗ ἐνέργειά ἐστι νόησις; Νόησις δὲ τὸ νοητὸν ὁρῶσα καὶ πρὸς τοῦτο ἐπιστραφεῖσα καὶ ἀπ' ἐκείνου οἷον ἀποτελουμένη καὶ τελειουμένη ἀόριστος μὲν αὐτὴ ὥσπερ ὄψις, ὁριζομένη δὲ ὑπὸ τοῦ νοητοῦ. Διὸ καὶ εἴρηται· ἐκ τῆς ἀορίστου δυάδος καὶ τοῦ ἑνὸς τὰ εἴδη καὶ οἱ ἀριθμοί· τοῦτο γὰρ ὁ νοῦς. Διὸ οὐχ ἁπλοῦς, ἀλλὰ πολλά, σύνθεσίν τε ἐμφαίνων, νοητὴν μέντοι, καὶ πολλὰ ὁρῶν ἤδη. Ἔστι μὲν οὖν καὶ αὐτὸς νοητός, ἀλλὰ καὶ νοῶν· διὸ δύο ἤδη. Ἔστι δὲ καὶ ἄλλο τῷ μετ' αὐτὸ νοητόν. Cf. V 1, 8.6–8: τοῦ αἰτίου δὲ νοῦ ὄντος πατέρα φησὶ τἀγαθὸν καὶ τὸ ἐπέκεινα νοῦ καὶ ἐπέκεινα οὐσίας (and since the Intellect is cause, he means by 'father' the Good, or that which is beyond Intellect and 'beyond substance'). Plotinus is referring to Plato, *Rep.* 509B.

to the One and not in its activity of thinking all that is intelligible. The 'object' of Intellect's thinking is the One. Since everything desires the One as the Good, and since Intellect's desire is entirely an intellectual desire, it desires to possess the Good in the only way possible, that is, by thinking it. Intellect, though, can only think the One, which is beyond being thought since it is beyond intelligibility, by thinking what the One is virtually, that is, all that which is intelligible, all the Forms.[74] So it is not exactly the case that Intellect creates the Forms by thinking them; rather, they 'already' exist in the One.[75] It creates distinct intelligible objects in its eternal (and successful) desire to be united with the Good in the only way it possibly can.

The most striking interpretative move made by Plotinus is that the Indefinite Dyad, as 'unformed' Intellect, is derived from the primary 'generator' of all. This is a decisive solution to what Konrad Gaiser called the central problem regarding Plato's doctrine of first principles, namely, whether the two principles are coordinate or is the second somehow derived from the first.[76] For Plotinus, the solution follows from the analysis of the exigencies of a first principle of all. Such a principle must be absolutely simple and,

---

74. See V 3, 11.1–8: Διὸ καὶ ὁ νοῦς οὗτος ὁ πολύς, ὅταν τὸ ἐπέκεινα ἐθέλῃ νοεῖ, ἓν μὲν οὖν αὐτὸ ἐκεῖνο, ἀλλ' ἐπιβάλλειν θέλων ὡς ἁπλῷ ἔξεισιν ἄλλο ἀεὶ λαμβάνων ἐν αὑτῷ πληθυνόμενον· ὥστε ὥρμησε μὲν ἐπ' αὐτὸ οὐχ ὡς νοῦς, ἀλλ' ὡς ὄψις οὔπω ἰδοῦσα, ἐξῆλθε δὲ ἔχουσα ὅπερ αὐτὴ ἐπλήθυνεν· ὥστε ἄλλου μὲν ἐπεθύμησεν ἀορίστως ἔχουσα ἐπ' αὐτῇ φάντασμά τι, ἐξῆλθε δὲ ἄλλο λαβοῦσα ἐν αὑτῇ αὐτὸ πολὺ ποιήσασα. (For this reason, this Intellect that is multiple, whenever it wishes to think that which is beyond it, then, thinks it as one, but wishing to attain it in its simplicity, ends up always grasping something else pluralized in itself. As a result, it impelled itself toward it not as Intellect, but as sight that is not yet seeing, and when it stopped, it had what it itself had pluralized, so that whereas it longed for something else having in an undefined way something like a sensory image, when it stopped it grasped something else in itself, making it multiple.) Cf. VI 7, 16.10–22.

75. See VI 7, 16.27–31: οὕτως καὶ ἡ τοῦ ἀγαθοῦ φύσις αἰτία οὐσίας καὶ νοῦ οὖσα καὶ φῶς κατὰ τὸ ἀνάλογον τοῖς ἐκεῖ ὁρατοῖς καὶ τῷ ὁρῶντι οὔτε τὰ ὄντα οὔτε νοῦς ἐστιν, ἀλλὰ αἴτιος τούτων καὶ νοεῖσθαι φωτὶ τῷ ἑαυτοῦ εἰς τὰ ὄντα καὶ εἰς τὸν νοῦν παρέχων (in this way, too, the nature of the Good, which is the cause of substance and of Intellect and light, according to our analogy, to the things in the intelligible world seen and to the seer, is neither the real beings nor Intellect, but is the cause of these and of thinking, providing by its own light thinking and being thought to the real beings and to Intellect).

76. See De Vogel 1954, 113, and Gaiser 1963, 12–13. Also, see Halfwassen 1997, 1, n. 1, for references to the considerable literature on the subject, including works of Gaiser and Krämer and others. The Plotinian solution is expressed in Krämer 1964a; 2nd ed., 1967, 332–34, and Halfwassen 2004, 218. It will be recalled that Eudorus has already tried to solve the problem by distinguishing a supreme One from the secondary coordinate principles of one and "the opposite nature" (τὴν ἐναντίαν φύσιν). See above, 216, n. 44. Eudorus, *ap.* Alexander of Aphrodisias, *In Meta.* 988a (= 58.25–59.8 Uesner), held that a reading of Aristotle's text that made the One and the Indefinite Dyad coprinciples was inferior to that which has the One alone as principle. Syrianus, *In Meta.* 165.33–166.14 Kroll, mentions a number of Pythagoreans, including Philolaus, "Archaenetus" (Archytas?), and Brotinus, who, while recognizing the principles of limit and unlimited, posited an absolutely first principle or "cause above a cause" (αἰτίαν πρὸ αἰτίας).

278 CHAPTER 10

hence, unique.⁷⁷ The derivation of the second principle from the first is not a deduction except in the sense that we can show that that which is first derived must be minimally complex. This minimal complexity, which Plotinus describes as a one-many, is also characterizable as an 'indefinite dyad.' It is, therefore, a principle of complexity that has, at the same time, a sort of unity, as, indeed, does everything derived from the One. In its own nature it is indefinite duality; when limited, it becomes a substantial Number, the Number Two, and so on.⁷⁸ This limitation is owing to the One, but only via the Forms that become distinct from Intellect itself.

Following Aristotle's account of the Platonic principles, Plotinus maintains that the Indefinite Dyad or the Great and the Small is a sort of matter, namely, intelligible matter apt for information by the One.⁷⁹ Plotinus's argument for the existence of intelligible matter is a stellar example of both his use of Aristotle for explicating Platonism and, more important, his seeing Platonism as a philosophy reflected in the dialogues not constructed out of them. Plotinus argues,

> If Forms are many, there is necessarily something common to them. And there is also something unique to each of them owing to which one differs from the other. That which is unique to each, the separating difference, is the proper shape of each. But if there is shape, there is that which is shaped, in which the difference occurs. Therefore, there is matter that is receptive of shape and is always the substrate.⁸⁰

Although nothing like intelligible matter occurs in the dialogues, Plotinus reasons that the Platonic system needs intelligible matter. In this he agrees with Aristotle, both regarding the first principles as in his testimony and in the general Aristotelian point that a shape or form requires a

---

77. As we saw in chapter 4, and as Halfwassen (1997, 5–12) shows, this exigency is recognized by Speusippus and ultimately is found in the first hypothesis of the second part of *Parmenides*.

78. See V 1, 5.7–9.

79. See Aristotle, *Meta*. A 6, 987b20–21: ὡς μὲν οὖν ὕλην τὸ μέγα καὶ τὸ μικρὸν εἶναι ἀρχάς, ὡς δ' οὐσίαν τὸ ἕν (as matter the Great and the Small are principles; as substance it is the One). In the following lines, 21ff., Aristotle contrasts Plato's doctrine with the Pythagoreans' on several points. This contrast throws light on the extremely important testimony of Sextus, *M*. 10.248–84, on the Pythagorean account of the principles of all things. For at least on the crucial issue of the Great and the Small or Indefinite Dyad, what Sextus says is a Pythagorean doctrine is exactly what Aristotle says is Platonic. Thus, Sextus appears to be using the term 'Pythagorean' in a sense that would allow the Platonic doctrine to be so designated. See Gaiser 2004, 240–62; Szlezák 2010b, on the passage from Sextus in relation to Plato and Aristotle's testimony.

80. II 4, 4.2–7: Εἰ οὖν πολλὰ τὰ εἴδη, κοινὸν μέν τι ἐν αὐτοῖς ἀνάγκη εἶναι· καὶ δὴ καὶ ἴδιον, ᾧ διαφέρει ἄλλο ἄλλου. Τοῦτο δὴ τὸ ἴδιον καὶ ἡ διαφορὰ ἡ χωρίζουσα ἡ οἰκεία ἐστὶ μορφή. Εἰ δὲ μορφή, ἔστι τὸ μορφούμενον, περὶ ὃ ἡ διαφορά. Ἔστιν ἄρα καὶ ὕλη ἡ τὴν μορφὴν δεχομένη καὶ ἀεὶ τὸ ὑποκείμενον.

substrate.[81] Intellect is *both* that which is common to the Forms because they are cognitively identical with it *and* that which provides the intelligible matter for each. That is why the Intellect is a one-many. Intelligible matter is the Intellect posterior to its generation as the Indefinite Dyad. It is the substrate that is 'shaped' by each and every Form. Intellect, by being cognitively identical with all intelligible reality, is 'shaped' by that reality analogous to the way that the bronze of the statue is shaped.

Plotinus adds an additional Platonic argument: everything in the sensible world must have its paradigm in the intelligible world. Call this the paradigm principle. So, if there is sensible matter, there must be intelligible matter.[82] Since sensible matter, as we have seen, is utterly unintelligible, it cannot be that a paradigm of matter is necessary to account for the intelligibility that matter has. Plotinus is applying the rationale for positing Forms in an interesting way. If sensible matter exists, then since the being of everything, including sensible matter, is to be explained by the One, and since apart from Intellect, the One acts through the instrumentality of Intellect, the existence of sensible matter indicates an instrumental role for Intellect in its production. So, in some way, Intellect must be the paradigm of sensible matter. Plotinus seizes on the natural conclusion: since Intellect must be complex, it must be the matter for the Forms that it eternally thinks. Intellect, as Indefinite Dyad, is the principle of intelligible matter, as well as the principle of sensible matter.[83]

The paradigm principle is a formalization of the claim in *Timaeus* that "that which comes to be must come to be by some cause."[84] As we learn in the following lines, this cause is the maker of the universe who uses an eternal paradigm as a model for producing the things that become.[85] But since Plato

---

81. Cf. Aristotle, *Meta.* Z 17, 1041b4–5: ἐπεὶ δὲ δεῖ ἔχειν τε καὶ ὑπάρχειν τὸ εἶναι, δῆλον δὴ ὅτι τὴν ὕλην ζητεῖ διὰ τί <τί> ἐστιν (since, then, something must have something else and the existence must be assumed, it is clear that one is seeking to know why this matter is something). It is worth emphasizing here that Plotinus agrees with Aristotle that any substance is a composite of form and matter. Hence, the separation of Forms from sensible matter is not the separation of form from matter altogether.

82. II 4, 4.7–9.

83. At II 4, 5.28–33 Plotinus seems to identify the kind Difference with the 'primal' difference the Indefinite Dyad has in relation to the One. I leave aside the problem of distinguishing this primal difference from the difference that Intellect has from its intelligible content. I will only point out that Plotinus speaks consistently of the "categories" of intelligible reality and the primal difference "prior" to there being an intelligible world in the proper sense. See Emilsson (2007, 78–80, 103–7) on the two types of difference.

84. See *Tim.* 28C2–3.

85. Cf. V 9, 5.17–23: Τὸ γὰρ πρῶτον ἕκαστον οὐ τὸ αἰσθητόν· τὸ γὰρ ἐν αὐτοῖς εἶδος ἐπὶ ὕλῃ εἴδωλον ὄντος, πᾶν τε εἶδος ἐν ἄλλῳ παρ' ἄλλου εἰς ἐκεῖνο ἔρχεται καί ἐστιν εἰκὼν ἐκείνου. Εἰ δὲ καὶ ποιητὴν δεῖ εἶναι τοῦδε τοῦ παντός, οὐ τὰ ἐν τῷ μήπω ὄντι οὗτος νοήσει, ἵνα αὐτὸ ποιῇ. Πρὸ τοῦ κόσμου ἄρα δεῖ εἶναι ἐκεῖνα, οὐ τύπους ἀφ' ἑτέρων, ἀλλὰ καὶ ἀρχέτυπα καὶ πρῶτα καὶ νοῦ οὐσίαν. (For the primary reality of each thing is not the sensible; for the form in the matter is an image of the real Form, and every form that is in something other comes to that from elsewhere and is an image of that from which it comes. But in

also says that the being of the intelligible realm, though it does not come to be, is dependent being, the One is in a way the archetype of Intellect.[86] As we have seen, it is the archetype in the precise sense that it is virtually what all the Forms are. Thus is the systematic structure of the Platonic universe affirmed.[87]

The Good Is Eros

There are many passages in the *Enneads* in which Plotinus claims that the Good or the One desires nothing or is in need of nothing.[88] This is hardly surprising given the self-sufficiency of the first principle of all. But Plotinus also says, quite astonishingly, that

> [the One] is itself the object of love, love, and love of itself, since it is beautiful not otherwise than by itself and in itself.[89]

That the One should be an object of love is, of course, unremarkable.[90] That it is identified with love is, to say the least, puzzling, given that Plato tells us in *Symposium* that love is a form of desire, in particular the desire for that which is good, and that love indicates a lack or deficiency.[91] If the One "loves itself," must it not also be deficient in some way with respect to the object of its love?[92]

The identification of the One with love is evidently parallel to its identification with the Good and with the virtuality or power of all things (δύναμις τῶν πάντων). The Good, as we have seen, is self-diffusive. This is a conclusion reached from the statements in *Timaeus* that the Demiurge is ungrudging because he is good.[93] But the Demiurge is not the Good

---

addition if there must be a maker of this universe, he will not think the things in the not yet existing universe in order to make it. Therefore, what he thinks must be prior to the cosmos, not representations from other things but archetypes, that is, primary things, and the substance of Intellect.)

86. See VI 8, 18.26–27: τὸ οἷον ἰνδάλματος αὐτοῦ ἀρχετυπον (in a way the archetype of its image).

87. So Krämer 1959, 516, "Das Eins Plotins und der Neuplatoniker erweist sich, geschichtlich betrachtet, als das Eins Platons."

88. See, e.g., V 3, 12.30–31; V 3, 13.16–17; V 3, 15.10; VI 8, 19.18–19, etc.

89. VI 8, 15.1–2: Καὶ ἐράσμιον καὶ ἔρως ὁ αὐτὸς καὶ αὐτοῦ ἔρως, ἅτε οὐκ ἄλλως καλὸς ἢ παρ' αὐτοῦ καὶ ἐν αὐτῷ.

90. See V 5, 12.7–9: Πάντα γὰρ ὀρέγεται ἐκείνου καὶ ἐφίεται αὐτοῦ φύσεως ἀνάγκῃ, ὥσπερ ἀπομεμαντευμένα, ὡς ἄνευ αὐτοῦ οὐ δύναται εἶναι. (For all things desire it [the Good] and long for it by a necessity of nature, as if divining that it is not possible to be without it.)

91. See *Symp.* 206A11–12.

92. *Ennead* III 5, 1, "On Love," to which I will return, is in part a commentary on the account of love in Plato's *Symposium*. Plotinus there does distinguish between love as an affection (πάθος) in the soul, that is, a type of desire (ἔφεσις), and Love as a god or daemon responsible for producing this affection. Whether this god or daemon is to be located at the level of Intellect or Soul is not entirely clear, but in either case it is distinct from the One. Plotinus adds, following Plato, that Love has a "mixed" nature, born of Plenty and Poverty. See III 5, 9.42–45.

93. See *Tim.* 29E1–2: ἀγαθὸς ἦν, ἀγαθῷ δὲ οὐδεὶς περὶ οὐδενὸς οὐδέποτε ἐγγίγνεται φθόνος.

itself, which is, accordingly, unqualifiedly ungrudging. Since it is virtually all things, it "has" all things to give, which it does unceasingly. Why, though, is this identical with ἔρως? The answer seems to be that "the soul loves that by which it was moved to love from the beginning."[94] So not only is the Good limitlessly bountiful, but its bounty includes the desire to return to the Good. The passive "was moved" is, I think, not to be confused with the motion produced by a final cause. The Good does indeed move as a final cause. But this is because it has moved productively, so to speak.[95] The love of the Good is a function of the being of all its products, which have, as products, been eroticized. It is not possible for something to have desire and at the same time not to desire the Good. The soul is moved to love the Good because the Good is virtually what it is. Love for the Good that is virtually all things is not love for a simulacrum of a real object of love; on the contrary, the being of anything that is not perfectly one is a simulacrum of its primary paradigm, the One. Its love for the Good is self-love, so long as the self is properly understood. Indeed, souls are capable of disliking (δυσχεραίνοι) themselves because they conceive of themselves as being other than that which produced them; by contrast, souls are satisfied with themselves only to the extent that they partake of the Good.[96]

This perhaps explains why Plotinus says that the One is not just love, but self-love. We have already looked at the passage in which Plotinus says that the three hypostases are "in us."[97] In particular, the One is said to be in a way "another self" (ἄλλον αὐτόν).[98] It is only "in a way" another self because it is not really other than anything. Everything is other than it but only in its diminished state of being.[99] So to say that the One is self-love is not to attribute any deficiency directly to it but rather to everything that the One is virtually. If the One were not love and self-love, then the love for it would not be, as Plotinus says it is, a "necessity of nature." Everything desires its own good. If this good did not amount to being identical with the Good, the love for the Good would be adventitious or perhaps "optional"; it would not be necessary. If the first principle of all were *merely* an object of love as

---

94. See VI 7, 31.17–18: τοῦτον τὸν τρόπον καὶ ψυχὴ ἐρᾷ μὲν ἐκείνου ὑπ' αὐτοῦ ἐξ ἀρχῆς εἰς τὸ ἐρᾶν κινηθεῖσα. Here the soul's love for the Good is analogous to the soul's love for any beloved.

95. See Denyer 2007, who argues that the Idea of the Good in *Republic* is exclusively a teleological cause. He argues that in accounting for "why something is as it is," the Good accounts for its existence as well as for its essence. But Denyer (307) clarifies the teleology of the Good as "seeing what is good about something." I fail to see, though, how seeing what is good about something explains either essence or existence, for 'it is good for Form F to be this way' presupposes the existence of the Form having the nature it has.

96. See VI 8, 13.42–47.

97. See V 1, 10–11.

98. See V 1, 11.10. Cf. III 8, 9.23–24: Ἔστι γάρ τι καὶ παρ' ἡμῖν αὐτοῦ· ἢ οὐκ ἔστιν, ὅπου μὴ ἔστιν, οἷς ἐστι μετέχειν αὐτοῦ. (For there is something of it in us, too; in fact, there is nowhere where it is not, in the things that participate in it.)

99. As Plotinus states elsewhere, this diminution occurs via the *addition* of something else, namely, nonbeing. See VI 5, 12.20–21.

perhaps the Unmoved Mover is, there would be no necessity for it to be the sole object of every love.[100]

Because the One is love and self-love, reversion to the One is as necessary as is the production of everything from the One. The so-called Neoplatonic triadic cycle of perdurance (μονή), procession (πρόοδος), and reversion (ἐπιστροφή), which is sometimes supposed to be an innovation, is for Plotinus a consequence of the principles of the Platonic system.[101] It should be clear that in claiming that the Good is love, Plotinus does not mean that the Good reciprocates the love that all things have for it. So his supposed innovation must be sharply distinguished from the authentic innovations of Christian theology. Against the imputation of innovation on Plotinus's part, it should be noted that reversion and procession are deeply woven into Platonism from the start. If all beings desire the Good, if the Good is the principle of the being of all things, and if the Good is undiminished in its giving, where is the innovation? I suspect that the charge of innovation rests on the systematization of Platonism itself. It is certainly true that Plotinus draws the parts of his reconstruction of Platonism from different dialogues, and from the direct and indirect testimony. As I tried to show in the second chapter, the prohibition on the use of material from one dialogue to interpret another leads manifestly to a dead end. In addition, the prohibition on the use of Aristotle's testimony rests on a circular argument that privileges the dialogues. The argument is circular because the use of the dialogues without the prohibition of using one to interpret another presumes that there is such a thing as Platonism apart from the dialogues or at the very least allows for the possibility. Aristotle is far more formidable as a witness to Platonism than as an exegete of individual dialogues.

In this chapter, I have focused on a number of difficult elements of the Platonic system according to Plotinus. Relying exclusively on the dialogues for the discovery of Plato's philosophy not surprisingly results in the charge that Plotinus is here innovating, perhaps wildly so. This exclusive reliance on the dialogues is not only based on an ungrounded assumption regarding the nature of Platonism, but it also invites us time and again—especially in dialogues like *Parmenides, Timaeus, Sophist,* and *Philebus*—to refrain from considering the philosophical implications of the specific arguments we find there. Such diffidence would be perfectly reasonable if in fact we did not possess an abundance of testimony regarding the Platonic system and a practically unbroken tradition of efforts to take it seriously.

---

100. See Aristotle, *Meta.* Λ 7, 1072b3–4: κινεῖ δὴ ὡς ἐρώμενον, κινούμενα δὲ τἆλλα κινεῖ (it moves as beloved; and the things moved, move other things).

101. See Proclus, *ET* Prop. 31.1–2: Πᾶν τὸ προϊὸν ἀπό τινος κατ' οὐσίαν ἐπιστρέφεται πρὸς ἐκεῖνο ἀφ' οὗ πρόεισιν. (Everything that proceeds from something reverts to that from which it proceeds according to its being.) Cf. Pigler 2003, 18–19, who in a very rich study of the self-love of the One, argues that this doctrine issues from a metaphysics profoundly different from that of Plato's.

CHAPTER 11

Plotinus as Interpreter of Plato (2)

In the previous chapter, I aimed to present the systematic structure of Platonism according to Plotinus as he found this in the dialogues, in the Aristotelian testimony, and, no doubt, in the oral tradition. It is widely held that what is distinctive about late Platonism and what makes it therefore really 'Neoplatonism' is the metaphysics. It is also the case that it is the metaphysics that provides the foundation for the interpretation of Plato's ethics and psychology. The metaphysical system of Platonism to which Plotinus adheres and which he is continually trying to articulate and defend is supposed by him to be the necessary basis for providing answers to what we might term, broadly speaking, human questions. In his treatises on happiness, virtue, evil, fate, providence, immortality, and freedom, he reveals himself responding to perennial student questions, to anti-Platonic philosophers old and new, and to contemporary intellectual issues, in particular those arising from the increasingly strained encounters with non-Greek religions. In almost all these cases, he goes back to first principles, trying to reason out the correct—that is, the Platonic—response.[1] Plotinus is well aware, even perhaps rueful, that Plato is not always so clear or even consistent in expressing the correct answer.[2] He is also aware that other Platonists

---

1. See IV 3, 1.1–6, where Plotinus seems to allow that there may be unsolvable problems in the realm of psychology.
2. E.g., see III 4, 5.2–4, where Plotinus admits that Plato is not so clear in *Rep.* 617D–E when he says that the gods are not responsible for the choices that humans make for themselves before they are embodied. Also, III 2, 7.19–20. Plotinus returns in the first six chapters of VI 8 to meditate on the proper Platonic account of what is "up to us." See Bobzien 1998a, 404, n. 101, for references to the widespread use of the *Republic* passage by Platonists.

differ in their own answers.³ The dissent among later Platonists from some of Plotinus's specific doctrines can be abundantly documented.

As I argued in the first chapter, the disagreements among Platonists arise from the fact that their shared fundamental Platonic principles are underdetermining with respect to the answers to many of the "human questions." In this last chapter, I would like to show that between the three hypostases on the one hand and the account of, say, culpable wrongdoing or the value of 'externals' to the good life on the other, there is something like a distinctive Platonic anthropology that, among other things, does define the limits on acceptable Platonic answers to human questions. This anthropology flows out of UP and is built on the armature of the metaphysics of the three hypostases. Plotinus's *Enneads* in general hardly ever disconnects the anthropology from the metaphysics. This is at least part of the reason why we sometimes find side by side in them quotations from dialogues of Plato like *Sophist* and *Symposium* that are infrequently juxtaposed. For Plotinus, at any rate, the harmony of the metaphysics and the anthropology is further evidence of the truth of Platonism.⁴

Human and Person

Plotinus follows Plato in distinguishing the human being (ἄνθρωπος), that is, the composite of body and soul, from the soul itself.⁵ Further, like Plato, he identifies the person or self with the soul.⁶ This identification is supposed to imply that the person is a nonbodily entity, that is, it is neither

---

3. E.g., see IV 8, 8.1–3, where Plotinus acknowledges that his own view that a part of our soul does not descend into the body but is eternally with Intellect is not a view shared by others. And, in fact, most later Platonists did not share it.

4. At II 9, 6.38–41, Plotinus lists among the doctrines found in Plato the immortality of the soul; the existence of the intelligible realm; the first god, that is, the One; the necessity for the soul to flee the body, that is, separation from it; and the necessity to flee from the realm of becoming to the realm of being. Note the juxtaposition of the metaphysical and the ethical.

5. See Plato, *Phdr.* 246C5–D2 for the mortality of the composite. See I 1, 7.14–24; VI 7, 5.1–2: Λόγον τοίνυν δεῖ τὸν ἄνθρωπον ἄλλον παρὰ τὴν ψυχὴν εἶναι. (The human being, then, must have an account other than that of the soul.)

6. See the canonical text at *Alc.* I 130C1–3: Socrates says: Ἐπειδὴ δ' οὔτε σῶμα οὔτε τὸ συναμφότερόν ἐστιν ἄνθρωπος, λείπεται οἶμαι ἢ μηδὲν αὐτ' εἶναι, ἢ εἴπερ τὶ ἐστι, μηδὲν ἄλλο τὸν ἄνθρωπον συμβαίνειν ἢ ψυχήν. (Since the human being is neither the body nor the combination of body and soul, I think it remains either that it is nothing or, if it is something, it follows that the human being is the soul.) Here, the word ἄνθρωπος is clearly being used differently from the *Phaedrus* passage cited above in n. 5. The difference is, I think, indicated by the words at the beginning of the passage, 129B1–3, where the question Φέρε δή, τίν' ἂν τρόπον εὑρεθείη αὐτὸ ταὐτό; (How can we come to know the self itself?) is answered in the conclusion, "The ἄνθρωπος is the soul." So the ἄνθρωπος is the composite of body and soul, but *really* it is only the soul, which is the self or person. This is the ἄνθρωπος within the ἄνθρωπος at *Rep.* 589A7–B1. I will not here discuss the question of the authenticity of *Alcibiades*. See Pradeau 1999, 219–20, for a convenient listing of the various arguments pro and con. No one in the ancient Platonic tradition doubted the authenticity of this dialogue (except perhaps the supposed forger!). Nevertheless, the claim made in this dialogue about the soul

a body nor an attribute of a body, including the body that it "inhabits."[7] There are, however, as Plotinus realized, numerous complications with this identification. The complications pertain largely to the problems of explaining how an immaterial entity can be related to a body and how the identical person can be the subject of bodily states and also exist separately from its body. The problems are, of course, not completely separate. For example, how can the immaterial person be the subject both of psychical and of bodily states? If the person can be shown to be such a subject, how can that person be identical with that which can have no bodily states at all, namely, the separate immaterial soul?[8] In the face of these problems, Plotinus seems to have been the first Platonist to assume that the appropriate metaphysical framework must be applied to their solution. He assumes both that in this he is following Plato and that, nevertheless, that framework may still be underdetermining for the solution to some particularly difficult and obscure problems. The latter include, for example, how personal identity is retained when a human soul inhabits a nonhuman body, how personal identity can be retained without memory of bodily states, how punishment for embodied behavior can fall upon the disembodied self, and why embodiment may lead us to evil.

According to this metaphysical framework, Plotinus takes embodiment to be a special case of the image-making labors of the Demiurge. The understanding of embodied persons is pursued analogous to the way the sensible world generally is understood as residing "between the really real and nothing," in principle, defective images of the intelligible world. For example, Helen is beautiful owing to the Form of Beauty, though the λόγος of Helen's beauty will be different from the λόγος of Beauty itself, since the former will necessarily contain as a constituent bodily attributes. Analogously, the λόγος of the embodied soul will contain constituents that do not

---

and the self is supported by many passages in other dialogues. Cf. *Lg.* 959B3–4 and 721B7–8, 773B5; *Phd.* 76C11–13, 92B5, 95C5–6; *Tim.* 90C2–3.

7. See IV 4, 18.11–15: Λέγω δὲ ἡμῖν τῇ ἄλλῃ ψυχῇ, ἅτε καὶ τοῦ τοιοῦδε σώματος οὐκ ἀλλοτρίου, ἀλλ' ἡμῶν ὄντος· διὸ καὶ μέλει ἡμῖν αὐτοῦ ὡς ἡμῶν ὄντος. Οὔτε γὰρ τοῦτό ἐσμεν ἡμεῖς, οὔτε καθαροὶ τούτου ἡμεῖς, ἀλλὰ ἐξήρτηται καὶ ἐκκρέμαται ἡμῶν, ἡμεῖς δὲ κατὰ τὸ κύριον, ἡμῶν δὲ ἄλλως ὅμως τοῦτο. (By "our self" I mean the rest of the soul, insofar as even the body so qualified is not another's, but belongs to us; wherefore, it is of concern to us, as belonging to us. For we are not this, nor yet have we been purged of it, but it depends on us and is suspended from us, whereas we exist in respect of our chief part, but nevertheless that other entity is ours, though in a different way.)

8. Notoriously, Plato seems to waver in holding, on the one hand, that the person or self is an immaterial intellect and, on the other, that it is or has 'parts' that are, at least when embodied, inseparable from bodies. See *Phd.* 78B4–84B4, the so-called Affinity Argument, which aims to show that the soul is like the immaterial Forms that it knows; *Rep.* 608C1ff., where the proof of the immortality of the soul depends on it being incomposite, that is, without the parts that seem to require embodiment; and *Tim.* 41C–D, 69C5–6, E1, 90A, where the immortal part of the soul seem fairly clearly to be identified as the intellect. And yet at *Phdr.* 246Aff., we have the myth of the charioteer and his two horses, evidently representing the disembodied tripartite soul. I have treated all these and related passages at length in Gerson 2003, chaps. 2, 3, 6.

belong to the disembodied soul, which, for Plotinus, is just the intellect. The essence or nature of beauty is in Helen just as the essence or nature of the human soul is in the body.[9]

Since the human soul is essentially rational, we should expect that it has no irrational attributes. And yet when Plato develops the account of the tripartite embodied soul in *Republic*, he seems to require one, if not two, irrational parts of the soul. For, as Socrates argues, that in our soul by which we learn and that by which we are angry and that by which we desire the pleasures of food and sex are activities of different parts of the whole soul.[10] The argument seems to rest on the intuitive principle that "one thing cannot do or experience opposites in the same respect in relation to the same thing at the same time."[11] For example, thirsty people are sometimes unwilling to drink. Plato infers the existence of different parts of the soul on the grounds that that which wants to drink must be different from that which wants to refrain from drinking. It is pretty clear that the part that wants to refrain from drinking makes this judgment as a result of reasoning (λογισμός), while that which commands the person to drink is the result of "pathological states and illnesses" (παθημάτων τε καὶ νοσημάτων).[12] The vexing problem faced by Plotinus as well as by modern scholars is how the identical person or embodied human soul can be the subject of these supposedly irrational appetites.

On the one hand, if reason can overcome or be overcome by appetite, then the appetitive part of the soul would seem to have its own capacity for reasoning. But if this is so, then this part of the soul will itself be divisible into its own rational and irrational part, threatening a regress of psychic divisions.[13] On the other hand, if appetite does not have its own capacity

---

9. See IV 3, 13.3–5, where the embodied soul is viewed as an εἴδωλον of the disembodied soul of *Republic* book 10 that has chosen a life according to its disposition. That disembodied soul is itself an image of an intellect.

10. See *Rep.* 436A8–B3.

11. *Rep.* 436B8–10.

12. *Rep.* 439C9–D2.

13. The threat of *'homunculi'* is well articulated by Annas 1981, 142–46; and Bobonich 1994; 2002, 216–57, who in fact thinks that Plato succumbs to this threat in *Republic* but circumvents it in *Laws* by abandoning tripartitioning of the soul. At *Phd.* 83D7, the rational soul is tempted to "share the opinions of" (ὁμοδοξεῖν) the body and so to become contaminated with it. Cf. *Rep.* 442C10–D1, where in the temperate individual, the two lower parts of the soul "share the belief" (ὁμοδοξῶσι) with τὸ λογιστικόν about who "should" (δεῖν) rule. But the "assent" to the rule of reason is just obedience to reason. It is not the employment of normative reasoning. Cf. Aristotle, *EN* A 13, 1102b27, where the part of the soul of the temperate man that "agrees with" (ὁμοφωνεῖ) reason is ἄλογος, though it participates in reason "in some way" (πῃ). In the continent individual, this part merely obeys reason. The idea of "sharing the opinions of the lower part(s) of the soul" is referenced by Plotinus at I 2, 3.11–19. On the multifarious use of "part" (μέρος) in Plato, see Shields 2010, 164–67. Shields usefully distinguishes between "compositional parts" and "aspectual parts," the latter being effectively equivalent to properties. If the parts of the soul are not *homunculi*, then it would seem more likely that they are aspectual, that is, properties of the embodied human being.

for reasoning, then how is it even possible to commensurate appetite and reasoning, that is, what possible grounds are there for a conflict?[14] In the course of the argument, Socrates distinguishes between the desire for drink and the desire to reject this desire. Presumably, though this is not made explicit, there might be a similar desire to endorse the appetite. The problem with this account is that it seems that if the desire to refrain from drinking is the work of the rational part of the soul, then the desire for drink must be an irrational desire. Accordingly, we have the above dilemma.[15]

By contrast, Plotinus assumes that the desire for drink is a rational desire just in the sense that it is the desire of an embodied rational soul.[16] What this means above all is that the desire can and must be conceptualized in order for it to factor into a process of practical reasoning. In effect, if the desire is construed exclusively as a bodily state, it is indeed nonrational. But the bodily state is not that which initiates a human action; the appetite or desire does that. Or, more accurately, the *subject* of the appetites does that. Analogously, if sense perception is construed as a bodily state or event, there is not necessarily anything like perceptual awareness of the sensible. The bodily states that are the raw material of desires are, in principle, available for inspection by someone other than the one whose body it is. By contrast, the full-fledged desire is only subjectively immediately available, though, of course, someone else can infer its presence from one's behavior.

The desire for drink is, then, rational, but it is not rational in the same way as is the desire, say, to refrain from drink or to endorse the primary desire. This 'second-order' rational desire is intrinsically normative as

14. Penner (1990) argues that the very idea of incontinence, or ἀκρασία, which entails some sort of conflict between reason and irrational appetite, is impossible. See Rudebusch 2009, 71–73, who acknowledges that the so-called brute desires are, in fact, no such thing and require conceptual contextualization. But it is not clear if Rudebusch thinks that this means that ἀκρασία is, counter to Plato, impossible or that Plato himself never actually accepted the possibility.

15. See Penner 1990, 55, who argues that desire for drink in *Republic* is "blind." See Brickhouse and Smith 2010, 202–10, who reject this view, arguing that the desire for drink is not "good-independent." But in making their case, they waver between making the appetites an independent judge of the goodness of their objects ("appetites make actual judgments of goodness," 205) and accepting that the actual judgment is done by reason ("we are not claiming that the appetites make actual judgments of value," 204), though the appetites "present" their objects as good. In the latter case, we would have all-things-considered judgments and so no ἀκρασία; in the former case we seem to have *homunculi* of a sort. See Moss 2008, 61–62, for the argument that desires of the appetitive part of the soul are not "good-independent," as was argued by Irwin 1995, 209–10. Moss, however, goes too far in maintaining that the lower parts of the soul make evaluative judgments.

16. See IV 3, 3.24–28: 'Ἀλλ' ὅτι ἕν γε πανταχοῦ, εἴρηται, καὶ ἐν τοῖς διαφόροις τῶν ἔργων....ὅταν δὲ καὶ λογικὴ ᾖ ψυχή, καὶ οὕτω λογικὴ ὡς <ἡ> ὅλη λέγεται...(But, as was stated, the soul is everywhere one, even in its different functions....But since the soul is rational, and rational in the sense in which the whole soul is said to be rational...) Cf. V 1, 3.17–19: Καὶ ταύτας μόνας δεῖ λέγειν ἐνεργείας ψυχῆς, ὅσα νοερῶς καὶ ὅσα οἴκοθεν. (And these alone should be called activities of soul, namely, those that are intellectual and those that belong to it.)

opposed to the 'first-order' desire which is not.[17] Because a desire for drink is nonnormative, one is tempted to think that it is nonrational. But it could not be such if the person is going to select the correct universal and particular premises in a practical syllogism. So reasoning that white meat is healthy and this is white meat indicates no action if one is not hungry. The hunger must be conceptualized in order to be taken to be an instance of that which the syllogism states.

Plotinus tends to distinguish a generic nonnormative rational desire from normative rational desire by different terms, ὄρεξις for the former and ἔφεσις for the latter.[18] The appetite for drink is a nonnormative rational desire, and the desire that, say, endorses this desire is a desire for drink as a good, that is, as an instance of the Good here and now. It is this second-order desire that, paradigmatically, characterizes Intellect. Nonnormative desires are, like all desires—even the desires of irrational animals—for that which is good. But the good is only apparent. It is the task of normative reasoning to determine if that which appears to be good is in fact so.[19] How, then, is the supposed conflict between appetite and reason parsed? It is a conflict within the rational soul between a desire for the apparent good and a distinct judgment that what appears to be good is or is not really so.

Here is a fairly obvious objection. Granted that what appears to be good is not really so, why prefer the former to the latter? Plotinus, quoting Plato, says that while people are often satisfied with the apparent beautiful, they are never satisfied with the apparent good.[20] Evidently, the reason for this

---

17. See VI 8, 6.38–39: Ἡ γὰρ βούλησις θέλει τὸ ἀγαθόν· τὸ δὲ νοεῖν ἀληθῶς ἐστιν ἐν τῷ ἀγαθῷ. (For will wants the Good; but thinking is truly in the Good.) The normativity is owing to the necessary orientation of βούλησις to the Good. It is βούλησις that enables us to judge primary or first-order desires as to whether their satisfaction is an instance of that which is good.

18. See I 1, 5.21 and esp. VI 7, 21.1–6; VI 7, 27.24–27: Νῦν δέ, εἰ ταῦτα ὀρθῶς λέγεται, καὶ ἡ ἐπανάβασις ἔχει τὸ ἀγαθὸν ἐν φύσει τινὶ κείμενον, καὶ οὐχ ἡ ἔφεσις ποιεῖ τὸ ἀγαθόν, ἀλλ' ἡ ἔφεσις, ὅτι ἀγαθόν. (Now if these conclusions are right, the ascent attains the good found in some nature, and it is not the desire that makes it good, but there is desire because it is good.)

19. Cf. Plato, *Gorg.* 467C5–8E5, where the distinction is between what seems (δοκεῖ) best to the tyrant and what he wills (βούλεται). Penner and Rowe (2005, 227–28) think that this distinction belongs to "Socratic intellectualism" because the tyrant who does what seems best to him is doing what he, mistakenly, thinks is best for him. By contrast, they think that the putative acratic acts on the basis of brute desires in opposition to what he thinks is best for him to do. But, on Plotinus's interpretation, the acratic no less than the tyrant acts on the basis of what he takes to be a (nonnormative) good in opposition to what he takes to be the normative good, the good of refraining from acting. This is possible and produces no contradiction because the embodied person is a divided self. Because the embodied person is a divided self, the tyrant's desire to do what "seems best" to him is really no different from Leontius's desire to gaze upon the naked corpses.

20. See V 5, 12.23–24: Καὶ καλοῖς εἶναι δοκεῖν ἀρκεῖ, κἂν μὴ ὦσι· τὸ δ' ἀγαθὸν οὐ δόξῃ ἐθέλουσιν ἔχειν. (And for them, it is sufficient if things seem beautiful, even if they are not. This is not how they stand in regard to that which is good.) Plotinus is here loosely quoting *Rep.* 505D5–9.

is that one might take the apparent beautiful for the real good. But there is no such inclination to take the apparent good for the real good, once a distinction between them is made.[21] And yet, according to Plotinus, most persons fail to make this distinction, and this is owing to a very specific cause, namely, they are confused about their real identities.

> What can it be, then, that has made the souls forget the god who is their father and be ignorant both of themselves and him even though they are parts of the intelligible world and are completely derived from it? The starting point for their evil is audacity, that is, generation or primary difference or wanting to belong to themselves. Since they then appeared to be pleased with their self-determination and to have made much of their self-motion, running as far away as possible and producing the maximum distance, they were also ignorant that they themselves came from the intelligible world. They were like children who at birth are separated from their fathers and, being raised for a long time far away, are ignorant both of themselves and of their fathers. Since they no longer can see their father or themselves, they dishonor themselves, owing to ignorance of their lineage, honoring instead other things, in fact, everything more than themselves, marveling at and being awestruck and loving and being dependent on these, and they severed themselves as much as possible from those things from which they turned away with their dishonor.[22]

There are many fascinating features of this well-known passage, several of which I will return to. Here, though, I want to emphasize Plotinus's claim that the source of human woe and wrongdoing is a failure to grasp or to grasp fully one's own true identity. That identity is found in a disembodied intellect. It is this intellect that is immortal, not the human being.[23] It is

---

21. Of course, it is true that even the virtuous person who knows what the real good is chooses what appears to him to be good. His virtue actually consists in this real identity between what appears good to him and what really is so. Thus the appetites of those other than the virtuous are not good-independent just in the sense that they are for apparent goods that in fact are not real goods.

22. V 1, 1.1-17: Τί ποτε ἄρα ἐστὶ τὸ πεποιηκὸς τὰς ψυχὰς πατρὸς θεοῦ ἐπιλαθέσθαι, καὶ μοίρας ἐκεῖθεν οὔσας καὶ ὅλως ἐκείνου ἀγνοῆσαι καὶ ἑαυτὰς καὶ ἐκεῖνον; Ἀρχὴ μὲν οὖν αὐταῖς τοῦ κακοῦ ἡ τόλμα καὶ ἡ γένεσις καὶ ἡ πρώτη ἑτερότης καὶ τὸ βουληθῆναι δὲ ἑαυτῶν εἶναι. Τῷ δὴ αὐτεξουσίῳ ἐπειδήπερ ἐφάνησαν ἡσθεῖσαι, πολλῷ τῷ κινεῖσθαι παρ' αὐτῶν κεχρημέναι, τὴν ἐναντίαν δραμοῦσαι καὶ πλείστην ἀπόστασιν πεποιημέναι, ἠγνόησαν καὶ ἑαυτὰς ἐκεῖθεν εἶναι· ὥσπερ παῖδες εὐθὺς ἀποσπασθέντες ἀπὸ πατέρων καὶ πολὺν χρόνον πόρρω τραφέντες ἀγνοοῦσι καὶ ἑαυτοὺς καὶ πατέρας. Οὔτ' οὖν ἔτι ἐκεῖνον οὔτε ἑαυτὰς ὁρῶσαι, ἀτιμάσασαι ἑαυτὰς ἀγνοίᾳ τοῦ γένους, τιμήσασαι τἆλλα καὶ πάντα μᾶλλον ἢ ἑαυτὰς θαυμάσασαι καὶ πρὸς αὐτὰ ἐκπλαγεῖσαι καὶ ἀγασθεῖσαι καὶ ἐξηρτημέναι τούτων, ἀπέρρηξαν ὡς οἷόν τε ἑαυτὰς ὧν ἀπεστράφησαν ἀτιμάσασαι· ὥστε συμβαίνει τῆς παντελοῦς ἀγνοίας ἐκείνου ἡ τῶνδε τιμὴ καὶ ἡ ἑαυτῶν ἀτιμία εἶναι αἰτία. Cf. IV 4, 3.1-3; IV 4, 18.15-19; IV 8, 5.28; VI 9, 8.31-32.

23. Cf. Plato, *Tim.* 90B1–C6. Cf. Aristotle, *EN* K 8, 1178a9-22. See Plotinus, I 1, 7.18-24: Κωλύσει δὲ οὐδὲν τὸ σύμπαν ζῷον λέγειν, μικτὸν μὲν τὰ κάτω, τὸ δὲ ἐντεῦθεν ὁ ἄνθρωπος ὁ ἀληθὴς σχεδόν· ἐκεῖνα δὲ τὸ λεοντῶδες καὶ τὸ ποικίλον ὅλως θηρίον. Συνδρόμου γὰρ ὄντος τοῦ ἀνθρώπου τῇ λογικῇ ψυχῇ, ὅταν λογιζώμεθα, ἡμεῖς λογιζόμεθα τῷ τοὺς λογισμοὺς

embodiment that brings with it 'forgetfulness' and confusion about one's identity.

Owing to embodiment, bodily desires arise. Their satisfaction appears to us to be a good thing. Insofar as we identify ourselves as human beings, that is, as soul-body composites, the only criterion we have for judging these apparent goods' claim to be the real thing is whether they are good for the human being. But this identification is deceptive and the criterion problematic. For the human being is a composite of body and soul. And most of the difficult choices and conflicts that arise in human life are between bodily goods and psychic goods. Why give preference to the latter over the former? One may, as we saw Penner doing in defense of a purely Socratic ethics, opt for a prudential employment of the criterion. Thus, unmeasured satisfaction of bodily desires is not a beneficial long-term policy for a human being, supposing, of course, that the long term is constitutive of the true human good. And crime does not pay. Yet in fact sometimes it does, and sometimes people prefer a shorter life to a longer one if it is packed with pleasures. Plato's tyrant in book 9 of *Republic* may, after all, have less pleasure than does the aristocratic person.[24] But crucially this is a determination that the latter makes, not the former. The tyrant has lost his true identity and so long as he does not discover it, he has no grounds for judging negatively his own life over against what must appear to him to be the life of a different kind of creature.

For the aristocratic person or philosopher, the criterion for judging the apparent goods of the body is, as we have already seen, normative reason. But normativity can cut both ways. That is, like a Thrasymachus or a Callicles, one can aspire to be a supremely rational practitioner of injustice. So normativity is not enough. One needs to recognize the uniqueness of the Good as objective first principle of all, thereby guaranteeing the distinction between real and apparent good. For with this recognition, one cannot imagine that there is a possibility of a conflict of goods such that something that is good for A is not good for B. But this is typically the nature of the apparent goods of the body. Indeed, if we consider A and B to be the same person at different times, many apparent goods are judged negatively now by A because they are not good later for B. If we then put together the recognition of the distinction between apparent and real goods and the further recognition that the Good is unique, it does not seem likely that someone could judge his real good to be a bodily good, at least insofar as this good is obtained at the expense of others.

We are still at least one step from the conclusion that our true identity is located in a disembodied rational soul, that is, in an intellect. Reflecting

---

ψυχῆς εἶναι ἐνεργήματα. (But there is nothing against calling the whole a "living being," with the lower parts being mixed in, although the true human being begins about there [with thought]. Those lower parts are the "lion-like" and, generally, the "multifaceted beast." Given that the human being coincides with the rational soul, whenever human beings reason, it is we who are reasoning with the acts of reasoning that are psychic products.)

24. See *Rep.* 587C–E.

on one's search for one's own identity, Plotinus claims that "he who knows himself will also know where he came from [ὁ δὲ μαθὼν ἑαυτὸν εἰδήσει καὶ ὁπόθεν]."[25] The opposite is equally true. The question of one's 'origin' must have resonated with any ancient reader. Am I really a 'pure' Greek? Do I descend from a divine race? In a Platonic framework, according to which the personal immortality of the soul is established, the question takes on an entirely different cast. According to *Timaeus*, the Demiurge, in his address to the created gods, informs them that there must be human beings if the cosmos is to be complete.[26] It is fitting, however, that these should have a share in immortality, and so the Demiurge sows the seed of immortality and hands over the product to the subordinate gods in order that they may add the mortal parts of human beings. So the origin of the immortal part of the human being is clearly the Demiurge. But this immortal part really is the self or person.

Plotinus, following Plato, rests this claim entirely on an epistemological argument:

> And the intellection of the 'in itself' of each thing, which the soul obtains by itself from the visions of things within itself or from recollection, yields the conclusion that the soul existed prior to the body and that it, having employed its eternal knowledge, is itself eternal.[27]

The immortal part of the soul is the intellect. This intellect, however, has eternal knowledge, knowledge that we can draw on in particular in making judgments that such intelligibility as the sensible world has is derived and deficient. Perhaps the immortal soul so characterized would be sufficient for reaching the conclusion that the true self is that intellect, and so its good is entirely an intellectual one. One might object, however, that intellectual goods are for separated intellects; human beings are different, and their true identity cannot ignore the goods of the body. Once, though, we admit this, the privileging of the goods of the intellect over the goods of the body or of the lower parts of the soul begins again to seem arbitrary. Why should we recognize our true identities here and now with an intellect that is separate only when the composite is gone?

In the face of such an objection, Plotinus makes a bold interpretative leap. Since we really do possess knowledge eternally, our intellects must not have descended into bodies:

> How, then, since the intelligible is separate, does the soul enter the body? It is like this: the part of it that is only intellect is impassive remaining always among the intelligibles and having an intellectual life only in the intelligible

---

25. VI 9, 7.33-34.
26. See *Tim.* 41A-D.
27. IV 4, 7.12. 8-11: Ἥ τε δὴ παρ' αὐτῆς ἐκ τῶν ἐν αὐτῇ θεαμάτων κατανόησις αὐτοεκάστου καὶ ἐξ ἀναμνήσεως γιγνομένη πρὸ σώματός τε αὐτῇ δίδωσι τὸ εἶναι καὶ ἀιδίοις ἐπιστήμαις κεχρημένην ἀίδιον καὶ αὐτὴν εἶναι. Cf. *Phd.* 72E-73A, 78C1-2.

world—for it has no impulse or desire—while that which acquires desire, following immediately on that intellect, by the addition of desire in a way extends further and desires to produce order according to what it saw in intellect, as if being pregnant by the intelligibles and laboring to give birth, and is eager to make and construct the world.[28]

The existence of Forms eternally contemplated by the Demiurge is not sufficient to account for our knowledge of them. Our ability to recollect Forms presumes that *we* know them now. This knowledge is not reducible to what we do and can achieve with our embodied discursive intellects since all embodied cognition is only an image of the paradigm of intellection.[29] When we judge sensible equals to be deficiently equal, we do so by comparing them to the Form of Equality. But our knowledge of this is not the word or concept we employ in making the judgment. For one thing, all the Forms are 'together' and our word or concept represents that Form as if it were separate.[30] So, we can 'access' the knowledge that we actually do possess, though the accessing is something we do via the images of Forms in our embodied intellects. We must, then, have undescended intellects that, here and now, are our true selves.[31]

For Plotinus, embodied human life is a struggle to recover our true identity, a struggle immensely complicated by the false images of the self thrown

---

28. IV 7, 13.1–8: Πῶς οὖν τοῦ νοητοῦ χωριστοῦ ὄντος ἥδε εἰς σῶμα ἔρχεται; ὅτι, ὅσος μὲν νοῦς μόνος, ἀπαθὴς ἐν τοῖς νοητοῖς ζωὴν μόνον νοερὰν ἔχων ἐκεῖ ἀεὶ μένει—οὐ γὰρ ἔνι ὁρμὴ οὐδ' ὄρεξις—ὃ δ' ἂν ὄρεξιν προσλάβῃ ἐφεξῆς ἐκείνῳ τῷ νῷ ὄν, τῇ προσθήκῃ τῆς ὀρέξεως οἷον πρόεισιν ἤδη ἐπιπλέον καὶ κοσμεῖν ὀρεγόμενον καθὰ ἐν νῷ εἶδεν, ὥσπερ κυοῦν ἀπ' αὐτῶν καὶ ὠδῖνον γεννῆσαι, ποιεῖν σπεύδει καὶ δημιουργεῖ. Cf. IV 8, 8, where Plotinus acknowledges that his view is not shared by others, that is, by other interpreters of Plato. I doubt that Plotinus believes he is contradicting the Platonism of Plato.

29. See I 8, 2.9–15:... νοῦ ἐκείνου ὄντος οὐ κατὰ νοῦν, ὃν οἰηθείη ἄν τις κατὰ τοὺς παρ' ἡμῖν λεγομένους νοῦς εἶναι τοὺς ἐκ προτάσεων συμπληρουμένους καὶ τῶν λεγομένων συνιέναι δυναμένους λογιζομένους τε καὶ τοῦ ἀκολούθου θεωρίαν ποιουμένους ὡς ἐξ ἀκολουθίας τὰ ὄντα θεωμένους ὡς πρότερον οὐκ ἔχοντας, ἀλλὰ κενοὺς ἔτι πρὶν μαθεῖν ὄντας, καίτοι νοῦς ὄντας (...intellect there [in the intelligible world] is not like the intellects we are said to have, intellects that are filled with propositions and are capable of understanding things that are said and of reasoning and so observing what follows, intellects that consequently observe realities that they did not formerly possess, since they were empty before learning them, despite being intellects.)

30. Cf. I 1, 8.6–8: ἔχομεν οὖν καὶ τὰ εἴδη διχῶς, ἐν μὲν ψυχῇ οἷον ἀνειλιγμένα καὶ οἷον κεχωρισμένα, ἐν δὲ νῷ ὁμοῦ τὰ πάντα (we have the Forms, then, in two ways: in the soul, as it were unfolded and separated, but in Intellect 'all together').

31. See VI 4, 14.16–22: ἡμεῖς δέ—τίνες δὲ ἡμεῖς; ἆρα ἐκεῖνο ἢ τὸ πελάζον καὶ τὸ γινόμενον ἐν χρόνῳ; Ἢ καὶ πρὸ τοῦ ταύτην τὴν γένεσιν γενέσθαι ἦμεν ἐκεῖ ἄνθρωποι ἄλλοι ὄντες καὶ τινες καὶ θεοί, ψυχαὶ καθαραὶ καὶ νοῦς συνημμένος τῇ πάσῃ οὐσίᾳ, μέρη ὄντες τοῦ νοητοῦ οὐκ ἀφωρισμένα οὐδ' ἀποτετμημένα, ἀλλ' ὄντες τοῦ ὅλου· οὐδὲ γὰρ οὐδὲ νῦν ἀποτετμήμεθα. (But we—who are we? Are we that which approaches and comes to be in time? In fact, even before this generated universe came to be we were in the intelligible world, being different sorts of human beings, some of us even gods, pure souls and intellect connected with the whole of being, parts of the intelligible, not separated off or cut off but belonging to the whole, for we are not cut off even now.) Cf. IV 8, 4.31–35. This view is rejected by virtually

up by experiencing embodied life.[32] The ideal self is an intellect. The endowed self, which we discover in every act of embodied existence and which we more or less effectively try to unify in some way, is an image of that ideal and, ultimately, a product of the first principle of all, the Good or the One.[33] This first principle, and Intellect, and our undescended intellects that constitute our immortal selves are the metaphysical framework for the Platonic answers to ethical and psychological questions. Plotinus's conviction that this framework is Plato's own shapes his interpretation of Plato's accounts of virtue, happiness, culpable wrongdoing, evil, and so on. Plotinus makes no distinction between a Socratic or Platonic ethics stripped of metaphysical presuppositions and one that is not, no doubt supposing that, for example, the so-called Socratic paradoxes would be question-begging without that framework.

Assimilation to the Divine

If there is one passage in Plato's dialogues that, for later Platonists, encapsulates the essence of Platonic anthropology, it is the so-called digression in *Theaetetus* where Socrates steps outside of the analysis of various definitions of knowledge, to reflect on the nature of philosophy and human life. The entire passage (172C3–177C2) is a rich source for reflection by later Platonists. Here I quote only the central thematic claim:

> Evils, Theodorus, can never be eliminated, for necessarily there must always be something in opposition to the good. Nor have evils any place among the gods; necessarily, though, they inhabit mortal nature and this realm. For this reason, it is necessary to try to flee from here to there as quickly as possible. And flight is assimilation to god as much as possible. And assimilation is becoming just and pious with wisdom. But, my good man, it is not at all an easy thing to persuade people that it is not for the reasons some say that it is necessary to flee wickedness and pursue virtue. It is not in order not to appear

---

all later Platonists. See, e.g, Proclus, *ET* Prop. 211.1–2; *In Parm.* 948.12–30; and on Proclus's report of Iamblichus as also rejecting this view, *In Tim.* 3.334.10–14. On the undescended intellect, see Szlezák 1979b, chap. 4.

32. See Remes 2007, chap. 4, for a particularly good discussion of the various aspects of this theme. Long (2005, 186–91) shows that Plato's "normative conception of the soul" leads him to identify person ideally with the impersonal, nonidiosyncratic rational faculty. This detachment from the individual viewpoint is at the center of Plotinus's interpretation as well. See VI 4, 15.32–40, and chap. 9, n. 112 above for the text. The distinction between ideal and endowed person, "*l'homme originel*" and "*l'homme adventice*," is also recognized by Aubry 2008, 109–10.

33. It is worth recalling that the seminal work of H. J. Krämer on the unwritten teachings of Plato is called *Arete bei Platon und Aristoteles*. Krämer's central thesis is that the doctrine of first principles is primarily an 'axiological' doctrine. See Beierwaltes 2002, 124–32, on the amalgamation of metaphysics and ethics in the identification of the Good and the One and on the idea of unification as a moral goal. By contrast, Vegetti (2003, 284–86), who focuses on the normativity of the first principle, excludes the metaphysical role. Also, see Fronterotta 2001, 137–39, with an exhaustive bibliography on the issue in the notes.

evil to others but to appear good that wickedness should be fled and virtue pursued. This is just an old wives' tale, or so it appears to me.

Let us state the truth in this way. God is in no way unjust; rather, he is as just as possible, and there is nothing more like him than one who would become as just as possible. It is in this matter that someone shows his true toughness or his insignificance and weakness. For the grasp of this is true wisdom and true virtue, whereas the ignorance of this is clearly folly and evil.[34]

Only in recent years has this passage received much attention from scholars, though in antiquity it was second to none in importance for expressing the heart of Platonism.[35] Perhaps the main reason for this neglect is the manifest otherworldliness of this passage, which is uncomfortably out of tune with a view of Plato that wishes to emphasize his supposed "earthier" Socratic side. But the otherworldliness is equally evident in the characterization of philosophy as "practice for dying and being dead" in *Phaedo*.[36]

We may begin by noticing that the "assimilation" (ὁμοίωσις) that Socrates exhorts his interlocutor to undertake is a term indicating a process of making something to be the same as or like a model or paradigm. The term ὁμοίωμα is the way Plato refers to a copy or image of a Form or other type of model or the result of a process of producing that copy.[37] So at first it is puzzling that one should strive to become an image or copy of the divine, given that we are, insofar as we are immortal intellects, already such

---

34. *Tht.* 176A5–C5: 'Ἀλλ' οὔτ' ἀπολέσθαι τὰ κακὰ δυνατόν, ὦ Θεόδωρε—ὑπεναντίον γάρ τι τῷ ἀγαθῷ ἀεὶ εἶναι ἀνάγκη—οὔτ' ἐν θεοῖς αὐτὰ ἱδρῦσθαι, τὴν δὲ θνητὴν φύσιν καὶ τόνδε τὸν τόπον περιπολεῖ ἐξ ἀνάγκης. διὸ καὶ πειρᾶσθαι χρὴ ἐνθένδε ἐκεῖσε φεύγειν ὅτι τάχιστα. φυγὴ δὲ ὁμοίωσις θεῷ κατὰ τὸ δυνατόν· ὁμοίωσις δὲ δίκαιον καὶ ὅσιον μετὰ φρονήσεως γενέσθαι. ἀλλὰ γάρ, ὦ ἄριστε, οὐ πάνυ τι ῥᾴδιον πεῖσαι ὡς ἄρα οὐχ ὧν ἕνεκα οἱ πολλοὶ φασι δεῖν πονηρίαν μὲν φεύγειν, ἀρετὴν δὲ διώκειν, τούτων χάριν τὸ μὲν ἐπιτηδευτέον, τὸ δ' οὔ, ἵνα δὴ μὴ κακὸς καὶ ἵνα ἀγαθὸς δοκῇ εἶναι· ταῦτα μὲν γάρ ἐστιν ὁ λεγόμενος γραῶν ὕθλος, ὡς ἐμοὶ φαίνεται· τὸ δὲ ἀληθὲς ὧδε λέγωμεν. θεὸς οὐδαμῇ οὐδαμῶς ἄδικος, ἀλλ' ὡς οἷόν τε δικαιότατος, καὶ οὐκ ἔστιν αὐτῷ ὁμοιότερον οὐδὲν ἢ ὃς ἂν ἡμῶν αὖ γένηται ὅτι δικαιότατος. περὶ τοῦτο καὶ ἡ ὡς ἀληθῶς δεινότης ἀνδρὸς καὶ οὐδενία τε καὶ ἀνανδρία. ἡ μὲν γὰρ τούτου γνῶσις σοφία καὶ ἀρετὴ ἀληθινή, ἡ δὲ ἄγνοια ἀμαθία καὶ κακία ἐναργής. Cf. *Rep.* 500D1, 517C7–9, 519C4–6, 613A4–B1; *Phdr.* 253A4–5; *Tim.* 68E7–69A2; *Lg.* 716C6–D1.

35. See Merki 1952; Roloff 1970; Annas 1999, chap. 3; Sedley 1997, 1999; Beierwaltes 2002, 138–42; Mahoney 2004; Lavecchia 2006. Dillon (1977, 44, 122–23) cites Eudorus (first century BCE) as the earliest Platonist to embrace "assimilation to god" as the central tenet of Platonic ethics. Aristotle seems a better candidate. See D.L., 3.78, where it is reported as the Platonic τέλος of human life.

36. See *Phd.* 81A1–2: [philosophy] μελέτη θανάτου. See Rowe 2007, 97, who, oddly, failing to mention the *Theaetetus* passage, thinks that the uniqueness of the "asceticism" of the *Phaedo* passage means that it can safely be taken as an "isolated thought-experiment." Peterson (2011, 59–89), reversing Rowe's position, ignores the *Phaedo* passage, and dismisses the *Theaetetus* passage as "philosophically pointless," although this pointlessness nevertheless has a point, namely, to draw out the implications of Theodorus's own position (59–60).

37. See *Parm.* 132D3; *Phdr.* 250A6, B3; *Rep.* 395B6; *Tim.* 51A2; *Lg.* 812C4. See Lavecchia 2006, 185–210, for a survey of the uses of ὁμοίωσις, ὅμοιος, ὁμοιότης, ὁμοιόω, ὁμοίωμα, and related concepts like μίμησις, εἰκάζω, and μετέχω in the dialogues.

images. But the puzzle disappears as soon as we realize that the "we" who are exhorted to become like the divine are human beings and we become like that which we really are already by identifying ourselves with the divine part of our souls, namely, our intellects.[38]

The more difficult puzzle is why assimilation to or appropriation of our true identity is to be undertaken by the practice of virtue. The text says that god is just, indeed, perfectly just. But this seems to indicate perfection analogous to the way a Form is perfect relative to its instances. If the Form of Justice cannot be just, one can still "assimilate" to the Form by being just. Similarly, if it is absurd to maintain that the Demiurge is just, simply because he can never owe anything to anyone, then the question remains why assimilation by means of virtue as opposed to, say, intense theoretical activity.[39] No doubt, the practice of the theoretical life is not irrelevant here; the philosopher may be virtuous, but he is more than that. The question, though, is why the practice of virtue is the focus of the assimilation.

For Plotinus, the interpretative key is Plato's identification of virtue as a kind of purification (κάθαρσις). In *Phaedo*, Socrates proclaims:

> In reality, temperance and justice and courage are a sort of purification of these things and wisdom itself is a kind of purifying ritual.[40]

"These things" refers to the "illusory facade" (σκιαγραφία) of virtue in the line above. This is the sort of virtue that seeks only to control bodily appetites. In contrast to these, true virtue is a kind of purification or purgation of them. So the implication is that there are at least two sorts of virtue, one

---

38. So Aristotle, *EN* K 7, 1177b30–1178a8. Cf. K 4, 1166a22–23; I 8, 1168b31–33. At I 2, 5.2 Plotinus takes assimilation to divinity as ταυτότης...θεῷ, identification with the divine, which is coincident with our self-identification. The self-identification results in self-knowledge. See V 3, 7.1–5. Beierwaltes (2002, 144) considers that in making assimilation into identification with the divine, Plotinus has "*radikalisiert*" the Platonic idea. I take this to be in fact equivalent to claiming that Plotinus has explicitly situated the assimilation within the metaphysical framework that is Plato's own. The 'radicalizing' is providing the metaphysical framework.

39. The Demiurge is good and without grudging. See *Tim.* 29D–30A. But this is not virtue. In any case, it is not the virtue of justice. Aristotle makes exactly this point at *EN* K 8, 1178b8–18. Plotinus follows him at I 2, 1.11ff.

40. *Phd.* 69B8–C3: τὸ δ' ἀληθὲς τῷ ὄντι ᾖ κάθαρσίς τις τῶν τοιούτων πάντων καὶ ἡ σωφροσύνη καὶ ἡ δικαιοσύνη καὶ ἀνδρεία, καὶ αὐτὴ ἡ φρόνησις μὴ καθαρμός τις ᾖ. Cf. 67C5. For Plotinus's reading of this passage and his association of it with the *Theaetetus* passage, see II 3, 9.19–24; III 6, 5.13–15; V 1, 10.24–32. Plotinus was no doubt aware of the anecdote recorded by Alexander of Aphrodisias, *De fat.* 171.11–17, where the physiognomist Zopyrus was heard to have said that Socrates had many bad character traits. When Socrates' associates ridiculed this, Socrates himself replied that it was true, but that the practice (ἄσκησις) of philosophy had caused him to become better than his own nature. Cf. *Lg.* 732B2–4: διὸ πάντα ἄνθρωπον χρὴ φεύγειν τὸ σφόδρα φιλεῖν αὑτόν, τὸν δ' ἑαυτοῦ βελτίω διώκειν ἀεί, μηδεμίαν αἰσχύνην ἐπὶ τῷ τοιούτῳ πρόσθεν ποιούμενον (for these reasons, human beings should flee the excessive love of self, and always follow that which is better than oneself, not letting embarrassment with such a position get in their way.)

that succeeds in self-restraint and a superior sort that purifies the states of one who has so succeeded. The purification is not of the unrestrained bodily states, but of those that have been held in check. According to Plotinus, Plato is not suggesting that the truly virtuous person will not feel pleasure or pain; rather, he achieves a distancing or alienation from them that is just the obverse of his identification of himself with his true self, his intellect.[41]

Plato calls the illusory facade "popular or political virtue" (τὴν δημοτικὴν καὶ πολιτικὴν ἀρετήν.[42] These, say Socrates, are developed from custom and practice without philosophy and intellect. This virtue is neither faux virtue nor is it hypocritical. It is manifested in socially accepted behavior. But without philosophy and intellect, it is deficient.[43] The deficiency is scarcely intelligible absent the positing of the ideal self. The reason that popular and political virtue is unsatisfactory is that one here still retains a false identity, that of the subject of the ameliorated or restrained bodily states.[44]

In *Republic*, Plato seems to identify this "popular or political virtue" with the virtue defined at the end of book 4.[45] This is, by implication, contrasted

---

41. See VI 8, 5.34–36: Εἰ οὖν οἷον νοῦς τις ἄλλος ἐστὶν ἡ ἀρετὴ καὶ ἕξις οἷον νοωθῆναι τὴν ψυχὴν ποιοῦσα. (If, then, virtue is in a way another kind of intellect, that is, a habit that in a way intellectualizes the soul.) Cf. Aristotle, *EE* Θ 3, 1249b13–21, where the exercise of φρόνησις consists in doing the things that make us unconscious of the irrational part of the soul. Also, *EN* H 13, 1145a6–11 where φρόνησις "gives orders for the sake of [ἕνεκα] wisdom." See Rist 1967.

42. See *Phd.* 82A10–B3. What Plato calls "popular or political virtue" is perhaps equivalent to what he elsewhere calls "continence" (ἐγκράτεια) or "mortal temperance" (σωφροσύνη θνητή). See *Phdr.* 256B1, with 256E5. Cf. Aristotle, *EN* Δ 15, 1128b33–34, where continence is explicitly distinguished from virtue. The characteristics of continence seem to be exactly the same as those of popular or political virtue, namely, behavioral. At *Rep.* 430E6–7, Socrates calls the virtue of temperance (σωφροσύνη) a sort of ἐγκράτεια of pleasures and appetites. Devereux (1995, 384) believes that when Aristotle in *EE* B 11, 1227B12–19 accuses "certain thinkers" of conflating virtue and continence, he must be referring to Socrates as opposed to Plato who, Devereux argues, separates them, like Aristotle. But Devereux's argument does not take into account the passages from *Phaedo, Phaedrus,* and *Republic.*

43. The words at *Tht.* 176B1–2, ὁμοίωσις δὲ δίκαιον καὶ ὅσιον μετὰ φρονήσεως γενέσθαι (and assimilation is becoming just and pious with wisdom), should be compared with *Rep.* 619D1, ἔθει ἄνευ φιλοσοφίας ἀρετῆς (virtue by habit without philosophy). The *Republic* passage occurs in the Myth of Er and describes the person who, despite his virtue, chooses the life of a tyrant. The words 'wisdom' and 'philosophy' are certainly being used synonymously, as confirmed by 613A7–B1, which is referencing the thought at *Tht.* 176B1–2 explicitly.

44. At II 9, 15.32–40, Plotinus gives voice to the skeptic who proposes that it is possible to acknowledge our divine identity while at the same time indulging in every pleasure. Plotinus rejects this as a possibility, saying that without true virtue, talk of god is a "name only" (ὄνομά ἐστιν). And, as he argues elsewhere, I 2, 7.10–11, it is not possible to have true virtue without having practical or political virtue at least "in potency" (δυνάμει).

45. Cf. *Rep.* 365C3–4 and especially 500D8 with 518D3–519A6, where the "popular" virtues are identified as the "so-called virtues of the soul," and especially 619C7–D1 for participation in virtue by "custom" (ἔθει) "without philosophy." At 430C3, courage is characterized as "political." At 443C10–D1, characterizing justice, Plato contrasts "external" behavior with "internal" virtue, which is concerned with what is "truly oneself and one's own." Only the

with the virtue of the aristocratic man (i.e., the philosopher) in books 7 and 8. His "divine virtue of intellect"[46] is precisely what justifies his rule in the ideal state. Of course, this virtue consists in more than intellectual achievement, as impressive as this might be after fifty years of education. It consists in transformation into one who has almost completely identified himself as a subject of thought—"as far as is possible for a human being." So identifying himself, he desires only what reason dictates; he desires his own good by desiring the Good.

In his treatise *On Virtues* Plotinus expresses what was to become the standard late Platonic interpretation of the virtues and their relation to assimilation to the divine.[47] The treatise begins with a reflection on the *Theaetetus* passage. Plotinus asks how the practice of virtue can make us like the divine and intelligible reality since there is no virtue there. The divine has no need of virtue because it is perfect.[48] In particular, it has no need of the popular or political virtues, which Plotinus identifies as achievements of an embodied tripartite soul. Assimilation to the divine consists in becoming like eternal intellect, absorbed in the contemplation of eternal reality.[49] All true virtues are understood as advancements toward identification of the person with the activity of a disembodied intellect.

Plotinus asks if the popular or political virtues are real virtues. And his answer is an insistence that whatever serves to make us godlike is a virtue.[50]

> These virtues do truly organize our lives and make us better by giving limit to and giving measure to our appetites and in general to all our feelings. And they eliminate false beliefs, by what is generally better and by limiting the unmeasured and unlimited.[51]

Eliminating false beliefs—that is, producing true beliefs—is a far cry from the achievement of a philosopher who, aiming for and achieving knowledge

---

philosopher is concerned with what is truly "his own." Cf. Vasiliou (2008, 259–67), who provides a similar argument for the claim that the virtue of nonphilosophers is a lower grade of virtue than the virtue of philosophers, though Vasiliou does not consider the achievement of true identity as that which distinguishes the one from the other.

46. *Rep.* 518E2.
47. See Dillon 1983, 93–102. Also, see O'Meara 1994.
48. I 2, 3.31.
49. See V 3, 4.29–30: Ἔστι δὴ νοῦς τις αὐτὸς γεγονώς, ὅτε τὰ ἄλλα ἀφεὶς ἑαυτοῦ τούτῳ καὶ τοῦτον βλέπει, αὐτῷ δὲ ἑαυτόν. Ὡς δὴ οὖν νοῦς ἑαυτὸν ὁρᾷ. (For someone has become intellect when he lets go of all of his other things and looks at this with this, and at himself with himself. It is, then, as intellect that he sees himself.)
50. I 2, 1.23–26.
51. I 2, 2.13–18: Αἱ μὲν τοίνυν πολιτικαὶ ἀρεταί, ἃς ἄνω που εἴπομεν, κατακοσμοῦσι μὲν ὄντως καὶ ἀμείνουι ποιοῦσιν ὁρίζουσαι καὶ μετροῦσαι τὰς ἐπιθυμίας καὶ ὅλως τὰ πάθη μετροῦσαι καὶ ψευδεῖς δόξας ἀφαιροῦσαι τῷ ὅλως ἀμείνονς καὶ τῷ ὡρίσθαι καὶ τῶν ἀμέτρων καὶ ἀορίστων ἔξω εἶναι κατὰ τὸ μεμετρημένον. These virtues are here understood according to a general account of *Philebus* 23Bff., esp. 26B–C, in which the imposition by the Demiurge of form on the sensible world is taken to be the imposition of limit on the unlimited.

rather than belief, knows why true beliefs are true. This achievement is supposed both by Plato and Plotinus to be self-transformative. Were this not the case, philosophy and the philosophical life would be a mere adornment to virtue rather than an expression of its highest form. The popular or political virtues are, therefore, a grade of virtue, but only of the lowest sort. They do not, as Plotinus points out, actually produce the sameness that is supposed to be the result of assimilation, presumably because they constitute only improvements in the life of the composite human being.[52]

What, then, of the 'higher' virtue that is a 'purification'? In contrast to the popular and political virtues that consist essentially in behavior, these virtues constitute a 'disposition' (διάθεσις) of the soul. According to this permanent state, the soul "thinks and is in this way free of affections" (ἀπαθής).[53] The reference here to "thinking" (τὸ νοεῖν) is not intended to suggest that there is no thinking in the practice of the lower virtues. As Plotinus explains elsewhere, the thinking is the orientation to the intelligible world.

> Looking to that which comes before it, it [the intellectual part of the soul] thinks, while when it looks into itself, it orders and arranges that which comes after it and rules it.[54]

Here the distinction between the higher and the lower virtue is clearly the manner in which the embodied intellect stands to the body, that is, to the animated body. Ruling the body is different from controlling it, since controlling it is a form of self-control. More precisely, one comes to rule over that which has been made alien to oneself, the obverse of assimilation to the divine by self-transformation in the direction of one's true identity.

The gradation of virtue that Plotinus associates with the doctrine of assimilation to the divine reflects the integrated hierarchical metaphysics that is always the starting point for his applications of Platonism.[55] Embodied rational souls are somewhere in the middle of this continuous hierarchy from the Good or One down to matter. 'Virtue' is the general name for self-development in the 'upward' direction; 'vice' is the name for the opposite. If the Idea of the Good as a metaphysical first principle and the identification of the true self with an immortal intellect are excluded from the framework of analysis of the Platonic account of what I am broadly

---

52. See I 2, 3.9–10. The word ὁμοίωσις is a process the result of which is sameness, or ὁμοιότης. The 'lower' virtues are still virtues because they are part of the process, but they do not achieve the result at which one aims by initiating the process. At V 9, 1.10–16, Plotinus criticizes Stoics for their focus on virtue in action. Owing to their materialism, they are unable to rise to true virtue, even though they tried to do so.

53. I 2, 3.19–20.

54. IV 8, 3.25–27: Βλέπουσα δὲ πρὸς μὲν τὸ πρὸ ἑαυτῆς νοεῖ, εἰς δὲ ἑαυτὴν τὸ μετ' αὐτὴν [ὃ] κοσμεῖ τε καὶ διοικεῖ καὶ ἄρχει αὐτοῦ.

55. Cf. Beierwaltes 2002, 132–37.

calling 'anthropology,' one may indeed be able to construct something like a 'prudentialist ethics' out of that account. Plotinus, as an assiduous student of the dialogues, seems right in rejecting out of hand such a truncated version of Platonism.

Moral Responsibility

Assume that Plotinus's interpretation of the nature of virtue and, by implication, of vice correctly carries the above metaphysical baggage. Assume that we are saved or doomed—whatever we take that to mean—by our success or failure to discover our true identities and thereby be united with the Good in the only way possible, by intellection. Does it make any sense to say that we are morally responsible for our fates?

On the one hand, we read the ringing proclamation in Plato's *Republic* that "the one who chooses is to blame; god is blameless" (αἰτία ἑλομένου· θεὸς ἀναίτιος).[56] The choice referred to is the choice of lives and of one's guardian spirit that we are to make prior to embodiment. It is true that in the passage in *Republic,* the opportunity to choose a life is arranged by lot, so that one chooses in an order over which he has no control. Yet any choice of life is said to be capable of bringing a measure of happiness. But the main point of the passage is that success in a choice of lives depends on the virtue that one brings to the task. And this virtue is, presumably, developed in a previous embodiment. So we read in *Laws* the passage in which the Athenian Stranger is considering divine providence that "all our actions are ensouled" (ἐμψύχους οὔσας τὰς πράξεις ἁπάσας), meaning, I think, that they are all a function of the state of the soul of the agent.[57] The Stranger then adds that the "King"

> made responsible the acts of willing of each individual for the generation of the state of the soul. This is so because in whatever way one manifests desire and whatever state his soul is in, it is almost always in this way that he acts each time and this is the way the state of the soul comes to be.[58]

Commenting on this passage, Plotinus says that

> there is a place for every man, one fit for the good and one fit for the bad. Each kind of man, then, goes according to nature and the expressed principle in him to the place that suits him, and holds the position he has chosen.

---

56. *Rep.* 617E4–5. Cf. III 2, 7.19–20; III 4, 5.1–3.
57. *Lg.* 904A6–7.
58. *Lg.* 904B8–C4: τῆς δὲ γενέσεως τοῦ ποίου τινὸς ἀφῆκε ταῖς βουλήσεσιν ἑκάστων ἡμῶν τὰς αἰτίας. ὅπῃ γὰρ ἂν ἐπιθυμῇ καὶ ὁποῖός τις ὢν τὴν ψυχήν, ταύτῃ σχεδὸν ἑκάστοτε καὶ τοιοῦτος γίγνεται ἅπας ἡμῶν ὡς τὸ πολύ. This passage provides the clarifying gloss for *Rep.* 619B7–C1 where the first one who chooses a new life in the Myth of Er does not notice that he who chooses this life is fated to eat his own children.

There one speaks blasphemies and commits crimes, the other speaks and acts in the opposite way; for the agents existed before the play and bring their own selves to it. Now in human plays the author provides the words, but the agents, each and every one of them, are responsible by themselves and from themselves for the good or bad acting of their parts. For there is action, too, which is theirs in addition to the words of the poet.[59]

Plotinus seems to concur with Plato that we are somehow responsible for the kind of persons we become when embodied and the kind of lives we lead. For this reason, punishments and rewards are just. This moral responsibility obtains regardless of the circumstances in which we find ourselves, and indeed, even the kinds of bodies.[60]

On the other hand, Plotinus's commitment to the Platonic idea of moral responsibility is made against the background of the consistently held Platonic principle: no one does wrong willingly (οὐδεὶς ἑκὼν ἁμαρτάνει).[61] Taken in one way, this claim is tautologous: no one willingly acts counter to their best interests as they conceive them to be. Taken in another, a paradox emerges: no one willingly acts counter to what are in fact their best interests, regardless of how they conceive of them. The quasi-tautology focuses on the meaning of "does wrong," or ἁμαρτάνει, for this implies one is trying to hit a target, this being one's own good. And, of course, no one willingly fails to hit that target. By contrast, the paradox relies on an implicit distinction between what one really wills and what one thinks one wills. But the paradox does not consist in this distinction, which is in itself banal. Nor does it even consist in the claim that if one believes that something is bad for oneself, then one cannot will it, as the existence of the phenomenon of ἀκρασία clearly shows. What turns the tautology into a paradox is the claim that one's own good is in fact never achievable at the expense of others. In that case, what one really wills is only the good simpliciter. And so if one errs it is always with respect to mistaking what appears to be good

---

59. III 2, 17.22-32: οὕτω τοι καὶ ἔστι τόπος ἑκάστῳ ὁ μὲν τῷ ἀγαθῷ, ὁ δὲ τῷ κακῷ πρέπων. Ἑκάτερος οὖν κατὰ φύσιν καὶ κατὰ λόγον εἰς ἑκάτερον καὶ τὸν πρέποντα χωρεῖ τὸν τόπον ἔχων, ὃν εἵλετο. Εἶτα φθέγγεται καὶ ποιεῖ ὁ μὲν ἀσεβεῖς λόγους καὶ ἔργα πονηρῶν, ὁ δὲ τὰ ἐναντία· ἦσαν γὰρ καὶ πρὸ τοῦ δράματος οἱ τοιοῦτοι ὑποκριταὶ διδόντες ἑαυτοὺς τῷ δράματι. ἐν μὲν οὖν τοῖς ἀνθρωπίνοις δράμασιν ὁ μὲν ποιητὴς ἔδωκε τοὺς λόγους, οἱ δὲ ἔχουσι παρ' αὐτῶν καὶ ἐξ αὐτῶν τό τε καλῶς καὶ τὸ κακῶς ἕκαστος—ἔστι γὰρ καὶ ἔργον αὐτοῖς μετὰ τὰς ῥήσεις τοῦ ποιητοῦ. Cf. III 2, 10.11-19; III 3, 3; IV 2, 24.11-16; IV 3, 15.20-23; 16.17-19; 24.8-10: Οὐ γὰρ μή ποτέ τις ἐκφύγοι, ὃ παθεῖν ἐπ' ἀδίκοις ἔργοις προσήκει. (For one will never escape that which it is appropriate to suffer for one's misdeeds.)

60. I take it that this is Plotinus's understanding of *Rep.* 379B15-16 where Plato says that what is good is not responsible for evils. In addition, at III 6, 2.65-66 and I 8, 8.3-4, Plotinus appears to be alluding to *Tim.* 86B-87B, where Plato says that psychic illnesses are owing to bodily dysfunction. This is in line with the identification of matter with evil. Plotinus here specifically distinguishes the vice of the appetitive part of the soul from that pertaining to the rational part, implicitly interpreting Plato as not attributing *all* vice to bodily constitution.

61. See Plato *Ap.* 37A5-6; *Gorg.* 488A3-4; *Protag.* 345D8, 358C6-7; *Rep.* 589C6; *Tim.* 86D1-E2; *Lg.* 731C-D.

as the real good. This is an intellectual error, to be sure. But it is highly misleading to characterize it exclusively thus. For we might well wonder why anyone would be convinced that there is never—absolutely never—a divergence between my own good and the good simpliciter. According to both Plato and Plotinus, such a conviction arises only in one who has radically reconceived his own identity. Such a person comes to think of his good only as the sort of thing that is obtainable without negative consequences for anyone else. In short, he comes to identify himself as an intellectual soul or simply an intellect whose only true good is enjoyment of cognition of all that is intelligible.[62]

Plotinus's most extensive treatment of the issues surrounding moral responsibility is in the treatise 6.8, a work that is principally focused on whether volition or will can be ascribed to the One. But Plotinus, reasonably enough, starts with human beings, analogous to the way that Aristotle starts with sensible substance on the way to understanding primary being. The specific question Plotinus begins by posing is "What is up to us?" (τὸ ἐφ' ἡμῖν). That is, what can we properly be held responsible for doing? The surprising answer at which Plotinus arrives is that the only thing that is up to us is our will (βούλησις).[63] Our will is for what is good. In our undescended intellects, the will for what is good and the will for the Good coincide.[64] For us, willing the Good alone is a kind of ideal that can never quite be achieved while embodied. But it is possible to will real goods, as opposed to apparent ones, here below.[65] So Plotinus interprets "no one does wrong willingly" as meaning that all wrongdoing results from a desire other than the will for the Good.

---

62. See IV 8, 1.4–5 for this dynamic sense of identification: ζωήν τε ἀρίστην ἐνεργήσας καὶ τῷ θείῳ εἰς ταὐτὸν γεγενημένος (I lived the best life and came to identify myself with the divine).

63. VI 8, 6.29–33: Ὅσα οὖν ἐκ ταύτης [βούλησις] καὶ διὰ ταύτην, ἐφ' ἡμῖν, ἔξω τε καὶ ἐφ' αὑτῆς· ὃ αὐτὴ βούλεται καὶ ἐνεργεῖ ἀνεμποδίστως, τοῦτο καὶ πρῶτον ἐφ' ἡμῖν. (All that comes from the will and through this is up to us, both in external action and internally; what it wills and actualizes without impediment, this is primarily what is up to us). Cf. III 1, 9. Plotinus thus appropriates Stoic insights via Epictetus's notion of προαίρεσις. See Gill 2000 for an argument that the Stoic understanding of moral responsibility provides the most plausible interpretation of *Tim.* 86B–87B. See also Bobzien 1998b, 167–73, on Plotinus's adoption of the Stoic idea that what depends on us is "one-sided and causative," meaning that for something to be "up to us" it does not follow that "we could have done otherwise."

64. See VI 8, 6.38–43: Ἡ γὰρ βούλησις θέλει τὸ ἀγαθόν· τὸ δὲ νοεῖν ἀληθῶς ἐστιν ἐν τῷ ἀγαθῷ. Ἔχει οὖν ἐκεῖνος, ὅπερ ἡ βούλησις θέλει καὶ οὗ τυχοῦσα ἂν ταύτῃ νόησις γίνεται. Εἰ οὖν βουλήσει τοῦ ἀγαθοῦ τίθεμεν τὸ ἐφ' ἡμῖν, τὸ ἤδη ἐν ᾧ θέλει ἡ βούλησις εἶναι ἱδρυμένον πῶς οὐ τὸ ἐφ' αὑτῷ ἔχει; (Will wants the Good; but thinking is truly in the Good. That Intellect has what its will wants and that by which it becomes thinking when it attains it. If, then, we place "up to us" in the will for the Good, does it not follow that that which is already seated in what its will wants has that?)

65. See VI 8, 6.22 and VI 6, 8.6.22, for virtue as τις ἄλλος νοῦς (a certain kind of other intellect). This is the superior virtue of the philosopher, not the popular or political virtue that consists in bodily self-restraint.

The obvious problem with this conclusion is that, according to Plato, the only cause for our desiring something other than that which is good is ignorance. Though we may well in fact desire that which is only apparently good, we do this owing to ignorance of the falsity of the belief that what seems good to us really is not. If this is so, how can we be held morally responsible for this ignorance? Stated otherwise, is all wrongdoing the result of culpable ignorance?

Culpable wrongdoing—*without* ignorance—seems particularly clear in cases where the wrongdoer acknowledges his culpability. This sort of culpability fits perfectly the description of the acratic who, by definition, knows that what he is doing is wrong, though he does it nonetheless.[66] Yet, because he knows that what he is doing is wrong, he does not seem to be ignorant. If the acratic is not ignorant of the truth of the universal moral proposition against which he acts, the vicious person may well manifest such ignorance, though he thereby seems to avoid the culpability of the acratic precisely because of this. So we have either a nonignorant and therefore culpable or an ignorant and therefore nonculpable vicious individual.

At the beginning of V 1, "On the Three Primary Hypostases," Plotinus dwells on the ignorance that is the result of embodiment.[67] The ignorance that people have of their "lineage" is the result of their "audacity" or "wanting to belong to themselves." As Plotinus explains elsewhere, the audacity itself is either nonculpable or minimally so.[68] Indeed, Plotinus reasons that if persons were not embodied, but rather remained in the intelligible world, the powers that are manifested here below would have been useless as mere quiescent paradigms.[69] So Plotinus seems to view embodiment as a necessary result of the operation of the primary principles, though the result of the operation is the ignorant human race. Given that embodiment

---

66. When at *Rep.* 439E6–440A4, Leontius berates himself for gazing on the naked corpse, he acknowledges his culpability.

67. See V 1, 1.1–17, quoted above, 289.

68. See IV 8, 5. See IV 3, 13.17–20: Ἴασι δὲ οὔτε ἑκοῦσαι οὔτε πεμφθεῖσαι· οὔ γε τὸ ἑκούσιον τοιοῦτον ὡς προελέσθαι, ἀλλ' ὡς τὸ πηδᾶν κατὰ φύσιν, ἢ <ὡς> πρὸς γάμων φυσικὰς προθυμίας ἢ [ὡς] πρὸς πράξεις τινὲς καλῶν οὐ λογισμῷ κινούμενοι. (The souls go neither voluntarily nor because they have been sent—or at least their volition is not such as would arise from a choice; it is more like a natural leap, as it might be toward a natural desire for marriage, or in another case toward the accomplishment of some noble exploits, not provoked by reasoned calculation.)

69. See IV 8, 5.27–33: κἂν μὲν θᾶττον φύγῃ, οὐδὲν βέβλαπται γνῶσιν κακοῦ προσλαβοῦσα καὶ φύσιν κακίας γνοῦσα τάς τε δυνάμεις ἄγουσα αὐτῆς εἰς τὸ φανερὸν καὶ δείξασα ἔργα τε καὶ ποιήσεις, ἃ ἐν τῷ ἀσωμάτῳ ἠρεμοῦντα μάτην τε ἂν ἦν εἰς τὸ ἐνεργεῖν ἀεὶ οὐκ ἰόντα, τήν τε ψυχὴν αὐτὴν ἔλαθεν ἂν ἃ εἶχεν οὐκ ἐκφανέντα οὐδὲ πρόοδον λαβόντα. (If [the embodied soul] escapes quickly, it is not harmed by acquiring knowledge of evil and coming to know the nature of vice, and manifesting its powers and displaying its deeds and actions, which had they remained quiescent in the disembodied soul, would have been there in vain, not ever being actualized; and the soul itself would not have known the powers it had if they had not been manifested and developed.)

is inevitable, and that it inevitably produces a loss of a clear sense of one's true identity, whence the culpability?

> For everything goes toward the worse unwillingly, but since they do it by their own impetus, when they experience the worse they are said to receive punishment for the things they did.[70]

The words "their own impetus" indicate that the desire in the agent is the origin of the action "toward the worse."[71] The action is unwilling because the agent is ignorant that he is pursuing the apparent good that is not real. The culpability is, then, to be located in ignorance of the fact that this apparent good is not real. This culpable ignorance leads the agent to do that which he does not truly will. As we learn from the passage above in V 1, this is supposed to be ignorance of one's true identity. Because one is ignorant of one's true identity, one engages in a process of reasoning that leads up to an action aimed at that which is worse.

The key to Plotinus's analysis is his insight that the acratic and the vicious person are on a continuum. That the former does and the latter does not accept a true moral proposition indicates only a different degree of confusion regarding one's own true identity. The vicious person has lost himself—perhaps irretrievably—while the acratic has a residual grasp on who he is.[72]

> Therefore, it is of concern to us when it [the human being] is experiencing pleasure and pain, and the more so the weaker we are, and to the extent that we do not separate ourselves from it, but hold this to be most valuable, and take it as the true man, and, as it were, submerge ourselves into it.[73]

We recall that only the person who acts κατὰ βούλησιν is unqualifiedly doing what is "up to him."[74] Everyone else is more or less acting in service to a counterfeit version of his true self. This ignorance of the true self is culpable because everyone, including the vicious individual, acknowledges his

---

70. See IV 8, 5.8–10: Πᾶν μὲν γὰρ ἰὸν ἐπὶ τὸ χεῖρον ἀκούσιον, φορᾷ γε μὴν οἰκείᾳ ἰὸν πάσχον τὰ χείρω ἔχειν λέγεται τὴν ἐφ' οἷς ἔπραξε δίκην. Cf. III 2, 7.20; IV 3, 24.15–16.

71. Cf. IV 3, 24.15–16: ἑκουσίῳ τῇ φορᾷ τὸ ἀκούσιον εἰς τὸ παθεῖν ἔχων (having to suffer that which is involuntary owing to voluntary impetus).

72. Cf. *Rep.* 550B–577D for the typology of psychic degeneration from the aristocratic man to his polar opposite, the tyrannical man. When the tyrant "makes a despot" (δεσπόζειν) of the worst part of his soul, he "identifies" with that part.

73. IV 4, 18.15–19: Διὸ καὶ ἡδομένου καὶ ἀλγοῦντος μέλει, καὶ ὅσῳ ἀσθενέστεροι μᾶλλον, καὶ ὅσῳ ἑαυτοὺς μὴ χωρίζομεν, ἀλλὰ τοῦτο ἡμῶν τὸ τιμιώτατον καὶ τὸν ἄνθρωπον τιθέμεθα καὶ οἷον εἰσδυόμεθα εἰς αὐτό.

74. See I 4, 4.13–15: τὸν δὲ εὐδαίμονα ἤδη, ὃς δὴ καὶ ἐνεργείᾳ ἐστί τοῦτο καὶ μεταβέβηκε πρὸς τὸ αὐτό, εἶναι τοῦτο (the one who has achieved happiness is this actually and has transformed himself in the direction of being identical with this). "This" is the intellect with which the happy person identifies himself.

essential rational nature when he endorses the desires he discovers in his embodied self. When the tyrant affirms his avaricious desires as constituting a good way to live, he implicitly pronounces his reason as sovereign, that is to say, as that which he most truly is. Even if the tyrant embraces the motto "Reason in the service of the passions!" that is, *malgré lui-même*, a revelation of reason's sovereignty. The vicious person, like the acratic, is culpably ignorant of his true identity. He is not less culpable than the acratic because he does not believe a universal proposition that the acratic does.[75] He is *more* culpable because he is more culpably ignorant of his identity.

The gradation of confusion about self-identity mirrors the gradation of the virtues. Someone who achieves popular or political virtue certainly has a clearer, that is, a more unified, sense of himself just insofar as he thinks he ought to moderate his appetites. Thinking that it is good for him to do so, he cannot continue to identify himself exclusively as the subject of those appetites. But the self-recognition so achieved is a relatively inferior achievement, as Plato spends the latter half of *Republic* spelling out.

Plotinus's account of moral responsibility eschews an imaginary conflict between 'Socratic intellectualism' and 'Platonic irrationalism.' The key to overcoming this conflict is the idea of the divided embodied self. This division follows the generation of the human soul in *Timaeus*.[76] In particular, souls are composed of a mixture of divisible and indivisible οὐσία along with divisible and indivisible identity and difference. Divisible οὐσία belongs to bodies; indivisible οὐσία belongs to intelligibles and intellect. Plotinus takes the 'mixture' of the two to result in multiple loci of subjectivity, so to speak.[77] But these all belong to one kind of οὐσία, to one kind of soul, namely, the rational soul of a human being. The acratic, no more or less than the vicious individual, possesses just such a soul. On this basis, ethical and psychological issues are appropriately situated within the Platonic metaphysical framework.[78]

---

75. The psychology of the acratic is identical if he acts on a virtuous desire over against his belief in the truth of a false universal moral proposition. His culpability does not reside in the content of what he does or does not believe.

76. See *Tim.* 41D–E with 35A.

77. See IV 2, 2.52–55: ἔστιν οὖν ψυχὴ ἓν καὶ πολλὰ οὕτως· τὰ δὲ ἓν τοῖς σώμασιν εἴδη πολλὰ καὶ ἕν· τὰ δὲ σώματα πολλὰ μόνον· τὸ δ' ὑπέρτατον ἓν μόνον (soul is, then, one and many in this way: the forms in bodies are many and one; bodies are only many, the highest is only one). The phrase "forms in the body" evidently alludes to "three forms *of soul* in the body" in *Rep.* 440E9.

78. Cf. *Phdr.* 270C1–2: Ψυχῆς οὖν φύσιν ἀξίως λόγου κατανοῆσαι οἴει δυνατὸν εἶναι ἄνευ τῆς τοῦ ὅλου φύσεως; (Do you think it possible to understand properly the nature of the soul without understanding the nature of the universe as a whole?) At *Tim.* 34A8–B9 the World's Soul, added to the body of the world, constitutes the "whole" (ὅλον) of the universe.

Conclusion

I began with the question: Was Plato a Platonist? My answer to this question is yes, with what I hope to have shown is a reasonable qualification. 'Platonism' refers to any version of a positive construct on the basis of UP. For all soi-disant followers of Plato from the Old Academy onward, Plato's version takes the crown. Nevertheless, recognition of the superiority of Plato's version of Platonism did not preclude disagreements—some subtle and some not so subtle—regarding the accounts of the elements of the construct. Nor did it preclude the formulation of responses to the enemies of Platonism that required the application of general principles to the solution to problems hitherto unappreciated or at least underappreciated.

As I have argued, the unification of the elements of UP into a single positive construct was of paramount importance. That is why Platonism is first and foremost a metaphysical doctrine. Without metaphysics, it is no doubt possible to consider the multitude of ethical, political, psychological, and epistemological claims in the dialogues each in some degree of isolation from the rest. Accordingly, the strength or weakness of one argument in one area need not reflect positively or negatively on another argument in another area. For example, it is evident that many proponents of something called 'Socratic moral philosophy' are eager to disassociate that from what they take to be unnecessary or even disastrous metaphysical accretions whether actually endorsed by Plato himself or not. I have found not the slightest bit of evidence either in the dialogues or in the indirect tradition that Plato ever contemplated such a disassociation. Indeed, there is no evidence that Plato ever contemplated something like a firewall separating his metaphysics from any of his other philosophical concerns.

The elements of UP—antinominalism, antimaterialism, antimechanism, antirelativism, and antiskepticism—frame Platonism generally. Versions of Platonism, including Plato's own, are positive constructs based on UP. The unifying element of each positive construct is a 'first principle of all,' called in *Republic* the Idea of the Good, and otherwise named, according to the testimony of Aristotle and others, 'the One.' The unification that this first principle was supposed to provide was primarily explanatory. That is, in trying to answer the array of questions formulated in ancient Greek philosophy going back to the earliest Pre-Socratics, the first principle of all was supposed to provide ultimate explanatory adequacy. That is at least in part how the Platonic tradition understood the identification in *Republic* of the Good as 'unhypothetical.' For even Forms—*hypothetical* entities in *Phaedo*—do not provide ultimate explanations. It is indeed the case that, say, the Form of Justice is the instrumental cause of the presence of the property of justice in some act or other. There is thus a conditional adequacy in this explanation. But justice is desirable only because justice is good, the explanation for which depends on showing how the being of the Form of Justice is eternally dependent on the first principle, the Good.

The postulation of a first principle of all is not unproblematic. Just to list some of the problems recognized by Platonists themselves, including the dissident Platonist Aristotle, is to provide a topical index to the early history of metaphysics. Here is a list that does not pretend to be exhaustive: How can the first principle of all *have* being in any sense without having a sort of complexity that undermines its explanatory ultimacy? How does the first principle cause anything else to be, including things that are utterly unlike it? How, again, if it does cause anything else to be, is its absolute simplicity not compromised? How is the first principle cognitively available to us such that it can be explanatorily ultimate in anything more than purely formal terms? Indeed, how does the first principle make anything else cognitively available or intelligible to us? Why is the first principle a normative principle?

Reflection on any one of these questions should make it obvious that virtually any answer is going to appear to be underdetermining. That is, the account given will never preempt variations on itself. That in a nutshell is the explanation for disagreement among the Platonists. It is also the explanation for the fact that opponents of UP, like the Stoics, can produce philosophical doctrines that converge with those taken by Platonists to be entailments of their accounts of first principles. It is, I think, illuminating to see Aristotle's own response to these questions as within the Platonic tradition, even though they were made explicitly against Plato's own responses and were rejected by all Platonists up to the advent of Christian theology. The guiding rule for this ongoing dialectical enterprise lasting more than eight hundred years was a commitment to UP. It is worth noting that philosophers like Numenius and Plotinus had no doubt that the ranks of those sharing this commitment included many who were separated by a considerable distance both in space and time from Plato. In this regard, philosophy was also seen to transcend culture.

In addition to the quite general questions listed above, a further seemingly technical question opened up an array of complex new issues. What is the first 'product' of the first principle of all? Or is there a first? The question of an ordering of production raises the issue of a hierarchy of being, and insofar as the first principle is a normative principle, that hierarchy has significant ethical import. The possibility that there is no first is evidently a nonstarter among Platonists because such a view would efface the distinction between the eternal and the temporal. Not only would this go directly against the text of Plato, but it would make nonsense of the very idea of an absolutely first and simple principle of all. The easiest answer to the question is: the Forms. Aristotle's testimony is clear that even if this was at one stage an answer endorsed within the Academy, it was apparently not the considered view of Plato or of his successors. Neither the testimony of Aristotle nor that of any other Platonist up to Plotinus explains why the Indefinite Dyad is the first product. Plotinus argues that the Indefinite Dyad is first because it is minimally complex. This is strictly a logical point. Whether Plotinus learned of this explanation from the oral tradition or whether he himself deduced its necessity is unknown. The critical point is that with the postulation of a second principle that is minimally complex we have a criterion of hierarchization: the less complex, the 'closer' to the first principle; the more complex, the further away from it. On the axis simple–complex or, in other terms, unified–dispersed, all things that exist can be arrayed. In addition, the account of desire, logically connected to the Good itself, can be given a more nuanced account and subjected to normative judgment.

The hypothesis that the first and second principles of all—the One and the Indefinite Dyad—yield to a mathematical account of the intelligibility of all that there is seems to have been on the Academic table, so to speak, right up until Plato's death. It also appears that most later Platonists approached this hypothesis with less than unbounded enthusiasm. The evidence here is sketchy to say the least, which is after all what we would expect if there were in fact no definitive word by Plato himself on how to reduce Form to Numbers. The precise role of mathematics in the positive construct remains the great unfinished research project within Platonism.

The philosophical position that is the precise contradiction of UP is the matrix out of which are built various forms of what is today called 'naturalism.' Examples of 'pure' Platonism and 'pure' naturalism are rare in the history of philosophy since the seventeenth century. Most of philosophy since then may be usefully seen as efforts by naturalists to accommodate one or another of the claims of Platonists and vice versa. I offer by way of a speculative conclusion that many, if not most, of the philosophical disputes today can be traced to one side or the other supposing that the elements of UP and of their contradictions are radically independent of each other, and therefore that, for example, it is possible to eschew relativism or skepticism

308 CONCLUSION

at the same time as one embraces nominalism or materialism. Most of the Platonists of antiquity resisted the allure of a rapprochement with various forms of naturalism; indeed, the exceptions, like Antiochus of Ascalon and perhaps Philo of Larissa, stand out by their negligible influence. For contemporary Platonists—most of whom today are in fact found among religious believers—the challenge remains exactly the same as it was for Plato: provide a compelling, integrated, positive construct on the basis of UP. For naturalists, the challenge is equally clear: show how acceptance of any one of the contradictories of the elements of UP entails all the rest. Visionary philosophers like the late Richard Rorty could see plainly that a recognition of the unbridgeable gap between pure Platonism and pure naturalism ought to frame or at least inform all nontrivial philosophical debate.[1]

I have argued in this book that Proclus's praise of Plotinus as leading the way in the exegesis of the Platonic revelation is essentially correct. Although this is a view shared by scholars of Platonism and by Platonists, too, well into the nineteenth century, it is a view that is today, especially in the English-speaking world, mostly either ridiculed or ignored. Surely, one main reason for this dramatic change is the hermeneutical approach to the dialogues initiated by Friedrich Schleiermacher at the beginning of the nineteenth century. After Schleiermacher, scholarly focus has gradually shifted from Platonism as a philosophical system or worldview to the dialogues themselves. This shift has come to seem so salutary because it is, of course, true that a careful reading of each dialogue in its dramatic context is a *good thing*. No doubt, the bad odor left by nineteenth-century idealistic system building in the twentieth century also contributed to a wish to pursue a more enlightened or perhaps less grandiose approach to Plato. Yet from the perspective of ancient Platonists, the flaw in this procedure is obvious: no single dialogue can be adequately understood as philosophical writing without drawing support from elsewhere, especially from other dialogues. Some few scholars have inferred from this fact that the dialogues must therefore not be philosophical writings after all, that is, there must be no doctrine in them that the author intends to communicate to anyone in any way. The radical nature of this interpretation does not in itself disqualify it. What disqualifies it is the fact that by using all the dialogues for the purpose of

---

1. See Rorty 1999, xii: "Most of what I have written in the last decade consists of attempts to tie my social hopes—hopes for a global, cosmopolitan, democratic, egalitarian, classless, casteless society—with my antagonism towards Platonism." By 'Platonism' Rorty means the "set of philosophical distinctions (appearance/reality, matter/mind, made/found, sensible/intellectual, etc.," that, in his view, continue to bedevil the thinking of philosophers today. Other important 'Platonic dualisms' rejected by Rorty are knowledge/belief, cognitional/volitional, and subject/object. These binary oppositions match up pretty well with the elements of UP and with the positive constructs made on this foundation.

interpreting any one it is possible to discern in the dialogues philosophical doctrine as well as, we must admit, philosophical doubt.

Rejecting the arbitrary philosophical atomizing of the dialogues, we can avail ourselves of the indirect evidence. The utility of this evidence from Aristotle onward is immense. Not only does it fill out the picture of Platonism in the dialogues, but it reinforces the claim that Platonism is not primarily what we might term a 'dialogic artifact.' It was primarily a way of life. And the focus of that way of life, at least within the Academy, was the positive construction of a theoretical framework on the foundation of UP. This does not make the dialogues irrelevant; it makes them what all Platonists took them to be, namely, λόγοι of that way of life. Altering our optic from the dialogues to Platonism as a way of life enables us to give both developmentalists and unitarians their due. Indeed, it also enables us to account for the privileged position of Socrates in the dialogues and even the connection between the dialogic Socrates and the historical one. Socrates, we could say, was taken by his admirers to have had an *anima platonica naturaliter*, even if as a matter of historical fact he never attained to the theoretical basis for this.

Plotinus was the inheritor of some six hundred years of Platonic exegesis when he resolved, late in his own life, to present his understanding of Platonism. Some of the salient features of that exegesis have been treated in the third part of this book. Plotinus would have no doubt been mortified to hear the charge that he was doing something other than accurately representing and setting forth in a systematic fashion what Plato himself taught. But as Plotinus himself recognizes, there are loose ends in the Platonic construct and there are obscurities that are as often as not likely to be the result of doubt over the correct resolution of an issue. All the more reason, Plotinus probably held, that a systematic expression of Platonism was desirable precisely so that these loose ends could be tied up and these obscurities eliminated. In evaluating the cogency of this systematic expression we should not lose sight of these six hundred years that separated him from Plato and that naturally resulted in a philosophical climate different from the one found in the middle of the fourth century BCE in Athens. Nevertheless, we should really acquit Plotinus of the charge of deviating from Plato solely on the grounds of this six-hundred-year gap. To suppose that Plotinus simply *must* be the product of something called philosophical 'development' is, I maintain, to underestimate the philosophical acumen both of him and of his master.

Bibliography

Primary Sources

Aëtius. 1879. *De placitis reliquiae*. In *Doxographi Graeci*, edited by H. Diels. Berlin.
Alcinous. 1990. *Alcinoos: Enseigement des doctrines de Platon*. Edited by J. Whittaker. Paris.
Alexander of Aphrodisias. 1887. *De anima liber cum mantissa*. Edited by I. Bruns. *CAG*, supp. 2.1. Berlin.
———. 1891. *In Aristotelis "Metaphysica" commentaria*. Edited by M. Hayduck. *CAG* 1. Berlin.
———. 1892. *Praeter commentaria scripta minora: Quaestiones de fato, de mixtione*. Edited by I. Bruns. *CAG* 2.2. Berlin.
Anonymous. 2003. *Prolégomènes à la philosophie de Platon*. Edited and translated by L. Westerink and J. Trouillard. Paris.
Aristotle. 1866. *Aristotelis Qui Ferebantur Librorum Fragmenta*. Edited by V. Rose. Leipzig.
———. 1884. *Aristotelis Ethica Eudemia*. Edited by F. Susemihl. Leipzig.
———. 1894. *Aristotelis Ethica Nicomachea*. Edited by I. Bywater. Oxford.
———. 1924. *Aristotle's Metaphysics*. 2 vols. Edited by W. D. Ross. Oxford.
———. 1933. *Aristotelis Qui Fertur Libellus De Mundo*. Edited by W. L. Lorimer. Paris.
———. 1949. *Aristotelis Categoriae et Liber de Interpretatione*. Edited by L. Minio-Paluello. Oxford.
———. 1950. *Aristotelis Physica*. Edited by W. D. Ross. Oxford.
———. 1955. *Aristotelis Fragmenta Selecta*. Edited by W. D. Ross. Oxford.
———. 1957. *Aristotelis Metaphysica*. Edited by W. Jaeger. Oxford.
———. 1958. *Aristotelis Topica et Sophistici Elenchi*. Edited by W. D. Ross. Oxford.
———. 1961. *Aristotle: De Anima*. Edited by W. D. Ross. Oxford.
———. 1961. *Aristotle's Protrepticus*. Edited by I. Düring. Stockholm.
———. 1964. *Aristotelis Analytica Priora et Posteriora*. Edited by W. D. Ross. Oxford.
———. 1965. *Aristote: Du ciel*. Edited by P. Moraux. Paris.
———. 1965. *Aristotelis De Generatione Animalium*. Edited by H. J. Drossart-Lulofs. Oxford.
———. 1966. *Aristote: De la génération et de la corruption*. Edited by C. Mugler. Paris.

Asclepius. 1888. *In Aristotelis Metaphysicorum libros a–z commentaria*. Edited by M. Hayduck. *CAG* 6.2. Berlin.
Atticus. 1977. *Fragments*. Edited by É. Des Places. Paris.
Cicero. 1933. *De natura deorum, Academica*. Edited by H. Rackham. London.
———. 1966. *De re publica, De legibus*. Edited by C. Keyes. London.
———. 1984. *M. Tulli Ciceronis Tusculanae disputationes*. Edited by M. Giusta. Turin.
———. 1998. *M. Tulli Ciceronis De finibus bonorum et malorum libri quinque*. Edited by L. D. Reynolds. Oxford.
Damascius. 1977. *The Greek Commentaries on Plato's "Phaedo."* Vol. 2, *Damascius*. Edited by L. Westerink. Amsterdam.
———. 1986–91. *Traité des premiers principes*. 3 vols. Edited by L. Westerink and J. Combès. Paris.
———. 1997–2003. *Commentaire du Parménide de Platon*. Edited by L. Westerink, J. Combès and A. P. Segonds. Paris.
Diogenes Laertius. 1980. *Lives of the Eminent Philosophers*. Edited by R. D. Hicks. 2 vols. Cambridge, MA.
Doxographi Graeci: Collegit recensuit prolegomenis indicibusque instruxit. 1965. 4th ed. Edited by H. Diels. Berlin.
Iamblichus. 1922. *Theologumena Arithmeticae*. Edited by V. de Falco. Stuttgart.
———. 1973. *In Platonis Dialogos Commentariorum Fragmenta*. Edited by J. Dillon. Leiden.
———. 1975. Repr. of 1891 ed. *Iamblichi Protrepticus*. Edited by H. Pistelli. Leipzig.
———. 1975. *Iamblichi De Communi Mathematica Scientia Liber*. Edited by U. Klein (post N. Festa). Stuttgart.
———. 1989. *Jamblique: Protreptique*. Edited by É. Des Places. Paris.
Numenius. 1973. *Numénius: Fragments*. Edited by É. Des Places. Paris.
Olympiodorus. 1956. *Olympiodorus: Commentary on the First Alcibiades of Plato*. Edited by L. G. Westerink. Amsterdam.
———. 1968. *Olympiodori Philosophi Platonis "Phaedonem" Commentaria*. Edited by W. Norvin. Hildesheim.
Photius. 1959–77. *Biblioteca*. 8 vols. Edited by R. Henry. Paris.
Plato. 1900–1902. *Platonis Opera*. 5 vols. Edited by J. Burnet. Oxford.
———. 1995. *Platonis Opera*. Vol. 1. Edited by E. Duke, W. Hicken, W. Nicoll, D. Robinson, and J. Strachan. Oxford.
———. 2003. *Platonis Rempublicam*. Edited by S. Slings. Oxford.
Plotinus. 1964, 1977, 1983. *Opera*. 3 vols. Edited by P. Henry and H.-R. Schwyzer (*editio minor*). Oxford.
Plutarch. 1959–. 9 vols. *Moralia*. Edited by C. Hubert et al. Leipzig.
Porphyry. 1993. *Porphyrii Philosophi Fragmenta*. Edited by A. Smith. Stuttgart.
Proclus. 1873. *Procli Diadochi in Primum Euclidis Elementorum Librum Commentarii*. Edited by G. Friedlein. Leipzig.
———. 1899, 1901. *Procli Diadochi in Platonis Rem Publicam Commentarii*. 2 vols. Edited by W. Kroll. Leipzig.
———. 1903–6. *Procli in Platonis Timaeum Commentaria*. 3 vols. Edited by E. Diehl. Leipzig.
———. 1933. *Proclus: The Elements of Theology*. Edited by E. R. Dodds. Oxford.
———. 1954. *Commentary on the First Alcibiades of Plato*. Edited by L. G. Westerink. Amsterdam.
———. 1960. *Tria opuscula: De providentia, libertate, malo*. Edited by H. Boese. Berlin.
———. 1965. *Procli Diadochi in Platonis Timaeum Commentaria*. 3 vols. Edited by E. Diehl. Amsterdam.
———. 1968. *Proclus: Théologie platonicienne*. 5 vols. Edited by D. Saffrey and L. G. Westerink. Paris.
———. 2007–9. *Procli in Platonis Parmenidem Commentaria*. 3 vols. Edited by C. Steel. Oxford.
Seneca. 1965. *Ad Lucilium epistulae morales*. Edited by L. Reynolds. Oxford.

Sextus Empiricus. 1914–58. *Opera*. Edited by H. Mutschmann and J. Mau. 4 vols. Leipzig.
Simplicius. 1882, 1895. *Simplicii in Aristotelis Physicorum Libros Commentaria*. 2 vols. Edited by H. Diels. *CAG* 9 and 10. Berlin.
———. 1907. *In Aristotelis Categorias Commentarium*. Edited by K. Kalbfleisch. *CAG* 8. Berlin.
Stobaeus. 1884. *Anthologii Libri Duo Priores Qui Inscribi Solent Eclogae Physicae et Ethicae*. Edited by K. Wachsmuth. 2 vols. Berlin.
Stoicorum Veterum Fragmenta. 1903–5. 4 vols. Edited by H. von Arnim.
Syrianus. 1892. *Syriani in Metaphysica Commentaria*. Edited by H. Rabe. *CAG* 6.1. Berlin.
Theophrastus. 1993. *Théophraste: Métaphysique*. Edited by A. Laks and G. Most. Paris.
Xenocrates. 1892. *Xenocrates: Darstellung der Lehre und Sammlung der Fragmente*. Edited by R. Heinze. Leipzig.
———. 1982. *Senocrate-Ermodoro: Frammenti*. Edited by M. Isnardi Parenti. Naples.

Secondary Sources

Abbate, M. 2003. "Il Bene nell' interpretazione di Plotino e di Proclo." In *Repubblica: Traduzione e commento*, vol. 5, edited by M. Vegetti, 625–78. Naples.
Ackrill, J. L. 1981. *Aristotle the Philosopher*. Oxford.
———. 1997. *Essays on Plato and Aristotle*. Oxford.
Adam, J. 1902. *The "Republic" of Plato*. 2 vols. Cambridge.
Adams, R. 2007. "Idealism Vindicated." In *Persons: Human and Divine*, edited by P. Van Inwagen and D. Zimmerman, 35–54. Oxford.
Allen, D. 2010. *Why Plato Wrote*. Chichester.
Allen, R. E. 1983. *Plato's "Parmenides": Translation and Analysis*. Minneapolis.
Alline, H. 1915. *Histoire du text de Platon*. Paris.
Altman, W. H. F. 2010. "The Reading Order of Plato's Dialogues." *Phoenix* 64:18–51.
Annas, J. 1976. *Aristotle's "Metaphysics": Books M and N*. Oxford.
———. 1981. *An Introduction to Plato's "Republic."* Oxford.
———. 1982. "Aristotle on Inefficient Causes." *Philosophical Quarterly* 32:311–26.
———. 1985. "Self-Knowledge in Early Plato." In *Platonic Investigations*, edited by D. O'Meara, 111–38. Washington, DC.
———. 1992. "Plato the Sceptic." In *Methods of Interpreting Plato and the Dialogues*, edited by J. Klaage and N. D. Smith, 43–72. Oxford.
———. 1999. *Platonic Ethics, Old and New*. Ithaca, NY.
———. 2006. "Ethics and Argument in Plato's Socrates." In *The Virtuous Life in Greek Ethics*, edited by B. Reis, 32–46. Cambridge.
Armstrong, H. A. 1940. *The Architecture of the Intelligible Universe in the Philosophy of Plotinus*. Cambridge.
———. 1960. "The Background of the Doctrine 'That the Intelligibles Are Not Outside the Intellect.'" In *Sources de Plotin*, 393–413. Entretien Hardt V. Vandoeuvres/Geneva.
———. 1970. 'Plotinus.' In *Cambridge History of Late Greek and Early Medieval Philosophy*, edited by H. A. Armstrong, 195–268. Cambridge.
Atkinson, M. 1985. *Ennead V 1: On the Three Principal Hypostases: Commentary with Translation*. Oxford.
Aubry, G. 2006. *Dieu sans la puissance: Dunamis et energeia chez Aristote et chez Plotin*. Paris.
———. 2008. "Un moi sans identité? Le *hemeis* plotinien." In *Le moi et l'intériorité*, edited by G. Aubry and F. Ildefonse, 107–25. Paris.
Bailey, D. T. J. 2006. "Plato and Aristotle on the Unhypothetical." *Oxford Studies in Ancient Philosophy* 30:101–26.
Baltes, M. 1974. "Numenios von Apamea und der platonische Timaios." In *Festgabe für Otto Hiltbrunner zum 60. Geburtstag (29.12.1973)*, 4–37. Münster.

———. 1975. "Numenios von Apamea und der platonische Timaios." *Vigiliae Christianae* 29:241–70.
———. 1976. *Die Weltentstehung des Platonischen Timaios nach den antiken Interpreten.* Leiden.
———. 1988. "Zur Theologie des Xenokrates." In *Knowledge of God in the Graeco-Roman World,* edited by R. E. A. van den Broek, 43–68. Leiden. Reprinted in Baltes 1999, 191–222.
———. 1992. "Was ist antiker Platonismus?" In *Studia Patristica 24: Papers Presented to the Eleventh International Conference on Patristic Studies Held in Oxford,* edited by E. A. Livingstone, 219–38. Leuven.
———. 1996. "Gegonen (Platon, Tim. 28B7): Ist die Welt Real Entstanden oder Nicht?" In *Polyhistor: Studies in the History and Historiography of Ancient Philosophy,* edited by K. Algra, P. W. Van der Horst, and D. Runia, 76–96. Leiden.
———. 1997. "Is the Idea of the Good in Plato's *Republic* beyond Being?" In *Studies in Plato and the Platonic Tradition,* edited by M. Joyal, 1–23. London.
———. 1999. "Was ist antiker Platonismus?" In *Dianoēmata: Kleine Schriften zu Platon und zum Platonismus,* edited by A. Hüffmeier, 223–46. Stuttgart.
Baltzly, D. 1996. "To an Unhypothetical First Principle in Plato's *Republic.*" *History of Philosophy Quarterly* 13:149–65.
———. 2004. "The Virtues and 'Becoming Like God': Alcinous to Proclus." *Oxford Studies in Ancient Philosophy* 26:297–321.
Barnes, J. 1989. "Antiochus of Ascalon." In *Philosophia Togata I: Essays on Philosophy and Roman Society,* edited by Jonathan Barnes and Miriam Griffin, 51–96. Oxford.
———. 1995. "Review of H. Cherniss' *L'énigme de l'ancienne Académie.*" *Classical Review* 45:178.
Baudy, G. J. 1986. *Adonisgarten: Studien zur antiken Samensymbolik.* Frankfurt am Main.
Bechtle, G. 1999. *The Anonymous Commentary on Plato's "Parmenides."* Bern.
———. 2000. "The Question of Being and the Dating of the Anonymous *Parmenides* Commentary." *Ancient Philosophy* 20:393–414.
Beierwaltes, W. 1985. *Denken des Einen: Studien zur neuplatonischen Philosophie und ihre Wirkungsgeschichte.* Frankfurt am Main.
———. 1999. "Causa Sui: Plotins Begriff des Einem als Ursprung des Gedankens der Selbstursachlichkeit." In *Traditions of Platonism: Essays in Honour of John Dillon,* edited by J. Cleary, 191–226. Aldershot.
———. 2002. "Das Eine als Norm des Lebens: Zum metaphysischen Grund neuplatonischer Lebensform." In *Metaphysik und Religion: Zur Signatur des Spätantiken Denkens,* edited by T. Kobusch and M. Erler, 121–51. Munich.
Benson, H. H. 2000. *Socratic Wisdom: The Model of Knowledge in Plato's Early Dialogues.* New York.
Berti, E. 1983. "Il Platone di Krämer e la metafisica classica." *Rivista di filosofia neoscolastica* 75:313–26.
———. 2003. "Il dibatto odierno sulla cosiddetto 'teologia' di Aristotele." *Paradigmi* 21:279–97.
———. 2004. "Is There an Ethics in Plato's 'Unwritten Doctrines'?" In *Plato Ethicus: Philosophy Is Life,* edited by M. Migliori and L. Napolitano Valditara, 35–48. Sankt Augustin.
———. 2009. "La cause du mouvement dans les êtres vivants." In *Ancient Perspectives on Aristotle's "De Anima,"* edited by G. Van Riel and P. Destrée, 141–53. Leuven.
———. 2010. "Il rapporto tra causa motrice e causa finale nella *Metafisica* di Aristotele." In *La scienza e le cause a partire dalla Metafisica di Aristotele,* edited by F. Fronterotta, 351–82. Naples.
Besnier, B. 1996. "Aristote et l'enseignement écrit et non-écrit de Platon." In *Platon et l'objet de la science,* edited by P.-M. Morel, 123–46. Bordeaux.
Beversluis, J. 2006. "A Defense of Dogmatism in the Interpretation of Plato." *Oxford Studies in Ancient Philosophy* 31:86–111.

Bianchi, U. 1986. "Plutarco e il dualismo." In *International Plutarch Society, Sezione italiana. Miscellanea Plutarchea. Atti del I Convegno di studi su Plutarco (Roma, 23 novembre 1985)*, 111–20. Ferrara.
Blondell, R. 2002. *The Play of Character in Plato's Dialogues*. Cambridge.
Blyth, D. 2000. "Platonic Number in the *Parmenides* and *Metaphysics* XIII." *International Journal of Philosophical Studies* 8 (1): 23–45.
Bobonich, C. 1994. "Akrasia and Agency in Plato's *Laws* and *Republic*." *Archiv für Geschichte der Philosophie* 76 (1): 3–36.
———. 2002. *Plato's Utopia Recast: His Later Ethics and Politics*. Oxford.
Bobzien, S. 1998a. *Determinism and Freedom in Stoic Philosophy*. Oxford.
———. 1998b. "The Inadvertent Conception and Late Birth of the Free-Will Problem." *Phronesis* 43:133–75.
Bolton, R. 1998. "Plato's Discovery of Metaphysics." In *Method in Ancient Philosophy*, edited by J. Gentzler, 91–111. Oxford.
Bonazzi, M. 2005. "Eudoro di Alessandria alle origini del platonismo imperiale." *Elenchos* 45:115–60.
———, ed. 2011. *Commentary and Tradition: Aristotelianism, Platonism, and Post-Hellenistic Philosophy*. Berlin.
———. 2012. "Antiochus and Platonism." In *The Philosophy of Antiochus*, edited by D. Sedley, 303–33. Cambridge.
Bonazzi, M., and J. Opsomer, eds. 2009. *The Origins of the Platonic System: Platonisms of the Early Empire and Their Philosophical Context*. Louvain.
Boys-Stones, G. R. 2001. *Post-Hellenistic Philosophy: A Study of Its Development from the Stoics to Origen*. New York.
———. 2012. "Antiochus' Metaphysics." In *The Philosophy of Antiochus*, edited by D. Sedley, 220–36. Cambridge.
Boys-Stones, G. R., and C. Rowe, eds. and trans. 2013. *The Circle of Socrates*. Indianapolis.
Brandwood, L. 1990. *The Chronology of Plato's Dialogues*. Cambridge.
Brickhouse, T. C., and N. D. Smith. 1994. *Plato's Socrates*. New York.
———. 2004. *Routledge Philosophy Guidebook to Plato and the Trial of Socrates*. New York.
———. 2010. *Socratic Moral Psychology*. Cambridge.
Brisson, L. 1993. "Présupposés et conséquences d'une interprétation ésoteriste de Platon." *Les études philosophiques* 4:473–95.
———. 1997. "De quelle facon Plotin interprete-t-il les cinq genre du *Sophiste*? (*Enneades* 6.2 (43) 8)." In *Études sur le Sophiste de Platon*, edited by P. Aubenque and M. Narcy, 449–73. Naples.
Brisson, L., and J.-F. Pradeau, eds. 2002–10. *Plotin. v. 1 Traités 1–6; v. 2, Traités 7–21; v. 3, Traités 22–26; v. 4, Traités 27–29; v. 5, Traités 30–37; v. 6, Traités 38–41; v. 7, Traités 42–44; v. 8, Traités 45–50; v. 9, Traiteé 51–54*. Paris.
Brittain, C. 2001. *Philo of Larissa: The Last of the Academic Sceptics*. Oxford.
———. 2006. *On Academic Scepticism*. Indianapolis.
———. 2011. "Plato and Platonism." In *The Oxford Handbook to Plato*, edited by G. Fine, 526–49. Oxford.
———. 2012. "Antiochus' Epistemology." In *The Philosophy of Antiochus*, edited by D. Sedley, 104–30. Cambridge.
Brown, J. R. 2012. *Platonism, Naturalism, and Mathematical Knowledge*. New York.
Brucker, J. 1742–44. *Historia critica philosophiae a mundi incunabulis ad nostram usque aetatem deducta*. Vols. 1–4. Leipzig.
Brunschwig, J. 1970. "*EE* I 8, 1218a15–32 et le ΠΕΡΙ ΤΑΓΑΘΟΥ." In *Untersuchungen zur Eudemischen Ethik*, edited by P. Moraux and D. Harlfinger, 197–222. Berlin.
———. 1994. "The Stoic Theory of the Supreme Genus and Platonic Ontology." In *Papers in Hellenistic Philosophy*, 92–157. Translated by J. Lloyd. Cambridge.

Burge, E. L. 1971. "The Ideas as Aitiai in the *Phaedo.*" *Phronesis* 16:1–13.
Burnet, J. 1914. *Greek Philosophy: Thales to Plato.* London.
———. 1928. *Platonism.* Berkeley.
Burnyeat, M. 1980. "Can the Skeptic Live His Skepticism?" In *Doubt and Dogmatism,* edited by M. Schofield, M. Burnyeat, and J. Barnes, 20–53. Oxford.
———. 1990. *The "Theaetetus" of Plato.* Indianapolis.
———. 1999. "Culture and Society in Plato's *Republic.*" In *The Tanner Lectures on Human Value,* edited by G. B. Peterson, 217–324. Salt Lake City.
———. 2005. "Platonism in the Bible: Numenius of Apamea on Exodus and Eternity." In *Metaphysics, Soul, and Ethics in Ancient Thought: Themes from the Work of Richard Sorabji,* edited by Ricardo Salles, 143–69. Oxford.
———. 2006. "The Truth of Tripartition." *Proceedings of the Aristotelian Society* 106:1–23.
Büsching, A. F. 1772. *Grundriss einer Geschichte der Philosophie und einiger wichtigen Lehrsatze derselben.* Berlin.
Campbell, L. 1867. *The "Sophistes" and "Politicus" of Plato.* Cambridge.
———. 1896. "On the Place of the *Parmenides* in the Chronological Order of the Platonic Dialogues." *Classical Review* 10:129–36.
Carone, G. R. 1994. "Teleology and Evil in *Laws* 10." *Review of Metaphysics* 48:275–98.
Centrone, B. 2000. "Cosa significa essere Pittagoprico in età imperiale: Per una reconsiderazione della categoria storiografica del neopitagorismo." In *La filosofia in età imperiale: Le scuole e le tradizioni filosofiche,* edited by A. Brancacci, 137–68. Elenchos 31. Bibliopolis.
Charrue, J.-M. 1978. *Plotin lecteur de Platon.* Paris.
Cherniss, H. 1936. "The Philosophical Economy of Plato's Theory of Ideas." *American Journal of Philology* 57:445–56.
———. 1944. *Aristotle's Criticism of Plato and the Academy.* Baltimore.
———. 1945. *The Riddle of the Early Academy.* Berkeley.
———. 1957. "The Relation of the *Timaeus* to Plato's Later Dialogues." *American Journal of Philology* 78 (3): 225–66.
Code, A. 1985. "On the Origins of Some Aristotelian Theses about Predication." In *How Things Are: Studies in Predication and the History of Philosophy and Science,* edited by J. Bogen and J. E. McGuire, 101–31. Dordrecht.
Cooper, J. 1984. "Plato's Theory of Human Motivation." *History of Philosophy Quarterly* 1:3–21. Reprint, Cooper 1999, 118–37.
———. 1999. *Reason and Emotion.* Princeton.
Cornford, F. M. 1934. *Plato's Theory of Knowledge.* London.
———. 1939. *Plato and Parmenides.* London.
Dancy, R. M. 1991. *Two Studies of the Early Academy.* Albany.
Denyer, N. 2001. *Plato: Alcibiades.* Cambridge.
———. 2007. "Sun and Line: The Role of the Good." In *The Cambridge Companion to Plato's Republic,* edited by G. R. F. Ferrari, 284–309. Cambridge.
Des Places, É. 1971. "Les fragments de Numénius d'Apamée dans la *Préparation évangélique* d'Eusèbe de Césarée." *Comptes rendus de l'Académie des Inscriptions et Belles Lettres* 115:455–62.
De Strycker, E. 1950. "Socrate et l'au-dela après l'*Apologie.*" *Les Études Classiques* 17:269–84.
Devereux, D. 1995. "Socrates' Kantian Conception of Virtue." *Journal of the History of Philosophy* 33:381–408.
De Vogel, C. 1953. "On the Neoplatonic Character of Platonism and the Platonic Character of Neoplatonism." *Mind* 62:43–64.
———. 1954. "A la recherche des étapes précises entre Platon e le Néoplatonisme." *Mnemosyne* 7:111–22.

———. 1988. *Rethinking Plato and Platonism.* Leiden.
Dillon, J. 1977. *The Middle Platonists: 80 BC to AD 220.* Ithaca, NY.
———. 1983. "Plotinus, Philo and Origen on the Grades of Virtue." *Jahrbuch für Antike und Christentum Münster* 10:92–105.
———. 1988. "Orthodoxy and Eclecticism in Middle Platonism and Neopythagoreanism." In *The Question of Eclecticism: Studies in Later Greek Philosophy,* edited by J. Dillon and A. A. Long, 103–25. Berkeley.
———. 1993. *Alcinous: The Handbook of Platonism.* Oxford.
———. 2003. *The Heirs of Plato: A Study of the Old Academy (347–274 BC).* Oxford.
———. 2010a. "The Origins of Platonic Dogmatism." Address to the Athenian Academy, Athens. 121–39.
———. 2010b. "Speusippus and the Ontological Interpretation of the *Parmenides.*" In *Plato's "Parmenides" and Its Heritage,* edited by J. Turner and K. Corrigan, 1:67–78. Atlanta.
Dodds, E. R. 1928. "The *Parmenides* of Plato and the Origin of the Neoplatonic 'One.'" *Classical Quarterly* 22 (3/4): 129–42.
———. 1933; 2nd ed., 1963. *Proclus: The Elements of Theology.* Oxford.
———. 1960. "Tradition and Personal Achievement in the Philosophy of Plotinus." *Journal of Roman Studies* 1:1–7.
Donini, P. 1982. *Le scuole, l'anima, l'imperio: La filosofia antica da Antioco a Plotino.* Turin.
———. 1986. "Lo scetticismo accademico, Aristotele e l'unità della tradizione platonica secondo Plutarco." In *Storiografia e dossografia nella filosofia antica,* edited by G. Cambiano, 203–26. Turin.
———. 1988. "La connaissance de dieu et la hiérachie divine chez Albinos." In *Knowledge of God in the Greco-Roman World,* edited by R. van den Broek and T. Baarda, 118–31. New York.
———. 2011. "Testi e commenti, manuali e insegnamento: La forma sistematica e i metodi della filosofia in età posthellenistica." In *Commentary and Tradition: Aristotelianism, Platonism, and Post-Hellenistic Philosophy,* edited by M. Bonazzi, 211–81. Berlin.
Dorion, L.-A. 2011. "The Rise and Fall of the Socratic Problem." In *The Cambridge Companion to Socrates,* edited by D. Morrison, 1–23. Cambridge.
Dörrie, H. 1976. *Von Platon zum Platonismus.* Opladen.
Dörrie, H., and M. Baltes. 1987–2004. *Der Platonismus in der Antike.* Vols. 1–6.2. Stuttgart.
Emilsson, E. 2007. *Plotinus on Intellect.* Oxford.
Erler, M. 2007. *Platon: Die Philosophie der Antike.* Bd. 2/2. Basel.
Ferber, R. 1989. *Platons Idee des Guten.* 2nd ed. Sankt Augustin.
———. 2007. *Warum hat Platon die "ungeschriebene Lehre" nicht geschrieben?* Munich.
Ferrari, F. 1995. *Dio, idee e materia: La struttura del cosmo in Plutarco di Cheronea.* Naples.
———. 1999. "Πρόνοια platonica e νόησις νοήσεως aristotelica: Plutarco e l'impossibilità di una sintisi." In *Plutarco, Platón y Aristóteles. Actas del V Congreso Internacional de la I.P.S.,* edited by A. Pérez Jiménez, J. García López, and R. Aguilar, 63–77. Madrid.
———. 2003a. "Causa paradigmatica e causa efficiente: Il ruolo delle idee nel *Timeo.*" In *Plato Physicus: Cosmologia e antropologia nei "Timeo,"* edited by Carlo Natali and Stefano Maso, 83–96. Amsterdam.
———. 2003b. "L'idea del bene: Collocazione ontologica e funzione causale." In *La Repubblica: Traduzione e commento,* edited by M. Vegetti, 5:287–325. Naples.
———. 2006. "*Poietes kai pater:* Esegesi medioplatoniche di *Timeo* 28C3." In *Tradizione, ecdotica, esegesi,* edited by G. Di Gregorio and S. Medaglia, 43–58. Naples.
———. 2007a. "La potenza del 'Buono.'" In *The Ascent to the Good,* edited by F. Lisi, 187–98. Sankt Augustin.
———. 2007b. "La *chora* nel *Timeo* di Platone: Riflessioni su 'materia' e 'spazio' nell' ontologia del mondo fenomenico." *Quaestio* 7:3–23.

———. 2010. "L'esegesi medioplatonica del *Timeo:* Metodi, finalità, risultati." In *Il Timeo: Esegesi greche, arabe, latine,* edited by F. Celia and A. Ulacco, 81–131. Pisa.
———. 2012. "Quando, perché e come nacque il Platonismo." *Athenaeum* 100:47–68.
Findlay, J. N. 1974. *Plato: The Written and Unwritten Doctrines.* New York.
———. 1978. *Plato and Platonism: An Introduction.* New York.
Fine, G. 1990. "Knowledge and Belief in *Republic* V–VII." In *Companions to Ancient Thought: Epistemology,* edited by S. Everson 1:85–115. Cambridge.
———. 1993. *On Ideas: Aristotle's Criticism of Plato's Theory of Forms.* Oxford.
———. 2003. *Plato on Knowledge and Forms: Selected Essays.* Oxford.
Fortenbaugh, W., P. Huby, R. Sharples, and D. Gutas, eds. 1993. *Theophrastus of Eresus: Sources for His Life, Writings, Thought and Influence.* 2 vols. Leiden.
Franklin, L. 2012. "Inventing Intermediates: Mathematical Discourse and Its Objects in *Republic* VII." *Journal of the History of Philosophy* 50:483–506.
Frede, D. 2006. "Platons Dialoge als Hypomnemata: Zur Methodik der Platondeutung." In *Platon in nachmetaphysischen Zeitalter,* edited by G. Schiermann, D. Mersch, and G. Boehme, 41–58. Darmstadt.
Frede, M. 1987. "Numenius." *Aufstieg und Niedergang der römischen Welt* 11 (36.2): 1034–75. Edited by W. Haase and H. Temporini. New York.
Frede, M., and D. Charles, eds. 2000. *Aristotle's "Metaphysics" Lambda.* Oxford.
Froidefond, C. 1987. "Plutarque et le platonisme." *Aufstieg und Niedergang der römischen Welt* 36 (1): 184–233. Edited by W. Haase and H. Temporini. New York.
Fronterotta, F. 2001. *Methexis: La teoria platonica delle idee e la partecipazione delle cose empiriche: Dai dialoghi giovanili al Parmenide.* Pisa.
———. 2006. "Questioni eidetiche in Platone: Il sensible e il Demiurgo, l'essere e il bene." *Giornale Critico della Filosofia Italiana* 87:412–36.
———. 2007. "The Development of Plato's Theory of Ideas and the 'Socratic Question.'" *Oxford Studies in Ancient Philosophy* 32:37–62.
———. 2008. "Alcune critiche alla concezione aristotelica della Νόησις Νοήσεως nella tradizione medioplatonica e neoplatonica: Plutarco, Alcinoo e Plotino." In *Aristotle and the Aristotelian Tradition/Aristotele e la tradizione aristotelica,* edited by E. De Bellis, 189–201. Soveria Manelli.
Furley, D. 1989. "The Cosmological Crisis in Classical Antiquity." In *Cosmic Problems,* edited by D. Furley, 223–35. Cambridge.
Gadamer, H.-G. 1985. *Gesammelte Werke.* Tübingen.
Gaiser, K. 1963; 2nd ed. 1968. *Platons ungeschriebene Lehre: Studien zur systematischen und geschichtlichen Begründung der Wissenschaften in der platonischen Schule.* Stuttgart.
———. 1968. "Quellenkritische Probleme der indirekten Platonüberlieferung." In Gaiser 2004, 205–63. Sankt Augustin.
———. 1980. "La teoria dei Principi in Platone." *Elenchos* 1980, 45–75. Reprinted as "Prinzipientheorie bei Platon," in Gaiser 2004, 295–315.
———. 2004. *Gesammelte Schriften.* Edited by T. Szlezák. Sankt Augustin.
Gallop, D. 1975. *Plato's "Phaedo."* Oxford.
Ganson, T. 2009. "The Rational/Non-Rational Distinction in Plato's *Republic."* *Oxford Studies in Ancient Philosophy* 36:179–97.
Gersh, S. 1986. *Middle Platonism and Neoplatonism: The Latin Tradition.* Notre Dame, IN.
Gerson, L. 1993. "Plotinus' Metaphysics: Creation or Emanation?" *Review of Metaphysics* 46:559–74.
———. 2003. *Knowing Persons: A Study in Plato.* Oxford.
———. 2004. "Platonism in Aristotle's Ethics." *Oxford Studies in Ancient Philosophy* 27:217–48.
———. 2005. *Aristotle and Other Platonists.* Ithaca, NY.
———. 2006. "The 'Holy Solemnity' of Forms and the Platonic Interpretation of the *Sophist."* *Ancient Philosophy* 26:1–14.

———. 2008. "From Plato's Good to Platonic God." *International Journal of the Platonic Tradition* 2:93–112.
———. 2009. *Ancient Epistemology*. Cambridge.
———, ed. 2010. *The Cambridge History of Philosophy in Late Antiquity*. Cambridge.
Gigon, O. 1944. "Zur Geschichte der sogenannten neuen Akademie." *Museum Helveticum* 1:47–64. Reprint in Gigon, *Studien zur antiken Philosophie* (Berlin, 1972), 412–31.
Gill, C. 2000. "The Body's Fault? Plato's *Timaeus* on Psychic Illness." In *Reason and Necessity: Essays on Plato's "Timaeus,"* edited by M. R. Wright, 59–84. London.
———. 2002. "Dialectic and the Dialogue Form." In *New Perspectives on Plato, Modern and Ancient*, edited by J. Annas and C. Gill, 145–71. Washington, DC.
Glucker, J. 1978. *Antiochus and the Late Academy*. Göttingen.
Gonzalez, F. 1995. "Self-Knowledge, Practical Knowledge, and Insight: Plato's Dialectic and the Dialogue Form." In *The Third Way: New Directions in Plato Studies*, edited by F. Gonzalez, 155–88. Lanham, MD.
Göransson, T. 1995. *Albinus, Alcinous, Arius Didymus: Studia graeca et latina Gothoburgensia* (61). Göteborg.
Griswold, C. L. 1977. "Logic and Metaphysics in Plato's *Sophist.*" *Giornale di Metafisica* 6:550–70.
———. 1986. *Self-Knowledge in Plato's "Phaedrus."* New Haven.
———. 1988. "Plato's Metaphilosophy: Why Plato Wrote Dialogues." In *Platonic Writings: Platonic Readings*, edited by C. Griswold, 143–67. London.
———. 1999. "E Pluribus Unum? On the Platonic Corpus." *Ancient Philosophy* 19:361–97.
Grote, G. 1865. *Plato and the Other Companions of Sokrates*. London.
Guthrie, W. K. C. 1975. *Plato: The Man and His Dialogues: Earlier Period*. Vol. 4 of *A History of Greek Philosophy*. Cambridge.
Hadot, P. 1960. "Etre, vie, pensée chez Plotin et avant Plotin." In *Les sources de Plotin*, 5:107–41. Fondation Hardt. Vandoeuvres-Geneva.
———. 1995. *Philosophy as a Way of Life: Spiritual Exercises from Socrates to Foucault*. Oxford.
———. 2002. *What Is Ancient Philosophy?* Cambridge, MA.
Hager, F.-P. 1987. *Gott und das Böse im antiken Platonismus*. Amsterdam.
Halfwassen, J. 1992. *Der Aufstieg zum Einen: Untersuchungen zu Platon und Plotin*. Stuttgart.
———. 1993. "Speusipp und die metaphysische Deutung von Platons *Parmenides.*" In *HEN KAI PLETHOS / Einheit und Vielheit: Festschrift für Karl Bormann zum 65. Geburtstag*, edited by L. Hagemann and R. Glei, 330–73. Echter.
———. 1997. "Monismus und Dualismus in Platons Prinzipienlehre." *Bochumer Philosophisches Jahbuch für Antike und Mittelalter* 2:1–21.
———. 2000. "Der Demiureg: Seine Stellung in der Philosophie Platons und seine Deutung im antiken Platonismus." In *Le "Timée" de Platon: Contributions à l'histoire de sa réception*, edited by A. Neschke-Hentschke, 39–62. Louvain.
———. 2002a. "Monism and Dualism in Plato's Doctrine of Principles [Monisme et dualisme dans la doctrine des principes chez Platon]." *Graduate Faculty Philosophy Journal* 23 (2): 125–44.
———. 2002b. "Metaphysik und Transzendenz." *Jahrbuch für Religionsphilosophie* 1:14–27.
———. 2004. "Platons Metaphysik des Einen." *Philotheos* 4:207–21.
Halliwell, S. 2006. "An Aristotelian Perspective on Plato's Dialogues." In *New Essays in Plato*, edited by F. G. Herrmann, 189–211. Swansea.
Heitsch, E. 2002. "Dialoge Platons vor 399 v. Chr.?" In *Nachrichten der Akademie der Wissenschaften zu Göttingen*, 1:303–45. Philologisch-Historisch Klasse. Göttingen.
Helmig, C. 2012. *Forms and Concepts: Concept Formation in the Platonic Tradition*. Berlin.
Hermann, K. 1839. *Geschichte und System der platonischen Philosophie*. Vol. 1. Heidelberg.
Herrmann, F.-G. 2005. "Plato's Answer to Democritean Determinism." In *La catena delle cause*, edited by C. Natali and S. Maso, 37–55. Amsterdam.

———. 2007. *Words and Ideas: The Roots of Plato's Philosophy*. Swansea.
Hicks, R. D. 1907. *Aristotle: De Anima*. Cambridge.
Holzhausen, J. 1992. "Eine Anmerkung zum Verhältnis von Numenios und Plotin." *Hermes* 120:250–55.
Horn, C. 1995. "Der platonische Parmenides und die Möglichkeit seiner prinzipientheoretischen Interpretation." *Antike und Abenland* 41:95–114.
Hubler, J. 2010. "Moderatus, E. R. Dodds, and the Development of Neoplatonist Emanation." In *Plato's "Parmenides" and Its Heritage*, edited by J. Turner and K. Corrigan, 1:115–28. Atlanta.
Huffman, C. A. 1993. *Philolaus of Croton: Pythagorean and Presocratic: A Commentary on the Fragments and Testimonia with Interpretive Essays*. Cambridge.
———. 2005. *Archytas of Tarentum: Pythagorean, Philosopher, and Mathematician King*. Cambridge.
———. 2008. "Two Problems in Pythagoreanism." In *The Oxford Companion to Presocratic Philosophy*, edited by P. Curd and D. Graham, 284–304. Oxford.
Hussey, E. 2012. "Aristotle on Earlier Natural Science." In *The Oxford Handbook of Aristotle*, edited by C. Shields, 17–45. Oxford.
Irwin, T. 1977. *Plato's Moral Theory: The Early and Middle Dialogues*. Oxford.
———. 1983. "Euripides and Socrates." *Classical Philology* 78:183–97.
———. 1988. *Aristotle's First Principles*. Oxford.
———. 1995. *Plato's Ethics*. New York.
———. 2008. "The Platonic Corpus." In *The Oxford Handbook of Plato*, edited by G. Fine, 63–87. Oxford.
Isnardi Parente, M. 1980. *Speusippo: Frammenti*. Naples.
———. 1982. *Senocrate—Ermodoro: Frammenti*. Naples.
Jackson, H. 1882–97. "Plato's Later Theory of Ideas," 1–7. 1: *Journal of Philology* 10 (1882): 253–98; 2: 11 (1882): 287–331; 3: 12 (1883): 1–40; 4: 13 (1885): 242–72; 5: 14 (1885): 173–230; 6: 15 (1886): 280–305; 7: 25 (1897): 65–82.
Jaeger, W. W. 1948. *Aristotle: Fundamentals of the History of His Development*. Oxford.
Johansen, T. K. 2004. *Plato's Natural Philosophy: A Study of the Timaeus-Critias*. Cambridge.
Kahn, C. 1981. "Did Plato Write Socratic Dialogues?" *Classical Quarterly* 31 (2): 305–20.
———. 1992. "Vlastos' Socrates." *Phronesis* 37:233–58.
———. 1996. *Plato and the Socratic Dialogue: The Philosophical Use of a Literary Form*. Cambridge.
———. 2000. "Response to Griswold." *Ancient Philosophy* 20:189–93.
———. 2002. "On Platonic Chronology." In *New Perspectives on Plato, Modern and Ancient*, edited by J. Annas and C. Rowe, 93–127. Cambridge, MA.
Karamanolis, G. E. 2006. *Plato and Aristotle in Agreement? Platonists on Aristotle from Antiochus to Porphyry*. Oxford.
Kennedy, J. B. 2011. *The Musical Structure of Plato's Dialogues*. Durham.
Knab, R. 2006. *Platons siebter Brief: Einleitung, Text, Übersetzung, Kommentar*. Hildesheim.
Krämer, H. J. 1959. *Arete bei Platon und Aristoteles: Zum Wesen und zur Geschichte der platonischen Ontologie*. Heidelberg.
———. 1964a; 2nd ed., 1967. *Der Ursprung der Geistmetaphysik: Untersuchungen zur Geschichte des Platonismus zwischen Platon und Plotin*. Amsterdam.
———. 1964b. "Die platonische Akademie und das Problem einer systematischen Interpretation der Philosophie Platons." *Kant-Studien* 55:69–101.
———. 1969. "ΕΠΕΚΕΙΝΑ ΤΗΣ ΟΥΣΙΑΣ: Zu Platon, Politeia 509B." *Archiv für Geschichte der Philosophie* 51:1–30.
———. 1972. *Platonismus und hellenistische Philosophie*. Berlin.
———. 1973. "Aristoteles und die akademische Eidoslehre: Zur Geschichte des Unversalienproblems im Platonismus." *Archiv für Geschichte der Philosophie* 51:119–90.
———. 1986. *La nuova immagine di Platone*. Naples.

———. 1990. *Plato and the Foundation of Metaphysics.* Translated by J. Catan. Albany.
———. 1994. "Das neue Platonbild." *Zeitschrift für philosophische Forschung* 48:1–20.
Kraut, R. 1984. *Socrates and the State.* Princeton.
———. 1992. "Introduction to the Study of Plato." In *The Cambridge Companion to Plato,* edited by R. Kraut, 1–50. Cambridge.
Kremer, K. 1987. "Bonum est diffusivum sui: Ein Beitrag zum Verhältnis von Neuplatonismus und Christentum." In *Aufstieg und Niedergang der Römischen Welt* 36.2, edited by W. Haase and H. Temporini, 994–1032. New York.
Kretzmann, N. 1997. *The Metaphysics of Theism.* Oxford.
Lamm, J. 2000. "Schleiermacher as Plato Scholar." *Journal of Religion* 80:206–39.
Lavecchia, S. 2006. *Una via che conduce al divino: La homoiosis theo nella filosofia di Platone.* Milan.
Ledger, G. R. 1989. *Re-Counting Plato: A Computer Analysis of Plato's Style.* Oxford.
Lee, J. S. 1982. "Omnipresence, Participation, and Eidetic Causation in Plotinus." In *The Structure of Being,* edited by R. B. Harris, 90–103. Norfolk.
Lennox, J. 2001. *Aristotle: On the Parts of Animals I–IV.* Oxford.
Little, A. 1949. *The Platonic Heritage of Thomism.* Dublin.
Loenen, J. H. 1957. "Albinus' Metaphysics: An Attempt at Rehabilitation, II." *Mnemosyne* 10:35–56.
Long, A. A. 1998. "Plato's Apologies and Socrates in the *Theaetetus.*" In *Methods in Ancient Philosophy,* edited by J. Gentzler, 113–36. Oxford.
———. 2005. "Platonic Souls as Persons." In *Metaphysics, Soul, and Ethics in Ancient Thought,* edited by Ricardo Salles, 173–91. Oxford.
Magrin, S. 2010. "Sensation and Scepticism in Plotinus." *Oxford Studies in Ancient Philosophy* 39:249–97.
Mahoney, T. 2004. "Is Assimilation to God in the *Theaetetus* Purely Otherworldly?" *Ancient Philosophy* 24:321–38.
Mann, W.-R. 2006. "Plato in Tübingen: A Discussion of Konrad Gaiser, *Gesammelte Schriften.*" *Oxford Studies in Ancient Philosophy* 31:349–98.
Mansfeld, J. 1972. "Three Notes on Albinus." *Theta-Pi* 1:61–80.
———. 1992. *Heresiography in Context: Hippolytus' Elenchos as a Source for Greek Philosophy.* Leiden.
McCabe, M. M. 2000. *Plato and His Predecessors: The Dramatisation of Reason.* Cambridge.
McDowell, J. 1973. *Plato's "Theaetetus."* Oxford.
McPherran, M. 1996. *The Religion of Socrates.* University Park, PA.
Meijer, P. A. 1992. *Plotinus on the Good or the One (Enneads VI.9): An Analytic Commentary.* Amsterdam.
Meinwald, C. 2002. "Plato's Pythagoreanism." *Ancient Philosophy* 22:87–101.
Menn, S. 1992. "Aristotle and Plato on God as *Nous.*" *Review of Metaphysics* 43:543–73.
Merki, H. 1952. *Homoiosis Theo: Von der platonischen Angleichung an Gott zur Gottähnlichkeit bei Gregor von Nyssa.* Freiburg.
Merlan, P. 1953; 3rd ed., 1968. *From Platonism to Neoplatonism.* The Hague.
———. 1967. "Greek Philosophy from Plato to Plotinus." In *The Cambridge History of Late Greek and Early Medieval Philosophy,* edited by H. A. Armstrong, 14–132. Cambridge.
Miller, D. 2003. *The Third Kind in Plato's "Timaeus."* Göttingen.
Miller, M. 1995. "'Unwritten Teachings' in the *Parmenides.*" *Review of Metaphysics* 48:591–633.
———. 2004. *The Philosopher in Plato's "Statesman."* Las Vegas.
———. 2007. "Beginning the 'Longer Way.'" In *The Cambridge Companion to Plato's "Republic,"* edited by G. R. F. Ferrari, 310–44. Cambridge.
Morel, P.-M. 1992. "Atome et nécessité: Démocrite, Épicure, Lucrèce." In *Platon, source des présocratiques: Exploration,* edited by M. Dixsaut and A. Brancacci, 129–50. Paris.

Morrison, D. 2000. "On the Alleged Historical Reliability of Plato's *Apology.*" In *Plato's "Euthyphro," "Apology," and "Crito": Critical Essays*, edited by R. Kamtekar, 97–126. Lanham, MD.

Morrow, G. R. 1962. *Plato's Epistles: A Translation with Critical Essays*. Indianapolis.

Moss, J. 2008. "Appearances and Calculations: Plato's Division of the Soul." *Oxford Studies in Ancient Philosophy* 34:35–68.

Mueller, I. 1984. "Aristotle's Approach to the Problem of Principles in *Metaphysics M and N.*" In *Mathematics and Metaphysics in Aristotle / Mathematik und Metaphysik bei Aristoteles*, edited by A. Graeser, 241–59. Bern.

Mulhern, J. J. 1969. "Treatises, Dialogues, and Interpretation." *Monist* 53:631–41.

———. 1971. "Two Interpretative Fallacies." *Systematics* 9 (3): 168–72.

Nails, D. 1995. *Agora, Academy, and the Conduct of Philosophy*. Dordrecht.

———. 2000. "Mouthpiece, Schmouthpiece." In *Who Speaks for Plato?* edited by G. A. Press, 15–26. Lanham, MD.

———. 2002. *The People of Plato: A Prosopography of Plato and Other Socratics*. Indianapolis.

Narbonne, J.-M. 2006. "Plotinus and the Gnostics on the Generation of Matter (33 [II 9], 12 and 51 [I 8], 14)." *Dionysius* 24:45–64.

———. 2007. "La controverse à propos de la génération de la matiere chez Plotin: L'énigme résolue?" *Quaestio* 7:123–65.

Nehemas, A. 1999. *The Virtues of Authenticity*. Princeton.

Nehemas, A., and P. Woodruff. 1995. *Plato: "Phaedrus."* Translation with introduction and notes. Indianapolis.

Nightingale, A. 1995. *Genres in Dialogue: Plato and the Construct of Philosophy*. Cambridge.

Nyvlt, M. 2012. *Aristotle and Plotinus on the Intellect*. Lanham, MD.

O'Brien, D. 1971. "Plotinus on Evil: A Study of Matter and the Soul in Plotinus' Conception of Human Evil." In *Le Néoplatonisme: Colloques internationaux du centre national de la recherche scientifique, Royaumont 9–13 juin 1969*, edited by P. M. Schuhl and P. Hadot, 113–46. Paris.

———. 1981. "Plotinus and the Gnostics on the Generation of Matter." In *Neoplatonism and Early Christian Thought*, edited by H. J. Blumenthal, 108–23. London.

———. 1991. *Plotinus on the Origin of Matter: An Exercise in the Interpretation of the "Enneads."* Naples.

———. 1996. "Plotinus on Matter and Evil." In *The Cambridge Companion to Plotinus*, edited by L. P. Gerson, 171–95. Cambridge.

———. 1999. "Plato and Empedocles on Evil." In *Traditions of Platonism*, edited by J. Cleary, 3–27. Aldershot.

———. 2011. "Plotinus on the Making of Matter, Part I: The Identity of Darkness." *International Journal of the Platonic Tradition* 5:6–57.

———. 2012. "Plotinus on the Making of Matter, Part III: The Essential Background." *International Journal of the Platonic Tradition* 6:27–80.

O'Meara, D. J. 1975. *Structures hiérarchiques dans la pensée de Plotin*. Leiden.

———. 1993. *Plotinus: An Introduction to the "Enneads."* Oxford.

———. 1994. "Political Life and Divinization in Neoplatonic Philosophy." *Hermathena* 157:155–64.

———. 2005. "The Metaphysics of Evil in Plotinus: Problems and Solutions." In *Agonistes: Essays in Honour of Denis O'Brien*, edited by J. M. Dillon and M. Dixsaut, 179–85. Aldershot.

Opsomer, J. 1998. *In Search of the Truth: Academic Tendencies in Middle Platonism*. Brussels.

———. 2001. "Proclus vs. Plotinus on Matter." *Phronesis* 46:154–88.

———. 2004. "Plutarch's *De animae procreatione in Timaeo*: Manipulation or Search for Consistency?" In *Philosophy, Science and Exegesis in Greek, Arabic and Latin Commentaries*, edited by Peter Adamson, Han Baltussen, and M. W. F. Stone, 1:137–62. Bulletin of the Institute of Classical Studies, supp. 83.1. London.

———. 2005a. "Demiurges in Early Imperial Platonism." In *Gott und die Götter bei Plutarch: Götterbilder—Gottesbilder—Weltbilder,* edited by R. Hirsch-Luipold, 51–99. Berlin.

———. 2005b. "The Place of Plutarch in the History of Platonism." In *Plutarco e la cultura della sua età: Atti del X Convegno plutarcheo Fisciano—Paestum, 27–29 ottobre 2005,* edited by P. Cacciatore and F. Ferrari, 281–309. Naples.

———. 2005c. "Plutarch's Platonism Revisited." In *L'eredità platonica: Studi sul Platonismo da Arcesilao a Proclo,* edited by M. Bonazzi and V. Celluprica, 163–200. Naples.

———. 2007a. "Plutarch on the One and the Dyad." In *Greek and Roman Philosophy 100BC–200AD,* 2:379–95. London.

———. 2007b. "Some Problems with Plotinus' Theory of Matter/Evil: An Ancient Debate Continued." *Quaestio* 7:165–89.

Owen, G. E. L. 1953. "The Place of the *Timaeus* in Plato's Dialogues." *Classical Quarterly* 3:79–95.

Penner, T. M. 1990. "Plato and Davidson: Parts of the Soul and Weakness of Will." *Canadian Journal of Philosophy* (supp.) 16:35–74.

———. 1991. "Desire and Power in Socrates: The Argument of *Gorgias* 466A–468E That Orators and Tyrants Have No Power in the City." *Apeiron* 24:147–202.

———. 1992. "Socrates and the Early Dialogues." In *The Cambridge Companion to Plato,* edited by R. Kraut, 121–69. Cambridge.

———. 2002. "The Historical Socrates and Plato's Early Dialogues: Some Philosophical Questions." In *New Perspectives on Plato, Modern and Ancient,* edited by J. Annas and C. Rowe, 189–212. Washington, DC.

———. 2004. "Towards a Prudential Reading of the *Crito.*" In *Socrates: 2400 Years since His Death: International Symposium Proceedings,* edited by V. Karamanlis, 13–21. Delphi.

———. 2005. "Socratic Ethics, Ultra Realism, Determinism, and Ethical Truth." In *Virtue, Norms, and Objectivity: Issues in Ancient and Modern Ethics,* edited by C. Gill, 157–87. Oxford.

———. 2011. "Socratic Ethics and the Socratic Psychology of Action: A Philosophical Framework." In *The Cambridge Companion to Socrates,* edited by D. Morrison, 260–92. Cambridge.

Penner, T., and C. J. Rowe. 2005. *Plato's "Lysis."* Cambridge.

Perl, E. 1998. "The Demiurge and the Forms: A Return to the Ancient Interpretation of Plato's *Timaeus.*" *Ancient Philosophy* 18:81–92.

Pépin, J. 1956. "Éléments pour une histoire de la relation entre l'intelligence et l'intelligible chez Platon et dans le néoplatonisme." *Revue Philosophique* 81:39–64.

Peterson, S. 2011. *Socrates and Philosophy in the Dialogues of Plato.* Cambridge.

Petty, R. 2012. *Fragments of Numenius of Apamea.* Wiltshire, UK.

Phillips, J. 2009. "Plotinus on the Generation of Matter." *International Journal of the Platonic Tradition* 3 (2): 103–37.

Pigler, A. 2003. *Plotin, une métaphysique de l'amour: L'amour comme structure du monde intelligible.* Paris.

Polansky, R. M. 2007. *Aristotle's "De Anima."* Cambridge.

Politis, V. 2010. "Explanation and Essence in Plato's *Phaedo.*" In *Definition in Greek Philosophy,* edited by D. Charles, 62–114. Oxford.

Polito, R. 2012. "Antiochus and the Academy." In *The Philosophy of Antiochus,* edited by D. Sedley, 55–79. Cambridge.

Pradeau, J.-F. 1999. *Alcibiade.* Paris.

Praechter, K. 1909. "Die Philosophie des Altertums." In *Grundriss der Geschichte der Philosophie,* edited by F. Ueberweg, 1:536–68. Berlin.

Press, G. A. 1996. "The State of the Question in the Study of Plato." *Southern Journal of Philosophy* 34:507–32.
———. 2000. *Who Speaks for Plato? Studies in Platonic Anonymity*. Lanham, MD.
———. 2007. *Plato: A Guide for the Perplexed*. London.
Prior, W. J. 1985. *Unity and Development in Plato's Metaphysics*. LaSalle, IL.
———. 2004. "Socrates Metaphysician." *Oxford Studies in Ancient Philosophy* 27:1–14.
———. 2006. "The Socratic Problem." In *A Companion to Plato*, edited by H. Benson, 25–35. Malden, MA.
Reale, G. 1997. *Toward a New Interpretation of Plato*. Translated from the 10th Italian edition (1991) by J. Catan and R. Davis. Washington, DC.
Remes, P. 2007. *Plotinus on Self: The Philosophy of the "We."* Cambridge.
Reshotko, N. 2006. *Socratic Virtue*. Cambridge.
Richard, M.-D. 1986. *L'enseignement oral de Platon: Une nouvelle interprétation du platonisme*. Paris.
Rist, J. 1964. *Eros and Psyche: Studies in Plato, Plotinus, and Origen*. Toronto.
———. 1965. "Monism: Plotinus and Some Predecessors." *Harvard Studies in Classical Philology* 69:329–44.
———. 1967. "Integration and the Undescended Soul in Plotinus." *American Journal of Philology* 88:410–22.
Robin, L. 1908. *La théorie platonicienne des idées et des nombres d'après Aristote: Étude historique et critique*. Paris.
———. 1935. *Platon*. Paris.
Roloff, D. 1970. *Gottähnlichkeit, Vergöttlichung und Erhöhung zu seligem Leben: Untersuchungen zur Herkunft der platonischen Angleichung an Gott*. Berlin.
Rorty, R. 1999. *Philosophy and Social Hope*. London.
Ross, W. D. 1924. *Aristotle's Metaphysics*. 2 vols. Oxford.
———. 1951. *Plato's Theory of Ideas*. Oxford.
———. 1955. *Aristoteles: Fragmenta Selecta*. Oxford.
Rossetti, L. 1991. "Logoi Sokratikoi anteriori al 399 a.c." In *Logos e logoi*, edited by L. Rossetti, 21–40. Naples.
Rowe, C. J. 2007. *Plato and the Art of Philosophical Writing*. Cambridge.
Rudebusch, G. 1999. *Socrates, Pleasure, and Value*. Oxford.
———. 2009. *Socrates*. Chichester, UK.
Ryle G. 1966. *Plato's Progress*. Cambridge.
Saffrey, H. D. 1955; 2nd ed., 1971. *Le peri philosophias d'Aristote et la théorie platonicienne des idées nombres*. Leiden.
Santa Cruz, M. I. 1997. "L'exegese plotinienne des megista gene du Sophiste." In *The Perennial Tradition of Platonism*, edited by J. Cleary, 105–18. Leuven.
Santas, G. X. 1979. *Socrates: Philosophy in Plato's Early Dialogues*. London.
———. 2002. "The Form of the Good as Paradigm and Its Essence." In *New Images of Plato*, edited by G. Reale and S. Scolnicov, 359–78. Sankt Augustin.
Sattler, B. 2012. "A Likely Account of Necessity: Plato's Receptacle as a Physical and Metaphysical Foundation for Space." *Journal of the History of Philosophy* 50:159–95.
Sayre, K. M. 1988. "Plato's Dialogues in Light of the *Seventh Letter*." In *Platonic Writings: Platonic Readings*, edited by C. Griswold, 93–109. London.
———. 1995. *Plato's Literary Garden*. Notre Dame, IN.
———. 2005. *Plato's Late Ontology: A Riddle Resolved: With a New Introduction and the Essay "Excess and Deficiency at 'Statesman' 283C–285C."* Las Vegas.
———. 2006. *Metaphysics and Method in Plato's "Statesman."* New York.
Schaefer, C. 2004. "Matter in Plotinus' Normative Ontology." *Phronesis* 49 (3): 266–94.
Scharle, M. 2009. "A Synchronic Justification for Aristotle's Commitment to Prime Matter." *Phronesis* 54 (4–5): 326–45.

Schefer, C. 2001. *Platons unsagbare Erfahrung.* Basel.
Schleiermacher, F. 1836; original German edition 1817. *Introductions to the Dialogues of Plato.* Translated by W. Dobson. London.
Schofield, M. 2000. "Plato in His Time and Place." In *The Oxford Handbook to Plato,* edited by G. Fine, 36–62. Oxford.
Schoppe, C. 1994. *Plutarchs Interpretation der Ideenlehre Platons.* Münster.
Scott, D. 1995. *Recollection and Experience.* Cambridge.
Scott, G. A. 2007. *Philosophy in Dialogue: Plato's Many Devices.* Evanston, IL.
Sedley, D. 1993. "Chrysippus on Psychophysical Causality." In *Passions and Perceptions: Studies in Hellenistic Philosophy of Mind: Proceedings of the Fifth Symposium Hellenisticum,* edited by J. Brunschwig and M. Nussbaum, 313–31. Cambridge.
———. 1996. "Three Platonist Interpretations of the *Theaetetus.*" In *Form and Argument in Late Plato,* edited by C. Gill and M. M. McCabe, 79–103. Oxford.
———. 1997. "'Becoming Like God' in the *Timaeus* and Aristotle." In *Interpreting the "Timaeus"-"Critias,"* edited by T. Calvo and L. Brisson, 327–39. Sankt Augustin.
———. 1998. "Platonic Causes." *Phronesis* 43:114–32.
———. 1999. "The Idea of Godlikeness." In *Plato,* edited by G. Fine, 2:309–28. Oxford.
———. 2004. *The Midwife of Platonism: Text and Subtext in Plato's "Theaetetus."* Oxford.
———. 2010. "Teleology, Aristotelian and Platonic." In *La scienza e le cause a partire dalla Metafisica di Aristotele,* edited by F. Fronterotta, 313–49. Naples.
———, ed. 2012a. *The Philosophy of Antiochus.* Cambridge.
———. 2012b. "Antiochus as Historian of Philosophy." In *The Philosophy of Antiochus,* edited by D. Sedley, 80–103. Cambridge.
Seel, G. 2006. "If You Know What Is Best, You Do It: Socratic Intellectualism in Xenophon and Plato." In *Remembering Socrates,* edited by L. Judson and V. Karasmanis, 21–49. Oxford.
Sharma, R. 2009. "Socrates' New Aitia: Causal and Metaphysical Explanations in Plato's *Phaedo.*" *Oxford Studies in Ancient Philosophy* 36:137–77.
Sharples, R. W. 1989. "The Criterion of Truth in Philo Judaeus, Alcinous, and Alexander of Aphrodisias." In *The Criterion of Truth,* edited by P. M. Huby and G. Neal, 231–56. Liverpool.
Shields, C. 1994. "Socrates among the Sceptics." In *The Socratic Movement,* edited by P. Vander Waerdt, 341–66. Ithaca, NY.
———. 2010. "Plato's Divided Soul." In *Plato's Republic: A Critical Guide,* edited by M. McPherran, 147–70. Cambridge.
Shiffman, M. 2010. "Erotic Wisdom and the Socratic Vocation in Plutarch's *Platonic Questions 1.*" *Greek, Roman, and Byzantine Studies* 50:243–71.
Shorey, P. 1904. *The Unity of Plato's Thought.* Chicago.
———. 1933. *What Plato Said.* Chicago.
———. 1938. *Platonism, Ancient and Modern.* Berkeley.
Sider, D. 1980. "Did Plato Write Dialogues before the Death of Socrates?" *Apeiron* 14:15–18.
Silverman, A. 2002. *The Dialectic of Essence.* Princeton.
Slings, S. R. 1994. *Plato's Apology of Socrates: A Literary and Philosophical Study with a Running Commentary.* Edited and completed from the papers of the late É. De Strycker. Leiden.
Smith, N. 2004. "Did Plato Write *Alcibiades I?*" *Apeiron* 37:93–108.
Sorabji, R. 1988. *Matter, Space, and Motion: Theories in Antiquity and Their Sequel.* Ithaca, NY.
Staab, G. 2009. "Das Kennzeichen des neuen Pythagoreismus innerhalb der kaiserzeitlichen Platoninterpretation: 'Pythagoreischer' Dualismus und Einprinzipienlehre im Einklang." In *The Origins of the Platonic System: Platonisms of the Early Empire and Their Philosophical Contexts,* edited by M. Bonazzi and J. Opsomer, 55–88. Brussels.

Steel, C. 1989. "L'un et le bien: Les raisons d'une identification dans la tradition platonicienne." *Revue des Sciences Philosophiques et Théologiques* 73:69–84.

———. 2012. "Plato as Seen by Aristotle." In *Aristotle's "Metaphysics" Alpha: Symposium Aristotelicum,* edited by C. Steel, 167–200. Oxford.

Steinthal, H. 1998. "L'enseignement oral dispensé par Platon." *Études Philosophiques* 1:57–68.

Stemmer, P. 1985. "Das Kinderrätsel von Eunuchen und der Fledermaus: Platon über Wissen und Meinung in Politeia V." *Philosophisches Jahrbuch* 92:79–97.

Szlezák, T. A. 1979a. "The Acquiring of Philosophical Knowledge according to Plato's Seventh Letter." In *Arktouros,* edited by G. W. Bowerstock, 354–63. Berlin.

———. 1979b. *Platon und Aristoteles in der Nuslehre Plotins.* Basel.

———. 1985. *Platon und die Schriftlichkeit der Philosophie.* Berlin.

———. 1999. *Reading Plato.* New York.

———. 2003. *Die Idee des Guten in Platons Politeia.* Sankt Augustin.

———. 2010a. "Von Brucker über Tennemann zu Schleiermacher: Eine folgenreiche Unwälzung in der Geschichte der neuzeitlichen Platondeutung." In *Akten des internationalen symposions vom 27–29 april 2006 in istituto svizzero di Roma,* edited by A. Neschke-Hentschke, 412–33. Basel.

———. 2010b. "The Indefinite Dyad in Sextus Empiricus's Report (*Adversus Mathematicos* 10.248–83)." In *Plato's "Parmenides" and Its Heritage,* edited by J. Turner and K. Corrigan, 1:79–91. Atlanta.

Tarán, L. 1981. *Speusippus of Athens: A Critical Study with a Collection of the Related Texts and Commentary.* Leiden.

Tarrant, H. 1979. "Numenius Fr. 13 and Plato's *Timaeus.*" *Antichthon* 13:19–29.

———. 1983. "Middle Platonism and the *Seventh Letter.*" *Phronesis* 28:75–92.

———. 1985. *Scepticism or Platonism? The Philosophy of the Fourth Academy.* Cambridge.

———. 1993. *Thrasyllan Platonism.* Ithaca, NY.

———. 2000. *Plato's First Interpreters.* Ithaca, NY.

———. 2006. "Platonic Interpretation and Eclectic Theory." In *Reading Plato in Antiquity,* edited by H. Tarrant and D. Baltzly, 9–18. London.

———. 2007. "Antiochus: A New Beginning?" In *Greek and Roman Philosophy 100BC–200AD,* 2:317–32. London.

Tarrant, H., D. Baltzly, D. Runia, and M. Share. 2007–. 5 vols. *Proclus: Commentary on Plato's "Timaeus."* Cambridge.

Taylor, A. E. 1928. *A Commentary on Plato's "Timaeus."* Oxford.

Taylor, C. C. W. 1992. "Socratic Ethics." In *Socratic Questions,* edited by B. S. Gower and M. C. Stokes, 137–52. London.

———. 2002. "The Origins of Our Present Paradigms." In *New Perspectives on Plato, Modern and Ancient,* edited by J. Annas and C. Rowe, 73–84. Cambridge, MA.

Tejera, V. 1984. *Plato's Dialogues One by One: A Structural Interpretation.* New York.

Theiler, W. 1930; 2nd ed. 1964. *Die Vorbereitung des Neuplatonismus.* Berlin.

Thesleff, H. 2009. *Platonic Patterns: A Collection of Studies.* Las Vegas.

Thiel, D. 2006. *Die Philosophie des Xenokrates im Kontext der alten Akademie.* Munich.

Tigerstedt, E. N. 1974. *The Decline and Fall of the Neoplatonic Interpretation of Plato: An Outline and Some Observations.* Helsinki.

Tomin, J. 1997. "Plato's First Dialogue." *Ancient Philosophy* 17:31–45.

Töplitz, O. 1929. "Der Verhältnis von Mathematik und Ideenlehre be Platon." *Quellen und Studien zur Geschichte der Mathematik* 1:3–33.

Trabattoni, F. 2003. "Il dialogo come 'portavoce' dell'opinione di Platone." In *Platone e la tradizione platonica,* edited by M. Bonazzi and F. Trabattoni, 151–78. Milan.

Vasiliou, I. 2008. *Aiming at Virtue in Plato.* Cambridge.

Vegetti, M. 2003. "Megiston mathema: L'idea del 'buono' e le sue funzioni." *La Repubblica: Traduzione e commento,* edited by M. Vegetti, 5:253–86. Naples.
Vlastos, G. 1939. "The Disorderly Motion in the *Timaeus*." *Classical Quarterly* 3:71–83. Reprinted in R. E. Allen, 1965, *Studies in Plato's Metaphysics,* London, 379–99.
———. 1954. "The Third Man Argument in the *Parmenides*." *Philosophical Review* 63: 319–49.
———. 1963. "On Plato's Oral Doctrine." *Gnomon* 41:641–55. Reprinted in Vlastos 1973, 379–98.
———. 1973. *Platonic Studies.* Princeton.
———. 1991. *Socrates, Ironist and Moral Philosopher.* Ithaca, NY.
Vogt, K. 2009. "Sons of the Earth: Are the Stoics Metaphysical Brutes?" *Phronesis* 54:136–54.
———. 2012. *Belief and Truth: A Skeptic Reading of Plato.* Oxford.
von Fritz, K. 1966. "Die philosophische Stelle im siebten platonischen Brief und die Frage der 'esoterischen' Philosophie Platons." *Phronesis* 11:117–53.
———. 1971. "The Philosophical Passage in Plato's Seventh Letter and the Problem of Plato's 'Esoteric' Philosophy." In *Essays in Ancient Greek Philosophy,* edited by J. P. Anton and G. L. Kustas, 407–49. Albany.
Vorwerk, M. 2010. "Plotinus and the *Parmenides*: Problems of Interpretation." In *Plato's "Parmenides" and Its Heritage,* edited by J. Turner and K. Corrigan, 2:23–33. Atlanta.
Wedin, M. V. 2000. *Aristotle's Theory of Substance: The "Categories" and "Metaphysics" Zeta.* Oxford.
Wehrli, F. 1967. *Die Schule des Aristoteles: Texte und Kommentare.* 10 vols. Basel.
Whittaker, J. 1967. "Moses Atticizing." *Phoenix* 27:196–201.
———. 1969. "Epekeina nou kai ousias." *Vigiliae Christianae* 23:91–104.
———. 1978. "Numenius and Alcinous on the First Principle." *Phoenix* 32:144–54.
———. 1990. *Alcinous: Enseignement des doctrines de Platon.* Paris.
Wimmer, F. 1862. *Theophrasti Eresii Quae Supersunt Opera.* Vol. 3, *Fragmenta.* Leipzig.
Witt, R. E. 1937. *Albinus and the History of Middle Platonism.* Cambridge.
Wolfsdorf, D. 1999. "Plato and the Mouth-Piece Theory." *Ancient Philosophy* 19:13–24.
———. 2004. "Socrates' Avowals of Knowledge." *Phronesis* 49:75–140.
Woodruff, P. 1992. "Plato's Early Theory of Knowledge." In *Essays in the Philosophy of Socrates,* edited by H. Benson, 86–106. Oxford.

General Index

Abbate, M., 275n.71
absoluteness of Socrates' ethics, 43, 48
absolute simplicity, 141, 201, 217, 231, 233
Academici, 4n.2
Academics, 25
Academy, 79
Ackrill, J., 192n.50
Adam, J., 21n.39
Adams, R., 128n.114
Aenesidemus, 165, 172
Affinity Argument (*Phd.*), 285n.8
αἵρεσις, 10n.12
ἀκρασία, 49, 52, 69–70
Allen, D., 92n.48
Allen, R. E., 12n.17, 78n.14, 231n.15
ἀλήθεια, 173
Altman, W., 93n.53
Anaxagoras, 23
Annas, J., 45n.27, 90n.44, 108n.40, 114n.67, 127n.111, 180n.4, 180n.5, 294n.35
anonymous (*Commentary on Plato's Theaetetus*), 26n.51
antimaterialism, 10–11, 15, 178, 180, 186, 187
antimechanism, 10–11
antinaturalism, 16
antinominalism, 10, 12, 14, 17
Antiochus of Ascalon, 61
antirelativism, 10, 13, 15, 28–29
antiskepticism, 10, 13, 164–65, 178
aporetic dialogues, 75

Arcesilaus, 166–67, 171, 171n.22
argument from illusion, 170
Argument from Relatives, 109
Aristotle on materialism, 112
Aristotle on nominalism, 110, 267
Aristotle on relativism, 111
Aristotle's testimony, 35, 99–100
Armstrong, A. H., 30n.59, 196n.67, 231n.15
assimilation to divine, 178, 204–6, 293–99
Atkinson, M., 258n.11
Atomism, 15n.24, 23
Atticus, 216n.44
Aubry, G., 236n.41, 293n.32
autoexplicability/heteroexplicability, 104–5, 107, 139, 140–41, 147, 233, 264
αὐτοόν, 211, 235

Bailey, D., 85n.32
Baltes, M., 154n.72, 155n.76, 156n.82, 157n.85, 193n.51, 199n.77, 214n.33, 215n.35, 216n.40, 216n.43, 218n.52, 259n.16, 275n.71
Baltzly, D., 54n.44, 85n.32
Barnes, J., 176n.43, 179n.3, 182n.10, 184n.15, 184n.17
Baudy, G., 92n.48
Bechtle, G., 209n.5
Beierwaltes, W., 233n.27, 293n.33, 294n.35, 295n.38, 298n.55
Benson, H., 41n.15, 60n.61
Berti, E., 267n.37
Besnier, B., 93n.53

General Index

Beversluis, J., 36n.3, 38n.9, 75n.7
Bianchi, U., 192n.48
βίος, 19–20
Blondell, R., 59n.57, 88n.38
Blyth, D., 127n.111
Bobonich, C., 286n.13
Bobzien, S., 12n.15, 283n.2, 301n.63
Bonazzi, M., 31n.60, 180n.5, 216n.44
bonum est diffusivum sui, 236
Boys-Stones, G., 19n.33, 184n.17, 185n.18, 186n.25
Boys-Stones, G./Rowe, C., 82n.21
Brandwood, L., 74n.4
Brickhouse, T./Smith, N., 41n.15, 43n.21, 57n.51, 63n.67, 65n.74, 67n.81, 287n.15
Brisson, L., 93n.50, 272n.58
Brittain, C., 6n.6, 134n.3, 176n.43, 182n.11, 182n.9, 187n.27
Brown, J., 3n.1, 16n.26
Brucker, J., 32n.81
Brunschwig, J., 19n.31, 86n.34
Burge, E., 108n.40
Burnet, J., 78n.13, 98n.4
Burnyeat, M., 62n.63, 91n.46, 117n.79, 152n.62, 164n.6, 172n.24, 211n.20
Büsching, A. F., 32n.61

Campbell, L., 74n.4
Carneades, 166, 174–75, 174n.33, 192n.49
causal closure, 11
Charrue, J.-M., 230n.11, 256n.4
Cherniss, H, 16n.25, 75n.6, 76n.10, 93n.50, 98n.2, 99n.5, 99n.6, 99n.7, 103n.20, 115n.70, 116n.78, 121n.95, 155n.75, 259n.16
Clitomachus, 166
Code, A., 266n.34
cognitive identity, 157, 159
compositeness, 111
Cooper, J., 41n.15, 53n.42, 67n.82
Cornford, F. M. 11n.13, 231n.15, 273n.62
Crantor, 258
creation in time, 194, 259n.16
criterion of truth, 175, 187
culpable ignorance, 302

Dancy, R., 135n.5, 139n.21, 150n.56
Decad, 121n.95,
Demiurge, 23, 120, 126, 127, 150, 155, 156, 177, 191, 194, 194n.60, 199, 212n.25, 218, 222, 258, 291
Democritus, 9n.10
Denyer, N., 21n.39, 45n.27, 281n.95
Des Places, É., 211n.20, 222n.73, 240n.63
De Strycker, É., 51n.41
developmentalism, 10, 28, 38–39, 42n.20, 46, 73–74, 75–76, 91, 100–101

Devereux, D., 296n.42
De Vogel, C., 7n.8, 93n.50, 209n.5, 259n.16, 277n.76
dialogues: as "enactments," 38n.7; fictive chronology of, 4n.12; literary form of, 35–36, 83–84, 87–88; as occasional pieces 80–81; as protreptic 37–38, 87; as ὑπομνήματα, 91–92
διάνοια, 151
Dillon, J., 80n.16, 137n.15, 141n.29, 142n.32, 153n.66, 154n.70, 154n.72, 158n.88, 161n.104, 161n.109, 184n.17, 185n.18, 186n.24, 188n.28, 201n.87, 202n.90, 207n.111, 211n.20, 214n.33, 216n.44, 294n.35, 297n.47
disorderly motion (*Tim.*), 191–93, 259n.16, 261
Divided Line (*Rep.*), 21, 70n.96, 119, 39n.20, 145, 164n.5, 173
divided self, 51, 288n.19, 304
Dodds, E.R., 30n.59, 198n.74, 201n.87, 209n.9, 240n.64, 257n.5
Donini, P., 31n.60, 184n.17, 192n.48, 197n.68
Dorion, L.-A., 39n.11, 53n.43, 55n.48
Dörrie, H., 7n.8, 31n.60, 32n.61
Dörrie, H./Baltes, M., 197n.69, 227n.4
δόξα, 153
dualism/monism, 214–15

'early' dialogues, 41, 56n.49, 57–59, 57n.51
early Stoa, 16n.28
Eleatic monism, 12n.17
elements of Forms, 116
'elenctic knowledge,' 59
Emilsson, E., 239n.59, 273n.60, 279n.83
eminence, 212–13, 216, 224
ἐνέργεια, 234
ἐνέργεια νοῦ, 110n.47
Epicureans, 238n.52
epistemic/nonepistemic appearances, 18, 175
epistemological holism, 26, 148, 149n.51, 151–53
ἐπιστήμη, 118, 144, 163–78
Erler, M., 45n.27, 94n.57
essentialism, 270
Eudorus of Alexandria, 216n.44, 277n.76
evil distinct from vice, 252
explanatory framework of UP, 15

Ferber, R., 93n.52, 116n.78
Ferrari, F., 31n.60, 155n.76, 179n.1, 194n.59, 195n.61, 235n.39, 245n.87
Findlay, J. N., 93n.50, 99n.6, 121n.96, 149n.55
Fine, G., 59n.53, 70n.96, 108n.41

first principle, proof of existence, 229–33
Forms: as divine thoughts, 199; as explanatory entities, 138, 264–65; as generated, 141; as Numbers, 114–15, 119, 121, 126, 128, 138, 148, 159; as one-over-many 117; as paradigmatic causes 160; independence of, 109–110; separate existence of, 59
Franklin, L., 21n.39, 114n.67
Frede, M., 92n.49, 212n.23, 214n.33, 218n.51, 219n.56
Froidefond, C., 192n.48
Fronterotta, F., 59n.53, 74n.22, 204n.98, 235n.39, 293n.33
Furley, D., 104n.22

Gadamer, H.-G., 5n.4
Gaiser, K., 81n.19, 93n.50, 93n.51, 93n.554, 94n.57, 95n.59, 277n.76, 278n.79
Gallop, D., 85n.29, 85n.30
generation of cosmos, 192
Gersh, S., 157n.84
Gerson, L., 8n.9, 44n.24, 50n.37, 70n.96, 103n.16, 104n.21, 109n.45, 118n.84, 142n.33, 146n.45, 164n.2, 167n.11, 177n.44, 199n.80, 231n.17, 241n.66, 245n.87, 266n.36, 271n.52, 284n.8
Gigon, O., 171n.22
Gill, C., 36n.3, 301n.63
Glucker, J., 4n.2, 10n.12, 171n.22, 174n.32, 179n.2
Gonzalez, F., 88n.38, 96n.62
'good' as second-order predicate, 47
Good: Good/Demiurge/Forms conflated, 190n.37, 196, 199, 207; as One, 98n.1, 212, 217; as unhypothetical first principle, 25n.49
good-independent desires, 287n.15
Görannson, T., 179n.2
graded synonymy, 109, 266
greatest kinds (Soph.), 271–76
Griswold, C., 36n.3, 38n.7, 40n.12, 274n.67
Grote, G., 36n.3
Guthrie, W. K. C., 78n.13

Hadot, P., 20n.35, 94n.55, 271n.53
Hager, F. 190n.40, 252n.111
Halfwassen, J., 17n.29, 141n.27, 141n.28, 148n.50, 155n.75, 237n.50, 256n.5, 277n.76, 278n.77
Halliwell, S., 39n.10
harmony among ancients, 210
harmony of Plato and Aristotle, 103
Heitsch, E., 57n.50
Helmig, C., 185n.21
Heracliteanism, 9n.11, 13n.18
Hermann, K., 57n.50
Herrmann, F.-G., 9n.10

Hicks, R. D., 159n.94
hierarchy of being, 246
historical Socrates, 53n.42, 53n.43, 63n.68
homunculi, 286n.13
Hubler, J., 257n.5
Huffman, C., 78n.13, 113n.64, 121n.96, 158n.89
Hussey, E., 9n.10, 103n.20
hypostases, 227–28

Idea of the Good, 29, 44, 46, 85, 140n.23, 147–48, 189, 191
Ideal Numbers as ordinals, 121n.111
Ideal Ratios, 123–24, 126, 159, 160
identity, degrees of, 238
identity of person with soul, 66–67, 284–85
Indefinite Dyad, 114, 116–17, 151, 215, 257–58, 278
infallibility, 146, 168, 177, 182
instrumental causality, 59, 213–14, 240, 242, 244–45, 260
Intellect one/many, 239
intelligibles, 25, 29
internal/external/activity, 236
Irwin, T., 41n.15, 42n.20, 44n.44, 53n.42, 60n.61, 102n.15, 287n.15

Jackson, H., 55n.49
Jaeger, W., 104n.21, 104n.23, 106n.27
Johansen, T., 173n.28

Kahn, C., 40n.12, 56n.49, 58n.52, 59n.57, 60n.59, 62n.63, 74n.4, 75n.6, 78n.14, 93n.53, 97n.1, 173n.29
Karamanolis, G., 176n.41, 183n.13, 185n.20, 188n.218, 194n.59, 184n.15, 210n.13
Kennedy, J., 53n.43, 78n.13, 114n.64
κίνησις νοῦ, 110n.47, 157, 193n.54, 244, 272
Knab, R., 94n.57
knowledge: as justified true belief, 168; as necessary and sufficient for virtue, 42; by acquaintance, 118, 151; knowledge not propositional, 146
knowledge of Forms, 167
Kramer, H. J., 15n.24, 16n.25, 30n.59, 32n.62, 59n.53, 93n.50, 94n.56, 96n.62, 98n.2, 101n.12, 113n.63, 116n.76, 121n.95, 140n.23, 154n.72, 155n.75, 155n.77, 158n.88, 160n.95, 166n.10, 190n.40, 203n.95, 209n.8, 211n.16, 214n.33, 218n.52, 233n.31, 277n.76, 289n.87, 293n.33
Kraut, R., 41n.15, 96n.62
Kremer, K., 236n.42
Kretzmann, N., 6n.27

Lamm, J., 35n.1, 99n.6
Lavecchia, S., 294n.35, 294n.37
Ledger, G., 58n.52, 74n.4
Lee, J., 245n.84
Lennox, J., 153n.65
literary Socrates, 63n.68
Living Animal (*Tim.*), 22, 115, 193, 199, 213-14, 239
Loenen, J., 196n.65
Λόγοι Σωκρατικοί, 39n.11
Long, A. A., 82n.21, 293n.32

Magrin, S., 9n.10
Mahoney, T. 294n.35
Mann, W.-R., 81n.19, 93n.50, 103n.17
Mansfeld, J., 188n.30, 192n.48, 196n.68
materialism, 18n.31
Mathematical Intermediaries, 21, 124, 127n.12, 142
matter: being of, 250; as evil, 246, 250-52; as generated, 248; generation of, 259; as necessary condition, 252; as privation, 248, 262
McCabe, M. M., 89n.40
McDowell, J., 152n.62
McPherran, M., 41n.15, 57n.51
Meijer, P., 229n.7
Meinwald, C., 113n.64
Menn, S., 203n.95
Merki, H., 294n.35
Merlan, P., 17n.29, 136n.11, 136n.7, 160n.94, 212n.22
metaphor as ontological concept, 21-22
metaphysical hierarchy, 17
Middle Platonism, 5, 179
Miller, M., 21n.39, 127n.112, 156n.80, 236n.42, 257n.5, 257n.6
Moderatus of Gades, 209, 219n.56, 257n.5
Monad/Dyad, 155, 220
monism/dualism, 247
moral paradox, 65n.73
Morel, P.-M., 9n.10
Morrison, D., 53n.43
Morrow, G., 95n.60
Moss, J., 287n.15
Mueller, I., 114n.67
Mulhern, J., 37n.6
Myth of Er (*Rep.*), 296n.43, 299n.58

Nails, D., 37n.6, 38n.9, 39n.11, 40n.12, 41n.14, 54n.44, 74n.2, 101n.10, 133n.1
Narbonne, J.-M., 246n.88, 247n.96, 248n.98
naturalism, 16n.26
Nehemas, A., 37n.5, 62n.63
Neoplatonism, 5, 7, 32, 179
Neo-Pythagoreanism, 209

Nightingale, A., 88n.37
nominal essences, 269
nominalism, 24
noncombinable/combinable numbers, 127, 127n.111
nonentailing evidence, 182-83
no one does wrong willingly, 49, 64, 300
normative/nonnormative rationality, 243n.78, 288
Νοῦς, 193
Nyvlt, M., 274n.66

O'Brien, D., 215n.36, 247n.96, 250n.104, 252n.113, 253n.117, 251n.106, 251n.107
Olympiodorus, 219n.57
O'Meara, D., 229n.5, 239n.5, 239n.59, 246n.91, 258n.11, 274n.66, 297n.47
ὁμοίωμα, 294-95
One, explanatory role of, 232; as unlimited, 259; One/Good, 235; One/Indefinite Dyad, 86, 128, 276-77; self-causality of, 236, 259; self love of, 281
one/many, 274
ontological priority, 105-6, 110
ontological/semantic truth, 173-74, 177
Opsomer, J., 31n.60, 188n.28, 190n.40, 191n.41, 192n.48, 194n.59, 194n.60, 196n.67, 213n.26, 246n.88, 249n.101
οὐσία, 140
Owen, G. E. L., 76n.8, 76n.10

paradigmatic causality, 267
paradigm principle, 279
Penner, T., 43n.21, 62-68, 97n.1, 287n.14, 287n.15
Penner, T./Rowe, C., 39n.11, 41n.15, 62n.63, 64n.69, 288n.19
Pépin, J., 237n.50
Perl, E., 155n.75
per se/per accidens causality, 241
Peterson, S., 58n.52, 68n.84, 294n.35
Petty, R., 219n.56
Phillips, J., 247n.96, 261n.20, 261n.22
Philolaus, 121n.96
Philo of Alexandria, 4n.3
Philo of Larissa, 176-77, 181-82
philosophy as a βίος, 94
physics a 'likely story' (*Tim.*), 172-73
Pigler, A., 282n.101
Plato: anonymity, 5n.5; anthropology of, 284-93; as authority, 20; oral doctrine of, 30; 'Socratic phase,' 28
Platonici, 4n.2
Platonism: of Aristotle, 8, 23; of Plato, 35-36; versions of, 3-8, 38, 74, 79, 103, 129, 256

Polemo, 161n.109
popular or political virtue, 296–97
Porphyry, 208n.3
possessing/having knowledge (*Tht.*), 27, 145, 164, 185–86
Pradeau, J.-F., 45n.27, 284n.6
Praechter, K., 179n.1, 184n.15
pre-Academic dialogues, 78
Press, G., 5n.5, 38n.7, 73n.1, 84n.26
prime matter, 262
Prior, W., 53n.42, 59n.53
priority by nature, 29n.58
Proclus, 245–46
prudentialism, 43, 44, 61, 290, 299
prudential paradox, 65n.73
Pyrrhonism, 23
Pyrrho of Elis, 165, 166n.8
Pythagoreanism, 136, 278n.79

rational/irrational desires, 286–88
rationality of belief, 171
Reale, G., 17n.29, 35n.1, 91n.47, 83n.50, 245n.87
Receptacle (*Tim.*), 120, 189, 257
Recollection Argument (*Phd.*), 14n.20, 27, 108n.41, 14–145, 164, 171, 178
reductivism, 104, 117, 152, 158, 162
Remes, P., 293n.32
Reshotko, N., 41n.15, 43n.21, 43n.23
reversion to One, 282
Richard, M.-D., 93n.50, 137n.14
Rist, J., 231n.15, 252n.111
Robin, L., 7n.7, 7n.8, 100n.8, 100n.9, 115n.75
Roloff, D., 294n.35
Ross, W. D., 63n.68, 76n.11, 98n.1, 102n.13, 105n.26, 137n.14, 294n.36
Rowe, C., 38n.7, 41n.15, 68–72
Rudebusch, G., 41n.15, 51n.39, 57n.51, 287n.14
Ryle, G., 5n.4, 74n.2, 80n.17

Santa Cruz, M., 272n.58
Santas, G. 43n.21, 65n.73, 235n.39
Sattler, B., 257n.6
Sayre, K., 81n.17, 94n.58, 116n.77, 140n.26
Schaefer, C., 252n.112
Scharle, M., 262n.24
Schefer, C., 96n.62
Schleiermacher, F., 34n.1, 40n.12, 57n.50, 78n.13, 83n.23, 99n.6
Schleiermacher's paradigm, 91n.47
Schofield, M., 55n.49, 81n.21, 97n.1
Scott, D., 89n.39, 167n.14
Sedley, D., 12n.15, 26n.51, 82n.21, 108n.41, 110n.47, 166n.10, 184n.15, 186n.22, 187n.27, 206n.106, 294n.35

Seel, G., 43n.21, 49n.35, 62n.63
self-predication, 77
self-transformation, 298
Sharma, R., 98n.3
Shields, C., 164n.3, 286n.13
Shorey, P., 36n.3, 75n.6, 99n.7, 227n.1
Sider, D., 57n.50
Silverman, A., 263n.25, 273n.61
Slings, S., 51n.41
Smith, N., 45n.27
Socrates$_E$ vs. Socrates$_M$, 54–60
Socratic intellectualism, 288n.19, 304
Socratic paradoxes, 41, 43, 44, 82;
Socratic philosophy in dialogues, 44–45
Socraticists, 49–50, 53, 61
Sorabji, R., 189n.32
Sosus Affair, 181
soul as moving number, 160
soul care, 45, 65–66
space/matter, 191
Staab, G., 216n.40, 216n.44
Steel, C., 56n.49, 259n.16
Steinthal, H., 80n.17, 99n.4
Stemmer, P., 70n.96
Stoic epistemology, 165–66; 169, 176
Stoic ethics, 28
Stoic incorporeals, 11n.15
stylometric analysis, 58n.52, 74–75
σύγγραμμα, 94–95
συμφόρησις, 269
suspension of judgment, 170–71
systematization of Platonism, 31–32, 80, 102, 112–13, 143–44, 188, 220, 256, 270, 282
Szlezák, T., 32n.61, 92n.48, 93n.50, 95n.59, 147n.47, 203n.95, 239n.59, 278n.79, 293n.31

Tarán, L. 135n.5, 137n.11
Tarrant, H., 63n.68, 88n.37, 94n.57, 175n.37, 179n.3, 187n.27, 196n.64, 205n.103, 209n.5, 211n.20
Taylor, A. E., 86n.35
Taylor, C., 41n.15, 78n.13
Tejera, V., 36n.3, 84n.27
teleology in nature, 18
Tetraktys, 150
Theophrastus, 162
Thesleff, H., 41n.13, 75n.5, 80n.17, 83n.23
Thiel, D., 156n.78
Third Man Argument (*Parm.*), 77
Tigerstedt, E., 32n.61, 32n.63. 99n.6
τὸ ἐφ' ἡμῖν, 301–3
Tomin, J., 57n.50
Töplitz, O., 121n.96

Trabattoni, F., 36n.3
'transitional' dialogues, 59n.58
tripartition of soul, 50, 68

undescended intellects, 291–92
unhypothetical first principle, 85, 119
unitarianism, 10, 46, 68, 71, 75, 100–101
Unlimited/Limit, 123
Unmoved Mover, 25, 25n.49, 29, 127, 142, 155, 210
unwritten teachings, 92–93, 96, 98, 98n.2, 101n.12, 156
Ur-Platonism (UP), 9–19 and *passim;* as framework for positive construct 20, 22; as Pythagorean, 113–14

Vasilou, I., 297n.45
Vegetti, M., 147n.48, 293n.33
via negativa, 9–10

virtuality, 206, 213, 216, 235–36, 240–41, 258, 280
virtue is knowledge, 41–49, 204
virtue sufficient for happiness, 204
Vlastos, G., 53–61, 77n.12, 101n.12, 192n.50, 259n.16
Vogt, K., 19n.31, 26n.52, 146n.46
von Fritz, K., 94n.57
Vorwerk, M., 256n.5

Wedin, M., 111n.50
Wehrli, F., 112n.61
Whittaker, J., 195n.62, 198n.74, 201n.87, 202n.91, 211n.20, 216n.44
Witt, R. E., 199n.80
Wolfsdorf, D., 57n.51, 60n.61
World Soul, 160, 219–20

Xenocrates, 190n.40

Index Locorum

AËTIUS

Placita (Diels)

1.7.20	142n.31
	155n.76
1.7.30	154n.71
17.31	211n.16
288.2–6	200n.82

ALCINOUS

The Handbook of Platonism (*Didask.*) (Whittaker)

153.6	197n.82
163.32–33	202n.90
163.14–15	197n.82
163.30–31	197n.82
164.18–27	202n.92
164.25	197n.69
	217n.47
164.27	211n.16
164.29–165.4	197n.68
	199n.82
165.5–16	201n.86
165.27–34	200n.84
165.34–166.7	201n.89
166.40ff	199n.81
169.32–35	200n.85
169.39–40	199n.82
178.1–12	205n.103
179.34–42	203n.97
	204n.101
180.16–28	205n.102
181.44–45	207n.110
189.28–29	195n.63

ALEXANDER OF APHRODISIAS

Commentary on Aristotle's Metaphysics (*In Meta.*) (Hayduck)

58.25–59.8	277n.76
82.11–83.7	108n.39

De fato

22.191.30–192.8	11n.15
22.192.21–24	11n.15

Anonymous Prolegomena to Plato's Philosophy (Westerink)

10.57–72	26n.51
15–16	83n.24

ARISTOTLE

Categories (*Cat.*)

3b11ff	267n.38

De anima (*DA*)

403b7–16	125n.106
404b16–21	121n.95
404b27–28	160n.98
408b32–33	160n.98
412b15–17	161n.102
413b25–26	157n.86
	220n.59
415a11–12	157n.86
	220n.59
429a22–24	157n.86
429a27–29	125n.105
	159n.94
429b5–9	239n.57
430a19–20	239n.57
430a22–23	221n.65
431a1–2	239n.57
431a16–17	119n.85
431a23	121n.96
431b17	239n.57
432a9	119n.85

De caelo (*DC*)

298b23	112n.60

De generatione animalium (*De gen. an.*)

731b24–732a1	142n.33

De generatione et corruptione (*GC*)

330b16–17	98n.1
335b10	98n.2
335b18–21	245n.84

De memoria (*De mem.*)
449b31–450a1   119n.85
De motu animalium (*De motu an.*)
699b32–700a6   142n.33
De mundo (*De Mun.*)
397b16–398a6   142n.33

Eudemian Ethics (*EE*)
1216b3–8   63n.68
1218a15–32   86n.34
                141n.30
1227b12–19   296n.42
1249b13–21   296n.41

Magna Moralia (*MM*)
1182a15–23   63n.68
1182a27–30   98n.2
1190b28–32   63n.68
1198a10–12   63n.68

Metaphysics (*Meta.*)
982a1–3   106n.28
982b7–10   106n.28
983a2–3   21n.40
983a5–10   106n.29
986b31–34   189n.32
987a13–19   114n.68
987a17–18   114n.65
987a29–31   19n.34
                113n.64
                209n.7
987a32–b1   28n.57
                114n.69
987b14–18   21n.39
                114n.66
987b18–22   114n.68
987b18–25   86n.34
987b18ff   258n.8
987b20–21   278n.79
987b21–22   276n.72
987b215–26   115n.77
987b33   275n.70
987b9–10   98n.3
988a12–14   189n.34
988a7–10   102n.14
988a7–17   258n.8
988a8–14   115n.76
988a18ff   228n.3
990a29–32   114n.69
990a34–990b9   29n.58
991a8–11   245n.84
991b18–21   121n.96
991b27–992a1   138n.16
991b9–21
992a10–15
992a20–22
993a28–31
993b23–31

993b26–31
994a1–2
999a7
1003b22–24
1009a36–38
1009b12–15
1010a1–3
1010a15–
  1010b1
1010a3–4
1016b20–21
1017b14–16
1018a4–9
1019a1–4

1022a14–15
1024b24–
  1025a1
1024b32–33
1025b3–18
1027b24–25
1028b2–4

1028b12
1028b18–21
1028b19
1028b21–24
1029a20–26
1029a27–30
1029a30–32
1029b13–14
1031a18
1031a31–b9
1031b1–2
1031b6–7
1035b14–16
1035b32
1036b13–25
1037a33–b2
1037b4–7
1038b14–15
1038b35–
  1039a3
1040a1–2
1041b11–33
1040b26–30
1041b11–33
1041b4–6
126n.109
121n.95
97n.1
139n.18
106n.27
235n.39
266n.35
198n.71
105n.25
237n.50
159n.92
112n.55
112n.60
111n.55

112n.57
112n.56
124n.104
107n.36
159n.92
97n.1
105n.26
265n.32
109n.43

103n.19
24n.46
139n.20
118n.84
110n.48
268n.42

107n.35
21n.39
29n.58
135n.4
111n.53
111n.51
110n.49
263n.27
109n.43
267n.38
128n.113
270n.47
128n.113
128n.113
114n.69
267n.38
268n.39
263n.27

71n.98
50n.37
232n.22
71n.98
128n.113
279n.81
1041b7–9
1042a10
1043a3
1043b13
1045a31–33
1045b27–
  1046a4
1046a16–19
1048a30–32
1049b23–25
1050b2
1050b28–29

1050b6–
  1051a3
1050b6–7

1054b23
1069a30–31
1069a34
1070a18–19
1071b14–16
1071b17
1071b19–20
1071b3–22
1072a19ff
1072a26
1072a26–b4
1072b13–14

1072b20–21
1072b24–25
1072b26–27

1072b30–
  1073a3
1072b30–34
1072b3–4
1072b35–1073a2
1073a18–19
1073a20–21

1074a31–38
1074b15–
  1075a12
1074b15–35
1074b28–35
1074b33–35
1075a11–13
1075a14
1075a18–22
1075a34–b1
1075a4–5
263n.27
107n.35
107n.36
107n.36
268n.40

197n.70
234n.33
234n.35
111n.52
111n.52
161n.108
267n.37

110n.46
162n.111
266n.33
150n.60
107n.35
29n.58
97n.1
102n.14
110n.47
142n.34
106n.31
161n.108
194n.60
197n.69
135n.3
142n.33
244n.82
125n.105
125n.105
220n.61
242n.70
272n.57

136n.8
135n.6
282n.100
198n.71
114n.69
121n.95
149n.55
197n.70

274n.66
197n.68
234n.36
125n.105
25n.48
210n.13
244n.82
86n.34
125n.105
239n.55

INDEX LOCORUM 337

1075b37–1076a3	135n.4 162n.110	1166a22–23	125n.105 158n.87 295n.38	*Topics* (*Top.*)		
				130b15–16	168n.15	
1076a20–21	135n.4 159n.91	1168b31–33 1169a2	295n.38 125n.105 158n.87	133b28ff 134b16–17 136b7 146b1–2	168n.15 168n.15 194n.59 168n.15	
1077b1–9	266n.33					
1078b15	112n.60	1177b26–				
1078b17–34	98n.1	1178a4	158n.87 295n.38	**ARISTOXENUS**		
1078b30–1079a4	29n.58	1177b33	206n.105	*Harmonic Elements*		
1078b9–12	114n.69	1178a2–8	125n.105	2.30–31 (=Aristotle, *On the Good*, p.111 Ross) 98n.2		204n.97
1079b12–15	245n.84	1178a9–22	289n.23			
1080b11–14	114n.69	1178b8–18	295n.39			
1080b14	135n.4	*On the Good* (Ross)				
1080b37–1083a17	127n.110	p.111	204n.97			
1081a13–15	276n.72	*On the Ideas*		**ATTICUS**		
1081a22	115n.77	*On Philosophy* (Ross)		*Fragments* (*Des Places*)		
1081a5–7	114n.69	Fr.16	202n.92	28.2	195n.61	
1083a18	114n.69	*Parts of Animals* (*PA*)		**AUGUSTINE OF HIPPO**		
1083b26–1084a13	121n.95	642b5–644a11	153n.65	*Against the Academics* (*C. Acad.*)		
1084a10–13	149n.55	*Physics* (*Phys.*)				
1084a29–32	121n.95 149n.55	188a27–28	233n.28	3.43	171n.22	
1084a34–35	161n.105	191a7–8	120n.93	**CICERO**		
1084a7–8	114n.69	192a3–8	248n.100			
1085b34–1086a16	134n.2	192a22–25	190n.38	*Academica* (*Acad.*)		
1086a11–13	114n.69	192a27ff	262n.23			
1086a32–35	71n.98	194a18–27	103n.19	1.13	176n.41 181n.7	
1087b4–12	141n.27	195b36–196b5	103n.19	1.14	185n.19	
1090a16	114n.69	198a24–25	237n.50	1.17	180n.5 183n.12	
1090a25–28	144n.35	201b19–21	161n.105			
1090a4–5	114n.69	206b32	149n.55	1.24	186n.25	
1090b19–20	162n.110	209b11–17	92n.50 189n.34	1.30	184n.16	
1090b20–24	121n.95			1.33	184n.17	
1091b13–15	115n.76	209b13–14	98n.2	1.39	11n.15	
1091b30–35	141n.30	266a10–b24	106n.33	1.41	167n.11	
1092a5–11	86n.34	*Poetics* (*Poet.*)		1.42	183n.14	
1092a11–16	106n.27 135n.7	1447a28–b13	39n.11	1.43 1.46	183n.13 35n.2 171n.22	
Nicomachean Ethics (*EN*)		*Politics* (*Pol.*)				
1095a323–33	97n.1	1265a10–13	39n.10	2.11–12	176n.41 179n.2 181n.7	
1096b5–7	136n.9	*Posterior Analytics* (*Post. An.*)				
1102b27	286n.13					
1116b3–5	63n.68	75b24	50n.37 144n.35	2.15	180n.5 183n.12	
1128b33–34	296n.42					
1139b19–24	50n.37 144n.35	81b5–7 88b30–37	50n.37 50n.37 144n.35	2.16 2.18	185n.19 176n.42 176n.41 181n.8	
1144b17–21	63n.68					
1144b28–30	63n.68	97a6–11	150n.58			
1145a6–11	296n.41	*Rhetoric* (*Rhet.*)		2.23	182n.9 185n.21	
1145b25–26	63n.68					
1150b19	49n.35	1417a19–22	39n.11	2.29	187n.26	

2.33	182n.9	**HERMODORUS**		28.6–12	181n.8
2.34	182n.11	APUD SIMPLICIUS,		39	220n.62
2.36	182n.11	*In Phys.*		42	220n.64
2.40	170n.20			46	219n.57
2.69	183n.13	247.30–248.18	114n.65	46c	211n.17
2.145	168n.16			52.1–14	215n.34
		IAMBLICHUS		52.33–44	215n.36
De finibus (De fin.)		*De communi mathematica*		52.64–75	215n.36
3.74	180n.5	*scientia* (Festa/Klein)		52.96–99	215n.35
4.36	186n.24				
5.29.87	78n.13	4.15–23	138n.17	**OLYMPIODORUS**	
			236n.46	*Commentary on Plato's*	
De natura deorum (ND)		4.32–49	141n.30	*Alcibiades (In Alc.).*	
1.11	164n.3	4.106–7	137n.11		
1.73	4n.2			12.12–14	26n.51
		NUMENIUS			
De re publica (Rep.)		*Fragments (Des Places)*		**PANAETIUS**	
1.10.16	78n.13	1a	210n.10	Frs. 127–129 (=Asclepius, *In*	
		2.13–16	210n.11	*Meta.* 90) 46n.29	
Tusculan Disputations (TD)			211n.15		
1.57	176n.41	2.23	211n.14	**PHILOLAUS**	
Cleomedes (=*SVF* 2.363)		3	215n.37	(HUFFMAN)	
11n.15		4a11–12	215n.37	*Fragments*	
		4b	221n.68	2–3	121n.97
DAMASCIUS		4b31–34	219n.54	4	158n.89
		6	221n.67		
Commentary on Plato's		7.4–7	209n.6	**PHILOPONUS**	
Phaedo (In Phd.)		8.14	208n.1	*Commentary on Aristotle's*	
1177, p.124.13ff		11.12–13	211n.21	*Physics (In Phys.)*	
Norvin	158n.87	11.11–20	218n.53		
			221n.70	521.9–15	92n.50
DIOGENES LAERTIUS		12.1–10	212n.23		
		13.4	211n.20	**PHOTIUS**	
Lives and Opinions of the			213n.27	*Bibliotheca* (Henry)	
Philosophers (D.L.)		14.6–7	214n.32	212	166n.8
1.20	9n.12	15	240n.63		
3.6	78n.13	15.3–5	217n.45	**PLATO**	
3.25	9n.10	15.8–9	217n.46	(?) *2nd Epistle*	
3.38	57n.50	16.1–4	215n.39		
3.48	82n.21	16.3	211n.19	312E–313A	95n.60
3.57–61	84n.25	16.9–10	215n.38	312E1–4	156n.81
3.63–4	80n.15	16.10–11	214.31		199n.79
3.78	294n.35	16.11–12	222n.73		218n.51
4.7–8	134n.3	16.16–17	221n.69		230n.8
4.18	161n.109	17.4	211n.16		
4.28–67	26n.50	18.13	222n.71	*7th Epistle*	
4.33	171n.22	19.13	212n.22		
4.62	176n.40	20.5–6	211n.18	324A–344D	94n.58
5.16	154n.68	21.1	216n.43	340B1–345D	94n.57
7.38	61n.62	21.1–5	217n.50	341C4–5	95
7.46	176n.42	22.1–5	213n.29	342D2–E2	115n.74
7.49–52	167n.13		218n.50	343D5–9	94n.58
8.28	220n.58	23	212n.22	344C1–E2	95
9.70	166n.8	24.5–12	209n.9	344D9–E2	152n.64
9.72	35n.2	24.68–73	221n.66		

INDEX LOCORUM 339

Alcibiades I (Alc.)

129B1–3	284n.6
129C–E	213n.29
130C1–3	284n.6
	66n.77
130C5–6	66n.77

Apology (Ap.)

20A–B	65n.74
24C–25C	65n.74
29B6–7	65n.72
29D7–E3	45n.26
	66n.78
31B5	45n.26
	66n.78
36C	65n.74
36C5–7	45n.26
	66n.78
37A5–6	300n.61
	41n.16
38A	38n.8
40C–41D	67n.83

Cratylus (Crat.)

387A–B	160n.97
393C2	160n.97
396A7f	155n.73
423E1–5	200n.83
440B4–C1	56n.49

Crito (Cr.)

47E–48A	45n.26
47E6–48A1	66n.79
49A6–7	65n.72
49A–E	66n.76
49B8	65n.72
49C10–E3	42n.19

Epinomis (Epin.)

991D–992A	114n.65

Euthydemus (Euthyd.)

278D–E	90n.45
301A1–4	59n.55
	244n.83

Euthyphro (Eu.)

6D10–11	59n.54
11A6–B1	171n.21

Gorgias (Gorg.)

467C5–468E5	42n.18
	288n.19
468B	90n.45
469B13–C2	65n.72
472C–481B	66n.76
488A3–4	41n.16
	300n.61
493A1–C3	67n.82
493A–B	113n.64
494E	60n.60
497D8–499B3	47n.31
499A–B	60n.60
499B4–500A6	47n.31
508C4ff	65n.72

Hippias Minor (Hip. Mi.)

374E3–4	66n.75

Laws (Lg.)

689A5–E3	253n.119
716C	204n.99
716C6–D1	294n.34
721B7–8	67n.80
	285n.6
731C–D	41n.16
	300n.61
732B2–4	295n.40
773B5	285n.6
773E5ff	67n.80
812C4	294n.37
856C10	95n.60
891C1–4	11n.13
892aff	243n.73
894A1–5	93n.51
895E10–896A2	161n.103
896A5–B1	191n.46
896A–B	192n.50
896E4–6	192n.49
	215n.36
	261n.22
897D1	215n.36
897D3	157n.85
897E4–6	161n.108
898A3–6	161n.106
904A6–7	299n.57
904B8–C4	299n.58
959B3–4	67n.80
	285n.6

Meno (Men.)

71B2–8	171n.21
76E–77B1	93n.51
77B2–78B6	90n.45
81A–B	113n.64
86A3–4	66n.77
98B1–5	55n.48

Parmenides (Parm.)

127D–128D	12n.17
130Eff	90n.42
132A1	90n.44
132A1–4	117n.80
132B–133C	159n.94
132B3–7	199n.82
132B3ff	185n.20
132D1–4	120n.92
132D3	294n.37
132D2	59n.54
135B6–C3	76n.9
	124n.104
	173n.29
136D4–E3	93n.51
140E3–4	238n.51
141E10–11	232n.21
142S–8	140n.83
142B5–7	200n.83
	272n.56
142B5–C2	230n.9
142D4–5	140n.22
143A–144A	127n.111
143A2	140n.26
143A4–B8	201n.88
143A6–8	141n.29
143B1–2	150n.59
143B8–144A4	127n.111
144E5	230n.14
147E3–148A3	150n.59
158C5–6	248n.100
	275n.70
158D5–6	275n.70

Phaedo (Phd.)

61D	113n.64
63B4–5	46n.30
63D8–9	46n.30
64A	46n.30
65Dff	90n.41
65E1–4	163n.1
66D7–E2	163n.1
66E4–6	163n.1
66E4–67B2	26n.53
67A2–6	163n.1
67C5	295n.40
67E	38n.7
69B8–C3	295n.40
72E3–77A5	27n.54
72E3–78B3	14n.20
	108n.41
	144n.36
	157n.84
72E–73A	291n.27
75D2	108n.41
76C11	67n.80
76C11–13	285n.6
76D8	90n.41

340   INDEX LOCORUM

76E	45n.28	276D3	92n.20	476D8–478E6	144n.37
78B4–84B4	285n.8	278A1	92n.20	477B10–11	90n.43
78C1–2	291n.27	279B	57n.50	477E6–7	90n.43
79C2–4	213n.29				144n.38
81A1–2	294n.36	*Philebus (Phil.)*		478B1–2	145n.38
82A10–B3	296n.41	15A4–7	90n.44	478D5–8	145n.39
82A–C	204n.99	15A4–B2	115n.73		263n.25
83A7–8	207n.109	15B1–2	124n.104	478E7–	
83D7	51n.39		240n.62	480A13	144n.37
	286n.13	16C1–17A5	116n.77	500C4–5	121n.96
84A8	71n.96		269n.44		150n.57
92B5	67n.80	16C9–10	220n.63	500D1	294n.34
	285n.6	17D7–E3	117n.81	500D8	296n.45
92E4–93A10	51n.39	17E3	140n.26	504E8	124n.104
94B4–95A3	51n.39	20D1	252n.110	505A2–4	119n.88
95C5–6	67n.80	22C6	202n.93		124n.104
	285n.6	23Bff	297n.51		148n.49
95E–105E	9n.10	23C–27C	116n.77	505A–506B	62n.65
95E7–102A2	107n.34	26B–C	297n.51	505B5–6	70n.96
96E6–97B3	109n.42	26E–30E	216n.44	506D2–507A2	93n.51
99A–B	11n.15	28D–E	156n.79	508B6–7	139n.19
99D4–100A3	11n.14	30C9–10	156n.79	508E1	173n.27
100B6	85n.29		193n.54	509A2–5	191n.44
100C9ff	85n.28	54C10	252n.110		198n.76
100D5–6	265n.30	60B4	252n.110	509B	276n.73
100D7–8	59n.55	62B5ff	270n.48	509B6–10	119n.86
100D–E	244n.83	65A1–5	199n.78		145n.41
100E5–6	59n.55			509B7–8	200n.84
101C2–9	98n.3	*Protagoras (Protag.)*		509B8–9	206n.108
101D5–E1	85n.29	345D8	41n.16	509B9–10	109n.44
105B8–C2	107n.37		300n.61		230n.11
107B4–10	93n.51	345Dff	42n.17		234n.34
		353A8–D3	49n.33	509C1–11	93n.51
Phaedrus (Phdr.)		356E8–357C1	93n.51	509D	199n.79
245C	261n.22	358C6–7	300n.61	509E–510A	21n.36
245C5	219n.57	358C–D	90n.45	510A9	173n.26
245C5–9	191n.46			510B2ff	85n.31
245C–E	192n.50	*Republic (Rep.)*		510B7	25n.49
245D3	230n.13	365C3–4	296n.45		86n.32
245E6–246A2	160n.98	379B15–16	189n.35		105n.24
246Aff	285n.8		300n.60	510B–E	21n.37
246C5–D2	284n.5	379C5–6	189n.35	510C1–D3	149n.54
247C7–9	193n.56		246n.88	510Cff	126n.108
	202n.91	395B6	294n.37	511B3–C2	119n.87
247D5–E2	148n.51	430C3	296n.45		206n.107
248A	204n.99	430E6–7	296n.42		270n.48
250A6	294n.37	433E1	207n.109	511B6	85n.32
250B3	294n.37	436A8–B3	286n.10		105n.24
253A4–5	294n.34	436B9–10	286n.11	511B7	145n.42
254D1	50n.38	439C9–10	286n.12	511B7–C2	149n.52
256A6	50n.38	439E6–440A2	49n.34	511B–D	164n.5
256B1	295n.42		301n.66	511C8–D2	164n.5
256B2–3	253n.119	440E9	304n.77	511E2	21n.38
256E5	295n.42	442A10–D1	51n.39	515D3	106n.30
257B	57n.50		286n.13		108n.40
259E–274B	14n.21	443C10–D1	296n.45	517C7–9	294n.34
272D2–273A1	14n.21	476A9–D7	144n.37	518C9	210n.12
275A5	92n.50	476A9ff	50n.36	518D3–519A6	296n.45

INDEX LOCORUM 341

518E2	297n.46	259E4–6	76n.9	29A2–3	222n.72
519C4–6	294n.34	270C1–2	304n.78	29B1–D3	173n.23
522C1–6	270n.48	*Statesman (Sts.)*		29C3	173n.26
525E–526A	21n.39				270n.48
526E3–4	210n.12	273B–E	192n.49	29D2	27n.56
527E8–D3	118n.83	273C6–D1	189n.33	29D–30A	295n.39
530D–E	113n.64	283C11–284B2	122n.98	29E1–3	21n.40
532B1	85n.32	283D8–9	124n.103		155n.75
533C7–E2	164n.2	284A1–E4	93n.51		197n.72
533C9	85n.32	284C2	123n.100		197n.73
533E4–534A2	145n.43	284E2–8	123n.99		237n.50
534A	21n.39	285B6–C2	123n.101		280n.93
534A3–5	21b.38	*Symposium (Symp.)*		30A2	197n.72
534B8–C1	119n.86			30A3–6	193n.51
534C6–8	118n.83	205D	90n.45	30A4–5	191n.45
550B–577D	302n.72	206A11–12	280n.91	30B3	193n.54
554D9–10	207n.109	206D6	247n.95	30C2–D1	115n.72
587C–E	290n.24		247n.97		155n.75
589A7	186n.23	210A–D	200n.84	30C–31B	150n.56
589A7–B1	284n.6	211B1	240n.62	30D1–31A1	22n.41
589C6	300n.61	211B2	184n.16		197n.72
589C–D	41n.16	*Theaetetus (Tht.)*		30D2	237n.50
608C1ff	285n.8			30D3	155n.74
611B9–612A6	67n.90	152C5–6	90n.43	34A8–B9	304n.78
612A3–6	253n,119		145n.40	35A	243n.77
613A4–B1	294n.34	161C3	13n.19		304n.76
	296n.43		111n.55	35A1–6	271n.51
613A–B	204n.99	176A5–C5	294n.34	35A–C	160n.99
617D–E	283n.2	176A8–B3	178n.46	36C3	161n.106
617E4–5	299n.56	176A–B	204n.99	37A1–2	22n.42
619B7–C1	299n.58	176B1–2	296n.43		194n.60
619D1	296n.43	176B2–3	204n.100	37A2–C5	161n.107
		183E	9n.11	37A–B	219n.54
Sophist (Soph.)		184E–186B	112n.58	37B9	173n.28
		185C9–10	165n.7	37C7	155n.74
238C8–10	250n.104	186A–E	15n.22	37D1–2	197n.75
243D–244	200n.84	187A–201C	112n.59	39E–40A	150n.56
244B–245E	9n.11	196D–199C	145n.44	39E7	155n.74
	140n.23	197B8–9	145n.44	39E8	214n.30
245A8–9	232n.24	197B–D	27n.55	41A	219n.54
245E8ff	217n.48		164n.4	41A7	155n.74
246A–248A	11n.13	202B5–6	117n.79	47A–D	68n.90
247B–C	18n.331	202E1	117n.79		206n.105
247C–E	18n.31	204A–B	140n.22		243n.77
248A–249D	24n.45	206E–208B	151n.61		285n.8
248E7–249A1	106n.30	*Timaeus (Tim.)*			291n.26
	156n.79			41D4–7	160n.100
249B5–10	271n.52	24B8	218n.51	41D–E	304n.76
249C10–D4	271n.52	28A	187n.27	42C2–6	245n.87
251A–C	12n.17	28A1–2	174n.30	46C	214n.29
252D6–10	273n.62		202n.91	46C7–E2	107n.34
254B7–D3	93n.51	28A6–B2	213n.29	46D5–6	193n.54
254B7ff	271n.50	28B4–C1	270n.48	46E4	193n.53
254D4–10	273n.62	28C1–4	155n.74	47E4	142n.32
255D9–E1	275n.69		174n.30		193n.53
254D14–15	150n.59		190n.37		237n.77
255E4–6	274n.68		216n.43	47E–48B	11n.15
256B6	273n.62		279n.85	48A1	155n.74
258A11–B3	250n.104				

342 INDEX LOCORUM

48A5	193n.53	86C7–D1	41n.16	I 8, 8.20	247n.96
48B3–4	216n.41	86D1–E2	300n.61	I 8, 8.3–4	300n.60
48B3–52D4	257n.7	89A1–3	156n.85	I 8, 9	253n.116
48C2–6	86n.33	90A	68n.90	II 3, 9.19–24	295n.40
	197n.69		285n.8	II 3, 9.22	261n.22
	203n.96	90A–B	51n.40	II 4, 13.22–24	251n.106
	216n.42	90A–C	220n.60	II 4, 16.3–4	248n.100
	216n.43	90B1–C6	289n.23		258n.14
	259n.15	90C	206n.105	II 4, 4.2–7	278n.80
48C2–E1	93n.51	90C2–3	67n.80	II 4, 4.7–9	279n.82
49A–50A	120n.89		285n.6	II 4, 5.18	250n.105
49D–E	269n.44			II 4, 5.25–26	240n.65
50C5	193n.58	**Plotinus**		II 4, 5.28–33	279n.83
51A2	294n.37			II 5, 5.20–22	251n.106
51A7–B1	193n.58	*Enneads (Enn.)*		II 6, 1.48–49	269n.43
51B–52A	263n.26	I 1, 5.21	288n.18	II 7, 3.4–5	269n.43
51B–E	15n.23	I 1, 6.14–18	238n.52	II 9, 1.40–41	272n.55
51D3–E6	145n.43	I 1, 7.14–24	284n.5	II 9, 2.31–44	247n.96
51D5–E4	176n.39	I 1, 7.18–24	289n.23	II 9, 3.11–12	259n.16
51D6	173n.28	I 1, 8.14–23	245n.85	II 9, 3.12–21	248n.98
51E4	169n.19	I 1, 8.6–8	292n.30	II 9, 6.38–41	284n.4
51E–52D	245n.87	I 2, 1.11ff	295n.39	II 9, 12.44	251n.106
	216n.41	I 2, 1.23–26	297n.50	II 9, 15.32–40	296n.44
52A4	120n.92	I 2, 2.13–18	297n.51	II 9, 18.15	243n.72
52A4–7	120n.91	I 2, 3.11–19	286n.13	III 1, 1.1–8	233n.26
52A5	173n.26	I 2, 3.19–20	298n.53	III 1, 8.4–8	242n.72
52A7	174n.30	I 2, 3.31	297n.48	III 2, 10.11–19	300n.59
52A8–B1	257n.6	I 2, 3.9–10	298n.52	III 2, 16.19–20	244n.80
52B2	120n.90	I 2, 5.2	295n.38	III 2, 17.22–32	300n.59
	193n.58	I 2, 7.10–11	298n.45	III 2, 2.15–18	240n.61
52B5	257n.7	I 3, 4	270n.49		240n.64
52C–E	178n.47	I 3, 4.13	270n.49	III 2, 3.33–37	244n.82
52D2–3	191n.41	I 3, 4.18–20	270n.49	III 2, 7.19–20	283n.2
52D2–52C3	260n.18	I 3, 5.17–19	239n.60		299n.56
52D3–4	257n.6	I 3, 6.1–5	270n.48		303n.70
52D4–53A2	191n.45	I 4, 3.33–40	242n.71	III 3, 2.3–6	244n.82
53B5	86n.35	I 4, 4.13–15	303n.74	III 3, 3	300n.59
	115n.71	I 4, 6.17–21	243n.75	III 3, 4.1	247n.96
53C4–D7	93n.51	I 6, 5.31–34	247n.96	III 3, 8.27–34	250n.105
	216n.42	I 7, 2	241n.68	III 4, 1.11–13	247n.96
53C5	115n.71	I 8, 14.1–13	253n.116	III 4, 1.12–17	248n.99
53D4–7	86n.33	I 8, 14.24	247n.96		260n.17
54C2	245n.86	I 8, 14.44–54	247n.96	III 4, 5.1–3	299n.56
54D4–5	115n.71	I 8, 2.9–15	292n.29	III 4, 5.2–4	283n.2
55D8	115n.71	I 8, 3.6–7	250n.104	III 4, 5.4ff	23n.44
68B3	155n.74	I 8, 4.1–2	253n.116	III 5, 1	280n.92
68D2	27n.56	I 8, 4.2	261n.20	III 5, 3.1	229n.6
68E7–69A2	294n.34	I 8, 5.14–17	252n.114	III 5, 9.24–28	193n.51
69A6	245n.86	I 8, 5.17	247n.96	III 5, 9.42–45	280n.93
69B2–5	191n.45	I 8, 5.30–34	253n.117	III 6, 2.65–66	300n.60
69B–D	261n.21	I 8, 5.8–13	252n.109	III 6, 5.13–15	295n.40
69C5–6	68n.90	I 8, 6.19–20	253n.115	III 6, 9.18–19	262n.24
	285n.8	I 8, 6.33–34	252n.111	III 6, 11.37–38	251n.106
69E1	68n.90	I 8, 6.36–41	246n.92	III 6, 11.41–43	251n.106
	285n.8	I 8, 7.1–7	249n.101	III 6, 14.1–2	249n.101
73B–C	124n.102	I 8, 7.19–20	246n.89	III 6, 14.18–23	250n.103
86B–87B	190n.40	I 8, 7.21–23	246n.92	III 7, 3.7–11	271n.53
	301n.63	I 8, 8.1–28	253n.116	III 7, 13.49	229n.6

Index Locorum 343

III 8, 2.25-27	260n.19		246n.90	V 5, 4.4-7	240n.65
III 8, 2.27-34	261n.22	V 1, 10-11	281n.97	V 5, 6.17-20	235n.40
III 8, 7	136n.7	V 1, 10.24-32	295n.40	V 5, 6.26-27	232n.21
III 8, 8.12-16	260n.19	V 1, 11.10	281n.98	V 5, 9.1-18	241n.67
III 8, 9.5	274n.66	V 1, 3.15-16	246n.93	V 5, 11.1-2	241n.67
III 8, 9.23-24	281n.98	V 1, 3.17-19	287n.16	V 5, 12.7-9	280n.90
III 8, 10.29-35	229n.7	V 1, 5-7	258n.11	V 5, 12.23-24	288n.20
III 8, 10.1-2	233n.30	V 1, 5.7-9	278n.78	V 5, 12.38-39	233n.30
	240n.65	V 1, 6.30-39	236n.43	V 5, 12.40-49	236n.47
III 9, 3.7-16	247n.96	V 1, 6.38	234n.37	V 5, 15.33	233n.30
III 9, 4.1-6	249n.101		246n.91	V 6, 2.134	234n.37
IV 2, 2.52-55	304n.77	V 1, 7.1-4	241n.69	V 6, 5.9-10	258n.12
IV 2, 24.11-16	300n.59	V 1, 7.9-10	233n.30	V 8, 7.45	233n.28
IV 3, 1.1-6	283n.1	V 1, 7.21-22	237n.49	V 8, 9.24-25	241n.67
IV 3, 2.50-59	243n.72	V 1, 7.42	246n.93	V 9, 1.10-16	298n.52
IV 3, 12.30-31	240n.64	V 1, 7.47-48	247n.96	V 9, 3.4-8	238n.54
IV 3, 13.17-20	302n.68	V 1, 8.1-10	256n.2	V 9, 5.17-23	279n.85
IV 3, 15.20-23	300n.59	V 1, 8.5	237n.50	V 9, 6	136n.7
IV 3, 16.17-19	300n.59	V 1, 8.6-8	276n.73	V 9, 7.14-16	200n.82
IV 3, 24.8-10	300n.59	V 1, 8.10-14	227n.2	V 9, 8.13-15	236n.43
IV 3, 24.15-16	303n.70	V 1, 8.22-28	232n.24	V 9, 10	253n.116
	303n.71	V 1, 8.26	239n.56	VI 1 26.1ff	259n.16
IV 3, 3.24-28	287n.16	V 1, 9.30-32	256n.2	VI 2, 2.2	239n.56
IV 4, 13.3-7	244n.79	V 2, 1.14	241n.69	VI 2, 10.11	239n.56
IV 4, 13.19-22	245n.85	V 2, 1.7	246n.94	VI 2, 7.1-24	271n.53
IV 4, 14.8-11	245n.84	V 2, 2.29-31	247n.96	VI 2, 7.16-20	272n.59
IV 4, 16.26-27	243n.74	V 2, 2.9-11	244n.81	VI 2, 7.31-32	273n.63
IV 4, 18.11-15	284n.7	V 3, 11.1-8	277n.74	VI 2, 7.6	272n.57
IV 4, 18.15-19	289n.22	V 3, 11.27	230n.14	VI 2, 8	271n.53
	303n.73	V 3, 12.26-33	235n.41	VI 2, 8.14	271n.54
IV 4, 18-20	261n.22	V 3, 12.30-31	280n.88	VI 2, 8.43-49	273n.63
IV 4, 3.1-3	289n.22	V 3, 13.16-17	280n.88	VI 2.15.11-13	274n.64
IV 4, 44.20-32	253n.116	V 3, 13.9-11	274n.64	VI 2, 11.20-29	258n.12
IV 4, 7.8-11	291n.27	V 3, 13.25	274n.65	VI 2, 15.14	239n.56
IV 4, 7.12	291n.27	V 3, 15.10	280n.88	VI 2, 19.20	271n.54
IV 4, 22.10-12	23n.44	V 3, 15.11-13	232n.24	VI 2, 21.39-40	271n.54
IV 5, 7.15-17	243n.76		249n.56	VI 2, 21.46-47	239n.56
IV 7, 10.11-12	247n.96	V 3, 15.22	239n.56	VI 2, 22.1	258n.13
IV 7, 13	253n.118		274n.64	VI 2, 22.10	239n.56
IV 7, 13.1-8	292n.28	V 3, 15.26-33	240n.65	VI 2, 22.11-13	270n.46
IV 8, 1.4-5	301n.62	V 3, 15.28	232n.24	VI 3, 2.1-4	269n.43
IV 8, 3.10	239n.56	V 3, 15.32-35	234.n32	VI 3, 7.4-5	249n.101
IV 8, 3.25-27	298n.54		235n.41	VI 3, 8.20	269n.43
IV 8, 4.1-24	253n.118	V 3, 15.37-40	275n.70	VI 3, 9.23-26	265n.31
IV 8, 4.31-35	292n.31	V 3, 16.2-3	233n.30	VI 3, 15.24-38	269n.43
IV 8, 4.40-42	259n.16	V 3, 17.10-14	232n.24	VI 3, 15.27-37	264n.28
IV 8, 5	302n.68		240n.65	VI 4, 14.16-22	292n.31
IV 8, 5.27-33	302n.69	V 3, 4.29-30	297n.49	VI 4, 15	261n.22
IV 8, 5.28	289n.22	V 3, 5.22-23	239n.55	VI 4, 15.1-6	261n.21
IV 8, 5.8-10	303n.70	V 3, 7.1-5	295n.38	VI 4, 15.32-40	253n.119
IV 8, 6.1-6	240n.65	V 3, 7.23-24	236n.43		293n.32
IV 8, 6.18-23	251n.106	V 4, 1.1-21	230n.14	VI 5, 1.1-14	258n.12
IV 8, 8.1-3	284n.3	V 4, 1.5-13	229n.7	VI 5, 5.13-17	249n.102
IV 9 1.10-13	243n.72	V 4, 1.24-25	233n.30	VI 5, 6.1-2	239n.56
IV 9, 4.15-20	243n.72	V 4, 2.1-13	276n.73	VI 5, 9.1-13	245n.84
V 1, 1.1-17	253n.118	V 4, 2.27-30	243n.76	VI 5, 12.1	245n.84
	289n.22	V 4, 2.38	233n.30	VI 5, 12.20-21	281n.99
	302n.67	V 5, 3.23-24	231n.16	VI 6, 6.13	239n.56

VI 6, 14.27–30	244n.83	*On Isis and Osiris*		*On the Delays of Divine*	
VI 6, 16.41	229n.6	(*De Is.*)		*Vengeance* (*De sera*)	
VI 7, 16.10–22	277n.74	351Dff	188n.28	371A	190n.39
VI 7, 16.27–31	277n.75	351E	191n.42		
VI 7, 21.1–6	288n.18	352A	211n.16	*Platonic Questions*	
VI 7, 23.19–20	241n.69	354E	188n.29	(*Plat. Quaest.*)	
VI 7, 23.19–25	232n.24	360E	188n.29	1000E	190n.37
	240n.65	363Dff	188n.29	1000E–1001B	190n.37
VI 7, 27.24–27	288n.18	369A–B	191n.43	1002B	194n.60
VI 7, 28.12	246n.92	369D	189n.36		
VI 7, 31.17–18	281n.94	3372E–373A	190n.38	*Table Talk* (*Quaest. conv.*)	
VI 7, 32.31	233n.30	370F	192n.47	719A	195n.61
VI 7, 36.12	271n.54		193n.57		
VI 7, 39.11–14	239n.56	371A	190n.39	**PORPHYRY**	
VI 7, 39.5	271n.54	371A–B	193n.53		
VI 7, 40.13–14	233n.30	372F	189n.33	*Life of Plotinus*	
VI 7, 42.11	240n.65		211n.16	3.32–34	256n.3
VI 7, 42.21–24	240n.64	373A	211n.16	14.4	16n.28
VI 7, 5.1–2	284n.5	373F	194n.60	17.1–2	208n.2
VI 7, 8.17–18	239n.56	375B	190n.39		
VI 8, 5.34–35	301n.65	375C	211n.16	**PROCLUS**	
VI 8, 5.34–36	298n.41	376C	193n.53		
VI 8, 6.22	301n.65	377E–F	193n.53	*Commentary on Euclid's*	
VI 8, 6.29–33	301n.63	377F	193n.55	*Elements* (*In Euc. Elem.*)	
VI 8, 6.38–39	288n.17	381F	188n.29	4.18	21n.39
VI 8, 6.38–43	301n.64			11.5–7	21n.39
VI 8, 7.53–54	236n.48	*On the Face Which Appears*			
VI 8, 8.12–13	234n.38	*in the Orb of the Moon*		*Commentary on Plato's*	
VI 8, 9.30–31	271n.54	(*De fac.*)		*Alcibiades* (*In Alc.*)	
VI 8, 13.6–7	235n.40			170.28–171.6	26n.51
VI 8, 13.42–47	281n.96	943A	193n.56		
VI 8, 14.39	234n.40	*On the Generation of the*		*Commentary on Plato's*	
VI 8, 14.41–42	233n.27	*Soul in the Timaeus*		*Parmenides* (*In Parm.*)	
VI 8, 15.1–2	280n.89	(*De proc. an.*)		630.15dd	22n.43
VI 8, 15.9	236n.48	1012F	155n.73	688.10ff	204n.97
VI 8, 18.26–27	280n.86	1012E–F	161n.101	888.18–19	160n.96
VI 8, 18.51–52	236n.43	1012F–1013B	258n.10	1057.20–25	21n.39
VI 8, 19.18–19	280n.88	1014F–1015D	190n.39	1064.7–10	246n.88
VI 9, 1.1	232n.21	1015C–D	189n.33	1083.1–1088.3	21n.43
	240n.65	1015D–E	192n.47	1135.17–21	234n.38
VI 9, 11.5–38	250n.104	1016B	194n.60		
VI 9, 2.36–37	274n.66	1016C	193n.53	*Commentary on Plato's*	
VI 9, 5.29–33	232n.21	1023D	193n.53	*Timaeus* (*In Tim.*)	
VI 9, 5.33–34	258n.13	1024A–C	193n.53	1.375	198n.74
VI 9, 5.36–37	233n.30	1026E	193n.53	1.394.2–4	195n.61
VI 9, 5.38–40	232n.21			1.219.2–13	200n.85
VI 9, 5.38–46	229n.7	*On the Obsolescence*		1.277.8–10	200n.85
VI 9, 7.33–34	291n.25	*of Oracles* (*De def. or.*)			258n.10
VI 9, 8.31–32	289n.22	414D	190n.39	1.304	234n.38
VI 9, 9.17	242n.70	414F–415A	245n.86	1.305.6–9	216n.44
		423D	190n.37	1.356.5–7	246n.88
PLUTARCH OF		426D	194n.60	1.383.1–22	260n.19
CHAERONEA		435F–436E	188n.28	1.384.19–	
				385.13	246n.88
Against Colotes (*Adv. Col.*)		*On the E at Delphi* (*De E.*)			249n.101
1114C–E	188n.31			1.388.1–15	260n.19
1115A–1116E	188n.28	392A–393A	188n.28	2.276.30–277.32	193n.51
1121F–1122A	171n.22	393C–D	188n.29	3.334.10–14	293n.31

INDEX LOCORUM   345

Elements of Theology (ET)

31.1–2	282n.101
57	246n.88
72	246n.88
211.1–2	293n.31

On the Existence and Origin of Evil (De mal. subst.)

31–33	252n.111
34.1–6	249n.101

Platonic Theology (PT)

1.1.16ff	30n.59
	227n.1
1.83.12–85.5	198n.74

Ps.–Galen

History of Philosophy

3.18 = *Doxographi Graeci*, 599.16ff Diels 154n.68

Seneca

Epistles (Ep.)

65.11	11n.15

Sextus Empiricus

Against the Dogmatists (M)

7.16	154n.69
7.60	13n.19
	111n.54
7.141–45	187n.26
7.150	174n.31
7.151–153	166n.11
7.153–154	167n.12
7.158.5–12	172n.23
7.159	176n.40
7.166	175n.35
7.174	175n.36
7.175	175n.38
7.248.1–4	176n.42
7.402	170n.20
8.263	11n.15
10.248–84	278n.79
10.276	121n.95

Outlines of Pyrrhonism (PH)

1.220–35	166n.9
1.221	84n.25
1.222	35n.2
1.226–32	175n.34
1.232	171n.22
1.235	176n.41
	181n.8
	183n.14

Simplicius

Commentary on Aristotle's Categories (In Cat.)

6.19–32	153n.67

Commentary on Aristotle's On the Heavens (In De Caelo)

485.19–23	203n.95

Commentary on Aristotle's Physics (In Phys.)

151.6–19	92n.50
	258n.9
181.7–30	216n.44
230.36–231.7	219n.56
453.22–30	258n.9
545.23–25	92n.50
1359.6–8	110n.47

Sophocles

Women of Trachis

1123	42n.17

Speusippus

Fragments (Isnarde Parente)

53	136n.8
63	136n.9
72	137n.11
	138n.18
28 (Tarán)	150n.56
58 (Tarán)	142n.31
63a (Tarán)	150n.58
67 (Tarán)	153n.65

Stobaeus

Eclogues (Ecl.) (Wachsmuth)

1.2.7b	158n.89
1.37.6–15	204n.98
1.138.14–139.4 (=SVF 1.89 and 2.336)	11n.15
2.73.19	167n.11
2.88.4	169n.18

Stoicorum Veterum Fragmenta (SVF)

1.60	167n.11
1.65	185n.18
1.66	168n.16
1.89	11n.15
1.90	11n.15
1.529	206n.104
1.564	206n.104
2.52	167n.13
2.336	11n.15
2.360	185n.18
2.361	181n.6
2.363	11n.15
2.365	185n.18
2.541	11n.15
3.149	206n.104
3.171	169n.18
3.245–52	206n.104
3 Antipater 56	186n.22

Syrianus

Commentary on Aristotle's Metaphysics (In Meta.)

82.20	21n.39
104.17–23	181n.6
105.19–106.13	185n.18
147.29–148.7	121n.95
165.33–166.14	277n.76

Theophrastus

Fragments (Wimmer)

48	197n.69
	245n.87

Metaphysics (Laks/Most)

4a9–17	162n.111
4b18ff	155n.77
6a22–b23	114n.65

Xenocrates

Fragments (Isnarde Parente)

82	154n.69
94	160n.98
164–187	160n.98
188	155n.73
	161n.101
211	158n.87
213	154n.71
265	154n.68

Xenophon

Memorabilia (Mem.)

1.2.35	56n.50
4.5.6–11	49n.35

www.ingramcontent.com/pod-product-compliance
Lightning Source LLC
Chambersburg PA
CBHW030303240426
43673CB00040B/1038